THE ECOLOGY OF SUMATRA

THE
ECOLOGY
OF
SUMATRA

Anthony J. Whitten
> Institute for Resource- and Environmental Studies (IRES), Dalhousie University, Halifax, Nova Scotia, Canada.

Sengli J. Damanik
Jazanul Anwar
Nazaruddin Hisyam
> Centre for Resource and Environmental Studies (CRES), University of North Sumatra, Indonesia

GADJAH MADA UNIVERSITY PRESS
1984

ACKNOWLEDGEMENTS

The preparation of this book would not have been possible without the wonderful support of those involved with the running of UNDP/IBRD project INS/78/056 'Education and Training in Environment and Resources'; namely, Gamil Hamdy (UNDP, Jakarta), Koesnadi Hardjasoemantri (KLH, Jakarta), Soeratno Partoatmodjo (PSL, Bogor Agricultural University), Arthur Hanson, Nancy Blair (IRES, Dalhousie University, Halifax), Albert Howlett (IBRD, Washington), A.P. Parlindungan and Abu Dardak (University of North Sumatra, Medan). Their firm support, particularly during the uncertain periods, is much appreciated. Thanks are also due to Gabriel Horn and Ken Joysey of the Zoology Department, University of Cambridge, who provided space and facilities for A.J.W. for five months.

The whole of the book was conscientiously criticized by Kuswata Kartawinata, and a number of people, Ruth Chambers, Jim Davie, Kathy MacKinnon, Adrian Marshall, Edmund Tanner and Jane Whitten, read one or more chapters.

Great thanks are expressed to Koesoemanto, Executive Director of Gadjah Mada University Press for his enthusiasm and encouragement.

Trips and expeditions made by teams from the Centre for Resource and Environmental Studies (CRES) at the University of North Sumatra were greatly assisted by the following: P.T. Semen Andalas Indonesia particularly Malcolm Llewellyn; P.T. Caltex Pacific Indonesia particularly Wisaksono Noeradi, L.L. Tobing, and R.B. Pulono Wahjukusumo; the present and former District Officers (Camat) of Muara Tembesi, A. Wahab Moehib and K.P.T. Ismail; P.T. Tambang Timah particularly Sumardekar and Iwa Wardiman; and staff of the Directorate-General of Nature Conservation in Medan, Pekanbaru, Jambi, and Sungaipenuh. The authors also wish to thank staff attached to CRES for their assistance in the field, namely Djuharman Arifin, Usman Rasyid and Hardy Guchi.

Many people have helped by sending material which was unpublished, not yet published or simply hard to obtain, by advising, by making helpful suggestions or by identifying specimens. They are: Hans Bänzinger, Eamonn Barrett, Roger Beaver, C.G.G. van Beek, Elizabeth Bennett, David Benzing, Philip Chapman, the Earl of Cranbrook, Glyn Davies, Geoffrey Davidson, John Dransfield, John Flenley, Ian Glover, Peter Grubb, Larry Hamilton, John Edwards Hill, Frank Howarth, Robert Inger, Daniel Janzen, Patricia Jenkins, Andy Johns, A.J. Kostermans, Yves Laumonier, Colin McCarthy, E. Edwards McKinnon, John MacKinnon, Bernard Maloney, Joe Marshall, Willem Meijer, John Miksic, Mohammad Amir, Robert Morley, Francis Ng, Harald Riedl, Yarrow Robertson, Carel van Schaik, John Seidensticker, George Sherman, Ian Spellerberg, C.G.G.J. van Steenis, Michael Tweedie, H.Th. Verstappen, Peter Waterman, David Wells, Tim Whitmore, W.J.J.O. de Wilde, Jane Wilson and the librarians of the Institute for Resource and Environmental Studies (Halifax), Rijksherbarium (Leiden), British Museum (Natural History) (London), Universiti Malaya (Kuala Lumpur), Environmental Studies Centre, National Biological Institue, Central Agriculture and Biology Library, Herbarium Bogoriense (all at Bogor), Scientific Periodicals Library, University Library, Balfour Library, Haddon Library, and Botany Library (all at Cambridge).

The typists for this book, Pam Ismail, Meribeth Schmidt, Jesaya Hutapea, Gladys Pudduck and Pat Reay, have worked with great diligence and care.

Finally, and mainly, we thank Almighty God for his caring love shown throughout the preparation of this book without which it would never have been completed.

Medan,   May, 1984.   Anthony J. Whitten
                                              Sengli J. Damanik
                                              Jazanul Anwar
                                              Nazaruddin Hisyam

COUNTIES OF SUMATRA BY PROVINCE

ACEH
1. Greater Aceh
2. Pidie
3. North Aceh
4. West Aceh
5. Central Aceh
6. East Aceh
7. Southeast Aceh
8. South Aceh

NORTH SUMATRA
9. Langkat
10. Deli Serdang
11. Dairi
12. Tanah Karo
13. Simalungun
14. Asahan
15. Central Tapanuli
16. North Tapanuli
17. Labuhan Batu
18. South Tapanuli
19. Nias

WEST SUMATRA
20. Pasaman
21. Limapuluh Kota
22. Agam
23. Padang Pariaman
24. Tanah Datar
25. Solok
26. Sawahlunto Sijunjung
27. Pesisir Selatan

RIAU
28. Kampar
29. Bengkalis
30. Upper Indragiri
31. Lower Indragiri
32. Riau Archipelago

JAMBI
33. Kerinci
34. Bungo Tebo
35. Tanjung Jabung
36. Bangko Sarolangun
37. Batanghari

BENGKULU
38. North Bengkulu
39. Rejang Lebong
40. South Bengkulu

SOUTH SUMATRA
41. Musi Rawas
42. Musi Banyuasin
43. Bangka
44. Belitung
45. Lahat
46. Muara Enim
47. Lower Ogan Komering
48. Upper Ogan Komering

LAMPUNG
49. North Lampung
50. Central Lampung
51. South Lampung

FOREWORD

Indonesia, a country which is developing rapidly, is actively engaged on a wide variety of development projects. The evertual aim of Indonesian National Development is to achieve harmony between man and his God, between mankind and his environment, between races and between human ideals in this world and joy in the world hereafter.

The increase in the pace of development brings the risk of pollution and environmental degradation such that the structure and function of ecosystems which support life can be irretrievably damaged. Wise development must be based on a knowledge of the environment as an entity so that we can achieve a guarantee for the well-being of this generation and for those generations to come.

Many ecology books have been written but until now there has been no book available specially written for a part of south-east Asia. *The Ecology of Sumatra* is therefore extremely important for, armed with this, readers will be better able to understand the physical and biological characteristics of this island. If the environment is better understood then the exploitation of natural resources in the context of development can be managed in a more rational way.

The team which produced this book was comprised of the following authors: Dr. Jazanul Anwar, Ir. Sengly Janus Damanik, M.Sc and Ir. OK. Nazaruddin Hisyam, MS together with Dr. Anthony J. Whitten. The first three are Staff at the Centre for Environmental and Resource Studies, University of North Sumatra, and the last was consultant to the above centre under a United Nations Development Program/World Bank project (No. INS/78/056) for environmental education. The project was administered for the Government of the Republic of Indonesia by the State Ministry of Population and Environment.

viii

We express great thanks to the authors for their many hours of work in the production of this book. We specially thank Dr. A.J. Whitten and his wife, Jane Whitten M.Phil who have worked extremely hard in encouraging, guiding and helping the staff of the Centre for Environmental and Resource Studies and in producing the English edition of *The Ecology of Sumatra*. They receive our sincere congratulations.

Finally, we hope that this book will encourage the execution of detailed ecological investigations on Sumatra by a wide range of investigations.

Medan, April 1984.   Prof. Dr. A.P. Parlindungan, S.H.
                                      Rector,
                                      University of North Sumatra.

PREFACE

It is with great pleasure that I write the preface to *The Ecology of Sumatra* because it has been one of the major activities of the Centre for Resource and Environmental Studies at the University of North Sumatra over the last two years.

At this time in Indonesia's history when environmental awareness has penetrated so far both into the minds of the common man and into government policy at the highest levels, we must remind ourselves that although ecology (unlike environmental science) does not always directly influence policy making, legislation, politics or planning, it is the *foundation* of environmental science [5]. An understanding of the components of ecosystems and the manner in which they interact is central to studying the environment and to conducting resource management. The study of those interactions and their effects is the study of ecology.

The book has been written primarily for those concerned with conducting environmental impact analyses and related studies in Sumatra. Before now it has been more or less impossible for such people to find relevant information on Sumatran ecosystems to help them with their work and as such we hope that this book represents a significant step in the history of Indonesian environmental science. It is hoped that the book will also be enjoyed by those with a general interest in Sumatra and Southeast Asian national history, such as lecturers, school teachers, students and travellers.

The Ecology of Sumatra describes the island's ecosystems one by one and it has not been possible to cover all ecological principles in the text. We would recommend the textbooks by Cox [1], Krebs [2], Putman and Wratten [3] and Ricklefs [4] to those readers wishing to know more about general ecology. We are well aware that, because of limited time and resources, this book is far from perfect. We therefore invite comments, suggestions and criticisms as well as reports or papers not uncovered by our literature searches. It is hoped that a second edition of *The Ecology of Sumatra* will be produced before 1990. We would be grateful if all such letters and information could be directed to this Centre and to Dr. A.J. Whitten at the Institute for Resource and Environmental Studies, Dalhousie University, Halifax N.S., Canada.

Prof. Dr. Abu Dardak
Director
Centre for Resource and
Environmental Studies,
University of North Sumatra,
Medan

1. Cox, G.W. (1980). *Laboratory Manual of General Ecology* 4th Edition. Brown, Dubuque, (23.2.6).
2. Krebs, C.J. (1978). *Ecology: The Experimental Analysis of Distribution and Abudance.* Harper and Row, New York. (23.2.7).
3. Putnam, R.J. and Wratten, S.J. (1984). *Principles of Ecology.* Croom Helm, London.
4. Ricklefs, R.E. (1979). *Ecology* 2nd Edition. Chiron, London. (23.2.1).
5. Soeriaatmadja, R.E. (1981). *Ilmu Lingkungan.* Institut Teknologi Bandung, Bandung. (23.1.6).

NOTES

All the references used in the preparation of this book are, or soon will be, in the Documentation and Information Unit collection at the Centre for Resource and Environmental Studies, University of North Sumatra. It is hoped that this material will be consulted by readers to deepen their knowledge of particular aspects of Sumatran ecology, and to improve the standard of environmental impact analyses and similar studies. Readers are encouraged to consult or order this material; to assist them, the three-number classification of each book, paper or report is shown after the reference. Details of costs, etc., can be obtained by writing to the Centre's Director.

Figures 1.11—1.19 were drawn by Peggy McCalla and the aerial photo of a logging area is by Dr. Gerard Persoon; to both these people thanks are expressed. The other illustrations are by A.J. Whitten.

CONTENTS

PART A

INTRODUCTION

The processes of land formation, land movements, climatic change and evolution have been operating for thousands of millions of years and we see the result of them as natural ecosystems and as ecosystems disturbed or created by man. The chapter in this first section summarizes what is known about these processes in relation to Sumatra in order to provide a background against which later chapters can be viewed. As we learn about the past and its influence on the present we can better predict and understand the possibilities for the future.

CHAPTER 1
BACKGROUND

1.1 GEOMORPHOLOGICAL AND GEOLOGICAL HISTORY

About 250 million years ago, at the beginning of the Mesozoic era (Table 1.1), the Earth's continents formed a single land mass called Pangea. During the Triassic, roughly 230 million years ago, Pengea broke into two, with Laurasia (North America, Europe and Asia) splitting off from Gondwanaland (India, Australia, Africa, South America and Antartica). Gondwanaland began to split into its separate parts 200 million years ago during the Jurassic, and India floated towards Asia at about 10—18 cm per year (Figures 1.1 and 1.2). By the early Tertiary, about 70 million years ago, India and the plate on which it lay began to collide with and move under Asia. Its major thrust caused the uplift of the Himalayas, and one of the associated thrusts caused the uplift of the Barisan mountains that run the length of Sumatra. The movement of the Indian plate under Asia caused great earthquakes, and although the rate of movement is now less, almost all the earthquakes experienced in Sumatra (and Java, Burma, etc.) today are caused by those continuing movements. The main parts of south-east Asia remained in more or less their present relative positions throughout this period although their absolute positions moved north and south of the equator.

As the Barisan Range buckled upwards, so the corresponding downward thrust formed the deep channel to the west of Sumatra and the secondary upward thrusts that occurred at different times along its length formed the chain of islands from Simeulue to Enggano. A very deep

Table 1.1 Summary of geological timescale and events

Era	Period	Epoch	Years from begin Period/ Epoch to present
	Quaternary	Holocene	10,000
		Pleistocene	1 million
Cenozoic	Tertiary	Pliocene	10 million
(age of mammals)		Miocene	25 million
		Oligocene	40 Million
		Eocene	60 million
		Palaeocene	70 million
Mesozoic	Cretaceous		145 million
(age of reptiles)	Jurassic		215 million
	Triassic		250 million
	Permian		280 million
Palaeozoic			
Carboni-ferous		350 million	
	Devonian		400 million

Geological & Geomorphological events	Biological Events
Volcanic activity based on mountains & usually associated with faults	Man appears
Some sedimentation & folding in E. Sumatra. Final mountain building faulting, rift valleys major upthrust, violent volcanic activity	Man's earliest ancestors appear
	Modern species of mammals evolve, extinction of large forms e.g. mammoths; monkeys appear
Sumatra subsides, formation of sedimentary rocks	in Oligocene
Barisan Range starts to be uplifted	Rise of birds and placental mammals
	Dominance of angiosperm plants, extinction of large reptiles
	Reptiles dominant; first birds and archaic mammals
Sedimentary rock of Barisan Range forming	First dinosaurs. Cycads & conifers dominant plant groups
	Increasing variation of reptiles displace amphibians as dominant group
	Ferns dominant plant group; sharks abundant; first reptiles
	Age of fishes (mostly fresh-water), first trees, amphibia insects
	Invasion of land by plants & arthropods; primitive vertebrates appear

6

Figure 1.1 Geographical distribution of continents in the Triassic-Jurassic periods (± 160—140 million years ago). (After Smith and Briden [101]).

Figure 1.2 Geographical distribution of continents in the Palaeocene period (± 70 million years ago). (After Smith and Biden [101]).

trough falling to the Indian plate itself was formed to the west of these islands. A smaller trough was formed to the north-east of the Barisan Range and is represented today by low hills and plains (Figure 1.3). The alluvial eastern plains are narrower in the north of Sumatra either because sedimentation was slower or because subsequent subsidence of the land was faster [111].

Figure 1.3   A generalized cross-section through Sumatra and the western islands to show the folding caused by the Indian Plate colliding with the Asian Plate.

The south-east of Sumatra, including the islands of Bangka and Belitung, forms part of the stable Sunda Shelf (see Figure 1.8) and occasional ancient granite outcrops, particularly on Bangka, are indications that the geological foundation of the Sunda Region[1] is not far below the surface.

The rocks of the Barisan Range are largely sedimentary, laid down over about 100 million years between the late Palaeozoic and early Mesozoic eras up to 180 million years ago. The Barisan Range began to be lifted and formed in the early Palaeocene some 60 million years ago, but between the Oligocene and Miocene Epochs, 35 million years later, there was considerable subsidence. Sedimentary rocks laid down by the sea then covering much of Sumatra can be found today in west and east Sumatra and at some places inland. At about that time andesitic vulcanism was important in south Sumatra. A major upthrust occurred 20 million years ago and this mountain building activity was accompanied by considerable faulting and violent volcanic activity. No significant faulting has occurred

1. The Sunda Region comprises the present-day land areas of Sumatra, Peninsular Malaysia, Borneo, Palawan, Java, Bali and their neighbouring islands.

since then. A final period of mountain building activity occurred between the Pliocene and Pleistocene about 3 million years ago, and some faulting, block-faulting, creation of rift valleys and horizontal offsetting of land accompanied this. The Semangko fault zone, traceable from Semangko Bay in the south to Weh Island in the north, is the largest. At the same time there was sedimentation and folding in eastern Sumatra, generally parallel to the island's axis [111].

The volcanoes of the Quaternary Period (the last 3 million years are located in the mountainous areas and are usually associated with faults. Ash and other products from these volcanoes cover great areas of the higher Barisan area, particularly in the south. In general, the most recent volcanoes are in the northern half of Sumatra - Lembuh in Aceh; Sinabung, Sibayak and Sorikmerapi in North Sumatra; Merapi and Talong in West Sumatra—but volcanic activity continues at Kaba near Pasemah, hot springs occur in parts of Bengkulu and the most famous of contemporary volcanic eruptions (1883) occurred at Krakatau (section 11.2). In the same way that the andesitic products of the Krakatau eruption fertilized many of the previously infertile areas of Lampung, so the products of the (geologically) recent volcanic activity north-west of Lake Toba flowed both south and far to the east to give fertility to the Karo highlands and the plantation areas respectively.

One of the greatest ever volcanic eruptions occurred 75,000 years ago when Lake Toba was formed [96]. This is very recent in geological terms and stone-age axes have been found below the 'ash' that reached Peninsular Malaysia. The deep Semangko Fault allowed molten material to flow up towards the earth's surface. This created enormous pressures and the land rose up as a result between where the Wampu and Baruman rivers now flow and formed the Batak Tumour. Eventually the tumour exploded and the 'ash', or Toba tuff, ejected during the eruptions spread over $20,000-30,000$ km^2, reaching Sri Lanka, the Bay of Bengal and the Andaman Islands. In some areas near Lake Toba the tuff is 600 m thick. About $1500-2000$ km^3 of material was ejected - the greatest amount known from any explosion-and it has been estimated that over 1000 km^3 of this ash was deposited in just nine days [32]. With so much material removed, the top of the volcano collapsed forming a huge crater. A second minor series of eruptions built up a second volcano inside the crater and when this too collapsed the volcano split into two halves - the western slope forming Samosir Island and the eastern slope forming the peninsula between the towns of Parapat and Porsea (Figure 1.4). The second explosion probably occurred as recently at 30,000 years ago [32]. The Toba crater and island are correctly called a resurgent caldera, and at 100 km long Toba is easily the largest such in the world. For comparison, the extensively reported explosion of Mount St Helen's in Washington State, U.S.A., ejected only 0.6 km^3 of material and left a crater only 2 km in diameter [32]. Many of the lakes in Sumatra such as Maninjau and Ranau occupy the tops of old volcanoes [4, 47].

Figure 1.4 The formation of Lake Toba. (a) After pressure has caused the earth's crust to bend upwards, a major vent opens and the major eruption occurs. (b) The loss of so much magma causes the volcanic cone to fall and a lake is formed. Pressure builds up again and the old volcanic cone is forced up again, a minor explosion occurs. (c) The second cone breaks in two forming Samosir Island and the Parapat Peninsula. (After Hehuwat [47]).

1.2. SOILS

The first ever soil map produced for a tropical region was of part of Sumatra (*Groondsoortenkart van een gedeelte van Deli*) published in 1901 [132]. Soil maps of various scales now exist for most of the island and convenient maps with text have been published by BPPP/Soepraptohardjo *et al.* [8] and Scholz [136]. A detailed description of the soil of Sumatra is outside the scope of this book and only a summary of soil types will be attempted here. Descriptions, uses and limitations of the various soils can be found elsewhere [8, 132].

The eastern fringe of Sumatra and the land either side of the major rivers are dominated by alluvial hydromorphic soil, frequently with alluvial soils or grey hydromorphic soils (so important for the plantation industry) behind that. The swampy eastern portions of Riau, Jambi and South Sumatra are dominated by organosols but these soils also occur in parts of south-east and south North Sumatra, west Aceh, north-west and south West Sumatra. The majority of lowland Sumatra is covered by red-yellow podzolic soils formed from a variety of parent materials. The soils of the mountainous areas have very complex distributions but, again, various forms of red-yellow podzolic soils associated with altosols or litosols predominate. Over the limestone areas brown podzolic and renzina soils occur, and andosols and brown-grey podzolic soil appears over the volcanic rocks. The western coast is fringed with sandy regosols for most of its length. Both the western and eastern islands are largely overlain by red-yellow podzolic soils, but the soils on the eastern islands are associated with podzols overlying Tertiary sandstone and with litosols over the intrusive granite.

Table 1.2 summarizes the distributions of the different soil types.

1.3. CLIMATES

1.3.1 Palaeoclimate

During the last two million years there has been a world-wide alternation of colder and warmer climates. The colder periods, or glacials, were associated with lower sea levels (Figure 1.5) because cooling of areas

Table 1.2 The area of different soil types in each province and in the whole of Sumatra.

Soil Type	Aceh Ha	%	North Sumatra Ha	%	West Sumatra Ha	%	Riau Ha	%
1. Organosol	436,508	7.9	402,359	5.7	435.542	8.7	4,827,972	51.0
2. Organosol and Gley humus association	—	—	—	—	—	—	145,542	1.5
3. Hydromorphic alluvium	66,689	1.2	216,905	3.1	—	—	498,857	5.2
4. Aluvium	277,869	5.0	178,947	2.5	158,930	3.2	—	—
5. Alluvium and Gley humus association	—	—	46,635	0.6	47,315	0.9	39,146	0.4
6. Grey Hydromorphic	145,503	2.6	412,120	5.8	—	—	—	—
7. Grey Hydromorphic and regosol association	—	—	80,255	1.1	—	—	—	—
8. Regosol	112,159	2.0	129,059	1.8	420,984	2.7	—	—
9. Andosol	205,118	3.7	244,019	3.5	420,984	8.5	—	—
10. Andosol and regosol association	—	—	54,226	0.8	—	—	—	—
11. Brown Forest Soil	—	—	81,339	1.1	—	—	—	—
12. Renzina	238,462	4.3	78,086	1.1	—	—	—	—
13. Brown podzolic	—	—	156,172	2.2	—	—	—	—
14. Grey-brown podzolic	—	—	339,457	4.8	—	—	—	—
15. Lateritic	—	—	—	—	—	—	—	—
16. Latosol	306,162	5.5	471,769	6.7	1,185,306	23.8	26,097	0.2
17. Latosol and regosol association	—	—	—	—	—	—	—	—
18. Latosol and andosol association	—	—	—	—	66,727	1.3	3,011	0.1
19. Latosol and red-yellow podzolic association	—	—	36,874	0.5	57,021	0.1	—	—
20. Red-yellow podzolic	1,458,056	26.3	1,980,343	28.0	1,023,949	20.5	3,162,773	33.4

(Adapted from BPPP/Soepraptohardjo *et al.* [8]).

Jambi Ha	%	South Sumatra Ha	%	Bengkulu Ha	%	Lampung Ha	%	Sumatra Ha	%
866,986	19.3	1,966,035	19.0	4,246	0.1	—	—	8,985,678	19.0
32,580	1.5	32,340	0.3	—	—	—	—	210,463	0.5
141,179	3.1	1,363,846	13.2	—	—	163,444	4.9	2,450,920	5.2
319,464	7.1	588,807	13.2	161,826	7.6	52,300	1.6	1,598,224	3.4
64,255	1.4	353,507	3.4	—		290,218	8.7	841,076	1.8
—	—	107,056	1.0	—	—	79,627	2.4	744,306	1.6
—	—	—	—	—	—	—	—	80,255	0.1
2,715	0.1	249,796	2.4	8,503	0.4	80,674	2.4	807,573	1.7
293,219	6.5	162,814	1.6	262,339	12.4	209,544	6.3	1,798,037	3.8
—	—	—	—	—	—	—	—	54,226	0.1
—	—	10,036	0.1	3,015	0.2	—	—	94,390	0.2
—	—	16,728	0.1	11,056	0.5	8,382	0.2	352,714	0.2
—	—	215,226	2.0	—	—	31,432	0.9	402,830	0.9
—	—	—	—	—	—	—	—	339,457	0.7
—	—	—	—	—	—	8,382	0.2	8,382	0.1
712,231	15.8	419,302	4.0	501,559	23.7	719,783	21.6	4,342,209	9.2
—	—	4,461	4.0	—	—	—	—	4,461	9.2
35,295	0.8	68,025	0.7	—	—	—	—	173,058	0.3
19,910	0.4	37,916	0.3	255.302	12.1	97,438	2.9	504,461	1.1
1,397,314	31.0	2,968,568	28.6	309,579	14.6	1,522,336	45.7	13,522,918	29.2

21. Red-yellow podzolic and grey hydromorphic association	—	—	30,367	0.4	—	—	—	—
22. Red-yellow podzolic and regosol association	—	—	175,693	2.5	—	—	—	—
23. Red-yellow podzolic and litosol association	—	—	—	—	—	—	116,433	1.2
24. Red-yellow podzolic and litosol association	—	—	—	—	—	—	355,323	3.7
25. Red-yellow podzolic, latosol and litosol complex	—	—	156,171	2.2	—	—	40,149	0.4
26. Red-yellow podzolic, latosol and litosol complex	1,436,837	25.9	967,397	13.7	922,040	18.5	240,897	2.5
27. Red-yellow podzolic, brown and grey podzolic and litosol complex	12,125	0.2	10,845	0.1	12,132	0.2	—	—
28. Litosol, latosol and regosol complex	—	—	—	—	—	—	—	—
29. Brown podzolic, podzol and litosol complex	843,712	15.2	386,091	5.5	505,908	10.1	—	—
30. Other	—	—	443,571	6.3	7,279	0.1	—	—
TOTAL	5,539,200		7,078,700		4,977,800		9,456,200	

—	—	761,658	7.3	—	—	—	—	792,025	1.7
—	—	—	—	—	—	—	—	175,693	0.4
—	—	—	—	—	—	—	—	116,433	0.2
—	—	907,744	8.7	—	—	—	—	1,263,067	2.7
184,619	4.1	53,528	0.5	22,113	1.0	67,054	2.0	523,634	1.1
337,563	7.5	—	—	—	—	—	—	3,904,734	8.2
—	—	28,994	0.2	141,273	6.7	—	—	205,819	0.4
—	—	40,146	0.4	—	—	—	—	40,146	0.1
85,070	1.9	12,267	0.1	263,344	12.4	—	—	2,096,392	4.4
—	—	—	—	38,195	1.8	—	—	489,045	1.0
4,492,400		10,368,800		2,116,800		3,330,700		47360,600	

Figure 1.5 The location of past (thicker lines) and present (thinner lines) coastlines. Number represent years before present.

that are now temperate locked up a great deal of water as ice, thus preventing its return to the sea (Figure 1.6). Minor changes in sea level have probably continued up to the present (Figure 1.7). The maximum sea level duing the last interglacial was only 3 to 6 metres higher than present levels [33,39,129], but Tjia reports sea levels up to 50 m higher than present at various times during the last two million years [109]. The minimum sea level was about 180 metres lower than at present, more or less outlining the Sunda Shelf and exposing three times more land in the Sunda Region than is visible now. The Sunda Shelf is an extension of the

Figure 1.6 Hydrological cycles (a) in warm conditions, and (b) in cold conditions. Note the fall in sea level because water cannot flow to the sea.

18

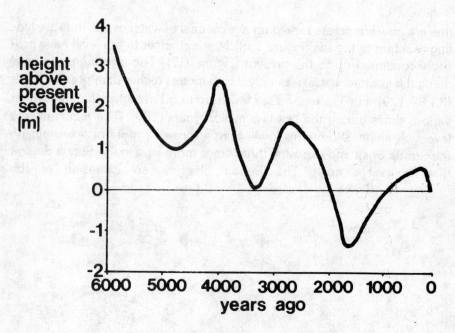

Figure 1.7   Changes in sea level during the last 6000 years. (After Tjia [109]).

Figure 1.8   The Sunda Shelf showing greatest area of land exposed during
the driest periods of the last two million years, major rivers and
present-day coastlines. (After Tjia [109]).

Asian continent (Figure 1.8) and lies between 40—200 m below present sea level. When exposed the shelf was bisected by the Great Sunda River, which arose between Belitung Island and Borneo and flowed north-east between the North and South Natuna Islands [109]. The extremes of sea level did not last very long and for most of the Quaternary the sea lay only some 30—80 m below present sea level.

There is no information about climates for any low-water (glacial) period other than the most recent, about 15,000 years ago. It has been estimated that the regional sea surface temperature was only about 2° to 3°C below today's temperature [14] so that the lowlands, at least, remained quite warm. On the highest mountains, however, where ice very occasionally forms today, large glaciers formed [114]. Until recently glaciers had been confirmed only on Mt. Kinabalu (Sabah) and on various peaks in New Guinea. Now, however, it has been shown that glaciers once existed on Mt. Leuser, Mt. Kemiri and Mt. Bandahara in the Mt. Leuser National Park [3]. The largest of these, on Mt. Leuser, measured about 100 km^2 and it is calculated that the temperature at the snowline (then about 3100 m) was 6°C colder than now. When the glaciers melted, peat began to form and the oldest peat at the bottom of a small lake near the summit of Mt. Kemiri has been given a radio-carbon date of 7590 ± 40 years before present. This thus gives us some indication of when the climate began to warm up again.

During the low-water periods the greater land area and consequent deflection of ocean currents changed weather patterns and air circulation, with the result that total annual rainfall almost certainly decreased and fell more seasonally [114].

1.3.2 Present climate

The climate of Sumatra is characterized by abundant rainfall moderately well distributed through the year with the wet and dry seasons much less clearly defined than in Java and eastern Indonesia.

a) Rainfall

Rainfall in Sumatra is very variable, dependent somewhat on the topography, and ranges from over 6,000 mm per year in areas to the west of the Barisan Range, to less than 1,500 mm per year in some areas of the east which are blocked from humid winds by the Barisan Range and the

Malay Peninsula. Out of 594 rainfall stations in Sumatra, 70% have an annual rainfall of over 2500 mm. Over much of the island the driest months are normally associated with the north-easterly monsoon between December and March, and the main rainy season usually falls during the transition period before the north-easterly monsoon and after the south-westerly monsoon which last from May to September. A rainy period of secondary importance occurs in about April which is after the north-easterly and before the south-westerly monsoon. Southern Sumatra, however, has the typical Java patterns of rainfall with a single pronounced dry season around July, and the northern tip of Aceh has the Asiatic type of climate with a pronounced dry season in February [136]. Figure 1.9 shows the distribution of climatic zones, the definitions of which are as follows:

Zone A — more than nine consecutive wet months, and two or less consecutive dry months.

Zone B — seven to nine consecutive wet months and three or less consecutive dry months.

Zone C — five to six consecutive wet months and three or less consecutive dry months.

Zone D — three to four consecutive wet months and two to six consecutive dry months.

Zone E — up to three consecutive wet months and up to six consecutive dry months.

'Wet' and 'dry' are defined as more than 200 mm rainfall/month and less than 100 m/month respectively [98].

An important point to note is the considerable difference bettween the climates of Sumatra and Java (Table 1.3). On Sumatra 71% of the land area has seven or more consecutive wet months and up to three consecutive dry months whereas only 27% of Java experiences similar conditions [94].

b) Temperature

The annual fluctuations in temperature are very small for almost all locations in Sumatra. Daily variations are greatest in the drier months when the sun is not obscured by clouds and when the heat escapes quickly at night because there are no clouds to insulate the earth. The differences in temperature between locations are caused mainly by altitude and this discussed further in section 9.2.1.

21

Figure 1.9 Climatic zones. (After Oldemann *et al.* [94]).

Table 1.3 **Summary of land area on Sumatra and Java in five agroclimatic zones.** (After Oldeman *et al.* [94]).

	A	B	C	D	E
		Climatic zone			
Sumatra	24	47	15	12	2
Java	4	23	39	25	9

c) Wind

There is great variablity in the winds but in general the winds blow from the north from December to March, and from the south from May to September. Where there are breaks in the Barisan mountains, monsoon winds are channelled and wind speed may be greatly increased. Some westerly winds of Sumatra are particularly famous. For example:

Angin Depek — at Air Tawar near Takengon between April and October. This stormy wind is named after a fish that comes to the surface at this time and is easily caught.

Angin Bohorok — in areas of North Sumatra. It is not feared because of its strength but because it is very dry and can damage crops, particularly tobacco. Angin Bohorok is a föhn wind - that is, a depression (low atmospheric pressure) moving to the east of the Barisan range, draws air into itself from the west of the range. The air ascends the western slopes, clouds form and there is heavy rain. When it reaches the eastern slopes, the air is still warm but it has lost most of its moisture, so it blows down as a very warm, dry wind. It starts in the Karo Highlands and is funnelled into upper Langkat and upper Deli Serdang through the Bohorok depression.

Angin Padang Lawas — east of Padang Sidempuan is a particularly serious föhn wind, drying the soil and making most forms of agriculture virtually impossible [94].

1.4 VEGETATION

1.4.1 Palaeovegetation

The oldest Sumatran forests of which we have evidence are those that formed the coal seams during the Carboniferous Period, about 300 million years ago. Coal is the highly compressed remains of undecayed swamp vegetation sandwiched between layers of marine sedimentary deposits. These primeval swamp forests covered much of the earth many millions of years before the first gymnosperm (e.g. conifer) or angiosperm (flowering) trees evolved. The earliest 'trees' were in fact primitive ferns and some, such as the giant club-moss *Lepidodendron*, reached 30 m in height. By the Tertiary many of the plants now found in forests had developed; for example, a leaf imprint of a *Dipterocarpus* leaf and a fossil dipterocarp fruit have been found in southern Sumatra dating from this era [2].

The tropical rain forests of today have been commonly regarded as relics from the Tertiary Era, a kind of living museum, and phrases such as 'unchanged for thousands of years' are often written. Evidence from many tropical regions now show that this is wrong [30]. The climate has changed during at least the last 30,000 years (section 1.3.1) both in temperature and rainfall and this in turn affected the vegetation.

In the drier, more seasonal periods of the Pleistocene the areas with a wet, non-seasonal climate would have contracted as the area of seasonal climate extended, but the exact amount of change is unknown. Populations of plants restricted to the wet, non-seasonal forests would therefore have had their ranges constricted but contact between populations could have been maintained to indeterminate degrees by occasional transfer between patches of suitable forest in the seasonal areas, as indeed occurs today in parts of Java [120]. It is possible that monsoon forest and perhaps even dry savannah forest [119] would have occupied some of Sumatra and other parts of the Sunda Region. There is, however, no evidence from the few studies of preserved polled from lowland sites in the region, of any replacement of non-seasonal forest by seasonal forest during or since the Tertiary [68,88,89,120], but this may yet be revealed by future research.

The palaeovegetation of Sumatra has been studied by investigating fossil pollen preserved in sediments of small lakes in the Kerinci and Toba regions. The sediment core taken from Lake Padang at 950 m south of Lake Kerinci revealed evidence of vegetation changes over the last 10,000 years. About 8,300 years ago an upper montane forest characterized by *Myrica* trees and the conifer *Podocarpus* gave way to a lower montane forest with abundant oaks (Fagaceae), suggesting that as the climate warmed up, so the upper montane species[2] retreated up the mountains [88, 89].

2 .A 'species' is a group of actually or potentially interbreeding populations that are

The sediment core from Pea Sim-Sim at 1,450 m on the Siborong-borong plateau south of Lake Toba covered the last 18,500 years. Up to 16,500 years ago a mosaic of sub-alpine and upper montane forest probably existed on the plateau [68]. Oak forest became established about 16,500 years ago and persisted until ± 12,000 years ago and 7,500 years ago montane vegetation becomes less important in the samples and *Eugenia* species, possibly from swamp forest, predominate. From these studies it appears that before the climate began to warm about 8,000—9,000 years ago, the vegetation zones (next section) had been lowered by 350—500 m.

The above results are more or less confirmed by analysis of sediments from Lake di-Atas [118] east of Padang, and Lake Bento [55] in the Kerinci Valley. The former, as yet unpublished, study is particularly interesting because it covers the last 31,000 years, and it appears that the montane vegetation revealed in the oldest samples from the core was quite different in composition and structure to that found today.

A review of the late Pleistocene vegetation in Sumatra has recently been published by Maloney [70].

---

reproductively isolated from all other types of organisms [96]. Within a species, populations can sometimes be recognized as being distinct on the basis of colour, shape or behaviour; these are called 'subspecies'. Similar species are grouped within a 'genus' and every known organism is named using its genus and species and these are correctly written either in italics or underlined. The genus begins with a capital letter, the species (and subspecies if necessary) with a small letter. Thus most cats are in the genus *Felis* which has various species such as the domestic cat *Felis domesticus*, the jungle cat *Felis bengalensis*, and the flatheaded cat *Felis planiceps*. The tiger *Panthera tigris* and the clouded leopard *Neofelis nebulosa* belong to different genera (plural of genus) but are in the same 'family', Felidae, as the *Felis* cats. Family names are written in normal script, starting with a capital, and usually ending in -dae for animals and -ceae for plants. Felidae is just one family in the 'order' Carnivora which includes dogs, civets and bears. Order names are written in normal script starting with a capital letter and generally end in -a. Thus, to summarize, the levels of classification used in this book are:

Order
Family
Genus
Species
Subspecies

The use of these names may seem complicated but it is a very elegant system conforming to many rules and is recognized and used by scientists throught the world.

1.4.2 Present vegetation

Sumatra supports a wide range of vegetation types and, due to its recent connection to Asia (section 1.3.1 and 1.6.2), these are very rich in species. For species diversity the Sumatran forests are comparable to the richest forests of Borneo and New Guinea and are far richer than those found on Java, Sulawesi and other small islands [82]. Sumatra has 17 endemic genera of plants (compared with 41 in Peninsular Malaysia/southern Thailand; 59 in Borneo; and 10 in West Java), and has some unique and spectacular species such as *Rafflesia arnoldi*, the largest flower in the world, and *Amorphophallus titanum* the tallest flower in the world featured on the Rp 500 banknote (section 7.3.7).

Sumatra supports a broad altitudinal range of vegetation types (Chapter 9), and some other distinctive vegetation types characteristic of the soils or topography on which they occur (Chapter 8). Dipterocarp trees such as *Shorea*, *Dipterocarpus* and *Dryobalanops* dominate much of the tall lowland forest, forming a continuous canopy and are capable of producing over 100 cubic metres of high quality logs per hectare (Chapter 7). The peat swamps of the east coast show characteristic forest formations of great commercial importance and botanical interest (Chapter 5). The sandy west coast supports various types of coastal forest (Chapter 3) but on the east the coast is dominated by very extensive areas of mangrove forests (Chapter 2). In the south, large peaty freshwater swamps are found (Chapter 6). These vegetation types are summarized in Table 1.4 and the distribution of the natural vegetation (i.e. not disturbed by man) of Sumatra is shown in Figure 1.10.

The bibliographies by Tobing [110] and Jacobs and de Boo [54] are very useful as preliminary means of exploring the literature on Sumatran vegetation and plants.

The distribution of vegetation types between provinces is not even (Table 1.5) - for instance, Riau has no montane forest but has the largest areas of peatswamp and mangroves, and West Sumatra has almost no mangroves and little swamp but considerable areas of montane forest.

The natural, remaining and protected areas of different vegetation types are shown in Table 1.6. The figures for the remaining areas have been calculated by FAO/MacKinnon [26] from the most recent available air photos (1973), more recent land use maps from the Indonesian Army

Table 1.4 Major vegetation types found on Sumatra. (After van Steenis [106] and Whitmore [119]). For a more detailed division see the chart by Kartawinata [58].

Soil water	Location	Soils		Vegetation Type
Dryland	Inland	Zonal soils	Lowlands, up to 1200 m	Lowland forest
			Mountains 1200 – 2100m	Lower montane forest
			Mountains 2100 – 3000m	Upper montane forest
			Mountains, 3000 +	Subalpine forest
		Podzolized sands	Mostly lowland	Heath Forest
		Limestone	Mostly lowland	Forest over limestone
	Coastal			Beach vegetation
	Saltwater			Mangroves
Watertable high (at least periodically)	Brackish water			Brackish water forest
	Freshwater	Oligotrophic peats		Peatswamp forest
		Eutrophic (muck and mineral soils)		Freshwater/Seasonal swamp forest

0 50 100 150 200km

LEGEND

- ■ mangrove forest
- ▨ peat swamp forest
- ▤ freshwater swamp forest
- ▦ heath forest
- ▩ ironwood forest
- ▨ lowland forest on alluvium
- □ "   "   " other soils
- ▽ lower montane forest (1000–1500)
- ○ upper   "   " (1500+ m)
- ○ coral

Figure 1.10 Natural vegetation. (After FAO/MacKinnon [26]).

Table 1.5 Approximate areas of natural vegetation types in each province (in 1,000 ha). (After FAO/MacKinnon [26]. 'Wet', 'Moist' and 'Dry' correspond to Zones A/B, C and D/E in Figure 1.9.* The figure for heath forest may be a considerable overestimate (see section 8.2.5.).

Vegetation type	Aceh	North Suma-tra	West Suma-tra	Riau	Jambi	South Suma-tra	Beng-kulu	Lam-pung
Moss forest	80	30	30	—	—	10	10	6
Montane forest on volcanic soils	950	250	230	—	—	—	—	20
Montane forest on limestone	310	120	560	—	350	570	220	170
Montane forest on other rocks/soils	330	1300	320	—	160	110	220	—
'Wet' lowland forest on:								
volcanic soils	100	360	950	—	780	980	240	240
limestone	1340	480	710	150	110	—	—	—
alluvium	30	120	80	100	200	690	260	20
other rocks/soils	450	2130	1160	3100	1020	1740	1120	260
'Moist' lowland forest on:								
volcanic soils	70	20	80	—	20	50	10	320
limestone	120	—	160	—	—	—	—	20
alluvium	230	330	—	—	40	140	—	180
other rocks/soils	450	620	320	320	170	440	—	1640
'Dry' lowland forest on:								
volcanic soils	60	—	—	—	—	—	—	—
alluvium	260	50	—	—	—	—	—	—
other rocks/soils	110	—	20	—	—	—	—	30
Ironwood forest	—	—	—	—	500	820	—	—
Heath forest*	—	—	—	—	—	1090	—	—
Peat swamp	20	200	—	4500	840	1720	—	—
Freshwater swamp on alluvium	—	460	20	380	110	1640	10	250
Freshwater swamp on other soils	450	400	330	140	20	530	20	150
Mangrove forest	170	200	—	680	170	230	—	20
Beach vegetation	2	2	3	—	—	2	2	2
Totals	5532	7072	6973	9450	4490	10362	2112	3328

Table 1.6 Natural, remaining and protected areas of vegetation types (in 1000 ha). (After FAO/MacKinnon [26]). *The estimate for heath forest may be too high - see section 8.2.5.

Vegetation type	Natural Area	Remaining area (and % of original area)	Area included in reserves (and % of original and remaining areas)
Moss forest	169	159 (94)	36 (21 23)
Montane forest on volcanic soils	1,946	1,469 (75)	419 (21 28)
Montane forest on limestone	1,225	1,078 (88)	357 (29 33)
Montane forest on other rocks/soils	2,340	1,245 (53)	179 (7 14)
'Wet' lowland forest on:			
volcanic soils	3,934	1,177 (30)	231 (6 20)
limestone	2,790	1,663 (60)	423 (15 25)
alluvium	1,500	282 (19)	33 (2 12)
other rocks/soils	11,180	4,065 (36)	800 (8 22)
'Moist' lowland forest on:			
volcanic soils	500	114 (23)	21 (4 18)
limestone	300	154 (51)	40 (13 26)
alluvium	940	364 (39)	17 (2 5)
other rocks/Soils	4,010	897 (22)	84 (2 9)
'Dry' lowland forest on:			
volcanic soils	60	18 (30)	(0 0)
alluvium	320	23 (7)	(0 0)
other rocks/Soils	160	40 (25)	6 (4 15)
Ironwood forest	1,320	440 (33)	20 (2 5)
Heath forest*	1,090	200 (18)	(0 0)
Peat swamp	7,280	4,613 (63)	131 (2 3)
Freshwater swamp	4,910	1,090 (22)	293 (6 26)
Mangrove forest	1,340	385 (29)	53 (4 14)
Beach vegetation	13	7 (54)	2 (15 29)

(TNI-Topografi) and the national mapping agency (BAKOSURTANAL), and the new vegetation maps being produced by BIOTROP [60].[3] The BIOTROP maps were particularly useful for documenting vegetation in South Sumatra and Lampung where considerable changes have occurred recently as a result of planned and unplanned transmigration. The remaining forest areas, existing reserves and proposed reserves in each of the provinces are shown in Figures 1.11 to 1.18 and the remaining forest for the whole of Sumatra in Figure 1.19. This can be compared with a similar map prepared 50 years ago by van Steenis (Figure 1.20).

It should be noted that it is very difficult to differentiate selectively logged/disturbed forest from primary forest by analysis of air photos. The forest areas given are, therefore, where tree cover exists rather than were unspoilt natural ecosystems may be found. Most types of forest which have suffered limited disturbance are able to regenerate successfully if left alone (section 11.2.1) and so the forest areas shown do have ecological meaning. Table 1.6 shows clearly that certain vegetation types have been reduced in area far more than others and that some vegetation types still have no protection. Montane forests have lost an average of one third of their natural area, whereas between two-thirds and four-fifts of lowland forest have disappeared. This reflects the severity of land-use conflicts. Note that the lowland forests-which have been reduced the most are those on the fertile alluvial and volcanic soils. Generally less than 10% of the natural vegetation types currently receive any protection and those vegetation types with the least area in reserves are generally those that have been reduced in area the most.

In terms of the loss of genetic diversity the figures in Table 1.7 show that in general the vegetation types under most pressure, such as lowland forests and heath forests, are also the richest/most diverse in terms of plant species. Similarly, the vegetation types under most threat support the greatest diversity of animal species. For example, 245 Sumatran bird species live in lowland forest, 158 species in lower montane forest, 62 species in upper montane forest, and only two commonly live in the sub-alpine zones (section 9.5) [28].

---

3. A small-scale land-use map for Sumatra is available [83], and a coloured vegetation map of Sumatra land the rest of Southeast Asia will be published in late 1984 [121].

31

Figure 1.11 Remaining forest, reserves and proposed reserves in Áceh.
(After FAO/MacKinnon [26]). *1, 2 and 3. Gunung Leuser; 4 and
5. Serbojadi; 6. Lingga Isaq; 7. Kuala Langsa; 8. Jantho; 9. Gunung Seulawah Agam; 10. Aneuk Laut; 11. Langsa Kemuning;
12. Kuala Jambu Air; 13. Rantau Pala Gadjah; 14. Singkit Barat;
15. Pulau Bangkaru; 16. Perairan P. Weh and P. Beras; 17. Per-
luasan Gunung Leuser Bengkong; 18. Pulau Simeulue; 19. Curah
Serbolangit.*

32

Figure 1.12 **Remaining forest, reserves and proposed reserves in North Sumatra.** (After FAO/MacKinnon [26]). *1. Sekundur; 2. Langkat Selatan; 3. Langkat Barat; 4. Lau Debuk-debuk; 5 dan 14. Sibolangit; 6. Dolok Tinggi Raja; 7. Dolok Surungan; 8, 9, 10 and 11. Nias; 12. Karang Gading/Langkat Timur Laut; 13. Padang Lawas; 15. Bandar Baru; 16. Sibolga; 17. Dolok Sembelin; 18. Dolok Sepirok; 19. Sei Prapat; 20. Lau Tapus.*

Lake Padang, Kerinci, the site of a fossil pollen study.

Tiangko Panjang cave, Sarko, inhabited by man 10,000 years ago.

33

Figure 1.13 Remaining forest, reserves and proposed reserves in West Sumatra. (After FAO/MacKinnon [26]). *1. Rimbo Panti; 2. Batang Palupuh; 3. Beringin Sati; 4. Lembah Anai; 5. Megamendung; 6. Lembah Harau; 7 and 10. Indrapura (Gunung Kerinci); 8 and 9. Teitei Batti; 11. Lunang; 12. Malampah-Alahan Panjang; 13. Lembah Anai extension; 14. Lembah Harau extension; 15. Danau Maninjau; 16. Gunung Singgalang; 17. Gunung Merapi; 18. Gunung Sulasihtalang; 19. Bukit Sebelah and Batang Pangeran; 20. Bajang Air Tarusan Utara; 21. Kambang/Lubuk Niur; 22. Gunung Sago/Malintang/Karas; 23. Muara Siberut.* Legend as for Figure 1.11.

Figure 1.14 Remaining forest, reserves and proposed reserves in Riau (After FAO/MacKinnon [26]). *1. Kerumutan Baru; 2. Pulau Berkeh; 3. Pulau Burung; 4. Pulau Laut; 5. Danau Bawah and Pulau Besar; 6. Bukit Mancung and Sei Gemuruh; 7. Muara Sungai Guntung; 8. Seberida; 9. Bukit Baling Baling; 10. Kerumutan Lama; 11. Peranap; 12. Siak Kecil; 13. Pantai Cermin; 14. Pulau Bulan; 15. Pulau Penyengat; 16. Istana Sultan Siak; 17. Candi Muara Takus; 18. Pulau Pasir Panjang; 19. Gian Duri; 20. Buaya Bukit Batu; 21. Danau Tanjung Padang; 22. Danau Belat/Besar Sekak/ Sarang Burung; 23. Air Sawan; 24. Bakau Muara; 25. Bakau Selat Dumai; 26. Tanjung Sinebu/Pulau Alang Besar; 27. Natuna Besar. Legend as for Figure 1.11.*

Figure 1.15 Remaining forest, reserves and proposed reserves in Jambi. (After FAO/Mac Kinnon [26]). 1. Berbak; 2. Gunung Indrapura; 3. Bukit Tapan; 4. Gunung Tujuh; 5. Batang Marangin Barat/Menjuta Ulu; 6. Sangir Ulu/Batang Tebo/Batang Tahir; 7. Kelompok Hutan Bakau Pantai Timur; 8. Bukit Besar; 9. Gunung Sumbing/Masurai; 10. Hutan Sinlah; 11. Batang Bungo; 12. Singkati Kehidupan. Legend as for Figure 1.11.

36

Figure 1.16   Remaining forest, reserves and proposed reserves in
South Sumatra. (After FAO/Mac Kinnon [26]). *1. Gumai
Pasemah; 2. Isau-Isau Pasemah; 3. Gunung Raya; 4. Rawas
Hulu Lakitan; 5. Subanjeriji; 6. Benakat; 7. Dangkau; 8. Ben-
tayan; 9. Paraduan Gistang; 10. Sungai Terusan Dalam;
11. Bukit Halal; 12. Gunung Patah; Bepagut, Muara Duakisan;
13. Bukit Natiogan Hulu/Nantikomering Hulu; 14. Bukit
Dingin/Gunung Dempo.* Legend as for Figure 1.11.

Figure 1.17 Remaining forest, reserves and proposed reserves in Bengkulu (After MacKinnon [26]). *1. Sumatera Selatan I (part); 2. Semidang Bukit Kabu; 3. Nanuua; 4. Bukit Gedang Seblat; 5. Bukit Gedang Seblat (northern extension); 6. Bukit Gedang Seblat (southern extension); 7. Taba Penanjung; 8. Pungguk Bingin; 9. Dusun Besar; 10. Bukit Raja Mandara/Kaur Utara; 11. Bukit Hitam/Sanggul/Dingin; 12. Bukit Balairejang; 13. Hulu Bintuanan/Palik Lebang/Lair/Wais Hulu/Lekat/Bukit Daun; 14. Bukit Reges/Hulu Sulup; 15. Bukit Kaba.* Legend as for Figure 1.11.

38

Figure 1.18   Remaining forest, reserves and proposed reserves in Lampung.   (After FAO/MacKinnon [26]).   *1. Way Kambas;
2. Sumatera Selatan I; 3. Gunung Betung; 4. Krui Utara/Bukit
Punggul; 5. Tangkitebak/Kota Agung Utara/Wai Waja; 6. Tang-
gamus; 7. Rebang.* Legend as for Figure 1.11.

Figure 1.19 Remaining forest in 1982. (After FAO/MacKinnon [26]).

Figure 1.20 Remaining forest in 1932. (After van Steenis [104]).

Table 1.7 Average number of tree species greater than 15 cms trunk diameter found in 0.5 ha. plots in different habitat types. (After FAO/MacKinnon [27]).

Vegetation type	Tree species
Upper montane forest	18
Fertile lower montane forest	66
Infertile lower montane forest	35
Fertile hill forest	75
Infertile hill forest	38
Fertile lowland forest	80
Infertile lowland forest	51
Heath forest	50
Beach forest	21
Volcanic scrub	20
Complex mangrove	14
Simple mangrove	6
Peat/Freshwater swamp forest	46

1.5 FAUNA

1.5.1 Palaeofauna

Nothing is know for certain about the Sumatran Pleistocene fauna or its fauna of any earlier period. Dubois investigated some caves in the Padang Highlands in 1890 and found subfossils of fifteen mammal species from several thousand years ago (Table 1.8) [21]. The prehistoric remains of orang-utan, gibbons, leaf monkeys, long- and pig-tailed macaques, tapir, banteng cattle and Javan rhinoceros indicate that all these species were somewhat larger in size than at present, and similar size differences have been found for animal remains in Niah caves, Sarawak [51]. This reduction in size is probably a response to the warmer temperatures now prevailing [23]. Larger animals have a lower area:volume ratio thus reducing the rate of heat loss. As a result, larger animals are better able to survive at lower temperatures.

Orang-utan are now found only north of Lake Toba, leopard and banteng are now extinct in Sumatra and the Javan rhinoceros is almost certainly extinct in Sumatra. Inhabitants of Deli, near what is now Medan, are said to have known a 'buffalo rhinoceros' (peaceful) and a 'pangolin rhinoceros' (savage). The latter was probably the Javan rhinoceros and would doubtless have been hunted to ensure people's safety. Two Javan

Table 1.8   Mammal species remains of which were found in central Sumatra caves by Dubois [21].

Leaf monkey	*Presbytis* sp.
Banded leaf monkey	*Presbytis melalophos*
Pig-tailed macaque	*Macaca nemestrina*
Long-tailed macague	*Macaca fascicularis*
Siamang	*Hylobates syndactylus*
Gibbon	*Hylobates* sp.
Orang-utan	*Pongo pygmaeus*
Common porcupine	*Histrix brachyura*
Sun bear	*Helarctos malayanus*
Leopard	*Panthera pardus*
Tiger	*Panthera tigris*
Tapir	*Tapirus indicus*
Javan rhinoceros	*Rhinoceros sondaicus*
Elephant	*Elephas maximus*
Wild cattle/banteng	*Bos javanicus*

rhinoceros were shot at Tanjung Morawa (just outside the present limits of Medan) in 1883, and the last eight known for Sumatra were shot in South Sumatra between 1925 and 1928 [43]. An unconfirmed shooting of a Javan rhinoceros on the southern boundary of the Way Kambas Reserve in 1961 has been reported [25].

Some mammals of the Sunda Region used to be more widespread than they are today [52] (Table 1.9), perhaps because the flooding of land bridges has prevented recolonization by a species after it had become extinct on one island. It is important to remember that the low sea levels were accompanied by lower temperatures, thus allowing plants and animals of cooler regions, such as the mountain goat *Capricornis sumatraensis* which is nowadays restricted to mountains, to expand their range and cross over to Sumatra from the Asian mainland (section 9.4.4).

The Niah caves of Sarawak have revealed similar finds to the Padang caves but in the lowest (= oldest = 30—40,000 years old) levels of cave sediment at Niah, remains of a giant pangolin *Manis palaeojavanica* have been found [42, 76]. This had previously been found in Java at the famous fossil sites of Trinil, Rali Gajah, Jebis, Ngandong and Sampung. These sites give the best impression in south-east Asia of what the Pleistocene fauna was like.

Table 1.9 Extant (x) and extinct (o) mammals of the Sunda Region. (After Hooijer [52] and the Earl of Cranbrook [16]).

	Java	Sumatra	Borneo
Orang-utan	0	x	x
Siamang	0	x	—
Tiger	x	x	0
Leopard	x	0	—
Sun bear	0	x	x
Elephant	0	x	x
Tapir	0	x	0
Javan rhinoceros	x	0	x
Sumatran rhinoceros	—	x	x
Wild cattle/banteng	x	0	x

Fossils only sample part of the fauna; for example, the larger animals are emphasized because they have more robust bones. In addition, fossils only form under certain conditions; most bones rot in tropical rain forest and so forest fauna are under-represented, but preservation can occur in open plains, along lake shores, along rivers and in dry caves. Considering the land bridges which have existed between Java and Sumatra, some if not most of the Javan fossil fauna probably once lived on Sumatra and it is therefore worthwhile to consider the palaeofauna of Java.

Among the most interesting finds in the Javan fossil beds dating from about 700,000 years ago were various forms of man's immediate forbear, *Homo erectus*, who had probably arrived from southern China. *Homo erectus* was, as the name suggests, erect in stature, and ate mainly seeds and fruit, hunted opportunistically or scavenged, used simple stone tools and lived in groups. His demise was probably caused by an inability to compete with the more advanced *Homo sapiens*.

Remains of eight species of elephants, as many as three coexisting at one time, were found in the same fossil beds as the human remains together with remains of tapir and three species of rhinoceros. There were usually three species of pig living in the same area at any one time, two species of antelope, a hippopotamus and three or four species of deer. These forms are preyed upon by hyaenas, wild dogs, early forms of the tiger and leopard as well as sabre-toothed cats [52, 67, 76].

In the absence of relevant information from Sumatra itself one is left with many questions about the changes - man-made, climate, etc. - that have formed the fauna existing today. One particular question is: why should the leopard have become extinct when it occurred on Sumatra until only a few thousand years ago, still exists on Java and in Peninsular Malaysia, is excellently adapted to hunting in mountains, forests or plains, and when there is an abundance of monkeys and other suitable prey?

1.5.2 Present fauna

Sumatra is one of the richest islands in Indonesia for animals. It has the most mammals (196 species) and its bird list (580 species) is second only to New Guinea. Indeed, new mammal species are still being discovered or recognized [5, 90]. This great wealth is due both to the large size of Sumatra, its diversity of habitats and also its past links with the Asian mainland (sections 1.3.1 and 1.6.2). Nine species of mammal are endemic to mainland Sumatra and a further eleven species are endemic on the isolated group of Mentawai Islands (Table 1.10). Sumatra has fifteen other

Table 1.10 Endemic mammals of Sumatra. (Adapted from FAO/van der Zon [29]).
 * = endemic to the Mentawai islands.

*Pagai Islands horseshoe bat	*Hipposideros breviceps*
Herman's mouse-eared bat	*Myotis hermani*
Sumatran free-tailed bat	*Tadarida doriae*
*Mentawai macaque	*Macaca pagensis*
Thomas' leaf-monkey	*Presbytis thomasi*
*Mentawai leaf-monkey	*Presbytis potenziani*
*Snub-nosed monkey	*Simias concolor*
*Mentawai gibbon	*Hylobates klossii*
Sumatran rabbit	*Nesolagus netscheri*
Aceh squirrel	*Callosciurus albescurus*
*Loga squirrel	*Callosciurus melanogaster*
*Jirit squirrel	*Sundasciurus fraterculus* (?*Lowii*)
*Soksak squirrel	*Lariscus obscurus*
*Mentawai black-cheeked flying squirrel	*Iomys sipora*
*Mentawai orange-cheeked flying squirrel	*Hylopetes sipora*
Hoogerwerf's rat	*Rattus hoogerwerfi*
Kerinci rat	*Maxomys hylomyoides*
Kerinci rat	*Maxomys inflatus*
*Mentawai pencil-tailed tree mouse	*Chiropodomys karlkoopmani*
Sumatran weasel	*Mustela hamakeri*

species confined only to the Indonesian region, including orang-utan. The island also harbours 22 species of Asian mammals found nowhere else within Indonesia (Table 1.11). In addition, Sumatra has populations of several mammals which are virtually extinct in other parts of Indonesia -e.g. Sumatran rhinoceros, elephant, tiger, and the dhole or forest dog *Cuon alpinus* [29].

Table 1.11 Non-endemic Sumatran mammals not found elsewhere in Indonesia.

Dayak fruit bat	*Dyacopterus spadiceus*
big-eared horseshoe bat	*Rhinolophus macrotis*
glossy horseshoe bat	*Rhinolophus refulgens*
arcuate horseshoe bat	*Rhinolophus arcuatus*
Sumatran pipistrelle	*Pipistrellus annectens*
Malaysian noctule	*Pipistrellus stenopterus*
groove-toothed bat	*Phoniscus atrox*
koka leaf monkey	*Presbytis femoralis*
white-handed gibbon	*Hylobates lar*
siamang	*Hylobates syndactylus*
bamboo rat	*Rhizomys sumatrensis*
Singapore rat	*Rattus annadalei*
Edwards giant rat	*Leopoldamys edwardsi*
Sumatran giant rat	*Sundamys infraluteus*
Kinabalu rat	*Rattus baluensis*
mountain spiny rat	*Niviventer rapit*
brush-tailed porcupine	*Atherurus macrourus*
hog badger	*Arctonyx collaris*
smooth-coated otter	*Lutra perspicillata*
Asian golden cat	*Felis temmincki*
tapir	*Tapirus indicus*
mountain goat	*Capricornis sumatraensis*

Sumatra has an extremely rich bird fauna. Of its 580 species, 465 are resident but only 14 are endemic (Table 1.12). The Sumatran list includes 138 bird species confined to the Sunda Region including 16 species found only on Java and Sumatra and 11 species occurring only on Borneo and Sumatra. Thirty-one Asian species found in Sumatra are not found on any other Indonesian islands, e.g. the Great Hornbill *Buceros bicornis* [28].

A phenomenon exhibited by birds is that of migration or making

Table 1.12 Endemic birds of Sumatra (After Bishop [7]). *The male of the northern subspecies is known only by a single tail feather.

English name	Scientific name	Distribution	Habitat
Red-billed partridge	Arborophila rubirostris	northern and central	montane forest
Salvadori's pheasant	Lophura inornata	West Sumatra and Aceh	montane forest
Bronze-tailed peacock pheasant*	Polyplectron chalcurum	northern	montane forest
Island Scops owl	Otus umbra	Enggano and Simeulue Islands	lowland forest
Mentawai Scops owl	Otus mentawi	Mentawai Islands	lowland forest
Kerinci Scops owl	Otus stresmani	Mt. Kerinci	montane forest
Schneider's pitta	Pitta schneideri	northern	montane forest
Striated bulbul	Pycnonotus leucogrammicus	northern	montane forest
Olive-crowned bulbul	Pycnonotus tympanistrigus	northern	montane forest
Blue-masked leafbird	Chloropsis venusta	eastern and southern	hill forest
Shiny whistling thrush	Myiophoneus melanurus	widespread	montane forest
Vanderbilt's jungle babbler	Tricastoma vanderbilti	northern	hill forest
Sumatran wren-babbler	Napothera rufipectus	northern	hill forest
Sumatran niltava	Niltava ruecki	northern	montane forest

regular seasonal movements between alternate areas.[4] Sumatra has about 120 species of migrant birds [29, 59] but very little has been confirmed about their movements. Studies have been conducted in Peninsular Malaysia for several decades, however, and we can be sure that the general principles found for migrant birds there apply also for Sumatra. The majority of the information below comes from Medway [79] and Nisbet [92].

About 60% of the migratory species that visit Peninsular Malaysia breed only in the Palaearctic (see Figure 1.21), 25% breed in the Palaearctic and tropical south and/or south-east Asia, and 15% breed elsewhere in the Oriental Realm. It is estimated that perhaps 12—15 million birds leave the eastern Palaearctic for the south every year, although many species do not come further south than 10°N (e.g. India, Philippines and Indochina). The reason they fly south is to avoid the winter of the northern regions when food is in short supply, and therefore they would be expected to be seen in Sumatra from September to February with a few in March and August. It seems likely that many species merely pass through Peninsular Malaysia on migration and that Sumatra is their ultimate destination. It has been suggested by Nisbet that eleven species make Peninsular Malaysia and/or Sumatra their principal wintering areas (Table 1.13) [92].

Most birds migrate by night since they need the day to feed but some, such as birds of prey which have to use hot air currents to gain height in the air, and barn swallows *Hirundo rustica* which feed on small insects while flying, migrate by day. Huge congregations of swallows can be seen roosting along telephone or electricity wires in many towns (section 13.7.2), for example, along Jl. Prof. M. Yamin in Jambi and Jl. Sutomo in Medan. Barn swallows have been studied in urban and rural Peninsular Malaysia by Medway [78] and comparative studies from Sumatra would be valuable.

The actual mechanism of migration has been studied a great deal and it seems that birds orientate themselves with reference to both star patterns and the earth's magnetic field [115, 116, 129]. Part of the knowledge of migration is inherited but young birds frequently make errors of direction and distance. For these young birds in particular, migration is hazardous

---

4. Bearded pigs *Sus barbatus* are also known to migrate, probably in response to changes in food availability, but records of this seem to be confined to Borneo.

Table 1.13 Palaearctic and temperate Oriental migrants for which Peninsular Malaysia and/or Sumatra provide principal wintering areas. (After Nisbet [92]).

English Name	Scientific Name	Breeding Area
Chinese egret	Egretta eulophotes	Southeast China and Korea
Crested honey buzzard	Pernis apivorus	Northeast Asia
Black-crested baza	Aviceda leuphotes	Northern oriental tropics
Asian dowitcher	Limnodromus semipalmatus	South Siberia
Spotted greenshank	Tringa guttifer	Sakhalin
Eastern crowed leafwarbler	Phylloscopus coronatus	Northeast Asia
Korean flycatcher	Ficedula zanthopygia	North China, Koera, East Siberia
Blue-throated flycatcher	Cyornis rubeculoides	Himalayas to southern China
Migratory jungle flycatcher	Rhinomyias brunneata	Temperate South-east China
Japanese paradise flycatcher	Terpsiphone atrocaudata	Japan, Taiwan
Rufous-headed robin	Erithacus ruficeps	Central Cina
Thick-billed shrike	Lanius tigrinus	North China, East Siberia

because they have no experience of the destination yet have to find a suitable location, find food in sufficient quantities to build up fat stores to last the trip back north, and to leave on time. In the few species that have been studied in Peninsular Malaysia, the date of departure of a species varies by only three or four days from year to year. It seems that some environmental cues such as high or low insect abundance, leaf-fall of trees (see section 7.4) or some climatic feature must be responsible. There is no shortage of possible environmental cues: what is needed is an investigation of their reliability and observations of whether birds actually respond to them.

Reptiles, amphibians and fishes, have been studied taxonomically in depth by authors such as de Beaufort, Bleeker, Fowler, van Kampen, Koumans, de Rooij, Tate Regan and Weber, but the amount of ecological knowledge on these animals is extremely small. There are enormous gaps in our knowledge of invertebrates, not just in knowing something about their ecology, but also in knowing simply what exists [124]. An exception to the latter problem is the large hawkmoths (Sphingidae) [19].

The bibliographies by Tobing [110] and Jacobs and de Boo [54] are extremely useful as preliminary means of exploring the literature on the Sumatran fauna.

1.6 BIOGEOGRAPHY

1.6.1 Differences between realms/zones

For the purposes of zoogeography the world is divided into six realms (Figure 1.21) and Sumatra falls within the Oriental Realm. The majority of animal species in the Oriental Realm are not found elsewhere and in some cases whole subfamilies, families, and even orders are confined within its boundaries, such as leaf monkeys (Cercopithinae), gibbons (Hylobatidae), and flying lemurs (Dermoptera). Only one family of birds (which are obviously more mobile than mammals) is endemic to the Oriental Realm and that is the Irenidae (fairy blue-birds *Irena*, leafbirds *Chloropsis* and ioras *Aegithina* [59]). This family seems to have its centre of evolution in Sumatra [22].

Within the Oriental Realm there are distinct differences between

Figure 1.21 Zoogeographical realms of the world.

regions and the Isthmus of Kra in southern Thailand, which is usually taken as the boundary between the Sunda Region, which includes Sumatra, and mainland Asia, is one of the more obvious regional boundaries. It coincides with a change in vegetation (dry to the north and wet to the south) which is reflected in the fauna (Figure 1.22).

A peculiar zoogeographic distribution has been described by Hoffman [50]. The millipede *Siphoniulus albus* used to be the only species of a monotypic genus, family and order, and until recently was known from only one specimen found near Lake Maninjau in 1890. A second member of the genus has now been found in Guatemala and Hoffman argues that human intervention in this distribution is extremely unlikely. How one explains this widely separated distribution has not yet been established.

Sumatra falls within the floral region of Malesia (which includes all the Indonesian Islands, northern Borneo, Papua (eastern) New Guinea, southern Thailand and the Philippines) and its flora is distinct from that of

Figure 1.22 Range limits of lowland forest birds in the Malay Peninsula. The length of the horizontal bars is proportional to the number of species/subspecies reaching their limit at the different latitudes. (After Wells [117]).

Asia and Australia. The disjunction at the Isthmus of Kra is very marked with 375 genera of plants reaching their northern limit there and 200 genera their southern limit. Within the Malesian region, Sumatra is classified as being part of West Malesia together with the Philippines, Borneo, part of southern Thailand, and Peninsular Malaysia [105] (Figure 1.23). There are some similarities with the western part of Java but that is classified as a sub-region of South Malesia.

52

Figure 1.23 Floral regions of South-east Asia. (After van Steenis [105]).

1.6.2 Differences within the Sunda Region

It has already been shown that the flora and fauna of the Sunda Region are similar largely because of the land bridges that once connected the various parts (section 1.3.1, 1.4.1, 1.5.1). When the sea level last rose, Sumatra was cut off first from Java, then Borneo, and lastly Peninsular Malaysia, and this is reflected in the degree of similarities between the biota (Figures 1.24, 1.25, 1.26). For both animals and plants Java is more different from Sumatra than either Borneo or Peninsular Malaysia.

Not all species arrived in, or moved through, the Sunda Region by the same routes or at the same time, and this is reflected in their distributions (Table 1.14). With our present knowledge it is not possible to state precisely why the tiger never managed to get to Borneo or the lesser mousedeer to Java but the information available about climate, sea levels and vegetation allows hypotheses to be formulated.

Care must be taken when discussing the apparent absence of a species. For instance, it was only recently that one particular biogeographical anomaly was resolved. *Isoetes* is a type of aquatic fern with a world-wide distribution but it had never been seen on Sumatra until found at the small lakes of Danau Sati and Danau Landah Panjang near

Figure 1.24 Percentage of combined totals of plant species shared between the major parts of the Sunda Region. (After FAO/MacKinnon [27]).

Figure 1.25 Percentage of combined totals of birds species shared between the major parts of the Sunda Region. (After FAO/MacKinnon [27]).

Figure 1.26 Percentage of combined totals of mammal species shared between the major parts of the Sunda Region. (After FAO/MacKinnon [27]).

Table 1.14 Examples of mammal distribution in the Sunda Region

	Sumatra	Peninsular Malaysia	Java	Borneo
Tiger	+	+	+	−
Greater mouse deer	+	+	+	+
Lesser mouse deer	+	+	−	+
Mountain goat	+	+	−	−
Orang-utan	+	−	−	+

Kerinci in 1972 [31]. Similarly, the bent-winged bat *Miniopterus pusillus* was known from most of the Oriental Realm except Sumatra [61] until a team from CRES caught one in a cave in North Sumatra in 1982 [49].

Many animals are dependent on walking or being carried on rafts for their dispersal from one area to another but birds, bats, and many insects can fly and can be blown to new areas by strong and perhaps freak winds. Strangely, perhaps, some spiders can also be dispersed by wind. For example, three small nets were held 18 m above the sea surface from a boat sailing in part of the East China Sea, 400 km from the nearest land, and in about two weeks 105 young spiders had been caught. Many of the species caught which are known from Sumatra are also known from Sri Lanka, China, the Philippines and even Australia and Africa, thereby illustrating the effectiveness of their means of dispersal [93].

1.6.3 Differences within Sumatra

It is well known that remote, small islands support fewer species than large islands close to the mainland. After a certain length of time the total number of species on an island will remain more or less constant and this total represents an equilibrium between the colonization of the island by immigrant species and the extinction of its existing species. The rate of colonization is clearly higher when an island is near the mainland because more species stand a chance of crossing the gap. Also, the rate of extinction is clearly greater when an island is smaller because the population of any species will be smaller and the chance of disease and other events

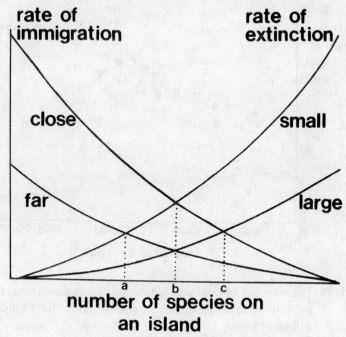

Figure 1.27 The relative number of species on small, distant islands (a) and large, close islands (c). The number of species on large, distant islands or small, close islands, (b) is intermediate.

reducing the population to zero or an unviable number will be greater. These effects are illustrated in Figure 1.27 and represent the foundation of the Theory of Island Biogeography.

The relationship between island size and number of species is relatively constant for a given group of animals and plants. An example for birds is shown in Figure 1.28 and an analysis for mammals has recently been published [45]. In general, however, reducing the island area by ten, halves the number of species. The depauperization of species is not random and the large animals (which have relatively large range requirements and low population densities) are usually the first to be lost. Thus there are no tigers, clouded leopard, elephant or Sumatran rhinoceros on any of the islands west of Sumatra. It often happens on islands, however, that a few species are more abundant and fill a wider niche than they do on the nearby mainland where they have more competitors for the same resources [122, 126].

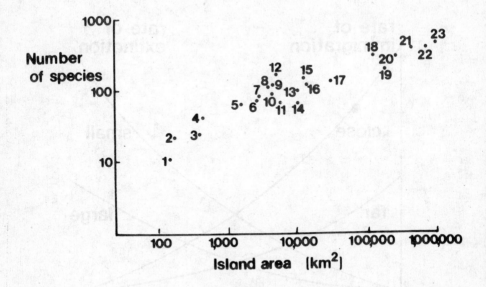

Figure 1.28 The number of land and freshwater birds on various island and archipelagos of Indonesia, together with the Philippines and whole of Irian. *1. Christmas; 2. Bawean; 3. Enggano; 4. Sawa; 5. Simeulue; 6. Alor; 7. Wetar; 8. Nias; 9. Lombok; 10. Belitung; 11. Mentawai; 12. Bali; 13. Sumba; 14. Bangka; 15. Flores; 16. Sumbawa; 17. Timor; 18. Java; 19. Sulawesi; 20. Philippines; 21: Sumatra; 22. Borneo; 23. New Guinea.*

Another effect of island size is the differences in body size of a particular species. For Prevost's squirrel *Callosciurus prevosti*, for example, which is found in Sumatra, Peninsular Malaysia and Borneo, the smallest individuals are found on the smallest islands. Body size increases with island size and the largest individuals are found on Penyilir Island (280 km[2]) and Rupat Island (1360 km[2]) in Riau. On larger islands body size decreases again but the Prevost's squirrels found on mainland Sumatra and Borneo are not as small as those found on very small islands. The reasons for this ∧-shaped curve are the differences found between islands in predation pressure, food limitations, competition between species, and selection for physiological efficiency [44].

It was clear from Table 1.10 in section 1.5.2 that the Mentawai Islands have a large number of unique mammals found nowhere else in the world. In fact, 80% of the non-flying mammals are endemic at some level [1]. The reason for this is can be seen in Figure 1.5: it is more than half a million years since the Mentawai Islands had a land connection via the Batu Islands to the mainland. Long geographical isolation of the Mentawai Islands has allowed the evolution of endemic species and the survival of relicts of an early Indo-Malayan fauna and these 'primitive' forms are extremely significant in studies of the evolution of present Sumatran and Asian biota [1].

The islands to the east of Sumatra have recent connections with the larger land masses [17]. They may even have acted as stepping stones to other islands for animals drifting across the sea on rafts of rotting vegetation carried down rivers during floods. From island biogeographic theory we would expect these islands to have relatively few species and not a great number of endemic forms. This appears to be the case: the Riau/Lingga archipelago and Anambas/Natuna archipelago have no endemic mammals species (although they have some endemic subspecies), and their mammals are far more similar to those on Sumatra and Borneo than are those of Mentawai (Table 1.15). It also appears that the mammals of Bangka and Belitung Islands and the Anambas/Natuna archipelago have a greater affinity with Borneo than with Sumatra.

Table 1.15 Number (and percentage of the combined totals) of mammals on four groups of Sumatran islands shared with the Sumatran mainland and Borneo (Data from FAO/van der Zon [29]).

	Sumatra	Borneo
Riau/Lingga archipelagoes	48 (26)	39 (25)
Bangka and Belitung islands	39 (26)	36 (32)
Anambas/Natuna archipelagoes	50 (21)	48 (24)
Mentawai islands	26 (13)	21 (13)

Two Sumatran islands, Simeulue and Enggano, have probably never had land connections with the mainland and have extremely impoverished faunas - for instance there are no squirrels on either island. Simeulue has three endemic species of snake, one endemic bird (and twenty endemic subspecies - one of a species not found on the Sumatran mainland) and a type of macaque and a type of forest pig that may be distinct species [87]. Enggano has seventeen species of mammal (a similar number to Simeulue) of which three are endemic [18, 102]. Two of the 29 bird species are endemic [56] as is one of the snakes [62].

The contrast between the biota of Sumatra's islands and that of Sumatra itself is by no means the only variation that exists. Within the mainland of Sumatra there are barriers caused by rivers that are too wide, or mountains that are too high, for animals to cross. One of the best illustrations of this is the distribution of the many species and subspecies of leaf monkeys. In fact there are no less than 26 zoogeographic regions on Sumatra and these are shown in Figure 1.29. The major boundaries limit the distributions of whole species or separate ecologically equivalent species. The minor boundaries limit gene exchange and separate subspecies.

Perhaps the most surprising zoogeographic boundary, because it is not obviously caused by a river or strait, is that which runs SW/NE through Lake Toba. Seventeen bird species are found only to the north of Lake Toba and ten only to the south [64]. Table 1.16 shows some examples of split distributions among the mammals. In the cases of the tapir and tarsier there is nothing that entirely replaces them in their ecological niche in the north, but Thomas' leaf monkey is more or less the ecological equivalent to the banded leaf monkey, as the white-handed gibbon is to the dark-handed gibbon [34]. Clearly there must have been a cessation of gene flow along the island that led to such isolated and differentiated faunas. The division between the northern and southern faunas approximately coincides with the position of Lake Toba, and it is possible that the huge eruption caused a wide barrier of bare, volcanic material. Alternatively, the area affected by drying föhn winds (section 1.3.2) near Padang Lawas which may once have been covered with species-poor heath forest (section 8. 11) may have represented a significant barrier to animal movements particularly during the drier periods of the Pleistocene. Presumably the tapir (now found also in Peninsular Malaysia) and the tarsier (now found also in Borneo) never reached the northern part of Sumatra.

Many species of plants and animals are restricted to specific habitats within a zoogeographic region, such as dry lowland, mountain tops or mangrove either because they are unable to compete successfully against other species in other habitats, or because they are tolerant of only a

59

Distribution of four species and twenty one subspecies of leaf monkey to illustrate the zoogeographic zones.
(Based on Chasen [12], Chasen and Kloss [13], Medway [75], Miller [85], Pocock [135], Whitten [125] and Wilson and Wilson [127, 128]. From top left: *Ptn - Presbytis thomasi nubilis; Ptt - P.t . thomasi; Pmm - P. melalophos margae; Pfpa - P. femoralis paenulata; Pfpe - P.f. percura; Pfn - P.f. natuna; Pfr -P.f. rhionis; Pm? - P. melalophos (subspecies not yet named); Pfc - P. femoralis canus; Pm? - P. melalophos (subspecies not yet named); Pmfu[1] - P.m. fuscomurina (lowland form); Pmfu[2] - P.m. fuscomurina (highland form); Pmfl -P.m. fluviatilis; Pmme - P.m. melalophos; Pmm -P.m. nobilis; Ppp - P. potenziani; Pps - P.p. siberu; Pmf - P. melalophos ferruginea; Pmb - P.m. batuana; Pma - P.m. aurata; Pms - P.m. sumatrana.* **The only leaf monkey that lives in the stippled area is the silvered leaf monkey** *Presbytis cristata,* **which is also common throughout the rest of Sumatra in coastal and riverine areas.**

Figure 1.29 Zoogeographic boundaries and units. Thicker lines indicate major boundaries, thinner lines indicate minor boundaries. (After MacKinnon [65]).

Table 1.16 Some examples of split distributions of mammals north and south of the zoogeographic boundary through Lake Toba.

North Only		South Only	
Thomas' leaf monkey	*Presbytis thomasi*	tarsier	*Tarsius bancanus*
white-handed gibbon	*Hylobates lar*	banded leafmonkey	*Presbytis melalophos*
orang-utan	*Pongo pygmaeus*	Sumatran rabbit	*Nesolagus netscheri*
		tapir	*Tapirus indicus*

certain range of conditions. An example of a plant with subtle restrictions to its distribution is the handsome palm *Johannesteijsmannia altifrons*. This palm has been collected from various localities in the northern half of Sumatra but it is most accessible in the Sekundur portion of the Mount Leuser National Park around which local people use the leaves for roofing their houses. It is found only on hillsides, not ridges or valley bottoms, and may be present in one valley but absent in the valleys either side, despite seemingly identical geology, vegetation and topography [20].

1.7 PREHISTORY AND HISTORY

1.7.1 Prehistory of man

The prehistory of Sumatra is poorly known even by comparison with that of neighbouring land masses. Unlike Java, Sumatra has as yet produced no fossil remains of early hominids (human ancestors). Unlike Java, Borneo, the Malay Peninsula, Sulawesi, Flores and Luzon it contains few if any non-marine fossil deposits of pre-Holocene/post-Mesozoic date.

It is not known when stone-age man arrived in Sumatra but rough stone tools found in Peninsular Malaysia beneath ash from the Toba eruption some 75,000 years ago indicate the presence of stone-age man in the Sunda Region from at least that time. What effect the fall of dust had on those people is hard to imagine.

Early man throughout the world inhabited caves. Caves provide shelter, warmth during the periods of lower temperatures, a certain degree of security, and were the focal points of activity [40]. In the Sunda Region the most extensive archaeological excavations of caves have been at Niah, Sarawak, but a similar body of knowledge could result from work at Tiangko Panjang cave in western Jambi. This is just one of about ten sites in southern Sumatra discovered at the start of this century that has revealed stone and wood tools (Figure 1.30) but surveys showed it was the site most likely to contain information spanning a long period [9].

Tiangko Panjang cave is about 13 m above the valley of the Tiangko River, a tributary of the Mesumai River. The rock face above the cave entrance is steep and although the descent to the valley floor is less steep, it is difficult enough to make the location secure from unwanted intrusions. The cave is a tunnel 24 m long and 5—8 m high and wide. With almost 200 m² of floor space, clear headroom, good ventilation, and a well-lighted and sheltered courtyard as well as a secure location, the cave would seem to be a desirable dwelling for early men.

A few small pits have been dug in the cave floor and radiocarbon dating of charcoal samples from different depths showed that man was inhabiting the cave at least 10,000 years ago when the cave floor was 135—160 cm below its present level.

The floor deposits contained hundreds of small stone flakes many of which had been used as tools. This indicates a culture rather more advanced than that which produced large rough flakes (palaeolithic), but not as advanced as that which produced, for example, smooth axe heads (neolithic). Remains of vertebrate animals included a single human tooth, a few deer teeth, a few bone fragments (usually burned) from deer-sized animals, numerous bat bones, many turtle shell fragments, moderate numbers of bird vertebrae and long bones of approximately small-chicken size, a moderate number of fish vertebrae, and teeth of rat-sized rodents. The most common invertebrate remains were snails, the majority of them two edible fresh water species, Brotia costula and Pila sp. (Figure 1.31). Pila is now uncommon near the Tiangko River but Brotia is often eaten by the present inhabitants of the area. Remains of freshwater snails have also been found in Niah cave [40] and in caves in Peninsular Malaysia [24, 74].

There is no sign of agriculture or domestication of animals in any of the remains. We do not know if these early men had begun to experiment

Figure 1.30 Sites in southern Sumatra where prehistoric stone tools have been found. (After Bronson and Asmar [9]). Caves in the Payakumbuh region were probably inhabited by prehistoric man; a CRES team visiting caves at Lho'Nga, North Aceh, found sea shells in cave deposits which were probably taken there by prehistoric man.

Figure 1.31 **Shells** of *Brotia* and *Pila,* both of which were eaten by prehistoric man. Each is about 1 cm long.

with agriculture or animal husbandry as there are no archaelogical remains to offer proof. Indications of rice in cave deposits are generally clear enough and have been found in caves in Sulawesi dating from 6000 years ago [37]. It seems that the inhabitants of Tiangko Panjang were successful enough at exploiting wild forest produce not to need true agriculture until long after other peoples of the region had fully entered the Neolithic culture.

Exploration and analysis of data from Tiangko Panjang cave is not complete but it has many similarities to Niah cave where considerable data have been collected. Because of this it is felt justifiable to consider findings from Niah. The stages of man's development there have been described as Early Stone Age (30—60,000 years ago) with chopping tools; Intermediate I (± 12,000 years ago) with advanced flake tools; Neolithic (± 4,000 years ago) with round axes, quadrangular edges, pottery, mats, and nets; Intermediate II (± 2,000 years ago) with elaborate pots and the first metal, and Iron Age (± 1,3000 years ago) with iron, glass beads, and imported ceramics [40].

At Niah, remains of 58 species of mammals have been found among the archeological remains [81]. It is assumed that no large animals other than flying or scansorial (climbing) types, or natural cave-dwellers, could freely enter the Niah cave (which is more difficult to enter than Tiangko Panjang cave) and hence that all remains of such large animals owe their presence in the cave to the intervention of man. In addition, the skeletal remains are dispersed and fragmented and many of them are

A shell midden of the Hoabinhian culture being mined for lime. Near Stabat, Langkat.

A Hoabinhian knife found in a shell midden by a CRES team.

charred - all suggesting that man was the cause of their presence. Most of the orang-utans were juveniles and this can also be interpreted as proof that they were killed by man since while it is possible that old, dying animals might climb into the cave, it is difficult to imagine why young ones would enter and die there [81].

It has been suggested by palaentologists working in different parts of the world that man has played a significant role in the late Pleistocene or early Holocene extinction of certain animal species - particularly of the gigantic types (either absolutely large, or large by comparison with modern relatives) collectively called the Pleistocene 'mega-fauna'. Opinion is not unanimous but man is now often accepted as a central contributive factor in the progressive decline of many species that occurred in late- and post-glacial Europe and northern Asia, and in the abrupt elimination of the North American mega-fauna about 11,000 years ago and of giant birds in New Zealand much more recently.

What impact did early man in the Sunda Region have on the fauna? Palaeolithic people would probably have set traps and snares to catch medium and large-sized mammals, and bearded pig *Sus barbatus* was consistently the most commonly caught. Other prey were rhinoceros, tapir, mouse deer, and sambar deer. As with any trapping effort, as distinct from deliberate hunting, success depended on an animal coming into the trap and the impact on even local populations of a species was probably negligible.

With the advent of Mesolithic technology, with perhaps a greater use of bone as tips for arrows and spears, there was an increase in the numbers of arboreal mammals (such as monkeys and squirrels) caught. Even so, pigs remained the major source of meat. With the exception of the pigs (which are anyway very fecund), the pre-Neolithic man did not concentrate on any one species and his prey species were taken in an opportunistic rather than deterministic fashion. It seems likely that his impact on the wild populations was trivial [81].

By the time the Neolithic culture had begun (about 4,000 years ago at Niah) [40], man was beginning to make use of a few crop plants such as sago, and to have domestic animals such as pigs *Sus scrofa* [77] and dogs *Canis familiaris* [15, 80]. He then needed to clear land for his agriculture but as the human population was still very low this probably had little impact on the forest. It was, however, the beginning of the end.

As the population grew, so a greater area of land had to be cleared and loss of forest is the single greatest threat to the majority of forest biota and should not be underestimated [95]. In Java, for example, less than half the mammal fauna survived the mid-Pleistocene and the arrival of modern man *Homo sapiens* [67]. For some species, however, there would have been benefits from limited clearance. Herbivores such as deer, tapir, Javan rhinoceros and elephant seek the succulent plants of secondary growth and are relatively common in 'edge habitats', but their presence in or near crops would have encouraged a certain amount of hunting.

There is evidence of forest clearance 11,000 years ago on Taiwan, and of agriculture between 14,000 and 8,000 years ago in Thailand. Archaeological evidence for agriculture dating from about 9,000 years ago has been found in New Guinea and rice was probably cultivated in Sulawesi 6,000 years ago [37]. There is little data available on the early activities of man in Sumatra but the studies of pollen samples from Sumatran lakes described in section 1.4.1. provide some information. Morley found some evidence of forest disturbance near Kerinci from about 7,500 years ago but firmer evidence was found from about 4,000 years ago [88, 89]. Whitehead found evidence of forest clearance around lake Di Atas from about 6,000 years ago [118]. Maloney, studying in the Toba highlands, found strong evidence of forest clearance about 6,200 year ago but changes in the pollen record 8,000 and 9,200 years ago may have been a result of man's activities. Rather less convincing evidence from one of the small lakes in the Toba highlands suggests forest clearance began about 17,800 years ago, but this may have been due to fire rather than felling. However, the possibility that man was using fire to clear forest in order to make hunting game easier should not be discounted [68, 71] (section 9.4.1).

Another set of sources of information about pre-historic man are a number of sites in East Aceh and eastern North Sumatra where enormous middens (rubbish piles) consisting largely of cockle shells have been found [100]. These are the remains of the distinctive 'Hoabinhian' culture which is known from sites in southern China, through Indochina to Peninsular Malaysia and Sumatra [35]. Amongst the millions of cockle shells are found stone tools, bones of both animals and man, and other artifacts such as pottery in the upper (newer) layers. The range of dates for the Sumatran sites are not certain but 8,000 — 3,000 years before present seems likely. Very little is known about these people but their culture seems to have spanned the stages of hunting-gathering (hunting a wide range of animals and harvesting useful wild or semi-domesticated plants) in the early period, to being the prime movers for the development of agriculture in South-east Asia. The information from the sites is not unequivocal but the people do seem to have brought many species of plants such as candlenut *Aleurites*, betel nut *Areca*, kenari *Canarium*, cucumber *Cucumis*, gourd *Lagenaria*, betel pepper *Piper*, and mentalun *Terminalia* into cultivation [37]. Their exploitation of cockles probably resulted in changes in the cockle populations [108] and this may have caused the settlements to move to seek unexploited areas. Most of these middens have been more or less destroyed for the manufacture of slaked lime for whitewash [134].

In later prehistoric periods, the story of Sumatra is no more complete or clear; many finds do not have recorded locations and the total is relatively few. Bronze-Iron Age bronze kettledrums have been found near Lake Kerinci, Bengkulu and Lake Ranau, other bronze vessels from the Kerinci area, and statues from Bangkinang in West Riau [46].

Megaliths - large stones either set standing, hollowed out or carved into a bas relief showing scenes of animals and men - have been found in Lampung (e.g. at Kenali and Bojong), Riau and West Sumatra (on the banks of the River Kamparkanan), and in Jambi (near Kerinci), but the most famous megaliths are those on the Pasemah Plateau (Bengkulu/South Sumatra), and on Samosir and Nias Islands. It used to be thought that the stones at Pasemah dated from historic times, but it is now known that they were made much earlier (perhaps 100 A.D.) during the Bronze-Iron Age [38, 46, 48]. The megalithic culture of Samosir continued until quite recently and on Nias certain vestiges remain today. Virtually nothing is known of how people in the Bronze-Iron Age culture lived in Sumatra nor how they interacted with their environment, other than that they were agriculturists.

The last remaining living elements of the megalithic culture on Nias, of hunter/gatherer culture of the Kubu people of Jambi/Riau/West Sumatra [63], and of Neolithic/Bronze age culture on Siberut Island [97, 123], are still available for environmental study now. They represent opportunities to study the responses to change of physical and biological resources such as drugs, rotan, semi-domesticated crops and other pro-

68

ducts. Although there is a new awareness of the information that can be
learnt from people who live close to, and rely upon, the natural environment, it is already too late to learn anything much from the orang Mamaq
of Indragiri, the orang Sakai and Akit of Siak, the orang Lubu and Ulu of
South Tapanuli, the orang Benua or Mapur of the Riau/Lingga archipelago and Bangka Island or from the orang Enggano [63, 133].

1.7.2 History - its effects on natural ecosystems

The transition between prehistory (no written records) and history
(written records) will clearly depend upon the people being considered; for
some, such as those on Sumatra's east coast, history began perhaps a
thousand years before it began for some of the inland tribes. In comparison
with Java, there is as yet relatively little know about the early historical
period of Sumatra, except about the economics and politics of the Srivijaya
Empire [130]. A recent review of Sumatra's early history is given in Miksic
[84].

Sumatra became known to Indian traders as the Island of Gold and
settlements may have been established on the Sumatran coast by 200 A.D.
The earliest Hindu-Buddhist artefact found in Sumatra (in Palembang) is a
statue of Buddha which dates from the late 5th century. The earliest
known written inscriptions (in fact the oldest in Indonesia) date from
683—686 A.D. (i.e. the early period or Sailendra Dynasty of the Srivijaya
Empire) and were found near Palembang and at Kota Kapur on Bangka
Island [48].

A few statues of Buddha and other remains from before 1000 A.D.
have been found in Jambi, Simangambat (South Tapanuli) and by the
Lematang River near Palembang, but most Hindu or Hindu-Buddhist
remains of temples or insribed stones on Sumatra date from the 11th to
13th centuries. Two sites with remains of temples or biara are worthy of
particular mention: Muara Takus on the Kampar Hulu River near
Bangkinang, Riau, and Padang Lawas in South Tapanuli [98]. Sumatra
also had close trading ties with South India, and a Tamil inscription written
in 1088 A.D. found near Barus, now a small port in Central Tapanuli, describes one such commercial relationship [48]. In about 1281 the first Islamic kingdoms were established on Sumatra's northern coast (although Islam
probably entered Sumatra through Barus) but it was a few centuries before

A long Islamic grave of an early Indian nobleman at **Barus, Central Tapanuli**.

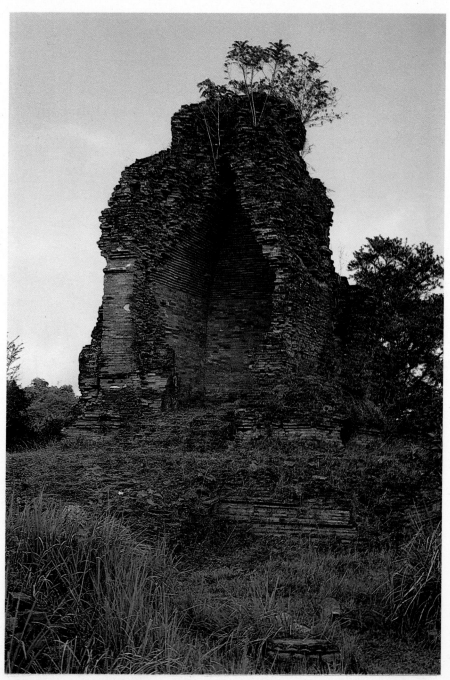

One of the Hindu-Buddhist temples near Padang Lawas, South Tapanuli.

their influence affected the rest of Sumatra [63].

The environmental impact of those and other inland kingdoms during the first half of the second millenium is not certain. The temple sites at Muara Takus and Padang Lawas were not centres of population and probably had only a ceremonial function although they may have lain on trading routes [84]. Hindus from India introduced wet rice culture, the plough, cotton and the spinning wheel to Sumatra. We may therefore envisage small, more or less permanent, rural communities surrounded by a limited area of sawah. A gold mine may have been nearby. Around these there would have been some areas in which people practised genuine shifting agriculture (i.e. leaving fields fallow for 25—30 years before using them again) (section 11.9.2). This type of land use creates a floristically diverse forest edge and favours many species of animals as well as maintaining and conserving soil structure and nutrients. Towns probably only existed as trading centres, primarily on the east coast.

The earliest substantial settlement found in the whole of Indonesia is Kota Cina, half-way between Medan and Belawan in North Sumatra [72]. This may date back to 1000 A.D. At that time, seagoing vessels would have been able to anchor in the immediate vicinity of Kota Cina itself, but coastal accretion, a common phenomenon at many places on Sumatra's east coast (section 2.5) has resulted in the site being progressively isolated from navigable waters. Chinese documents written in 1282 mention a locality that is possibly Kota Cina. It was a dependency of Srivijaya (although by then Srivijaya had lost most of its power), and was known as a source of fragrant resins (damar) [86]. Kota Cina appears to have been a very cosmopolitan town for remains of Chinese and Persian ceramics and other pottery, Chinese coins, Indian Buddha statues, and coins from Sri Lanka have been found. Kota Cina was abandoned by the late 14th century at the same time that Islam was beginning to become established, Malaca was becoming the region's major trading centre, and relations between Sumatra and Java were disturbed because of the increasing power of the Majapahit Empire.

It is not known precisely what products were exported from Kota Çina but damar resin, camphor and beeswax from the highlands are likely, and gold, lead ore, ivory and fine timber probably contributed to the trade. There is no evidence of Sumatran agricultural produce being exported, and the impact of Kota Cina and similar settlements on natural ecosystems was probably minimal.

A settlement from the same period as Kota Cina may have existed at Muara Kumpeh, 72 km downstream along the Batanghari from the city of Jambi (section 2.5). This settlement may have been similar in its function then as Sungsang, at the mouth of the Musi River in South Sumatra, is now [66].

In northern South-east Asia, archaeological remains have been found for many cities, their satellite towns and hinterlands. In southern South-east Asia, however, with the exception of Java, no such early cities have been found. Yet Srivijaya, the hypothetical capital of the Sumatra-based empire of the same name, should rival central Java and southern Thailand for producing the first capital city in the Sunda Region. It was the administrative and intellectual centre of an empire which is known from Chinese historical records to have ruled the seas of South-east Asia and to have lasted for over five hundred years from before 700 A.D.

Palembang has always been identified as the location of Srivijaya. It used to be a port nearer the sea, it has a strategic position for local and international trade, Chinese sailing directions indicate Srivijaya was in the Palembang area, and some ancient inscriptions had been found there that mention Srivijaya. In 1974, however, thorough archaelogical excavations were conducted and not a single piece of evidence could be found for a settlement or related hinterland dating from before the 14th century - when the empire had already begun to crumble [10].

This has some important environmental/historical implications. Palembang was supposed to be the only early (pre-1000 A.D.) urban site south of the Thailand/Malaysian border. Now that Palembang, and probably the whole area drained by the Musi River, has been ruled out, there remains no example, even supposed, of an early urban culture in Sumatra.

Srivijaya *did* exist, but it must have been a form of habitation that would have been described as a city by a visitor, yet not leave obvious remains. One of the four requirements suggested by Bronson and Wisseman for such a city is that it exist in comparative isolation from its hinterland [10]. This seems unlikely at first but at the peak of the history of Malacca in the 15th-16th century, this important port was surrounded by uninhabited forest, and its population of about 20,000 people depended on supplies from Java and Thailand for its subsistence. Thus, even though the Srivijaya empire was being coordinated from Sumatra, its emphasis was on controlling and profiting from trade rather than on controlling the interior, and so the impact on the natural environment may have been very slight. Some trade in Sumatran goods may have been conducted from the town of Srivijaya (as at Kota Cina later) but it could have served as an entrepot, similar to Singapore at its founding.

The ineffectiveness of Srivijaya as a cultural missionary, except at a few places along the coast, is illustrated by the survival in nearby areas of forest people with primitive cultures: the orang Mapur in the interior of Bangka Island, the Kubu of the Jambi/Riau forests, the Akit of the Siak and Bengkalis region, and the nomads of Batam Island [103].

The history of the islands to the east of Sumatra was also not greatly affected by the Srivijaya Empire: as stated before, Srivijaya was more concerned with trade than with territory. Instead, the Orang Laut, specifically the Celates, were far more important. These were groups of nomadic people, not necessarily pirates, whose culture and economy were based on the coasts and seas. They tended to build settlements away from established centres of population [103] and because they were concerned only with marine products they never strayed inland from the coast. For example, the hilly interior of Belitung Island was completely deserted until tin mining began in 1851, although there were numerous settlements of Orang Laut around the coast [103].

So, it was with the arrival of Portugese, Dutch and British in the 16th, 17th, 18th and 19th centuries that most of the natural ecosystems of Sumatra received their first major shocks. Before then the majority of the landscape probably consisted of low-density, small-scale agriculture among a scarcely-disturbed forest and with virtually no urbanization [73]. To supply the spice tade, land had to be cleared and early plantations of tobacco and other crops were also established. However, not all large-scale and clearance was directed towards the plantation industry or even conducted in response to Christian missionary influence. Burton and Ward were the first Europeans to enter the Toba region and the description of their journey from Sibolga in 1824 makes instructive reading because they depict a largely deforested land much of it planted with rice. For example:

> "The woodland had already given place to grassy plains; and the mountain on which we stood had been cleared on every side for cultivation, merely retaining its original forest in a tuft at the top . . . The soil now became san-

dy and grey and the hills were entirely free from wood, and planted with the sweet potatoe in many instances to the very tops . . . The principal object of the picture was an uneven plain, ten or twelve miles long and three broad, forming a vast unbroken field of rice . . . The plain was surrounded by hills from five hundred to one thousand feet high, in a state of cultivation; and the whole surrounding country was perfectly free from wood, except the summits of two or three mountains said to be the abode of monstrous serpents and evil spirits" [11].

Descriptions, land-use maps and photographs of the Toba, Alas and Karo areas at the turn of the century are surprisingly similar to today [53, 112, 113].

1.8 PRESENT STATE OF NATURAL ECOSYSTEMS

Before beginning the description of the various ecosystems of Sumatra, it is instructive to consider the pressure on forested land in the provinces. It has already been shown (section 1.4.2) that the provinces have different areas of the different natural vegetation types and that the proportion remaining in reserves varies. To complete the picture we need to include information on the most important component of Sumatran ecosystems, Man (Table 1.17). The figures do not show what we would hope to find, namely that provinces with most cleared land produce the most food. The flatter provinces of Riau, Jambi, and South Sumatra have a relatively large area of cleared land *per capita* but their rice production *per capita* is the lowest. This is to be compared with the figures for Aceh and North Sumatra where the areas of cleared land are low but the apparent productivity of the land for rice is the greatest. What relationship is there between these findings and the protection of natural ecosystems in watershed and other areas? What can be learned from the workings of natural ecosystems that might help to increase the efficiency of land use and land productivity? These questions will have to be answered in the future by resource managers with knowledge of Sumatra and of the intricacies of its natural and man-made ecosystems.

Table 1.17 Land, man, rice and timber. (Data from Biro Pusat Statistik [6] and FAO/MacKinnon [26]).

	Area (1000s ha)	Official area of forest (1000s ha)	Actual area of remaining forest (1000s ha)	% of province under maintaining forest	Population (1000s)	Trans-migration grants 1980 planned	Area per capita	Cleared land per capita	Forest left per capita	1976 rice production (1000s tons)	Rice production per ha cleared land	Rice production per capita (tons)	1976 Timber export (1000 m³)
Aceh	5,539	4,135	3,967	72	2,608	16,550	2.1	0.60	1.5	921	0.59	0.40	738
North Sumatra	7,079	2,347	2,489	35	8,357	15,700	0.8	0.55	0.5	1.916	0.41	0.27	651
West Sumatra	4,976	2,634	1,983	39	3,402	13,600	1.5	0.88	0.6	957	0.31	0.32	366
Riau	9,456	7,333	4,873	52	2,163	53,000	4.4	2.12	2.3	322	0.07	0.17	1,026
Jambi	4,492	3,470	2,103	47	1,439	25,250	3.1	1.66	1.5	417	0.17	0.37	1,239
South Sumatra	10,369	4,221	2,491	24	4,521	100,600	2.2	1.70	0.5	959	0.12	0.24	765
Bengkulu	2,117	1,612	1,206	57	768	13,000	2.8	1.19	1.6	222	0.24	0.37	30
Lampung	3,331	659	659	20	4,622	—	0.7	0.58	0.1	705	0.26	0.21	83
Total/Average	47,361	26.902	19,771	42	27,980	237,700	1.7	0.99	0.7	6.423	0.23	0.29	4.892

REFERENCES

1. Anon. (1980). *Saving Siberut: A Conservation Masterplan.* World Wildlife Fund, Bogor. (10.2.1)
2. Ashton, P.S. (1982). Dipterocarpaceae. *Flora Malesiana I* 9: 237—552.
3. Beek, C.G.G. van (1982). *A Geomorphological and Pedological study of the Gunung Leuser National Park, North Sumatera, Indonesia.* Wageningen Agricultural University, Wageningen, (23.3.5)
4. Bemmelen, R.W. van (1929). The origin of Lake Toba. In *Proc. 4th Pac. Sci. Cong. (Java, 1929). Vol. IIA* (Physical papers), pp. 115—124. (3.1.1)
5. Bergmans, W. and Hill, J.E. (1980). On a new species of *Rousettus* Gray, 1921, from Sumatra and Borneo (Mammalia: Megachiroptera). *Bull. Br. Mus. Nat. Hist.* 38: 95—104. (12.8.66)
6. Biro Pusat Statistik (1980). *Statistik Indonesia.* Biro Pusat Statistik, Jakarta. (19.6.1)
7. Bishop, D. (in press). *Endemic Island Birds of the World.* ICBP, Cambridge.
8. BPPP/Soepraptohardjo, M., Soekardi, M., Kurnia, H.D. and Suhardjo, S. (1979). *Sumber daya lahan/tanah dan potensinya di Pulau Sumatera.* Konsultasi Penelitian Pertanian Menunjang Pembangunan Sumatera. Lembaga Penelitian Tanah, Bogor. (23.4.14)
9. Bronson, B. and Asmar, T. (1976). Prehistoric Investigations at Tiangko Panjang cave, Sumatra: An Interim Report. *Asian Perspectives* 18: 128—145. (23.7.14)
10. Bronson, B. and Wisseman, J. (1978). Palembang as Srivijaya. *Asian Perspectives* 19: 220—239. (23.7.6)
11. Burton, R. and Ward, N. (1827). Report on a journey into Batak country in the interior of Sumatra in the year 1824. *Trans. R. As Soc.* 1: 485—513. (23.7.3).

75

12. Chasen, H.N. (1940). A handlist of Malayan mammals. *Bull. Raff. Mus. S'pore* 15. (12.8.32)
13. Chasen, F.N. and Boden Kloss, C. (1927). Spolia Mentawiensia - Mammals. *Proc. Zool. Soc.Lond.* 1927: 797—840. (12.8.63)
14. Climap (1976). The surface of the ice-age earth. *Science* 191: 1131—1137.
15. Clutton-Brock, J. (1959). Niah's Neolithic dog. *Sarawak Mus. J.* 9: 142—145. (12.13.36)
16. Cranbrook, Earl of. Personal communication.
17. Dammerman, K.W. (1926). The fauna of Durian and Rhio-Lingga Archipelago. *Treubia* 8: 281—326. (12.13.9)
18. De Jong, J.K. (1938). Een en ander over Enggano. *Natuur Tijd. Ned.-Indie* 98: 3—46. (12.13.39)
19. Diehl, E.W. (1980). *Heterocera Sumatrana. Band 1: Sphingidae.* Distributor: E.W. Classey Ltd., London. (12.4.27)
20. Dransfield, J. (1972). The genus *Johannesteijsmannia* H.E. Moore Jr. *Gdns' Bull. S'pore* 26: 63—84. (12.1.44)
21. Dubois, E. (1891). Voorloopig bericht omtrent het onderzoek naar de Pleistocene en tertiarire vertebraten-fauna van Sumatra en Java, gedurende heb jaar 1890. *Natuur. Tijd. Ned.-Indie* 51: 93—100. (23.6.11)
22. Dunn, D.F. (1974). Zoogeography of the Irenidae (Aves: Passeres). *Biotropica* 6: 165—174. (12.7.18)
23. Edwards, W.E. (1967). The late-pleistocene extinction and diminution in size of many mammalian species. In *Pleistocene Extinc tions: A search for a cause.* (ed. P.S. Martin and H.E. Wright), pp. 141—154. Yale University Press, New Haven. (23.6.9)
24. Evans, J.H.N. (1918). Preliminary report on cave exploration, near Lenggong, Upper Perak. *J. Fed. Malay States Mus.* 7: 227—234.
25. FAO/Wind, J., Soepomo, D. and Isnan, W. (1979). *Way Kambas Game Reserve Management Plan 1980/81—1984/5.* Field Report No. 5, INS/78/061, FAO, Bogor. (10.2.9)
26. FAO/MacKinnon, J. (1982). *National Conservation Plan for Indonesia, Vol. II. Sumatra.* FAO, Bogor. (10.2.16)

27. _____: (1982). *National Conservation Plan for Indonesia, Vol. 1. Introduction: Evaluation Methods and Overview of National Nature Richness.* FAO, Bogor. (10.2.10)

28. FAO/MacKinnon, J.R. and Wind, J. (1979). *Birds of Indonesia* (draft). UNDP/FAO, Bogor. (12.7.41)

29. FAO/Zon, A.P.M. van der (1979). *Mammals of Indonesia.* FAO, Bogor. (12.8.36)

30. Flenley, J.R. (1980). *The Equatorial Rain Forest: a geological history.* Butterworths, London. (23.6.13)

31. Flenley, J.R. and Morley, P.J. (1978). *Isoetes* in Sumatra. *J. Biogeog.* 5: 57—58. (12.1.102)

32. Francis, P. (1983). Giant volcanic calderas. *Scient. Amer.* 248: 60—70. (23.3.10)

33. Geyh, M.A., Kudrass, H.R. and Streif, H. (1979). Sea level changes during the late Pleistocene and Holocene in the Strait of Malacca. *Nature, Lond.* 278: 441—443.

34. Gittins, S.P. (1978). The species range of the gibbon *Hylobates agilis.* In *Recent Advances in Primatology vol. 3. Evolution* (ed. D.J. Chivers and K.A. Joysey), pp. 319—321. Academic Press, London.

35. Glover, I.C. (1977). The Hoabinhian: hunter-gatherers or early agriculturalists in SE Asia? In *Hunters, Gatherers and First Farmers Beyond Europe* (ed. J.V.S. Megaw), pp. 145—166. Leicester Univ. Press, Leicester. (23.6.2)

36. _____: (1978). Report on a visit to archaeological sites near Medan, Sumatra Utara, July 1975. *Bull. Indo-Pacific Prehistory Ass.* 1: 56—60. (23.6.19)

37. _____: (1979). Prehistoric plant remains from Southeast Asia, with special reference fo rice. *South Asian Archaeology* 77: 7—37. (23.6.7)

38. _____: (1979). The Late Prehistoric Period in Indonesia. In *Early South-East Asia* (ed. R.B. Smith and W. Watson), pp. 167—184. Oxford Univ. Press, Oxford. (23.6.3)

39. Haile, N.S. (1975). Postulated late Cainozoic high sea level in the Malay Peninsula. *J. Malay. Br. R. Asiatic Soc.* 48: 78—88. (23.6.20)

40. Harrisson, T. (1958). The Caves of Niah: A History of Prehistory Sarawak Mus. J. 8: 549—595. (23.6.21)
41. _____:(1967). Niah caves Progress Report to 1967. Sarawak Mus. J. 15: 95—96. (23.6.22)
42. Harrisson, T., Hooijer, D.A. and Medway, Lord (1961). An extinct giant pangolin and associated mammals from Niah Cave, Sarawak. Nature, Lond. 189: 166. (12.13.35)
43. Hazewinkel, J.C. (1933). Rhinoceros sundaicus in Zuid Sumatra. Trop. Natuur. 22: 101—109. (12.8.17)
44. Heaney, L.R. (1978). Island area and body size of insular mammals: Evidence from the tri-coloured squirrel (Callosciurus prevosti) of Southeast Asia. Evolution 32: 29—44. (12.8.31)
45. _____: (1984). Mammalian species richness on islands on the Sunda Shelf, Southeast Asia. Oecologia 61: 11—17.
46. Heekeren, H.R. van (1958). The bronze-iron age of Indonesia. Verh. Kon. Inst. Taal- Land- Volkenkunde 22. (23.7.8)
47. Hehuwat, F. (1982). Tao Toba: Tumor Batak, Tufa Toba, Depresi Vulcanotektonik; Sejarah Terjadinya Danau Toba. Suara Alam 16: 18—20. (3.1.6)
48. Heine-Gelde R. (1972). The archaeology and art of Sumatra. In Sumatra: Its History and People (by E.M. Loeb), pp. 305—331. Oxford Univ. Press, London. (23.7.13)
49. Hill, J.E. (1983). Bats (Mammalia: Chiroptera) from Indo-Australia. Bull. Brit. Mus. Nat. Hist. (Zool.) 45: 103—208
50. Hoffman, R.L. (1979). A siphoniulid millipede from Central America. Rev. Suisse Zool. 86: 535—540. (12.4.54)
51. Hooijer, D.A.: (1962). Prehistoric bone: The gibbons and monkeys of Niah Great Cave. Sarawak Mus. J. 9: 428—449.
52. _____: (1975). Quaternary mammals west and east of Wallace's Line. Neth. J. Zool. 25: 46—56. (23.6.8)
53. Hügel, A von (1896). The land of the Bataks. Geog. J. 7: 75—82, 175—183. (23.7.2)
54. Jacobs, M. and Boo, T.J.J. de (1983). Conservation Literature on Indonesia: Selected Annotated Bibliography. Rijksherbarium, Leiden.
55. James, F. (in prep.). The late Quaternary vegetational history of the upper Kerinci valley, Sumatra, Indonesia. MSc thesis, Univerity of Hull, Hull.

57. Kartawinata, K. (1974). *Report on the State of Knowledge on Tropical Forest Ecosystems in Indonesia.* Herbarium Bogoriense LBN-LIPI, Bogor. (12.10.87)

58. _____: (1980). Classification and utilization of Indonesian forests. *BioIndonesia* 7: 95—106. (10.4.20)

59. King, B., Woodcock, M. and Dickinson, E.C. (1975). *A Field Guide to the Birds of S.E. Asia.* Collins, London. (12.7.45)

60. Laumonier, Y., Gadrinab, A. and Purnajaya (1983). *Southern Sumatra: Map of Vegetation and Environmental Conditions, 1:1,000,000.* Institut de la Carte International du Tapis Végétal/ SEAMEO-BIOTROP, Bogor.

61. Lekagul, B and McNeely, J.A. (1977). *The Mammals of Thailand.* Association for the Conservation of Wildlife, Bangkok. (12.8.21)

62. Lieftinck, M.A. (1984). The Odonata of Enggano. *Treubia* 19: 279—300. (12.4.53)

63. Loeb, E.M. (1972). *Sumatra: Its History and People.* Oxford Univ. Press, Oxford. (23.7.13)

64. MacKinnon, J. Personal communication.

65. _____: unpublished.

66. McKinnon, E.E. (1982). A brief note on Muara Kumpeh Hilir: An early port site on the Batang Hari? *SPAFA Digest* 3: 37—40. (23.6.18)

67. McNeely, J.A. (1978). Dynamics of extinction in Southeast Asia. *BIOTROP Spec. Publ.* 8: 137—158. (12.11.2)

68. Maloney, B.K. (1980). Pollen analytical evidence for early forest clearance in North Sumatra, Indonesia. *Nature, Lond.* 287: 324—326. (23.6.6)

69. _____: (1981). A pollen diagram from Tao Sipinggan, a lake site in the Batak Highlands of North Sumatra. *Modern Quatern. Res. S.E. Asia.* 1981: 57—76.

70. _____: (1983). The terminal Pleistocene in Sumatra, Indonesia. *Quatern. Newsl.* 39: 1—9

71. _____: (in press). Man's impact on the rain forests of West Malesia: the palynological record. In *Proc. 7th Aberdeen-Hull Symp. Malesian Ecol.*

72. Manning, A., McKinnon, E.E. and Treloar, F.E. (1980). Analysis of

79

gold artifacts from the Kota Cina site near Medan, Sumatra. J. Malay. Br. R. Asiatic Soc. 53: 102—113. (23.7.4)

73. Marsden, W. (1811). *The History of Sumatra*. Republished by Oxford Univ. Press, Kuala Lumpur, 1966.

74. Medway, Lord: (1966). Animal remains from Lobang Angus. *Sarawak Mus. J.* 14: 184—216.

75. _____: The monkeys of Sundaland: ecology and systematics of the cercopithecids of a humid equatorial environment. In *Old World Monkeys: Evolution, Systematics and Behaviour* (ed. J.R. and P.H. Napier), pp. 513—553. Academic Press, London.

76. _____: (1972). The Quaternary mammals of Malesia. In *The Quaternary Era in Malasia* (ed. P. Ashton and M. Ashton), pp. 63—98. Univ. Hull, Hull. (23.6.15)

77. _____: (1973). The antiquity of domesticated pigs in Sarawak. *J. Malay. Br. R. Asiatic Soc.* 46: 169—178.

78. _____: (1973).A ringing study of migratory barn swallows in West Malaysia. *Ibis* 115: 60—86. (12.7.43)

79. _____: (1974). Migratory birds. In *Birds of the Malay Peninsula* (by Lord Medway and D.R. Wells), pp. 35—55. Witherby, London. (12.7.42)

80. _____: (1977). The ancient domestic dogs of Malaysia. *J. Malay. Br. Royal Asiatic Soc.* 50: 14—27. (12.13.37)

81. _____: (1979). The Niah excavations and an assessment of the impact of early man on mammals in Borneo. *Asian Perspectives* 20: 51—69. (23.6.5)

82. Meijer, W. (1981). Sumatra as seen by a botanist. *Indonesia Circle* 25: 17—27. (10.12.89)

83. Meijer, W. and Withington, W.A. (1981). A map of vegetation and land use in Sumatra. *Indonesia Circle* 24: 29—37. (10.4.12)

84. Miksic, J. (1979). *Archaeology, Trade and Society in Northeast Sumatra*. PhD thesis, Cornell University. (23.7.9)

85. Miller, C.S. Jr. (1942). Zoological results of the George Vanderbilt Sumatran Expedition, 1936—1939.Part V - Mammals collected by Frederick A. Ulmer Jr. on Sumatra and Nias. *Proc. Acad. Nat. Sci. Phil.* 94: 107—165. (12.8.64)

86. Milner, A.C., McKinnon, E.E. and Luckman, S. (1978). Aru and Kota Cina. *Indonesia* 26: 1—42. (23.6.23)

80

87. Mitchell, A.H. (1981). *Report on an survey of Pulau Simeulue, Aceh, with a proposal for a Suaka Margasatwa.* World Wildlife Fund, Bogor. (10.1.12)
88. Morley R.J. (1980). Changes in dry-land vegetation in the Kerinci area of Sumatra during the late Quaternary period. *Proc. IV Intern. Palynol. Conf., Lucknow (1976-77)* 3: 2—10.
89. —————: (1982). A palaeoecological interpretation of a 10,000 year pollen record from Danau Padang, central Sumatra, Indonesia. *J. Biogeog.* 9: 151—190.
90. Musser, G.G. (1979). Results of the Archbold Expeditions. Part 102. The species of *Chiropodomys* arboreal mice of Indochina and the Malay Archipelago. *Bull. Am. Mus. Nat. Hist.* 162: 377—446. (12.8.34)
91. Ninkovich, D., Shackleton, N.J., Abdel-Monem, A.A., Obradevich, J.D. and Izett, G. (1978). K-Ar age of the later Pleistocene eruption of Toba, North Sumatra. *Nature, Lond.* 276: 574—577.
92. Nisbet, I.C.T. (1974). The eastern palearctic migration system in operation. In *Birds of the Malay Peninsula* (by Lord Medway and D.R. Wells), pp. 57—69. Witherby, London. (12.7.44)
93. Okuma, D. and Kisimoto, R. (1981). Air-borne spiders collected over the East China Sea. *Jap. J. appl. Ent. Zool.* 25: 296—298. (12.4.49)
94. Oldeman, L.R., Las, I. and Darwis, S.N. (1979). An Agroclimatic Map of Sumatra. *Contr. Centr. Res. Inst. Agric. Bogor* 52: 1—35. (1.1.1)
95. Olson, S.L. and James, H.F. (1982). Fossil birds from the Hawaiian Islands: Evidence for wholesale extinction by Man before Western contact. *Science* 217: 633—635. (23.6.1)
96. Ricklefs, R.E. (1979). *Ecology.* Chiron, London. (23.2.1)
97. Schefold, R. (1980). *Spielzeug für die Seelen.* Museum Rietberg, Zurich. (15.1.10)
98. Schnitger, F.M. (1938). The archaeology of Hindoo Sumatra. *Int. Archiv. v. Ethnogr.* 35 (Suppl.): 1—44. (23.7.5)
99. —————: (1939). *Forgotten Kingdoms in Sumatra.* Brill, Leiden. (23.7.7)

100. Schurmann, H.M.E. (1931). Kjökkenmöddinger und paläolithicum in Nord Sumatra. *Tijd. Kon. Ned. Aard. Gen.* 48: 905—923.

101. Smith, A.C. and Briden, J.C. (1977). *Mesozoic and Cenozoic Palaeocontinental Maps.* Cambridge University Press, Cambridge.

102. Sody, H.J.V. (1940). On the mammals of Enggano. *Treubia* 17: 391—401. (12.8.30)

103. Sopher, D.E. (1977) *The Sea Nomads.* National Museum, Singapore. (2.5.15)

104. Steenis, C.G.G.J. van (1935). Maleische vegetatiescheten. *Tijd. Kon. Ned. Aard. Gen.* 52: 25—67, 171—203, 363—398.

105. _____: (1950). The delimitation of Malaysia and its main plant geographical divisions. *Flora Malesiana* 1: 70—75. (12.1.97)

106. _____: (1957). Outline of vegetation types in Indonesia and some adjacent regions. *Proc. Pac. Sci. Cong.* 8: 61—97. (12.10.51)

107. Strien, N.J. van (1977). *Sumatran Birds: Supplement to the Field Guide to the Birds of South east Asia.* Agriculture Dept., Wageningen. (12.7.45)

108. Swadling, P. (1976). Changes induced by human exploitation in prehistoric shellfish population. *Mankind* 10: 156—162. (23.6.16)

109. Tjia, H.D. (1980). The Sunda Shelf, Southeast Asia. *Z. Geomorph.* 24: 405—427. (23.3.6)

110. Tobing, D.H. (1968). *A Preliminary Bibliography on Fauna, Flora, Vegetation Conservation of Nature and Natural Resources of Sumatra.* Nature Conservation Dept., Agricultural University, Wageningen. (27.1.16)

111. Verstappen, H.T. (1973). *A Geomorphological Reconnaisance of Sumatra and Adjacent islands (Indonesia).* Wolters - Noordhoff, Groningen. (23.3.1)

112. Volz, W. (1909). *Nord-Sumatra. Band I - Die Batakländer.* Dietrich Reimer, Berlin.

113. _____: (1912). *Nord-Sumatra. Band II - Die Gajoländer.* Dietrich Reimer, Berlin.

114. Walker, D. (1982). Speculations on the Origin and Evolution of Sunda Sahul Rain Forests. In *Biological Diversification in the*

Tropics (ed. G. Prance), pp. 554—575. Columbia Univ. Press, New York. (23.6.14)

115.Wallraf, H.G. (1978). Proposed principles of magnetic field perception in birds. *Oikos* 30: 188—194. (12.7.19)

116.Wallraf, H.G. and Gelderloos, O.G. (1978). Experiments on migratory orientation of birds with simulated stellar sky and geomagnetic field: method and preliminary results. *Oikos* 30: 207—215. (12.7.20)

117.Wells, D.R. (1974). Resident birds. In *Birds of the Malay Peninsula* (by Lord Medway and D.R. Wells). Witherby, London. (12.7.23)

118.Whitehead, J.C. (in prep.). *Late Quaternary Vegetational History of the West Sumatran Highlands*. PhD thesis, University of Hull, Hull.

119.Whitmore, T.C. (1975). *Tropical Rainforests of the Far East*. Clarendon, Oxford. (12.10.8)

120._____: (1982). Palaeoclimate and vegetation history. In *Wallace's Line and Plate Tectonics* (ed. T.C. Whitmore), pp. 36—42. Oxford University Press. Oxford. (23.6.12)

121._____: (in press). Vegetation map of South-east Asia. *J. Biogeog.*

122.Whitten, A.J. (1982). Possible niche expansion in the spangled drongo on Siberut Island, Indonesia. *Ibis* 126: 122—193. (12.7.7)

123._____: (1982). *The Gibbons of Siberut*. J.M. Dent, London. (12.13.3)

124._____: (1983). Compendium of abstracts from papers concerning Sumatran invertebrates. (27.2.8)

125._____: unpublished.

126.Whitten, J.E.J. (1980). Ecological separation of three diurnal squirrels in tropical rainforest on Siberut Island, Indonesia. *J. Zool., Lond.* 193: 405—420. (12.8.5)

127.Wilson, C.C. and Wilson, W.C. (1973). Census of Sumatran primates. Final report to LIPI, Jakarta. (12.8.40)

128. Wilson, W.L. and Wilson, C.C. (1975). Species-specific vocalizations and the determination of phylogenetic affinities of the *Presbytis aygula-melalophos* group in Sumatra. *Contemp. Primatol,* pp. 459—463. Karger. (12.8.51)

129. Wiltschko, R. and Wiltschko, W. (1978). Relative importance of stars and the magnetic field for the accuracy of orientation in night migrating birds. *Oikos* 30: 195—206. (12.7.21)

130. Wolters, O.W. (1970). *The Fall of Srivijaya in Malay History.* Oxford Univ. Press, Kuala Lumpur. (23.7.11)

131. Jancey, T.E. (1973). Holocene radiocarbon dates on the 3 meter wave cut notch in northwestern peninsular Malaysia. *Geol. Soc. Malaysia Newsl.* 45: 8—11.

132. Young, A. (1976). *Tropical Soils and Soil Surveys.* Cambridge Univ. Press, Cambridge. (23.4.16)

133. Jaspan, M.A. (1973). A note on Enggano. *Sumatra Res. Bull.* 3: 54—63.

134. McKinnon, E.E. (1974). A brief note on the current state of certain of the kitchen middens of East Sumatra. *Sumatra Res. Bull.* 4: 45—50.

135. Pocock, R.I. (1934). The monkeys of the genera *Pitheus* (or *Presbytis*) and *Pygathrix* found to the east of the Bay of Bengal. *Proc. Zool. Soc. Lond.* 1934: 895—961.

136. Scholz, U. (1983). *The Natural Regions of Sumatra and their Agricultural Production Pattern: A Regional Analysis.* Two vols. Central Research Institute for Food Crops Bogor.

PART B

NATURAL ECOSYSTEMS

Sumatra, area 476,000 km^2, probably has over 10,000 species of higher (seed) plants, most of which are found in lowland forest. For comparison, the British Isles is 65% of the area but has only about 13% of the number of species. The number of tree species per unit area in the lowland forests (section 7.1.1) of Malesia and particularly Western Malesia (which includes Sumatra) is probably greater than in similar forests in West Africa or South America. Indeed, these Sunda Region forests are probably the most species-rich plant communities in the World [15].

Part of the reason for the very large number of plant species is that in the near-perfect growing conditions of warmth and adequate moisture, the tall trees provide a large framework for a wide and environmentally-diverse range of structural niches. These are filled by smaller trees, shrubs, herbs, scramblers, climbers, epiphytes, parasites, etc. The underlying causes of high plant diversity are discussed in section 7.1.1.

The vast number of plant species present in Sumatra and elsewhere in the Sunda Region represent a magnificatly rich source of natural resources many of which have proven or potential economic value [17]. About one-third of the 7500 species of plants known from Peninsular Malaysia are listed by Burkill [3] as having some economic value and a similar proportion would be expected from Sumatra's plants. The dipterocarp timber trees are the most obvious example and these constitute about one-quarter of all the hardwood timber in international markets. Unfortunately, this indicates productivity of timber companies rather than the productivity of the trees themselves and accessible supplies of dipterocarp timber will be exhausted by the end of this century or before [1]. In addition to the timber species already exploited, there are many tree species whose potential for timber, fibre or cellulose remains unexploited. In addition to these there are hundreds of species in the forests whose economic potential for food or chemicals remains unassessed [16]. People of rural areas generally have a deeper understanding of the value of wild or semi-domesticated forest plants but, as Sastrapradja and Kartawinata [11] have pointed out, knowledge of these can be lost within the timespan of a generation. Useful summaries of species with economic potential in Southeast Asian forests and of the need for genetic resource conservation are given by Sastrapradja *et al* [12], Whitmore [16] and Jacobs [7].

The economic value of forest vertebrates is less well studied but the vital role that macaque species played in the early stages of the mass production of polio vaccine should not be forgotten [10]. That role was largely unanticipated and it would be a brave person who would claim now that some other wild vertebrate could not be of similar value to human welfare. In addition, cave bats are vital to the production of durians (section 10.6). The potential uses and values of invertebrates - which are more numerous, more diverse, less well known - are clearly even greater (section 7.1.2). The economic value of the goods and services provided by coastal swamps and other natural ecosystems, particularly, lowland forest, is described elsewhere [2, 5, 8].

Considering the economic importance, aesthetic value and diversity of Sumatra's forests and other natural ecosystems, it is surprising that studies of their components and the way these components function and interact has not been particularly intense or widespread. From discussions with university staff there seem to be three major reasons for this situation - tigers, snakes and leeches - all of which have reputations unrelated to the facts.

a) Tigers - The tigers reported in the newspapers as killing stock animals or even humans are rogue individuals and are not typical of the species. Adventurous young or ailing old animals may take to seeking food around villages, at least in part because their forest habitat is being reduced in area. Field workers who have spent over two years conducting research in the forests of the Mount Leuser National Park, where tigers are regarded as common, have counted themselves 'lucky' to have had a fleeting glimpse of a fleeing tiger. It is worth reporting that during the CRES ascent of Mt. Kemiri, one or two tigers visited the first camp site (at 1500m) on two consecutive nights - passing within 30 and 50 cms of the sleeping party - and the only loss was a pair of flipflops, later found thoroughly chewed at the side of the path.

b) Snakes - It surprises many people to learn that less than 18% of the world's 2300—2700 snakes species are poisonous, and only a fraction of these actually endanger human life [4, 9]. Sumatra has about 150 snake species [6]. Of this total 6% are poisonous seasnakes, 13% are harmless freshwater of brackish water snakes, 67% are harmless land snakes, and 14% are poisonous land snakes. Of this last group, however, most are too small or weak to present any hazard to humans. In addition to these the adult reticulated python. *Python reticulatus* which constricts its prey must be regarded as dangerous to man. In fact, the percentage and density of snakes that pose any sort of threat to people is probably considerably higher in towns and villages than in forest. The percentages stated above should not be allowed to lead to carelessness with snakes in forests; in any case, snakes are only rarely seen.

    c) Leeches - Most leeches, whose closest relatives are earthworms, are found in freshwater but some species have adapted to life on land or in the sea. Some of the larger freshwater (swamp) species are known to transmit protozoan blood parasites to their hosts (usually mussels, fish and frogs), or cause serious blood loss to cattle or buffalo which drink from infested water. The leeches seen in lowland forest are small (2—4cms) and are not known to transmit any disease to humans or other animals [13]. Of the two commonest species, the dull-coloured *Haemadipsa zeylandica* gives a paintless bite, but the brighter coloured *H. picta* has a fiery bite. Bleeding from a land leech bite looks spectacular but the amount of blood lost is very small. Proper dress and perhaps a repellent (based on dimethylphthalate) provides protection, but if a leech manages to bite, a dab of antiseptic to prevent secondary infection is all that is required.

    The concern for and interest in natural ecosystems expressed by some people (often foreigners) baffles others. "Why bother?" they might ask. Van Steenis [14] has replied to such a rhetorical question by answering, "Come with an observant eye and the question will answer itself." In the next nine chapters it is hoped that the reader will be able to 'observe' a little from his chair and then be sufficiently enthused to venture out and find out more himself about the forests and other natural ecosystems of Sumatra.

REFERENCES

1. Ashton, P.S. (1980). The biological and ecological basis for the utilization of dipterocarps. *Bio Indonesia* 7: 43—53. (9.1.25)

2. Burbridge, P.R. (1982). Valuation of tidal wetlands. In *Man, Land and Sea* (ed. C. Soysa, L.S. Chia and W.L. Collier) pp. 43—64. Agricultural Development Council, Bangkok. (2.4.29).

3. Burkhill, I.H. (19). *A Dictionary of the Economic Plants of the Malay Peninsula.* Department of Agriculture, Kuala Lumpur.

4. Duellman, W.E. (1979). The numbers of amphibians and reptiles. *Herp. Review* 10: 83—84. (12.6.27).

5. Farnworth, E.G., Tidrick, T.H., Jordan, C.F. and Smathers W.M. (1981). The value of natural ecosystems: an economic and ecological framework. Environ. Conserv. 8: 275—282. (9.2.10).

6. Hass, C.P.J. de (1950). Checklist of the snakes of the Indo-Australian Archipelago, *Treubia* 20: 575—653.

7. Jacobs, M. (1980). Significance of the tropical rain forests on 12 points. *BioIndonesia* 7: 75—94. (12.10.73).

8. Krutilla, J.V. and Fisher, A.C. (1975). *The Economics of Natural Environments: Studies in the Valuation of Commodity and Amenity Resources.* John Hopkins University Press, Baltimore. (23.8.1).

9. McCarthy, C. *Personal communication.*

10. *Medway, Lord. (1980). Tropical forests as a source of animal genetic resources. BioIndonesia* 7: 55—63. (12.10.80).

11. Sastrapradja, S. and Kartawinata, K. (1975). Leafy vegetables in the Sundanese diet. In *South-east Asian Plant Genetic Resources* (ed. J.T. Williams), pp. 166—170. Lembaga Biologi Nasional, Bogor. (9.2.15).

12. Sastrapradja, S., Soenartono, A., Kartawinata, K. and Tarumingkeng, R.C. (1980). The conservation of forest animal and plant genetic resources. *BioIndonesia* 7: 1—42. (12.13.10).

13. Sharma, R.E. and Fernando, C.H. (1961). Leeches and their ways. *Malay. Nat. J.* 15: 152—159. (12.3.29).

14. Steenis, C.G.G.J. van. (1971). Plant conservation in Malaysia. *Bull. Jard. Bot. Nat. Belg.* 41: 189—202. (12.12.9)

15. Whitmore, T.C. (1975). *Tropical Rain Forests of the Far East.* Clarendon, Oxford. (12.10.8)

16. _____: (1980). Potentially economic species of Southeast Asia forests. *BioIndonesia* 7: 65—74. (9.1.26)

17. Williams, J.T. (ed.) (1975). *Southeast Asian Plant Genetic Resources.* Lembaga Biologi Nasional, Bogor. (9.2.15)

CHAPTER 2

MANGROVE FORESTS

2.1 INTRODUCTION

Mangrove forests[1] are frequently regarded as a very distinct ecosystem virtually requiring a separate discipline of science. In fact, mangrove forests are just one of the many types of forest in Sumatra having a closed, even canopy made up of tree species which are predominantly evergreen. The environmental conditions in which they grow are extreme, however, because they are subject to soil-water salinity and waterlogging. Mangrove forests have various important environmental roles concerned with land, wildlife and fisheries (Table 2.1.) and have been exploited by man for numerous natural products (Table 2.2). This exploitation by man has had important effects on the ecosystem (section 2.3.2).

On Sumatra, mangrove forests have been studied more than almost any other natural ecosystem. Every Sumatran province has mangroves fringing some of its shores, if only in a few sheltered bays or river entrances or around offshore islands, but of the 1,470,000 ha of mangrove forests over 60% are in Riau and South Sumatra (section 1.4.2) and this is where the studies have concentrated. Major studies have been conducted by Sabar *et al.* [69], Soeriaatmadja [76], Sukardjo [85], and Sukardjo and Kartawinata [81]. Unfortunately, none of these authors is based on Sumatra and there is a need to develop local expertise so that comprehensive

---

1. In this chapter the term 'mangrove forests' includes not only the vegetated area but also the exposed land or silt area between it and the sea.

Table 2.1 Roles of mangrove ecosystems (From Saenger *et al.* [70]).

Physical functions

> Stabilizer of coastlines
> Accelerator of land extension
> Buffer against waves and storms
> Protector of beaches and river banks
> Assimilator of waste material

Biological functions

> Nursery ground for fish, prawns and shellfish of the open sea
> Sanctuary for large nesting birds
> Natural habitat for many forms of wildlife

Potential commercial functions

> Aquaculture
> Salt ponds
> Recreation
> Timber

studies such as that conducted by Hardjosuwarno *et al.* [30] for the Cilacap region can be started.

Mangrove forests form a protective and productive margin to much of Sumatra's coastline. It is important, from many points of view, that the ecology of mangrove areas should be understood as fully as possible and as soon as possible, but particularly because so many development projects are in the coastal region and create serious conflicts of land use.

An excellent review of the present state of knowledge of mangrove ecosystems in Indonesia is given by Kartawinata *et al.* [36]. They conclude: "Almost all species of plant which make up Indonesian mangrove swamps are now known. However, many fields such as variations in species composition, forest structure, seed dispersal, phenology, biology, flowering and fruiting, composition of the fauna, mineral cycling, productivity and ecosystem dynamics are barely understood. Because of this, studies of the above topics need to be encouraged. Exploration, inven-

Table 2.2 Products of the mangrove ecosystem. (From Saenger *et al.* [70]). **See also Table 27 in Soegiarto and Polunin [75] for a species by species list.**

A. MANGROVE FOREST PRODUCT

FUEL
Firewood (cooking, heating)
Charcoal
Alcohol

CONSTRUCTION
Timber, scaffolds
Heavy construction (e.g. bridges)
Railfoad ties
Mining pit props
Boat building
Dock pilings
Beams and poles for buildings
Flooring, panelling
Thatch or matting
Fence posts, water pipes, chipboards, glues

FISHING
Poles for fish traps
Fishing floats
Wood for smoking fish
Fish poison
Tannins for net and line preservation
Fish attracting shelters

AGRICULTURE
Fodder, green manure

OTHER PRODUCTS
Packing boxes
Wood for smoking sheet rubber
Wood for burning bricks
Medicines from bark, leaves and fruits

TEXTILES, LEATHER
Synthetic fibres (e.g. rayon)
Dye for cloth
Tannins for leather preservation

FOOD, DRUGS & BEVERAGES
Sugar
Alcohol
Cooking Oil, Vinegar
Tea substitue
Fermented drinks
Dessert topping
Condiments from bark
Sweetmeats from propagules
Vegetables from propagules, fruit or leaves
Cigar substitute

HOUSEHOLD ITEMS
Furniture
Glue
Hairdressing oil
Tool handles
Rice mortar
Toys
Matchsticks, Incense

PAPER PRODUCTS
Paper of various kinds

B. OTHER NATURAL PRODUCTS

Fish
Crustaceans
Shellfish
Honey
Wax

Birds
Mammals
Reptiles and reptile skins
Other fauna (amphibians, insects)

torization and mapping must be given priority too." As with other chapters, results of studies from Peninsular Malaysia and elsewhere are used below in order to increase the depth of the information.

Although there is no generally accepted definition of a mangrove ecosystem, Saenger *et al.* proposed that it should consist of the following:

1) one or more of the exclusive mangrove tree species (see section 2.3.1 and Table 2.4);
2) any non-exclusive plant species growing with (1);
3) the associated biota - the terrestrial and marine animals, the lichens, fungi, algae, bacteria, etc., whether temporary, permanent, casual, incidental or exclusive in the area of (1);
4) the processes essential for its maintenance whether or not within the area of (1) [70].

To this should be added:

5) and the foreshore below the margin of vegetation where colonization by pioneer mangrove trees will occur and where the fauna has a terrestrial component.

An extremely comprehensive bibliography[2] of references to mangroves totalling 5,608 entries has been published by UNESCO [68].

2.2 IMPORTANT PHYSICAL FEATURES

2.2.1 Tides

The most important feature of the physical environment for the mangrove biota is the tide. Tides usually occur twice each day and are caused by the gravitational pull of the moon and to a lesser extent the sun. In the open ocean the amplitude (height) of the tides is not more than about 0.5 m but in shallow seas around Sumatra it is commonly up to 3 m. The tides of greatest amplitude, the spring tides, occur when the earth, sun and moon are in a straight line - i.e. about the times of the new moon and the full moon. Neap tides, those of smallest amplitude, occur when the sun is opposed (is at right angles) to the gravitational pull of the moon - i.e.

---

2. Bodies undertaking research mangrove ecosystems should make obtaining this book a high priority.

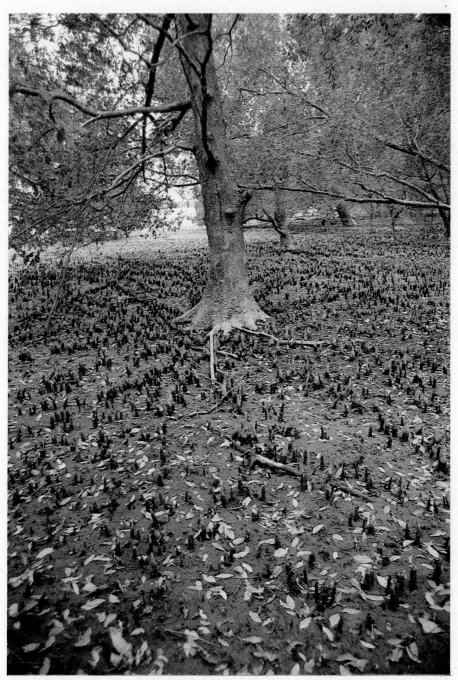

Pneumatophore roots radiating from *Sonneratia alba;* near Bubun, Langkat.

Avicennia marina saplings in the pioneer zone near Perbaungan, Deli Serdang.

Barnacles are commonly found on tree trunks in mangrove forest.

about the times of the first and last quarters of the moon. As the moon orbits the earth in the same direction as the earth's rotation, a period of rather more than one day (in fact, 24 hours 50 minutes) elapses between successive occasions when the moon is vertically above the same meridian. Thus, the interval between successive high or low tides is generally half this period, i.e. about 12½ hours. This general pattern is modified when the tidal waters move through complex archipelagos or irregularities in the coastline, and the fauna and flora of different locations will respond to these different regimes of inundation.

The tidal regimes for the waters around Sumatra are shown in Figure 2.1 and it can be seen that Sumatra experiences four types of tide which are described below and illustrated in Figure 2.2.

Semi-diurnal tide - two high waters and two low waters daily with similar amplitudes;

Mixed tide, mainly semi-diurnal - two high waters and two low waters daily with different amplitudes;

Mixed tide, mainly diurnal - sometimes only one high water and one low water daily, but sometimes also two high waters which differ greatly in height;

Diurnal tide - only one high water and one low water daily.

Some of the mangrove fauna do not avoid the alternate wetting and exposure caused by tides. Others climb into the trees during high tides and then descend to feed during low tides. One such animal is the snail *Cerithidea decollata* whose pattern of activity follows the tidal rhythm and is not associated with light or dark [22]. The snails descend during low tide periods and ascend before the next high tide. Note that the rising tide does not *force* them up, but that the tidal rhythm is part of their own internal rhythm.

2.2.2 Salinity

As might be expected, the salinity of sea water around the coast decreases during the rainy season because of the increased volumes of freshwater flowing out of the rivers, and is greatest during the dry seasons. The average annual variation in surface salinity (in parts per thousand or ‰ NaCl) for the waters around Sumatra is shown in Figure 2.3. Patterns of water movement in estuaries are extremely complex. Where freshwater

A ⬛ — semi-diurnal   C ⬛ — mixed tide, mainly diurnal

B ⬛ — diurnal   D ☐ — mixed tide, mainly semi-diurnal

Figure 2.1 Distribution of tidal types around Sumatra. (After Wyrtki [102]).
Legend as in Figure 2.2.

Figure 2.2 Fluctuations in tide level through a cycle of sixteen days for four different tidal regimes. A-semi-diurnal tide; B-mixed tide, mainly semi-diurnal; C-mixed tide, mainly diurnal; D-diurnal tide. (After Wyrtki [102]). **Refer to text for further explanation.**

Figure 2.3 Average annual variation of surface salinity (‰). (After Wyrtki [102]).

meets sea water, mixing does not automatically occur but rather the heavy sea water sinks below the fresh water to form a 'salt-water wedge'. This configuration varies with tides and also with river flow.

For most of the mangrove forest trees and burrowing fauna, the salinity of tidal water is probably less important than the salinity of the soil water. The salinity of this interflow (section 4.3.1) is generally less than the water above it because of dilution by fresh (rain) water seeping through the soil. To investigate this water it is necessary to dig holes and collect the water in them. For tree roots and burrowing fauna the crucial factor is not so much the concentration of NaCl alone but the osmotic potential. This depends partly on soil type, being greater in clayey soils than in sandy soils. If it is not feasible to measure osmotic potential with the equipment available, then salinity and conductivity measurements represent a good second best.

2.2.3 Temperature

In tropical coastal waters the surface temperature is generally between 27° and 29°C. In shallow water, however, temperatures can reach at least 30°, and the mudflats may become much hotter than this [78]. Inside the actual mangrove forest the temperature is lower [23] and the variation is more or less the same as for other shaded coastal areas. The forest areas therefore represent a rather more equitable environment for the mangrove biota than the mudflats.

2.2.4 Surface currents

In general terms, sea water currents change with the rainy seasons but Figure 2.4 shows that the Straits of Malacca experience a south-east current throughout the year and the west coast of Sumatra a north-west current. However, the coast of southeast Sumatra has a north/north-west current in February and a south/south-east current in August. The western coast of Aceh and some of North Sumatra experience the opposite change in current. It can be seen that most of the water from rivers on the east coast will flow to the north-west, and water from rivers on the west coast to the south-east.

Figure 2.4 Surface currents around Sumatra in February and August. (After Wyrtki [102]).

2.2.5 Nutrients and dissolved oxygen

The greatest concentration of dissolved oxygen in the coastal environment is at the open water edge where wave action repeatedly agitates the water. Oxygen concentration also fluctuates with tides with highest values being found at high tide. The abundance of life in mangrove forests and the constantly replenished supply of nutrients, leads to a very high biological demand for oxygen and this tends to lower the levels of available oxygen. Nevertheless, neither oxygen concentrations in free water nor nutrient levels impose any limitations on the productivity of the mangrove biota.

2.2.6 Summary of water quality in a mangrove forest

Variations in water quality at different locations from open sea to land through mangrove forest are shown in Table 2.3. In general there is a gradient of decreasing nutrient concentrations moving from the mangrove area to the open sea [60]. This is caused by dilution in the greater volume of water and increasing incorporation of the nutrients into the sediments.

Table 2.3 Average measurements of water quality in a mangrove forest. (After Gomez [29]).

	Open Area	Forest Margin	m from forest margin						
			20 m	40 m	60 m	80 m	100 m	120 m	140 m
Temperature	29.5	29.1	28.7	28.2	27.9	27.8	27.6	27.5	27.6
pH	7.2	7.0	6.9	6.8	6.7	6.7	6.7	6.6	6.6
Salinity	22.21	22.04	21.46	21.18	20.96	20.67	19.87	18.62	19.49
Dissolved Oxygen (mL/L)	4.40	3.37	2.99	2.68	2.36	2.15	1.99	1.55	1.70
COD (mg/L)	16.00	17.91	18.88	17.73	16.48	16.82	19.88	19.82	20.62
PO_4 (mg P/L)	1.18	1.29	0.97	0.97	0.82	0.84	0.87	0.83	0.86
NO_3 (mg N/L)	2.03	2.22	2.39	2.53	2.42	2.36	2.46	2.41	2.59

2.3 ENERGY FLOW AND THE IMPORTANCE OF MANGROVE VEGETATION TO FISHERIES

Mangrove forests are highly productive ecosystems but only about 7% of their leaves are eaten by herbivores [35]. Most of the mangrove

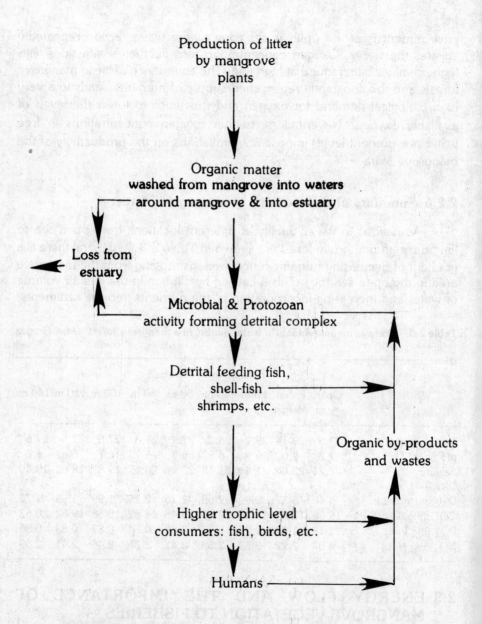

Figure 2.5 **Major pathways of energy flow in a mangrove-fringed estuary.**
(After Saenger *et al.* [70]).

forest production enters the energy system as detritus or dead organic matter (Figure 2.5). This detritus plays an extremely important role in the productivity of the mangrove ecosystems as a whole [42, 58, 59] (see section 2.4.3). Its importance to offshore ecosystems is not clear [54]. Leaves and other small litter (twigs, flowers, and fruit) fall throughout the year and are broken down by macro-organisms (mainly crabs) and micro-organisms (mainly fungi) into smaller particles that form the detritus. The detritus becomes rich in nitrogen and phophorus because of the fungi, bacteria and algae growing on and within it and is therefore an important food source for many 'detritivore' animals such as zooplankton, other small invertebrates, prawns, crabs, and fish. These detritivores are eaten in turn by carnivores which are dependent to varying degrees on these organisms. Those carnivores not dependent on detritivores would be directly or indirectly dependent on planktonic benthic algae (section 4.4.1). It is known that in the turbid coastal waters characteristic of at least the northern half of the Malacca Straits, the productivity of phytoplankton is low. It is probable, therefore, that most of the micro- and macro-fauna in the mangroves and surrounding coastal areas are dependent on the productivity of litter from mangrove forests [58, 59]. Studies on energy flow through mangrove forests are not known from Sumatra but a study has begun in the Seribu islands near Jakarta [11].

The high productivity of mangroves and the physical structure and shading they provide forms a valuable habitat for many organisms, some of which are of commercial importance. At present the most valuable mangrove-related species in Indonesia are the penaeid prawns which support an export market worth over $150,000,000 annually [1]. The juvenile stages of several of these prawn species live in mangrove and adjacent vegetation, while the adults breed offshore [75]. As elsewhere in the world [87] the commercial production of penaeid prawns in different parts of Indonesia is positively correlated with the associated area of mangrove forest. It should be said that certain species of prawn do not conform to this relationship but the overall correlation is valid [49, 50].

The influence of mangroves extends far beyond the prawn fisheries themselves. In Sumatra, for example, the profits from the export of prawns subsidizes the sale of fish which are caught in trawlers' nets [87]. The average coastal fishpond (tambak) produces 287 kg fish/ha/year which is more than the offshore shrimp yield, but the loss of one hectare of mangrove to tambak actually leads to an approximate net loss of 480 kg offshore fish and shrimp per year. Thus, widespread loss of mangrove to tambak is likely to cause the loss of jobs [87]. An assessment of the impact of a mangrove reclamation project of the south Java coast conservatively estimated that the development would lead eventually to loss of employment for 2400 fishermen in the area and the loss of $5.6 million in annual income [86].

Apart from the prawns, many other species of economic importance are associated with mangrove. These include the edible crab *Scylla serrata*, the shrimp *Acetes* from which 'belacan' paste is made, and fishes such as *Chanos*, *Mugil* and *Lates* [47, 75].

2.4 THE VEGETATION

2.4.1 Tree species

Mangrove forests are found in almost all tropical areas and it is likely that the centre of evolution was the Indo-Malesian region. This region (India, Burma, Thailand, Malaysia, Indonesia and northern Australia) has the most species-rich mangrove forests [20, 21], but even so contains many fewer species than other natural forest types. There are only seventeen tree species (belonging to seven genera and only four families) which would be generally encountered in Sumatran mangroves (Table 2.4) but over 20 different plant communities, many dominated by a single tree species, have been identified in South-east Asian mangroves [21]. Details of the species found at different locations along the east coast of Sumatra and west coast of Peninsular Malaysia can be found elsewhere [9, 13, 24, 26, 36, 42, 44, 58, 71, 76, 79, 80, 81, 82, 89]. Further Dutch references can be found in Kartawinata *et al.* [37]. A practical key to mangrove and estuarine trees is available [101].

Mangrove trees are 'halophytes'. That is, they are able to withstand the saline soil in which they are rooted, and repeated inundation by sea water. This does not imply that they can grow only under such conditions and three species thrive next to a freshwater pond at the Botanic Gardens in Bogor [25]. The occurrence of mangrove forest only along coasts indicates that the species concerned exist there because of a lack of successful competition from plant species which have not adapted to the salty

Table 2.4 Principle species of mangrove trees in Sumatra. For fullers lists, see Kartawinata *et al.* **[37]. Old names which are sometimes still used are shown in brackets.**

Rhizophoraceae
  Rhizophora apiculata (conjugaga)
  R. mucronata

  Bruguiera cylindrica (caryophylloides)
  B. gymnorrhiza
  B. parviflora
  B. sexangula (eriopetala)

  Ceriops tagal (candolleana)
  Kandelia candel

Sonneratiaceae
  Sonneratia acida
  S. alba
  S. caseolaris
  S. griffithii

Avicenniaceae
  Avicennia alba
  A. marina (intermedia)
  A. officinalis

Meliaceae
  Xylocarpus (Carapa) granatum (obovata)
  X. moluccensis

environment. Clearly the mangrove species are in turn unable to compete successfully against freshwater vegetation in other locations. This illustrates well the difference between fundamental niche and realized niche which is discussed in section 4.8.5. Some mangrove trees can be found growing on river banks over 100 km from the sea. The water they grow in may appear to be fresh but a wedge of salt water (heavier than fresh water) may extend to great distances inland. Thus the roots of a plant may be in saline water although it grows through fresh water. A review of the response of mangrove plants to salt water is given fresh water. A review of the response of mangrove plants to salt water is given by Walsh [93].

A number of mangrove forest trees have peculiar rooting systems (Figure 2.6). *Rhizophora* spp. have stilt roots which help to support the trees and possibly prevent other seedlings from becoming established too close. The spike pneumatophores (roots that stick out of the ground) of *Sonneratia* and *Avicennia*, and the bent pneumatophores of *Bruguiera* allow oxygen to enter the root system. The mangrove soil is generally waterlogged and unless there is extensive burrowing by crabs and other animals, roots a few centimetres below the soil surface are essentially in anoxic (no oxygen) conditions.

The roots of *Sonneratia* and *Avicennia* are composed of four distinct parts. The cable root runs beneath the soil surface and is held in place by anchor roots which grow downwards. The pneumatophores grow up from the cable root and small nutritive roots grow horizontally from these (Figure 2.6). In addition to the function of pneumatophores in gas exchange, it is thought that they also allow nutritive roots to grow quickly into new sediments should the soil surface suddenly rise causing the nutritive roots to be within the anoxic layer [47, 85].

The pollination ecology of mangrove trees is extremely diverse with wind, bats, birds, butterflies, moths and other insects all being pollinators. The pollination ecology of Rhizophoraceae (*Rhizophora, Bruguiera* etc.) is described by Tomlinson *et al.* [84].

A few mangrove tree species have evolved an unusual, though not unique, form of reproduction. Generally speaking, fruit develops on a plant and when it is ripe or fully developed, the fruit or the seed(s) inside it is then dispersed and the seed germinates when or if it comes to rest in suitable conditions. In most of the Rhizophoraceae such as *Rhizophora* and *Bruguiera*, however, the fruits ripen and then, before leaving the parent tree, the seeds germinate inside the fruit, possibly absorbing food from the tree. The embryonic root or hypocotyl of the seedling pierces the wall of the fruit and then grows downwards. The cotyledons (first leaves) remain inside the fruit. Eventually, in *Rhizophora mucronata* for example, the root may reach a length of 45 cm. When the seedling is fully grown it drops off by separating itself from the cotyledon tube, the scar of which forms a ring around the top of the fallen seedling, and the small leaf-bud can be seen above this scar (Figure 2.7). *Bruguiera* behaves similarly, but the break occurs at the stalk of the fruit. These types of fruit are described in more detail by MacNae [47].

103

Figure 2.6 Different types of roots in mangrove trees: a- knee roots as found in *Bruguiera* spp.; b- spike roots as found in *Sonneratia* spp., *Avicennia* spp. (and sometimes *Xylocarpus moluccensis*); and c- stilt roots as found in *Rhizophora* spp.

2.4.2 Zonation

Watson recognized five major divisions of mangrove forest in Peninsular Malaysia based on tidal regimes, such that the first division (nearest the sea) was inundated by all tides, and the fifth division was inundated only by abnormal tides [96]. These tidal zones supported different types of vegetation, the species composition of which varied with the position relative to rivers and the sea (Figure 2.8). The major divisions were:

1) Forest nearest the sea dominated by *Avicennia* and *Sonneratia*, the latter growing on deep mud rich in organic matter. *A. marina* grows on comparatively firm clayey substrate which is easy to walk on, whereas *A. alba* grows on softer mud [25, 81, 85].

2) Forest on slightly higher ground is often dominated by *Bruguiera cylindrica* and can form virtually pure stands behind *Avicennia* forest. It grows on firm stiff clays out of the reach of most tides.

3) Forest further inland dominated by *Rhizophora mucronata* and *R. apiculata*, the former preferring slightly wetter conditions and deeper mud. These trees can be 35—40 m tall [25]. Also present are *Bruguiera parviflora* and *Xylocarpus granatum*. Mounds of mud built up by the mud lobster are often colonized by the large fern *Acrostichum aureum*.

4) Forest dominated by *Bruguiera parviflora* can occur in pure stands and whereas it often invades *Rhizophora* forest after it has been clearfelled, this is not the only condition in which it occurs.

5) The final mangrove forest is that dominated by *Bruguiera gymnorrhiza*. The seedlings and saplings of this tree are tolerant of shade in conditions where *Rhizophora* cannot perpetuate itself. Like the she-oak *Casuarina* (section 3.2.1) however, seedlings of *B. gymnorrhiza* will not develop under the canopy of their parents. The transition between this type of forest and inland forest is marked by the occurrence of *Lumnitzera racemosa*, *Xylocarpus moluccensis*, *Intsia bijuga*, *Ficus retusa*, rattans,pandans and at the inland margin the tall palm *Oncosperma tigillaria*. This succession is not always visible, particularly where man has disturbed the forest; in such conditions the fern *Acrostichum aureum* is very common (section 11.4).

The above descriptions refer mainly to gently sloping, accreting shores but where there are creeks, bays or lagoons, *Rhizophora* is usually the tree found as the pioneer. This is common in areas near coral reefs

Mangrove forest in Pulau Baai, Bengkulu showing *Rhizophora apiculata*, *Bruguiera gymnorrhiza* and (the pale trunks) *Xylocarpus granatum*.

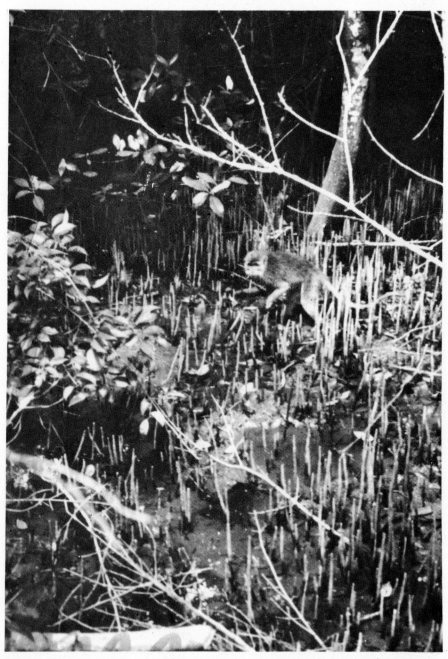

Long-tailed macaque searching for crabs in mangrove forest near Belawan, Langkat.

105

Figure 2.7 The propagule of *Rhizophora mucronata* showing the root (often
mistaken for part of the fruit) and the top of the part that
detaches itself from the parent plant.

Figure 2.8 Typical but not invariable distribution of mangrove tree species near the mouth of a large river. (After Watson [96]).

Aa- *Avicennia alba*, Am- *A. marina*, Bc- *Bruguiera cylindrica*, Bg- *B. gymnorrhiza*, Bp- *B. parviflora*, Bs- *B. sexangula*, Ct- *Ceriops tagal*, Fr- *Ficus retusa*, Ir- *Intsia bijuga*, Ot- *Oncosperma tigillaria*, Ra- *Rhizophora apiculata*, Rm- *R. mucronata*, Sa- *Sonneratia alba*, Sg- *S. griffithii*, Xg- *Xylocarpus granatum*, Xm- *X. moluccensis*. Note that some of the names used by Watson have been modernized for this diagram. See Table 2.4.

(section 3.5.1). The succession generally followed by mangrove vegetation under different conditions is shown in Figure 2.9.

The tendency of the mangrove forest to occur in distinct floral zones has been interpreted by various authors in many different ways. These have been summarized by Snedaker in the following four categories: plant succession, geomorphology, physiological ecology, and population dynamics [74].

Plant succession

Plant succession is a classic ecological concept and is defined as being the progressive replacement of one plant community with another; e.g. bare ground - alang-alang - scrub - secondary forest - primary forest (see section 11.2). Much of the early work on mangrove forests focused on its supposed land-building role. It seemed clear from this that one species colonized an exposed bank of mud, and as conditions changed (such as an increase in the organic debris of the mud) so other species took over. Thus at any one spot a succession of species or communities of species would be observed over a period of time. It is clear however that in most places, including Sumatra, the stages of succession are not always consistent and different local environmental conditions and man's impact on those have an influence.

Budowski compiled a list of 20 characteristics of secondary succession in tropical forests which distinguish between early and late stages [13]. If this is compared with the stages of succession for mangroves, only seven of the characters apply, nine do not, and four are inconclusive. This suggests that attributing the apparent zonation to succession is not the whole story [74].

Geomorphological change

Early workers on mangrove felt that it was mangroves that 'built land'. However, it is clear from observations that in some areas such as the huge deltas of the Ganges, Indus and Irrawaddy, it is the process of sediment decomposition that builds land (section 2.4). It appears to most workers now that mangroves do not have any influence on the initial development of the land forms. Mangroves may accelerate land extension but they do not seem to cause it (section 2.5). Van Steenis tells of engineers working at Belawan (the port north of Medan) who planted mangrove seedlings on a new port extension to stabilize it. The attempt failed, thereby demonstrating that it is not possible to force accumulation of silt [25].

From a geomorphological perspective, it is the shape, topography and history of the coastal zone that determine the types and distributions of mangrove trees in the resulting habitats. The position of species relative to tidal levels (and thus soil type) is obviously important and Watson considered the pattern of tidal inundation and drainage to be the major factor in mangrove zonation [96]. This idea was developed by Lugo and Snedaker to include variation in the salinity of the tidal water and the direction of its flow into and out of the forest [42]. Although good correlations exist between salinity and zonation, they are not proofs of direct cause and effect.

Physiological response to soil-water salinity

If salinity is an actual cause of zonation in mangrove forests it needs to be shown that the plants actually respond through their physiology to salinity gradients and not to a factor such as oxygen levels which under certain conditions will fall with decreasing salinity [25]. It has already been mentioned that mangroves are able to live in freshwater (i.e. they are facultative not obligate halophytes) but each species probably has a definable optimum range of salinity for its growth. Indeed, Lugo *et al.* found that within each zone the characteristic species had apparently maximized its physiological efficiency and therefore had a higher metabolic rate than any invading species [43]. These invading species would be at a competitive disadvantage due to their lower metabolic efficiency in that habitat. Similarly, it has been found that each species of the mangrove forest grows best under slightly different conditions such as the amount of water in the mud, the salinity, and the ability of the plant to tolerate shade [41]. This means that the various species are not mingled together in a haphazard way but occur in a fairly distinct zonation.

As was shown in sections 2.2.2 and 2.2.6, salinity can vary considerably between high and low tides and between seasons, and thereby

OPEN COAST   CREEKS, BAYS, LAGOONS

(Silt)   (Sand)

Sonneratia   *Avicennia*   *Rhizophora mucronata*
alba   *alba*   ± *Rhizophora apiculata*
Ceriops tagal
                    Avicennia marina

Rhizophora   *Bruguiera*   *Rhizophora apiculata*
mucronata   *cylindrica*   ± *Bruguiera spp.*
                                                Xylocarpus
                                                    granatum
                          (depressions)
                          Bruguiera   (brackish)
                          parviflora

                    Ceriops tagal   *Sonneratia*
                                                    caseolaris
                                                Nypa fruticans
                                                Heritiera littoralis

Bruguiera
gymnorrhiza
± *Acrostichum aureum*

Lumnitzera racemosa

Figure 2.9 Succession in mangrove forests. (After Chapman (1970) in Walsh
[93]).

presents a confusing picture to a scientist conducting a short-term study.
Thus, to identifity the salinity levels to which the different species are op-
timally adapted requires long-term and detailed measurements to determine long-term averages and ranges of salinity.

Differential dispersal of propagules

The suggestion that differential dispersal of propagules (fruit etc.)
influence zonation of mangroves rests on the idea that the principal propagule characteristics (e.g. size, weight, shape, buoyancy, viability,
numbers, and location of source areas) result in differential tidal sorting
and therefore deposition. There are as yet few data to support this
hypothesis [63] and interested readers should refer to Snedaker [74] for a
thorough discussion.

Geomorphology and environmental physiology thus appear to be the most relevant of the topics discussed above to further the understanding of zonation and plant succession in the mangrove forest. However the impact of human activities, so ubiquitous in coastal regions, plays a major role in modifying species composition, and physical conditions, and so should also be considered in any study of zonation.

The term 'zone' itself needs to be clarified. Bunt and Williams suggest that recognizable zones may arise through at least two causes: situations where neighbouring vegetation associations have little or no floristic affinity although growing in the same environmental conditions (continuous variation); and situations where environmental gradients exist at a scale to permit sudden changes between related vegetation associations (discontinuous variation) [14]. Thus vegetational changes can be continuous, discontinuous or a combination of both. This, they argue, is why it is crucial to consider scale before attempting an analysis of mangrove forest and why, in the absence of such consideration, data from isolated transects, even from the same area, are so hard to interpret. Comparisons of transect data from different sites are useful in compiling inventories and noting similarities but are not a basis for a discussion of zonation.

2.4.3 Biomass and productivity

Biomass is a term for the weight of living material, usually expressed as a dry weight, in all or part of an organism, population or community [67]. It is commonly expressed as the biomass density or biomass per unit area. Plant biomass[3] is the total dry weight of all living plant parts and for convenience is sometimes divided into above-ground plant biomass (leaves, branches, boughs, trunk) and below-ground plant biomass (roots). It appears that no study of mangrove biomass has been conducted in Sumatra but several studies have been conducted on the other side of the

---

3. The measurement of dry weight biomass of a forest requires access to drying ovens, time and patience. If one or more of these is not available it is possible to use the allometric relationships determined by Ong et al. [58]. In these the above-ground dry weight (wa.g.) for Bruguiera trees is:

Wa.g. = 0.0033 π (diameter at chest height)$^{2.767}$ and for Rhizophora trees is:
Wa.g. = 0.0277 π (diameter at chest height)$^{2.167}$

Relationships for other species can be determined from first principles using a number of samples.

Straits of Malacca in Peninsular Malaysia. Thus the biomass of trees in the Sungai Merbok Forest Reserve was between 122 and 245 t/ha [58]. In the Matang Forest Reserve, however, which has been exploited for timber on a sustained basis for eighty years, and which receives silvicultural management, the biomass of trees was 300 t/ha [59]. As is explained below, the higher biomass in managed forest is not unexpected.

Biomass is a useful measure but it gives no indication of the dynamics of an ecosystem. Ecologists are interested in productivity because if the dry weight of a community can be determined at a given moment and the rate of change in dry weight can be measured, these data can be converted into the rate of energy flow through an ecosystem. Using this information different ecosystems can be compared, and their relative efficiencies of converting solar radiation into organic matter can be calculated [10].

Plant biomass increases because plants secure carbon dioxide from the atmosphere and convert this into organic matter through the process of photosynthesis. Thus, unlike animals, plants make their own food. The rate at which biomass increases is the 'gross primary productivity'. This depends on the leaf area exposed, amount of solar radiation, temperature and upon the characteristics of individual plant species [97]. During the day and during the night, plants, like all other living organisms, respire and use up a proportion of the production formed through photosynthesis. What remains is called 'net primary productivity' and over a period of time this is termed 'net primary production'. Net primary productivity is obviously greatest in a young forest which is growing and it should be remembered that a dense, tall forest with a high biomass does not necessarily have a high net primary productivity. Large trees may have virtually stopped growing. Indeed in an old 'overmature' forest, the death of parts of the trees and attacks by animals and fungi may even act to reduce the plant biomass while net primary productivity remains more or less constant. The major aim of silvicultural management in forests or timber plantations is to maximize productivity and the trees are usually harvested while they are still growing fast and before the net primary productivity begins to decrease.

One means of assessing net primary production is to mesure the rate at which litter is produced. The production of litter at Merbok Forest Reserve was found to be 8.1 t/ha/year for leaf litter and 12.0 t/ha/year for total small litter (mainly leaves but with twigs, flowers and fruit) [58]. At Matang, Ong *et al.* obtained figures for production of 8.2 and 10.4 t/ha/year [59]. These figures are similar to those obtained in lowland forest (section 7.2.8).

The approximate annual accumulation of litter on the mangrove forest floor at Merbok was calculated to be 0.33 t/ha for leaf litter and 1.13 t/ha for total litter. An experiment at the same site revealed that 40—90% of fallen leaves were lost after 20 days on the forest floor. The major agents in the disappearance were probably crabs which either bury them (eventually to form peat) or eat them, latter to be excreted as detritus. At Matang, the time required for total leaf decomposition in areas with virtually no crabs (i.e. with only micro-organisms involved in decomposing) was 4—6 months [58].

In calculations of total productivity the contribution made by soil algae, algae growing on roots, and phytoplankton should not be overlooked as the combined total can be quite significant [93].

2.4.4 Tannins

It used to be thought that the leaves of mangrove trees were exceptionally rich in tannins, a view originating perhaps from the commercial use of mangrove bark for producing tannins for the leather industry [93, 94]. Recent analyses, however, suggest that the tannin content of mangrove tree leaves exhibit a wide spectrum of concentrations with *Bruguiera* having the highest levels. It may well be that mangroves have a higher than average concentration of tannins, but not significantly more than in other forests growing under somewhat adverse conditions [95] (sections 5.5, 8.2.3). Bark of trunks usually contains more tannins than bark of twigs which has in turn more tannins than the leaves. Mangrove barks often contain 20—30% dry weight of tannins [94], and although high this it is not outside the range found in lowland forest barks [99].

Tannins play an extremely important role in the interactions between herbivores and leaves (section 2.6.4, 5.6, 7.6, 8.2.4).

2.5 THE COASTLINE OF EASTERN SUMATRA AND THE ROLE OF MANGROVES IN LAND EXTENSION

It used to be thought that in historical times the southern Sumatran coast comprised a series of large bays. Obedeyn studied old maps dating from 1030 to 1600 AD and proposed that both Jambi and Palembang had been ports at the end of promontories [56, 57]. Thus the dashed line in Figure 2.10 would correspond to the coast in about 1000 AD and the dot-dash line to the coast in about 1600 AD. The supposed infilling of the bays by silt since those times required that the shore line had been advancing at over 100 m per year, but recent studies in the Musi-Banyuasin area had shown that present rates of accretion were over five times less, at only 20 m per year [18]. This discrepancy was not easy to explain but Chambers suggested debris from volcanoes active during earlier periods could have caused the higher accretion rate [17].

It now seems, however, that the coastlines proposed by Obedyn certainly did once exist but in geological rather than historical time. Investigations have shown that areas near the coast of Jambi had habitation at times when, according to Obedyn, no land would have existed. Cultural remains found 1.75 m below the soil surface at Muara Kumpeh, for example, have revealed stoneware from the 12th to 14th centuries, and a coin from the 7th or 8th century. Chinese sources mention 'Kompei' or 'kumpeh' during the 6th century [46]. These and other archaeological finds suggest that early rates of coastal accretion were not nearly as fast as were supposed, and may even have been slower than present rates. Indeed, the current high rates of soil erosion caused by extensive bad land use have doubtless dramatically increased the rates of coastal accretion.

In the southern part of Sumatra, the areas of maximum accretion are not, strangely, directly related to the major drainage systems. For example, opposite Bangka Island lies one of the broadest stretches of 'tidal swamp' in Sumatra, extending over 100 km inland. This appears to be because of the long-shore drift carrying sediment eastwards from the Musi/Banyuasin drainage system and such eastward currents occur in the region for nine months of the year [102]. Chambers and Sobur suggest that over half of the deposition of sediment from Musi/Banyuasin may occur outside the river delta itself, because the relatively exposed delta experiences considerable erosion [18]. Thus, no conventional delta can be

Figure 2.10. **Changes in the coastline of part of easter Sumatra.** (After Obedeyn [56, 57]).

formed [17].

As described in section 2.4.2, mangrove forests do not 'build' land but they do have a vital role in colonizing emerging mud banks, consolidating sediments and thereby accelerating the process of land extension [7, 8, 93]. The pioneer colonization by species of *Sonneratia* produces a network of pneumatophores which have three indirect functions:
- they help to protect the young trees from wave damage,
- they entangle floating vegetation, and
- they provide a habitat for burrowing crabs which help to aerate the soil [17].

If the mud banks were not colonized, it is likely that shifting currents, seasonally increased flows, or strong wave action could wash them away. Thus, at the mouth of rivers, deposition which typifies coastal extension is in the form of gradually enlarging off-shore islands which ultimately coalesce (although occasionally separated from the mainland by small tidal channels [17]). This phenomenon can be seen near the mouths of the rivers Besitang, Bile/Barumun, Rokan, Siak, Kampar, and Inderagiri, as well as in the Musi/Banyuasin area.

Along the shoreline between the major rivers the sediment deposition is more or less parallel to the established shoreline, particularly in sheltered bays where wave action is minimal. Species of *Sonneratia* in these areas area are again important as pioneer colonizers [17].

2.6 FAUNA

The fauna of mangrove forests can be divided conveniently into two groups: the essentially aquatic component of crabs, snails, worms, bivalves and others which depend directly upon the sea in various ways, and the terrestrial, often 'visiting', component including insects, spiders, snakes,lizards, rats, monkey and birds (see section 2.6.4, 2.6.5) which do not depend directly upon the sea. The majority of what follows, based on Berry [4], deals with the aquatic component.

The animals mentioned below represent only a fraction of the total mangrove fauna but the important points to be understood are that there are many different habitats within the mangrove forest each of which supports a distinct community of animals, and that a proportion of the fauna in mangrove forests is more or less restricted to mangroves. Knowledge of the coastal fauna of the Sunda Region is not yet sufficiently advanced to decide whether any of the mangrove fauna is absolutely restricted to mangroves [19, 20, 32, 47].

2.6.1 The challenges of living in mangroves

In comparison with other shore fauna, the mangrove forest fauna is heavily dominated by many species of crabs and snails. There are few types of worms, and very few bivalve molluscs, coelenterates (sea anenomes), echinoderms (starfish, sea urchins), etc. (Figure 2.11.) The dominance of crabs and snails may be largely ascribed to the peculiar conditions found in mangrove forests to which these two groups of animals have evolved successful adaptations.

Animals living on the soil of the inter-tidal area are subjected to long periods during which they are not covered by the sea. At the mean high water level of spring tides (MHWS), for example, the soil is left exposed for about 270 days per year, and for up to 25 consecutive days; at the lower terrestrial margin, soil is left exposed for about 320 days per year, and for up to 30 consecutive days. Most marine animals cannot stand this because:
- they quickly dry out,
- most cannot respire in air,
- many can only feed on water-borne food, and
- many must release spermatozoa, eggs and larvae into seawater

Crabs and snails, however, have:
- impervious exoskeletons/shells to restrict water loss,
- many can breathe air,
- many feed on micro-organisms or organic materials,
- many climb into the trees to find these foods, and
- they have internal fertilization and protect their eggs and early developing young in capsules or brood pouches (see section 4.6.2).

The soil in mangrove forests is subjected to salinities ranging from nearly zero to 50‰ [72]. During spring tides, salinities approximate those of tidal seawater, that is about 27–32‰. During neap tides, however, when the landward mangrove soil is not covered by the sea for days at a time, rainfall may reduce salinity to less than 15‰. Conversely, evaporation

117

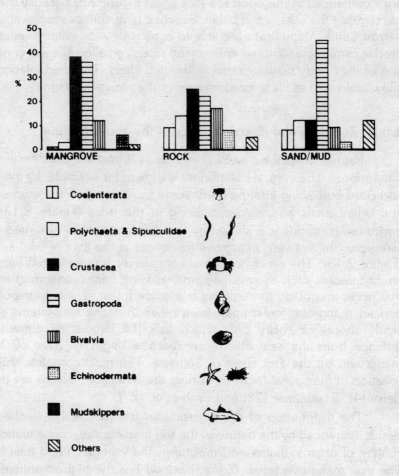

Figure 2.11 Percentages of total aquatic animal taxa recorded at three types of shore (omitting microscopic forms). Note that crustaceans and gastropod molluscs account for 74% of the total on the mangrove shore. Data from Berry [4]. Note that these data are not based on *complete* lists or on equally exhaustive surveys but they serve to illustrate the major differences.

without rainfall can increase salinity to more than 32‰. Most marine animals are only able to withstand very minor variations in salinity such as are experienced in the open sea (see again Figure 2.3) because they cannot regulate the salts/water balance of their body fluids except within quite narrow limits. Many crabs are able to cope with wide salinity variation by precise osmoregulation, whereas many snails can allow the salt concentration of their body tissues to vary without ill effect. These adaptations thus allow crabs and snails to predominate in the mangrove fauna.

2.6.2 Zonation and characteristics of the aquatic fauna

Faunal zonations within mangrove forest are effectively three-dimensional. The vertical component is shown, for example, by the worms and crabs burrowing into the mud, some snails living on the mud surface, and other snails and barnacles living in the trees (Figure 2.12). One horizontal component is shown by the different species observed on the foreshore, the seaward mangrove forest and at the limit of tidal influence (Figure 2.13). The other horizontal component is represented by the different features such as small streams, eroding banks, and mud mounds that occur irregularly through the mangrove forest. These forms of zonation set mangrove forest apart from other shoreline ecosystems such as sandy shores or rocky cliffs which lack the large-scale dimension of distance from the sea which can reach a depth of over 50 km for mangroves on the east coast of Sumatra. The most complete studies of zonation of mangrove fauna in or near the Straits of Malacca are those of Berry [4], Sasekumar [72] and Frith et al. [27].

The distribution of the macrofauna (animals visible to the naked eye) is influenced by the nature of the soil (particle size, consolidation, and content of organic matter and moisture), the vegetation and tidal factors. The true mangrove forest (Zone 4 below) has the highest animal abundance and species diversity because of its shade, complexity and abundance of organic detritus [27].

Ecologists have found that dividing ecosystems into recognizable subdivisions or zones is fraught with difficulties because vegetation types often intergrade with each other. Nevertheless, as long as the subdivisions are not regarded as rigid, and it is clear on what criteria they are based, such an approach provides a convenient means of describing the different

Figure 2.12 **Relative density of several species of tree-dwelling fauna distributed vertically on trees in an *Avicennia* forest, 10 m from the sea. (After Tee [82]). a- snail *Thais tissoti*; b- barnacle *Balanus amphitrite*; c- bivalve mollusc *Crassostrea cucullata*; d- barnacle *Chthamalus withersii*; e- mussel *Brachyodontes variabilis*.**

Figure 2.13 **Relative abundance of several species of tree-dwelling fauna along a transect through mangrove forest. (After Tee [82]). a- barnacle *Balanus amphitrite*; b- snail *Nerita birmanica*; c- snail *Littorina scabra*; d- barnacle *Chthamalus withersii*; e- polychaete worm *Nereis* spp.**

areas (Figure 2.14). The mangrove zones described by Berry [4] are as follows:

Zone 1: Seaward foreshore

As those field scientists who have tried to work in mangroves know to their discomfort, the seashore below the mangrove tree edge is usually extremely soft mud. This soil commonly comprises about 75% very fine sand (particles of $20-210\mu$), most of the remainder being even finer silt [72]. It extends down from the mean low water level of neap tides (MLWN) and so is covered by every tide of the year and never left exposed for many hours. The fauna is essentially marine with certain crab species, a few snails such as *T. telescopium* (Figure 2.15) and two or three species of polychaete worms (Figure 2.16) predominating. A variety of mudskippers - an unusual group of fish capable of living out of water for short periods - occur commonly along the water's edge and in burrows in the mud. An excellent review of general mudskipper biology can be found in MacNae [47].

Underwater, mudskippers breathe just like other fishes but in air they obtain oxygen by holding water and air in their gill chambers. This is supplemented by gas exchange through their skin and fins [78]. On land mudskippers move in a variety of ways: they lever themselves forward on their pectoral fins which move in synchrony with each other (i.e. not true walking) leaving characteristic tracks in the mud, they skip over the mud by flicking their tails, and they climb on vegetation using their pectoral and pelvic fins.

Although they look very similar, the different species of mudskipper have very different diets; some take mud into their mouths, retain algal material, and blow out the rest; some are omnivorous, eating small crustaceans as well as some plant material; and some are voracious carnivores feeding on crabs, insects, snails and even other mudskippers [15, 45].

It can be safely assumed that the modern mudskippers evolved from the same single ancestral mudskipper. It is not possible to determine what its feeding habits were, but it is likely to have been a generalized, detritus feeder. Genetic variations in individuals of this mudskipper made it possible for them to specialize in exploiting one particular food resource or group of food resources with more efficiency and thus greater competitive advantage. Although a taxonomic/ecological study of Sumatran mudskip-

Isopod crustaceans in a *Rhizophora* root tip.

Defoliated *Excoecaria agallocha* trees near Belawan, Langkat.

The defoliator: the caterpillar of the moth *Ophiusa serva*.

121

Figure 2.14 Major zones in a mangrove forest. Horizontal distances extremely reduced for clarity. Streams (Zone 5 in the text) are omitted. Figures represent tide coverings per year and days per year with tidal wetting. An eroded bank (Zone 3 in the text) is shown superimposed in dashed lines. Common tree species are indicated above. EHW = extreme high water, MHWS = mean high water of spring tides, MHWN = mean high water of neap tides, MSL = mean sea level, MLWN = mean low water of neap tides. (After Berry [4]).

pers has not been undertaken, a study in Queensland has shown that at least five species of predatory mudskippers can live in the same area by successfully partitioning their habitat and its resources between them [55] (see also section 4.8.5, 7.8.3 and 10.6).

If an observer stands still on the foreshore, animals which have been scared into their burrows by his approach will start to reapear. Hundreds of fiddler crabs *Uca* emerge, in densities as high as 50 per m². The larger mudskippers are their main predators (others include snakes, spiders, birds and monkeys) [45] and it would seem reasonable to ask why the mudskippers 'allowed' such high populations of potential food to exist.

Rates of prey exploitation depend upon the adaptations of both predator and prey. If predators evolved prudence so that they deliberatly avoided over-exploiting their prey, it would both oppose the pre-eminent goal of evolution which is to maximise the fitness or advantage of the individual, and also require that predator populations were regulated altruistically to maintain an optimum density. Natural selection should favour maximum exploitation of prey by each individual mudskipper at the expense of optimum prey management.

Figure 2.15 *Telescopium telescopium*

The level of exploitation of a prey population is determined by the ability of the predator to capture prey, balanced by the ability of the prey to avoid being captured (section 12.4.4). In this case, the speed of attack by mudskippers is balanced by the awareness and speed of retreat into burrows by the crabs. Both of these skills are evolved and tend to result in a

Figure 2.16 A polychaete worm common in mangrove soil - *Leiochrides australis;* this species commonly reaches 14 cm long.

Figure 2.17 Fiddler crab *Uca dussumieri.* (After Berry [4]).

more or less stable equilibrium between the numbers of predators and prey.

In an area of mangrove foreshore, 10 m wide and 20 m from the sea edge to the first mangrove seedlings, it would not be unusual to find an average of about 10 *Uca dussumieri* fiddler crabs (Figure 2.17) per square metre - therefore 2000 over the entire area - and a total of four large mudskippers *Periophthalmodon schlosseri.* This gives a predator-prey ratio of numbers of 1:500. Ricklefs lists various predator-prey ratios taken from the literature, and their range is 1:30 — 1:1263 [67].

Most mudskippers occupy deep burrows the tops of which are turretted in some species. Their inter-and intraspecific relationships are complex but burrows are usually evenly spaced on the mud thereby reducing the likelihood of conflicts [78]. Males seem to dig the burrows and make displays to attract passing females by jumping, and by erecting their dorsal fin. After pairing, eggs are laid on the sides of the burrow which is then defended by the male. Such territorial defence is rare or absent outside the breeding season [55].

Zone 2: Marine pioneer zone

Actively accreting pioneer zones rise gently through the region of neap low tide and mid-tide levels as bare mud gives way to seedlings and saplings, often of *Avicennia* and *Sonneratia*. The soil differs little from the of Zone 1. Most of this zone except the highest parts is covered by all the high tides of the year. This zone includes fever common marine animals and begins the more typical mangrove fauna. Snails such as *Syncera*, *Salinator*, and *Fairbankia* may occur on the wet soil (Figure 2.18). Mud-skippers are common, and the large fiddler crab *Uca dussumieri* and the smaller *U. mani* can be very numerous.

Horseshoe crabs (Figure 2.19) are periodically seen in this zone. They are distantly related to spiders but are the sole representatives of a group of animals which dominated the sea during the Palaeozoic Period over 250 million years ago. Fossil horseshoe crabs from the Silurian period

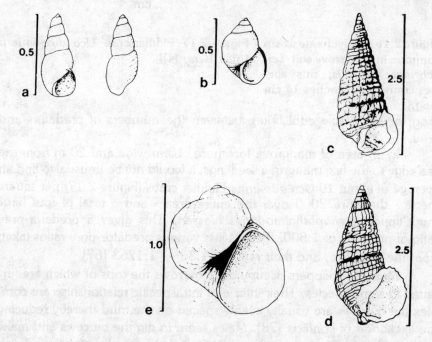

Figure 2.18   Some snails from mangrove soil. a- *Fairbankia* sp.; b- *Syncera brevicula*; c- *Cerithidea cingulata*; d- *Terebralia sulcata*; = e-*Salinator burmana* (a lung-bearing pulmonate snail). (From Berry [4]).

400 million years ago are virtually indistinguishable from the five species surviving today. The reason for the lack of change in these animals is hard to explain but it may be that they simply have not experienced effective competition or predation from other species to select for refinements or other adaptations.

Horseshoe crabs live in shallow water along sandy or muddy shores. They can swim through the water by flapping appendages on their abdomens. They feed on soft-shelled molluscs and worms, digging for them using shovelling movements of their shell. When the moon is full and the tide is high, horseshoe crabs come up to the beach to breed. The females, which are larger than the males [51], dig a shallow nest for their thousand or so eggs. The male clings to the back of the females shell, ready to release his sperm when the eggs are laid. One month later, again at high tide, the eggs hatch and the small larvae join the other marine zooplankton. Sumatran horseshoe crabs are of two species: those with a tail triangular in cross-section are *Tachypleus gigas,* and those with a tail circular in cross-section are *Carcinoscorpius rotundicauda.*

An extract of horseshoe crab tissue assists medical science in two unlikely ways. It is used in an extremely sensitive test for checking whether vaccines and intravenous fluids are contaminated by bacterial toxins and in a test for gonorrhoea.

Various species of polychaete worms, occasional bivalve molluscs and the peculiar sipunculid peanut-worm (Figure 2.20) live permanently in

Figure 2.19 Horseshoe crab.

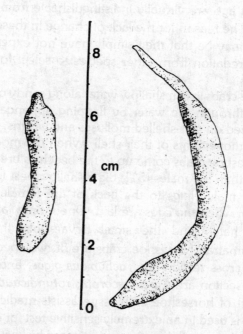

Figure 2.20 Peanut worm *Phascolosoma*. (After Berry [4]).

the soil of this zone. Peanut worms rest vertically in the soil and sweep their long proboscis over the soil surface picking up particles of organic matter.

The abundance and type of fauna living on the vegetation depends largely on the age of the tree - older ones have denser populations of more species. *Littorina* snails (Figure 2.21) occur on almost all the vegetation [40]; sometimes up to 2 m above the soil surface. Populations of sedentary animals encrust the lower stems of trees as they grow. These animals typically include barnacles with larger ones *Balanus amphitrite* below and the smaller *Chthamalus withersii* extending higher; oysters, commonly *Crassostres cucullata*; and the small black mussels *Brachyodontes* sp. which are attached to the tree by 'byssus' threads. A total of 15,401 animals. 9,199 of which were mussels of the genus *Brachyodontes*, were found on a single *Avicennia* tree [83]. These attached fauna may be eaten off the lower stems by the carnivorous snails *Thais* and *Murex* (Figure 2.22). Barnacles and mussels sometimes suffer 50% mortality in the first

Figure 2.21 Four species of *Littorina* commonly found in mangrove forest near the seaward edge. a- *L. melanostoma;* b- *L. scabra;* c- *L. nudulata;* d- *L. carinifera.* (From Berry [4]).

Figure 2.22 Two predatory snails *Thais* sp. and *Murex* sp.

10 m above the soil surface but the number of dead animals decrease upward indicating that predation higher up the tree is less [83]. Figure 2.23 shows the effect of predation by *Thais tissoti* on the barnacle *Balanus amphritrite*.

Figure 2.23 The numbers of the barnacle *Balanus amphritrite* found dead and alive at different heights up a mangrove tree stem, with the percentage of dead animals. The shaded portion indicated by the arrow represents those animals probably predated upon by the predatory snail *Thais tissoti*. (After Tee [83]).

Two or three species of hermit crab are found in this zone. These crabs have lost the hard protective carapace over the rear part of their bodies and depend on finding empty shells for protection. The combination of security and mobility of the adopted shells is clearly advantageous and hundreds of hermit crabs can sometimes be seen on a beach. Suitable shells are, unfortunately for the crabs, a limited resource and this affects growth and reproduction. It has been found that crabs with roomy shells put their energy into growth and do not reproduce, whereas crabs with tight shells, stop growing and put their energy into reproduction [5]. The scarcity of shells leads to active competition between species of hermit crabs and this is described by Bertness [6]. A review of hermit crab ecology is given by Hazlett [31].

Zone 3: Eroded banks

The seaward edge of mangrove forest is often marked by a nearly vertical bank 1—1½m high instead of a sloping pioneer zone. This is caused by current sweeping away the silt and is most obvious on the outer bend of rivers near the sea, where the current flows faster than on the inner bend (Figure 2.24). The bank may be broken in places and mangrove trees at its edge often fall into the sea as the soil is slowly eroded away. The top of this bank is usually at or slightly above the mean high water of neap tides, and may sometimes be left 9 — 10 days without tidal cover. The soil of an eroded bank resembles that of the mangrove forest floor behind it, with less fine sand (commonly about 65%) than in Zones 1 and 2.

The bank is burrowed into by various crab species [3].

Figure 2.24. Schematic diagram of a meandering river near the sea to illustrate the position of eroded banks (heavy lines).

Zone 4: True mangrove forest

The mangrove fauna of this zone differs in several respects from the preceding zones. Most of this zone is very flat and the soil surface is exposed to the air for an average of 27 days per month. However, since the trees provide heavy shade the humidity is very high, so the soil rarely dries out. There is also abundant leaf litter and other organic matter so that detritus feeders abound. The soil contains even less fine sand and more of the finer silt and clay particles. There is also more organic matter than in soils near the water's edge.

About 75% of the fauna of this zone is not found in the other zones [27], and is best divided into three groups: tree fauna, soil surface fauna and burrowing fauna.

Tree fauna

Perhaps the most striking change is the rapid decrease of encrusting animals, which rely on frequent inundation, on the lower stems and trunks of the trees. The remaining (mobile) tree fauna is largely composed of snails such as species of *Littorina* and *Nerita birmanica* (Figure 2.25) which are also found in Zone 2. Further back from the sea *Cerithidea obtusa* and *Cassidula* are found, and even further inland species of *Ellobium* occur. (Figure 2.26) [40]. Most of these feed on algae and move up trees when tides wet the soil but *Littorina* very rarely leaves the tree trunks. All these

3
cm

Figure 2.25 *Nerita birmanica.*

Figure 2.26 Two ellobid snails. a- *Ellobium aurisjudae*; b- E. *aurismidae*.
(From Berry [4]).

snails are able to breathe efficiently in air and some, the pulmonates such
as *Ellobium*, have lungs.

Soil surface fauna

These animals comprise mostly crabs (see below) and snails,
although the medium mudskippers *Periophthalmus vulgaris* can be common. Among the snails, actual distance from the sea seems to matter less
than details of ground conditions. In wetter areas such as where water
drain into small gullies, *Syncera brevicula* is more common than anywhere
else in the mangrove forest.

Molluscs at the seaward edge (Zone 1 and 2) of the mangrove forest
comprise a mixed sample of gastropods and bivalves. Further back in the
mangrove forest, however, carnivores and filter-feeding molluscs disappear. The vast majority of the molluscs in the true mangrove forest feed by
grazing on algae or micro-organisms on the soil surface. Little is known
about mollusc reproductive behaviour in mangrove forests but most have
internal fertilization of eggs and, unlike many aquatic snails, have eggs that
develop into tiny baby snails rather than water-borne larvae.

Burrowing fauna

Nearly all the mangrove crustaceans and worms make burrows
which reach down to the water table. Many different types of tunnels are
constructed (Figure 2.27) and the elliptical tunnels of the edible crab may

slope down from the bank of a river for as far as 5 m.

In general, these burrows serve as:
- a refuge from predators at the surface,
- a reservoir of water,
- a source of organic food,
- home for pairing and mating, to be defended, and
- a place for brooding eggs and young,

although no one species uses a burrow for all these purposes.

As mentioned in section 2.6.1, most mangrove crabs are able to tolerate long periods out of water and their respiratory systems are obviously specialized. Typical crabs inhale water under the sides of the carapace, between the legs and into the gill chambers. Deozygenated water is expelled either side of the mouth. When water is scarce for this, sesarmid crabs (small crabs with a characteristic square carapace) allow air into the moist gill chambers. Sesarma (Figure 2.28) can even recirculate the water around the carapace where it becomes reoxygenated [48].

The most abundant, though largely invisible, source of food on the forest floor is a mixture of organic deposits, much of it originating from decomposed leaves and other vegetable material, mixed with a flora of diatoms, bacteria and other micro-organisms growing on the deposits. Many crabs and other mangrove animals feed upon either the organic matter, the micro-organisms, or both, picking up this 'mud' with their pincers or chelipeds. Male fiddler crabs have one huge pincer which is useless for feeding and the forced to eat half as fast as the females which have a pair of normal-sized pincers; presumably the males have to eat for twice as long. This seemingly unnecessary encumbrance is used for attracting females for mating and for warning away males. It would serve a mutant male fiddler crab little if its larger pincer was reduced in size and could be used for feeding, if it could not then attract females for mating.

In the landward areas of true mangrove forest, the first signs are seen of an animal that is itself rarely seen. the mud lobster. This animal builds volcano-like mounds of mud which can reach over a metre high (see again Figure 2.27), and feeds on mud, digesting algae, protozoa and organic particles [34]. The burrow below the mound is one to three metres long, extending down to the water table. The entrance leading to the main burrow is generally plugged with layers of earth. The habit of burrowing deeply in anoxic mud, closing itself off in poorly oxygenated air and water

Figure 2.27 Different types of animal burrows in mangrove soil. This horizontal line indicates the water table. A- crab *Scylla serrata* (with transverse section of burrow); B- mud lobster *Thalassina anomala* (not all burrows open below ground as shown here); C- crab *Uca* spp. (burrows may reach water table nearer the low-tide level); D- crab *Sesarma* spp.; E- peanut worm *Phascolosoma;* F- large mudskipper *Periophthalmodon schlosseri;* G-smaller mudskipper *Boleophthalmus bodaerti;* H- pistol prawns *Alphaeus* spp.; smaller mudskipper *Periophthalmus vulgaris.* (From Berry [4]).

1.5 — 4.5 cm

Figure 2.28 *Sesarma* sp.

suggests that it may have evolved means of anaerobic respiration [48]. Research into this secretive creature would not simply be for academic interest, because it mounds are often regarded as a nuisance. Managing the numbers of distribution of mud lobsters requires a knowledge of their biology and ecology.

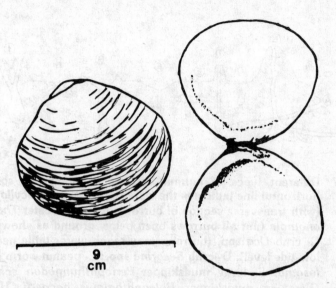

Figure 2.29 The bivalve mollusc *Geloina ceylonica*. (From Berry [4]).

The bivalve mollusc *Geloina* (Figure 2.29) lives buried in mud and can occasionally be found in this zone, but is more common in mangrove forests on islands in or near river deltas. *Geloina* is remarkable in its ability to feed, respire and breed so far from open water and at levels where it is sometimes not covered by tidal seawater for several weeks at a time.

Zone 5: Rivers, streams and gullies
The banks and beds of water courses in the mangrove forest have a fauna which is generally distinct from that on the general forest floor. For example, many of the forest floor species of polychaete worms and crabs are missing, whereas juvenile fiddler crabs and some snail species are more common. The edible crab with the paddle-like rear legs occurs in the larger streams and rivers in the mangrove forest where it is caught in traps.

Zone 6: The terrestrial margin
Far back from the sea, mangrove soil is covered by fewer and fewer tides and suffers longer and longer intervals of exposure. Unlike other types of shore, there is virtually no wave action in mangrove swamps to carry seawater higher than the true tidal level, because the wave energy is absorbed by the abundant vegetation. Thus, animals in this zone live on a

135

salt-impregnated soil but are covered by seawater only at irregular and infrequent intervals.Insects, snakes, lizards and other typically terrestrial animals are much more common here than further seaward. *Sesarma* and-some large crabs occur here and in the *Nypa* palm swamps behind. Their basic requirement is that their burrows must reach down to the water table. The mud lobster has one of the deepest burrows and is therefore seen some distance from the mangrove forest, for instance in coconut plantations. Where there is moving water some snails, such as *Fairbankia* and *Syncera*, and the large mudskipper *Periophthalmodon schlosseri* may be found.

2.6.3. Biomass of aquatic fauna

Only one estimate of biomass of aquatic mangrove fauna seems to have been determined in the Sunda Region. Tee calculated the dry-tissue biomass of tree-dwelling aquatic fauna in four mangrove forest zones in Selangor, Peninsular Malaysia (Table 2.5). The results show a general reduction of biomass with increasing distance from the sea. It is supposed that the turnover rate (time for one generation to replace another) must be quite fast because most of the tree-dweling aquatic fauna are in the lower trophic group (i.e. filter feeders) none of which have long life spans [80].

Table 2.5 Estimated biomass of tree-dwelling aquatic fauna in four types of mangrove forest. (From Tee [83].

FOREST TYPE

	Avicennia forest	Sonneratia forest	Bruguiera forest	Rhizophora forest
Distance from sea (m)	10	235	310	445
Estimated biomass (kg)	1014.0	272.4	29.7	37.9

2.6.4 Terrestrial fauna

Insects, birds and mammals live chiefly in the canopy of mangrove forest. Ground living animals such as wild pig, mousedeer, wild cats, rats, and lizards only venture into the landward edge of mangrove for brief periods. The two mangrove mammals seen most often are the silvery leaf monkey *Presbytis cristata* and the long-tailed macaque *Macaca fascicularis*. The leaf monkeys are largely arboreal and eat leaves, shoots and fruit, whereas the macaques are mainly ground-dwelling and eat crabs, peanut worms and small vertebrates as well as some leaves, shoots and fruit. Faecal analyses have also shown that both species eat the nectar rich flowers of *Sonneratia* [39].

Leaves are a poor source of food for most mammals because the cellulose molecules are very long and are therefore hard to break down without special digestive adaptations. Leaf monkeys have evolved a highly sacculated stomach, like a cow's, in which special bacteria ferment and break down cellulose so that it becomes digestible.

Many tree leaves are defended against being eaten by herbivores by defence compounds, the most common of which are fibre (lignin) and phenols, particularly tanins (section 2.4.4). In a normal acidic digestive tract (the content of a human stomach are generally at pH 3), tannins will bind strongly onto any protein, both food and enzymes, thereby hindering the digestive process.[4] In the leaf monkey's complex stomach, however, the pH is probably maintained between 5.0 and 6.7 [2], and in such conditions not only are the fermentation bacteria able to thrive, but the attachment of tannins onto proteins is weaker. Both silvery leaf monkeys and long-tailed macaques have been observed to eat bark from the twigs of *Bruguiera* [39], which have considerable quantities of tannins - perhaps 30% dry weight. For the macaques, which have a simple stomach, this may have been eaten as a stomach purgative (section 7.6).

Fruit bats, particularly the flying fox *Pteropus vampyrus*, roost in the mangrove forest canopy and other bats such as the cave fruit bat *Eonycteris spelaea* and the long-tongued fruit bat *Macroglossus sobrinus* are very important in the pollination of the flowers of *Sonneratia* [77] (section 10.5).

The mangrove frog *Rana cancrivora* is exceptional among

---

4. The binding of tannins onto protein is what is felt when one bites through unripe banana or banana skin. Bitter tastes, such as coffee and papaya leaves, are caused by compounds called alkaloids.

Colonization of a sandy shore by the creeping *Ipomoea pes-caprae* and seedlings of *Casuarina equisitifolia*. Near Singkil, South Aceh.

Animals both within the sand and thrown up by the waves attract birds to feed on sandy shores. These are redshanks, white-winged terns and ruddy turnstones.

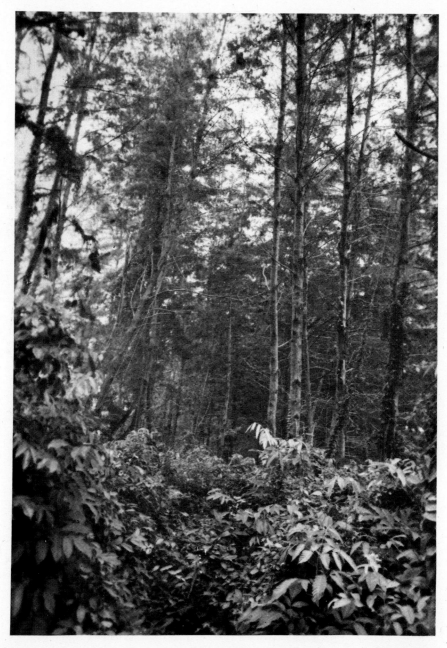

Inside a *Casuarina* forest; note the absence of *Casuarina* seedlings. Near Singkil, South Aceh.

amphibians in being able to live and breed in weakly saline water. The tadpoles are more resistant to salt than the adults and metamorphosis into adults will only occur after considerable dilution of the salty water [47].

Mangroves are inhabited by a variety of reptiles such as the monitor lizard *Varanus salvator*, the common skink *Mabuya multifasciata*, mangrove pit viper *Trimeresurus pupureomaculatus* and the common catsnake *Boiga dendrophila*. Most snakes seen in or near mangroves are not in fact sea snakes (Hydrophidae) which live primarily in open water [90, 91, 92]. Potentially the largest animal of the mangrove swamps is the estuarine crocodile *Crocodilus porosus*. Persecution for centuries has reduced its numbers to a very low level and it is possible that large specimens (they can exceed 9 m) no longer exist around Sumatra (section 6.4).

The most conspicuous of the insects are mosquitoes, but only one of these, *Anopheles sundaicus*, carries malaria. The larvae of this species can live in water with a salinity of 13‰ [21]. Species of *Aedes* mosquitoes have been seen feeding on mudskippers but they are also attracted to human skin. Another potential insect hazard is the leaf-weaving ant *Oecophylla smaragdina* the workers of which, if their nest is disturbed, can inflict a very painful bite. The making of the nest is extraordinary because the adult ants have no means of producing silk to join the leaves of the nest together. The larvae do have silk glands, however, originally intended so they could weave cocoons to pupate within, but they are not now used for this. Instead, when a leaf is to be added to the nest or a tear repaired, some of the worker ants seize the edges to be joined and hold them in the required position. Other workers enter the nest and collect a larva. The larva is held in the workers' jaws and while it produces the sticky silk it is moved back and forth between the leaf edges, like a tube of quick-drying glue [88].

One insect, the caterpillar of the moth *Olethreutes leveri*, has managed to extend its niche and avoid competition by spinning together leaves of *Sonneratia alba*. It is able to survive periodic immersion in sea water because air is trapped within the web. Experiments showed it could withstand 8½ hours immersion within the web, but died quickly if immersed in sea water without the web [38].

2.6.5 Birds

Mangrove forests on the west of Peninsular Malaysia are used by at least 121 species of birds which are probably almost identical to those found in Sumatran mangroves. The most important trees for nesting are probably *Sonneratia*, which are both tall (± 30 m) and have occasional holes in their trunks which are used by woodpeckers. The landward side of a mangrove forest generally has more birds of more species than the seaward side but birds are found throughout.

Nesbit divided the list of bird species observed in mangrove forests on the west coast of Peninsular Malaysia into ten groups (Table 2.6) according to the manner in which they use the ecosystem [53]. Mangroves are thus important to birds in at least four ways:

Table 2.6. **The number and percentage of birds observed in mangrove forest in Peninsular Malaysia grouped according to the manner in which they use the habitat.** (From Nisbet [53]).

GROUP A.		
Species which are confined exclusively to mangroves	4 %	(5)
GROUP B.		
Residents confined to mangrove but migrants found elsewhere	2.5%	(3)
GROUP C.		
Nesting more or less exclusively in mangroves but feeding outside	7.5%	(9)
GROUP D.		
Migrants which depend largely on mangroves for roosting	7.5%	(9)
GROUP E.		
Coastal species for which mangrove is a major habitat	14 %	(17)
GROUP F.		
Species which make seasonal movements to and from mangroves	7.5%	(9)
GROUP G.		
Migrants which use mangroves as well as lowland areas	14 %	(17)
GROUP H.		
Aerial species which feed over mangroves as well as land	4 %	(5)
GROUP I.		
Species of semi-open country which are also found in mangroves	28 %	(34)
GROUP J.		
Species of forest which are also found in mangroves	11 %	(13)
Total	121 species	

Figure 2.30 Storks, egrets ad herons commonly seen near mangrove forests. a- woolly-necked stork *Ciconia episcopus*; b- little egret *Egretta garzetta*; chinese egret *Egretta eulophotes*; d- plumed egret *Egretta intermedia*; e- great egret *Egretta alba*; f- grey heron *Ardea cinerea*; g- purple heron *Ardea purpurea*; h- great-billed heron *Ardea sumatrana*.

- they provide nesting sites for a number of large species of herons and storks (Figure 2.30), and also for at least three birds of prey and two owls. Many of these species nest nowhere else, and presumably would be subjected to much greater predation (certainly by young humans) if they attempted to do so.

- they provide roosts for many migrant species (and a few residents) which feed on or over the tidal mudflats. These roosts are particularly important for the migrant waders.

- they are visited seasonally by a number of pigeons and parrots, both from inland and outlying islands. One of these, the pied imperial pigeon *Ducula bicolor* (Figure 2.31) is thought to be the main source of seeds reaching Jarak Island in the Straits of Malacca. Of the plants growing on the island, 90% have fruit dispersed by birds [100].

Figure 2.31 **Pied Imperial Pigeon** *Ducula bicolor.*

- they support a varied fauna of resident and migrant land-birds. Eight species (groups A and B in Table 2.6) occur in no other habitat and seventeen others (group E) occur largely within mangrove forest. This assemblage of birds is distinctive in that it is largely made up of predatory kingfishers, insectivorous woodpeckers and warblers and nectar-drinking sunbirds and some of the dominant frugivores of adjacent forest (pheasants, hornbills, barbets, leaf-birds, bulbuls and babblers) are more or less absent. Interestingly, most of the species in group A and B occur outside mangrove forests in other parts of their range.

A significant feature of the resident land-bird fauna is that most of the common species (in groups E and I, e.g. tree sparrows *Passer montanus*) are those which, in other parts of Malaysia, and indeed Sumatra, are characteristic of semi-open habitats - villages, towns, gardens, riversides and clearings. This is perhaps most surprising because mangrove forest is dense and much more similar in structure to secondary forest. Since semi-open habitats are largely man-made it is likely that many of these species were, until recently, confined to a narrow coastal strip of mangroves and scrub and to clearings and river banks in the forest. It should be said, however, that the species which have benefited most from the clearance of inland forest are not very numerous in mangroves, while most of the dominant mangroves species are still primarily coastal in distribution.

Some of the species which are most specialized for life in mangrove forest are replaced in inland areas by an obvious potential competitor. For example, the Ruddy kingfisher *Halcyon coromanda* breeds in forest in the northern part of its range (India, E. China, Japan, Taiwan) but is confined to mangroves as a breeding species in Peninsular Malaysia and Sumatra where the forest is inhabited by the Rufous-collared kingfisher *Halcyon concreta*. Thus it seems that as inland forest was opened up by man, the unspecialized coastal species (group I) were able to spread inland, whereas the species which were more specialized to live in mangrove forest remained confined to the mangroves and nearby coastal scrub.

2.7 EFFECTS OF THE FAUNA ON THE VEGETATION

Very little is known about the effects of the activities of animals on the mangrove forest. The holes constructed by crabs and mudskippers may affect rates of accretion or erosion and increase aeration of the soil, the mounds of the mud lobster and the activities of polychaete worms may significantly influence the rate of nutrient/energy flow in the ecosystem, inshore fish that graze on yung seedlings may cause slower colonization etc., but there have been no studies in the Sunda Region on these or related topics.

Some of the known effects are rather surprising. Root tips of *Rhizophora* trees which have not yet reached the ground are sometimes attacked by small isopod crustaceans. They burrow into the soft root tip, form a chamber and breed. Such destruction of growing points, as with most plants, results in the formation of multiple side roots. It had been suggested that the activity of these isopods may benefit *Rhizophora* by increasing the number of roots and therefore the number of channels by which nutrients can reach the tree. A higher production of roots per tree would either result in a faster expansion of adjacent areas of *Rhizophora* or in a higher number of roots per unit area. In Florida, the number of roots per unit area was indeed higher where these trees were parasitized by isopods than at sites where they were absent [64, 65]. The effect of the increased root density on silt settlement and thence on land formation has not been measured but it could be quite significant.

As far as can be ascertained, only two large-scale natural defoliations have been reported from mangrove forest, both in Southeast Asia. One was in southern Thailand where caterpillars of the geometrid butterfly *Cleora injectaria* defoliated an area of *Avicennia alba* [60]. The second defoliation of mangroves was recorded in the Belawan area of North Sumatra in early 1983. In this case caterpillars of the noctulid moth *Ophiusa serva* were responsible for defoliating a large area of *Excoecaria agallocha* [98]. Interestingly, *Excoecaria* is a member of the family Euphorbiaceae and has a poisonous white sap which, if it comes in contact with eyes, can cause blindness [16]. Neither case of mangrove defoliation caused the death of the plants.

Rhizophora may avoid defoliation by insects by exuding a clear, thick, sticky, sweet substance from the base of leaf buds which have either been slightly damaged or are above young flowers. This substance is licked by sunbirds which, apart from weating sweet substances such as nectar, also eat insects. Thus, attracting sunbirds with the sugary solution may benefit the plant if the sunbirds also feed on damaging insects [51].

Defoliation and other local effects of fauna on the mangrove should be recorded by responsible scientists and reports sent to the National Oceanological Institute, Jakarta, and to the National Biological Institue Bogor. Only in this way will the understanding of ecosystems develop and grow so that distinctions can be drawn between natural phenomena and the impact of industrial development.

143

REFERENCES

1. Anon. (1979). *Fisheries Statistics of Indonesia 1977.* Direktorat Jenderal Perikanan, Jakarta. (Referred to in Soegiarto and Polunin, 1980).

2. Bauchop, T. and Marrucci, R.W. (1968). Ruminant digestion of the langur monkey. *Science* 161: 698—700. (12.8.8)

3. Berry, A.J. (1963). Faunal zonation in mangrove swamps. *Bull. natl. Mus. Singapore* 32: 90—98. (12.9.22)

4. —————. (1972). The natural history of West Malaysian mangrove faunas. *Malay. Nat. J.* 25: 135—162. (12.9.11)

5. Bertness, M.D. (1981). Competitive dynamics of a tropical hermit crab assemblage. *Ecology* 62: 751—761. (12.3.37)

6. —————. (1981). Pattern and plasticity in tropical hermit crab growth and reproduction. *Am. Nat.* 117: 754—773. (12.3.36)

7. Bird, E.C.F. (1982). Coastal landforms of the Asian humid tropics. In *Man, Land and Sea* (ed. C. Soysa, L.S. Chia, W.L. Collier), pp. 3—14. Agricultural Development Council, Bangkok. (2.4.25)

8. Bird, E.C.F. and Barson, M.M. (1977). Measurement of physiographic changes on mangrove-fringed estuaries and coastlines. *Mar. Res. Indonesia* 18: 73—80. (2.4.7)

9. Bodegom, A.H. van (1929). De Vloedbosschen in het gewest Riouw en onderheerigheden. *Tectona* 22: 1302—1332. (12.9.31)

10. Brock, T.D. (1981). Calculating solar radiation for ecological studies. *Ecol. Modelling* 14: 1—19. (19.5.18)

11. Brotonegoro, S. and Abdulkadir, S. (1979). Penelitian pendahuluan tentang kecepatan gugur daun dan penguraiannya dalam hutan bakau Pulau Rambut. In *Prosiding Seminar 'Ekosistem Hutan Mangrove'* (ed. S. Soemodihardjo, A. Nontji, A. Djamali), pp. 81—85. Lembaga Oseanologi Nasional, Jakarta. (12.9.2)

12. Boudowski, G. (1963). Forest succession in tropical lowlands. *Turrialba* 13: 42—44. (12.10.109)

13. Bunning, E. (1944). Botanische Beobachtungen in Sumatra. *Flora N.S.* 37: 334—344. (12.1.12)

14. Bunt, J.S. and Williams, W.T. (1981). Vegetational relationships in the mangroves of tropical Australia. *Mar. Ecol. Prog. Ser.* 4: 349—359. (12.9.48).

15. Burhanuddin and Martosewojo, S. (1979). Pengamatan terhadap ikan gelodok, *Periophthalmus koelreuteri* (Pallas) di Pulau Pari. In *Prosiding Seminar 'Ekosistem Hutan Mangrove'* (ed. S. Soemodihardjo, A. Nontji, A. Djamali), pp. 86—92. Lembaga Oseanologi Nasional, Jakarta. (12.9.2).

16. Burkill, I.H. (1966). *Dictionary of the Economic Products of the Malay Peninsula.* Department of Agriculture, Kuala Lumpur. (. .)

17. Chambers, M.J. (1980). The environment and geomorphology of deltanic sedimentation. (Some examples from Indonesia). In *Tropical Ecology and Development* (ed. J. Furtado), pp. 1091—1095. University of Malaya, Kuala Lumpur. (2.4.27).

18. Chambers, M.J.G. and Sobur, A. (1977). *Problems of Assessing the Rates and Processes of Coastal Changes in the Province of South Sumatra.* Research Report 3, Centre for Natural Resource Management and Environmental Studies, IPB, Bogor. (2.4.28).

19. Chapman, V.J. (1976). *Coastal Vegetation,* 2nd Edition. Pergamon, Oxford. (2.4.32).

20. _____. (1977). Introduction. In *Wet Coastal Ecosystems* (Red. V.J. Chapman), pp. 1—29. Elsevier, Amsterdam. (2.4.28)

21. _____. (1977). Wet coastal formations of Indo-Malesia and Papua New Guinea. In *Wet Coastal Ecosystems* (ed. by V.J. Chapman), pp. 261—270. Elsevier, Amsterdam.

22. Cockcroft, V.G. and Forbes, A.T. (1981). Tidal activity rhythms in the mangrove snail *Cerithidea decollata* (Linn.) *S. Afr. J. Zool.* 16: 5—9. (12.3.16).

23. Cruz, A.A. dela and Banaag, J. F. (1967). The ecology of a small mangrove patch in Matabungkay Beach, Batangas Province. *Natur. Appl. Sci. Bull.* 20: 486—494. (12.9.33).

145

24. Dinas Kehutanan Propinsi Dati I Riau. (1979). Hutan mangrove di Propinsi Riau. In *Prosiding Seminar 'Ekosistem Hutan Mangrove'* (ed. S. Soemodihardjo, A. Nontji, A. Djamali), pp. 176—185. Lembaga Oseanologi Nasional, Jakarta. (12.9.2)

25. Ding Hou (1958). Rhizophoraceae. *Flora Malesiana I* 5:429—493. Introductory section on ecology (pp. 431—441) by C.G.G.J. van Steenis.

26. Endert, F.H. (1920). De woodboomflora van Palembang. *Tectona.* 13: 113—160. (12.9.34)

27. Frith, D.W., Tantanasiriwong, R. and Bhatia, O. (1976). Zonation of macrofauna on a mangrove shore, Phuket Island. *Phuket Mar. Biological Center, Res. Bull. No. 10.* (12.9.49)

28. Glocek, G.S. and Voris, H.K. (1982). Marine snake diets: prey composition diversity and overlap. *Copeia.* 1982: 661—666. (12.6.4)

29. Gomez, E.D. (1980). *The Present State of Mangrove Ecosystems in southeast Asia and the Impact of Aquatic Pollution.* South China Sea Fisheries Development and Coordinating Programme, Manilla. (12.9.24)

30. Hardjosuwarno, S., Shalihuddin, D.T., Slukahar, A., Pudjoarinto, A., and Purwoto (1978). *Studi mengenai ekosistem dari mangrove community Cilacap (Jawa Tengah).* Study Group Pencemaran, LEMIGAS, Jakarta. (12.9.4)

31. Hazlett, B.A. (1981). The behavioural ecology of hermit crabs. *Ann. Rev. Ecol. Syst.* 12: 1—22. (12.3.38)

32. Hutchings, P.A. and Reicher, H.F. (1982). The fauna of Australian mangroves. *Proc. Linn. Soc. N.S.W.* 106: 83—121. (12.9.50)

33. IPB/Team Kehutanan (1975). Laporan survei kehutanan di Delta Upang-Banyuasin. IPB, Bogor.

34. Johnson, D.S. (1961). The food and feeding of the mudlobster *Thalassina anomala* (Herbst). *Crustaceana* 2: 325—326. (12.3.35)

35. Johnstone, I.M. (1981). Consumption of leaves by herbivores in mixed mangrove stands. *Biotropica*. 13: 252—259. (12.9.36)
36. Jonker, H.A.J. (1933). De vloedbosschen van den Riaw Lingga Archipel. *Tectus* 26: 717—741 (12.9.51)
37. Kartawinata, K., Adisoemarto, S., Soemodihardjo, S., and Tantra, I.G.M. (1979) Status pengetahuan hutan bakau di Indonesia. In *Prosiding Seminar 'Ekosistem Hutan Mangrove'* (ed. S. Soemodihardjo, A. Nontji, A. Djamali), pp. 21—39. Lembaga Oseanology Nasional, Jakarta. (12.9.2)
38. Lever, R.J.U. (1955). Notes on a mangrove caterpillar from Port Dickson. *Malay. Nat. J.* 10: 13—14. (12.4.2)
39. Lim, B.H. and Sasekumar, A. (1979). A preliminary study on the feeding biology of mangrove forest primates. Kuala Selangor. *Malay. Nat. J.* 33: 105—112. (12.8.73)
40. Lim, C.F. (1963). A preliminary illustrated account of mangrove molluscs from Singapore and S.W. Malaya. *Malay. Nat. J.* 17: 235—240. (12.3.17)
41. Lind, E.M. and Morrison, M.E.S. (1974). *East African Vegetation*. Longman, London. (Referred to in Rabinowitz, 1978).
42. Lugo, A.E. and Snedaker, S.C. (1974). The Ecology of Mangroves. *Ann. Rev. Syst. Ecol.* 5: 39—64. (12.9.9)
43. Lugo. A.E., Evink, G., Brinson, M.M., Broce, A., and Snedaker, S.C. (1975). Diurnal rates of photosynthesis, respiration and transpiration in mangrove forests of south Florida. In *Tropical Ecological Systems* (ed. F.B. Golley and E. Medina), pp. 335—350. Springer-Verlag, New York. (12.9.37)
44. Luythes, A. (1923). De vloedbosschen in Atjeh. *Tectona*. 16: 575—591. (12.9.38)
45. MacIntosh, D.J. (1979). Predation of fiddler crabs (*Uca* spp.) in estuarine mangroves. In *Mangrove and Estuarine Vegetation in Southeast Asia* (ed. P.B.L. Srivastrava, A.M. Ahmad, G. Dhanarajan and I. Hamjah). BIOTROP Special Publication No. 10, pp. 101—110. BIOTROP, Bogor. (12.9.26)
46. McKinnon, E.E. (1982). A brief note on Muara Kumpeh Hilir: An early port site on the Batang Hari? *SPAFA Digest* 3: 37—40. (23.6.18)

147

47. MacNae, W. (1968). A general account of the fauna and flora of mangrove swamps and forests in the Indo-Pacific region. *Adv. mar. Biol.* 6: 73—270. 612.9.32)

48. Mallley, D.F. (1977). Adaptations of decapod crustaceans to life in mangrove swamps. *Mar. Res. Indonesia.* 18: 63—72. (12.3.10)

49. Martosubroto, P. (1979). Sumbangan hutan mangrove terhadap perikanan. In *Prosiding Seminar 'Ekosistem Hutan Mangrove'* (ed. S. Soemodihardjo, A. Nontji, A. Djamali), pp. 109—113. Lembaga Oseanologi Nasional, Jakarta. (12.9.2)

50. Martosubroto, P. and Naamin, N. (1977). Relationship between tidal forests (mangrove) and commercial shrimp production in Indonesia. *Mar. Res. Indonesia.* 18: 81—86. (2.2.7)

51. Meer Mohr, J.C. van der (1941). On two species of Malaysian King-Crabs. *Treubia* 18: 201—205. (12.3.39)

52. Meijer, W. (1974). *Field Guide for the Trees of West Malesia.* Univ. Kentucky Press.

53. Nisbet, I.C.T. (1968). The utilization of mangrove by Malayan birds. *Ibis.* 110: 345—352. (12.7.3)

54. Nixon, S.W., Furnas, B.N., Lee, V., Marshall, N., Ong, J.E., Wong, C.H., Gong, W.K. and Sasekumar, A. (1980). The role of mangroves in the carbon and nutrient dynamics of Malaysian estuaries. Paper presented at the UNESCO Symposium on *'Mangrove Environment: Research and Management'.* Universiti Malaya, Kuala Lumpur. (2.4.19)

55. Nursall, J.R. (1981). Behaviour and habitat affecting the distribution of five species of sympatric mudskipper in Queensland. *Bull. Mar. Sci.* 31: 730—735. (12.5.16)

56. Obdeyn, V. (1941). Zuid Sumatra volgens de oudste berichten. I. de geomorfologische gesteldheid van Zuid Sumatra in verband met de opvatting der ouden. *Tijd. K. ned. Aardrijksk;* 58: 190—216. (2.4.40)

57. _____. (1942). De oude zeehandelsweg door de straat van Malaka in verband mat de geomorfologie der selateilanden. *Tijd. K. ned. Aardrijksk.* 59: 742—770 (2.4.41).

58. Ong, J.E., Gong, W.K., and Wong, C.H. (1980). *Ecological Survey of the Sungei Merbok Estuarine Mangrove Ecosystem*. Universiti Sains Malaysia, Penang. (12.9.21)

59. Ong. J.E., Gong, W.K., Wong, C.H. and Dhanarajan, G. (1980). Contribution of aquatic productivity in a managed mangrove ecosystem in Malaysia. paper presented at the UNESCO Symposium on *'Mangrove Environment: Research and Management'*. University Malaya, Kuala Lumpur. (12.9.20)

60. Piyakarnchana, T. (1981). Severe defoliation of *Avicennia alba* Bl. by larvae of *Cleora injectaria* Walker. *J. Sci. Soc. Thailand* 7: 33—36. (12.9.43)

61. Primack, R.B. and Tomlinson, P.B. (1978). Sugar secretions from the buds of *Rhizophora*. *Biotropica* 10: 74—75. (12.9.52)

62. Purchon, R.D. and Enoch, I. (1954). Zonation of the marine fauna and flora on a rocky shore near Singapore. *Bull. Raffles Mus. S'pore*, No. 25. (12.4.38)

63. Rabinowitz, D. (1978). Early growth of mangrove seedlings in Panama and an hypothesis concerning the relationship of dispersal and zonation. *J. Biogeogr.* 5: 113—133. (12.9.46)

64. Ribi, G. (1981). Does the wood boring isopod *Sphaeroma terbrans* benefit red mangroves *(Rhizophora mangle)? Bull. Mar. Sci.* 31: 925—928. (12.9.4)

65. _____. (1982). Differential colonization of roots of *Rhizophora mangle* by the wood-boring isopod *Sphaeroma terebrans* as a mechanism to increase root density. *Mar. Ecol.* 3: 13—19. (12.9.42)

66. Richards, P.W. (1952). *The Tropical Rain Forest: An Ecological Study*. Cambridge University Press. Cambridge.

67. Ricklefs, R.E. (1979). *Ecology*. Chiron, London. (23.2.1)

68. Rollet, B. (1981). *Bibliography on Mangrove Research 1600—1975*. UNESCO, Paris. (27.1.14)

69. Sabar, F., Djajasasmita, M., and Budiman, A. (1979). Susunan dan penyebaran moluska dan krustasea pada

beberapa hutan rawa payau: suatu studi pendahuluan. In *Prosiding Seminar 'Ekosistem Hutan Mangrove'* (ed. S. Soemodiharjo, A. Nontji, A. Djamali), pp. 120—125. Lembaga Oseanologi Nasional, Jakarta. (12.9.2)

70. Saenger, P., Hegerl, E.J. and Davie, J.D.S. (1981). *First Report the Global Status of Mangrove Ecosystems.* Commission on Ecology, IUCN, Gland. (12.9.23)

71. Samingan, M.T. (1980). Notes on the vegetation of the tidal areas of South Sumatra, Indonesia, with special reference to Karang Agung. In *Tropical Ecology and Development* (ed. J. Furtado), pp. 1107—1112. University Malaya, Kuala Lumpur.

72. Sasekumar, A. (1974). Distribution of macrofauna on a Malayan mangrove shore. *J. Anim. Ecol.* 43: 51—69. (12.9.16)

73. Snedaker, S. (1982). A perspective on Asian mangroves. In *Man, Land and Sea* (ed. C. Soysa, L.S. Chic, W.L. Collier), pp. 65—74. Agricultural Development Council, Bangkok. (12.9.45)

74. ──────────. (1982). Mangrove species zonation: why? In *Tasks for Vegetation Science, vol. 2* (ed. D.N. Sen and K.S. Rajpurohit). Junk, The Hague. (12.9.44)

75. Soegiarto, A. and Polunin, N.V.C. (1980). *The Marine Environment of Indonesia.* IUCN, Gland. (2.5.3)

76. Soeriaatmadja, R.E. (1979). Plant inventory and vegetational analysis at proposed tidal reclamation project areas in Siak and Rokan, Riau, Sumatera, Indoensia. In *Mangrove and Estuarine Vegetation in Southeast Asia* (ed. P.B.L. Srivestrava, A.M. Ahmad, G. Dhanarajan and I. Hamzah). BIOTROP Special Publication No. 10., pp. 155—179. BIOTROP, Bogor. (12.9.26)

77. Start, A.N. and Marshall, A.G. (1975). Nectarivorous bats as pollinators of trees in West Malaysia. In *Tropical Trees: Variation, Breeding and Co. servation* (ed. J. Burley dan B.T. Styles), pp. 141—150. Academic, London. (12.8.37)

78. Stebbins, R.C. and Kalk, M. (1961). Observations on the natural history of the mudskipper, *Periophthalmus sobrinus. Copeia* 1961: 18—27. (12.5.31)

150

79. Steup, F.K.M. (1941). Botanische aanteekeningen wit Riouw. *Trop. Natuur* 30: 88—94. (9.1.35)

80. Sukarjo, S. (1979). Hutan payau di Kuala Sekampung, Lampung Selatan, Sumatra. In *Prosiding Seminar 'Ekosistem Hutan Mangrove'* (ed. S. Soemodihardjo, A. Nontji, A. Djamali), pp. 59—68. Lembaga Oseanologi Nasional, Jakarta. (12.9.2).

81. Sukarjo, S. and Kartawinata, K. (1979). Mangrove forest of Banyu-asin, Musi River Estuary, South Sumatra. In *Mangrove and Estuarine Vegetation in Southeast Asia* (red. P.B.L. Srivestava, A.M. Ahmad, G. Dhanarajan, and I. Hamzah). BIOTROP Special Publication No. 10., pp. 61—79. BIOTROP, Bogor. (12.9.8)

82. Tee, A.C.G. (1982). Some aspects of the ecology of the mangrove forest at Sungei Buloh, Selangor I. Analysis of environmental factors and the floral distribution and their corelationship. *Malay. Nat. J.* 35: 13—18. (12.9.40)

83. _____. (1982). Some aspects of the ecology of the mangrove forest at Sungai Buloh, Selangor II. Distribution pattern and population dynamics of tree-dwelling fauna. *Malay. Nat. J.* 35: 267—278. (12.9.47)

84. Tomlinson, P.B., Primack, R.B. and Bunt, J.S. (1979). Preliminary observations on floral biology in mangrove Rhizophoraceae. *Biotropica* 11: 256—277. (12.9.34)

85. Troll, D. and Dragendorf, O. (1931). Uber die Luft wurzeln von *Sonneratia* Linn. f. und Ihre biologische Bedeutung. *Planta* 13: 311—473.

86. Turner, R.E. (1975). Referred to in Soegiarto and Polunin (1980).

87. _____. (1977). Intertidal vegetation and commercial yields of penaeid shrimp. *Trans. Am. Fish. Soc.* 106: 411—416. (2.2.26)

88. Tweedie, M.W.F. and Harrison, J.L. (1970). *Malayan Animal Life*. Longman, Kuala Lumpur. (12.13.2)

89. Versteegh, F. (1951). Proeve van een bedrijfsregeling voor de vloedbossen van Bengkalis. *Tectona* 41: 200—258. (9.1.27)

90. Voris, H.K., Voris, H.H., and List, L.B. (1978). The food and feeding behavior of a marine snake, *Enhydrina schistosa*

(Hydrophiidae). *Copeia* 1978: 134—146. (12.6.11)

91. Voris, H.K. and Jayne, B.C. (1979). Growth, reproduction and population structure of a marine snake, *Enhydrina schistosa* (Hydrophiidae). *Copeia* 1979: 307—318. (12.6.10)

92. Voris, H.K. and Moffett, M.W. (1981). Size and proportion relationship between the beaked sea snake and its prey. *Biotropica* 13: 15—19. (12.6.9)

93. Walsh, G.E. (1974). Mangroves: a review. In *Ecology of Halophytes* (ed. R.J. Reinmold and W.M. Queen), pp. 51—174. Academic, New York. (12.1.98)

94. _____. (1977). Exploitation of mangal. In *Wet Coastal Ecosystems* (ed. V.J. Chapman), pp. 347—362. Elsevier, Amsterdam.

95. Waterman, P.G. Personal communication.

96. Watson, J.G. (1928) Mangrove forests of the Malay Peninsula. *Malay. For. Rec. No. 6.* (12.9.1)

97. Whitmore, T.C. (1975). *Tropical Rainforests of the Far East.* Clarendon, Oxford. (12.10.8)

98. Whitten, A.J. and Damanik, S.J. (in press.). Defoliation of mangrove by noctulid moths in Sumatra. *Biotropica.*

99. Whitten, J.E.J. Unpublished.

100. Wyatt-Smith, J. (1951). Distribution of the Pied Imperial pigeon. *Malay. Nat. J.* 5: 208.

101. Wyatt-Smith, J. (1979). Pocket Check List of Timber Trees. Revised by K.M. Kochumen. *Malay. Forest Rec.* No. 17. (12.1.70)

102. Wyrtki, K. (1961). *Physical Oceanography of the Southeast Asian Waters.* Scripps Institute for Oceanography, La Jolla. (2.5.7)

CHAPTER 3

OTHER COASTAL ECOSYSTEMS

3.1 INTRODUCTION

In addition to mangrove forests, five other types of ecosystems are found around the coasts of Sumatra. These are beach vegetation on accreting coasts (pes-caprae formation), beach vegetation on abrading coasts (Barringtonia formation), brackish water forests, rocky shores and coral reefs. The last of these is not strictly within the scope of this book as it is a marine ecosystem, but it is included as background material for the reader who may wish to pursue studies on coral reefs.

None of the coastal ecosystems is known particularly well, except for the economically important coral reefs, and so the following sections serve only as introductions upon which further investigations can be based.

3.2 BEACH VEGETATION

3.2.1 Pes-caprae formation

Along accreting coasts, that is, where new sand is being deposited, the sandy beach is colonized by a form of vegetation known as the 'pes-caprae' formation. Such vegetation is found throughout the Indonesian archipelago and the western Pacific [29]. The name refers to *Ipomoea pes-caprae*, a purple-flowered creeper related to convolvulus, which is just one of a number of low, sand-binding herbs, grasses and sedges which advance over the sand with long, deep-rooting stolons or stems. Other species expected in this formation would include the legume *Canavalia*, sedges *Cyperus pedunculatus* and *C. stoloniferus*, and the grasses *Thuarea involuta* (Figure 3.1) and the prickly *Spinifex littoreus*. Full lists are given by Whitmore [41], Wong [53] and Soegiarto and Polunin [33].

Seaweeds can only grow on the permanently wet lower parts of a rocky shore. Near Painan, Pesisir Selatan.

The force of the constant wave action demands that animals and plants living on a rocky shore have well-developed means of attachment.

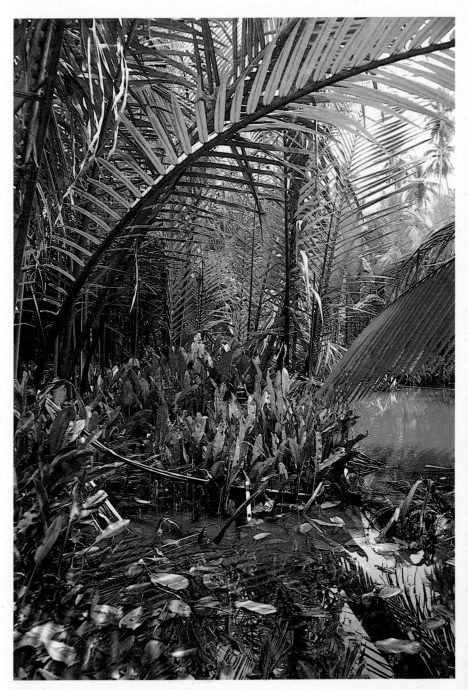

Nypa forest near Sicanggang, Langkat.

153

Figure 3.1 *Thuarea involuta* a creeping species of grass found in the pes-caprae association. (From Holttum [15]).

These plants are well-adapted, being tolerant of periodic drought, salt spray (although dependent on non-saline ground water), wind, low levels of soil nutrients and high soil temperatures. They also produce small seeds which are dispersed by floating on water; for example, the small seed of *Thuarea* is surrounded by an air-filled chamber which floats easily and is dispersed by tidal currents [15]. The mat of low vegetation of the parent plants traps dead leaves and other organic material blown by the wind or tossed there by the tides, and provides a little shelter for animals. Thus nutrients increase and later stages of the plant succession (section 2.4.2, 11.2.1) can occur and the landward fringe is colonized anew. She-oak *Casuarina equisetifolia* is found at the inner edge of the pes-caprae formation where it represents a late stage in the plant succession. She-oak can form pure stands but is unable to regenerate in closed forest or even in open forest on the carpet of litter formed by its own dead twigs. Thus, unless the coastline advances and provides fresh habitat, the belt of she-oak forest will be supplanted by other species [7]. The 30m-wide mature she-oak forest examined by a CRES team near Singkil, South Aceh, had a basal area of 32.7 m^2/ha for trees of 15cm diameter and over.

The environment of exposed sandy beaches is particularly hostile to animals because of the instability of the sand, and the wide variations in temperature, salinity and humidity. A great many small animals live permanently within the sand where they have some protection, but they have to cope with the difficulties of finding food, reproductive partners and the low oxygen concentrations in the spaces of air between the sand grains [46]. Near the high water level burrows about 8 cm across can be found with small piles of sand around them. Their occupants are adult, beige-coloured sand crabs *Ocypode ceratophthalma* which are rarely seen during the day. It is difficult to dig one of these crabs out of its burrow or to catch it as it runs across the sand. Young *Ocypode* are very numerous and can be seen on the sand surface both by day and night. *Ocypode* feed mainly on organic material from the sand but are sometimes predatory [39].

On wider beaches the small ghost crabs *Dotilla mictyroides* may occur in thousands with densities of over $100/m^2$ [13, 21]. Although some of the larger individuals are coloured light blue with pinkish legs, the majority are sand-coloured. As the tide rises and covers the beach each ghost crab builds a shelter of wet sand pellets over its back. The crab traps air beneath itself and as it burrows down so the air pocket is carried down with it. When the crabs emerge as the tide falls, they are followed by a stream of small bubbles [39]. Isopod crustaceans can be found by careful examination of the sand and the organic material washed ashore onto the upper sandy reaches [17], and wading birds can sometimes be seen feeding on these and other small animals.

Lower down the beach a variety of molluscs occur but are rarely seen because they burrow beneath the surface. Examples of the bivalves are the white and pinkish *Tellina*, the large *Pinna*, and the economically important edible cockle *Arca granosa*.

The sandy beaches are used as nesting sites by sea turtles. Sumatra is visited by at least three species which nest on its sandy beaches:
- the most abundant is the Green turtle which weighs up to 100 kg and has a carapace up to 1m long. Its eggs are commonly seen on sale in western towns such as Padang;
- the Hawksbill turtle, also common, is exploited for its shell, with the main trading centre at Sibolga. This species is slightly smaller than the Green turtle, weighing up to 80 kg and with a carapace length of 90 cm;
- the rarer, massive Leatherback turtle which can weigh up to 1 ton.

The distribution of a fourth species, the Loggerhead turtle, may include Sumatra (Figure 3.2). There is hardly any information on nesting

155

Figure 3.2 Shells of four species of sea turtles found around Sumatra.
a - green turtle - *Chelonia mydas,* b - hawksbill turtle - *Ereto-chelys imbricata,* c - leathery turtle - *Dermochelys coriacea,* d - loggerhead turtle - *Caretta caretta.* (From Anon [3]).

sites of turtles on Sumatra but the more important areas are almost certainly on the offshore islands and the west coast of the mainland [33, 50, 51]. However, in an article on the shore life of Pantai Cermin in Deli Serdang, Meer Mohr shows a picture of Green turtle tracks on the beach indicating that some turtles bred there in 1940 [23]. Turtles used to lay eggs on Berhala, a small island off the coast of North Sumatra in the Straits of Malacca [16, 50], but there is no recent information. Turtles also nest at a small beach near Kuala Kambas, eastern Lampung, but since all the eggs are taken for local consumption, the turtles may not return for much longer [11] (section 11.5.1). Any information on nesting turtles in Sumatra is valuable so that their distribution and conservation status can be more accurately determined. Any such details should be sent to the National Oceanological Institute and the National Biological Institute.

3.2.2. Barringtonia formation

The Barringtonia formation is found behind the pes-caprae formation on sandy soils. It is also found on abrading coasts where sand is either being removed by unhindered ocean swells or where sand has at least ceased to accumulate; in such areas a beach wall about 0.5—1 m tall is formed. On and inland from this wall the second type of vegetation, the Barringtonia formation, is found. It is also tolerant to salt spray, nutrient-deficient soil and seasonal drought. This belt of vegetation is not very wide, usually between 25 and 50 m where the lie of the land allows it, but narrower where the coast is steep and rocky. This type of forest merges with lowland rainforest inland. Large trees sometimes sprawl across the upper parts of the beach, and as the beach wall is eroded away so these eventually fall over and die. The larger trees of the *Barringtonia* association are of two main species: *Barringtonia asiatica* [40] which has huge 15 cm wide feathery flowers and unusual fruit (Figure 3.3.), and *Calophyllum inophyllum* which has transparent yellow sap and 3-cm round fruit, the seeds of which are dispersed by bats. It should be noted that *Barringtonia* itself is not invariably present in the formation which bears its name [35, 36]. The plants found in this (and also the pes-caprae) type of beach vegetation are found in similar locations throughout the Indo-Pacific region and some are typical of sandy shores throught the tropics. Many of the species are not found outside these formations. In addition to the trees mentioned above, other typical species include the large bush *Ardisia elliptica* with its pink young twigs and leaves, *Heritiera littoralis* with its peculiar boat-shaped

cm
0   4

Figure 3.3 The fruit of *Barringbonia asiatica*

Figure 3.4 The fruit of *Heritiera littoralis*

floating fruit (Figure 3.4), and other trees such as *Excoecaria agallocha,* pandans [37] particularly *Pandanus tectorius, Scaevola taccada, Terminalia catappa* and two types of hibiscus *Hibiscus tiliaceus* and *Thespesia populnea.* Both hibiscus have large yellow flowers with purple bases but the former species has slightly hairy lower leaf surfaces, heart-shaped leaves as long as they are broad, flowers which fall off as soon as they have dried and smaller fruit. The latter has smooth leaves longer than they are broad with a sharper tip, flowers which remain on the plant for some days after they have died and larger fruit (Figure 3.5). *Hibiscus tiliaceus* is commonly planted in towns and villages.. The cycad *Cycas rumphii* is also sometimes found in the Barringtonia formation. Despite their appearance cycads are not palms, neither are they ferns, but they are related to the now-extinct seed-ferns that flourished roughly between 280 and 180 million years ago [8]. Cycads are commonly planted in gardens. In addition to the species above, certain species from the pes-caprae association can also be found, particularly on the beach wall.

Barringtonia formation forests have been cleared in many areas to make way for coconut groves but some excellent examples still exist on the west coast of Siberut [2, 44] and in remote parts of the western coast of northern Sumatra.

Almost nothing has been written about the animals of Barringtonia formation forests but Simakobu leaf monkeys *Simias concolor* have been observed in them on Siberut Island [44], and the CRES team investigating the rocky shores near Painan, West Sumatra, observed silvered leaf

Figure 3.5 The fruit of *Hibiscus tiliaceus* (left), *Thespesia populnea* (right)

monkeys *Presbytis cristata* in the *Barringtonia* trees. The fauna of the sand in front of the *Barringtonia* formation is more or less the same as that described for the sand in and below the pes-caprae formation.

3.2.3 Productivity

Little is known about the productivity of beach vegetation but there are obviously great differences between the low-lying pes-caprae and the trees and shrubs of the Barringtonia formations. On the beach below the vegetation zone the majority of energy inputs originate from the sea, and flotsam such as wood, sea-grass leaves and algal fronds may be an important source of food at the upper limit of tides [33]. Details of plant succession on the shores of Krakatau are given in section 11.3.

3.3 BRACKISH WATER FORESTS

Brackish water forest can be found at the inner boundary of mangrove forest, and at the upper tidal limit of rivers. It may also occur where the seaward beach is merely a sand barrier thrown up by the waves and formed by the currents. Behind such barriers the land is usually flat and low and streams often flood, thus creating marshy lagoons suitable for brackish water forest. Examples of these are shown in Figure 3.6. Brackish

159

Figure 3.6 Locations of three brackish water forests behind sand bars:
a) River Rangau, Bangka Island, b) River Perbaungan, Deli
Serdang, c) River Lebekiu, Siberut Island. The arrows point
north.

water forest is characterized by nipa *Nypa fructicans* which forms pure, often extensive stands, but most of the other elements of the vegetation are commonly found in either mangrove forests or the Barringtonia formation [41, 45]. Only one plant, the Mangrove date palm *Phoenix paludosa*, appears to be restricted to this type of forest. It is easily recognized because it is the only feather-palm in Sumatra whose leaflets, when viewed from above form a trough rather than a ridge at the junction with the midrib [49]. The Mangrove date palm is the most easterly relative of the date palm of north Africa and Arabia. Although brackish water and deserts are very different habitats, neither has fresh water freely available to plant roots [42].

3.4. ROCKY SHORES

Rocky shores occur where hard and resistant rock faces the sea in such a manner that the results of weathering are swept out to sea rather than deposited to form a wide beach. Such shores are usually steep with the scarp face continuing below the sea surface. There is commonly, however, a narrow shelf or beach with shingle rather than sand in the upper tidal regions. Such steep coasts and cliffs are usually formed of old limestone (e.g. west of Banda Aceh), volcanic rock (e.g. south of Padang), granites and Tertiary sandstone (e.g. Bangka, Belitung and Bintan Islands and the Riau/Lingga, Anambas, Natuna and Tambelan archipelagos [34].

There is no one type of vegetation peculiar to rocky shores but a few specimens of trees normally found in the Barringtonia formation, such as *Barringtonia*, *Casuarina*, and *Calophyllum*, and pandans may be seen clinging to the rocks. Where the slope lessens and the salt spray are less, some form of lowland forest would be expected to grow.

The fauna of rocky shores is rather poor but has representatives from a very wide range of phyla. The animals are adapted to withstand the force of the waves, periodic desiccation, high temperatures and variable salinity. They all have efficient means of retaining a grip on the rocks; some are permanently fixed but others can move around to forage or graze. Barnacles are common and, among the molluscs, small oysters, cap-shaped limpets and *Nerita* snails are usually found [39]. Medium-sized, long-legged rocky crabs (probably *Grapsus grapsus*) will be seen near the water's edge, and at the rocky shore examined by a CRES team near Painan, small blenny fish jumped from rock to rock in the spray zone. The zonation of animals up a rocky shore has been studied in Singapore [28], and the principles of zonation are discussed by Brehaut [47].

Most of the limestone or granite cliffs that have clefts or small caves in them will usually support colonies of swiflets (section 10.3.1). One species, *Aerodramus fuciphaga*, build its cup-like nest purely from hardened saliva but others mix in bits of vegetable material [22].

3.5. CORAL REEFS

The conditions necessary for coral to grow are:
- warm water (above 22°C).
- clear water
- water with near to normal sea-water salinity, and
- light.

All the seas around Sumatra are warm enough for coral but the second and third conditions are not met where large rivers flow into the sea. These rivers reduce the salinity and their sediment loads cause increased turbidity which in turn reduces light penetration. Thus the coasts of eastern Sumatra, and the coasts along the plains in western Sumatra have no coral (Figure 3.7).

Most of the reefs around Sumatra are fringing reefs i.e. growing out from land, but atolls (islands formed by waves throwing up piles of coral fragments) and barrier reefs (away from land where the sea bed is near enough to the surface for coral to form) are found between the west coast of Sumatra and the islands of Simeulue, Nias and the Mentawai Islands. The fringing reefs found around the islands of the Riau/Lingga, Natuna, Anambas and Tambelan archipelagos are shelves exposed briefly at low tide. The surface is flat and slopes gently towards the open sea [34]. Loosened coral blocks are tossed by the breakers and are piled up to form a low ridge at the edge of the coral shelf.

The animal life of the coral reef is stunningly beautiful in colour and shape, and astoundingly diverse. Corals themselves are examples of colonial animals. The outer layer of a block of coral is made up of numerous 'polyps'. Each polyp removes calcium carbonate from the sea water and secretes its own skeleton of limestone but is connected to its neighbours by strands that extend laterally through minute holes in their skeletons. As the colony develops so new polyps form, often on the connecting sections between the older polyps, and the new skeletons grow over and stifle the polyps below. Thus the reef-building corals grow. Each species of coral has its own characteristics pattern of budding and so constructs its own particular and characteristic shape. Many of the species around Sumatra's coasts can be readily identified [48, 52].

The reason corals cannot live deeper than light can penetrate is because they are dependent upon single-celled algae, called zooxanthellae, which grow within their bodies. The algae need light to photosynthesize and thus provide food for themselves and for the polyp. During photosynthesis they release oxygen which helps the coral to respire.

Figure 3.7 Distribution of coral reefs in Sumatra

During the day the corals may appear to be nothing but dead lumps of limestone, some of which are coloured, but most of which are rather dull. At night and under certain other conditions, however, the millions of polyps extend their brightly coloured, feathery tentacles into the water, blurring the shape of the coral block they form as they sift the water for food particles. Optimum growth conditions for reef-forming coral occur when vigorous wave action causes turbulence and a continuous supply of food is available to the polyps.

Polyps are not the only organisms involved in reef building because a peculiar group of pink-coloured algae, known as coralline algae (Corallinaceae), also contribute. These plants are red algae which deposit calcium carbonate in their cell walls. Coralline algae exist as crusts, fronds, segmented branches, epiphytes, parasites on other coralline algae, or as gravelly nodules, and are the world's hardest plants; it is impossible even to scratch them with a fingernail. Nearly 22% of the surface of a coral reef off Hawaii was found to be covered by several species of coralline algae each of which had its own distinct habitat preference [17].

There are innumerable types of organisms associated with a coral reef. Some of these are attached, such as sedentary worms and sea anenomes, and some, such as certain fish and molluscs, hide in crevices. Inshore fish and other wide-ranging organisms live close to the reef and exploit its high biological productivity [10]. Of 132 fish species listed as being of 'economic' in Indonesia, 32 are associated with coral reefs [33].

Green plants can also be found on and around coral reefs. Some are green seaweeds, such as *Ulva, Hallineda* and *Padina*, but more commonly seen are seed-plants known collectively as seagrasses. Most of the seagrasses to be found off the coast of Sumatra, particularly in the Riau Archipelago, belong to the family Hydrocharitaceae which includes the cosmopolitan Canadian pond weed *Elodea canadensis*. Unlike *Elodea*, however, most seagrasses look remarkably grasslike with long, narrow leaves (one important exception to this is *Halophila* which has spoon-shaped leaves). Seagrasses form mixed-species meadows, particularly of *Thalassia hemprichii* and *Enhalus acoroides* [14], or pure stands depending on the substrate. Distinct zonation of species can also be observed [19].

Seagrass leaves may carry very heavy loads of epiphytes, so many in fact that half the above-ground biomass of a seagrass meadow can be accounted for by epiphytes such as bacteria, algae and various sedentary marine animals. These epiphytes tend to thrive in nutrient-enriched water caused by human activity, but the enhanced growth of epiphytes reduces the amount of light reaching the seagrass, sometimes to its ultimate demise.

The flowers of seagrasses open underwater and the pollen is dispersed either by water current or, if floating, by being blown across the water surface. Some seagrasses do, however, exhibit various forms of self-pollination.

Seagrass meadows have a high standing crop, high productivity (about one-third of a lowland forest), and they are able to concentrate available nutrients. They would therefore be expected to be important in food chains and this is indeed the case, but primarily through their detritus rather than through being grazed. The detritus is eaten by crabs and molluscs which are in turn eaten by fishes. Seagrass is grazed by green turtles and dugong *Dugong dugon* but they take only a small proportion of the productivity [20]. Dugong are now extremely rare and it is doubtful whether a viable population exists anywhere off Sumatra.

3.5.1 Productivity

The net primary productivity of coral reef ecosystems can be as much as 2000 g carbon per m^2 per year. This is higher than almost any other terrestrial or aquatic ecosystem anywhere in the world. For example, the equivalent average figure for tropical forest and estuaries is 1800, for open ocean 125 and for savanna 700 [43]. In reef lagoons, i.e. where there is little turbulence and thus little mixing of water, the net primary productivity is much lower. For example, Nontji and Setiapermana recorded values of 39—96 g carbon per m^2 per year for lagoons in the Seribu archipelago off Jakarta [24].

3.5.2 Coral reef studies

Apart from recording the distribution of coral reefs, no studies have been made on any aspect of coral reef ecology in Sumatra. Considering their economic importance for food fish, other edible animals such as clams, for pearl oysters, for ornamental fish, and for tourism, this situation should be rectified. No two coral reefs are the same and they provide an unsurpassed natural laboratory for ecological studies. A selection of recent papers for those wishing to study coral reefs is given in the reference list [3, 4, 5, 6, 9, 10, 12, 24, 26, 31, 32, 38].

REFERENCES

1. Anon. (1979). Jenis penyu laut di Indonesia. *Suara Alam* 5: 34-36. (12.6.34)
2. Anon. (1980). *Penyelamatan Siberut: Rencana Induk Konservasi.* World Wildlife Fund, Bogor. (10.2.1)
3. Ayal, Y. and Safriel, V.N. (1982). Spesies diversity of the coral reef - a note on the role of predation and of adjacent habitats. *Bull. Mar. Sci.* 32: 787-790. (12.3.21)
4. Birkeland, C. and Neudecker, S. (1981). Foraging behaviour of two Caribbean Chaetodontids. *Copeia* 1981: 169-1787. (12.5.17)
5. Borowitzka, M.A. (1981). Algae and grazing in coral reef ecosystems. *Endeavour* 5: 99-106. (12.3.22)
6. Bull, G.D. (1982). Scleractinian coral communities of two inshore high island fringing reefs at Magnetic Island, N. Queensland. *Mar. Ecol. Prog. Ser.* 7: 267-277. (12.3.18)
7. Corner, E.J.H. (1952). *Wayside Trees of Malaya.* 2 vols. 2nd. Ed. Government Printer, Singapore. (12.1.15)
8. _____: (1964) *The Life of Plants.* University of Chicago Press, Chicago. (12.1.13)
9. Dahl, A.L. (1981). Monitoring coral reefs for urban impact. *Bull. Mar. Sci.* 31: 544-551.
10. De Silva, M.W.R.N., Betterton, C. and Smith, R.A. (1980). Coral Reef Resources of the East coast of Peninsular Malaysia. In: *Coastal Resources of East Coast Peninsular Malaysia: An Assessment in Relation to Potential Oil Spills* (ed. Chua T.E. and J.K. Charles), pp. 95-158. Universiti Sains Malaysia, Penang. (2.4.3)
11. FAO/Wind, J., Soepomo, D. and Isnan, W. (1979). *Way Kambas Game Reserve Management Plan, 1980/81 — 1984/85.* Field Report No. 5, INS/78/061. FAO, Jakarta. (10.2.9)

12. Goh, A.H. and Sasekumar, A. (1980). The community structure of a fringing coral reef, Cape Rachado. *Malay. Nat. J.* 34: 25—37. (12.3.19)

13. Hails, A.J. and Yaziz, S. (1982). Abundance, breeding and growth of the ocypodid crab *Dotilla myctiroides* (Milne-Edwards) on a West Malaysian beach. *Estuar. Coast. Shelf Sci.* 15: 229-239.

14. Hartog, C. den (1958). Hydrocharitaceae. In *Flora Malesiana, I.* 5: 381—413.

15. Holttum, R.E. (1977). *Plant Life in Malaya*, 2nd ed. Longman, Kuala Lumpur. (12.1.14)

16. Jazanul, A.: Personal communication.

17. Johansen, H.W. (1981). *Coralline Algae: A First Synthesis.* CRC, Florida.

18. Jones, D.A. (1979). The ecology of sandy beaches in Penang, Malaysia, with special reference to *Excirolana orientalis* (Dana). *Est. Coast. Mar. Sci.* 9: 677-682. (2.4.37)

19. Kartawinata, K.: Personal communication.

20. McComb, A.J., Cambridge, M.L., Kirkman, H. and Kuo, J. (1981). The biology of Australian seagrasses. In *The Biology of Australian Plants* (ed. J.S. Pate and A.J. McComb), pp. 258-293. University of Western Australia Press, Perth.

21. McIntyre, A.D. (1968). The microfauna and macrofauna of some some tropical beaches. *J. Zool., Lond.* 156 377-392. (2.4.34)

22. Medway, Lord. (1968). Field characters as a guide to the specific relations of swiftlets. *Proc. Linn. Soc. Lond.* 177: 151-172 (12.7.4)

23. Meer Mohr, J.C. van der. (1941). Biologisene waarnamingen bij Pantai Tjermin (III). *Trop. Natuur.* 30: 49-55. (2.4.31)

24. Nontji, A. and Setiapermana, D. (1980). Phytoplankton productivity and related aspects of the Pari Islands Lagoons. Makalah yang disajikan pada 'Symposium on Recent Research Activities on Coral Reefs in South-east Asia', BIOTROP, 6-9 May, 1980. (12.2.15)

25. Pichon, M. and Morrissey, J. (1981). Benthic zonation and community structure of South Island Reef, Lizard Island (Great Barrier Reef). *Bull. Mar. Sci.* 31: 581-593. (12.3.20)

26. Polunin, N.V.C. (1980). Guidelines for a BIOTROP project on reef

fishes and fisheries. Paper given at the *'Symposium on Recent Research Activity on Coral Reefs in South-east Asia'*, BIOTROP, 6—9 May, 1980.

27. Pugh, D.T. and Rayner, R.F. (1981). The tidal regimes of three Indian ocean atolls and some ecological implications. *Estuar. Coast Shelf Sci.* 13: 389-407. (12.3.34)

28. Purchon, R.D. and Enoch, I. (1954). Zonation of the marine fauna and flora on a rocky shore near Singapore. *Bull. Raffles Mus. S'pore* No. 25. (2.4.38)

29. Richards, P.W. (1952). *The Tropical Rain Forest: An Ecological Study.* Cambridge Univ. Press, Cambridge.

30. Rosen, B.R. (1983). The recovery of the corals of the Krakatau region. Paper given at the symposium *'Krakatoa: 100 Years On'*, British Museum (Natural History), 21 September 1983.

31. Sale, P.F. and Douglas, W.A. (1981). Precision and accuracy of visual census technique for fish assemblages on coral patch reefs. *Environ. Biol. Fish.* 6: 333-339. (12.3.25)

32. Sheppard, C.R.C. (1981). Coral populations on reef slopes and their major controls. *Mar. Biol.* 7: 83-115. (12.3.23)

33. Soegiarto. A. and Polunin, N.V.C. (1980). *The Marine Environment of Indonesia.* IUCN/WWF, Gland. (2.5.3)

34. Sopher, D.E. (1977). *The Sea Nomads.* National Museum, Singapore. (2.5.15)

35. Steenis, C.G.G.J. van. (1959). Discrimination of tropical shore formations. In *Proc. Symp. Humid Tropics Vegetation, Tjiawi,* 1958, pp. 215-217. UNESCO, Paris. (2.4.30)

36. Steup, F.K.M. (1941). Botanische anteekeningen uit Riouw. *Trop. Natuur* 30: 88-94. (12.1.16)

37. Stone, B.C. (1983). The genus *Pandanus* in Sumatera. *Fed. Mus. J.* 28: 101-122. (12.1.101)

38. Tay, S.W. and Khoo, H.W. (1980). The distribution of coral reef fishes at Pulau Salu, Singapore. Paper given at the *'Symposium on Recent Research Activities on Coral Reefs in South-east Asia'*, BIOTROP, 6—9 May, 1980. (12.5.32).

39. Tweedie, M. and Harrison, J.L. (1970). *Malayan Animal Life.* Longman, Kuala Lumpur. (12.13.2)

40. Wallwork, F. (1982). The autecology of *Barringtonia asiatica* on Rakata. In *The Krakatoa Centenary Expedition* (ed. J.R. Flenley and K. Richards), pp. 127-141. University of Hull, Hull. (12.1.92)

41. Whitmore, T.C. (1975). *Tropical Rain Forests of the Far East.* Clarendon, Oxford. (12.10.8)

42. _____: (1977). *Palms of Malaya.* Oxford University Press, Oxford. (12.1.3)

43. Whittaker, R.H. and Likens, G.E. (1973). Primary productvity: The Biosphere and Man. *Human Ecol.* 1: 357-367. (9.2.9)

44. Whitten, A.J. (1982). *The Gibbons of Siberut.* J.M. Dent, London. (12.13.3)

45. Wyatt-Smith, J. (1963). Manual of Malayan silviculture for inland forests (2 vols). *Malay. For. Rec.* No. 23. (9.1.17)

46. Brafield, A.E. (1978). *Life in Sandy Shores.* Studies in Biology No. 89. Edward Arnold, London.

47. Brehaut, R.N. (1982). *Ecology of Rocky Shores.* Studies in Biology No. 139. Edward Arnold, London.

48. Henry, L.E. (1980). *Coral Reefs of Malaysia.* Longman, Kuala Lumpur.

49. Jochems, S.C.J. (1927). De boeging der vloedbosschen van Noord Sumatra. *Trop. Natuur* 15: 145—150.

50. Meer Mohr, J.C. van der (1928). Poelaoe Berhala. *Trop. Natuur.* 17: 85—97.

51. Rappart, F.W. (1936). Een schildpaddenstrand in het wildreservaat Zuid Sumatra. *Trop. Natuur* 25: 124—126.

52. Searle, A.G. (1956). An illustrated key to Malayan hard corals. *Malay. Nat. J.* 11: 1—28.

53. Wong, P.P. (1978). The herbaceous formation and its geomorphic role, East Coast, Peninsular Malaysia. *Malay. Nat. J.* 32: 129—141.

CHAPTER 4

RIVERS AND LAKES

4.1 INTRODUCTION

Sumatran lakes (together with those in Java and Bali) have the distinction of being the first tropical lakes to be studied in great detail. In contrast to many other aspects of Sumatran biology the amount written about a number of Sumatra's lakes is enormous. Between 1928 and 1929 a German Expedition spent 10 months conducting thorough studies of lakes (and to a lesser extent rivers) in Java, Sumatra, and Bali. The results, written by over 100 experts, total an amazing 7920 text pages with 3055 tables and figures and were published in *Archiv für Hydrobiologie (Supplement)* between 1931 and 1958. Most of the papers are taxonomic (over 1100 new species were described) and this gives a wonderful base for freshwater ecology studies. Very little work has been conducted on Sumatran rivers and lakes since that expedition, except the work by the National Biological Institute on the River Alas [39], and by the Bogor Agricultural Institute on the largely brackish Upang-Banyuasin delta [26].

One of the major values of the German work for Sumatran environmental science today is in studying changes due to human settlement, irrigation schemes, etc. Studies of lakes in Java and Bali 45 years after the German surveys showed surprisingly little change, but the impact of settlements and recent introductions of foreign fish species was evident [22, 23].

It is unfortunate that almost all these papers are in German and therefore unavailable to most Indonesians. The comprehensive, comparative summary of the hydrography and hydrochemistry written by

Ruttner [64] is, however, thorugh the generosity of the Honorary Consul of the Federal Republic of Germany in Medan, being translated into Indonesian for the purposes of this book and for use by interested parties.

Taxonomy of life forms is obviously fundamental to ecology and a great deal of the early work on the biota of Sumatran rivers and lakes was taxonomic. In 1907, for example, Volz wrote a 215-page 'Catalogue of Sumatran fishes' but it is not possible to use the list either to identify fishes or to gather meaningful information on habitat selection etc. The massive standard work on Indonesian fishes[1] has recently been republished but its purchase could not be justified for the purposes of this book. The aquatic fauna of the Sunda Region is among the richest in the world [31, 35] but in addition to not knowing which species live in the major rivers of Sumatra, not enough is known even to decide whether some species are found only in very restricted areas.

Very little recent work has been conducted on the ecology of Sumatran freshwaters (with the obvious exception of that conducted by the Faculty of Fisheries, University of Riau and papers that appear in their journal *Terubuk* [24]) so it has been necessary to seek information from other parts of the Sunda Region. The detailed book on the limnology of the Gombak River in Peninsular Malaysia by Bishop is especially useful [7].

Identification keys and information in English are available on various aquatic plant and animal groups of the Sunda Region: Euglenidae [57], Flagellata [59], Desmida [56], bluegreen algae [28], Rotifera [37], snails and bivalve molluscs [5], bivalve molluscs [5, 6], leeches [70], Cladocera (water fleas) [29, 33], Gerridae (water skaters) [12], cyprinoid fishes (which represent a third of all freshwater fishes) [45, 46], and general fishes [1, 2]. The Indonesian key to fishes by Saanin [66] and for freshwater turtles by Iskandar [27] are also very useful.

4.2 SUMATRAN RIVERS AND LAKES

Major lakes occur in every province in Sumatra and these are

---

1. Weber, M. and de Beaufort, L.F. (1913—1964). *The Fishes of the Indo-Australian Archipelago. (Including an Index to the Ichthyological papers of P. Beecker).* Eleven volumes. Reprinted 1981. Brill, Leiden. Dfl. 1800.

Table 4.1 The major lakes of Sumatra.

Province	Lake	Area (km^2)	Depth (m)
Aceh	Kawar	55	—
	Realoib	3	—
North Sumatra	Toba	1146	450+
	Hulu Batumundam	2	—
West Sumatra	Maninjau	98	169
	Singkarak	110	269
	Di Bawah	15	—
	Di Atas	12	44
Riau	Lakes along the Siak Kecil River	—	—
Jambi	Kerinci	42	—
Bengkulu	Tes	2	—
	Dusun Besar	2	—
South Sumatra	Ranau	80	229
	Jemawan	8	—
Lampung	Ranau	45	229

listed in Table 4.1 with their approximate surface areas and depths. It is important to remember that no two lakes and no two rivers are the same since their biological and physical characteristics are strongly affected by geological, topographical, and climatic factors. The Indonesian saying, *"Lain lubuk, lain ikannya"* ("Different ponds have different fish") is absolutely true and should be remembered by those conducting studies of aquatic ecosystems.

The 'lebak' lakes of South Sumatra, along the Ogan and Komering rivers near Padamaran, Tanjungraja and Kayuagung are particularly interesting. True lebaks are situated close to and connected with a river, and thus receive an annual flow of silty water during the rainy season when the adjacent river level rises and water flows over the banks [70]. The use that man has made of these special lakes for rice growing and fish farming is also worthy of further study.

When Sumatra and the other parts of the Sunda Region were conneted by dry land the present rivers in western Peninsular Malaysia and eastern Sumatra were tributaries of the same, much larger river system that flowed towards the east (see Figure 1.8). This is now reflected in the similarity between the aquatic fauna of the regions. For example, Taniuchi found the same species of freshwater stingray *Dasyatis bennetti* in the Indragiri River (eastern Sumatra) and the Perak River (western Peninsular Malaysia) [74], although it is intolerant of seawater [49]. When the sea level was lower the Indragiri and Perak Rivers were tributaries of the same northwest-flowing river, and the present two populations of stingray would have been one. Another interesting example of fish distribution is provided by the distribution of certain species of freshwater eels which breed in the Indian Ocean in water several thousand metres deep. The young larvae swim towards land and when they reach water about 200 m deep they metamorphose into 'elvers'. These then enter rivers and grow into adults before swimming back to the ocean to breed. It appears that only rivers immediately adjacent or near to the ocean are entered by eels (Figure 4.1). Lake Toba contains no such eels because the Siguragura falls are a barrier to the young fish, but eels do occur in Lake Tawar and Lake Maninjau. Lakes Ranau, Dibawah, Diatas, Kerinci and Singkarak are drained by rivers that flow in the shallow east coast and so contain no eels [17].

4.3 EFFECTS OF THE CATCHMENT AREA ON RIVERS AND LAKES

The geology, geography and human use of a catchment area are extremely important to considerations of freshwater ecosystems because they influence the chemical composition of the water and the rate of water input. These in their turn will influence the composition of the biota.

4.3.1 Water input

The major input to most rivers and lakes in from groundwater discharge (Figure 4.2). The water table - the top of the groundwater zone - rises until it is exposed in the bottom of the deepest depression in the area, and this usually forms a river. Water entering a river may have fallen as rain days or even weeks beforehand. Even in Sumatra, rivers can run dry, particularly in the headwater regions, and the resident biota are forced to bury themselves in the moist substrate, to find permanent pools, or, for

Grapsus crabs on a rocky shore.

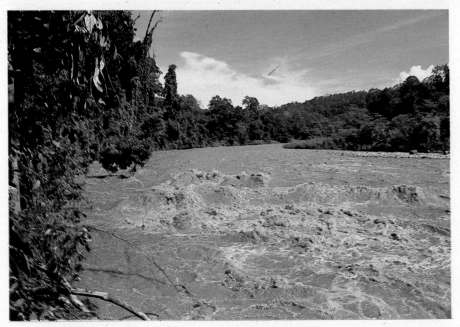

A river in flood transports material and living organisms downstream; Alas River, South-east Aceh.

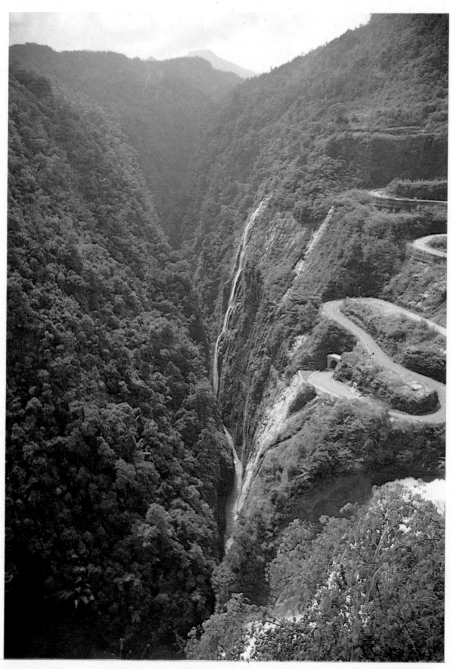

Waterfalls are barriers to animals moving upstream, Siguragura Falls near Lake Toba.

Figure 4.1   Rivers in which freshwater eels are recorded. (After Delsman [17]).

smaller forms, to form a cyst or some other resistant body that can begin to develop again when conditions become favourable.

At the other extreme, floods occur. Heavy rain does not usually cause serious flooding where the ground is covered with forest and most of the rain can permeate the ground to join the ground-water or the interflow (water that flows beneath the ground but above the water table). Only some rain water normally enters rivers and lakes via the surface runoff. However, where forest cover is removed, unobstructed rainfall causes the

174

Figure 4.2 Diagram of the various pathways of water after arrival in a catchment area (After Townsend [76]).

ground to compact, water is not held in the trees' root mat, and very little water enters the transpiration stream of plants so that most of the rain water flows along the soil surface into streams. This causes erratic streamflow and frequent floods which deplete the groundwater resources. As the groundwater is depleted, so the likelihood of rivers running dry increases. At times of high water flow, the substratum of the stream bed is likely to be scoured out and many animals and plants are removed with it, thus also depleting the biological resources.

4.3.2 Water chemistry

Freshwater contains chemicals which affect the nature of the biological communities within it. All plants, both micro- and macro-scopic, require a large number of elements but particularly nitrogen, phosphorus and potassium. Aquatic animals also have specific chemical requirements, for instance, molluscs are dependent on sufficient supplies of calcium for shell growth [5]. The effects of high levels of phenolic compounds in water draining from nutrient-poor sites are described in section 5.6.2.

The concentrations of dissolved oxygen and carbon dioxide have important effects on all aquatic organisms. A proportion of these gases enter the water through diffusion from the atmosphere or, in fast-flowing rivers, by natural aeration in turbulent water. However, photosynthesis and respiration within the stream itself also have significant effects on gases in solution. For example, the marked diurnal pattern of photosynthesis may be reflected by considerable changes in oxygen and carbon dioxide concentrations, and in situations where large amounts of organic waste enters a stream (e.g. near habitation or a palm oil processing factory), its decomposition by microorganisms causes severe depletion of dissolved oxygen.

Minerals can also enter rivers and lakes from rainwater which is by no means pure and which may contain quite appreciable quantities of many inorganic compounds, and from the groundwater. Much of the latter will have been in intimate contact with both soil and unweathered parent rock and as a result will have incorporated inorganic and organic substances in solution or suspension. Thus the chemistry of river water is largely determined by the mineral nature of the catchment area. If it consists of easily eroded sedimentary rock, the concentration of minerals will be high. Conversely, if the rock is resistant to weathering, the river water will be relatively low in minerals [76].

4.4 BIOTIC COMPONENTS

4.4.1 Plants

The major groups of macrophytes, as the larger aquatic plants are known, are the flowering plants and mosses. Those macrophytes which do not float or have most of their leaves above water survive by being adapted to low oxygen levels, slow rates of diffusion and low light intensity of their environment. A good supply of large-celled aerenchyma tissue (through which gases can pass easily) is often found in these plants, thus facilitating adequate internal aeration. Adaptations allowing relatively high rates of photosynthesis under conditions of low light intensity include the absence of cuticle from stems and leaves and high concentrations of chloroplasts in the epidermal layer. Many plants, however, such as water lilies *Nymphoides*, duckweed *Lemna*, and the smallest of all flowering plants *Wolffia*,[2] avoid these problems by having floating leaves which are in contact with the atmosphere. Some macrophytes such as mosses may be found attached to rocks while others, such as water hyacinth *Eichhornia crassipes*, are free-floating. Most of the flowering plants, however, are rooted in the substrate.

The macrophytes of four of Sumatra's lakes have been described in detail by van Steenis and Ruttner [72]. In each of the lakes (Toba, di Atas, Singkarak and Ranau) *Hydrilla verticillata*, a submerged plant with whorls of three to eight leaves along the stem, was common. In Lake Singkarak it was found 8m below the lake surface. Other plant species were common to different degrees in the four lakes.

Algae are the major primary producers in lakes and rivers. Attached algae are found on stones or on macrophytes and although they are generally microscopic in size, larger attached filamentous algae (such as *Spirogyra*) are also found. The other main group of algae is the phytoplankton, which consists exclusively of microscopic forms. Phytoplankton is rarely found in rivers and any free-floating microscopic algae found in upstream regions are almost certainly not phytoplankton but attached algae which have become detached [76]. Examples of phytoplankton are shown in Figure 4.3, and a description of the plankton in the Pekanbaru area is given by Anwar *et al.* [3]. A methodology for determining the population size of phytoplankton in ponds, where it is much more common, is given by Humner [25]. Studies of chlorophyll-*a* and chlorophyll-*b* in phytoplankton are extremely useful in assessing the primary productivity of aquatic ecosystems [62].

4.4.2 Fungi and bacteria

The major role of fungi and bacteria is as decomposers of dead organic matter (corpses, faeces, dead plant material etc.). The fungi and actinomycetes (a common group of bacteria) are best suited to coping with solid matter because they adhere to and penetrate the surface, and often produce extracellular degrading enzymes, and the smaller molecules released during this metabolism are rapidly consumed by bacteria. The ubi-

---

2. The entire *Wolffia* plant is less than 0.5 × 1 mm.

Figure 4.3 Examples of aquatic microorganisms. a- filamentous algae; b-fungal spore; c, j- diatoms; d, e, i- green algae; f, h- blue-green algae; g, l- desmid; k- dinoflagellate. (After Townsend [76]).

quitous nature of fungal spores and bacteria in most fresh water means that dead material is rapidly colonized. Many aquatic fungi have four long straight 'arms' diverging from the centre of the spore and these probably act like anchors to allow efficient attachment even in turbulent water (Figure 4.3b). These spores are sometimes concentrated by bubbles and the persistent foam below waterfalls or rapids is a good source of them. If this foam is collected the spores can easily be examined under a microscope [76].

4.4.3 Animals

Animals of lakes and rivers can be roughly categorized by habitat.

A few species, such as water skaters (Gerridae) [12], live on the water surface supported by surface tension and this group of animals is known as the neuston. The species living in the mid-water are divided into two groups; those which are capable of swimming are called the nekton, the others swim weakly if at all and are called the zooplankton. The commonest zooplankton are the Rotifers [37], and the small crustaceans Cladocera and Copepoda [33]. Like the phytoplankton, zooplankton are concentrated in lakes or downstream sections of rivers. Plankton can be useful subjects in environmental studies, but identification, particularly of zooplankton, is often extremely difficult. Keys with pictures for the major plankton groups in Sumatra are urgently needed. There are considerable (and not always easily explicable) fluctuations in the abundance of plankton at different levels in a body of water from hour to hour, day to day and season to season and so the best method of sampling is by vertical pulls of a plankton net.

Most species of invertebrates are associated with river and lake beds and are known as the benthos. The majority of this benthos comprises insects but, in certain habitats, oligochaete worms, leeches, molluscs or crustaceans may predominate.

4.4.4 Food Webs

Constructing a food web for an aquatic or any other ecosystem demands more than just the compilation of an inventory and decisions on likely connections. Some links in the web may require considerable detective work to elucidate them. For example, the most successful ponds raising chinese carp *Cyprinus carpio flavipennis* are generally those in which the waters have been heavily fertilized with pig manure. Under such conditions the dominant organisms is often the red protozan *Euglena sanguinia* (Figure 4.4), the numbers of which are sometimes so dense as to form an orange-red film on the water surface. Since carp usually feed on macrophytes it is not immediately obvious what role *Euglena* plays in the food web [58]. An example of a carefully produced food web is shown in section 4.8.2. and the methods used to produce it are given by Green *et al.* [22].

Figure 4.4   *Euglena sanguinia* - **a protozoan common in some fish ponds.**

4.5 PHYSICAL PATTERNS IN LAKES

One way to view lakes is as very slow moving rivers in which the river bed has become very wide and very deep. Many of the same species of animals and plants live in both lakes and rivers, and many of the adaptations they require are also the same. However, so great are some of the structural differences of lakes and rivers that their behaviour and characteristics require separate attention. Lakes are dealt with first because they are simpler than rivers.

The German Sunda Expedition studied fifteen lakes in Sumatra, Java and Bali, and those studied in Sumatra were:

Lake Diatas,
Lake Ranau,
Lake Maninjau,
Lake Singkarak, and
Lake Toba [64].

In addition to these, Lake Kawar and Lake Mardingding were studied briefly by a team from CRES in order to collect data to illustrate topics discussed in this section (Figure 4.5).

4.5.1 Lake Kawar and Lake Mardingding

Lake Kawar in the Karo highlands was formed several thousand years ago when a lava flow from the volcano Mount Sinabung blocked the

Figure 4.5 Locations of Lake Kawar and Lake Mardingding relative to Mt. Sinabung.

River Tupin [79]. A small dam was built at the outflow in about 1954 for an irrigation scheme and this raised the level by about 2 m. Its present area is 116 ha and this is only slighly greater than before the dam was built because the lake sides slope steeply. North of the lake is undisturbed forest and to the south, there is low-intensity agricultural activity.

The CRES team recorded depth, gradients of temperature, conductivity and dissolved oxygen, benthos, and concentrations of nitrogen,

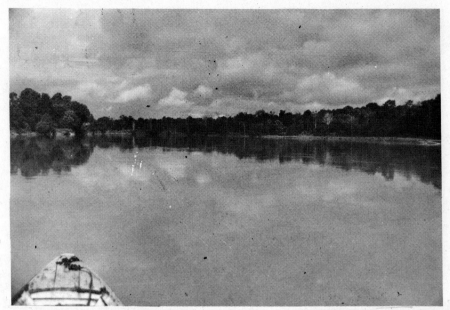

A slow-moving wide river has much in common with lakes. River Singkil, South Aceh.

Lake Dusun Besar, Bengkulu.

River Alas, South-east Aceh.

Lake Kerinci showing a mat of water hyacinth directly abutting a rice field.

potassium and phosphorus at 25 locations on the lake. From the depth soundings a map showing the approximate location of depth contours was produced (Figure 4.6). From these data the capacity of the lake could be calculated [50] and was found to be 41.5 million m³ (equivalent to a cube with sides 346 m long). The outflow over the dam was measured

Figure 4.6 Height contours (every 25 m) around, and depth contours (every 5 m) within Lake Kawar with the locations of the 25 sampling points.

and was found to be 25.8 m³ per minute. Assuming, for the sake of simplicity, that this is an average flow rate, it is clear that the volume of the lake is 'replaced' every three years. This fails to take account of seepage from the lake in the groundwater and the fact that deeper water is replaced slower than surface water but it provides some indication of the time taken for water to pass through the lake.

Lake Mardingding lies on the southwest slope of Mount Sinabung. Its formation has not been described but it may have formed in a small hole left by a minor crater. Its edges were reinforced with cement some years ago, presumably to aid irrigation. The same parameters studied on Lake Kawar were examined at ten locations on Lake Mardingding. Its area is

0.4 ha and has a volume of 4,200 m³. Outflow was not measured but was estimated to be 1 m³ per minute. Thus the lake volume would be exchanged in about three days (again, this does not take account of seepage into the groundwater).

4.5.2 Temperature

The sun's rays penetrate to a certain depth in all lakes and the surface water is therefore warmed. Warm water is less dense than colder water and so a layer of warm water 'floats' on top of the cold layer. The warm layer is called the 'epilimnion', and the cold layer is the 'hypolimnion'. Separating the two is a fairly thin layer called the 'metalimnion', across which there is a sharp temperature gradient called the 'thermocline' (Figure 4.7). Dark-coloured water absorbs more heat than light-coloured water. Thus the CRES team investigating the black-water lake of Lake Pulau

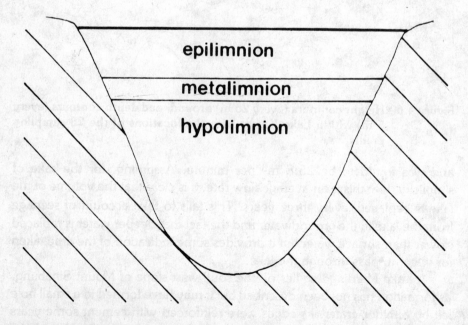

Figure 4.7 Hypothetical vertical section of a lake showing the layers.

183

Besar in the peatswamps of eastern Riau found the surface temperature to be 30.5°C, one or two degrees higher than would normally be expected. Even within a lake surface temperatures can vary. In Lake Ranau, for example, the western end is 4°C warmer than the eastern end because of the influence of hot spring [82].

The temperature profile from one of the deepest parts of Lake Kawar is shown in Figure 4.8. The thermocline occurred at about

Figure 4.8 Temperature profile near the middle of Lake Kawar showing the thermocline at about 8 m.

8.5 m and although the temperature probe was only 12 m long, the hypolimnion appears to have begun 10 m below the lake surface and to have had an even temperature of 21°C. No thermocline or any other stratification was observed in the shallow Lake Mardingding. Sections through the middle and outflow end of Lake Kawar (Figure 4.9) show that the thermocline depth was more or less the same across the body of the lake but the increased flow near the dam caused a certain amount of disturbance.

In none of the 15 lakes studied by the German Sunda Expedition did the temperature difference between top and bottom exceed 5.5°C. At maximum depth in the hypolimnion the temperature was between 20.1°C and 27.0°C, being lowest in the mountain lakes, and increasing 0.4—0.6°C for every 100 m decrease in altitude [64] (see section 9.2.1).

TEMPERATURE

Figure 4.9   Sections through Lake Kawar (between locations 6—9 and 22—25) showing temperature readings every two metres.

4.5.3   Dissolved oxygen

Thermal stratification has interesting consequences for the hypolimnion. Photosynthetic organisms thrive in the epilimnion near the light, thus keeping the epilimnion well supplied with oxygen. In the darker waters of the hypolimnion, however, there may be almost no photosynthesis and so almost no oxygen is produced there. A few animals live in the sediments at the bottom of the lake, however, and remove the oxygen by their respiration. This oxygen deficit is made worse by the continual action of decomposers because the biota of the lighted surface will be continually dropping faeces, corpses and other debris into the hypolimnion, and these will be processed by bacteria as they fall. Bacterial respiration can quickly reduce the oxygen dissolved in the hypolimnion to virtually zero and there is no way the oxygen can reach these layers unless the layers overturn (section 4.5.6).

The dissolved oxygen profile from one of the deepest parts of Lake Kawar is shown in Figure 4.10. This shows the boundary between oxygenated and deoxygenated water to be between 6.5 and 7 m. The dissolved oxygen probe was only 8 m long but the readings suggested the water would have been anoxic at about 10 m.

Figure 4.10 Dissolved oxygen profile near the middle of Lake Kawar showing a boundary at about 7 m.

Sections through the middle and outflow end of Lake Kawar (Figure 4.11) show the boundary between the oxygenated and almost deoxygenated water to be at nearly the same depth across the body of the lake, and about 2 m shallower at the outflow end. It is interesting that the readings for dissolved oxygen 10 cm below the surface were an average of 7.1 ppm on the northern edge and an average of 7.5 ppm on the southern edge. Unlike the northern side, the south is not protected from the wind by projecting ridges and coves and so is better able to take up oxygen.

Figure 4.11 Sections through Lake Kawar (between locations 6—9 and 22—25) showing dissolved oxygen readings every two metres.

4.5.4 Nutrients and conductivity

As described above, much of the living matter in the epilimnion eventually finds its way to the hypolimnion when the animals or plants die or when their consumers defaecate their remains into the water. Thus, the epilimnion experiences a net loss of nutrient minerals while the hypolimnion experiences a net gain. The profile of conductivity (concentration of electrolytes) for one of the deepest parts of Lake Kawar is shown in Figure 4.12. This shows that the boundary between the low concentration of dissolved minerals in the surface water and high concentration of dissolved minerals in the deeper water occurred at 7.5 m. Figure 4.13 reveals that this boundary was more or less constant across the body of the lake and slightly shallower and more disturbed at the outflow end.

Oxygen consumption (rate of respiration) is about 4—9 times faster in Sumatran lakes than in lakes in the temperate regions because the

Figure 4.12 Conductivity profile near the middle of Lake Kawar showing a boundary at about 75 m.

because the temperature of the Sumatran hypolimnions are 15—20° higher. Thus carbon dioxide and other solutes are released very fast and in deeper lakes much of the settling organic matter is mineralized before it even reaches the bottom. In the deepest lakes examined by the German Sunda Expedition, the deep bottom sediment consisted of almost pure silica in the form of diatom shells and spongilla needles [64]. Ruttner also

Figure 4.13 Sections through Lake Kawar (between locations 6–9 and 22–25) showing conductivity readings every two metres.

found very high levels of phosphate and ammonium in some hypolimnions and suggested that water from deeper layers rather than the surface should be siphoned and used for rice field irrigation to save using artificial fertilizers. Algal growth in the euphotic zone (section 4.5.5) is limited by the levels of nitrates and phosphorus and the relative importance of these differs, depending on the catchment area.

Ecologists classify lakes between two extremes based on their nutrient content and organic productivity. 'Oligotrophic' lakes have low concentrations of nutrient minerals and harbour relatively little plant and animal life. The water in oligotrophic lakes is generally clear and unproductive. 'Eutrophic' lakes are rich in nutrient minerals and support an abundant fauna and flora (see section 11.6.2). As a result of the dense plankton populations, water clarity is reduced.

4.5.5 Light penetration

Light entering a water body is absorbed by the water itself, dissolved substances and particles (mainly phytoplankton) in suspension. In theory, light is never *totally* absorbed at any depth but where it is reduced to about 1% of the surface intensity, this represents the approximate depth at which the energy used by algae in respiration is balanced by the energy they gain by photosynthesis. This is known as the 'compensation point', and the water above the compensation point is known as the 'euphotic' zone. The depth of this zone depends to a large extent on the nutrient status of the lake because high nutrient levels lead to high phytoplankton populations which cause surface shading and so reduce light penetration. If a black and white disc (a Secchi disc) is lowered into water, the mean depth of where it disappeared from view and where it reappeared is equivalent to 0.3—0.5 of the depth of the euphotic zone. Secchi disc readings at Lake Kawar were between 1.9 and 2 m and the fact that dissolved oxygen was found down to almost 8 m suggests that there was some mixing within the epilimnion rather than that photosynthesis occurred down to that depth. Ruttner found that the euphotic zone was generally the same as the epilimnion and varied from 20—30 m in Lake Toba to 2—5 m in smaller lakes [64].

4.5.6 Stability

In temperate regions, lake water is mixed in the autumn when the top layer starts to cool and strong winds exert a force on the lake water sufficient to overturn the layers. In most tropical lakes, however, the layering of water is more or less stable although overturns are known (see the paper by Green et al. for a lake in Java [22]) and when they occur the low oxygen concentration of the new surface water can cause the death of fish and other animals.

Most of the 15 lakes investigated by the German Sunda Expedition were stratified and Ruttner found that their stabilities (resistance to mixing) and depth of thermoclines were related to surface area roughly according to the following proportions [64]:

area	1 :	100 :	1000
depth of thermocline	1 :	3 :	6
stability (0—20 m)	50 :	10 :	1

Thus the thermocline of Lake Toba (over 1000 km^2) is over six times the depth found in Lake Kawar (1.16 km^2) and needs less than onefiftieth the wind force to mix the top 20 m. So large is Lake Toba and so strong the winds that blow across it, that oxygen was found down to 425 m in the northern basin [51, 64].

4.6 BIOTIC PATTERNS IN LAKES

4.6.1 Layers - light and oxygen

As would be expected, the distribution of biota in a lake is determined principally by the physical conditions, particularly the layers.

The distribution of plankton in lakes (and other bodies of water) is governed by a wide range of variables: water density and viscosity, nighttime cooling, turbulence, temperature, light intensity and time of day. In addition, the form of feeding or photosynthesis has an effect [16]. Ruttner found that differences in plankton abundance did not only occur between the epi-, meta-, and hypolimnion but that considerable variation also existed within the epilimnion itself; those differences were not easy to explain [65]. Phytoplankton were not usually found below the thermocline but in the very clear Lake Toba, for instance, some phytoplankton were even present in the hypolimnion.

Many fish obviously depend on the plankton but would be unable to feed on them if they were in the hypolimnion because of the low levels of oxygen found there. In Lake Kawar, for example, more than half the volume of the lake would not support fish because of the virtual absence of oxygen and about 70% of the lake bed would not support benthos-eating fish because the lake bed is below the thermocline. Benthic animals either have to be able to cope with very little oxygen (such as the red, haemoglobin-filled chironomid fly larvae) or with no oxygen (and usually no light) such as anaerobic saprophytic[3] fungi and bacteria. In the low-oxygen, dark environment these organisms have few predators. Some animals make vertical migrations, coming to the surface epilimnion for oxygen and descending to feed. At Lake Kawar a total of 78 hauls of lakebed samples resulted in just one snail *Melanoides tuberculata* being found. Even when sampling in shallower water closer to the edge only an occasional snail could be found. This scarcity was probably caused by the low nutrient levels in the lake which were also reflected in the absence of submerged macrophytes around those parts of the lake that were surveyed.

---

3. Saprophytes are organisms that derive their energy from dead organic matter and are the chief agents in the process of decay.

The high altitude (and therefore low temperature), deep water, and low nutrients of Lake Kawar do not recommend it for fisheries. Carp have been introduced with limited success but introductions of *Sarcotherodon* (formerly *Tilapia*) *mossambica* and gourami *Osphronemus goramy* failed. See the report by Ondara for an excellent account, in Indonesian, of the introductions into Lake Toba which is also nutrient-poor [51], and the paper by Schuster for a discussion of the successes and failures of fish introductions into Indonesia [69].

At Lake Mardingding, the water was almost choked with water weeds and floating on the surface were quantities of duckweed *Lemna*. The nutrient levels at Lake Mardingding were much higher than at Lake Kawar and the oxygen levels at the bottom (1 m) of this well-mixed small lake were ± 7 ppm. This resulted in a considerably richer invertebrate (and probably fish) fauna, particularly amongst the water plants.

4.6.2 Water hyacinth community ecology

One of the best known of Sumatra's lake plants is the water hyacinth *Eichhornia crassipes*. It is distributed throughout the tropics and sub-tropics (although it originated in Brazil) and has caused serious and expensive problems in many water management schemes because of its rapid growth. At the new Asahan River hydroelectric site, water hyacinth floating out of Lake Toba has to be held back by floating pontoons and then collected to prevent the plants entering the various sections of the hydro-scheme. Water hyacinth used to cover most of Lake Kerinci but a control program has reduced it considerably.

The above examples give the impression that water hyacinth is nothing but a pest. In fact, it can be a useful plant: Indonesian conservation groups have used it to make rough paper and efforts have been made to use it as cattle feed. It can also reduce levels of inorganic pollutants [67], and in moderate quantities plays an important role in lake fisheries.

At Lake Lamongan, one of the crater lakes on Mount Lamongan, East Java, water hyacinth forms a girdle around three sides of the lake up to 30 m wide, held in position by bamboo stakes. Around the fourth side, at the eastern end, there is a much more extensive mat. In the study by Green *et al.* it was found that there was fairly free movement by epilimnion water beneath the girdle of water hyacinth and thus the temperature, oxygen and pH up to 2 m beneath the mat was more or less the same as that in the open water [22]. At the eastern end, however, there was evidence of oxygen depletion. This was presumably caused by shading which prevented phytoplankton and macrophytes from photosynthesizing.

The loose meshwork of water hyacinth roots extending 20—30 cms below the lake surface supported an abundance of aquatic organisms. The leaves reaching up to one metre above the lake surface formed a habitat that was essentially terrestrial and was occupied by such air-breathing animals as could swim or fly to it. An analysis of animal stomach contents showed that few animal species seemed to feed directly on the tissue of the water hyacinth roots, but many fed on the organic debris and diatoms that covered the roots. Micro-invertebrates were abundant having been attached to, crawling on, or swimming among the roots, but unfortunately small protozoans and some rotifers are rarely recognizable in gut contents and so their role in the food web cold be not be completely determined (Figure 4.14). The water hyacinth root community forms the basis for an important trap-fishery for the people living around Lake Lamongan.

4.7 PHYSICAL PATTERNS IN RIVERS

Longitudinal patterns in the intensity or concentration of physical factors occur down the length of almost all rivers, but not necessarily in a smooth, continuous fashion. Large waterfalls, for instance, can cause a major change in the concentration of dissolved oxygen. Variation also exists across a stream in depth, substrate composition and current velocity, and these also have their effects on the biological communities.

4.7.1 Current velocity

Despite what one may intuitively believe, the mean velocity of water (section 4.7.2) increases from the headwaters to the lower streches of a river. Less surprisingly, the discharge of a river (water volume per unit time) also increases downstream as a product of the cross-sectional area and the mean velocity. This is due partly to additional water entering from tributaries and a reduction of friction on the riverbed caused by the change from large, irregular boulders to fine silt.

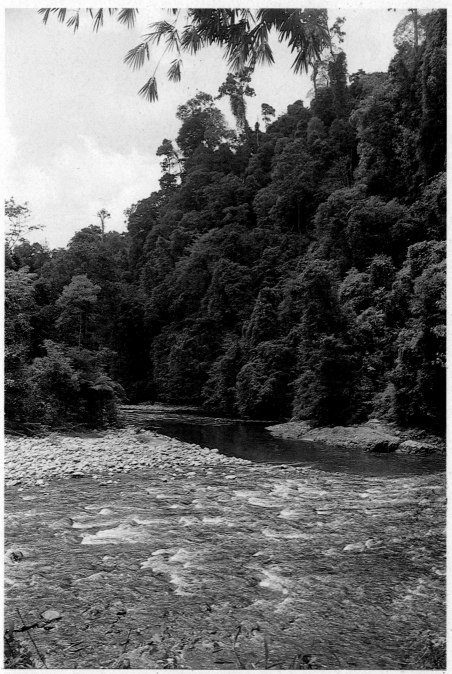
The fauna in the stony reaches is different from that in the pools; River Bohorok, Langkat.

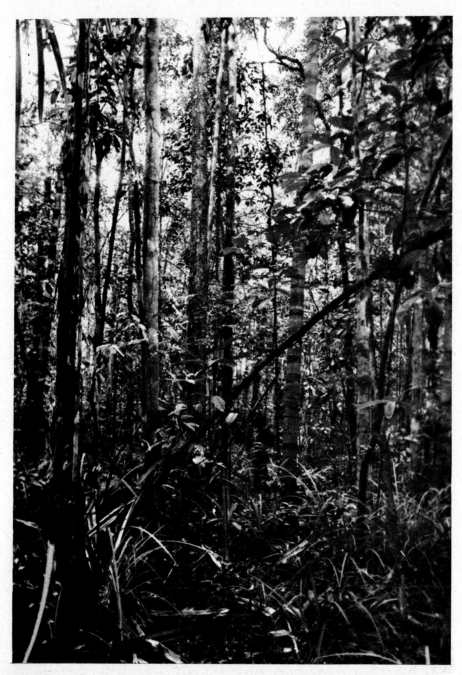

Peatswamp forest on 30m of peat near Lake Pulau Besar, Bengkalis.

193

Figure 4.14 A simplified food web for part of the water hyacinth root-mat community in Lake Lamongan. The diagram is based on the gut contents of animals caught in or near the water hyacinth, or known to have fed there because of fragments of water hyacinth roots in the gut; or, in the case of *Ophiocephalus*, because the gut contained so many species from the water hyacinth community. The link between a consumer and its food is thick if the food item was ever recorded as the main gut contents of the consumer. Links based on indirect evidence are marked with a question mark. (After Green et al. [22]).

Current velocity also varies across the width of a river being greatest near the middle and greatly reduced among macrophytes and varies along the length of short stretches. In small streams, for example, shallow sections with fast water alternate with deeper pools where the water flows more sluggishly.

4.7.2 Shear stress on the river bed

Current velocity decreases in a logarithmic manner from water surface to river bed (Figure 4.15). The average velocity of the whole column of water is equivalent to that occurring at about 60% depth and this may be an important factor in investigations of plankton and nekton which live in that region. This average velocity is, of course, of little relevance to animals living on the river bed. They are subject to the force of 'shear stress' (t_o) on the bed. The greater the shear stress on the river bed the greater the chance that a benthic organism will be dislodged and washed downstream. Shear stress is calculated as follows:

Figure 4.15 Relationship between current velocity and depth in an open channel. (After Townsend [76]).

$$t_o = yds$$

where y is the specific weight of water, d is depth and s is slope. Slope declines more quickly than depth increases (there could easily be a hundred-fold decrease in slope but only a ten-fold increase in depth) and thus for a given discharge frequency, t_o decreases downstream. It is clear then that the shear stress experienced by benthic organisms is likely to be a more important factor nearer the headwaters, despite the lower average velocity there [76] (section 4.7.1).

4.7.3 River bed particle size

Shear stress affects not only animals and plants but also inorganic particles which can be dislodged. The particles which remain in a location will be those that are larger than the flowing water is able to carry away. The smallest ones will be carried in the water as 'suspended load' while the larger particles roll along the bottom as 'bed load'. As shear stress decreases downstream, so particle size also decreases downstream.

4.7.4 Temperature

Soil is well buffered against the effects of changing air temperature and solar radiation and so its temperature is much more stable than that of air. Headwater streams fed primarily by groundwater will be at temperatures close to that of the surrounding soil. The water is gradually warmed as it moves downstream by contact with the air and by being warmed directly by sunlight. The rise is approximately proportional to the logarithm of the distance travelled [76].

Although water temperature is frequently measured in river or lake research programmes, full use is rarely made of the data and its usefulness to environmental science is often underestimated. A survey of midday temperatures was conducted in three areas in western Peninsular Malaysia [14] and this highlighted the wide range of thermal regimes encountered in quite a small area and showed that river temperatures are strongly influenced by the environmental characteristics of the catchment area. As would have been predicted from the theoretical discussion of temperature in rivers above, water temperatures were lower where there was major input from groundwater and where the river was shaded, than they were in open plains where input from surface water was important and there was no obstacle to solar radiation. The thermal regime of a river might provide a useful measure of the environmental impact of land use changes. Forest clearance, for example, would lead both directly and indirectly to increased temperatures and greater temperature fluctuations. The direct effects would be to reduce the amount of shade along the river and to increase surface and soil temperatures by allowing more sunlight to reach the ground. Indirectly, felling would increase surface runoff, thereby reducing the groundwater component which has a low temperature and low variability. Also, by favouring high rates of soil erosion, the sediment load would be increased, thus enhancing the rate at which the river absorbs solar radiation [14].

The ecological consequences of the above are discussed in section 4.8.3.

4.7.5 Dissolved oxygen

The concentration of dissolved oxygen in rivers is determined by a number of physical and biological factors. A rise in temperature reduces the solubility of gases so the increase in temperature downstream causes a decrease in dissolved oxygen concentration. This pattern is reinforced because in the headwaters the water is turbulent and well mixed, whereas downstream it is calmer and less mixed. There is also likely to be more decomposition of organic debris (consumption of oxygen) downstream, and if the water is turbid the rate of photosynthesis (production of oxygen) is lower. Striking daily patterns can be found because photosynthesis can produce oxygen-saturated water during the day, while decomposition of organic matter and plant respiration at night can greatly deplete oxygen levels [76].

4.7.6 Mineral nutrients

The concentration of ecologically important mineral nutrients or dissolved salts generally increases downstream. Rocks in the headwaters are generally resistant to weathering and the concentration of minerals will thus be low. Downstream, in areas of alluvium and sedimentary rock, the inflow of minerals and therefore the conductivity of the water, will increase. This trend is amplified by the inputs of mineral nutrients from the wastes of human activities [76].

4.8 BIOTIC PATTERNS IN RIVERS

Longitudinal sequences in the distribution of many riverine animal

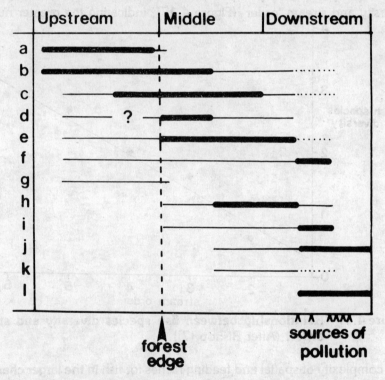

Figure 4.16 Longitudinal distribution of twelve species of fish in R. Gombak. Horizontal dotted lines denote rare occurrence; narrow lines denote constant species; wide lines denote 10% or more of the fish catch. a- *Tor soro;* b- *Acrossocheilus deauratus;* c- **spiny eel** *Mastacembelus maculatus;* d- **catfish** *Silurichthys hasseltii;* e- *Glyptothorax major;* f- **barb** *Puntius binotatus;* g- **snakeshead** *Channa gachua;* h- *Mystacoleueus marginatus;* i- **rasbora** *Rasbora sumatrana;* j- **halfbeak** *Dermogenes pusillus;* k- *Acrossocheilus sp.;* l- **guppy** *Poecilia reticulata.* (Adapted from Bishop [7]).

and plant species are commonly found - presumably at least partly related to the changes in the abiotic factors discussed above. One of the few detailed studies on this topic in the Sunda Region was conducted by Bishop along the Gombak River [7]. His data are extremely complex but the longitudinal distribution of just twelve fish species is shown in Figure 4.16. Note the change in species at the forest edge and where pollution sources become frequent. Bishop also found a significant correlation between fish diversity and stream 'order' (Figure 4.17), indicating the greater number

Figure 4.17 **Relationship between fish species diversity and stream order.** (After Bishop [7]).

and complexity of spatial and feeding niches for fish in the larger channels. The method for assigning stream orders in shown in Figure 4.18.

4.8.1 Current

Current velocity increases in a downstream direction but shear stress is greatest in the shallow, turbulent headwaters (section 4.7.1), and so those organisms possesing adaptations enabling them to resist being swept away are usually found upstream. Examples of animals living in headwater rivers are shown in Figure 4.19.

199

Figure 4.18 Hypothetical river basin showing system of assigning stream orders. Thus, 1 + 1 = 2, 2 + 2 = 3, but 2 + 1 = 2, 3 + 2 = 3 and so forth. (See Strahler [73]).

Plants

The only plants found in very fast-flowing water are encrusting algae, unbranched filamentous algae, and mosses. These are usually squat species which resist shear stress, but this habit makes them more suscepti- ble to smothering by sand. Despite these adaptations, the stones they are attached to can, of course, be washed away if the river bed is unstable.

The adaptations which enable higher plants to live in fast flowing water include a low resistance to water flow, high anchoring strength, and high resistance to abrasion. The ability to propagate from small fragments is also a common feature of plants of these zones. Plants especially adapted to living on the sides of rivers are called rheophytes and are typically shrubs with narrow leaves and brightly coloured fruit which are dispersed either by water or by fish [71]. Clearly, plants growing at the sides of fast streams (or growing amongst resistant species) are subject to less battering, and so variation in plant density occurs across the stream. Since discharge varies with the time, plants at any point will, at least in part, show adaptations to the periods of maximum spate [76]. Dudgeon, working on a river in a Hong Kong forest, found that floods caused a great reduction in epilithic

Figure 4.19 A selection of animals from torrent rivers in the Sunda region. Relative sizes correct; about ⅓ natural size. a-pied suckerloach *Homaloptera ocellata*; b- catfish *Glyptothorax majus*; c- leech *Hirudinea*; d- catfish *Acrochordonichthys melanogaster*; e- torrent prawn *Atya spinipes*; f-giant water stick insect *Cercometus* sp.; g- hellgrammite larva (Corydalidae); h-mayfly nymph (Ecdyonuridae); 1-mayfly nymph *Baetis* sp.; j-waterpenny larva *Eubrianax* sp.; k-stonefly nymph *Perta* sp.; l-dragonfly nymph (Gomphidae); m- caddis worm (Rhyacophilidae). (After Johnson [30]).

algae (algae growing on stones or rock), but not in detritus, because detritus washed downstream was replaced by more detritus washed down from further upstream [19]. Dependence on detritus as an energy source thus leads to a more stable existence than dependence on attached algae.

Invertebrates

There are many ways in which invertebrates have adapted to the conditions in turbulent headwater rivers. Many species have extremely flat bodies which allow them to live and move about in the relatively motionless layer just about the riverbed, or to live under stones thereby avoiding the current. Other species hang on by means of hooks or suckers, or have streamlined shapes offering very little resistance to stream flow. Lieftinck, writing about a lowland stream in West Java, states that at a meander in a river, the slow-flowing inside of the bend has an almost lake-like invertebrate fauna, whereas the fast-flowing outer bend has species with adaptations for the torrents of headwaters [40]. The same paper also describes the many and varied adaptations of dragonfly larvae to life on the river bed.

Fish

Many species of fish are adapted to life in fast-flowing water in ways which are similar to those evolved by invertebrates. Most are stream-lined and round in cross-section, so offering little resistance to flow, and are frequently strong swimmers. These fish are components of the nekton but many fish of headwaters are effectively part of the benthos, spending most of their time on the river bed. These fish are not such strong swim-mers, are frequently flattened, live amongst stones and rocks, often have their eyes rather close to the dorsal surface and their mouth located ven-trally. Many of these fish have suckers or friction pads to prevent them be-ing washed away. Most of these fish also have the swim-bladder, an air-filled organ acting as a buoyancy control, much reduced in size.

4.8.2 Substratum

The current determines the occurence of boulders in the headwaters and of silt near the river mouth (section 4.7.3). Such differences obviously influence the distribution of invertebrates: species which are adapted to live under stones or in crevices only occur where the bed is stony, those that re-ly on their own hooks or nets for anchorage can only occur where the substratum is relatively stable, and the burrowing aquatic larvae of flies re-quire a river bed of fine particles. In the light of this, it is interesting to con-sider the impact on the river biota of removing middle-sized boulders from river beds for use as hard core for roads and other constructions.

In regions of a river where there is sufficient silt, rooted macrophytes can occur. These have a direct influence on the distribution of many in-vertebrates because more species and larger numbers tend to occur on plants than on the nearby mineral substratum, and some species or groups are confined to macrophytes. Most invertebrates on aquatic macrophytes do not in fact feed on the plant tissue (section 9.4.10). Instead, some graze on epiphytic algae growing on the macrophytes, others use the plant as an anchorage from which to filter food from the passing water, and others are predators. Artificial aquatic plants made from plastic string would probably be colonized by the same invertebrate community that colonize the plants and this method can be used for sampling [43]. This emphasizes the role of macrophytes as a living substrate rather than as a food [76].

The importance of particle size on a river bed in determining species distribution was shown in a study of two species of freshwater crayfish *Orconectes* that inhabit the same river in the USA. The rocky parts of the river were inhabited by *O. virilis* and the stretches with finer particles were inhabited by *O. immunis;* both species were found in the middle stretches of the river. Various factors such as dissolved oxygen levels were investigated to explain this distribution but most important was the nature of the river bed. Figure 4.20 shows the results of laboratory experiments in which both species were offered three types of river bed independently and then with both species together. When separate it is clear that both species preferred a rocky river bed and avoided a muddy river bed. When both species were present, however, the 'preference' of *O. immunis,* but *not* of *O. virilis* apparently reversed, because *O. virilis* consistently drove *O. immunis* away from the prime, safe, rocky sites [9] (see section 4.8.5).

4.8.3 Temperature and dissolved oxygen

It has been shown that river temperature increases with distance from the river source (section 4.7.4). Distribution of animals that do not seem to be related to current or nature of the river bed might be explicable in terms of temperature, but there is such an intimate relationship between temperature and dissolved oxygen that these are better considered together.

The solubility of oxygen decreases with increase in temperature and so dissolved oxygen levels are generally lower downstream. This effect is exaggerated because water is less turbulent downstream so that the oxygen removed from the water by respiration of organisms is less easily replaced than in the aerated headwaters. This is especially important for organisms inhabiting the sediment where most of the decomposition of organic matter occurs. In this respect, a slow-moving river resembles a lake (section 4.5.4). Special adaptations to these conditions include the high haemoglobin levels in the bodies of bloodworms (larvae of chironomid

Figure 4.20   Substratum preferences (R = rocky, G = Gravel, M = Mud) for the crayfish species *Orconectes virilis* and *O. immunis* when alone and when together, expressed as a percentage of total positions recorded. (After Bovbjerg [9]).

flies) which enables them to live at very low oxygen levels, and movements of other animals which come up to the surface to take in gaseous air.

Most studies of the environmental tolerances and preferences of fish and other aquatic organisms have focused chiefly upon chemical parameters [47, 52], including pollutants, and the possibility of thermal controls has generally been overlooked. It is well established that the metabolic rates of fish (and some other aquatic animals), and hence their demand for oxygen, increase in proportion to temperature, whilst haemoglobin has a *lower* affinity for oxygen, and levels of dissolved oxygen in water *diminish* at higher temperature [76]. Some fish, such as goldfish[4] have a wide tolerance of temperature; the same species that lives in ornamental tanks in Sumatran homes can overwinter successfully in European, ice-covered ponds (Figure 4.21). Most fish and other aquatic organisms, however, have a narrow tolerance of temperature although optimum temperatures will vary between species.

In addition, aquatic life is poorly adapted to rapid and marked temperature changes. Thus, irrespective of other factors, temperature may cause short rivers arising out of mountains and with a significant ground-water component (such as the River Anai flowing through Padang) to have different numbers of different species from long rivers arising from lowland lakes (such as the River Indragiri arising from Lake Singkarak).

As a result of forest clearance on the plains and the development of,

Figure 4.21 **The relationship between standard metabolism and temperature for the goldfish. (After Varley, 1967 in Townsend [76]).**

---

4. The goldfish *Carassius auratus* is the popular aquarium fish; the goldfish of fishponds and lakes is in fact the golden carp *Cyprinus carpio flavipennis*.

for example, mining activities, many mean river temperatures have probably increased from 25 to 30°C. This leads to a 9.5% reduction in dissolved oxygen at saturation, and the effect would probably be compounded because the percentage saturation might well also fall. This, combined with a marked increase in temperature variability, is likely to have considerable impact on many species of aquatic animals and plants [14].

4.8.3. Mineral nutrients

It would not be surprising if the distribution of certain species were to some extent determined by the changes in concentration of dissolved salts along a river. Virtually all aquatic molluscs, for example, secrete shells of calcium carbonate and the majority of species are not found in water with less than 20 mg calcium/litre. Thus rivers running off volcanic areas are unlikely to have many, if any, molluscs. Also, plants which have adapted to growing in nutrient-poor (oligotrophic) conditions in mountain headwaters may often not be able to compete against species downstream which are not so adapted [76].

4.8.5. Biotic factors

There is more to understanding the distribution of an organism than simply determining physical factors such as temperature and water flow. Every organism fares better within a certain range for each of a set of physical variables and the areas where these conditions are met may be called the organism's 'fundamental niche.' Unfortunately, another species may also be happiest in more or less the same conditions and this leads to competition between the species and the establishment of a species' 'realized niche'. Thus, taking the example of crayfish in section 4.8.2, the realized niche of Orconectes immunis was quite different from its fundamental niche because of the aggresiveness of O. virilis whose fundamental and realized niches were more or less the same. This type of competition is called 'interference competition'. Another type of competition, 'exploitation competition', is more subtle and refers to the indirect competition that takes place between species exploiting the same limited resource. Consumption of that resource by one species will reduce the amount available to the other species, and the one which is less able to convert the resource into reproductive output will either be forced to seek an alternative place to live or else perish. There are few detailed studies of this in any fresh waters but Pattee *et al.* [53] and Lock and Reynoldson [41] describe a series of experiments and observations concerning the role of exploitation competition in the distributions of three species of flatworms (Tricladida). These papers show the importance of competition but also stress that abiotic and biotic factors often interact in very complex ways and that distribution patterns may be influenced by different factors in different rivers. An account of resource partitioning among the fishes of rainforest rivers in Sri Lanka has recently been published [83].

4.9 ENERGY FLOW IN RIVERS

At the level of communities or whole ecosystems, the study of ecology can be broadened to include the flow of energy through the ecosystem or part of an ecosystem. In this approach organisms are therefore regarded as transformers of energy and this energy flow can be traced through the intricate webs of interaction. The biotic community relies on an energy base for the successive trophic levels and in most ecosystems this base for the successive trophic levels and in most ecosystems this base is provided by plants converting solar radiation through photosynthesis into high-energy organic molecules. Exceptions are caves (section 10.3.1.) where there is not enough light for green plants, and rivers in which a substantial proportion of the energy base is provided by dead organic matter. This organic matter can be divided into two components: 'allochthonous' (originating outside the system) and 'autochthonous' (originating within the system). The latter is a relatively minor component. The available organic matter, living and dead, is processed by a wide range of organisms, which include fungi, invertebrates and fish, all interacting in a highly complex manner.

The living organisms of a river can be classified according to their role in energy transfer. Thus, there are:

autotrophs   - photosynthesizing plants which represent the starting point for energy in most ecosystems;

microorganisms - fungi and bacteria whose major role is in the decomposition of organic material;

and four groups of invertebrates and vertebrates:

    grazers   - herbivores feeding on attached algae;

    shredders   - animals feeding on large units of plant material;

    collectors   - animals feeding on loose organic particles either on the river bed or free in the water;

    predators   - animals which (usually) kill and eat other animals [15].

Interactions between these groups and three classes of organic materials are shown in Figure 4.22.

Figure 4.22 A simplified model of energy flow in a river ecosystem. To preserve clarity some arrows have been omitted. For example, all the animals contribute to FPOM in the form of faeces, dead bodies etc; some of the allochthonous input contributes directly to FPOM; the principal food of many fish in rivers consists of invertebrates so the 'predator' category includes fish. However, some fish feed on macrophytes and detritus.

The classes are:

- dissolved organic matter (DOM) arbitrarily defined as smaller than 0.00045 mm diameter,
- fine particulate matter (FPOM), less than 1 mm diameter, and
- coarse particulate organic matter (CPOM), more than 1 mm diameter and including whole leaves, twigs, etc.

The FPOM and CPOM components include the microorganisms associated with them. For more detailed discussion of and information relating to energy flow in rivers see the papers by Petersen and Cummins [55], Barlocher & Kendrick [4], and Mann [44].

4.9.1 Longitudinal patterns

The actual details of the workings of a particular community depend greatly on the nature of its energy base. A hypothetical model is shown in Figure 4.23 that represents the relative importance of the allochthonous

Figure 4.23 Hypothetical representation of the relative contributions of potential energy inputs to a river. (After Townsend [76]).

and various types of autochthonous inputs. The majority of river headwaters, particularly if undisturbed by man, flow through forested catchment areas and receive a substantial allochthonous input from material that simply falls in from the forest canopy. The low level of light reaching the river naturally prevents or at least hinders the growth of attached algae or macrophytes. Lower down the river the shading only occurs at the margins and the autotrophic component increases. The attached algal component, which is generally better adapted to extreme flows and less dependent on a substrate of sediment, would be expected to reach its maximum role nearer the headwaters than the macrophytes. Both macrophytes and attached algae should continue to make significant contributions to the river energy budget until the depth and turbidity are such that light can no longer reach the river bed, and then these plants will be restricted to the margins [76]. Phytoplankton will usually only make a significant contribution where the river is long enough for this component to build up. The generation time for phytoplankton is one or two days (at least three or four days and frequently more for zooplankton) and since rivers generally flow between 20—60 km per day, it is clear that only rivers on the east of Sumatra will commonly have well-developed populations of phytoplankton.

Such longitudinal patterns have not been studied in S.E. Asia. The scheme illustrated is, it is repeated, hypothetical but it seems to fit the known facts from other regions. If it applies to Sumatran systems it can be seen that forest clearance in headwater areas can seriously disturb a river's energy input (and therefore the life that depends on it).

4.10 BENTHOS DYNAMICS IN RIVERS

When a heavy fall of rain causes increased flow, the shear stress exerted on the river bed intensifies and the substrate is scoured, often with the loss of organisms on or in it, and as the flow subsides so organisms from upstream will be deposited in their place. When the river flow is normal, however, benthic organisms are still moving, either on the river bed or in the flowing water, and examination of the contents a net which has been placed in a river and held above the river bed confirms this. This phenomenon is called 'invertebrate drift'.

4.10.1 Invertebrate drift

Bishop found that an average of 222,800 individual invertebrates would drift past a transect in a major headwater stream in just 24 hours [7]. This is equivalent to about 160 individuals per 100 m^3 of river water. The drift varies not just with river flow but also through the day. Studies from various parts of the world including Peninsular Malaysia have shown that drift is highest at night, particularly just after sunset [7]. This appears to be related to light levels rather than to chemical changes. Many invertebrates spend much of the day hiding under stones etc. and only forage when darkness falls. It is logical that when they start to move they are more susceptible to being swept away [11].

An index has been devised that expresses the percentage of the benthos drifting over a unit area of river bed at an instant in time. Various studies in a number of rivers have shown that this value varies from 0.01 to 0.5% and Bishop found values of 0.013—0.018% for headwater streams [7]. These figures may appear low but for a river flowing at 1 m per second, a value of 0.01% means that in one day at least 86400 (seconds) × 0.01 = 864 times as many benthic organisms flow over a 1 m^2 area of river bed as were in that area of river bed. A study by Townsend and Hildrew showed that 2.6% of benthic invertebrates shifted their position each day by drifting [75]. It is important to note that McLay showed that 60% of drifting invertebrates travel for less than 10 m before regaining a foothold [42].

Whether or not losing contact with the river bed and drifting downstream is accidental, there may be adaptive significance in doing so. A river bed, as with most habitats, is composed of 'patches' some favourable for a particular organism and some unfavourable. The patch may be a food resource, a form of substrate, an area experiencing a certain set of biotic and/or abiotic conditions, etc. In some cases a patch may change its suitability, such as when a food resource is depleted or when a flood occurs [7, 74]. Drifting, although it has certain risks, is an energy-efficient way of moving from an unfavourable to a possibly favourable patch, for a journey of 10 m along a river bed is not inconsiderable for many river invertebrates. It has been shown for some invertebrates that if the substrate landed upon is not a favourable one there is a high probability of the animal re-entering the drift within a short time (5-30 minutes) [80], suggesting that invertebrate drift is not entirely passive.

4.10.2 Colonization cycles

Sections above have stressed the importance of the downstream movement of organisms. It seems very reasonable, therefore, to ask how the upstream regions remain populated. Do upstream movements by some organisms compensate for the downstream losses?

Firstly, a downstream displacement of organisms does not necessarily lead to the extinction of those species in upstream stretches. One way to view drift is as a dispersal mechanism for removing animals (possibly as eggs or as larvae) which, had they stayed in the headwaters, would have exceeded the habitat's carrying capacity. It is obvious that not all young invertebrates could remain in the area where their eggs were laid because they would soon exhaust the initial food resource [54].

The above explanation is not the whole story, however, because an organism drifting downstream is likely to leave its zone of suitable environmental conditions. It would therefore be reasonable to suggest that adult invertebrates that managed somehow to reach regions upstream of their optimum habitat to breed would have an evolutionary advantage because their young would have a greater chance of developing in that optimum habitat [76]. A 'colonization cycle' is thus envisaged with eggs being laid in the headwaters, dispersal of larvae occurring downstream and an upstream flight or other movement of adults to the headwaters to complete the cycle. This is commonly known as Müller's Hypothesis.

The first two stages of this hypothesis are irrefutable but evidence for the upstream movemet of adults is less convincing and a review of early work on this subject has been written by Bishop and Hynes [8]. Twin traps set to catch insects flying upstream and those flying downstream along the Gombak River, revealed that the predominant direction of flight was in fact downstream [7]. As a rule, winged adults of invertebrate species with aquatic larval forms are not strong fliers and their flight direction might simply reflect the prevailing wind direction. Strong winds occur most frequently in rainy seasons and these are the periods when insect dispersal is most common [21]. Adults of invertebrate species which spend their entire life cycle in freshwater are not usually strong swimmers or walkers but they may travel near the river edge where shear stress is least so that the upstream journey requires the least possible energy. Most studies have found that upstream movements represent only about 7—10% of the individuals that move downstream [48, 81]. It must be remembered, however, that if only a single female reaches the upstream regions, she may lay hundreds or thousands of eggs.

The study of invertebrate drift deserves more attention. If a factory is to be sited in the middle stretches of a river, and an environmental impact statement has been requested before it is built, one of the many problems that should be considered is the impact on the recolonization of upper stretches of the river by invertebrates (or, for that matter, fish). Is the effluent going to be poisonous or debilitating to adults moving upstream? Which months are the most critical? Since invertebrates are common food for fish, and fish are common food for humans, the problem of the mechanism of invertebrate drift is wider than that of esoteric biology.

REFERENCES

1. Alfred, E.R. (1961). Singapore fresh-water fishes. *Malay. Nat. J.* 15:1-19. (12.5.20)

2. _____, (1966). The freshwater fishes of Singapore. *Zool. Verh. Leiden* 78:1—68. (12.5.28)

3. Anwar, S., Mukhtar, A., Dasni, S., and Hamdan, A (1980). Plankton air tawar Pekanbaru. *Terubuk* 6:2-17. (12.2.12)

4. Barlocher, F. and Kendrick, B. (1975). Leaf conditioning by microorganisms. *Oecologia* 20: 359—362. (3.2.22)

5. Berry, A.J. (1963). An introduction to the non-marine molluscs of Malaya. *Malay. Nat. J.* 17:1-17. (12.3.27)

6. _____, (1974). Freshwater bivalves of Peninsular Malaysia with special reference to sex and breeding. *Malay. Nat. J.* 27: 99—110. (12.3.26)

7. Bishop, J.E. (1973). *Limnology of a Small Malayan River, Sungai Gombak.* Junk, The Hague. (3.2.15)

8. Bishop, J.E. and Hynes, H.B.N. (1969). Downstream drift of the iNvertebrata fauna in a stream ecosystem. *Arch. Hydrobiol.* 66: 59—90. (3.2.25)

9. Bovbjerg, R.V. (1970). Ecological isolation and competitive exclusion in two crayfish (*Orconectes virilis* and *Orconectes immunis*). *Ecology* 51: 225—236. (12.3.32)

10. Chaston, I. (1968). Endogenous activity as a factor in invertebrate drift. *Arch. Hydrobiol.* 64: 324-334. (3.2.37)

11. _____, (1969). The light threshold controlling the periodicity of invertebrate drift. *J. Anim. Ecol.* 38:171-180. (3.2.36)

12. Cheng, L. (1965). The Malayan pond skaters. *Malay. Nat. J.* 19: 115-123. (12.4.4)

13. Critchlow, R.E. and Stearns, S.C. (1982). The structure of food webs. *Am. Nat.* 20: 478-499. (12.13.8)

14. Crowther, J. (1982). The thermal characteristics of some West Malaysian rivers. *Malay. Nat. J.* 35: 99—109. (3.2.18)

15. Cummins, K.W. (1974). Structure and function of stream ecosystems. *Bioscience* 24: 631-641. (3.2.21)

16. Davis, C.C. (1955). *The Marine and Freshwater Plankton*. Michigan University Press, Michigan. (12.2.2)

17. Delsman, H.C. (1929). The distribution of freshwater eels in Sumatra and Borneo. *Treubia* 11:287-292. (12.5.21)

18. Dudgeon, D. (1982). Aspects of the hydrology of Tai Po Kau Forest Stream, New Territories, Hong Kong. *Arch. Hydrobiol. Suppl.* 64:1-35. (3.2.19)

19. _____, (1982). Spatial and seasonal variations in the standing crop of periphyton and allochthonous detritus in a forest stream in Hong Kong, with notes on the magnitude and fate of riparian leaf fall. *Arch. Hydrobiol. Suppl.* 64:189-220. (3.2.17)

20. Edmondson, W.T. (1970). Phosphorus, nitrogen and algae in Lake Washington after diversion of sewage. *Science* 169: 690-691. (3.1.10)

21. Fernando, C.H. (1963). Notes on aquatic insects colonizing an isolated pond in Mawai, Johore. *Bull. Nat. Mus. Singapore* 32: 80—89.

22. Green, J., Corbet, S.A., Watts, E. and Oey, B.L. (1976). Ecological studies on Indonesian lakes. Overturn and restratification of Ranu Lamongan. *J. Zool., Lond.* 180:315—354. (3.1.8)

23. _____, (1978). Ecological studies on Indonesian lakes. The montane lakes of Bali. *J. Zool. Lond.* 186: 15-38. (3.1.9)

24. Hamdan A. and Rasoel, H. (1980). Beberapa jenis ikan hias di S. Siak, Pekanbaru. *Terubuk* 6:30-43. (12.5.19)

25. Hummer, P.J. (1980). Determining the population size of pond phytoplankton. *Amer. Biol. Teach.* 42:545-548. (12.2.10)

26. IPB/Team Biologi Perairan (1975). Laporan Survei Biologi perairan Delta Upang-Banyuasin. PUSDI-PSL, IPB, Bogor.

27. Iskandar, Dj. T. (1978). Kunci identifikasi kura-kura. *Terubuk* 4:1-5. (12.6.26)

28. Johnson, A. (1970). Blue-green algae in Malayan rice-fields. *J. Sing. natn. Acad. Sci.* 1: 30-36.

29. Johnson, D.S. (1956). Systematic and ecological notes on the Cladocera of Lake Toba and the surrounding country, North Sumatra. *J. Linn. Soc. Zool.* 43: 79-91. (12.2.13)

30. _____, (1957). A survey of Malayan freshwater life. *Malay. Nat. J.* 12:57-65. (3.2.16)

215

31. —————, (1960). Some aspects of the distribution of freshwater organisms in the Indo-Pacific area, and their relevance to the validity of the concept of an Oriental region in zoogeography. In *Proc. Centenary & Bicentenary Cong. Biol. S'pore 1958.* (ed. R.D. Purcheon). Oxford University Press, Kuala Lumpur. (3.6.3.)

32. —————, (1961). An instance of sudden large-scale mortality of fish in a natural habitat in S. Malaya. *Malay. Nat. J.* 15: 160-162. (3.2.34)

33. —————, (1962). Water fleas. *Malay. Nat. J.* 16: 126-144. (12.3.33)

34. —————, (1967). Distributional patterns in Malayan freshwater fish. *Ecology* 48:722-730. (12.5.26)

35. —————, (1973). Equatorial forest and the inland aquatic fauna of Sundania. *IUCN Publ. New Ser.* 25:111-116. (3.2.26)

36. Johnson, D.S., Soong, M.H.H. and Wee, B.T. (1969). Freshwater streams and swamps in the tree country of southern and eastern Malaya with special reference to aquarium fish. In *Natural Resources of Malaysia and Singapore* (ed. B. Stone). University of Malaya, Kuala Lumpur. (3.2.33)

37. Karunakaran, L. and Johnson, A. (1978). A contribution to the rotifer fauna of Singapore and Malaysia. *Malay. Nat. J.* 32: 173-208. (12.2.11)

38. Kitchener, H.J. (1951). Diatoms. *Malay. Nat. J.* 8:152-156. (12.2.18)

39. LBN (1980). Laporan Teknik. Bogor.

40. Lieftinck, M.A. (1950). Further studies of S.E. Asiatic species of *Macromia* Rambur. *Treubia* 20: 657-716. (12.4.3)

41. Lock, M.A. and Reynoldson, T.B. (1976). The role of interspecific competition in the distribution of two stream-dwelling triclads. - *J. Anim. Ecol.* 45:581-592. (12.3.31)

42. McLay, C.L. (1970). A theory concerning the distance travelled by animals entering th drift of a stream. *J. Fish. Res. Board Can.* 27: 359-370. (3.2.20)

43. Macan, T.T. and Kitching, A. (1972). Some experiments with artificial substrata. *Verh. Int. Verein theor. angew. Limnol.* 18:213-220.

44. Mann, K.H. (1975). Patterns of energy flow. In *River Ecology* (ed. B.A. Whitton), pp. 248-263. Blackwell, Oxford. (3.2.29)

45. Mochsin, Moh. A.K. (1980). Ecology and morphology of the freshwater fishes of Selangor. Part 1. Cyprinoid fishes of the subfamilies Abraminae, Rusborinae and Garrinae and Family Homalopteridae and Cobitidae. *Malay. Nat. J.* 34: 73-100. (12.5.23)

46. Mohsin, Moh. A.K. and Ambak, Moh. Azmi. (1982). Cyprinoid fishes of the subfamily Cyprinidae in Selangor. *Malay. Nat. J.* 35: 29—35. (12.5.25)

47. Mohsin, Moh. A.K. and Law, A.T. (1980). Environmental studies of Kelang River. II. Effects on fish. *Malay. Nat. J.* 33:189-199. (3.2.25)

48. Moss, B. (1980). *Ecology of Freshwaters.* Blackwell, Oxford.

49. Mukhtar, A. and Sonoda, S. (1979). Ekologi elasmobranchii air tawar 1. Tentang ikan pari S. Indragiri, Riau. *Terubuk* 5:2-11. (12.5.22)

50. Myers, M.L. and Shelton, R.L. (1980). *Survey Methods for Ecosystems Management.* Wiley, New York. (19.5.1)

51. Ondara (1969). *Laporan survey perikanan di Danau Toba.* Laporan Penelitian No. 3, Lembaga Penelitian Perikanan Darat, Palembang. (3.1.2)

52. Palmieri, M.D., Palmieri, J.R. and Sullivan, J.T. (1980). A chemical analysis of the habitat of nine commonly occurring Malaysian freshwater snails. *Malay. Nat. J.* 34: 39-45. (12.3.28)

53. Pattee, E., Lascombe, C. and Delolme, R. (1973). Effects of temperature on the distribution of turbellarian triclads. In *Effects of Temperature on Ectothermic Organisms* (ed. W. Wieser), pp. 201-207. Springer-Verlag, Berlin. (12.2.14)

54. Peckarsky, B.L. (1979). Biological interactions as determinations of distribution of benthic invertebrates within the substrate of stony streams. *Limnol. Oceanogr.* 24: 59-68. (3.2.24)

55. Petersen, R.C. and Cummins, K.W. (1974). Leaf processing in a wood land stream. *Freshwat. Biol.* 4:343-368.

56. Prowse, G.A. (1957). An introduction to the desmids of Malaya. *Malay. Nat. J.* 11:42-58. (12.2.9)

57. —————, (1958). The Euglenidae of Malaya. *Gards' Bull. Sing.* 16: 136-204.

58. —————, (1958). Fish and food chains. *Malay. Nat. J.* 12:66-71. (3.4.5)

59. —————, (1962). Further Malayan freshwater Flagellata. *Gards' Bull. Sing.* 19:105-145. (12.2.20)

60. —————, (1962). Diatoms of Malayan freshwaters. *Gards' Bull. Sing.* 19: 1-104. (12.2.21)

61. —————, (1964). Some limnological problems in tropical fish ponds. *Verh. Internat. Verein. Limnol.* 15: 480—484. (3.4.6)

62. Relevante, N. and Gilmartin, M. (1982). Dynamics of phytoplankton in Great Barrier Reef Lagoon. *J. Plank. Res.* 4:47-75. (12:2.16)

63. Ricklefs, R.E. (1979). *Ecology.* Chiron, London. (23.2.1)

64. Ruttner, F. (1931). Hydrographische und hydrochemische Beobachtungen auf Java, Sumatra und Bali. *Arch. Hydrobiol. Suppl.* 5:197-454. (3.1.11)

65. —————, (1943). Beobachtungan iiber die tagliche Verbikal wanderung des Planktons in tropischen Seen. *Arch. Hydrobiol.* 40:474-492. (12.2.14)

66. Saanin, H. (1968). *Taksonomi and Kuntji Identifikasi Ikan. Jilid I dan II.* Binatjipta, Jakarta. (12.5.1 and 12.5.2)

67. Sato, H. and Kondo, T. (1981). Biomass production of water hyacinth and its ability to remove inorganic minerals from water. I. Effect of the concentration of culture solution on the rates of plant growth and nutrient uptake. *Jap. J. Ecol.* 31:257-267. (25.1.14)

68. Schindler, D. (1974). Eutrophication and recovery in experimental lakes: implications for lake management. *Science* 184: 897-899. (3.1.12)

69. Schuster, W.H. (1950). Comments on the importation and transplantation of different species of fish into Indonesia. *Contr. gen. agr. Res. Stn. Bogor* 111: 1—31. (12.5.15)

70. Sharma, R.E. and Fernando, C.H. (1961). Leeches and their ways. *Malay. Nat. J.* 15: 152-159. (12.3.29)

71. Steenis, C.G.G.J. van (1952). Rheophytes. *Proc. R. Soc. Queensland* 62: 61-68.

72. Steenis, C.G.G.J. van and Ruttner, F. (1933). Die Pteridophyten und Phanerogramen den Deutschen Limnologischen Sunda Expedition. *Arch. Hydrobiol. Suppl.* 11:231-287.

73. Strahler, A.N. (1957). Quantitative analysis of watershed geomorphology. *Trans.Amer.Geophys. Union* 38:913-920. (23.3.17)

74. Taniuchi, T. (1979). Freshwater elasmobranches from Lake Naujan Philippines, Perak River Malaysia and Indragiri River Sumatra, Indonesia, South East Asia. *Japan. J. Ichthyol.* 25: 273-277. (12.5.24)

75. Thienemann, A. (1957). Die Fische der Deutschen Limnologischen Sunda Expedition. *Arch. Hydrobiol.* 23:471-477. (12.5.18)

76. Townsend, C.R. (1980). *The Ecology of Streams and Rivers.* Edward Arnold, London. (3.2.28)

77. Townsend, C.R. and Hildrew, A.G. (1976). Field experiments on the drifting colonization and continuous redistribution of stream benthos. *J. Anim. Ecol.* 45:759-772. (3.2.38)

78. Vaas, K.F., Sachlan, M. and Wiraatmadja, G. (1953). On the ecology and fisheries of some inland waters along the rivers Ogan and Komering in South-east Sumatra. *Contr. Inl. Fish. Res. Sta.* 3:1-23. (3.2.23)

79. Verstappen, H.T. (1973). *A Geomorphological Reconnaisance of Sumatra and adjacent Islands (Indonesia).* Wolters-Noordhoff, Groningen. (23.3.1)

80. Walton, O.E. (1978). Substrate attachment by drifting aquatic insect larvae. *Ecology* 59: 1023-1030. (12.4.25)

81. Williams, D.D. (1981). Migrations and distributions of stream benthos In *Perspectives in Running Water Ecology* (ed. M.A. Lock and D.D. Williams), pp. 155-207. Plenum, New York.

82. Forbes, H.O. (1885). *A Naturalist's Wandering in the Eastern Archipelago. A Narrative of Travel and Exploration from 1878 to 1883.* Sampson Low, London.

83. Moyle, P.B. and Senanayake, F.R. (1984). Resource partitioning among the fishes of rainforest streams in Sri Lanka. *J. Zool.* 202: 195—223.

CHAPTER 5

PEATSWAMP FORESTS

5.1. INTRODUCTION

Peat is a soil type with a very high organic content. It is defined, for the purposes of this chapter, as a soil at least 50 cm deep which, when dried and burned, will lose more than 65% of its mass [16], and is therefore more than 65% organic matter. Certain international agricultural-oriented criteria now define peat as a soil with more than 30% organic matter[1] [17] but peatswamp forests do not develop on such soils [6]. The natural area of peat soils in Sumatra is estimated to have been 7.3-9.7 million hectares [8] or about one-quarter of all tropical peat lands [16].

Peat deposits can be of two forms:

- ombrogenous peat: the most common type which has its surface above the surrounding land. Plants that grow on this peat utilize nutrients solely from within the plants themselves, the peat or directly from the rain. There are no nutrients entering the system from the mineral soil below the peat or from rain water running into it. This type of peat is generally found near the east coast behind the mangrove and is often very deep (± 20 m). The peat and its drainage water are very acid and poor in nutrients (oliogotrophic) particularly calcium.

- topogenous peat: a less common type formed in topographic depressions. Plants growing on this peat extract their nutrients from

---

1. Soil which contains 35—65% organic material is called 'muck.' [6].

mineral subsoil, river water, plant remains and rain. Topogenous peat can be found behind coastal sand bars and inland where free drainage is hindered, such as in mountain depressions (section 1.4.1) and extinct craters. The peat is usually found in a relatively thin layer (± 4 m) but a 9m core was taken from the bottom of a pond on the peaty plateau west of Siborongborong, south of Lake Toba (section 1.4.1). The peat and drainage water are slightly acid (pH 5.0) with relatively abundant nutrients (mesotrophic). Eutrophic peats, although present in temperate regions do not seem to occur in the Sunda region [14].

The surface of the peat is a fibrous crust, either hard and compacted or soft, overlying a semiliquid interior which contains large pieces of wood and other vegetable remains.

Much of the fundamental work on peat soils by Polak was conducted in Sumatra [36], and early vegetation studies concentrated on the potential of peatswamp forests for forestry [11, 12, 18, 38, 39]. More recently, studies have been conducted on vegetation ecology and soils of peatswamp forest in Riau [7, 16], Ahmad classified coastal swamps (probably topogenous) in West Sumatra [1]. Yamada and Soekardjo studied peatswamp forest in South Sumatra [45], and Whitten investigated a topogenous peatswamp on Siberut Island, West Sumatra [42]. Teams from the Environmental Studies Centre at IPB (Bogor) have conducted various studies on peat in the Upang delta and Banyuasin area of South Sumatra [37]. In addition, Morley et al. examined small peaty lakes in central Sumatra [47].

A CRES team visited the peatswamp forest around Lake Pulau Besar, Bengkalis, in the Caltex oil concession in order to collect some data for this chapter.

5.2 PEATSWAMP FORMATION

5.2.1 Formation of ombrogenous peatswamp

It was shown in section 2.3.2 that mangrove forest colonizes areas of recently deposited alluvium along the coast. As the coast, and therefore the mangrove forest, advances seawards, so other plant communities develop in its wake [6]. These are no longer inundated by tides and so

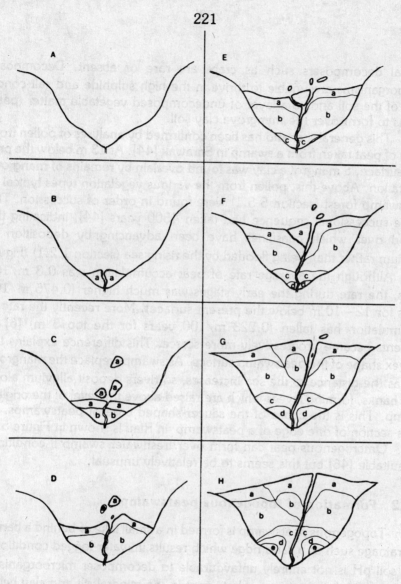

Figure 5.1 **Hypothetical formation of a coastal peatswamp forest. A - an estuary after the final rise in sea level (about 8000 years ago). B-H- deposition of alluvium, colonization by mangrove forests. a -mangrove pioneers (e.g. *Avicennia*), b - Late mangrove species (e.g. *Bruguiera*), c - peatswamp forest pioneers on thin peat and slightly brackish soils, d - mixed peatswamp forest on thicker peat soils above the level of adjacent rivers, e - dwarfed 'padang' forest on thick peat.**

coastal decomposers such as crabs are rare or absent. Decomposer microorganisms are unable to thrive in the high sulphide and salt conditions of the soil and so a layer of undecomposed vegetable matter (peat) begins to form over the mangrove clay soil.

This general scenario has been confirmed by analyses of pollen from cores of peat taken from a swamp in Sarawak [44]. At 13 m below the present surface, a mangrove clay was found overlain by remains of mangrove vegetation. Above this, pollen from the various vegetation types typical of peatswamp forest (section 5.5.1) were found in order of succession. The whole successional sequence had taken 4500 years [44], indicating the period over which coastlines have been advancing by deposition of alluvium rather than being flooded by the rising sea (section 1.2.1) (Figure 5.1). Although the average rate of peat accumulation was 0.3 m/100 years, the rate during the early stages was much higher (0.475 m/100 years for 12—10 m below the present surface). More recently the rate of accumulation has fallen (0.223 m/100 years for the top 5 m) [6] as nutrients became progressively more scarce. This difference explains the convex shape of the peatswamp surface. As swamps replace the mangrove and as the distance to the sea increases, so rivers deposit alluvium along their banks, forming levees which are raised above the level of the original swamp. This is the cause of the saucer-shaped base of peatswamps. A cross-section of one edge of a peatswamp in Riau is shown in Figure 5.2.

Ombrogenous peat can form over freshwater swamp if conditions are suitable [46] but this seems to be relatively unusual.

5.2.2 Formation of topogenous peatswamp

Topogenous peatswamp is formed in a small lake or behind a barrier to drainage such as a sand ridge which results in water-logged conditions. The soil pH is not entirely unfavourable to decomposer microorganisms and many of the plants are able to root in the mineral silt and clay below the peat. This means that peat accumulation is slow, great depths of peat are not formed, and that the brown humic acids characteristic of ombrogenous peat are not so pronounced.

The area of topogenous peatswamp in Sumatra is not large and small lakes only occurs in coastal western Sumatra and certain locations inland [20]. In the classification by Ahmad [1] topogenous peatswamp

Figure 5.2   **Vertical section through a peatswamp near Muara Tolam, near the River Kampar, Riau. Note the vertical and horizontal scales are different. a- peat layer (a matted crust above, looser below), b- peat remains and clay deposited beneath mangrove forest during an earlier time, c- clay deposited beneath the sea, d- clay deposited beneath river (After Driessen [16]).**

is described as shallow fresh water swamp and fringe brackish swamp. There is virtually nothing known about the vegetation or ecology of topogenous peatswamps in Sumatra.

5.3 DRAINAGE AND DRAINAGE WATER

Although the surface of an ombrogenous peat swamp is raised above the surrounding areas, rivulets form on its surface. This is probably so because the heavily compacted mass of woody peat, and the saucer-shaped mineral base of the swamp, prevent lateral drainage [6]. Water flowing out of such a peatswamp is generally clear but appears tea-coloured by transmitted light and opaque black by reflected light in the same way as does Coca-Cola. Such waters are known as blackwater rivers and are generally very acidic (pH 3—4.5). They contain many fewer inorganic ions than do clear, white or muddy waters even in the same drainage basin, have low concentrations of dissolved oxygen, and high concentrations of humic acids [22, 33, 34].

The low nutrient content of blackwater rivers is partially explained by the nature of the soil, for which the only source of nutrients is rainwater (section 5.1). The humic acids are chelating agents for inorganic ions, binding them into larger molecules, thus preventing their uptake by plants. The generally low oxygen levels are probably due to the scarcity of aquatic plants. The high acidity of the water is due to the humic acids.

Humic acids are phenolic compounds, which are one of the many groups of plant defence (or secondary[2]) compounds and have been found to be very important in plant-animal interactions. Phenolic compounds are generally toxic to animals and decomposers because they bind with protein (section 2.6.4. and 7.6.1), and are difficult to degrade. They therefore persist to a greater degree than other chemicals in plant debris. Humic acids would therefore be expected to have detrimental effects on organisms attempting to live in blackwater rivers.

It seems that the water draining into the blackwater rivers has high concentrations of phenolic compounds (and possibly other toxic compounds) because:
  - the leachate from the living vegetation and decomposing litter in the peat-swamp soils is exceptionally rich in phenols and other defence compounds, (but see the paper by St. John and Anderson [48]) and because
  - the soil leads indirectly, and high input of phenols directly, to a soil and litter decomposition community (of bacteria, fungi, etc.) which is unable to break down these compounds [22].

The effect of phenolic compounds on the soils, aquatic and forest communities, will be discussed further in section 5.6 after a description of peatswamp vegetation.

---

2. Secondary compounds are compounds which do not play a role in metabolism.

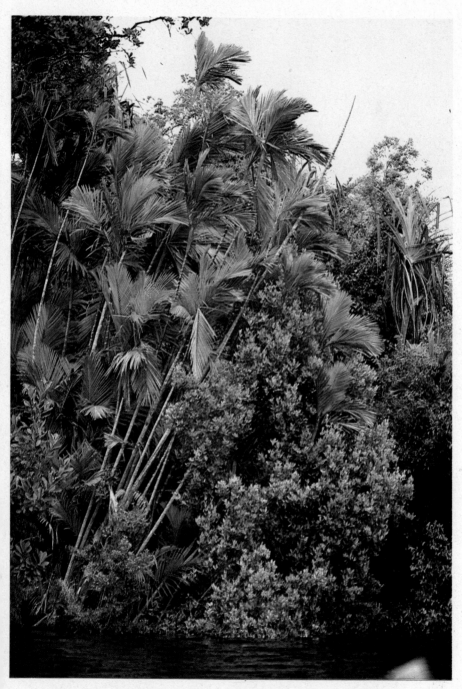

The sealing wax palm on the shores of Lake Pulau Besar, Bengkalis.

The palm *Licuala spinosa* in a topogenous peatswamp forest on Siberut Island.

5.4 VEGETATION

5.4.1 Compositon

Because the surface of an ombrogenous peatswamp is out of the reach of flood-water and because the only nutrient input comes from the nutrient-poor rain, there is a decrease towards the centre of a swamp in the amounts of mineral nutrients in the soil, and this is particularly marked for phosphorus and potassium [35]. The top 15 cm of a peatswamp soil, where a mat of roots is formed, generally has more nutrients than deeper down. This trend of increasing infertility towards the centre of a peat-swamp seems to be reflected in the vegetation by the:
- decreasing canopy height,
- decreasing total biomass per unit area,
- increasing leaf-thickness (an adaptation to poor soils) (see sections 8.2.3 and 9.4.2).
- decreasing average girth of certain tree species [40].

Thus there is no single type of peatswamp forest. Instead, in response to the changes in nutrients, depth of peat etc., a series of forest types develop which intergrade with each other. Anderson [5] has describ-ed the composition of forest types from certain peatswamp areas in Sarawak in great detail but considerable differences exist in species com-position of equivalent forest tyes [7], and not all forest types were found in each area.

In general, however, the sequential pattern of forest types (Figure 5.3) represents a change from:
- a high forest with an uneven canopy which is similar in general appearance to other Sumatran lowland forests, but with fewer species and stems per unit area, and a lower canopy (36-42 m); to:
- a dense forest with a relatively even canopy, but stunted and with various xeromorphic characters; to:
- a very dense 'pole forest' with a canopy barely 20 m high and trunks with a diameter rarely wider than 30 cm; to, in some areas:
- an open, savanna forest (padang) with few trees over 15 m high [6, 40].

Anderson examined trees of 30 cm girth (± 10 cm diameter) at breast height and over in three areas of peatswamp in Riau at Teluk

226

Figure 5.3 Sections through four types of peatswamp forest. a - high-canopy mixed forest, b - lower canopy forest, c - pole forest, d - padang forest. (After Anderson [4])

Kiambang, Muara Tolam and near the Siak Kecil River [7]. Although he had recognized six forest types in Sarawak forest, he divided these areas of Sumatran forest into just two[3]. The three locations had markedly different species compositions (Table 5.1), indicating that no generalizations should be made about the species present from this small sample. Further variation is indicated by the dwarf forest dominated by *Tristania* found by Polak in the central region of the Pareh Peninsula [36], and the dominance of

Table 5.1. Tree species found in two types of peatswamp forest at three locations in Sumatra (From Anderson [7]).

	Teluk Kiambang	Muara Tolam	R. Siak Kecil
Mixed Swamp Forest	*Durio carinatus** *Palaquium burkii* *Dyera lowii* *Shorea platycarpa* *Shorea uliginosa* *Shorea teysmanniana*	*Artocarpus rigidus* *Gonystylus bancanus* *Palaquium burkii*	*Strombosia javanica** *Mezzettia leptopoda* *Palaquium walsuraefolium* *Koompassia malaccensis*
Pole Forest	*Campnosperma coriacea*	*Eugenia elliptifolia* *Shorea teysmaniana* *Mangifera havilandii*	*Palaquium burckii** *Blumeodendron kurzii* *Palaquium walsuraefolium* *Campnosperma coriacea*

* = dominant species

somewhat stunted *Tristania obovata* and *Ploiarium alternifolium* found in peatswamp forest in the Musi delta region of South Sumatra by Endert [18]. *Tristania* is easily recognized by its smooth, peeling bark which varies from pale-grey to orange in colour. It is a member of the family Myrtaceae and like its relatives *Eucalyptus*, *Melaleuca* (paperbark tree) and *Eugenia* (e.g. rose apple, clove) its leaves smell when crushed. Yamada and

---

3. Anderson used the term 'padang' for peatswamp forest which contained many low trees (about 800/ha) [7]. 'Padang vegetation' (section 8.2.3) is poor in species dwarfed and relatively open, so in this chapter Anderson's padang forest is referred to as 'pole forest'. Anderson had used this term earlier in descriptions of Sarawak and Brunei peatswamp forests [3].

Soekardjo found that in their 0.01 ha central peatswamp plot, *Polyalthia glauca* was the most common tree [45]. The topogenous peatswamp examined on Siberut Island was dominated by *Stemonurus secundiflorus* (Icacinaceae) and *Radermachera gigantea* (Bignoniaceae) which together made up nearly 50% of the trees [42].

Palms are not common in peatswamp forest but a few species are more or less confined to this ecosystem. Both Endert [18] and Yamada and Soekardjo [45] mention *Salacca conferta,* a close relative of the edible salak *Salacca zallaca.* Salak is a stemless palm with long (6 m) leaves armed along the midrib with fans of long white spines [41]. Its habit of growing in dense clumps makes salak one of the most formidable natural barriers in Sumatran forest. The tall serdang palms *Livistona hasseltii* of Sumatran peatswamp forest often emerge above the forest canopy [15] and its crown of fan-shaped leaves can be seen clearly from the air. A total of 22 palm species have been found in the peatswamp Berbak reserve in Jambi, making it the most palm-rich peatswamp forest yet known [15]. The forest around Lake Pulau Besar examined by a CRES team had large numbers of the bright-red sealing-wax palm *Cyrtostachys lakka.*

The only epiphytes found in the pole forest and peat padang are those with some means of obtaining mineral nutrients other than just from mineral uptake from their substrate and the rain. Almost all these epiphytes provide shelter for small, non-aggressive ants *Iriodomyrmex,* and in return receive nutrients in the form of discarded food, dead ant remains and ant waste products [21, 23].

Muller investigated fossil pollen in coal (fossilized peat), and marine and coastal sediments in Sarawak [35]. He found that some of the tree genera present in peatswamps there today have been present since the Oligocene (26 million years ago) and that most have been present since at least the mid-Miocene (± 18 million years ago). The striking similarities between the ancient peatswamp and those of today indicates that the climatic changes of the Pleistocene did not influence the composition of the peatswamp communities to any great degree.

5.4.2 Structure

Structural and other data taken from peatswamps by Anderson are shown in Table 5.2. For some variables, such as number of trees, there is

Table 5.2 Characteristics of two types of peat swamp forest in 0.2 ha quadrats at three locations in Sumatra. (From Anderson [7]).

	Teluk Kiambang	Muara Tolam	R. Siak Kecil	Average
No. species				
Mixed Swamp				
Forest	37, 37, 31	49, 44	29, 32	37
Pole Forest	25, 49	46	32, 31	37
No. Trees				
Mixed Swamp				
Forest	163, 159, 110	137, 110	89, 89	122
Pole Forest	220, 123	176	169, 149	167
Average girth				
(cm)				
Mixed Swamp				
Forest	80, 85, 95	76, 85	86, 97	86
Pole Forest	69, 67	70	68, 69	69
Total Basal				
Area (m^2)				
Mixed Swamp				
Forest	8.3, 9.3, 8.0	6.3, 6.3	5.3, 6.7	7.2
Pole Forest	8.3, 4.4	6.8	6.3, 5.7	6.3
Average Basal				
Area (m^2)				
Mixed Swamp				
Forest	0.051, 0.059, 0.072	0.046, 0.058	0.060, 0.076	0.060
Pole Forest	0.038, 0.047	0.039	0.038, 0.038	0.036

considerable variation between plots in the same forest type and so the averages should be treated with caution. The number of species per plot is very similar between the forest types. This is not the pattern generally found in Kalimantan [6, 7] where pole forest is much poorer in species and may indicate that the soils of the Sumatran pole forests are not as nutrient-poor as those in Kalimantan. Other areas of Sumatran pole forest in peat swamp may well have a lower species diversity.

The number of trees, as expected, increases from mixed swamp forest to pole forest, but the average girth decreases. The total basal areas[4] (of the trees measured) was generally higher in mixed swamp forest than in pole forest, as was the average basal area (total basal area divided by number of trees). The single 0.01 ha plot investigated by Yamada and Soekardjo had a total basal area of 1.56 m² (3.1 m²/0.2 ha) one-third of which was contributed by a single large *Alstonia angustiloba* [45].

5.5 ECOLOGICAL CONSEQUENCES OF LOW NUTRIENT LEVELS

The low nutrient levels of the soils in mature peatswamp forest (section 5.3) almost certainly limit primary productivity. Although studies have yet to be conducted to investigate this, the low total basal area of pole forest (Table 5.2), and the doubtless even lower total basal area of stunted peat padang, indicate that their primary productivity is low. In such a habitat, but where climatic conditions are favourable for animal life, plants would be expected to defend their leaves and other edible parts as fiercely as possible against potential herbivores. The three main reasons for this are:

- The loss of a leaf or other part to a herbivore would be proportionately more serious for a plant growing in peatswamp than for a plant growing in a more fertile habitat. This is because of the greater 'cost' of replacing the eaten or damaged leaf part in infertile habitats. Thus it would be expected that proportionately more of the energy and nutrient resources of a peatswamp forest plant were used for defence.

- In a habitat with relatively low productivity, the plant should produce better-protected leaves in order to increase the life of each leaf. Leaves have a finite life, usually related to the amount of damage they sustain, and so it is advantageous to a plant to ensure this damage occurs as slowly as possible. It is possible that the relatively thick cuticle may reduce the leaching of nutrients from living leaves.

- In habitats with low productivity and containing vegetation whose

---

4. Basal area is a forestry term for the cross-sectional area of a trunk at breast height. The total basal area of trees in plot is a rough measure of the amount of forest present.

Table 5.3. Tree families in Sarawak peat swamp forest. The number of genera are shown in parentheses (From Anderson [5]).

Anacardiaceae (3)	Ebenaceae (1)	Oleaceae (1)
Anisophylleaceae (1)	Euphorblaceae (1)	Rubiaceae (1)
Annonaceae (5)	Fagaceae (1)	Rutaceae (1)
Apocynaceae (1)	Guttiferae (6)	Sapindaceae (1)
Aquifoliceae (1)	Leguminosae (1)	Sapotaceae (2)
Burseraceae (1)	Meliaceae (1)	Sterculiaceae (3)
Crypterioniaceae (1)	Myristicaceae (1)	Thymelaceae (1)
Dipterocarpaceae (5)	Myrtaceae (6)	Xanthophyllaceae (2)

seeding strategies involve anti-predator[5] measures such as extreme toxicity or gregarious fruiting (section 7.4.1) there is usually a low species richness of trees and noticeable grouping of species [22].

The trees over 30 cm girth at breast height found by Anderson in Sarawak peatswamp belong to families known to be particularly rich in defence compounds such as latex, essential oils, resins, tannins, and other phenolic or terpenoid compounds [4, 5] (Table 5.3). This indicates that most leaf-eating animals from lowland forest on good soils would find it difficult to live in peatswamp forest.

As stated above (section 5.4.1), many of the plants growing in the inner part of peatswamp forests have thick leaves. When these are crushed there is usually resinous, acrid or aromatic odour or taste. This is most atypical of tropical vegetation but common for plants growing in poor conditions [22], particularly where nitrogen and phosphorus are in short supply [9]. Thick leaves are probably not only a defence against harsh environmental conditions but also a means of deterring herbivores (section 9.4.7). Leaf samples were collected from trees around Lake Pulau Besar but the results of the analyses of their defence compounds are not yet available. Interested readers should contact the authors direct for further information.

The lack of ant-free epiphytes mentioned in section 5.5.1 has been interpreted by Janzen as a consequence of low productivity due to a low rate of inorganic ion input to tree crowns from bird faeces, insects, and falling leaves and twigs [22].

---

5. The term 'predator' is used because the seed represents a new individual which can be killed outright. A herbivore grazing on leaves or eating fruit is clearly not a predator.

5.6 ECOLOGICAL CONSEQUENCES OF HIGH LEVELS OF SECONDARY COMPOUNDS

5.6.1 Microorganisms

Some litter microorganisms can degrade phenolic compounds in soil and water [2, 28] but they do so slowly, requiring a well-oxygenated substrate and accessory energy sources [13]. It is not surprising that microorganisms have difficulty in degrading phenolic compounds because such chemical defences are the result of selection specifically favouring compounds which are difficult for microorganisms and higher animals to digest. As a result, a leaf from a peatswamp forest will probably lie on the ground for many weeks, unattacked by decomposers, until most of the defence compounds have been leached out by rain water. It is not unexpected, then, to find that phenolic compounds have negative effects on mycorrhizae, other fungi, bacteria, roots, vertebrates, insects and worms (for references see the paper by Janzen [22]).

The effects of these defence compounds on microorganisms will be enhanced in the pole forest and peat padang soils by:
- the initial low nutrient quality of the soil (section 5.3) making the microorganisms even more dependent on the litter itself for nutrients;
- the high acidity of the soil;
- the low nutrient quality of the litter because of selection favouring withdrawal of as many nutrients as possible from the leaves before they drop, especially on low-nutrient soils;
- a low rate of litter input because of low primary productivity.

5.6.2 Aquatic animals

Data from Peninsular Malaysia suggest that blackwater rivers have an impoverished and distinct fauna. Malayan blackwater rivers have only about 10% of the fish fauna of other rivers [25]. Cladocera (water fleas), annelid worms, rotifers, nematodes and protozoans are rare; algae are generally rare except for a few species which are locally abundant, and macrophytes may be absent [26]. Of the fifteen fish species found in blackwater rivers, nine were air-breathers or lived near the surface [24] and almost all the insects were air-breathers [25]. This may be due solely to the

A small inlet on the shore of Lake Pulau Besar, Bengkalis, used as a resting place by a false ghavial.

A view from Mt. Kerinci of 'Lake' Bento, the highest freshwater swamp in Sumatra, with Mt. Tujuh and its crater lake behind.

False ghavial.

difficulties of existing at low oxygen levels but it could also be that the protein-binding defence compounds such as tannins, deleteriously affect animals' gills. Thus the aquatic larvae of biting insects, such as mosquitoes, are rare in peatswamp forest. The productivity of animals and plants in these rivers is low and the biomass of fish may be only 0.5 g/m^2. Bishop estimated the fish biomass of a 'normal' small Malayan river to be about 18g/m^2 [10].

What factor is responsible for this distinct aquatic ecosystem? Low nutrient levels have been suggested, but Johnson [24] has shown that calcium levels (for example) in blackwater rivers are generally higher than in other types of river. The low pH cannot be the only factor because those blackwater rivers in Malaya which later flow over limestone have a pH over 6.0; these streams have snails, more insects and fish but the fish are restricted to blackwater rivers, rarely occurring in other rivers with a 'normal' pH [26]. The blackness of the water and hence low light penetration might be though to be an important factor but this would not explain why there are so few animals and plants at the water surface, nor why such animals and plants exist in very muddy water where light penetration is even less. So it would seem that the main factor infuencing this ecosystem is the high level of phenolic compounds.

5.6.3 Terrestrial animals

Peatswamp forests do not support an abundance of terrestrial wildlife. Morton said of an inland peatswamp in Peninsular Malaysia "it was the absence of animals rather than their presence which was so striking" [32]. Janzen described an animal collecting trip in peatswamp forest in Sarawak as "generally a waste of time" [22]. An investigation of primate densities in peatswamps of Peninsular Malaysia found that away from rivers, in the species-poor forests, few primate species existed and those species present lived at densities of less than three groups per km^2 [29]. Typical figures for lowland forest would be 10 groups per km^2 [28]. Similarly, in a study of one group of Mentawai gibbons on Siberut Island, it was found that these animals consistently under-used the area of inland peatswamp in their home range in comparison with the other forest types available to them [42, 43]. This behaviour is understandable because primates depend on tree and vine fruit for most of their diet and the generally low productivity of peatswamp forests would result in fruit being available only rarely.

REFERENCES

1. Ahmad, A. (1978. Klasifikasi rawa-rawa pesisir (coastal swamps) di Pasaman Barat. *Terubuk* 10: 30—36 (12.10.11)
2. Alexander, M. (1964). Biochemical ecology of soil micro-organisms. *A. Rev. Microbiol.* 18: 217—252. (12.4.59)
3. Anderson, J.A.R. (1959). Observations on the ecology of the peat-swamp forests of Sarawak and Brunei. In *Proc. Symp. Humid Tropics Vegetation, Tjiawi 1958,* pp. 141—148. UNESCO, Paris. (12.10.14)
4. _____. (1961). *The Ecology and Forest Types of the Peat Swamp Forest of Sarawak and Brunei in Relation to Their Silviculture.* Ph.D. thesis, Edinburgh University. (Referred to in Whitmore (1975))
5. _____. (1963). The flora of the peat swamp forests of Sarawak and Brunei, including a catalogue of all recorded species of flowering plants, ferns, and fern allies. *Gdns' Bull. S'pore* 29: 131—228. (12.10.18)
6. _____. (1964). The structure and development of the peat-swamps of Sarawak and Brunei. *J. Trop. Geog.* 18: 7—16. (12.10.12)
7. _____. (1976). Observations on the ecology of five peat swamps in Sumatra and Kalimantan. In *Proc. ATA 106 Midterm Seminar, Peat and Podzolic Soils and Their Potential for Agriculture in Indonesia.* pp. 45—55. Soil Research Institute, Bogor. (12.10.13)
8. Andriesse, J.P. (1974). *Tropical Lowland Peats in South-east Asia.* Koninklijk Instituut voor de Tropen, Amsterdam. (23.4.12)
9. Beadle, N.C.W. (1966). Soil phosphate and its role in molding segments of the Australian flora and vegetation with special reference to xeromorphy and sclerophylly. *Ecology* 47: 992—1007. (12.1.47)

10. Bishop, J.E. (1973). *Limnology of a Small Malayan River, Sungai Gombak*. Junk, The Hague. (3.2.15)
11. Bodegom, A.H. van (1929). De vloedbosschen in het gewest Riouw en onderheerigheden. *Tectona 22*: 1302—1332. (12.9.31)
12. Boon, D.A. (1936). De inrichting van de voor exploitatie in aanmerking komende bosschen in de afdeeling Bengkalis, benevens eenige ipmerkingen omtrent de samenstelling der terplaatse voorkomende moerabosschen. *Tectona 29*: 344—373. (12.10.113)
13. Burges, N.A. (1965). Biological processes in the decomposition of organic matter. In *Experimental Pedology*. (ed. E.G. Hallsworth and D.V. Crawford), pp. 189—199. Butterworth, London.
14. Coulter, J.K. (1957). Development of the peat soils of Malaya. *Malay. Agric. J.* 40: 161—175. (23.4.9)
15. Dransfield, J. (1974). Notes on the palm flora of Central Sumatra. *Reinwartia* 8: 519—531. (12.10.61)
16. Driessen, P.M. (1977). Peat soils. Soils and Rice Symposium, Manilla. (23.4.8)
17. Driessen, P.M. and Soepraptohardjo, M. (1974). *Soils for Agricultural Expansion in Indonesia*. Soil Research Institute, Bogor. (23.4.3)
18. Endert, F.H. (1920). De Woudboomflora van Palembang. *Tectona*. 13:113—160. (12.10.15)
19. Furtado, J.I and Mori, S. (ed.) (1982). *Tasek Bera: The Ecology of a Freshwater Swamp*, Junk, The Hague.
20. Hansell, J.R.F. (ed.) (1981). *Transmigration settlements in central Sumatra: identification, evaluation, and physical planning*. Land Resource Study No. 33. Land Resources Development Centre, Surbiton. (15.4.1)
21. Huxley, C.R. (1978). The ant-plants *Myrmecodia* and *Hydnophytum* (Rubiaceae), and the relationship between their morphology, and occupants, physiology, and ecology. *New Phytol.* 67: 231—268. (12.1.17)
22. Janzen, D.H. (1974). Tropical blackwater rivers, animals, and mast fruiting by the Dipterocarpaceae. *Biotropica* 6: 69—103. (12.10.59)

23. _____. (1974). Epiphytic mutualism in Sarawak: Mutualism through the feeding of plants by ants. *Biotropica* 6: 237—259. (12.1.18)

24. Johnson, D.S. (1967). On the chemistry of freshwaters in southern Malaya and Singapore. *Arch. Hydrobiol.* 63: 477—496. (3.3.5)

25. _____. (1967). Distributional patterns in Malayan freshwater fish. *Ecology* 48: 722—730. (12.5.26)

26. _____. (1968). Malayan blackwaters. In *Proc. Symp. on Recent Adv. Trop. Eco.* (ed. R. Misra and B. Gopal). Int. Soc. Trop. Ecol., Varanasi. (3.2.22)

27. Kartawinata, K.: Personal communication.

28. McConnell, W.J. (1968). Limnological effects of organic extracts of litter in a southwestern impoundment. *Limnol. Oceanogr.* 13: 343—349. (3.1.15)

29. Maloney, B.K. (1980). Pollen analytical evidence for early forest clearance in North Sumatra, Indonesia. *Nature* 287: 324—326. (23.6.6)

30. Marsh, C.W. (1981). Primates in Malaysian peat swamp forest. In *Conservation Inputs from Life Sciences*. (ed. M. Nordin, A. Latiff, M.C. Mahani and J.C. Tan), pp. 101—108. University Kebangsaan Malaysia, Bangi. (12.8.10)

31. Marsh, C.W. and Wilson, W.L. (1981). *A survey of primates in Peninsular Malaysian forests*. Universiti Kebangsaan Malaysia, Bangi. (12.8.9)

32. Merton, F. (1962). A visit to the Tasek Bera. *Malay Nat. J.* 16: 103—110. (12.10.17)

33. Mizuno, T. and Mori, S. (1970). Preliminary hydrobiological survey of some southeast Asian inland waters. *Biol. J. Linn. Soc.* 2: 77—117. (3.1.13)

34. Mohr, E.C.J. and Baren, F.A. van (1954). *Tropical Soils*, Mouton, The Hague. (23.4.6)

35. Muller, J. (1972). Palynological evidence for change in geomorphology, climate and vegetation in the Mio-Pliocene of Malesia. In *The Quaternary Era in Malesia* (ed. P. and A. Ashton), pp. 6—34. University of Hull, Hull. (23.6.15)

36. Polak, E. (1933). Uber Torf und Moor in Niederlandisch Indien. *Verh. K. Akad. Wet.* 30: 1—85. (23.4.11)
37. PSL-IPB (1977). Laporan Akhir. Penelitian daerah Upang-Banyuasin.
38. Rakoen, M.P. (1955). Beberapa pendapat mengenai daerah hutan Bengkalis/Kampar. *Rimba Indonesia.* 4: 223—248. (9.1.18)
39. Sewandono, M. (1938). Het veengebied van Bengkalis. *Tectona* 31: 99—135. (12.10.67)
40. Whitmore, T.C. (1975). *Tropical Rain Forests of the Far East.* Claredon, Oxford. (12.10.8)
41. _____. (1977). *Palms of Malaya.* Oxford Univ. Press, Oxford. (12.1.3)
42. Whitten, A.J. (1982). A numerical analysis of tropical rain forest using floristic and structural data and its application to an analysis of gibbon ranging behaviour. *J. Ecol.* 70: 249—271. (12.10.19)
43. _____. (1982). Home range use by Kloss gibbons (*Hylobates klossii*) on Siberut Island, Indonesia. *Anim. Behav.* 30: 182—198. (12.8.7)
44. Wilford, G.E. (1960). *Radiocarbon age determinations of Quaternary sediments in Brunei and north east Sarawak.* British North Borneo Geological Survey Annual Report, 1959. (Referred to in Whitmore, 1975).
45. Yamada, I. and Soekardjo, S. (1980). Ecological study of mangrove forests in South Sumatra. In *South Sumatra: Man and Agriculture.* (ed. Y. Tsubouchi, Nasruddin, I.Y. Takaya, and A.R. Hanafiah), pp. 1—33. Center for S.E. Asian Studies, Kyoto. (12.10.16)
46. Morley, R.J. (1981). Development and vegetation dynamics of a lowland ombrogenous peat swamp in Kalimantan Tengah, Indonesia. *J. Biogeog.* 8: 383—404.
47. Morley, R.J., Flenley, J.R. and Kardin, M.K. (1973). Preliminary notes on the stratigraphy and vegetation of the swamps and small lakes of the central Sumatran highlands. *Sumatra Res. Bull.* 2: 50—60.
48. St. John, T.V. and Anderson, A.B. (1982). A reexamination of plant phenolics as a source of tropical black water rivers. *Trop. Ecol.* 23: 151—154.

CHAPTER 6

FRESHWATER-SWAMP FORESTS

6.1 INTRODUCTION

Freshwater-swamp forest and related vegetation grow on soils where there is occasional inundation of mineral-rich freshwater of pH 6 and above and where the water level fluctuates so that periodic drying of the soil surface occurs. The floods may originate from rain or from river water backing up in response to high tides. The major physical differences between this and peatswamp forest are the lack of deep peat (a few centimetres thickness is sometimes found but this seems to have little effect on tree species composition), and the source of water being riverine and rainwater [20]. Although freshwater-swamp forest normally forms on riverine alluvium it can also be expected, under natural conditions, to form on alluvium deposited by larger lakes where wave action prevents the formation of peat, such as in 'Lake' Bento, Kerinci.

The high agricultural potential of their soils has meant that the freshwater-swamp forests of Sumatra have suffered considerably from human disturbance. Only 22% remains of the original area of freshwater swampforest in Sumatra (section 1.4.2) and very little of this is in an undisturbed state.

6.2 SOILS

Freshwater-swamp forest grows on recent freshwater alluvial soils. Such soils usually are more fertile than the soils on the surrounding slopes and, after draining, have obvious potential for agriculture, but they are less fertile then some of the soils on recent marine alluvium or volcanic ash [1]. Recent alluvium from rivers and lakes has had less time than most soils for soil formation and the absence of clear soil horizons are one of their characteristics. They are further characterized by their low position, close to the water table. The actual content of the soil varies greatly with the nature of the parent material but it is usually composed of relatively fine particles, the last to be deposited by a flooding river. Recent, waterlogged alluvial soils are usually grey (or mottled-grey and orange where the soil occasionally dries) as a result of 'gleying'. The main processes of gleying are the reduction of iron compounds to their ferrous forms and their partial reoxidation and precipitation [23]. The grey colour of these soils seems to arise from the lack of mixing of the often peaty soil surface with the lower layers. This is because soil animals that would normally take organic matter into the soil (such as termites and earthworms) are not tolerant of the frequent anaerobic conditions caused by waterlogging such as occur in swamp soils. Gley soils are amongst the most poorly-understood yet agriculturally most important tropical soils [23].

6.3 VEGETATION

6.3.1 Composition and Structure

The vegetation of freshwater-swamps varies considerably in response to the wide variation in its soils. In some areas grassy marshes may be the natural vegetation, in others some form of palm or pandan-dominated forest and in yet others forest which is similar in structure and species composition to lowland rainforest. Under certain conditions, long, winding tree buttresses, stilt roots and pneumatophores are common. Few plant species are restricted to the freshwater-swamp ecosystem but the tree species found there tend to be gregarious and to form species-poor associations.

Very little information appears to be available on the floristics of freshwater-swamp forests in Sumatra [13] but much can be learned from the highly readable account by Corner of freshwater swamp forests in South Johore and Singapore [3]. In an enumeration of various forest types on Siberut Island, it was found that freshwater swamp forest was more similar in species composition to neighbouring flat and non-swampy areas of lowland forest than it was to nearby peat swamp forest [21]. The total basal area, median basal area and height were not exceptional in comparison with other forest types but the trees tended to be smaller. The area examined was dominated by the extremely gregarious *Alangium ridleyi,* a medium-sized tree with sweet fruit, which accounted for 20% of the trees. Lake Bento, which lies south of Mt. Tujuh and north-west of Lake Kerinci, is surrounded by the highest (in elevation) forestclad marsh in West Malesia [5].

Unfortunately, the primary freshwater swamp forest in Way Kambas Reserve, set up to protect the swamp ecosystems, has been extensively logged [4]. Fragments remain elsewhere but it is likely that it will never now be possible to know exactly how such forests functioned in Sumatra.

6.3.2 Adaptations to floods

Trees of freshwater-swamp forest often have to endure prolonged periods of flooding. Inundation with water will flood air spaces in the soil which, in a normal moist top soil, can account for about 60% of the soil volume [2]. With these spaces filled, the soil soon becomes anaerobic and plants have difficulty in obtaining sufficient oxygen through their roots.

Very little is known about trees' tolerance of and responses to flooding. Where logging roads have dammed small rivers in forests, it is clear from the many surrounding tree skeletons that flood tolerance is not inherent to all trees. Information that does exist concerning the effects of flooding in tropical forests comes from South America. The flood tolerance of the swamp tupelo *Nyssa sylvatica,* for instance, depended on its capacity to accelerate anaerobic respiration and to oxidize the 'rhizosphere' (the immediate surroundings of the roots) [11, 14, 15, 16]. Another tree, *Sebastiana klotzchyana,* commonly found in South American freshwater swamp forests, was found to continue growing during flood conditions whereas growth of shoots from young trees of other species found in dry areas was inhibited during artificial flood conditions. After one month of flooded conditions the roots of *S. klotzchyana* showed a significant decrease in uptake of oxygen (indicating they had partially 'switched-over' to anaerobic respiration) whereas roots of trees from dry areas showed a significant increase (as though they were making up for a period of reduced respiration). Rates of anaerobic respiration and the levels of metabolic products such as ethanol, malate, lactate and succianate, varied between trees from flood-areas and dry areas, and showed that a range of responses are to be found even among flood-toolerant trees [12].

If the roots of a plant are under water, oxygen must reach them from the exposed parts of the plant. Some trees in freshwater swamps have strongly lenticellate bark — that is, the bark has large lenticels or holes through which diffusion of gases can occur. The submerged roots and pneumatophores of aquatic or semi-aquatic plants are usually very aerenchymatous (they heve large channels for air movement). To test whether a plant has aerenchymatous tissue, blow down one and of a cut section of root and watch for bubbles at the other end while it is held under water [3]. Bubbles will be seen if the root is from an aerenchymatous root. It should be emphasized that since the above characters are not common to all swamp species, there is clearly more than one way to adapt to the

Figure 6.1   Five types of pneumatophores found in freshwater-swamp forest. (After Corner [3]).

anaerobic soil conditions. In a freshwater-swamp forest in Johore, Peninsular Malaysia, Corner found 36 species (in 19 families) with pneumatophores and these pneumatophores were of five forms [3] (Figure 6.1.):

- erect conical pegs (similar to *Sonneratia*, section 2.4.1);
- erect plank buttresses degenerating into squat knee-roots where there was shallow tidal flooding (similar to *Bruguiera*, section 2.4.1);
- slender loop-roots formed by erect pneumatophores bending down into the soil;
- thick loop roots formed in the same way as the previous form;
- roots formed by a descending root growing laterally from a slanting ascending root. The top section may laterlly die.

6.4 FAUNA

The occasional high floods caused by heavy rain can create rather peculiar conditions. Corner described graphically the state of the animal life in freshwater swamp forest during a 6 m flood of the Sedili Besar River in Johore, Peninsular Malaysia. *"During the three days at Danau we paddled in a canoe through the flooded forest. The force of the flood was lost among the trees . . . . Whenever we touched leaf, twig, trunk of floating log, showers of insects tumbled into the canoe. Everything that could, had climbed above the water. Ants ran over everything that could, had climbed above the water, even scorpions, centipedes and frogs . . . . Lizards clung to the trunks; earthworms wriggled in the water . . . . I realized the importance of the hillocks in and around the swamp forest to animal life, for anything that could escape the flood must have fled there. We med no corpses. Pig, deer, tapir, rat, porcupine, leopard, tiger, monitor lizard and snakes must have congregated on those hillocks in disquieting proximity"* [3].

The fauna of freshwater-swamp forests is both much more diverse and more dense than the fauna of peatswamp forests, and is similar to that in lowland dry-land forests. Nothing is known in detail about the species inhabiting Sumatran (or even other Southeast Asian) freshwater swamps but Wind *et al.* report siamang, darkhanded gibbons, monkeys, rusa, barking deer, pigs, elephant, tapir and tiger from Way Kambas Reserve,

Figure 6.2 **Birds commonly found in grassy swamps a - tern** *Sterna hirundo*, **b - Chinese egret** *Ixobrychus sinensis*, **c - Java heron** *Ardeola speciosa*, **d - Java tree duck** *Dendrocygna javanica*, **e - pygmy goose** *Nettapus coromandelianus*, **f - long-billed stork** *Leptoptilus javanicus*, **g - milky stork** *Ibis cinereus*. (After King et al. [17]).

Lampung [4]. The areas of swamp grassland also appear to be utilized by most of these species.

The swamp grassland of the southern part of Way Kambas is used by herons, egrets (see Figure 2.30), terns, bitterns, pond-herons, whistling ducks, pygmy geese, lesser adjudants, milky storks (Figure 6.2) and occasionally the rare white-winged wood duck [4]. This species (Figure 6.3) is considered 'endangered' by the International Union for the Conservation of Nature and Natural Resources (IUCN) and has been reported in Sumatra only from the eastern side of Lampung in and around freshwater swamp and lowland forest [9, 10]. It may possibly live in peat swamp areas but no information is available. Its range used to include the swampy areas adjacent to lowland forest from Java to Burma but it seems to be extinct from all that area except for parts of Assam (N.E. India), possibly northern Burma, and southern Sumatra. In the northern parts of its range it appears to require dense forest but Holmes found the ducks in the much more open and disturbed forest of Lampung [10]. This ability to adapt to disturbed areas encourages some optimism regarding the security of its future.

Figure 6.3 **White-winged wood duck** *Cairina scutulata* (After MacKenzie and Kear [18]).

During the wetter seasons these ducks can live almost entirely within forest but when the slow-running streams they frequent begin to dry up they venture into areas of swamp or even rice fields. They fly to these areas just before dusk and, if not disturbed, may remain there until two or three hours after dawn. White-winged wood duck are omnivorous, eating floating aquatic plants, seeds, insects, worms, molluscs, frogs and even small snakes and fish [18]. They are usually seen in pairs but when the young are old enough to fly, family groups may be seen. One of the best ways to locate these birds is to listen for the evening light call which is described by MacKenzie and Kear as a "prolonged, vibrant, wailing honk sometimes breaking to a nasal whistle at the end" [18]. This call is never, it seems, given by birds flying alone. White-winged wood duck nest in the holes of swamp trees, particularly 'rengas' (probably *Melanorrhoea*) and their breeding season lasts from December to March or April [10].

The freshwater-swamp areas used to have large populations of the estuarine crocodile *Crocodylus porosus* and of the smaller false ghavial *Tomistomus schlegeli*. The false ghavial, which never exceeds five metres in length, resembles the true ghavials in having a snout which is much longer and more slender than the snouts of most crocodiles. The crocodiles are the last remaining members of the Archosaurs, the group of reptiles including dinosaurs that dominated the earth during the Mesozoic. They are the largest inhabitants of freshwater swamps and their movements inhibit the encroachment of aquatic plants into waterways. In areas with a prolonged dry season they maintain residual waterholes which serve as restocking reservoirs for smaller aquatic organisms which would otherwise perish. Crocodiles enrich the nutrient content of the water by converting prey into water-borne faecal particles which are food for a host of invertebrates and fish. Crocodiles have been mercilessly hunted partly through fear (unjustified in the case of the false ghavial which rarely eats anything but fish) and unbridled greed for their skins. Luckily, the remaining small populations of estuarine crocodiles are now protected throughout Indonesia.

Like all animals that can live in both seawater and freshwater, the estuarine crocodile has physiological adaptations which enable it to control the osmotic pressure of its plasma. In a marine environment the crocodile conserves water by reabsorbing it in its kidneys leading to a very concentrated urine, and by reabsorbing it from its faeces before these are passed.

Calcium, magnesium and potassium and salts such as ammonium, uric acid, and bicarbonates are excreted in the urine. Sodium chloride, however, does not pass through into the urine [8], but is excreted through the crocodile's external nasal gland near the nostril and lachrymal glands in the corner of the eyes.

When a female crocodile is ready to lay eggs, she seeks a shady location on land where she builds up a dome-shaped nest of leaves or tall grass [7]. The eggs, up to 50 or more, are laid in the middle of this nest, where they remain damp and are protected from direct sunlight. The heat generated by the decomposition of vegetable matter may help the incubation but if the mother senses the eggs are becoming too hot she will spray urine over the nest to cool it down.

Just before the eggs hatch, the young crocodiles make high-pitched croaks which are audible even outside the nest. The mother responds by scratching away the now hardened surface of nest material and as the young crocodiles wrestle their way out of their shells, she (and sometimes the father too) picks them up gently in her mouth and carries them away to to a secluded 'nursery' area in a swampy bank. They stay there for a month or two, catching large insects and small vertebrates such as fish and frogs, while their parents guard them closely.

Perhaps the most fascinating aspect of crocodile nesting behaviour is that the sex of the young animals is determined by the temperature of incubation. This has been known for various groups of reptiles [19] and although experiments have yet to be conducted on Asian crocodilians it has recently been determined for the Mississippi alligator of northern America [6]. Field and laboratory experiments have shown that alligator sex is fully determined and irreversible by the time of hatching and that incubation temperatures of up to and including 30°C produced all females, and 34°C and above produced all males. Since nests on exposed levees or other dry areas receive more sunlight and are hotter than those nearer wet, shaded swamp, the sex ratios of hatchlings will be different between these habitats [6]. It is likely that the sexes of Sumatran crocodiles are also determined by incubation temperature, and this is important for management of the species. Felling of swamp trees, particularly those near river banks, will reduce the amount of shading and may increase the average ambient temperature of any area. This in turn may increase the number of male crocodiles. However, the efficiency of nest temperature regulation by the female is unknown as are the social constraints to any alterations in sex-ratio.

REFERENCES

1. Burnham, C.P. (1975). The forest environment: Soils. In *Tropical Rain Forests of the Far East* (by T.C. Whitmore), pp. 103—120. Clarendon, Oxford. (12.10.8)
2. Bridges, E.M. (1970). *World Soils*. Cambridge University Press, Cambridge. (23.4.1)
3. Corner, E.J.H. (1978). The freshwater swamp-forest of South Johore and Singapore. *Gdns' Bull. S'pore Suppl.* No. 1. (12.10.10)
4. FAO/Wind, J., Soepomo, D., and Isnan, W. (1979). *Way Kambas Game Reserve Management Plan 1980/81 — 1984/85*. Field Report No. 5, INS/78/061. FAO, Bogor. (19.2.9)
5. FAO/Wulf, R. de, Djoko, S., and Kurnia, R. (1981). *Usulan Taman Nasional Kerinci-Seblat: Rencana Pengelolaan Pendahuluan 1982—1987*. UNDP/FAO National Parks Development Project, Bogor. (10.2.11)
6. Ferguson, M.W.J. and Joanen, T. (1982). Temperature of egg incubation determines sex in *Alligator mississippiensis*. *Nature* 296: 850—853. (12.6.12)
7. Greer, A.E. (1971). Crocodilian nesting habits and evolution. *Fauna* 3: 20—28.
8. Grigg, G.C. (1981). Plasma homeostasis and cloacal urine composition in *Crocodylus porosus* caught along a salinity gradient. *J. Comp. Physiol. B.* 144: 261—270. (12.6.13)
9. Holmes, D.A. (1976). A record of White-winged Wood Duck *Cairina scutulata* in Sumatra. *Bull. Brit. Orn. Club* 96: 88—89. (12.7.50)
10. _____. (1977). A report on the White-winged Wood Duck in southern Sumatra. *Wildfowl* 28: 61—64. (12.7.6)
11. Hook, D.D., Brown, C.L. and Kormanik, P.P. (1971). Inductive flood-tolerance in swamp tupelo (*Nyssa sylvatica* var. *biflora* Walt., Sarg.). *J. Exp. Bot.* 22: 78—89. (12.1.128)

12. Joly, C.A. and Crawford, R.M.M. (1982). Variation in tolerance and metabolic responses to flooding in some tropical trees. *J. Exp. Bot.* 33: 799—809. (12.10.9)

13. Kartawinata, K. (1974). *Report on the State of Knowledge on Tropical Forest Ecosystem in Indonesia.* Lembaga Biologi Nasional, Bogor. (12.10.87)

14. Keeley, J.E. (1978). Malic acid accumulation in roots in response to flooding: evidence contrary to its role as an alternative to ethanol. *J. Exp. Bot.* 29: 1345—1349. (12.1.129)

15. _____. (1979). Population differentiation along a flood frequency gradient: physiological adaptation to flooding in *Nyssa sylvatica. Ecol. Monogr.* 49: 89—108. (12.1.131)

16. Keeley, J.E. and Franz, E.H. (1979). Alcoholic fermentation in swamp and upland populations of *Nyssa sylvatica*: temporal changes in adaptive strategy. *Am. Nat.* 113: 587—592. (12.1.126)

17. King, B., Woocock, M. and Dickinson, E.C. (1975). *A Field Guide to the Birds of South-East Asia.* Collins, London. (12.7.45)

18. MacKenzie, M.J.S. and Kear, J. (1976). The White-winged Wood Duck. *Wildfowl* 27: 5—17. (12.7.5)

19. Vogt, R.C. and Bull, J.J. (1982). Temperature controlled sex determination in turtles: ecological and behavioural aspects. *Herpetologica* 38: 154—164. (12.6.18)

20. Whitmore, T.C. (1975). *Tropical Rain Forests of the Far East.* Clarendon, Oxford. (12.10.8)

21. Whitten, A.J. (1982). A numerical analysis of tropical rain forest using floristic and structural data and its application to an analysis of gibbon ranging behaviour. *J. Ecol.* 70: 249—271. (12.10.19)

22. Wyatt-Smith, J. (1954). A note on the freshwater swamp, low land and hill forest types of Malaya. *Malay. Forester* 24: 110—121. (12.10.115)

23. Young, A. (1976). *Tropical Soils and Soil Survey.* Cambridge Univ. Press, Cambridge. (23.4.16)

Estuarine crocodile.

A millipede, one of the many decomposers on the forest floor.

CHAPTER 7

LOWLAND FORESTS

7.1 INTRODUCTION

The lowland forests of Sumatra are among the most diverse, awe-inspiring, complex and exciting ecosystems on Earth. They are probably the best-studied forested natural ecosystem on the island, but for information on how these forests actually function it is frequently necessary to turn elsewhere in the Sunda Region. In many respects, the Sunda Region lags behind tropical America in unravelling and understanding ecological interactions. For this reason, occasional examples are taken from lowland forests in countries such as Costa Rica, when illustrations of particular aspects of ecology are required.

7.1.1 Diversity of plants

The diversity of tree species in Sumatran lowland forest is extremely high. In a valley area around the River Ranun in North Sumatra, the Simpson Index of Diversity[1] for trees of 15 cm diameter and over at breast height was 0.96, and in the neighbouring hills it was 0.93 (from data in Mackinnon [147]). In a hill forest on Bangka Island investigated by a CRES team, the index of diversity was 0.94. Both studies used local vernacular names which always underestimates actual species number, as explained

---

1. The Simpson Index of Diversity is given by: $D = 1 - \sum (p_i)^2$
where p_i is the proportion of species 'i' in a community. Zero is the lowest possible index (when only one species is present) and the highest index is $1 - \dfrac{1}{\text{number of species}}$

in section 7.2.3. Corresponding figures for a forest in Europe might be 0.4—0.6.

The problem of explaining the very high diversity of plants in tropical forests, particularly lowland forests, has taxed many minds. Before detailed investigations of fossil pollen began about 15 years ago it was thought that tropical forests had experienced climatic stability for millions of years and this had allowed time for the evolution of many species. This has now been shown to be false as it is known that tropical vegetation has experienced considerable changes (section 1.4.1). Other writers have suggested that the formation of isolated forest blocks or refuges during the peaks of glacial activity, when climates were cooler and drier, would have resulted in the species of each block following a course of evolution different from species in other blocks. When the climate ameliorated and the forest blocks were reunited, some of the closely related species would be incompatible for reproduction and thus a greater degree of diversity would exist than before the forest blocks were separated. This is generally known as the Refuge Theory [77] and has been useful in explaining diversity in certain taxa in Amazonia and Africa. It is less satisfying as a theory in South-east Asia however where the whole of Peninsular Malaysia, Sumatra, Borneo and West Java are suggested to have formed one 'refuge' and the majority of New Guinea the other. The Refuge Theory does not explain all species distributions [57] and it is clear that more detailed surveys are required [165].

An ecosystem with high diversity has, by corollary, a large number of rare species (Figure 7.1.) so, as Flenley suggests, instead of asking "why is lowland forest so diverse", we could equally well ask "why are there so many rare species?" [66]. Reproductive strategies adopted by living organisms can be described as falling within a spectrum within two extremes: r-selected strategies in which as many offspring are produced as possible, and K-selected strategies in which few offspring are produced but each has a great deal of care, attention and material resources devoted to it in order to ensure its survival and success. Thus, elephants, cows, and bats are K-selected, and rats, pigs, and many fish and insects are r-selected (section 12.3.2). If an organism adopts the K-strategy in a lowland forest it will almost certainly be relatively rare. It is then necessary to ask "under what circumstances can rarity be an advantage?". It is generally true that the herbivores on a plant species in lowland forest are

Figure 7.1 Relative abundance of tree species near the River Ranun, Dairi. Note that 73% of the species contribute only about 20% of the trees. (After Mackinnon [148]).

restricted to a few species which have evolved as the plant species evolved and found ways to circumvent whatever forms of physical or chemical defence the plant has adopted (see section 7.6). The chances of a pest finding an individual of a particular tree species are greater if that three is common, and so the pressure exerted by herbivores on an abundant or otherwise dominant tree species puts it at a disadvantage and permits subordinate species to coexist [104].

Rarity can also be an advantage if the parent tree produces toxic exudates from its roots to discourage competition for limited resources from both its own seedlings as well as from other species. Where the tree is common, there is little space for seedlings to establish themselves but where it is rare there is more chance of seedlings finding an unaffected patch [227]. This mechanism is probably not particularly common.

Pressure from herbivores and toxic root exudates are known from temperate as well as from tropical areas so there seems no reason why tropical flora and fauna in particular should have so many rare species. In temperate regions, however, seedlings survival is controlled largely by climatic effects such as extreme heat or cold, or extremes of soil water content. These effects would obviously show no selection in favour of rare species [66].

A hypothesis has been suggested by Ricklefs that greater heterogeneity in soil properties and surface microclimate in the tropics might be the basis of the trend of increasing tree species diversity from temperate to tropical regions [203]. He proposes that the ranges of angle and intensity of incident solar radiation, precipitation, temperature, and the partitioning of nutrients between soil and vegetation are wider in a tropical forest clearing than in a similar clearing in temperate regions. The differences are because:

a). the large biomass of a tropical forest modifies factors such as light levels, humidity, temperature, and environmental constancy to a greater extent than does a temperate forest of smaller biomass;

b) the higher proportion of nutrients in the vegetation compared with nutrients in the soil in tropical forests (section 7.2.1) suggest that the influx of nutrients to the soil from decaying vegetation in tree-falls compared to nitrient levels in soils under closed canopies may be greater in the tropics;

c). more rapid decomposition of leaf litter and other organic detritus in tropical forests accelerates the release of mineral nutrients and organic detritus from fallen trees and increases the flush of nutrients into the soil (see also Anderson and Swift [6]);

d) even if nutrient levels in soils under temperate and tropical forests were similar, the humus content of tropical forest soils is lower. Humus content influences the retention of soil moisture and the stability of other soil properties when exposed to more intense physical forces within forest gaps;

e) the higher rainfall of tropical areas increases the leaching of certain ions from exposed soils. This differential leaching would further increase variation across a forest gap;

f) for much of the day the sun is more or less overhead and so the light hits the soil in a tropical forest gap more directly and for a longer time each day than in a temperate forest.

These differences create a greater heterogeneity of environmental conditions for seedling establishment in tropical forests and it is this heterogeneity that provides the basis for resource partitioning and the coexistence of competing species.

The natural rarity of some plant species is compounded because some also are dioecious (bearing flowers of only one sex on one tree) and because many plants are endemic to quite restricted areas. One consequence of this is that reserves hoping to conserve these species have to be extremely large [174].

7.1.2 Diversity of animals

The large number of animal species in lowland forest is generally associated with structural and taxonomic heterogeneity of the plants. The number of animal species is high in Sumatra and other parts of the Sunda Region, but not as high as in other tropical regions. For example, the total number of birds in about 15 ha of primary lowland forest in seven sites is shown in Table 7.1 and it is clear that those for sites in the Sunda Region are considerably lower than for South America [190]. When tested against a wide range of environmental variables none of the data showed any significant relationship.

Table 7.1 The number of bird species found in 15 ha of primary lowland forest at seven locations. (Based on Pearson [190]: figure for Sumatra from Rijksen [204] and R. Eve and A.M. Gigue [61] for rather more than 15 ha at the Ketambe Research Station.)

	No. of species/15ha primary lowland forest
Ecuador	232
Peru	204
Bolivia	181
Gabon	158
Sumatra	151
Borneo	142
New Guinea	114

Significance was achieved, however, when the geological history of the localities was considered in terms of separations from, and connections to, other land masses. Since islands theoretically have higher extinction rates and lower immigration rates than similar continental areas (section 1.6.3), sites in Borneo, Sumatra, and New Guinea would be expected to have fewer species than sites in tropical continental South America.

Inger compared the densities of frogs and lizards in lowland forests in Borneo (the data are probably applicable to Sumatra) and Central America [98]. In Borneo about 1.5 individuals were found per 100 m^2 but in Central America the figures ranged from 15 to 45. He proposed (as Janzen [106, 109] had done earlier) that the low abundance was due to many major tree species in the Sunda Region exhibiting the phenomenon of gregarious fruiting at long intervals (section 7.4.1). This in turn would reduce the numbers of seed-eating insects available as frog and lizard food. The same argument would apply to other insect-eating animals.

7.2 VEGETATION

7.2.1 Characteristics

Tropical lowland forests are characterized by the huge amount of plant material they contain, and this can be measured in terms of the amount of carbon present. The tropical forests of the world (i.e. not just lowland forests but also montane, swamp and dry forests) cover 1838 million hectares or 11.5% of the earth's land surface, yet they contain 46% of the living terrestrial carbon [33]. The type of lowland forest found in Sumatra would certainly contain an even more disproportionate percentage of the carbon.

Of the total of organic matter in a lowland forest only about 1% is accounted for by the litter, about 40% by the soil, but about 60% is in the vegetation [33]. In temperate regions the corresponding biomass figures are about 10—20%, 35% and 50%.

Lowland forests are characterized by the conspicuous presence of thick climbers, large buttressed trees, and the prevalence of trees with tall, smooth-barked trunks. Although the canopy may occasionally be dominated by small-leaved leguminous tree (such as the magnificent *Koompasia excelsa* and *K. malaccensis*) the vast majority of trees have simple mesophyllsized leaves (section 9.4.2) between 8 and 24 cm long. The leaves of understory trees, including the immature individuals of large trees, often have larger leaves [187].

Leaves with smooth edges and 'drip-tips' (Figure 7.2) are particularly common in lowland forest and there is considerable convergence between plant families in leaf shape which, together with the high diversity of species, frequently makes identification somewhat difficult. Even so, characters such as sap, type of bark, size of buttresses, leaf vein arrangement and arrangement of leaves on twigs give ample characters to allow identification of the majority of specimens, even without flowers. For a convenient key see Wyatt-Smith and Kochumen [256] but see section

255

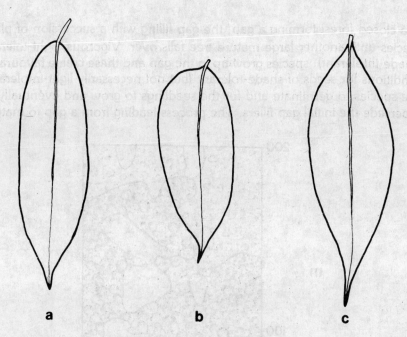

a   b   c

Figure 7.2 **Leaves of a)** *Dialium platysepalum,* **b)** *Dracontomelon mangiferum,* **and c)** *Sterculia foetida* **to show drip-tips characteristic of many lowland forest trees.**

7.2.3 for cautions. Since plant taxonomy is based on flower anatomy, final identification relies on the examination of flowers.

The drip-tips are most prevalent in understory saplings. Since one theory of the function of drip-tips is that they allow water to run easily off the leaf surface and thus prevent or hinder the growth of epiphylls (section 7.3.4), it is reasonable that these should be most common where the relative humidity is highest (i.e. rates of evaporation lowest).

7.2.2 Forest growth cycle

Different types of tropical rain forests, and indeed forests throughout the world, have many fundamental similarities because the processes of forest succession and the range of ecological strategies of tree species are more or less the same [21, 233]. These strategies form what is known as the forest growth cycle; that is, the events of a large mature tree falling over in a closed forest forming a gap, the gap filling with a succession of plant species until another large mature tree falls over. Vigorous, light-tolerant (shade-intolerant), species grow up in the gap and these create favourable conditions for seeds of shade-tolerant (but not necessarily light-intolerant) tree species to germinate and for the seedlings to grow and eventually to supersede the initial gap fillers. The process leading from a gap to mature

Figure 7.3 Mosaic of a) gap, b) building and c) mature phases at S. Menyala, Peninsular Malaysia. The extensive area of building phase was caused by partial clearance in 1917. (After Whitmore [233]).

257

forest is known as secondary succession. Whitmore divides the cycle into three phases - the gap, building and mature phases - which together form a mosaic throughout the forest which is continually changing in state and shape [233] (Figures 7.3. and 7.4). For example, a patch of forest in

Figure 7.4 Gaps near the River Pesisip, Batang Hari, formed within ten years preceding the study of Huc and Rosalina [96].

building phase may return to gap phase should a tree in a neighbouring mature patch fall across it. The size of a gap depends on its cause - from the falling of a single dead tree, to a landslide, a fire, or even a widespread drought. The floristic composition of a forest will depend on the size of former gaps because a large gap will be filled initially with tree species requiring light whereas small gaps will be filled by shade-tolerant tree species. Many of the latter may have grown slowly for many years to become part of the understory but have been unable to form part of the main canopy until a small gap was formed. It should be noted that since a single tree can contribute to gap, building, and mature phases, it is incorrect to refer to 'gap-phase' or any other phase species [234]. Terms which describe the behaviour of a species, such as pioneer, shade-tolerant or light-intolerant, are more useful. Since forest comprises a mosaic of gap, building and mature areas, it is a matter of debate whether the term 'climax' vegetation has any meaning in the field.

Gaps and their plants have been studied in Sumatra at various locations in West Sumatra, Jambi, South Sumatra and Lampung by Huc and Rosalina [95, 96]. Huc and Rosalina concluded that the size of gaps influences the duration of the forest growth cycle. Small gaps created by dead standing trees produced short cycles without a gap phase. That is, immature trees beneath the dead tree were able to grow up as soon as the light intensity increased. Large gaps created by the fall of several adjacent large trees allowed the full forest growth cycle to occur (Figure 7.5). Huc and Rosalina's findings confirmed those of Kramer on the slopes of Mt Gedeh [132]. Kramer made artificial clearings of 1000, 2000, and 3000 m^2. The first was soon filled by regenerating mature-forest trees but the larger clearings were swamped by vigorous pioneer species. This has also been observed in Mount Leuser National Park by Rijksen [204]. Huc and Rosalina calculated that the average duration of the growth cycle in the forests they examined was about 117 years [96], and at Ketambe Research Station an approximate duration of 108 years has been estimated by van Noordwijk and van Schaikk [177]. These results are comparable to estimates ranging from 80 to 138 years in Costa Rica [83] but rather less than the 250 to 375 years estimated by Poore for part of Peninsular Malaysia [193].

Within each of the different stages of the forest growth cycle the trees which are found have a number of ecological characteristics in common. For example, the first species that grow up in a gap (often called pioneer species) generally produce large numbers of small seeds frequently, if not continuously. These seeds tend to be easily dispersed (often by wind, squirrels or birds) and, probably because of this, these species tend to have wide geographical distributions [95]. They have high viability even in full light, and the seedlings grow rapidly. In addition, these species are often dioecious (each plant bearing flowers of only one sex) which leads to considerable genetic variablity. An index of the pioneering ability of different species has been devised [207].

Figure 7.5. Silvigenetic cycles. 1, 2 and 3 are short cycles due to the replacement of dead trees by trees below with no gap formation. 4 is a long cycle due to the formation of a gap in which pioneer vegetation grows. (After Huc and Rosalina [96]).

The trees of later stages in the succession are shade-bearers (that is, they tolerate growing in shade, but if more light is available they will grow faster) and can regenerate beneath their living parents. These species often have large seeds with rather specialized means of dispersal and a relatively restricted geographical distribution. Between these two extremes are large numbers of species of 'late-secondary growth' which are unable either to colonize open sites or to regenerate beneath their living parents [234].

Changes in species composition during succesion may be due to availability of nutrients, availability of seeds, suppression of some species by chemicals produced by the same or other species (allelopathy), crown competition or root competition [95], but there is still very little information available on how regeneration actually occurs. There are three ways in which trees can grow: from shoots growing out of roots, stumps or fallen trunks, from established seedlings, or from seeds. Beneath a mature forest there are clearly no seedlings of light-demanding species and, conversely, in gaps light-intolerant species will die. Seed may lie dormant in or on the soil surface (seed bank), or it can be brought into an area in the 'seed rain' (seeds dispersed from their parents). The existence of seed banks in rain forest in northern Thailand has been demonstrated by Cheke *et al.* [36]. They found dormant, viable seeds of pioneer species such as *Trema*, *Mallotus*, *Macaranga*, *Melastoma* and grasses in locations where those species were not represented. Similar findings are reported from Peninsular Malaysia [140, 173, 217]. Some of the seeds that were found 20 cm below the soil surface were still able to germinate although they must have arrived many years before. In addition, a long period of dormancy for these seeds is suggested by the low rate of seed input and the large numbers of seeds found.

Whereas trees of the gap and early building phases may have seeds which can lie dormant for many years, this is not so for many of the trees of the mature phase. These tend to fruit infrequently (section 7.4), to have poor dispersal and little or no potential for extended dormancy. Their continued existence in an area therefore depends on fruit from mature trees falling into a spot with the correct conditions for immediate germination. Dipterocarpaceae trees fall into this category (section 7.2.3). Secondary succession is discussed further in section 11.2.1.

7.2.3 Floristic composition and variation

As was stated in the introduction to Part B the lowland forests of West Malesia (section 1.4.2) are amongst the most diverse and species-rich ecosystems in the world. Vernacular names allow differentiation of some of the trees and represent a common and useful means of conduct-

261

ing a general forest survey [147, 204, 237]. It should, however, be realized that vernacular or commercial names generally greatly underestimate the number of species present. For example, 'meranti' describes the genus *Shorea* but the 'specific' names such as 'meranti merah', 'meranti putih' and 'meranti damar hitam' each represent a group of species. For example, in Sumatra there are over 26 true species of 'meranti merah' [168].

Figure 7.6 Fruits of Sumatran dipterocarp trees: a) *Shorea assamica,* **b)** *Hopea ferruginea,* **c)** *Vatica maingayi,* **d)** *Dipterocarpus cornutus,* **and e)** *Dipterocarpus palembanicus.* (After Symington [218]).

Most types of forest formation in West Malesia are dominated by a single family of tree called Dipterocarpaceae (Figure 7.6). These are the only forests in the world in which a single family has such a high density of genera, species and individuals [234]. This domination is usually, but not always, particularly marked in lowland forests. Sumatra has 112 species of dipterocarps including 11 endemic species [10, 168].

The emergent trees in Sumatran lowland forest, some of which can reach 70 m tall, are generally of the families Dipterocarpaceae (e.g. *Dipterocarpus, Parashorea, Shorea, Dryobalanops*), and Caesalpiniaceae (formerly part of Leguminosae) (e.g. *Koompasia, Sindora* and *Dialium*). An extensive and interesting enumeration of large trees in part of Peninsular Malaysia was conducted by Whitmore [232]. For indentification of large and medium-sized trees see Meijer [164], Symington [218] and Wyatt-Smith and Kochumen [256]. It must be remembered that the last two of these books were written for Peninsular Malaysia, and although most Sumatran tree species are included, an unknown tree should not be *forced* to become a particular species. It is generally quite satisfying to identity a tree to its genus.

Common families for the smaller trees are Burseraceae, Sapotaceae, Euphorbiacae, Rubiaceae, Annonaceae, Lauraceae, Myristicaceae and smaller species of Dipterocarpaceae but some will also be immature emergents.

Dipterocarp trees dominate much of the lowland forests of Sumatra. For example, on the hill ridges examined on Siberut Island, between 20% and 59% of all trees over 15 cm diameter at breast height were dipterocarps; Myristicaceae, Euphorbiaceae and Sapotaceae were the next most common families. On level ground between the ridges, Euphorbiaceae, Dipterocarpaceae and Myristicaceae ranked more or less first equal [242]. Other families may be dominant, however, such as at the Ketambe Research Station where Meliaceae accounts for 17% of the trees over 10cm diameter and dipterocarps are not particularly common, accounting for only 4% of the trees [135, 204]. Near the Pesisip River, Batang Hari, the dominant families are Dipterocarpaceae and Olaceae (particularly *Scorodocarpus borneensis*) [69].

Numerous surveys of Sumatra's lowland forests have been conducted for forestry evaluations but these are of limited use for ecological work because:
— they enumerate only those trees providing profitable timber, and
— they concentrate on areas where timber trees are likely to be most common.

There is thus very little ecologically-useful information concerning the composition of Sumatra's forests although total species lists have been produced for Mount Sagu near Payakumbuh [166], and are being produced by teams from the National Biological Institute for the forest around the Ketambe Research Station [135]. Lists for the forests around the former botanic gardens (now Tourist Park) at Sibolangit, Deli Serdang [62], must exist but have not yet been located.

Variation in the floristic composition of a given phase in the growth cycle of lowland forest can be quite considerable, but because the variation is often continuous (that is, there are no sharp boundaries, forest of one composition changes gradually into a forest with another composition) it is very hard to study. Poore was of the opinion that floristic composition was largely determined by chance factors, particularly at the times of fruit dispersal and seedling establishment [187]. Within a given area, however, composition is related to large-scale habitat features such as soils and topography [9, 11, 69]. A detailed study of species composition and various soil and other site variables in Sarawak showed that soil texture, levels of iron and aluminium oxides, and the acidity of the soil parent material were the most important factors determining species composition [11]. These effects are very subtle and occur more as a variation in the relative abundance of species rather than as the presence or absence of one or more species. This is partly because a particular soil type will not always exclude ill-adapted species, but adults of such species will be relatively rare and have reduced vigour. The minor variations between the forest type studied on Siberut Island were sufficiently clear to the gibbons occupying the area for it to be possible to detect differences in their behaviour and activity between the various forest types [241, 242].

A particularly noticeable variation in lowland forest occurs along streams, and certain tree species tend to be restricted to these areas. These species have been studied at the Ketambe Research Station by teams from the National Biological Institute [135] and as part of a wider study by van Noordwijk and van Schaik, but the results are not yet available. Below these trees, alongside fast-flowing rivers, rheophytes (river-plants) can be found. These are usually shrubs which, although diverse taxonomically, have narrow leaves and often brightly coloured fruits dispersed by either water or fish [100, 213, 214, 233].

7.2.4 Layering

The canopies of forest trees are often said to form several (usually three) 'layers'. While this is a convenient theoretical concept it has limited application in the field. An emergent layer is often quite clear but below that the supposed layers may be difficult to distinguish. Some trees are usually referable to a particular layer but many more are generally indefinable. Part of the difficulty in applying the concept of layering lies in the existence of the mosaic of gap, building and mature phases in the forest (section 7.2.2), each of which is in a dynamic flux. In an analysis of various forest types on Siberut Island each of 2459 trees along 11.5 ha of 20m-wide transects were scored for the position of its crown relative to the neighbouring canopy. 'Emergence' (defined as 0—25% of the crown in contact or enclosed by other crowns) did not correlate with tree height because, within a large area in building phase, a medium-sized tree can be emergent, and in mature forest a 40m high tree can be more or less completely enclosed by taller trees [242].

The shape of tree crowns changes as the trees grow and thus a certain amount of layering of crown shape occurs. Young trees tend to have monopodial stems (that is, a single main stem) and the crown is tall and narrow around that stem. Mature trees, however, tend to be sympodial (that is, without a single main stem) at the canopy level. This difference is shown in Figure 7.7. Layering is discussed more fully by Whitmore [233] and Richards [202].

7.2.5 Basal area

The basal area for trees of 15 cm diameter and over at breast height in seven lowland forest types on Siberut Island ranged from 16 to 42 m^2 per ha. The tree palm *Oncosperma horridum* was most common in the forest types with the lowest basal area of trees, and when this species was added, the range decreased to 23—42 m^2 per ha. It was suggested that the inclusion of all other woody plants (e.g. small trees, other palms, shrubs and climbers) in the basal area calculation would have resulted in the basal area of the forest types becoming very similar [242]. The basal area of trees in 17¼-ha plots at Ketambe Research Station was 16—45 m^2 per ha [177] and near the Pesisip River, Batang Hari, was 27.9 m^2 per ha [96]. Two

A community of epiphylls on a forest leaf.

Rafflesia arnoldi; Batang Palupuh near Bukittinggi.

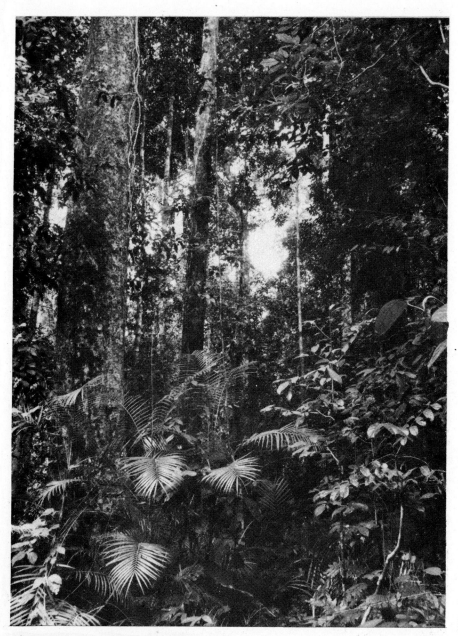

Lowland forest, Siberut Island.

265

adjacent forest areas of 0.5 ha examined by a CRES team on Bangka Island had basal areas equivalent to 24.7 and 25.7 m² per ha.

Figure 7.7 **Mature and building phases at Belalong, Brunei. Dipterocarps are stippled - note that in the building phase these have the tall, monopodial crown of youth. (After Ashton, 1964 in Whitmore [233] in which identification of each tree is given.).**

7.2.6. Biomass

The above-ground biomass of two areas of Pasoh Forest Reserve in Peninsular Malaysia was estimated using destructive sampling (felling, cutting and weighing) by Kato et al. [128]. The reslts were 475 and 664 ton per ha. Ogawa et al. have estimated root biomass as one-tenth of above-ground biomass [181] and so Kato et al. suggest that average total plant biomass for the Pasoh Forest Reserve was 500—550 t per ha [128]. The changes in biomass with height above ground are shown in Figure 7.8. The total plant biomass increment was found to be about 7 ton per ha per year. The ratio between leaf area and leaf dry weight (sometimes known as mean specific leaf area) varied with height above the ground; it decreased steadily from 13 m² per kg in ground layer seedlings to 7 m² per kg in the tallest trees, showing that leaves are generally thicker in the higher parts of the canopy.

Figure 7.8 Vertical distribution of leaf and wood biomass density in a plot at Pasoh Forest Reserve, Peninsular Malaysia. (After Kato et al. [128]).

7.2.7 Leaf area index

Leaf area index (total leaf area perpendicularly above a unit area of ground) was measured at Pasoh Forest Reserve in different height categories (Figure 7.9) [128]. It was relatively constant between 10 and

Figure 7.9 Vertical distribution of leaf area index in a plot at Pasoh Forest Reserve, Peninsular Malaysia. (After Kato *et al.* [128]).

35 m and the increase below this was caused by the plants in the shrub and herb layers. There were relatively few leaves between 5 and 10 m and leaves of climbers maintained a surprisingly constant contribution (average 10%). The total leaf area index in the two destructive plots was 7.15 and 7.99 m per ha.

7.2.8 Litter production

Litter production has been investigated at Ketambe Research Station and by teams from the National Biological Institute [135] and by van Noordwijk and van Schaik. Preliminary results from the second study indicate that 4.7—8.3 tons of leaves and 2.2—5.9 tons of other litter fall per ha per year with leaves accounting for about 65% of the litter fall. Litter production was lower in forests with lower pH (lower fertility) [176, 177]. Yearly production of all small litter (twigs, branches and leaves) at Pasoh Forest Reserve was found to be between 7.5 and 10.6 ton per ha per year [141, 180] with a likely average of 9.0 ton per ha per year. Similar values were obtained in lowland forest in Sarawak [194] and East Kalimantan [127]. The proportion of the litter in different forms at Pasoh was as follows: leaves 72%, twigs 17%, fruit and flower parts 6%, other 5% [141]. Ogawa found that the annual leaf fall (6.5 ton per ha) was less than the leaf biomass (8 ton per ha) and thus calculated the mean life of the leaves to be 15.2 months [180]. Litter usually accounts for only 1% of the organic carbon in a lowland forest compared with about 20% in a European forest [33].

7.2.9 Total primary production

Very few studies of total forest primary production (section 2.4.3) have been conducted anywhere in the Sunda Region largely because of the many methodological difficulties involved [233]. At Pasoh Forest Reserve three methods were used [130, 131, 258, 259]. The results suggested a net primary productivity of 25—50 ton per ha per year and a gross primary productivity of 70—100 ton per ha per year. Kato *et al.* remark that the net primary productivity is lower than for rubber and oil palm plantations [128]. As was described in section 2.4.3, however, a mature forest would not be expected to have as high a productivity as a managed, growing forest or an agricultural plantation.

7.2.10 Mineral cycling

Cycling of minerals through a lowland forest has not been investigated in its entirety in the Sunda Region, but relevant papers have been written on various stages of the cycle [7, 141, 153, 154, 180, 257, 258, 260, 262]. A review of mineral cycling in tropical forests has recently been published [269]. See section 9.4.6 for details of a study of mineral cycling in a lower montane forest.

7.3 ECOLOGY OF SOME FOREST COMPONENTS

7.3.1 Roots

A relatively small proportion of the organic carbon and other nutrients in a lowland forest is in the soil. Organisms such as fungi, bacteria, soil animals and roots therefore compete for what are probably limiting resources. It appears that almost all trees in lowland forests and almost all non-grain crops can develop a mutualistic relationship between their roots and fungi [101]. This is called a mycorrhiza. The most common form found in the tropics has the hyphae ('root' strands) of the fungus penetrating the plant's roots where they take up carbohydrates from the plant. For its part the fungus channels minerals into the roots [102, 103]. Many plant species with mycorrhiza appear not to possess root hairs because these structures are improved upon by the mycorrhizae. Mycorrhizae are probably common among trees in heath forest (section 8.2.3), but are poorly developed among plants of early successional stages which normally grow on soil enriched from fire ash, deposits left by flood water, or the decomposition products of fallen trees [107]. In such situations a plant would be at a disadvantage if it had to wait for its roots to be infected with fungus before it could start growing and competing [101, 103]. Some species cannot grow without mycorrhizae, whereas others grow better without mycorrhizae where mineral nutrients are not limited but better with mycorrhizae in poor soils [101, 103]. For trees that depend on mycorrhizae it is advantageous for their fruit to have large seed reserves because they provide a source of food upon which the seedling can draw before infection with fungus occurs. It is not surprising, then, that seedlings kept experimentally without mycorrhizae, stopped or slowed their growth after attaining a size correlated with the average dry weight of a seed for that species [102].

7.3.2 Buttresses and trunks

Buttresses are common features of trees in lowland forest. Setten found that 41% of 18067 large ('timber-sized') trees in a forest in Peninsular Malaysia had buttresses reaching more than 1.35 m up the trunk [209]. Different species are relatively constant in the presence, shape and surface characteristics of buttresses and these characters can be helpful in identification [256].

Buttresses are sometimes said to act as structural supports for trees whose roots are relatively shallow and where the substrate affords little anchorage [84, 210]. They are also said to be composed of 'tension wood' to reduce the pulling strain on the roots and so would be expected to form on the uphill side of a trunk, on the side of a trunk opposite a major congregation of heavy climbers, or on the side the wind blows from - that is, on the 'tension' side. Data to test this hypothesis would be easy to collect, but does not appear to have been published. From subjective impressions, however, it is clear that some trees do not 'obey' the rules and instead form buttresses on the 'compression' side of the trunk; see, for example, photographs by Corner [44]. In addition, of course, many trees grow well in similar conditions without buttresses.

Recent hypotheses on buttress formation have been unrelated to structural problems. It has been suggested, for example, that since buttresses increase the space of forest floor occupied by an individual tree, they could be viewed as a competitive mechanism [27]. The physical presence of a buttress prevents or hinders the establishment of neighbouring (i.e. competing) trees. If this hypothesis is correct then it should be possible to observe that:
- the density of trees near a buttressed tree are less than near a tree of similar bole size, canopy form and age without buttresses;
- the distance to the nearest neighbours of buttressed trees are greater on the average than from a non-buttressed tree to its nearest

neighbours;

- the density of trees around different individuals of a buttress-forming species bear a relationship to the age of the individual trees. Older buttressed trees should have both more distant and fewer neighbours in the smaller size classes;

- species diversity of trees around a buttressed tree are lower than around a non-buttressed tree because some species are likely to be less competitive against buttresses than others [27].

These hypotheses need testing and collecting appropriate data does not require in-depth botanical knowledge.

Trees with rotten, empty trunks are surprisingly common in lowland forest. This may appear to be unfortunate for the tree but it has been suggested that it is in fact a strategy of distinct advantage. Empty cores of large trees are inhabited by bats, porcupines and rats in addition to a host of invertebrates. Faeces and other products from these animals are broken down by microbes and thus provide an exclusive supply of nutrients for the tree in a generally nutrient-poor environment [64, 108, 119].

It is not generally known that tree trunks exhibit a daily fluctuation in girth being largest in the early morning and smallest in the late afternoon. These changes are presumably caused by water being drawn out of the plant by evapotranspiration during the day. Although measurable, the changes are quite small, being in the region of 0.1 mm around an average timber tree [261].

7.3.3 Climbing plants

Climbing plants abound in many types of lowland forest. The crown of a large climber may be as large as that of tree but because (with the exception of rattan) they do not possess any real commercial value, they have been little studied. Identifying climbers is very difficult but the coiled or convoluted ones with flattened stem sides are generally leguminous species, and the ones with regular hoops around the stem are members of the Gnetaceae, relatives of the conifers. The best known member of the Gnetaceae in Sumatra is the tree *Gnetum gnemon* from which *emping* crisps are made, but almost all members of the family are climbers.

When young, many species of free-hanging climbers in the forest understory can look very similar to young trees as they grow slowly, waiting for an opportunity to rise to the canopy. Such opportunities are afforded when a gap is formed and it is then that a young climber can attach itself to a rapidly growing tree and be carried upwards. During a similar period of apparent dormancy, some species are growing a large tuber below ground. In response to a particular cue the energy available in the tuber is suddenly used up in a rapid burst of upward growth whether or not a gap has formed [107]. Some climbers, such as rattans, have elaborate hooks by which they can climb their own way to the light at the top of the canopy. Other climbers begin to coil their way up their chosen host as soon as they have germinated. Some species have populations which coil in a left-handed manner in the northern hemisphere, and in a right-handed manner in the southern hemisphere so as to make most efficient use of the sun's rays [107]. It would be interesting to know whether this phenomenon exists in Sumatra, which is more or less equally divided by the equator.

The stems of climbers can sometimes be seen to loop down towards the forest floor and back again indicating that the major bough or the whole tree supporting the climber may have fallen and the climber then grew up again. Mature climbers are rarely supported by a single tree but rather grow horizontally through the canopy, sewing together the tree crowns. This may help to prevent trees from falling over in strong winds but, if a tree is felled, the climbers in its crown often pull over other trees as well (section 11.9.5).

A considerable portion of the apparent 'seedlings' of climbers (and a certain proportion for some forest trees) are in fact no more than shoots growing up from a horizontal root of an established climber [107]. This is a means by which a plant can increase the size of its crown and since these shoots are obviously genetically identical to their 'parent', the actual number of genetically distinct individuals in a given area may be extremely low.

Climbers compete with trees for light, nutrients and water and can cause mechanical damage to trees. In well-managed production forest this is the reason climber stems are cut (see section 7.3.7). In addition, bole diameter is often greater than average for trees with heavy climbers in their crown, indicating that trees have to divert resources away from vertical growth and reproduction in order to increase the strength of the supporting structure [244]. Where climbers are abundant, regeneration of trees can be seriously delayed and so for all these reasons it is an advantage to a tree to shed or to avoid climbers.

Fast-growing tress are better able to avoid climbers than are slow-growing trees. Trees which are able to rapidly increase their bole diameter as well as their height are also more likely to escape certain climbers which coil up the stem because such climbers are limited in the diameter of support they can ascend. Rapid growth of girth can also break potentially strangling plants. Some trees exhibiting a symbiotic relationship with ants (such as *Macaranga*, section 11.9.8) may benefit from the ants removing vines from the branches as they have been shown to do in Central America [103]. Other strategies used by trees to avoid climbers are suggested by Putz [195].

7.3.4 Epiphytes and epiphylls

An epiphyte is a perennial plant rooted upon, not in, a larger host, and one which does not have to produce or maintain massive woody stems and branches to live above the forest floor. Epiphytes are common in lowland forest, but even more common in certain montane and heath forests (section 8.2.3, 9.4.2), and they are thought to make a significant contribution to the totals of biomass and species-richness in a forest [22]. The major higher plant families of epiphytes in Sumatra are Gesneriaceae, Melastomaceae, Rubiaceae (including the ant-plants *Myrmecodia* and *Hydnophytum*), Asclepiadaceae and Orchidaceae. In addition to these are numerous epiphytic ferns, lichens and bryophytes (including mosses and liverworts).

Bryophytes are small but common epiphytes in lowland forest. Their small size makes them less restricted than other plants in the range of microhabitats they can occupy, and these are shown in Figure 7.10. The most luxuriant bryophyte communities in wet lowland forest are generally found on the bases of large trees (see Pocs [192] for detailed descriptions).

Epiphytes might seem to have an easy life but they live on a substrate which is extremely poor in nutrients. Most of them rely upon nutrients dissolved in rain, a small amount of litter fall, and occasional mineral inputs from animals. Epiphytes also have to contend with a very erratic water supply - being drenched when it rains, and parched when the sun is shining and the wind is blowing [107].

Epiphytes cope with growing in nutrient-poor conditions in various ways (although few species will exhibit all these features):

274

Figure 7.10. Bryophyte microhabitats in a lowland forest. 1. bases of large trees, 2. upper parts of trunks, 3. macro-epiphyte 'nests', 4. bark of main branches, 5. terminal twigs and leaves, 6. bark of climbers, shrub branches and thin trunks, 7. pandan stems 8. tree-fern stems, 9. palm trunks, 10. rotting trunks, 11. soil surface and termite mounds, 12. roadside cuttings, 13. rocks and stones, 14. submerged or emergent rocks in streams. (After Pocs [192]).

- their own tissues may have very low nutrient concentrations;
- juvenile stages are prolonged even though little growth is required to become mature;
- their vegetative parts are reduced in size;
- they may obtain nutrients from unconventional sources such as ants;
- their leaves tend to be long-lasting (due perhaps to some form of defence against herbivores) so that the replacement of nutrient-expensive leaves is required only infrequently; and
- their flowers are pollinated by animals because wind dispersal of the pollen would result in 'expensive' losses [22].

In addition, it has been observed that some epiphytes concentrate their roots on the underside of boughs where water and nutrients would remain longest [237].

The third strategy, vegetative reduction, has been studied by Benzing and Ott [23]. They investigated three species of shoot-less orchid; that is, orchids with no leaves and a shoot which merely initiates roots and produces occasional flowers (Figure 7.11). It was found that these orchid roots were green in colour and that they were capable of fixing carbon in their tissues, whereas roots of normal, leafy orchids, while able to photosynthesize, were unable to exhibit a net gain of carbon. Benzing and Ott consider that the shootless habit, by reducing the 'cost' of the vegetative body has evolved for reasons of nutrient economy so that maximum nutrient resources can be directed towards reproductive effort [23].

As Janzen has pointed out, epiphyte leaves seem to suffer very little damage from herbivores and he further suggests that those leaves may be defended chemically to prevent the loss of such valuable leaves [107]. There appears to be no data yet to confirm this. Some epiphytes notably *Myrmecodia* (section 8.2.3), harbour ants in their stems and these may well protect their leaves from caterpillars and other arthropod herbivores. It seem unlikely that the succulent leaves of *Myrmecodia* contain concentrations of chemical defences because on Siberut Island, Mentawai gibbons, whose diet indicated a marked avoidance of potential sources of defence compounds, ate *Myrmecodia* leaves [238, 240]. *Myrmecodia* on Siberut Island appeared to grow further away from the tree trunks than other species and it may have been helped in such extreme habitats by the nutrients provided through its relationship with ants [237].

Although epiphytes (by definition) do not take nutrients directly

Figure 7.11 *Taeniophyllum,* **an example of a leafless orchid.**

from the host plant, they have been called 'nutritional pirates' [21, 22]. This is because they can tie up nutrients in their own biomass from dust, leaf leachates and rain which would otherwise have fallen through to the soil to be utilized by the hosts. While this is true, Nadkarni has found that host trees can turn the tables at least partially back in their favour by producing small roots beneath the mats of dead and living epiphyte tissue [172]. These roots thus give the tree access to canopy nutrient sources. The main boughs of some tree species are almost invariably covered with epiphytes but it would appear that other species actively deter epiphyte growth, presumably because the relationship is disadvantageous. Thus, on Siberut Island, *Sterculia macrophylla* were always laden with epiphytes but *Endospermum malaccensis* bore none [237].

Epiphylls are mosses, liverworts, algae and lichens which grow on the living surface of leaves in shady situations where the air is almost continually saturated.[4] Thus they are generally restricted to the leaves of young trees, shurbs and long-lived herbs of the lowest layer of forest up to about 2—3 m and also near streams. Over ten species of epiphylls can occur on a single leaf and some of these are obligate; that is, they are found only on leaves [192]. Epiphylls are restricted to certain types of leaves and are possibly more common on leaves lacking drip-tips (section 7.2.1).

7.3.5 Gaps

Pioneer plants (section 7.2.2) are generally thought to be low in defensive compounds; their growth strategy is to grow and reproduce quickly because, in the nature of succession, they are limited in both space and time. Resources are not diverted into possibly unnecessary defence. Plants growing in gaps, the location of which is unpredictable, are able to avoid herbivores partly through that unpredictability of occurence and partly through relatively short life cycles [107]. Maiorana noticed that some species growing in shaded habitats suffered more from being eaten than did the same species in open habitats [152]. Strangely, when leaves from both habitats were presented to snails, generalist herbivores frequently used in palatability experiments [56, 254], it was found that the plants from open areas were preferred. It is suggested that the 'defence' used by pioneer plants might in fact be the hot, unshaded, low humidity of the gap environment itself.

The fast-growing often succulent plants of lowland forest gaps are food for the larger herbivorous mammals such as deer, tapir and elephant

---

4. Similar conditions are also found in moss forest (section 9.4.2)

(section 11.9.6). Studies of birds in forest gaps indicated that the number of species caught in nets in gaps was greater than those caught in surrounding forest. In addition, the assemblage of birds using the gaps was distinct from that in the forest (although there was of course some overlap in species) [208].

As described in section 7.1.1 gaps experience considerable differences in microclimate with mature forest [203] and this is reflected in the habits of some animals which are found in both habitats. For example, the orientation of webs of a particular spider was found to be north/south in closed habitats and east/west in open habitats. The longer a spider spends on the web, the more prey it captures (some prey manage to wriggle loose before being killed by the spider) and so presumably an orientation is chosen to allow maximum time on the web. Web orientation seems to be related to the body temperature of the spiders because both too little and too much heat can affect spider activity. Thus, in open habitats, the spiders' webs face east/west to reduce heat load and in closed habitats face north/south to increase body temperature [26].

7.3.6 Figs

Fig plants exhibit numerous interesting characteristics (e.g. the strangling habit of some species - Figure 7.12) and represent an extremely important source of food for many forest animals. Fig plants are, however, probably most interesting for the way in which pollination is effected.

According to botanical terminology, figs are syconia not fruit, but ecologically they *are* fruit and so that noun is retained [116]. The wall of the flowers arches over and around so that the flowers are inside a small, almost entirely enclosed, cup (Figure 7.13). The hole at the end of a fig is partially closed by scales formed by bracts.

Fig flowers are pollinated exclusively by tiny ($\pm$ 1 mm) fig-wasps (Agaonidae) (Figure 7.14), and both figs and wasps are entirely dependent on each other for their survival. In addition, one species of fig plant (and there are about 100 species in Sumatra [43]) will generally have only one species of pollinator wasp. The female flowers develop first and female wasps fly to the figs, probably attracted by a smell. One or more females climb inside the fig by forcing their way through the scales and in the process lose their wings and antennae. Once inside, a female pushes her

Figure 7.12 One means by which a strangling fig forms. A bird, squirrel or monkey deposits a seed in the crown of a tree. A small bush grows from which a long root descends to the ground. Side roots then form and grow around trunk, joining where they meet. The supporting tree eventually becomes encased in a basket of roots which eventually strangle the host to death. In time the fig will stand like a tree with a hollow trunk. (After Corner [42]).

Figure 7.13 A cross-section through a fig fruit showing the ring of male flowers (arrowed) around the end, and the bract scales partially closing the opening. (After Corner [42]).

Figure 7.14 Fig-wasps; female above, male below.

ovipositor down into the ovary of one of the female flowers and lays an egg. It used to be thought [42, 71] that females oviposted in ovaries of flowers specifically intended for developing larvae but various authors have shown that this is not so [116]. During oviposition and as she moves around inside of the fig, the female deposits pollen from the where she hatched onto other flowers and so effects pollination. Thus, although the wasps pollinate the flowers, they are also seed 'predators'. Janzen found that in a sample of 160 figs from four species, 98% of the figs had had more than 30% of their potential seeds killed by pollinating wasps [112, 114].

The larvae develop and pupate and the wingless males emerge first. They search for female pupae and fertilize them before they

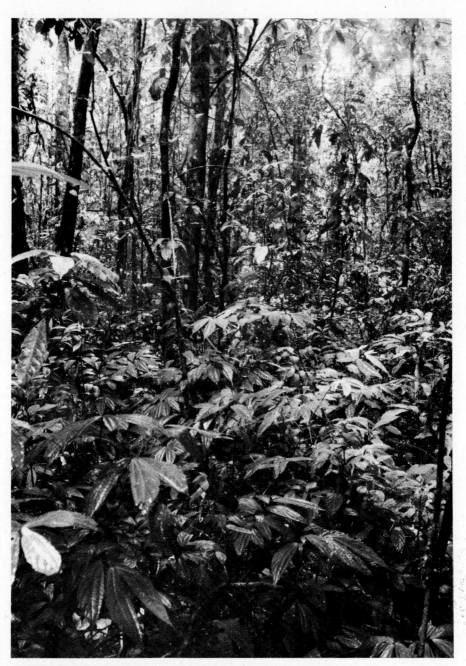

Lowland forest, Ketambe, South-east Aceh.

Mentawai gibbon eating the potentially toxic fruit of the wild sugar palm.

emerge. Janzen found that most figs are only entered by one or two females [115]. This means that there is a very high probability of brothers and sisters mating, a situation avoided in most other organisms. Implications of this have yet to be investigated in depth. The males' role is not yet completed because they then make a tunnel through the fig to the outside. The carbon dioxide level inside the fig is about 10% but when the hole is made the concentration drops to atmospheric levels (i.e. 0.03%). This change appears to stimulate the development of the male flowers, the emergence of the females and the process of ripening. In some species the females fly out through the tunnel made by the males and in other species both males and females eat away the scales at the fig entrance. Either way, the females fly off carrying pollen in search of a developing fig; and so the cycle continues. The males die within the fig.

Not all the insects emerging from a fig are fig-wasps because small parasitic wasps oviposit from the outside of the fig into a developing fig-wasp larva. How they locate a larva without seeing it is unknown. The story is further complicated by some of the parasites being parasitized themselves by other wasps (Figure 7.15).

Figure 7.15 Fig-wasps wasp parasite. (After Corner [42]).

7.3.7 Rafflesia

One of the best known wild flowers in Sumatra is *Rafflesia*, although it is rarely seen by most people except in photographs. It is a member of the family Rafflesiaceae which includes two other peculiar flowers found in Sumatra, *Rhizanthes* and *Mitrastemon* [186]. Sumatra has at least four species of *Rafflesia*: *R. atjehensis*, found in northern Sumatra, *R. hasseltii* in central Sumatra, *R. arnoldi* (the largest flower in the world) in Benkulu and West Sumatra [31, 32, 126], and *R. patma* in Lampung and South Sumatra [163, 167]. It is possible that hybrids form between *R. arnoldi* and *R. hasseltii*[168]. *Rafflesia* occurs mainly in lowland forest but van Steenis reports finding one at 1800 m on Mount Lembuh, Aceh. A bibliography for the Rafflesiaceae has been prepared by Meijer and Vangala [169].

Rafflesia is exceptional not just because of its size but because it is the most specialized of all parasitic plants - it has no stem, leaves or roots. Apart from the flower the plant consists of only strands of tissue growing inside the stem and larger roots of a few species of *Tetrastigma* climbers (family Vitaceae). Flower buds form on the stem and, for *R. arnoldi*, take about 19—21 months before they open as flowers. *R. arnoldi* buds of 10 cm diameter will take about 5 months to flower, of 15 cm diameter 2 to 3 months, and of 25 cm 20 to 30 days [163]. There appears to be no evidence for seasonal flowering but this has not been investigated in detail.

When *Rafflesia* flowers open (Figure 7.16), a smell of decaying meat arises from inside the flower and this attracts flies which presumably effect pollination. Male and female flowers are separate and for pollination to occur both need to be open simultaneously. Flowers may remain open for a week and then wither and decay. The fruits inside the flower are very small and their means of dispersal to other *Tetrastigma* is unknown [58, 126]. It seems feasible, however, that pigs, squirrels, rats and tree shrews may get *Rafflesia* fruits stuck in their feet while searching for food in the forest undergrowth. If they disturb the ground around another *Tetrastigma* climber, the seeds may be rubbed off onto the bark where they can germinate.

The name 'bunga bangkai' is sometimes given to *Rafflesia* but this name is also used for *Amorphophallus titanum*, the tallest flower in the world which is featured on the Rp500 banknote. *Amorphophallus* plants are quite easily recognized by their characteristic blotchy stems and

Figure 7.16 Cross-section of *Rafflesia arnoldi* on a *Tetrastigma* root. Arrow indicates location of sexual parts. (After Meijer [163]).

unusual leaves (Figure 7.17), but those seen in disturbed areas are generally smaller species. The flower of *Amorphophallus titanum* has a foetid odour which attracts small beetles and these effect pollination [191].

7.4 CYCLES OF FLOWER, FRUIT AND LEAF PRODUCTION

As far as is known, cycles of flower, fruit and leaf production have been studied in Sumatra only at the Ketambe Research Station [177, 204], and on Siberut Island [236]. None of the published accounts cover a period of more than two years. There is considerable variation within and between species, between months and between years and the patterns become clearer if the cycles are studied for longer periods such as the six years achieved at Ulu Gombak [160] and the long term but intermittent

Figure 7.17 The form of the stalk of *Amorphophallus* and detail from part of a leaf.

studies at Kuala Lompat [198], both in Peninsular Malaysia.

At Ulu Gombak 61 mature canopy trees representing 45 species were monitored. Only one of these flowered and fruited at consistent non-annual intervals and that was the large strangling fig *Ficus sumatrana* which had a cycle of 4 to 5 months. Strangely, that rhythm was unconnected with the weather and yet it always produced a heavy crop. Ten species were represented by two or more trees in the sample and only five of these synchronized their flowering and fruiting. In only ten species was flowering and fruiting consistent with annual cycles; the remaining 34 species flowered and fruited at irregular intervals usually exceeding one year and irrespective of weather. Ten species produced flowers each year but only six of these produced fruit every year. This illustrates the fact that flowering does not necessarily lead to fruiting. This can be caused by lack of pollination, fruit and seed predation or adverse weather conditions. In a recent review of this subject it is suggested that abortion of flowers or young fruit is often caused by a lack of necessary resources such as inorganic nutrients, water and products of photosynthesis [215].

Leaf flush was also variable between species. Three species produced new leaves almost all of the time and 21 species showed consistent annual patterns. Five other species exhibited irregular biannual patterns. Eight species were deciduous (lost all their leaves), four on an annual basis and four at intervals greater than a year.

Despite these variations, the tree community does show clear patterns of flower, fruit and leaf production (Figure 7.18). At the Ulu Gombak

Figure 7.18 Monthly percentages of trees with any fruit, with ripe fruit, with flowers and with leaf flush at Ulu Gombak, Peninsular Malaysia. Figures are averaged over six years. (Data from Medway [160]).

forest new leaves were produced twice each year with a major peak in March to June (just after the driest time of year) and a minor peak from October to December beginning just before and extending into the wettest time of year [160]. Flowering at Ulu Gombak peaked after the driest time of year, that is from March to July and, not surprisingly, fruiting peaked in

August to September just before the wettest time of year. The flowering of many lowland forest trees seems to be initiated by waterstress [233]. The apparent higher percentage of fruiting trees than flowering trees is caused by the fact that fruit remains on a tree longer than flowers and are thus counted in more months. For this reason the number of trees with ripe fruit is also shown.

The rainfall patterns in much of northern Sumatra are very similar to those of Ulu Gombak and so similar cycles of flower, fruit and leaf production would be expected. In the south of the island, however, where the driest months are usually June/July [182], the cycles are presumably adjusted accordingly.

7.4.1 Gregarious fruiting

Gregarious (or mast) fruiting is a term applied to the simultaneous mass fruiting of certain trees over wide areas at intervals in excess of one year and often in excess of five years. In the tropics, this phenomenon is only found in South-east Asia and virtually only among the Dipterocarpaceae. In sections 2.4.4, 5.5, 5.6 and 8.2.4 mention is made of the strategy of chemical defence of leaves by trees growing with low productivity on poor soils in climates favourable for animal life, leading to low numbers of animals. Janzen has proposed that gregarious fruiting is an indirect consequence of low productivity and, possibly, relatively low animal biomass (section 7.1.2) [106].

The primary purpose of gregarious fruiting is to escape seed predation. The trees produce so much seed that, after satiating the appetites of seed-predators which find the fruit, some seed still remains for germination. The synchrony also means that seed predators are unable to specialize on the particular fruit and so the population of potential seed predators is kept at a low level until gregarious fruiting begins. If only a single tree species adopted the strategy of gregarious fruiting there would be no chance of satiating the seed predators and the strategy only works because most of the family members fruit at the same time. It was shown in section 7.2.3 that dipterocarp trees often make up a considerable proportion of the trees in a lowland forest.

Dipterocarp seeds are eaten by squirrels, rats and probably also by larger animals such as pigs, tapir, deer, rhino and elephant [188, 193,

252]. They do not seem to be heavily defended with chemicals. Janzen suggests that if such oil-rich, defence-poor seeds lay on the floor of most African, Central or South American forests, none would escape predation [106]. It was shown in section 7.1.2 that there are fewer species of animals in the Sunda Region than in Central and South America and it is the subjective view that animal biomass is probably also less [106, 109]. This is due, at least in part, to:

— the long gaps between periods of fruiting which reduce the amount of regularly available food needed to sustain denser populations; and
— too much of the forest floor being occupied by immature dipterocarp seedlings and saplings which 'steal' resources from species which flower and fruit (produce animal food) at comparable heights.

If it is presumed that a fruiting interval for dipterocarps of only two years is sufficient to avoid most of the insects that might specialize on dipterocarp seeds [160] (section 7.5), and to reduce the populations of vertebrate seed predators, it is necessary to ask why they wait so much longer than two years. It is probably because the longer interval between fruiting seasons enables more products of photosynthesis to be stored, and thus more fruit to be produced. The longer the interval, the smaller is the percentage of the total seed crop consumed or lost. It appears that intervals of six years are common but the interval appears to be longer on poorer soil [106].

It is interesting that although fruiting time is synchronized between species, flowering time is not. This disparity is probably because pollinating insects are shared between species. However, fruit of late-flowering trees develop quickly and fruit of early-flowering trees develop more slowly. It will have been noticed by those accustomed to working in forests, that mast fruiting does not operate perfectly and trees sometimes make 'mistakes' [142, 160, 252]. Janzen suggests that since flowering appears to be triggered by climatic events (probably occasional, severe droughts) within a generally very uniform climate, minor localized droughts may sometimes cause flowering in a small population of a species [106]. Trees sometimes deal with such mistakes by absorbing flower buds or flowers, or by producing sterile fruit [160, 252]. None of the seeds produced in fertile fruit by a single tree or small population are likely to survive because the crop would be insufficient to satiate all the potential seed predators [252].

7.4.2 Effects of flower, fruit and leaf production cycles on animals

Since many of the trees in lowland forest are pollinted by insects, it is not surprising that peaks in abundance of certain insect species coincide with peaks of flower production. These peaks occur at the drier times of year and usually coincide with, or come slightly after, peaks of leaf production which are exploited by butterfly and moth caterpillars. Other insect species, particularly those associated with rotting wood, or those dependent on pools of water for breeding, become most abundant during the wetter months [144, 265].

These variations in insect abundance are probably reflected in the behaviour of insectivorous or partially-insectivorous birds. The second category is included because, for birds that feed largely but not entirely on fruit, seeds or nectar, insects represent a protein-rich source of food essential for the energy-expensive tasks of feeding their young and for moulting. The insectivorous and partially-insectivorous birds of Peninsular Malaysia breed and moult all year round but there are major peaks in March-May and July-August respectively (Figure 7.19). It is believed that these peaks

Figure 7.19 Percentage incidence of breeding and moulting birds of insectivorous of partial-insectivorous habit in the Malay Peninsular. (After Wells [228]. The heavy line describes the percentage of breeding birds and the light line the percentage of moulting birds.

depend on food availability [228] and similar results have been found for insectivorous birds in Sarawak lowland forest [68], and insectivorous bats [75].

Frugivorous mammals and birds differ in their response to changing fruit abundance depending on the degree to which they are restricted to particular areas (section 7.8.1). For example, animals such as bearded pigs, certain hornbills (section 7.8.3), mynahs, broadbills, small parrots and, to some extent, orangutans are free to move away from an area when food is scarce because they are either nomadic, migratory or have huge home ranges. Frugivores with fixed home ranges, however, such as squirrels, gibbons, some monkeys and certain hornbills, eat more non-fruit foods or take aseasonal fruit. Important among these aseasonal fruits are figs [138].

Variation in fruit abundance have been shown to affect the behaviour of gibbons [197]. During months when fruit was scarce the animals did not travel very far and stayed close to a few good fruit sources, but when fruit was abundant they travelled widely in their home range and ate a wide variety of foods.

The peak of pregnancy in Malaysian forest rats coincided with the seasonal peak in fruiting [79, 160], and this has been shown in more detail for rodents in a lowland forest in Zaire [54] (Figure 7.20).

7.5 SEED DISPERSAL

The dispersal of a seed is not simply the event of a mature fruit being released by its parent. Dispersal implies the carrying of a seed by some agent to a place where the seed will, perhaps, germinate, grow and reproduce. Most seeds die because the places they are dropped are unsuitable for growth; that is, they are not successfully dispersed. Seeds found directly below the parent tree are probably undispersed seeds, that is, they have simply dropped from the branches. Very few seeds and seedlings beneath their parent tree have any chance of survival because they will experience severe competition from others of their species. In addition, the parent tree and its offspring would represent a clumped food resource for seed predators. Thus dispersal of seeds can be envisaged as a means of escape from seed predators [90] as well as a method of colonizing widely

Figure 7.20 Relationship between rainfall (columns), reproductive activity as a percentage of 13 rodent species (upper graph), and percentage of trees in fruit (lower graph) ina lowland forest in Zaire. Note the similar shapes. (After Dieterlen [54]).

separated available sites. In the species-rich lowland forest where, as shown in sections 7.1.1 and 7.2.3, most species are rare, a seed dispersed away from its parent will stand a relatively low chance of being adjacent to a tree of the same species. A further advantage of dispersal away from the parent is that the biological and physical environment of the location where the parent germinated has in almost all cases changed by the time it has matured [107]. In general, this is the same as saying the environment below the parent tree is now unsuitable for its own seeds. Gap, building and mature forest areas (section 7.2.2) occur in more or less predictable proportions and patterns in a forest and the means of seed dispersal will aim to maximize the colonization of suitable areas with seeds.

The area over which seeds come to rest on the forest floor is known as a 'seed shadow'. The seed shadow of a tree is generally most dense close to the parent tree and much less dense overall when dispersd by an animal than when dispersed by wind. Whereas a wind-generated seed shadow is quite homogeneous, a seed shadow generated by animals will usually be heterogeneous. That is, animal-dispersed seeds will occur in dung piles, along animal paths, especially in certain vegetation types, etc. An exception are fig trees whose fruit is fed upon by many species of animals whose modes of living are so varied that a relatively homogeneous seed shadow can result. There is also variation in seed shadows for neighbouring individuals of the some species because access by the disperser into one tree may be easier than into another, and because other attractive food sources may be close to one but not to the other [107, 124]. These seed shadows are not simply of academic interest but are of major importance in determining future forest structure and composition [65].

Wind-dispersed fruits are generally borne by tall trees - the only forest treees to be affected by wind to any extent. Wind-dispersed fruits are either very light or have wings - in both cases their descent to the ground is delayed. Although wind does not disperse tree seeds particularly far from the parent, wind can at least be relied upon, whereas animals cannot.

The majority of forest tree seeds are dispersed by animals which eat the fruit and carry away the still-living seeds in their guts to be deposited some distance away when the animal defaecates. Seeds can be dispersed by animals in at least six different ways and the fruit can be classified accordingly [188, 189]. They are:
— bird fruits (divisible into opportunistic fruits, seed-eating bird fruits, specialist bird fruits and mimetic fruit),
— opportunistic fruits,
— arboreal mammal fruits,
— bat fruits,
— terrestrial rodent fruits, and
— large mammal fruits.

Thus fruits can usually be identified as being adapted for dispersal by a particular group of animals. It is worth considering what effect hunting and forest reduction has had on those species of tree whose fruits are adapted for dispersal by large mammals such as Sumatran rhino [216] and elephants [184].

The dispersal agent for a particular fruit depends on the nutritional requirements of the animals, the accessibility of the fruit, its shape and its size. The fruits produced by a tree vary in size and, in some species, the number of seeds they contain. Thus different portions of the fruit crop may be dispersed by different animals over different distances [90, 92, 120].

It is obviously to a plant's advantage to ensure that its fruit are dispersed to the right type of location and numerous means are used to selectively advertise their presence and to encourage certain dispersers while discouraging others. These characteristics have been shaped over evolutionary time by reciprocal interactions between animals and plants but, unlike the process of pollination, few species-specific relationships exist [122, 231]. Edible fruits are basically seeds covered with a bait of food, and Janzen has recently hypothesized that grasses and other herbs also encourage active dispersal by surrounding dry, small seeds with a bait of nutritious foliage. When the foliage is eaten, the seeds are too [266]. The fruit bait can vary greatly in nutritional value and plants tend to adopt one of two strategies. They can produce large numbers of 'cheap' fruit (small, sugary) most of which may be wasted or killed by the many species of frugivores attracted to them. Alternatively, a plant can produce smaller numbers of 'expensive' fruit (large, lipid-rich, oily) that have to be searched for by those few specialized species of frugivores which gain a balanced diet almost entirely from fruit [88, 89, 90, 91].

Fruits advertise their ripeness to dispersers using colour, texture, taste, conspicuous shapes, and odour. However, between ripening and being taken by a disperser, the fruit is also exposed to destructive animals and micro-organisms.

The destructive animals may be termed seed predators. It should be noted that a disperser animal can become a predator if it eats the fruit before the seeds are mature. Thus a fruit needs to be as unattractive as possible before the seed is viable and this is commonly achieved by the presence of defence compounds whose concentration is reduced as ripening progresses. For example, on Siberut Island the endemic gibbons eat the fruit of wild sugar palms *Arenga obtrusifolia*. These fruits contain water-soluble sodium oxalate which, if it comes into contact with mucous membranes (such as lips, mouth and throat), absorbs calcium and becomes water-insoluble needle-sharp crystals of calcium oxalate. The pain and the loss of calcium can kill. As the fruit ripens, however, the sodium oxalate is broken down and when fully ripe the fruit can be eaten safely [212].

Some fruit do not lose all their defence compunds when they are ripe and this is thought to be a means of protecting fruit from being eaten or destroyed by non-disperser animals or micro-organisms [86, 123]. Defence compounds can be divided into two groups: toxins which can debilitate or kill, and quantitative defences or digestion inhibitors such as resins, gums, volatile oils and phenols which deter potential seed predators or cause some mildly adverse physiological effect (such as feeling sick) [151, 225, 226]. A review of these defended ripe fruits concluded that the species producing them were at a competitive disadvantage for dispersal relative to species without defended ripe fruit. If the defences are viewed as means by which undesirable seed predators can be avoided, then extreme toxicity may be a 'last resort' [86].

Orang-utans are probably the sole fruit desperser for some plants amongst which is the climber *Strychnos ignatii* [204]. The large fruit contains the 'deadly' alkaloid strychnine but it appears to have no effect on orang-utans except for an excessive production of saliva. Indeed, strychnine appears to be dangerous only for carnivorous animals and for omnivores such as humans [111]. Orang-utans also eat the fruits of the ipoh tree *Antiaris toxicaria* which contain another poisonous alkaloid [204]. Ipoh latex is used by some peoples in the preparation of poisoned arrows and darts but it is actually not as deadly as popularly believed [34, 42]. It may be that these plants use their toxins to deter the 'wrong' dispersers.

Seed predators are commonly larvae of small beetles and these show a high level of specificity. Of over 975 species of shrubs and trees in an area of Costa Rica, at least 100 species regularly had beetle larvae in their mature or nearly-mature seeds. Three quarters of the 110 beetles species found (primarily from the family Bruchidae) were confined to a single species of plant; if a beetle species was found on more than one plant species, the plants were closely related. Of the 100 species of plants, 63 were legumes and 11 were Convolvulaceae [117]. This 'preference' for legumes might be because most plant families have had strong defences against attacks from bruchid beetles (Figure 7.21) whereas a few families have not. It seems more likely, however, that bruchid beetles became legume seed predators many millions of years ago and were able to counter whatever forms of defence the plant used. As the legumes evolved

Figure 7.21 A brucid beetle.

and diversified so the beetles evolved - a case of coevolution. Since plant defences appear to be so complex, the specializations required to predate on a particular species or genus are such that a beetle species would be unlikely to be able to also become a predator on seeds in another plant family.

In general, the larger the seed the longer the time between ingestion and excretion. In experiments with a tapir it was found that a considerable proportion of large, unchewed seeds were killed in the animal's gut because they germinated before being excreted and thus were acted upon by digestive juices [119].

Destructive micro-organisms (fungi and bacterial) represent a form of competition for frugivores. Fungi are not generally envisaged in this role but Janzen has suggested that this interpretation is valid [110, 113]. To a microbe, a ripe fruit is a considerable food resource which can be digested and converted into more microbes. It is obviously preferable, having started, to exploit the whole of the fruit and so competitors have to be dissuaded from using it as food. The microbe produces antibiotic substances to prevent other micro-organisms from colonizing the fruit and toxic and unpleasant tasting substances to deter larger frugivores. Producing tasteless toxins alone would not be a successful strategy because an animal may still eat the fruit, kill the microbe and later die itself. In that case neither party wins. Fruits invaded by microbes have to look, smell or taste different from untainted fruit or else the microbes have lost the battle.

Some fruits are known to produce their own antibiotics against decomposer micro-organisms [111] but this field of study has received little attention.

7.6 LEAVES AND BARK AS SOURCES OF FOOD

7.6.1 Leaves

About 50% of a leaf consists of cellulose, a complex sugar molecule which makes up the outer cell walls. Most animals lack the necessary enzymes to break down the cellulose into easily digestible, volatile fatty acids but some employ certain bacteria (or fungi - section 7.7.1) to conduct this first stage of digestion on their behalf. The possession of these bacteria allows access to a widely distributed and abundant food source. The bacteria themselves form an important source of protein for the host and can synthesize most vitamins except A and D. In vertebrates there are two major forms of bacteria-assisted digestion: foregut and hindgut fermentation. Foregut fermentation is found in, for example, cattle, deer and leaf-monkeys, and hindgut fermentation in, for example, rabbits, horses, koalas, rodents and flying lemurs [15, 171]. Leaves are eaten by a wide range of mammals and larval and adult insects, but not by amphibians and by very few reptiles or birds [170, 199]. It is estimated that 7—12.5% of leaf production is eaten by insects [136, 251] and only 2.4% by vertebrates [136]. However, as Janzen points out, these figures are usually calculated from the remains of fallen leaves and so do not necessarily include leaves or shoots eaten in their entirety [111].

The actual amount of leaf material eaten is not the most important ecological measurement because different parts have different values to the plant and hence different 'costs' for replacement. For example, the loss of a small shoot from a seedling is considerably more costly to the individual plant than the loss of a great many leaves on a mature plant. Leaves pay back their cost by photosynthesizing and contributing the products of photosynthesis to the plant. So, once a leaf has paid back its 'debt', its value to the plant decreases with time. It is clear, then, that for advanced ecological analysis of an ecosystem, a list of plant species eaten by a particular animal species is not nearly so useful as knowledge of what parts of each species are eaten and the likely cost to the individual plants of the material lost.

To the eyes of a human observer the leaves of a lowland forest, or indeed other tropical vegetation type, vary in shape and shade of green. To an animal which depends on leaves as a food source, however, they are 'coloured' "nicotine, tannin, lectin, strychnine, cannabinol, sterculic acid, cannavanine, lignin, etc., and every bite contains a horrible mix of these" [118]. These phenolic and alkaloid compounds [223] are just some of the toxic and digestion inhibiting chemicals used by plants to defend their leaves against herbivores [55]. Some of the ecological consequences of these chemicals are described in sections 5.6 and 8.2.4. See also section 7.3.5 for a discussion of the defence strategies of plants growing in gaps.

A recent laboratory study in North America has added a further dimension to the study of defence compounds. The response of tree seedlings was monitored before and after 7% of their leaf area was removed. Within two days the seedlings had increased the concentration of phenolic compounds in their remaining leaves - perhaps as a defence against futher loss of leaves. Strangely, however, nearby undamaged seedlings of the some species behaved similarly. This suggests that the damaged plants were able to communicate a warning to the other plants. How this is effected is as yet unknown [264].

Some animals may be able to eat leaves because they have coevolved with the plant - that is, changes in a plant's chemical defences will be met by changes in the animal's digestive capability [55, 254]. It could be, however, that an animal has evolved the ability to cope with the defences with no corresponding innovation in the plant's chemisty. Conversely a plant may produce defences which cause the partial 'defeat' of the herbivore with no response by the animal.

There is probably no plant whose defences preclude attack by all herbivores, and there is certainly no animal which can eat all types of leaves. A particular moth caterpillar in Costa Rica is able to eat leaves containing 40% by dry weight of phenolic compounds. This caterpillar eats almost only phenol-rich leaves from nearly twenty species but it grows at only about half the rate of moth caterpillars eating phenol-poor leaves from just a few species of plants [121]. Similar results were obtained in experiments with locusts [24, 25]. When eating a leaf rich in defence compounds a herbivore gains less usable food per unit effort (per mouthful) than when eating a leaf low in defence compounds, but it probably has more species to use as food and experiences relatively less competition from other herbivores unable to cope with the chemicals.

Experiments on the selection of leaves by a captive South American tapir showed that out of 381 species offered, only 55% were eaten, and only one of the 55 leguminous species was accepted. The tapir of the Sunda Region is also a very selective feeder in the wild, eating from saplings of only a fraction of the available tree species [161, 249].

Monkeys are also very selective in the plants they eat, choosing particular species, ages of leaves, parts (stem, tip or entire blade), and quantities. Recent studies of food selection by leaf-monkeys in Peninsular Malaysia and Sabah have shown that leaves selected as food are consistently low in lignin (fibre), and usually relatively high in protein; that is, the leaves are highly digestible. Tannin levels did not show consistent significant correlations with food selection [19, 49]. Similar results have been obtained in Africa and India [178, 179] and it is now generally felt that the role of tannins in food choice has been overemphasized [225]. They do, however, probably remain a potent force in ecosystems where poor soil conditions cause some form of strees in the trees growing on them (sections 5.6 and 8.2.4).

Tannins and lignins are classed as digestion-inhibiting phenolic compounds (although lignin is 10—20 times less effective than tannins), whereas others, such as the alkaloid strychnine, are classed as toxins. The term 'toxic' is really a measure of the energy expended by an animal in utilizing a food relative to the energy value of usable materials gained from the digestion process. Toxicity is therefore an outcome rather than an inherent property of a chemical, although some chemicals are more likely to be toxic than others. Whether a certain percentage composition of a potentially dangerous chemical is toxic or not will depend on the food value of the material eaten and on the efficiency of the animal's detoxification system. Thus, a leaf with a certain weight and concentration of defence compounds may be more toxic than a seed of the same weight and the same concentration of defence compounds *but* with more nutritive value [70, 111, 145]. Defence compounds should not be thought of as purely disadvantageous from the herbovore's point of view because they can have decidedly beneficial effects, as described in the next section.

7.6.2 Bark

Bark is, perhaps, an unlikely food but it has been recorded as a constituent of the diet of orang-utans [204], gibbons [203], elephants [184], Sumatran rhino [216] and squirrels [188, 246, 247]. Bark is not a rich food source and it may be eaten as a supplementary food to provide dietary fibre or trace elements.

On Siberut Island the small squirrel *Sundasciurus lowii* eats bark as a major item of its diet (section 7.8.3), and an analysis of the bark and bark-eating was conducted by J. Whitten [246]. Physical characteristics of trees (size, roughness of bark, ease of access for squirrels, etc.) food value and concentration of phenolic compounds in the bark of trees chosen as food sources were compared with similar data from trees not chosen as food sources. Trees on which the squirrels fed tended to be large, smooth-barked and relatively free of climbers, and certain tannins were absent in the barks eaten. These barks were not noticeably richer in food-value than those which were not eaten.

Defence compounds in bark, and indeed other food items, need not necesarily be selected against by animals; indeed, Janzen suggest that certain compounds may be actively sought for specific purposes [111]. For example, elephants have been reported to feed extensively on a certain leguminous creeper before embarking on a long period of travel and it may be that the plant contains some stimulating or sustaining chemical [94]. The high levels of tannins in some barks may be eaten to combat heavy parasite loads or upset stomachs. For example, Asian buffalo eat a plant with an informative scientific name *Holarrhena antidysenterica* [183] and Sumatran rhino have been observed to eat so much of the tannin-rich bark of the mangrove tree *Ceriops tagal* that their urine is stained bright orange [93]. It is worth noting, however, that the once-popular drug for diarrhoea 'Enterovioform' contains 50% (dry weight) tannin, a concentration not unknown in nature, but its role in combating diarrhoea has now been largely discredited.

7.7 SOIL AND ITS ANIMALS

The soil under the majority of lowland forest in Sumatra is red-yellow podzolic, and this has been described by Burnham [29], Soepraptohardjo et al. [35] and Young [263].

The majority of soil fauna in the Sunda Region is known very poorly and the only quantitative studies seem to have been conducted in Peninsular Malaysia and Sarawak [31, 39]. In 1 m² at Pasoh an average of 2000 ants, 300 termites, 30 earthworms, 30 fly larvae, 50 spiders and 100 beetles and their larvae were found. The total biomass of these invertebrates was about 3 g/m² (3000 kg/km²) but this and the proportions of different groups varied greatly from month to month. Similar results with more termites were obtained in Sarawak where the biomass was 4—6 g/m² [39]. To compare these figures with vertebrate biomass see section 7.8.5. Among the smaller animals at Pasoh, over 10,000 mites (Acarina) and about 56,000 nematode worms were found per m². These totals are not particularly high and some temperate areas would have greater densities but species diversity in the tropics is almost undoubtedly greater.

The soil animals about which most is known are termites.

7.7.1 Termites

Termites may look superficially like ants but they are classified in a completely different order which is more closely related to cockroaches. Termites are Isopterans, ants (together with bees and wasps) are Hymenopterans (Figure 7.22). Termites are like ants, however, in that they form enormous colonies with (at least in some parts of the world) possibly a million or more members. A colony is not a simple community of distinct individuals because all except two of the colony members are siblings. The other two, the 'royal pair', are the parents. The parents originated in other termite nests from which they flew along with thousands of others. Some manage to escape the hordes of ants, amphibians, reptiles, birds and mammals to which such a swarm is a food bonanza. After landing their wings drop off and if a male can find a female they will look for a suitable crack in the ground or a tree (depending on the species) and here they build their 'royal cell'. They copulate and the female begins laying eggs. The larvae, unlike the helpless larvae of ants, bees and wasps,

300

Figure 7.22. Typical termites (worker on left, soldier on right) and an ant.

are fully able to move around and undergo several moults (like cockroaches) rather than a single metamorphosis before becoming adults. These first larvae have to be fed by their parents but as soon as they are large enough to forage for food and to build walls for the nest, the royal pair devote themselves entirely to the production of eggs. The abdomen of the female, or queen, grows to grotesque proportions and a production rate of thousands of eggs per day is common.

A termite colony can be likened to a single, although sometimes disparate, organism because none of its components is capable of independent life. The workers are blind and sterile, and the soldiers which protect the columns of foraging workers and guard entrances to the colony's nest have jaws so large that they can no longer feed themselves and have to be fed by the workers. The king and queen are also fed by the workers. In the same way that communication between different organs or parts of a single body is effected by chemicals flowing through a body's tissues, so chemicals - pheromones[5] - link the different members of a termite colony into a coordinated and organized whole. All of the colony members continually exchange food and saliva which contain pheromones. Workers pass these materials from mouth to mouth and also consume one another's faeces to reprocess whatever partially digested food remains. Workers feed the soldiers, larvae and royal pair as well as collect the queen's faeces. There is thus a continual interchange of chemicals through the colony and this coordinates the operations of the colony. For example, larvae are potentially fertile termites of either sex but the food with which the workers feed them contains quantities of pheromone from the queen which inhibits the developement of larvae and produces workers. The soldiers also produce a pheromone which causes the larvae to develop into soldiers. When, for some reason, the number of soldiers falls, the level of 'soldier repression pheromone' circulating through the colony members falls and some eggs develop into soldiers. On other occasions the queen will reduce her repressive pheromones and her eggs will develop into fertile winged termites which, when the air is moist will leave the nest in a swarm and the cycle of colony formation begins again.

Most invertebrate decomposers of the lowland forest soil depend on free-living saprophytic fungi and bacteria to break down indigestible plant material into a digestible form before they can play their role, and termites are no exception. One subfamily of termites, the Macrotermitinae, represented in Sumatra by *Macrotermes, Odontotermes* and *Microtermes,* maintain a fungus in 'gardens' in their nests which releases them from competing for partially-decomposed material outside their nest. The workers of the above genera build complex frameworks, or combs, from their own round faecal pellets (not, as was once thought, from chewed food) - other groups of termites use faeces for building the fabric of their nests. (An identification key to genus level based on the head shape of soldiers has been written by Harris [78]). Since the main food of the Macrotermitinae is wood and leaf litter, the combs look like thin fragile pieces of moist, spongy, rotten wood. These combs are the food of a form of fungus called *Termitomyces* which is unknown outside termite nests. Small white dots which are clumps of asexual spores. can sometimes be seen on the combs if a

---

5. Pheromones are volatile chemicals produced by insects. The ingestion or smell of a pheromone produced by one individual of a particular species can determine or influence the behaviour of another individual of the same species.

nest is cut open. It takes up to two months for the fungus to process the combs [40].

This relationship with the fungus confers several advantages on the termites. No animal has the necessary digestive enzymes to digest lignin, a largely inert compound which is the main component of wood and thus one of the major items in a termite diet, and so lignin is excreted unchanged in the termite faeces. The fungus, however, can digest lignin. The termites are also unable to digest cellulose - the main component of plant cell walls - but the fungus does produce the necessary enzymes for breaking down cellulose. When the termites eat the fungus-permeated comb, these cellulose-digesting enzymes persist in the termite gut thereby improving the efficiency of its own digestion [40]. The fungus removes carbon from the comb during the digestion process and releases carbon dioxide as a result of its respiration. This has the advantage to the termite that the proportion of nitrogen in the combs increases roughly four-fold when processed by the fungus [156, 158]. The tremendous contribution the fungus makes to Macrotermitinae nutrition has resulted in these termites being unable to live without Termitomyces - an example of obligate symbiosis. It has made them so successful that they have been reported to be responsible for the removal of 32% of leaf litter in Pasoh Forest Reserve in Peninsular Malaysia [157]. In the same forest Abe studied the role of termites in the decomposition of fallen trees [1, 2]. He found that the rate of wood removal was higher for small branches (3—6 cm diameter) than for trunk wood (30—50 cm diameter) which is harder and more difficult to cut and remove. In a species of meranti Shorea parviflora, 81% of the tree's dry weight of small branches was removed in the first eighteen months after it fell compared with 18% of the trunk. Termites thus play a major role in the breakdown and cycling of plant material [253].

There are at least 55 species of termite at Pasoh [3, 4] and for population studies Matsumoto chose the four most abundant species with conspicuous mound nests part of which projected above the soil surface [156, 158]. Approximately 100 nests were found per hectare for three of the species but there were only 15 large nests of Macrotermes. The population size per nest for Macrotermes (about 88,000) was, however, at least twice that for the other species. The number of nests built by other genera in trees averaged four per species per hectare. Nests and the queen or queens they contain can survive for many years but some colonies may last less than a year [3, 4]. Colonies die for various reasons: because of extensive parasitism by small wasps, because the queen or king dies, or because the nest is destroyed by pangolins. Harrison examined the stomach of a pangolin *Manis javanica* and found approximately 200,000 ant workers and pupae within it [81]. If this is taken as an average daily diet (probably an underestimate) then a single pangolin could eat 73,000,000 ants or termites per year.

7.8 SPACING OF VERTEBRATE ANIMALS

The way in which different species organize the distribution and grouping of their members varies considerably. It is beyond the scope of this book to cover the theoretical reasons behind different kinds of social structure but the major patterns found in Sumatran lowland forest animals are described.

7.8.1 Social systems

Adult male orang-utans, slow loris, pangolins, shrews, tigers, bears, tapirs and Sumatran rhinos all live in more less exclusive ranges within which single female/offspring groups live in somewhat smaller, overlapping ranges. The male attempts to maintain exclusive breeding rights over these females and the extent of his claimed area is communicated to other males by loud calls, regularly-visited dung or urine sites or a combination of these two [28, 139, 148, 204, 216, 248]. Male pigs also live a largely solitary existence but several females and their offspring form groups of ten to twenty animals. When a female pig is ready to give birth she will go off on her own and remain alone until the piglets are old enough to run after her.

Mouse deer live singly for most of the year but form stable pairs for breeding [51]. Elephant males and females also live apart but the males will sometimes form bachelor groups and the females form herds with their young. Even when one or more males are attending the females and offspring, that group is still led by a matriarch [184].

The wild forest fogs *Cuon alpinus* live in mixed-sex packs of ten or more, led by a dominant male. They travel and hunt together and are

304

quite capable of killing a large deer even though its larger size, antlers and speed would make it unlikely prey in a one-to-one contest.

Almost all monkeys live in single- or multi-adult-male groups with more adult females than adult males (polygynous). The exception, unique among the world's monkeys, is the joja leaf-monkey *Presbytis potenziani* of the Mentawai Islands. It lives, like gibbons, siamang and tarsiers, in permanent, monogamous (one adult male and one adult female) groups within home ranges (the areas normally used by individuals or groups) containing territories which are defended against others of the same species [5, 47, 72, 73, 175, 197, 221, 240, 241, 245, 250]. The other Mentawai leaf monkey or simakobu *Simias concolor* lives in both monogamous and polygynous groups [22, 224, 240].

Most species of forest birds are more or less solitary for most of the year. Amongst these, the great argus pheasant *Argusianus argus* (Figure 7.23) is of particular interest. The male scratches conspicuous, cleared

Figure 7.23 Great Argus Pheasant *Argusianus argus*. (After King *et al.* [129]).

'dancing grounds' about 12 m² in area on the forest floor on the top of hills or knolls. He utters his well-known 'ki-au' call from the dancing grounds to attract females for breeding and when they arrive he performs a dramatic dance displaying his ornate, 1.5 m-long tail. After mating he plays no further role in the development of the chicks [52].

Most pigeons (Columbidae), small parrots (*Loriculus* and *Psittinus*), ioras and leafbirds (*Aegithina* and *Chloropsis* - see section 1.5.1), minivets

305

(*Pericrocotus*), some hornbills[6] (Bucerotidae) and some other birds are gregarious and form flocks for most of the year but separate into pairs for breeding. Drongos (Dicruridae) and some hornbills spend most of their adult life in pairs and these tend to be territorial. Other hornbills are territorial, communal breeders living in more or less permanent flocks of up to ten [137]. In addition, mixed-species flocks are found [46, 137]. These have been interpreted as a means by which relatively specialized insect-eating birds can increase their food supply, particularly during times of food shortage (section 7.4.2), because of the insects flushed by the activity of the other species in the flock. The different responses of insects to disturbance and the different specializations of the species could ensure benefit for all the flock members [46].

7.8.2 Niches

The type of niche discussed below is the realized niche (section 4.8.5) or that part of the total environment which a species actually exploits. A species' niche has been likened to its profession and this is a useful way to understand the term.

The enormous structural complexity and the high plant species diversity of lowland forest provides an uncountable number and often unexpected range of niches for possible exploitation by animals. For example, certain bark beetles (Scolytidae) (Figure 7.24) breed only in the leaf stalks of certain species of trees [17, 18]. The large number of animal species in turn provide a wealth of exploitation opportunities for other animals. For example, when spiders move about they leave behind them trails of fine 'silk' which may be on a substrate or suspended between two objects. Certain flies, wasps and moths habitually hang on these abandoned threads at night and are thus out of danger of walking predators (e.g. ants) and can effect a rapid escape from danger [133]. In addition, certain wasps have developed the ability to take flies out of spiders' webs before the fly is killed by the spider and without getting caught themselves [30].

Three Sumatran reptiles (the geckos *Cnemaspis kandianus* and *Peropus mutilatus* and the skink *Sphenomorphus cyanolaemus*) are

---

6. The remarkable nesting behaviour of hornbills has been described by various authors [13, 14, 125]).

306

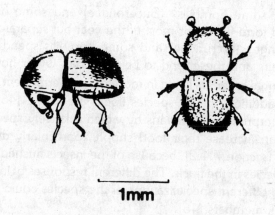

Figure 7.24 Side and dorsal views of a scolytid beetle.

'specialists' on buttress in lowland forests. That is, after reptiles were collected for six weeks at Bukit Lawang, Langkat, those three species were only caught on buttresses. There were even micro-habitat preferences within the 'buttress-niche' depending on the amount of litter present between the arms of the buttresses [222].

As stated elsewhere (section 10.4.3), although the niches of two species cannot be exactly the same, one species frequently shares part of its niche with another species (section 4.8.2). This can cause competition between two species such that the removal of one species will increase the abundance of the other. This has been shown for frogs found on the banks of lowland forest streams in Sarawak. Three species (two of which are found in Sumatra) were studied along three streams and each was found to range from the stream bank to different distances from the stream: thus *Rana blythi*, the largest of the three was found up to 10 m from the stream, *R. ibanorum* up to 7 m, and *R. macrodon* up to 3 m. The last two species were almost exactly the same size and only slightly smaller than *R blythi*. The prey of the three species also showed considerable overlap. After complete censuses of the frogs had been made along the three streams, *R ibanorum* was removed from along the stream where *R. blythi* was least common, *R. blythi* from the stream where *R. ibanorum* was least common, and the third stream was left as a control. The results are shown in Figure 7.25. Where *R. ibanorum* was removed, *R. blythi* increased its

Figure 7.25 Estimates of frog population size on three streams in Sarawak at five census periods distributed over one year, showing mean and one standard deviation either side of the mean: a) untampered with to act as a control, b) streams with *R. ibanorum* removed, after the first census, c) streams with *R. blythi* removed after the first census. (After Inger and Greenberg [99]).

population, but where *R.blythi* was removed, the *R. ibanorum* population fluctuated but did not increase. Thus *R. ibanorum* seemed to have been restricting the realized niche of *R blythi* but not *vice versa*. Exactly how the competition was effected is not known [97, 99].

7.8.3 Niche differentiation

The manner in which similar species are able to co-exist in the same area is termed niche differentiation. This can be effected by spatial separation, dietary separation, temporal separation, or, more usually, a combination of all three. To illustrate this, the niche differentiation within three groups of lowland forest animal communities will be described: primates, squirrels, and hornbills.

Primates

The greatest possible number of primate species in an area of mainland Sumatran lowland forest is eight[7]: orang-utan *Pongo pygmaeus* or tarsier *Tarsier bancanus*[8], siamang *Hylobates syndactylus*, white-handed gibbon *H. lar* or black-handed gibbon *H. agilis* (section 1.6.2), silvered leaf-monkey *Presbytis cristata*, Thomas' leaf-monkey *P. thomasi* or banded leaf-monkey *P. melalophos* or eastern leaf-monkey *P. femoralis*, long-tailed macaque *Macaca fascicularis*, pig-tailed macaque *M. nemestrina*, and slow loris *Nycticebus coucang*. The tarsier and slow loris have a very different niche from the others: they are both nocturnal, the slow loris eating fruit and insects [12], the tarsier mainly insects. The niche separation of the other six is not so obvious.

Spatial separation - The actual areas of lowland forest used by the diurnal primate species are more or less identical although long-tailed macaques and to some extent silvered leaf-monkeys are more common in riverine forest [250]. Wilson and Wilson also report that silvered leaf-monkeys rarely enter deep itno lowland forest but, on Bangka Island where banded and eastern leaf-monkeys are absent, they appear to be quite common inland [244]. Each species has its own altitudinal range (section 9.5.3). Marked separation also occurs in the use each species makes of the canopy (Figure 7.26). The difference between the two macaques is the most marked, with pig-tailed macaques being much more

---

7. A ninth species, 'orang pendek' or 'short man', which is supposed to live in the southern half of Sumatra is probably only a bear. The idea of its existence may go back to ancient times when the orang-utan was still found in southern Sumatra [48].
8. The distribution of tarsiers and orang-utan used to overlap in southern Sumatra before the orang-utan became extinct there. It is doubtful whether the range of the eastern leaf monkey has ever overlapped with that of the orang-utan.

Figure 7.26 Vertical use of the canopy by six primates at Ketambe Research Station, Mount Leuser National Park. Bars beneath each column represent 50% of total observations. (After Rijksen [204]).

terrestrial [45]. The two species do use the canopy in a similar manner for feeding but pig-tailed macaques are anatomically better suited to walking on the ground than to jumping or leaping. The siamang and gibbon are very similar in their use of the canopy [149] but the orang-utan uses the middle canopy more than either of them [204]. Orang-utans never leap between trees and often rock back and forth on trees in the middle canopy of the forest until they can reach a neighbouring tree.

Dietary separation - Representative diets of some of the diurnal primates are shown in Figure 7.27. These figures disguise considerable variations between days, months and seasons, but illustrate the major differences in the relative importance of fruit and leaves. The differences are clearer still if the actual food items are considered. In other words, different plant species and different parts of the same plant species are counted

Figure 7.27 Average diets for six Sumatran primates. The proportions are typical but disguise a wide variation between days and between months. (From data in MacKinnon [148]), Rijksen [204], MacKinnon and MacKinnon [149] and from E.L. Bennett [20] and A.G. Davies [50]). **Thomas' and Mentawai leaf monkeys probably have similar diets to banded leaf monkey. Silvered leaf monkeys probably eat more leaves than fruit.**

separately; this is shown in Figure 7.28. Thus, whereas in Figure 7.27 siamang and banded leaf-monkeys were apparently quite similar in their diet the actual overlap between the food items they eat is very small. Insufficient data are available for a complete analysis but in the Ranun River area of North Sumatra pig-tailed macaques have a high dietary overlap of 48% with their close relative, the long-tailed macaques [149] and the diets of orang-utan and white-handed gibbons overlap by 40% [148]. The orang-utan diet probably overlaps more with that of gibbons and siamang than with the diets of the other primates.

311

Figure 7.28 Number of different food items eaten by four primate species (in brackets), the number of shared items, and the percentage of dietary overlap between each pair of species. (Based on MacKinnon and MacKinnon [149]). E.L. Bennett believes the overlap between white-handed gibbons and banded leaf monkeys is only about 1% [20].

The greatest dietary overlap is between the siamang and gibbon, which also appear to have the most specialized diets (fewest types of items). The way in which they segregate food resources between them is a function of body size which influences their different foraging strategies. Siamang are twice as heavy as gibbons but travel only half as far each day and feed at only half as many feeding sites, but feed for twice as long at each site. Siamang have to travel direct routes between trees with abundant food but gibbons are able to exploit smaller, more dispersed food sources [73, 148, 149, 197]. These two species compete by depleting each other's food supplies and exploitation competition (section 4.8.2) is probably the major form of this competition. The larger siamang however, is able to dominate the gibbon if they meet at a food source (disturbance competition). The rarity of meetings between the two species, even when they occupy the same area of forest, is probably avoidance of this form of competition by the gibbons which are able to seek alternative food sources [196].

Temporal separation - The activity patterns of five Sumatran primates in shown in Figure 7.29. Different activity patterns have probably evolved so that food is eaten at optimally-spaced intervals through the day. Thus leaf-monkeys, which eat seeds and leaves both of which contain high levels of defence compounds, need to space their feeding more or less evenly through the day so that the effects of these compounds do not cause debilitating peaks. Conversely, gibbons and siamang eat mainly fruit and young leaves and feed more intensively during the early part of the day.

Figure 7.29 Daily activity patterns of five primate species. Note the relatively high proportion of travel for white-handed gibbons, the double peak of feeding and marked midday rest for orang-utan, and the relatively late start for banded leaf monkeys and long-tailed macaques. (After MacKinnon [148] and MacKinnon and MacKinnon [149]).

313

Since leaves are most nutritious at the end of the day when the products of photosynthesis (carbohydrates and sugars) have accumulated, it would be expected that these are eaten most in the afternoon. This is found in both leaf-monkeys [47], siamang and gibbons [73].

Temporal separation also occurs in the times at which the different primate species call (Figure 7.30) (see also section 7.8.4).

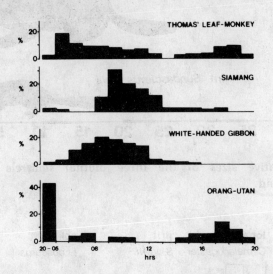

Figure 7.30 **Percentage of calls occurring through the day for four primate species around the River Ranun, Dairi.** (After MacKinnon [148]).

Squirrels

Ecological separation of three diurnal squirrels was investigated on Siberut Island by J. Whitten [247]. The species (relative sizes shown in Figure 7.31) were separated largely on their vertical use of the forest (Figure 7.32) but in the areas of overlap in the lower levels they were separated by both activity (as indicated by calling) (Figure 7.33) and by diet. The large *Callosciurus melanogaster* ate mainly fruit and insects, the small *Sundasciurus lowii* ate bark, moss, lichens, insects and earthworms, and the largely ground dwelling *Lariscus obscurus* ate mainly fruit (Figure 7.34).

314

Figure 7.31 Relative sizes of the three diurnal squirrels on Siberut Island.

Figure 7.32 Vertical distribution of three species of squirrel on Siberut Island. (After J. Whitten [247]).

Figure 7.33 Distribution of calling through the day by three species of squirrel on Siberut Island. Note that the vertical axis for *S. lowii* and *L. obscurus* are calls per hour, whereas for *C. melanogaster* the vertical axis is total number of calls heard. (After J. Whitten [247]).

Figure 7.34 Diets of three squirrels on Siberut Island. (Simplified from data in J. Whitten [247]).

Similar results were obtained in Peninsular Malaysia by Payne [188]. Peninsular Malaysia has the two very large diurnal squirrels *Ratufa affinis* and *Ratufa bicolor* which are both also found in Sumatra. These two species are almost exactly the same size and weight (factors which usually influence ecological separation) and exploit the forest in very similar ways. Their niche separation is thought to be due to minor differences in canopy use and diet [188].

Hornbills

Sumatra has ten species of hornbill and at least eight can be found in a single area of forest. The means by which available resources are divided between them so that these species can coexist have not been studied in Sumatra, but this subject was studied in East Kalimantan where seven species (all of which are found on Sumatra) live in the same forest [137]. Two of the species are nomadic, flocking species, three live as territorial pairs and two live in territorial but communal groups. Fruit forms the major part of all their diets but they will all also eat small animals. The two major classes of fruit eaten, sugary figs and lipid-rich fruits, differed in their abundance, distribution and profitability (net rates of energy gain for the hornbills). The economics of searching for these different foods together with the hornbills' body weight and competitiveness probably influence group size and the relative importance of figs or other fruit to the birds. The nomadic species travel large distances (i.e. expend considerable energy) but track temporary peaks in fruiting of lipid-rich fruits within localized habitats over a large area. The territorial species, living within fixed areas and thus with lower energy costs, supplement their diets with figs and animal prey between the periods of lipid-rich fruit availability.

7.8.4 Temporal separation of animal calls

The way in which sound transmits through forest, particularly the structurally complex lowland forest, is quite different from the way sound moves through open air. Foliage, air turbulence, air termperature gradients and ground effects can rapidly degrade the vocal signals which animals use to communicate with others of the same species. In brief, the principles governing sound transmission in lowland forest are:

a) sounds with wavelengths shorter than objects in their path will be reflected whereas longer wavelengths will not;

b) low frequency sounds are absorbed less rapidly by humid air than high frequency sounds;

c) animals calling from the forest canopy, above the range of ground effects and at times when other animals are not calling, increase the distance to which their calls will be carried;

d) complex structural properties of forests produce 'sound windows' through which certain frequencies can pass but others cannot;

e) temperature increases with height above the forest floor during the day and this causes sound to be trapped and attenuated within the forest [200, 239].

Given the above principles one would expect animals to call when conditions allow maximum transmission of their calls. Examination of the spacing of calls by cicadas [264], birds and other vertebrates [85, 159], and gibbons [239] have shown that calls are indeed given at the times and frequency that provide for best transmission.

7.8.5 Density of larger animals

Knowledge of the home range occupied by a single group cannot be used to calculate a density because for some species there are frequently gaps between home ranges or, for other species, home ranges overlap. The densities of selected larger mammals and birds in Sumatran lowland forest shown in Table 7.2 *must not* be used to calculate densities in a given patch of forest in, for example, an environment impact assessment. They are included in this book so that the reader can form an impression of the natural rarity of many of the larger animals and of the density that might be expected. Densities vary considerably between areas and between forest types [155, 255] and results from one area should not be applied indiscriminately to another area. The methodology of faunal surveys can be found elsewhere [63, 155, 255]. Data are currently available on numbers and biomass of insectivorous birds in lowland forest [229], on approximate ranges of forest rats [80] and of other mammals [72, 144] and on the density and biomass of squirrels [188].

Table 7.2 Approximate densities of various large birds and mammals in Sumatran lowland forest. [1]- long-tailed macaques are more or less restricted to riverine forest so figures given here are per km of river bank [176]. (After Chivers and Davies [38], Davison [53], Flynn and Abdullah [67], Lekagul and McNeely [139], MacKinnon [147, 148], MacKinnon and MacKinnon [149], Medway & Wells [162], van Noordwijk and van Schaik [176], Olivier [184], Payne [188], Poniran [267], Rijksen [204], Robertson [205], Seidensticker [268], van Strien [216], West [230], World Wildlife Fund (Malaysia)/Payne and Davies [255]).

Species	Individuals per km^2	Group size	Groups per km^2	Biomass (kg) per km^2
Great Argus pheasant *Argusianus argus*	3	—	—	?
Helmeted hornbill *Rhinoplax vigil*	0.4	2	0.2	?
Rhinoceros hornbill *Buceros rhinoceros*	1.1	2	0.4	?
Bushy-crested hornbill *Anorrhinus galeritus*	4	6	0.7	?
Black giant squirrel *Ratufa bicolor*	11	—	—	18
Banded leaf-monkey *Presbytis melalophos*	26	13	2	150
Thomas' leaf-monkey *Presbytis thomasi*	29	10	2.9	168
Long-tailed macaque *Macaca fascicularis*	30[1]	15	2[1]	120[1]
Pig-tailed macaque *Macaca nemestrina*	6	30	0.2	27
Gibbon *Hylobates lar/agilis*	6	3.5	1.5	22
Siamang *Hylobates syndactylus*	9	3.5	2.6	75
Orang-utan *Pongo pygmaeus*	1.5	—	—	36.5
Tiger *Panthera tigris*	0.02	—	—	4
Elephant *Elephas maximus*	0.1	15	0.007	300
Tapir *Tapirus indicus*	0.1	—	—	20
Rhinoceros *Dicerorhinus sumatrensis*	0.01	—	—	8

REFERENCES

1. Abe, T. (1978). The role of termites in the breakdown of dead wood in the floor of Pasoh study area. *Malay. Nat. J.* 30: 391-404. (12.4.31)
2. _____ (1979). Food and feeding habits of termites in Pasoh Forest Reserve, *Jap. J. Ecol.* 29: 121—136.
3. Abe, T. and Matsumoto, T. (1978). Distribution of termites in Pasoh Forest Reserve. *Malay. Nat. J.* 30: 325—335. (12.4.32)
4. _____ (1979). Studies on the distribution and ecological role of termites in a lowland rain forest of West Malaysia III. Distribution and abundance of termites at Pasoh Forest Reserve. *Jap. J. Ecol.* 29: 337—353.
5. Aldrich-Blake, F.P.G. (1980). Long-tailed macaques. In *Malayan Forest Primates: Ten Years' Study in Tropical Rainforest* (ed. D.J. Chivers), pp. 147—165. Plenum, New York. (12.8.25)
6. Anderson, J.M. and Swift, M.J. (1983). Decomposition in tropical forests. In *Tropical Rain Forest: Ecology and Management* (ed. S.L. Sutton, T.C. Whitmore and A.C. Chadwick), pp. 287—309. Blackwell, Oxford.
7. Anderson, J.M., Proctor, J. and Vallack, H.W. (1983). Ecological studies in four contrasting lowland rain forest in Gunung Mulu National Park, Sarawak III. Decomposition processes and nutrient losses from leaf litter. *J. Ecol.* 71: 505—527.
8. Ashton, P.S. (1964). Ecological studies in the mixed dipterocarp forest of Brunei State. *Oxf. For. Mem. No. 25.* (Referred to in Whitmore, 1975).
9. _____. (1976). Mixed dipterocarp forest and its variation with habitat in Malayan lowlands: a reevaluation at Pasoh. *Malay. Forester* 39: 56—72. (12.10.86).
10. _____. (1982). Dipterocarpaceae. *Flora Malesiana I, 9*: 237 —552.

320

11. Baillie, I.C. and Ashton P.S. (1983). Some aspects of the nutrient cycle in mixed dipterocarp forests in Sarawak. In *Tropical Rain Forest: Ecology and Management* (ed. S.L. Sutton, T.C. Whitmore and A.C. Chadwick), pp. 347—356, Blackwell, Oxford.
12. Barrett, E.M.: Personal communication.
13. Bartels, H. (1956). Waarnemingen bij een Broedhol van der Jaarvogel *Aceros u. undulatus* (Shaw) op Sumatra. *Limosa* 39: 1-18.
14. Bartels, M. and Bartels, H. (1937). Uit het leven der neushoornvogels (I), (II), (III). *Trop. Natuur* 26: 117—127, 140—147, 166-172. (12.7.49)
15. Bauchop, T. (1978). Digestion of leaves in vertebrate arboreal folivores. In *The Ecology of Arboreal Folivores* (ed. G.G. Montgomery), pp. 193-204. Smithsonian Institution, Washington, D.C. (12.8.47)
16. Bazzaz, F.A. and Pickett, S.T.A. (1980). Physiological ecology of tropical succession: a review. *Ann. Rev. Ecol. Syst.* 11: 287—310. (12.10.92)
17. Beaver, R.A. (1979). Leafstalks as a habitat for bark beetles. (Col.: Scolytidae). *Z. Entomol.* 88: 296—306. (12.4.40)
18. _____. (1979). Non-equilibrium 'island' communities. A guild of tropical bark beetles. *J. Anim. Ecol.* 48: 987—1002. (12.4.39)
19. Bennett, E.W. (1984). *The Banded Langur: Ecology of a Colobine in Colobine in West Malaysian rainforest*. PhD thesis, University of Cambridge, Cambridge.
20. _____. Personal communication.
21. Benzing, D.H. (1981). Mineral nutrition of epiphytes: an appraisal of adaptive features. *Selbyana* 5: 219—223. (12.1.85)
22. _____. (1983). Vascular epiphytes: a survey with special reference to their interactions with other organisms. In *Tropical Rain Forest: Ecology and Management* (ed. S.L. Sutton, T.C. Whitmore and A.C. Chadwick), pp. 11—24. Blackwell, Oxford.
23. Benzing, D.H. and Ott, D.W. (1981). Vegetative reduction in epiphytic Bromeliaceae and Orchidaceae: Its origin and significance. *Biotropica* 13: 131—140. (12.1.65)

321

24. Bernays, E.A. (1978). Tannins: an alternative viewpoint. *Ent. exp. appl.* 24: 44—53. (12.13.31)
25. Bernays, E.A. and Chamberlain, D.J. (1980). A study of tolerance of ingested tannin in *Schistocerca gregaria. J.* Insect Physiol. 26: 415-420. (12.4.55)
26. Biere, J.M. and Uetz, G.W. (1981). Web orientation in the spider *Micrathena gracilis* (Araneae: Araneidae). *Ecology* 62: 336—344. (12.4.38)
27. Black, H.C. and Harper, K.T. (1979). The adaptive value of buttresses to tropical trees: additional hypotheses. *Biotropica* 11: 240. (12.1.64)
28. Borner, M. (1979). *A Field Study of the Sumatran Rhinoceros* Dicerorhinus sumatrensis *Fischer 1914: Ecology, Behaviour and Conservation Situation in Sumatra.* Juris Druck, Zurich. (12.8.48)
29. BPPP/Soepraptohardjo, M., Soekardi, M., Kurnia, H.D. and Suharjo, S. (1979). *Sumber daya lahan/tanah dan potensinya di Pulau Sumatera.* Konsultasi Penelitian Pertanian Menunjang Pembangunan Sumatera 28 Nopember — 3 Desember 1979. Lembaga Penelitian Tanah, Bogor. (23.4.14)
30. Bristowe, W.S. (1976). Rare arachnids from Malaysia and Sumatra. *J. Zool.* 178: 7—14. (12.4.37)
31. Brown, R. (1822). An account of a new genus of plants named *Rafflesia. Trans. Linn. Soc. Lond.* 13: 201—234. (12.1.80)
32. _____: (1845). Description of the female flower and fruit of *Rafflesia arnoldi* with remarks on its affinities. *Trans. Linn. Soc. Lond.* 19: 221—247. (12.1.81)
33. Brown, S. and Lugo, A.E. (1982). The storage and production of organic matter in tropical forests and their role in the global carbon cycle. *Biotropica* 14: 161—187. (12.10.19)
34. Burkill, I.H. (1966). *Dictionary of the Economic Products of the Malay Peninsula.* Dept. Agriculture, Kuala Lumpur.
35. Burnham, C.P. (1975). Soils. In *Tropical Rainforests of the Far East* (oleh T.C. Whitmore), pp. 103—120. Clarendon, Oxford. (12.10.8)
36. Cheke, A.S., Nanakorn, W. and Yankoses, C. (1979). Dormancy and dispersal of seeds of secondary forst species under the

canopy of a primary tropical rain forest in northern Thailand. *Biotropica* 11: 88—95. (12.1.66)

37. Chiba, S. (1978). Numbers, biomass and metabolism of soil animals in Pasoh Forest Reserve. *Malay. Nat. J.* 30: 313—324. (12.10.87)

38. Chivers, D.J. and Davies, A.G. (1978). Abundance of primates in the Krau Game Reserve, Peninsular Malaysia. In *The Abundance of Animals in Malesian Rainforests* (ed. A.G. Marshall), pp. 9—36. University of Hull, Hull. (12.8.22)

39. Collins, N.M. (1980). The distribution of soil macrofauna of the West ridge of Gunung (Mount) Mulu, Sarawak. *Oecologia* 44: 263—275.

40. _____: (1982). The importance of being a bugga-bug. *New Scient.* 94: 834—837. (12.4.41)

41. _____: (1983). Termite populations and their role in litter removal in Malaysian rain forests. In *Tropical Rain Forest: Ecology and Management* (ed. S.L. Sutton, T.C. Whitmore, A.C. Chadwick), pp. 311—325. Blackwell, Oxford.

42. Corner, E.J.H. (1952). *Wayside Trees of Malaya.* 2 jilid, 2nd ed. Government Printer, Singapore. (12.1.15)

43. _____: (1962). An introduction to the distribution of figs. *Reinwardtia* 4: 325—355.

44. _____: (1978). The freshwater swamp-forest of South Johore and Singapore. *Grdns' Bull. S'pore Suppl. No. 1* (12.10.10)

45. Crockett, C.M. and Wilson, W.C. (1980). The ecological separation of *Macaca nemestrina* and *Macaca fascicularis* in Sumatra. In *The Macaques:* Studies in Ecology, Behaviour and Evolution (ed. D.G. Lindburg), pp. 148—181. van Nostrand Reinhold, London.

46. Croxall, J.P. (1976). The composition and behaviour of some mixed species bird flocks in Sarawak. *Ibis* 118: 333—346. (12.7.26)

47. Curtin, S.H. (1980). Dusky and banded leafmonkeys. In *Malayan Forest Primates: Ten Years' Study in Tropical Rainforest* (ed. D.J. Chivers), pp. 107—145. Plenum, New York. (12.8.25)

48. Dammerman, K.W. (1930). The orang pendek or ape-man of Sumatra. *Proc. 4th Pac. Sci. Cong., Java 1929,* 3: 1—6. (12.8.103)

323

49. Davies, A.G. (1984). *The Ecology and Behaviour of the Rufous Leaf-monkey* Presbytis rubicunda *in Sabah*. PhD thesis, University of Cambridge, Cambridge.
50. _____. Personal communication.
51. Davison, G.W.H. (1980). Territorial fighting by lesser mouse deer. *Malay. Nat. J.* 34: 1—6. (12.8.75)
52. _____. (1981). Sexual selection and the mating system of *Argusianus argus* (Aves: Phasianidae). *Biol. J. Linn. Soc.* 15: 91—104. (12.7.27)
53. _____. (1981). Diet and dispersion of the Great Argus *Argusianus argus*. *Ibis* 123: 485—494. (12.7.28)
54. Dieterlen, F. (1982). Fruiting seasons in the rain forest of Eastern Zaire and their effect upon reproduction. Poster presentation at Tropical Rain Forest Symposium, 1982. Leeds University, Leeds. (12.8.49)
55. Edwards, P.J. and Wratten, S.D. (1980). *Ecology of Insect-Plant Interactions*. Edward Arnold, London. (23.2.11)
56. _____. (1982). Wound induced changes in palatability in birch (*Betula pubescens* Ehrh. ssp *pubescens*). *Amer. Nat.* 120: 816—818. (12.1.87)
57. Endler, J.A. (1982). Pleistocene forest refuges: fact or fancy? In *Biological Diversification in the Tropics* (ed. G. Prance), pp. 641—657. Columbia University Press, New York. (23.6.17)
58. Ernst, A. and Schmidt, E. (1983). Uber Blüte und Frucht von *Rafflesia*. *Ann. Jard. bot. Buitenz.* 27: 1—58. (12.1.82)
59. Erwin, T.L. (1982). Tropical forests: their richness in Coleoptera and other arthropod species. *Coleopterists' Bull.* 36: 74—75. (12.4.46)
60. _____. (1983). Tropical tree canopies: the last biotic frontier. *Bull. ESA* 1983: 14—19. (12.4.47)
61. Eve, R. and Gigue, A.M.: Personal communication.
62. Fairchild, D. (1928). A jungle botanic garden. *J. Hered.* 19: 145—158. (12.13.17)
63. FAO/MacKinnon, J. (1981). *National Conservation Plan for Indonesia, Vol. VIII: National Park Development and General Topics*. FAO, Bogor. (10.2.15)

64. Fisher, J.B. (1976). Adaptive value of rotten tree cores. *Biotropica* 8: 261. (12.1.123)

65. Fleming, T.H. and Heithaus, E.R. (1981). Frugivorous bats, seed shadows and the structure of tropical forests. *Biotropica (Reprod. Bot. Suppl.)* pp. 45—53. (12.10.111)

66. Flenley, J.R. (1980). The Quaternary history of the tropical rain forest and other vegetation of tropical mountains. *IV Int. Palyn. Conf. Lucknow (1976—7)* 3: 21—27. (12.10.69)

67. Flynn, R. and Abdullah, M. (1983). Distribution and numbers of Sumatran rhinoceros in the Endau-Rompin region of Peninsular Malaysia. *Malay. Nat. J.* 36: 219—247.

68. Fogden, M.P.L. (1972). The seasonality and population dynamics of equatorial forest birds in Sarawak. *Ibis* 114: 307—343. (12.7.48)

69. Franken, N.A.P. and Roos, M.C. (1981). *Studies in lowland equatorial forest in Jambi Province, Central Sumatra.* Unpublished report, BIOTROP, Bogor. (12.10.103)

70. Freeland, W.J. and Janzen, D.H. (1974). Strategies in herbivory by mammals: the role of plant secondary compounds. *Amer. Natur.* 108: 269—289. (12.8.46)

71. Galil, J. (1977). Fig biology. *Endeavour N.S.* 1: 52—56. (12.1.109)

72. Gittins, S.P. (1980). Territorial behaviour in the Agile gibbon. *Int. J. Primatol.* 1: 381—399. (12.8.41)

73. Gittins, S.P. and Raemaekers, J.J. (1980). Siamang, lar and agile gibbons. In *Malayan Forest Primates: Ten Years' Study in Tropical Rain Forest* (ed. D.J. Chivers), pp. 63—105. Plenum, New York. (12.8.25)

74. Gould, E. (1978). Foraging behaviour of Malaysian nectarfeeding bats. *Biotropica* 10: 184—193. (12.8.43)

75. ⎯⎯⎯⎯⎯⎯⎯. (1978). Rediscovery of *Hipposideros ridleyi* and seasonal reproduction in Malaysian bats. *Biotropica* 10: 30—32. (12.8.57)

76. Groeneveldt, W (1938). Een overzicht van de vaste trekwegen in Zuid Sumatra alsmede enige gegevens over rhinocerossen. *Ned. Comm. Intern. Natturbesch. Med.* 12: 73—109.

77. Haffer, J. (1982). General aspects of the Refuge Theory. In *Biological Diversification in the Tropics* (ed. G. Prance), pp. 6—24. Columbia University Press, New York. (12.13.11)

78. Harris, W.V. (1957). An introduction to Malayan termites. *Malay. Nat. J.* 12: 20—32. (12.4.33)

79. Harrson, J.L. (1955). Data on the reproduction of some Malayan mammals. *Proc. Zool. Soc. Lond.* 125: 445—460. (12.8.58)

80. —————. (1958). Range of movement of some Malayan rats. *J. Mammal.* 39: 190—206. (12.8.44)

81. —————. (1962). The distribution of feeding habits among animals in a tropical rain forest. *J. Ecol.* 31: 53—63. (12.13.30)

82. —————. (1969). The abundance and population density of mammals in Malayan lowland forests. *Malay. Nat. J.* 22: 174—178.

83. Hartshorn, G.S. (1978). Tree falls and tropical forest dynamics. In *Tropical Trees as Living Systems* (ed. P.B. Tomlinson and M.H. Zimmermann), pp. 617—638. Cambridge University Press, Cambridge. (12.10.108)

84. Henwood, K. (1973). A structural model of forces in buttressed tropical rain forest trees. *Biotropica* 5: 83—93.

85. Henwood, K. and Fabrick, A. (1979). A quantitative analysis of the dawn chorus: temporal selection for communicatory optimalization. *Amer. Nat.* 114: 260—274

86. Herrera, C.M. (1982). Defense of ripe fruit from pests: its significance in relation to plant-disperser interactions. *Am. Nat.* 12: 218—241. (12.1.55)

87. Heurn, F.C. van (1937). Eerste registratie van de kudden olifanten die voorkomen op Sumatra's Oostkust, Westkust en Tapanoeli en van gegevens, die daarop betrekking hebben. *Ned. Comm. Intern. Natuurbesch. Med.* 11: 66—78.

88. Howe, H.F. (1980), Monkey dispersal and waste of a neotropical fruit. *Ecology* 61: 944—959. (12.1.72)

89. —————. (1981). dispersal of a neotropical nutmeg (*Virola sebifera*) by birds. *Auk* 98: 88—98. (12.1.71)

90. Howe, H.F. and Smallwood, J. (1982). Ecology of seed dispersal. *Ann. Rev. Ecol. Syst.* 13: 201—228. (12.1.54)

91. Howe, H.F. and Vande Kerckhove, G.A. (1980). Nutmeg dispersal by tropical birds. *Science* 210: 925—927. (12.1.51)

92. _____. (1981). Removal of wild nutmeg (*Virola surinamensis*) crops by birds. *Ecology* 62: 1093—1106. (12.1.52)

93. Hubback, T.R. (1939). The two-horned Asiatic rhinoceros (*Dicerorhinus sumatrensis*). *J. Bombay. nat. Hist. Soc.* 40: 594—617. (12.8.96)

94. _____. (1941). The Malay Elephant. *J. Bombay nat. Hist. Soc.* 42: 483—509. (12.8.97)

95. Huc, R. (1981). *Preliminary studies on pioneer trees in the dipterocarp forest of Sumatra.* **Unpublished report,** BIOTROP, Bogor. (12.10.104)

96. Huc, R. and Rosalina, U. (1981). *Chablis and primary dynamics in Sumatra.* Unpub. BIOTROP report, Bogor. (12.10.19)

97. Inger, R.F. (1969). Organization of communities of frogs along rain forest streams in Sarawak. *J. Anim. Ecol.* 38: 123—148. (12.6.16)

98. _____. (1980). Densities of floor dwelling frogs and lizards in lowland forests of Southeast Asia and Central America. *Am. Nat.* 115: 761—770. (12.6.17)

99. Inger, R.F. and Greenberg, B. (1966). Ecological and competitive relations among three species of frogs (Genus *Rana*). *Ecology* 45: 746—759. (12.6.15)

100. Jacobs, M. (1981). Review of *Rheophytes of the World* by C.G.G.J. van Steenis. *Flora Malesiana Bull.* 34: 3617—3620. (12.1.113)

101. Janos, D.P. (1980). Mycorrhizae influence tropical succession. *Biotropica (Trop. Succession Suppl.)* pp. 56—64. (12.1.62)

102. _____. (1980). Vesicular-arbuscular mycorrhizae affect lowland tropical rain forest plant growth. *Ecology* 61: 151—162. (12.1.57)

103. _____. (1983). Tropical mycorrhizas, nutrient cycles and plant growth. In *Tropical Rain Forest: Ecology and Management* (ed. S.L. Sutton, T.C. Whitmore and A.C. Chadwick), pp. 327—345. Blackwell, Oxford.

104. Janzen, D.H. (1970). Herbivores and the number of tree species in tropical forests. *Amer. Natur.* 104: 501—528. (12.10.119)

105. _____. (1973). Dissolution of mutualism between *Cecropia* and its *Azteca* ants. *Biotropica* 5: 15—28.

106. _____. (1974). Tropical blackwater rivers, animals and mast fruiting by the Dipterocarpaceae. *Biotropica* 6: 69—103. (12.10.59)

107. _____. (1975). *Ecology of Plants in the Tropics*. Edward Arnold, London. (12.1.93)

108. _____. (1976). Why tropical trees have rotten cores. *Biotropica* 8: 110. (12.1.125)

109. _____. (1977). Promising directions of study in tropical animal-plant interactions. *Ann. Missouri Bot. Gard.* 64: 706—736. (12.13.16)

110. _____. (1977). Why fruit rots, seeds mold and meat spoils. *Am. Nat.* 111: 691—713.

111. _____. (1978). Complications in interpreting the chemical defenses of trees against tropical arboreal plant-eating vertebrates. In *The Ecology of Arboreal Folivores* (ed. G.G. Montgomery), pp. 73—84. Smithsonian Institution, Washington, D.C. (12.1.63)

112. _____. (1978). A bat-generated fig seed shadow in rain forest. *Biotropica* 10: 121. (12.1.60)

113. _____. (1979). Why food rots. *Nat. Hist.* 88: 60—64. (12.13.13)

114. _____. (1979). How many babies do figs pay for babies? *Biotropica* 11: 48—50. (12.1.59)

115. _____. (1979). How many parents do the wasps from a fig have? *Biotropica* 11: 127—129. (12.4.35)

116. _____. (1979). How to be a fig. *Ann. Rev. Ecol. Syst.* 10: 13—51. (12.1.58)

117. _____. (1980). Specificity of seed-attacking beetles in a Costa Rican deciduous forest. *J. Ecol.* 68: 929—952. (12.4.34)

118. _____. (1981). The defenses of legumes against herbivores. In *Advances in Legumes Systematics* (ed R.M. Polhill and P.H. Raven), pp. 951—977. Royal Botanic Gardens, Kew. (12.1.68)

119. _____. (1981). Digestive seed predation by a Costa Rican Baird's tapir. *Biotropica (Reprod. Bot. Suppl.)*, pp. 59—63. (12.8.45)

120. _____. (1982). Variation in average seed size and fruit seediness in a fruit crop of a guanacaste tree (Leguminosae: *Enterolobium cyclocarpum*). *Amer. J. Bot.* 69: 1169—1178. (12.1.61)

121. _____. (1983). Food webs: who eats what, why, how and with what effects in a tropical forest? In *Tropical Rain Forest Ecosystems* (ed. F.B. Golley), pp. 167—182. Elsevier, Amsterdam. (12.13.14)

122. _____. (1983). Seed and pollen dispersal by animals: convergence in the ecology of contamination and sloppy harvest. *Biol. J. Linn. Soc.* 20: 103—113.

123. _____. (1983). Physiological ecology of fruits and their seeds. In *Physiological Plant Ecology III* (ed. O.L. Lange, P.S. Nobel, C.B. Osmond and H. Ziegler)', pp 625—655. Springer-Verlag, Berlin. (12.1.9)

124. Janzen, D.H., Miller, G.A., Hackforth-Jones, J., Pond, C.M., Hooper, K. and Janos, D.P. (1976). Two Costa Rican bat-generated seed shadows of *Andira inermis* (Leguminosae). *Ecology* 57: 1068—1075. (12.1.56)

125. Johns, A.D. (1982). Observations on nesting behaviour in the Rhinoceros hornbill, *Buceros rhinoceros*. *Malay. Nat. J.* 35: 173—177. (12.7.46)

126. Justessen, P.Th. (1922). Morphological and biological notes on *Rafflesia* flowers, observed in the highlands of mid-Sumatra (Padangsche Bovenlanden). *Ann. Jard. bot. Buitenzorg* 32: 64—87. (12.1.135)

127. Kartawinata, K., Rochadi, A. and Tukirin, P. (1981). Composition and structure of a lowland dipterocarp forest at Wanariset, East Kalimantan. *Malay. Forest.* 44: 397—406.

128. Kato, R., Tadaki, Y. and Ogawa, H. (1978). Plant biomass and growth increment studies in Pasoh forest. *Malay. Nat. J.* 30: 211—224. (12.10.76)

129. King, B., Woodcock, M. and Dickinson, E.C. (1975). *A Field Guide to the Birds of S.E. Asia*. Collins, London. (12.7.45)

130. Kira, T. (1978). Primary productivity of Pasoh Forest. *Malay Nat. J.* 30: 291—297. (12.10.75)

131. Koyama, H. (1978). Photosynthesis studies in Pasoh Forest. *Malay. Nat. J.* 30: 253—258. (12.10.74)

132. Kramer, F. (1933). De natuurlijke verjonging in het Goenoeng-Gegdeh-complex. *Tectona* 26: 155—185. (12.10.40)

133. Lahmann, E.J. and Zuniga, C.M. (1981). Use of spider threads as resting places by tropical insects. *J. Arachnol.* 9: 339—341. (12.4.42)

134. Langham, N.P.E. (1982). The ecology of the Common Tree Shrew *Tupaia glis* in peninsular Malaysia. *J. Zool.* 197: 323—344.

135. LBN (1983). *Laporan Teknis 1980—1982.* Lembaga Biologi Nasional, Bogor.

136. Leigh, E.G. (1975). Structure and climate in tropical rain forest. *Ann. Rev. Ecol. Syst.* 6: 67—86. (12.10.78)

137. Leighton, M. (1982). *Fruit Resources and Patterns of Feeding, Spacing and Grouping among Sympatric Bornean Hornbills.* Ph.D. thesis, University of California, Davis. (12.7.38)

138. Leighton, M. and Leighton, D.R. (1983). Vertebrate responses to fruit seasonality within a Bornean rain forest. In *Tropical Rain Forest Ecology and Management* (ed. S.L. Sutton, T.C. Whitmore and A.C. Chadwick), pp. 181—196. Blackwell, Oxford.

139. Lekagul. B. and McNeely, J.A. (1977). *The Mammals of Thailand.* Association for the Conservation of Wildlife, Bangkok. (12.8.21)

140. Liew, T.C. (1973). Occurrence of seeds in virgin forest top soil with particular reference to secondary species in Sabah. *Malay. Forester* 36: 185—193. (12.10.42).

141. Lim, M.T. (1978). Litterfall and mineral nutrient content of litter in Pasoh Forest Reserve. *Malay. Nat. J.* 30: 375—380. (12.10.79)

142. McClure, H.E. (1966). Flowering, fruiting and animals in the canopy of a tropical rain forest. *Malay. Forester* 29: 182—203. (12.10.116)

143. _____. (1967). The composition of mixed-species flocks in lowland and submontane forests of Malaya. *Wilson Bull.* 79: 131—154. (12.7.47).

330

144. _____. (1978). Some arthropods of the dipterocarp forest in Malaya. *Malay, Nat. J.* 32: 31—51. (12.4.43).

145. McKey, D. (1978). Soils, vegetation and seed eating by black colobus monkeys. In *The Ecology of Arboreal Folivores* (ed. S. Montgomery), pp. 423-437. Smithsonian Institution Press, Washington. (12.8.27).

146. McKey, D., Waterman, P.G., Mbi, C.N., Gartlan, J.S. and Struhsaker, T.T. (1978). Phenolic content of vegetaion in two African rain forests: ecological implications. *Science* 202: 61—64. (12.1.34).

147. MacKinnon, J.R. (1974). The behaviour and ecology of wild orang utans (*Pongo pygmaeus*). *Anim. Behav.* 22: 3—74. (12.8.53).

148. _____: (1977). A comparative ecology of Asian apes. *Primates* 18: 747—772. (12.8.61).

149. MacKinnon, J.R. and MacKinnon, K.S. (1980). Niche differentiation in a primate community. In *Malayan Forest Primates: Ten Years' Study in Tropical Rain Forest* (ed. D.J. Chivers), pp. 167—190. Plenum, New York. (12.8.25).

150. Maiorana, V.C. (1978). What kinds of plants do herbivores really prefer? *Amer. Nat.* 112: 631—635. (12.1.86).

151. _____. (1979). Non-toxic toxins: the energetics of coevolution. *Biol. J. Linn. Soc.* 11: 387—296. (12.13.23)

152. _____. (1981). Herbivory in sun and shade. *Biol. J. Linn. Soc.* 15: 151—156. (12.1.69).

153. Manokaran, N. (1978). Nutrient concentration in precipitation, through fall and stemflow in a lowland tropical rain forest in Peninsular Malaysia. *Malay. Nat. J.* 30: 423—432. (12.10.107)

154. _____: (1980). The nutrient contents of precipitation, through fall and stemflow in a lowland tropical rainforest in Peninsular Malaysia. *Malay Forester* 43: 266—289. (12.10.46).

155. Marsh, C.W. and Wilson, W.L. (1981). *A Survey of Primates in Peninsular Malaysian Forests*. University Kebangsaan Malaysia, Bangi. (12.8.9)

156. Matsumoto, T. (1976). The role of termites in an equatorial rain forest ecosystem of West Malysia I. Population density, biomass, carbon, nitrogen and calorific content and respiration rate. *Oecologia* 22: 153—178.

157. _____ (1978). The role of termites in the decomposition of leaf litter on the forest floor of Pasoh Study area. *Malay. Nat. J.* 30: 405—413. (12.4.45).

158. _____: (1978). Population density, biomass, nitrogen and carbon content, energy value and respiration rate of four species of termites in Pasoh forest Reserve. *Malay. Nat. J.* 30: 335—351. (12.4.44).

159. Medway, Lord (1969). The diurnal activity cycle among forest birds at Ulu Gombak. *Malay. Nat. J.* 22: 184—186. (12.7.29)

160. _____: (1972). Phenology of a tropical rain forest in Malaya. *Biol. J. Linn. Soc.* 4: 117—146. (12.10.81).

161. _____: (1974). Food of a tapir, *Tapirus indicus. Malay. Nat. J.* 28: 90—93. (12.8.52).

162. Medway, Lord and Wells, D.R. (1971). Diversity and density of birds and mammals at Kuala Lompat, Pahang, *Malay. Nat. J.* 24: 238—247. (12.13.19)

163. Meijer, W. (1958). A contribution to the taxonomy of *Rafflesia arnoldi* in West Sumatra. *Ann. Bogorienses* 3: 33—44 (12.1.108)

164. _____: (1974). *Field Guide to the Trees of West Malesia.* University of Kentucky Press, Kentucky.

165. _____: (1982). Plant refuges in the Indo-Malesia Region. In *Biological Diversification in the Tropics* (ed. G. Prance), pp. 576-584. Columbia University Press, New York. (23.6.10).

166. _____: (1982). *Provisional checklist of the flora of Mt. Sago near Payakumbuh - West Sumatra.* University of Kentucky, Kentucky. (12.10.79).

167. _____: (1983). Tentative key to the species of *Rafflesia.* Unpubl., University of Kentucky, Kentucky. (12.1.111).

168. _____. Personal communication.

169. Meijer, W. and Vangala, S. (1983). A bibliography of literature on Rafflesiaceae. University of Kentucky, Kentucky. (27.1.17).

170. Morton, E.S. (1978). Avian arboreal folivores: Why not? In *The Ecology of Arboreal Folivores*. (ed. G.G. Montgomery), pp. 123-130. Smithsonian Institution, Washington, D.C. (12.7.31).

171. Muul, I., and Lim, B.L. (1978). Comparative morphology, food habits and ecology of some Malaysian arboreal rodents. In *The Ecology of Arboreal Folivores*. (ed. G.G. Montgomery), pp. 361—368. Smithsonian Institution, Washingon, D.C. (12.8.59).

172. Nadkarni, N.M. (1981). Canopy roots: convergent evolution in rain forest nutrient cycles. *Science* 214: 1023-1024. (12.10.82).

173. Ng, F.S.P. (1980). Germination ecology of Malaysian woody plants. *Malay. Forester* 43: 406—437.

174. _____. (1983). Ecological principles of tropical lowland rain forest conservation. In *The Tropical Forest*. (ed. S.L. Sutton, T.C. Whitmore and A.C. Chadwick), pp. 359—375, Blackwell, Oxford.

175. Niemitz, C. (1979). Outline of the behaviour of *Tarsius bancanus*. In *The Study of Prosimian Behavior* (ed. G.A. Doyle and R.D. Martin), pp. 631-660, Academic, New York. (12.8.62).

177. Norrdwijk, M.A. von and Schaik, C.P. von (1983). A study concerning the relation between ecological and social factors and the behaviour of wild long-tailed macaques (*Macaca fascicularis*). Final Progress Report to LIPI, Jakarta. (12.8.105).

177. Noordwijk, M.A. van and Schaik, C.P.: In prep.

178. Oates, J.F., Swain, T. and Zantovska, J. (1977). Secondary compounds and food selection by colobus monkeys. *Biochem. Syst. Ecol.* 5: 317-321. (12.8.104).

179. Oates, J.F., Waterman, P.G. and Choo, G.M. (1980). Food selection by the South Indian leaf-monkey, *Prebytis johnii*, in relation to leaf chemistry. *Oecologia* 45: 45—56. (12.8.89).

333

180. Ogawa, H. (1978). Litter production and carbon cycling in Pasoh Forest. *Malay. Nat. J.* 30: 367—373. (12.10.106).

181. Ogawa, H., Yoda, K., Kira, T., Ogino, K., Shidei, T., Ratanawongse, D. and Apasutaya, C. (1965). Comparative ecological studies on three main types of forest vegetation in Thailand. II. Plant biomass. *Nature Life in S.E. Asia* 4: 49—80. (Referred to in Whitmore, 1975).

182. Oldeman, L.R., Las, I. and Darwis, S.N. (1979). An Agroclimatic Map of Sumatra. *Contr. Centr. Res. Inst. Agric. Bogor.* 52:1—35. (1.1.1).

183. Ogilvie, G.H. (1929). Bison eating bark. *J. Bombay nat. Hist. Soc.* 33: 706—707 (12.8.94).

184. Olivier, R.C.D. (1978). *On the Ecology of the Asian Elephant* Elephas maximus *with particular reference to Malaya and Sri Lanka.* Ph.D. thesis, University of Cambridge, Cambridge. (12.8.55).

185. _____: (1978). Distribution and status of the Asian elephant. *Oryx* 14: 379—424.

186. Palm, B.T. (1934). A *Mitrastemon* Rafflesiaceae from Sumatra. *Acta Horti. Gotoburgensis.* 9: 147—152.

187. Parkhurst, D.F. and Loucks, O.L. (1972). Optimal leaf size in relation to environment. *J. Ecol.* 60: 505—537. (12.1.116)

188. Payne, J.B. (1979). *Synecology of Malayan tree squirrels with special reference to the genus* Ratufa. Ph.D. thesis, University of Cambridge, Cambridge. (12.8.56)

189. _____: (1980). Competitors. In *Malayan Forest Primates: Ten Years' Study in Tropical Rain Forest* (ed. D.J. Chivers), pp. 261—277. Plenum, New York. (12.8.25)

190. Pearson, D.L. (1982). Historical factors and bird species richness. In *Biological Deversification in the Tropics.* (ed. G. Prance), pp. 441—452. Columbia University Press, New York. (12.7.39)

191. Pijl, L. van der (1937). Biological and physiological observations on the inflorescence of *Amorphophallus. Rec. trav. bot. neerl.* 34: 157—167. (12.1.106)

192. Pócs, T. (1982). Tropical forest bryophytes. In *Bryophyte Ecology* (ed. A.J.F. Smith), pp. 59—104. Chapman and Hall. London, (12.10.83)

193. Poore, M.E.D. (1968). Studies in Malaysian rain forest. I. The forest on triassic sediments in Jengka Forest Reserve. *J. Ecol.* 56: 143—196. (12.10.114)

194. Proctor, J., Anderson, J.M., Fogden, S.C.L. and Vallack, H.W. (1983). Ecological studies in four contrasting lowland rain forest in Gunung Mulu National Park, Sarawak. II. Litterfall, litter standing crop and preliminary observations on herbivory. *J. Ecol.* 71: 261—283. (12.10.21)

195. Putz, F.E. (1980). Lianas vs. trees. *Biotropica* 12: 224—225. (12.10.84)

196 Raemaekers, J.J. (1978). The sharing of food sources between two gibbon species in the wild. *Malay. Nat. J.* 31: 181—188. (12.8.53)

197. _____: (1979). Ecology of sympatric gibbons. *Folia primatol.* 31: 227—245. (12.8.54)

198. Raemaekers, J.J., Aldrich-Blake, F.P.G., and Payne, J.B. (1980). The forest. In *Malayan Forest Primates: Ten Years' Study in Tropical Rain Forest* (ed. D.J. Chivers), pp. 29—61. Plenum, New York. (12.8.25)

199. Rand, A.S. (1978). Reptilian arboreal folivores. In *The Ecology of Arboreal Folivores* (ed. G.G. Montgomery), pp. 115—122. Smithsonian Institution, Washington, D.C. (12.6.17)

200. Richards, D.G. and Wiley, R.H. (1980). Reverberations and amplitude fluctuations in the propagation of sound in a forest: implications for animal communication. *Am. Nat.* 115: 381—399. (12.13.33)

201. Richards, P.W. (1952). *The Tropical Rain Forest: An Ecological Study.* Cambridge University Press, Cambridge.

202. _____: (1983). The three-dimensional structure of tropical rain forest. In *Tropical Rain Forest: Ecology and Management* (ed. S.L. Sutton, T.C. Whitmore and A.C. Chadwick), pp. 287—309 Blackwell. Oxford.

203. Ricklefs, R.E. (1977). Environmental heterogeneity and plant species diversity: a hypothesis. *Amer. Nat.* 111: 376—381. (12.10.85)

204. Rijksen, H.D. (1978). *A Field Study on Sumatran Orang Utans* (Pongo pygmaeus abellii *Lesson 1827*). *Ecology, Behaviour and Conservation.* Veenman and Zonen, Wageningen. (12.8.88)

205. Robertson, J.M.Y. (1982). Behavioural ecology of *Macaca n. nemestrina.* Final progress report to LIPI. (12.8.90)

206. _____: Personal communication

207. Sakai, K.I., Budhiyono, B.E. and Iyama, S. (1979). Studies on pioneer trees and the pioneer index in tropical forest. Unpubl. report, BIOTROP, Bogor. (12.10.79)

208. Schemske, D.W. and Brokaw, N. (1981). Treefalls and the distribution of understory birds in a tropical forest. *Ecology* 62: 938—945. (12.7.22)

209. Setten, G.G.K. (1953). The incidence of buttressing among Malayan tree species when of commercial size. *Malay. Forester* 16: 219—221. (12.1.120)

210. Smith, A.P. (1972). Buttressing of tropical trees: a descriptive model and new hypotheses. *Am. Nat.* 106: 32—46. (12.1.122)

211. _____: (1979). Buttressing of tropical trees in relation to bark thickness in Dominica, B.W.I. *Biotropica* 11: 159—160. (12.1.47)

212. Steenis, C.G.G.J. van (1938). Exploraties in de Gajo-Landen. Algemeene resultaten der Löser Expeditie 1937. *Tijdschr. Kon. Ned. Aardr. Genootschap* 55: 728—801. (12.10.39)

213. _____: (1952). Rheophytes. *Proc. R. Soc. Queensland* 62: 61—68.

214. _____. (1978). Rheophytes in South Africa. *Bothalian* 12: 543—546.

215. Stephenson, A.G. (1981). Flower and fruit abortion: proximate causes and ultimate functions. *Ann. Rev. Ecol. Syst.* 12: 253—279. (12.1.48)

216. Strien, N.J. van (1974). *The Sumatran or Two-horned Asiatic Rhinoceros - A Study of Literature.* Veenman and Zonen, Wageningen. (12.8.95)

217. Symington, C.F. (1933). The study of secondary growth on rain forest sites in Malaya. *Malay. Forester* 2: 107—117. (12.10.118)

218. _____. (1943). *Foresters' Manual of Dipterocarps*. Malayan Forest Records No. 16. Republished by Penerbit Universiti Malaya, Kuala Lumpur, 1974. (12.1.110)

219. Thompson, K. (1977). Why organisms feed on the cores of tropical trees. *Biotropica* 9: 144. (12.1.124)

220. Tilson, R.L. (1977). Social behaviour of simakobu monkeys and its relationship to human predation. *J. Mammal.* 58: 202—212. (12.8.101)

221. Tilson, R.L. and Tenaza, R.R. (1976). Monogamy and duetting in an Old World monkey. *Nature* 263: 320—321. (12.8.100)

222. Voris, H.K. (1977). Comparison of herpetofaunal diversity in tree buttresses of evergreen tropical forests. *Herpetologica* 33: 375—380. (12.6.14)

223. Walker, J.R.L. (1975). *The Biology of Plant Phenolics*. Edward Arnold, London. (12.1.73)

224. Watanabe, K. (1981). Variation in group composition and population density of the two sympatric Mentawaian leaf-monkeys. *Primates* 22: 145—160. (12.8.70)

225. Waterman, P.G. (1983). Distribution of secondary metabolites in rain forest plants: toward an understanding of cause and effect. In *Tropical Rain Forest: Ecology and Management* (ed. S.L. Sutton, T.C. Whitmore and A.C. Chadwick), pp. 167—179. Blackwell, Oxford.

226. Waterman, P.G. and Choo, G.M. (1981). The effects of digestibility-reducing compounds in leaves on food selection by some Colobinae. *Malays. appl. Biol.* 10: 147—162.

227. Webb, L.J., Tracey, J.G. and Haydock, K.P. (1967). A factor toxic to seedlings of the same species associated with living roots of the non-gregarious sub-tropical rain forest tree *Grevillea robusta*. *J. appl. Ecol.* 4: 13—25. (12.1.127)

228. Wells, D.R. (1974). Resdident birds. In *Birds of the Malay Peninsula* (by Lord Medway and D.R. Wells). Witherby, London. (12.7.23)

229. _____. (1978). Numbers and biomass of insectivorous birds in the understory of rain forest at Pasoh Forest. *Malay. Nat. J.* 30: 353—362. (12.7.24)

230. West, K.L. (1979). The ecology and behaviour of the siamang *(Hylobates syndactylus)* in Sumatra. M.Sc. thesis, University of California, Davis. (12.8.69)

231. Wheelwright, N.T. and Orians, G.H. (1982). Seed dispersal by animals: contrasts with pollen dispersal, problems of terminology and constraints on coevolution. *Am. Nat.* 119: 402—423. (12.1.49)

232. Whitmore, T.C. (1973). Frequency and habitat of tree species in the rain forest of Ulu Kelantan. *Gdns' Bull. S'pore* 26: 195—210. (12.10.71)

233. _____. (1975). *Tropical Rain Forest of the Far East.* Clarendon, Oxford. (12.10.8)

234. _____. (1982). On pattern and process in forests. In *The Plant Community as a Working Mechanism* (ed. E.I. Newman), pp. 45—59. Blackwell, Oxford. (12.10.70)

235. Whitten, A.J. (1980). Arenga fruit as a food for gibbons. *Principes* 26: 143—146. (12.8.3)

236. _____. (1980). *The Kloss Gibbon in Siberut Rain Forest.* PhD. thesis, University of Cambridge, Cambridge. (12.8.60)

237. _____. (1981). Notes on the ecology of *Myrmecodia tuberosa* Jack on Siberut Island. *Ann. Bot.* 47: 525—526. (12.1.6)

238. _____. (1982). Diet and feeding behaviour of Kloss gibbons on Siberut Island, Indonesia. *Folia primatol.* 37: 177—208. (12.8.6)

239. _____. (1982). The ecology of singing in Kloss gibbons on Siberut Island, Indonesia. *Int. J. primatol.* 3: 33—51. (12.8.91)

240. _____. (1982). *The Gibbons of Siberut.* J.M. Dent, London. (12.13.3)

241. _____. (1982). Home range use by Kloss gibbons *(Hylobates klossii)* on Siberut Island, Indonesia. *Anim. Behav.* 30: 182—198. (12.8.7)

242. _____. (1982). A numerical analysis of tropical rain forest using floristic and structural data and its application to an analysis of gibbon ranging behaviour. *J. Ecol.* 70: 249—271. (12.10.19)

243. _____. (1982). The role of ants in selection of night trees. *Biotropica* 14: 237—238.
244. _____. Unpublished..
245. Whitten, A.J. and Whitten, J.E.J. (1982). Preliminary observations of the Mentawai macaque on Siberut Island, Indonesia. *Int. J. Primatol.* 3: 445—459. (12.8.93)
246. Whitten, J.E.J. (1979). *Ecological Isolation of an Indonesian Squirrel* (Sundasciurus lowii siberu). M. Phil. thesis, University of Cambridge, Cambridge. (12.8.61).
247. _____. (1980). Ecological separation of three diurnal squirrels in tropical rain forest on Siberut Island, Indonesia. *J. Zool. Lond.* 193: 405—420. (12.8.5)
248. Williams, K.D. (1979). Radio-tracking tapirs in the primary rain forest of West Malaysia. *Malay. Nat. J.* 32: 253—258. (12.8.39)
249. Williams, K.D. and Petrides, G.A. (1980). Browse utilization, feeding behaviour and management of the Malayan tapir in West Malaysia. *J. Wildl. Managt.* 44: 489—494.
250. Wilson, C.C. and Wilson, W.L. (1973). Census of Sumatran Primates. Final Report to LIPI, Jakarta. (12.8.40)
251. Wint, G.R.W. (1983). Leaf damage in tropical rain forest canopies. In *Tropical Rain Forest: Ecology and Management* (ed. S.L. Sutton, T.C. Whitmore and A.C. Chadwick), pp. 229—239. Blackwell, Oxford.
252. Wood, G.H.S. (1956). The dipterocarp flowering season in North Borneo, 1955. *Malay. Forester* 19: 193—201. (12.1.121)
253. Wood, T.G. (1978). The termite (Isoptera) fauna of Malesian and other tropical rainforests. In *The Abundance of Animals in Malesian Rain Forest* (ed. A.G. Marshall), pp. 113—132. University of Hull, Hull. (12.8.22)
254. Wratten, S.D., Goddard, P. and Edwards, P.J. (1981). British trees and insects: the role of palatability. *Amer. Nat.* 118: 916—919. (12.1.83)
255. WWF (Malaysia)/Payne, J.P. and Davies, A.G. (1981). *Faunal Survey of Sabah.* World Wildlife Fund (Malaysia), Kuala Lumpur. (12.13.29).
256. Wyatt-Smith, J. and Kochummen, K.M. (1979). Pocket check list of timber trees. *Malay. Forest Rec.* No. 17. (12.1.70)

257. Yoda, K. (1978). Organic carbon, nitrogen and mineral nutrients stock in the soil of Pasoh Forest. *Malay. Nat. J.* 30: 229—251. (23.4.13)

258. _____. (1978). Respiration studies in Pasoh forest plants. *Malay. Nat. J.* 30: 259—279. (12.1.50)

259. Yoda, K. and Kira, T. (1982). Accumulation of organic matter, carbon, nitrogen and other nutrients in the soil of a lowland rain forest at Pasoh, West Malaysia. *Jap. J. Ecol.* 32: 275—292.

260. Yoda, K. and Sato, H. (1975). Daily fluctuation of trunk diameter in tropical rain forest trees. *Jap. J. Ecol.* 23: 47—48.

261. Yoneda, T., Yoda, K. and Kira, T. (1978). Accumulation and decomposition of wood litter in Pasoh Forest. *Malay. Nat. J.* 30: 381—389. (12.10.72)

262. Young, A. (1976). *Tropical Soils and Soil Surveys.* Cambridge University Press, Cambridge. (23.4.16)

263. Young, A.M. (1981). Temporal selection for communicatory optimalization: the dawn-dusk chorus as an adaptation in tropical cicadas. *Am. Nat.* 117: 826—829. (12.4.32)

264. Baldwin, I.T. and Schultz, J.C. (1983). Rapid changes in three leaf chemistry induced by damage; evidence for communication between plants. *Science* 221: 277—279.

265. Hails, C.J. (1982). A comparison of tropical and temperate aerial insect abundance. *Biotropica* 14: 310—313.

266. Janzen, D.H. (1982) Dispersal of small seeds by big herbivores: foliage is the fruit. *Amer. Nat.* 123: 338—353.

267. Poniran, K. (1974) Elephants in Aceh. *Oryx* 12: 576—580.

268. Seindensticker, J. (in press). Large carnivores and the consequences of habitat insularization: ecology and conservation of tigers in Indonesia and Bangladesh. In *Proc. Intern. Cat Symp., Caesar Kleteny Wildlife Research Inst.,* Texas (ed. D.D. Everett and S.D. Miller). National Wildlife Federation, Washington, D.C.

269. Vitousek, P.M. (1984). Litterfall, nutrient cycling and nutrient limitation in tropical forests. *Ecology* 65: 285—298.

CHAPTER 8

UNCOMMON LOWLAND FORESTS

8.1 INTRODUCTION

In section 7.2.3 it was shown that lowland forests vary quite considerably in composition and three types are discussed individually below because they are so strikingly different. They are heath forest/padang vegetation, ironwood forest and forest on limestone. The first two types were investigated by a team from CRES and are discussed in detail below.

8.2 HEATH FOREST/PADANG VEGETATION

The only places where heath forest and padang vegetation can be found in Sumatra to any extent are on Bangka and Belitung Islands, but small areas also exist in parts of eastern Sumatra, the Lingga and Natuna Islands and Jemaja Island in the Anambas group [25, 38, 63, 64, 71, 72]. Heath forest is known by botanists as kerangas forest from an Iban (Sarawak) word which refers to forested land which, if cleared, would not grow rice. It has nothing to do with 'rengas' trees (e.g. *Gluta, Melanorrhoea*) although these may occasionally be found within the forest. Padang vegetation is often associated with heath forest and although its status as a completely natural vegetation type is still open to some debate (section 8.2.5) it is certainly a long-lasting and relatively stable secondary growth forming after heath forest is cut or burned.

8.2.1 Soil

Heath forest usually grows on soils derived from siliceous parent materials which are inherently poor in bases and commonly coarsely textured and free draining [7]. The soils in intact heath forest or under bushes in padangs have a covering of brownish-black, half-decomposed organic material. In the open padangs the surface is generally pure white sand about 0.5—5cm thick above a darker layer [7]. In the ecological literature the soils of both heath forests and padangs are called white-sand soils.

White-sand soils usually originate from ancient eroded sandstone beaches which were stranded due either to uplift of land or fall of sea level. If conditions are suitable for soil development, a hard iron-rich layer (podzol pan) forms a metre or so below the soil surface [7]. One of the first descriptions of a tropical podzol was by Hardon from a padang soil on Bangka Island (Table 8.1) [30]. The hard iron pan can cause temporary

Table 8.1 Description of a podzol from Bangka Island. (From Hardon [30]).

Horizon	Depth	pH	Description
A_0	0—10 cm	2.7	Black cover of half-decomposed organic material intermixed with coarse quartz sand.
A_1	10—25 cm	3.9	Loose greyish-black humic quartz sandy layer.
A_2	25—40 cm	6.1	Loose greyish-white quartz sandy layer.
B_1	40—70 cm	3.9	Dark brown very compact quartz sandy hardpan.
B_2	70—100 cm	4.6	Loose light brown quartz sandy layer.

waterlogging of the soil after heavy rain before the water is able to drain away.

The 'A-horizon' soils have a very high percentage of sand and only about 1% of clay [30]. This leads to high porosity, rapid leaching, and low ion retention properties so that white-sand soils are probably among the most nutrient-poor soils in the world [51]. Analyses of soils from a Sarawak heath forest are also given by Proctor et al [54] and Richards [56].

8.2.2 Drainage water

The water draining from heath forest is generally a blackwater (see section 5.3). A water sample taken from a small stream flowing out of the heath forst visited by the CRES team was very acid' (pH 4—4.5) and had low nutrient levels (2 ppm nitrogen, 1 ppm potasium and 1 ppm phosphorus). These results are characteristic of heath forest water [78]. A study of white-sand soils in the Rio Negro region of Amazonia concluded that, apart from iron, the concentration of nutrients in the river water draining from them was the same as the region's rainwater. This suggests that there are no nutrients being weathered from the parent material [70]. The ecological aspects of blackwaters in peatswamp areas described in section 5.5, 5.6, are all relevant to drainage water for heath forests/padang vegetation.

8.2.3 Vegetation

a) Heath forest

No detailed survey of heath forest ever seems to have been conducted on Bangka or Belitung Island and therefore much of the following is taken from studies conducted in Sarawak and Brunei. Heath forest can be strikingly different in its floral components and structure from usual lowland dipterocarp forest and it can itself show considerable variation [16,64]. In normal lowland forest, fresh, green-coloured vegetation evenly and loosely fills the space from the floor to the multi-layered canopy, whereas in heath forest a low, uniform single-storey canopy seems to be formed predominantly by crowns of large saplings and small 'pole' trees [4]. These sometimes form such dense vegetation that walking can be difficult. For example, in East Kalimantan forest, 454—750 trees of 10 cm diameter at breast height and over were found per ha [57,58]. Brown and reddish colours are common in the foliage of the upper part of the canopy [4]. Many of the tree species have thick leaves (section 9.4.2). The medium leaf thickness of twelve tree species measured by the CRES team was 0.25 mm (range 0.10—0.45 mm).

Trees of large girth or with buttresses, and large woody climbers are very rare. Palms are also found but the CRES team found several Giant mountain rattans *Plectocomia elongata*, a species which, as the name suggests, is normally found on mountains where the soils are also poor [77] (section 9.3). Thin, small climbers may be quite comon as may epiphytes, several of which have associations with ants or catch small insects. The ground flora is sparse and frequently consists of mosses and liverworts. The number of tree species is relatively low. Proctor *et al.* found 123 species in a 1 ha plot in Sarawak compared with 214 species in a 1 ha plot in nearby dipterocarp forest [54]. However, a total of 849 species from 428 genera are reported from the heath forests of Sarawak and Brunei [16].

Many of these features of heath forest vegetation have parallels in mountain and peatswamp vegetation, which also grow on poor, acid soils (section 5.3, 9.3). The similarities with peatswamp forests are particularly striking as many of the tree species are the same. In Figure 5.3 (section 5.4.1), the four types of peatswamp forest in Sarawak have, from tallest to shortest repectively, 27, 55, 54, and 70% of their species also recorded from heath forest [78].

Various aspects of heath forest suggest it is restricted in its productivity by the low nutrient content of the soil. First, heath forest generally has a lower biomass than lowland forests on usual latosols. For example, Proctor *et al.* calculated the above-ground biomass of heath forest in Sarawak to be 470 t/ha (dry weight) compared with 650 t/ha in nearby dipterocarp forest. These are probably both heavier than average for their type [53]. The basal area of trees in an East Kalimantan heath forest was 6.4—16.9 m^2/ha [57, 58] compared with 25—30 m^2/ha in a normal lowland forest. The heath forest examined by a CRES at Padang Kekurai, Bangka, had a basal area of 13.5 m^2/ha for trees of 15cm diameter and over. Second, plants with supplementary means of mineral nutrition are common, e.g. myrmecophytes and insectivorous plants [33, 34]. Third, heath forest is easily degraded into padang if burned or abandoned after brief cultivation; that is, heath forest does not seem to regenerate. This may be because the nutrient level of the soil has gone below some critical level for full regeneration. While the heath forest is intact, nutrients from the detritus are recycled into the vegetation efficiently by the plant's roots.

The small litterfall (leaves and small wood) in the plot of heath forest examined by Proctor *et al.* was relatively low in its concentration of nitrogen and this may be due to the very low soil pH which could limit the mineralization of the organic nitrogen [53]. They suggest that the small leaves typical of heath forest trees are likely to be an adaptation to low nitrogen levels but the mechanism of this adaptation is not explained. The leaf thickening had earlier been explained as an adaptation to periodic drought as well as to low levels of soil nutrients [15, 78]. Experiments by Peace and MacDonald have, however, shown that the heath forest species they examined had no special ability to avoid or resist desiccation [52]. However, if features of heath forest such as the relatively even canopy, and the small, often slanting and reflective leaves are seen as adaptations to reduce water loss, then the roots would not have to cope with such large volumes of water containing potentially toxic hydrogen ions (very acid soils have high concentrations of hydrogen ions) and phenolic compounds. Phenolic compounds can significantly inhibit the uptake of ions by certain crops [26, 27], and occur in high concentrations in heath forest leaves (section 8.4).

b) Padang vegetation

Padang is a shrubby vegetation in which the tallest trees usually reach only about 5 m, but trees reaching 25 m are not unknown. Plants from padangs on Bangka and Belitung have been collected by several botanists [63]. In the padang (Padang Kekurai) examined by the CRES team, the dominant small trees was Baeckia frutescens and Melaleuca cajuputih, but Calophyllum sp., Garcinia sp. and Syzygium sp. were quite common. The most notable absences were of trees normally common as colonizers of open groud such as Macaranga spp., Mallotus spp. and Melastoma spp. Bare patches of white sand were frequent and these were often bordered by the sedges Fimbristylus sp. Rhyncospora sp., Xyris microcephala, and Xyris sp., the lily Dianella and the bush Rhodomyrtus tomentosa was also locally common. Pitcher plants Nepenthes sp. were abundant and Valeton also records the presence in the damper parts of Bangka padangs of the small insectivorous plant Drosera burmanii [71]. The climbing epiphyte Dischidia sp. covered the lower trunks of some of the larger trees. This plant has yellowish leaves shaped like wrinkled inverted saucers. When the plant is pulled off a tree and the underside examined, numerous ants are found sheltering beneath the leaves which also cover the plant's roots. This mutualistic association is similar to that found in Myrmecodia (Figure 8.1) and Hydnophytum [33, 34] (both of which are also found in heath forests) with the plant providing

Figure 8.1 *Myrmecodia tuberosa*

protection and the ants supplying nutrients in the form of waste food, faeces and dead ants.

The leaf thickness of ten plant species were measured and the median value was 0.30 mm (range 0.25—0.70), thicker than leaves in normal lowland forest indicating an impoverished soil (section 9.4.2).

Padang has been regarded as degraded heath forest caused by fire or felling [35, 78], and as a natural ecosystem in its own right growing on extremely impoverished soils [43, 62]. The former is certainly true but it does not necessarily follow from that that the latter is false. Padang is very slow growing [58]. Janzen mentions 1-2 m of plant growth in 30 years on the padang at Bako National Park, Sarawak, and it seems unable to regenerate back into heath forest [35] (section 11.10.1). Decomposition of dead plant material (burned stumps, etc.) is also very slow and it is possible that a padang formed many decades (or even centuries) ago might show no signs of its heath-forest past. Kartawinata reports having found charcoal 50 cm below the soil surface in a heath forest in East Kalimantan [38]. This may indicate that heath forest regenerated from a padang vegetation formed by fire but the depth of the charcoal show that the fire was clearly a very long time ago.

From the work of Brunig, Specht and Womersley counted 83 plant species that had been recorded from padangs in Sarawak and Brunei, and 48 of these were *not* found in heath forest [62].

8.2.4 Fauna

Animals in heath forest and padang vegetation face very similar problems to those in peatswamp forest. Poor soils cause low productivity which causes plants to defend their edible parts with toxic or digestion-inhibiting compounds to make themselves unattractive to herbivorous animals [35]. Not only that, but the nutritive value of the vegetation can be less on white-sand soils than on normal soil. Hardon analysed the chemical composition of leaves of two species of plant, one set from padangs on Bangka Island and another from specimens growing at the Botanic Gardens in Bogor on an andesitic laterite soil [30]. The results are shown in Table 8.2. Low nutrient levels were also found in leaves of heath forest trees by Pearce and MacDonald [52].

Table 8.2 Nutrient levels in leaves from two plant species, one set grown on poor soils on Bangka Island, and the other set grown of fertile soils at the Botanic Gardens in Bogor. (From Hardon [30]).

	Dacrydium elatum		Rhodomyrtus tomentosa	
	Padang, Bangka Island	Botanic Gardens, Bogor	Padang, Bangka Island	Botanic Gardens, Bogor
ash	2.16	7.59	2.58	3.70
CaO	0.59	3.43	0,13	0.58
MgO	0.33	0.69	0.21	0.35
K_2O	0.52	0.57	0.36	0.50
Na_2O	0.08	0.05	0.24	0.14
MnO	0.02	0.15	0.07	0.45
P_2O_5	0.10	0.15	0.07	0.45

In view of the above it is hardly surprising that animal communities are considerably reduced in heath forest and padang vegetation. Wallace describes a visit to the port of Muntok on Bangka in 1861 and writes, "A few walks into the country showed me that it was very hilly and full of granite and lateritic rocks with a dry and stunted vegetation; and I could find very few insects" [75]. Janzen describes his intensive, but barely successful attempt to find vertebrates and invertebrates using baits and direct observations in the heath forests/padangs of Bako National Park, Sarawak, and writes that "the absence of bird calls was deafening" [35]. In the same area, Harrison estimated there was only one mammal per 2 ha and one bird per 0.4 ha [31]. The results of collecting frogs, lizards and snakes in three forest types is shown in Table 8.3. Heath forest had less than half the number of species found in the other forest types [46]. Similarly, in a comparison of a number of forest types at Mulu, Sarawak, heath forest had the smallest number of dung beetles (Scarabaeidae) [29].

Table 8.3 The number of different types of reptiles in three types of forest (After Lloyd *et al.* [45]).

	Frogs	Lizard	Snakes	Tortoises	Total
Heath forest	24	13	13	0	50
Alluvial forest	33	33	38	2	106
Hill forest	53	31	35	1	120

From what was written about the effects of nutrient-poor soils on the chemical defences of tree leaves in peatswamp forest (section 5.5), it would be reasonable to expect similar strategies to reduce the impact of herbivores in heath forest. Only two studies are known that have compared the levels of phenolic compounds in leaves between a forest growing on acid, nutrient-poor white-sand (heath forest) soil and a forest growing on more usual soil. In the first study, McKey showed that there was approximately twice the concentration of phenolic compounds in the leaves of trees growing on the white-sand soils. Monkeys living in forest on usual soils ate a wide range of leaves, whereas those living in the forest on white-sand soils avoided almost all the leaves expect the most nutritious ones where the benefit of eating a good source of food was greater than the cost of ingesting defence compounds [45, 48]. Although no sweeping generalizations should be made from the results of a single study, there is reason to suppose that the acute lack of animals in heath forest in Sumatra and adjacent regions is at least partly due to higher than normal concentrations of toxic phenolic and other defence compounds. The second study found that the mean value of total phenols in oven-dry heath foest leaf litter was 2.49 mg/100g, compared with 1.68 mg/100g in nearby dipterocarp forest [53]. It might be expected, then, that consumption of the heath forest leaves would be relatively low. In fact, the percent of leaf area missing from fallen leaves (22% with no damage, 50% with 20% damage, 15% with 20—40% damage) was similar to that found in the other three forest types examined [53]. This does not, however, necessarily negate the hypotheses of Janzen [35] because although leaves may fall after the same approximate degree of destruction, the *rate* of destruction of heath forest leaves may be much lower. Data are not yet available to examine this.

Leaf samples from padang and heath forest were collected by the CRES team but the results of the chemical analyses are not yet available.

Fauna of pitcher plants

Pitcher plants provide an excellent example of an ecological microcosm. It is well-known that insects are lured into the pitchers where they slip on the smooth, waxy lip and drown in the pool of water held in the bottom of the pitcher. Glands inside the pitcher secrete digestive enzymes and so the nutrients from the corpses are available to the plant although the mechanism of uptake has yet to be established.

It is less well-known, however, that the water inside a pitcher supports a community of insect larvae and other organisms which are resistant to the digestive enzymes. Most of these animals feed directly on the drowned insects or feed indirectly on them by being predators on bacteria and other microorganisms which have themselves fed on the corpses. Since many of these species spend only the early part of their life cycle inside pitchers, they represent an export of nutrients which would otherwise have been used by the plant [6, 7].

Thienemann documented the fauna of pitcher plants in Sumatra [66, 67] but the only study to consider the ecology of these unlikely communities is by Beaver who worked on Penang Island. In the three species of pitcher plants examined (*Nepenthes albomarginata, N. ampullaria* and *N. gracilis*) he found 25 species of insect and three species of arachnid. The predominant family was Culicidae or true mosquitoes, but eight other families of flies (order Diptera) were found as well as representatives of the Hymenoptera (bees, wasps, ants), Lepidoptera (butterflies and moths), Araneae (spiders) and Acari (mites). Bacteria, protozoans, rotifers, nematode worms, oligochaete worms and crustaceans are also known from pitcher plants but these occur most frequently in old pitchers which have been deserted by insects and arachnids. These old pitchers no longer attract prey and so the input of nutrients is low and population levels of these microorganisms can never become high. Microorganisms are probably infrequent in younger, attractive pitchers because of the filter-feeding activities of some mosquito larvae. A negative correlation between protozoa and mosquito larvae in such habitats in north America was shown by Addicott [1].

The fauna of pitcher plants can be divided into three groups using terms coined by Thienemann according to the frequency of use of pitchers [66]. Nepenthebiont species normally live *only* in pithers and these account for 66% of the pitcher fauna found in Peninsular Malaysia and Singapore [6]. A few species are considered nepenthephils because they are common in pitchers but are frequently found in other habitats, and other species are called nepenthexene. This last group occur in pitcher plants but are far more often found elsewhere. One such nepenthexene mosquite, *Aedes albopictus,* is the only medically important insect to have been found in pitchers.

The fauna of pitchers occupy a range of feeding and spatial niches. The drowned animals in the pitcher fluid are fed upon directly by the larvae of certain Diptera, the larger species of which generally only tolerate a single individual because of aggressive competition for limited food supply. Mosquito larvae generally feed by filtering the microorganisms from the pitcher fluid, but some will also browse over the surface of the corpses ingesting loosened particles. At the very bottom of the pitcher, finely divided detritus from the remains of animals and plants accumulate and this is fed upon by the larvae of biting midges (Ceratopogonidae) and by mites. The pitcher fluid is also inhabited by insect predators such as a predatory mosquito larva which preys on other mosquito larvae; because of its large size, only one is found per pitcher. Above the fluid, a thomisiid spider (Figure

8.2) waits, and the predatory larva of a mycetophilid fly spins a web, to intercept insects falling from the pitcher rim as well as adult insects emerging from the pitcher after developing in the fluid (Figure 8.3). Finally, small encyrtid and diapriid parastic wasps lay eggs in the pupae of phorid flies

Figure 8.2 A vertical section of a pitcher showing a thomasiid spider waiting for its prey. The round marks below it are glands on the inside of the pitcher wall from which digestive enzymes are secreted.

Figure 8.3 A horizontal cross-section of a pitcher showing the web of a mycethophilid fly larva.

(Figure 8.4).A simplified food web for the community in two species of pitcher plants is shown in Figure 8.5.

Figure 8.4 A phorid fly larvae of which are parasitized by small wasps in pitchers. Phorids are peculiar flies in that most species are virtually wingless and most are less than 1 mm long (After Mani [49]).

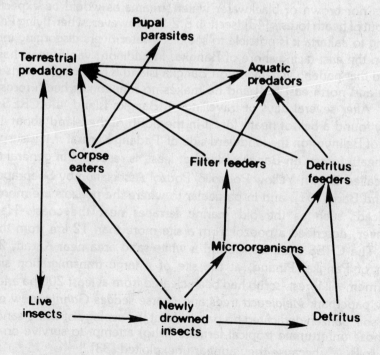

Figure 8.5 A simplified food web of the community living in a pitcher, showing the functional groups. (After Beaver [8]).

8.2.5 Distribution of heath forest on Bangka and Belitung Islands

It has been suggested or implied that the natural vegetation for the majority of Bangka and Belitung Islands would have been heath forest [23]. This may not be the case. Berkhout [11] and de Leeuw [45] described the forests and general situation of Bangka Island but make no mention of a forest like heath forest, nor of species that would be especially expected from heath forest or padang. Instead they describe the conventional dipterocarp forests that today clothe only the hills. Descriptions of birds [5], fishes [11] and snakes [77] from Bangka and Belitung Islands make no mention of an unusual forest type nor give any hint that the fauna was poor in species. Heath forests are notoriously poor in species (see section 8.2.4). Kostermans spent six months collecting botanical specimens primarily in the south of Bangka Island and found areas of padang but no heath forests nor brown or blackwater water streams as would be expected to flow out of heath forests [43] (section 8.2.2). However, when flying Pangkal Pinang to Jakarta it is possible to see blackwater rivers disgorging into the sea on the east-facing shore of Bangka. In addition, van Steenis has suggested that padang vegetation on Bangka Island is restricted to parts of the north and north-east [53] and he makes no mention of heath forest.

After several days of travelling on Bangka Island, the CRES team finally found a belt of heath forest in the north of the island about 10 km N.E. of Belinyu, on the landward side of 'Padang Kerurai'.[1] It is suspected that heath forest, on Bangka Island at least, is restricted in general to the soils called Brown Yellow Podzolic/Podzol Association by Soepraptohardjo and Barus [61], and in particular to where the podzols are more pronounced, such as the old marine terraces near the coast. Hardon, however, described a podzol from a site more than 12 km from the sea [30]. The CRES team also found a white-sand area near Kurau, 25 km south of Pangkal Pinang, at the site of a large transmigration site for fishermen. All forest/scrub had been cleared from at least 200 ha and only a few paperbark Melaleuca trees and coarse sedges Gahnia grew on the poor soil. Janzen dedicated his paper about the ecology of white-sand soils to "those unfortunate tropical farmers (who) attempt to survive on white sand soils . . . because they appear unexploited [33]."

---

1. Maps (1:50,000) redrawn in 1945 from older Dutch maps were made available to the CRES team by the Head, Bureau of Ecology and Land Affairs, Bangka Tin Mining Unit.

353

In inland areas of Bangka Island which are also shown on maps as having Brown Yellow Podzolic/Podzol Assocation soils and being over old sandstone parent material (e.g. around Poding and Petaling) small rubber plantations and fruit orchards are common. Large areas are used for pepper and this suggests the capability of the land is limited but not critical. In the descriptions of typical heath forest/padang soils, however, it is suggested that they are virtually unusable for permanent agriculture. This suggests that heath forest would not necessarily have covered these flat or undulating inland areas.

It is interesting that in the form of the Melayu language spoken on Bangka Island, the word 'ngarangas' (similar to kerangas) is used to describe the dead and dying trees around the tin tailings. It is possible that ngarangas used to refer to heath forest.

The present area of intact or partially disturbed heath forest is not known but it is probably much less than that estimated by FAO/MacKinnon [23]. *It is probably Sumatra's most endangered ecosystem,* and a thorough survey should be undertaken as soon as possible.

8.3 IRONWOOD FOREST

8.3.1 Introduction

Ironwood forest in Sumatra is of special interest because of its extremely low diversty of tree species, being dominated by the ironwood *Eusideroxylon zwageri.* The ecological interest centres on its apparently stable state despite its species-poor composition.

8.3.2 The Tree

Ironwood is a member of the laurel family (Lauraceae) and is distributed through Sumatra, Kalimantan, and southern Philippines. There used to be two members of the genus *Eusideroxylon* but the one called *melagangai* has recently been moved to its own genus *Potoxylon* by Kostermans [42]. Ironwood is a large tree (50 m tall and 2.20m diameter at breast height) with a warm red-brown bark, large leaves and heavy (± 300 g) fruits. Its timber is economically very valuable because of its strength and durability - it can resist rotting for up to eight years when in constant contact with wet soil, or decades in dryer conditions [40, 58, 65]. It is used for bridges, piers, road foundations, floors and, of course, the popular 'sirap' roofing tiles.

Ironwood seems to be restricted to southern Sumatra, having been found in Jambi, South Sumatra, and Bangka and Belitung Islands [21, 28, 41, 60], but its range has been greatly reduced by the heavy demand for its timber. It has been shown that ironwood could be an important plantation species and guidelines for its cultivation have been proposed [41]. Commercial germination of seeds and growth of seedlings can be quite successful if conducted in moist, shady places such as beneath secondary growth with a closed canopy [41, 68]. The main threat appears to be a certain amount of predation of the seeds by porcupines (section 8.3.6).

A characteristic feature of ironwood is that, when felled, numerous coppice shoots grow from its base. If cut carefully these can be used for plantation stock and Beekman found that these shoots grew faster than seedlings [9].

8.3.3 The forest

Ironwood forest can vary from forest in which it is virtually the only species of large tree present to forest in which it is one of many species but clearly the most dominant one. An example of the former was investigated by a team from CRES in Rimbo Kulim[2] near the River Kahidupan, north of Muara Tembesi in Jambi. It was difficult to find a patch of unexploited forest but eventually sufficient was found to enumerate 0.5 ha (10 × 500 m) of undisturbed forest. A total of 84 trees of 15cm diameter at breast height were found and 81 (96%) of these were ironwood (Figure 8.6). Two of the remainder were unidentified small trees, and the other was a large specimen of *Koompasia* sp. The Simpson Index of species diversity (section 7.1.1) for this situation is only 0.07. As many as 33 ironwood trees of 20cm diameter and over can be present per hectare in Kalimantan [44]. The equivalent figure for the forest examined by the CRES team was 126 indicating a perhaps unusual richness.

---

2. 'Kulim' is the local name for *Scorodocarpus borneensis* [2]. This also grows naturally in species-poor stand but because of its value, there are only a few damaged skeletons of it left north of Muara Tembesi.

355

Figure 8.6 Relative abundances of tree species (n = 84) at Rimbo Kulim, Muara Tembesi, Jambi. 96% of the sample comprises ironwood *Eusideroxylon zwageri*. Data collected by a CRES team.

When inside the forest at Rimbo Kulim it is not immediately obvious that the forest is species-poor because there is wide range of tree sizes. It is quite unlike, for example, being in a mangrove forest where the vegetation within a zone is relatively homogenous. The distribution of trunk diameters for ironwood trees at Rimbo Kulim is shown in Figure 8.7. The undergrowth consists of many ironwood seedlings as well as small palms (*Pinanga* sp. and *Licuala* sp.) and the tall palm *Livistona* sp.

The ironwood forest examined by Suselo was not far from Rimbo Kulim and was also dominated by ironwood, but it was only one of 37 tree species in his plot of 0.2 ha [65]; He found 65 trees of 10cm diameter or more but only 17 (26%) were ironwood (Figure 8.8). (A similar percentage was found in a nearby plot [24].) Ironwood, however, formed the main canopy of the forest. In ironwood forest examined by Greeser, *Koompasia*, *Shorea* or *Intsia* were the main emergents and ironwood was

Figure 8.7 The distribution of different diameter classes among the ironwood trees at Rimbo Kulim, Muara Tembesi, Jambi. Data collected by a CRES team.

a subdominant species [28].

In other areas where ironwood grows, such as Bangka Island, it can occur in mixed dipterocarp forests as just an occasional species.

8.3.4 Soils and topography

Witkamp considered that ironwood was generally restricted to sandy soils of Tertiary origins [82]. The ironwood forest examined by Suselo was, however, on a clay-loam (for the top 20cm) and on clay below that [65]. The soil analysis for three samples taken at Rimbo Kulim is shown in Table 8.4, and reveals a sandy silt loam (but close to a clay loam) top soil with clay below that. The soil is moderately acid with quite high carbon but a moderate C/N ratio. The soil contains very low concentrations of phosphorus, sodium and magnesium but a fairly high concentration of potassium. The total exchangeable bases are very low and the cation

357

Figure 8.8 Relative abundances of tree species (n = 65) at the forest
examined at Dusun Aro, Jambi. (Based on data from Suselo,
[69]). a- *Eusideroxylon zwageri*, b- *Hydnocarpus polypetala*, c-
Aglaia sp., d- *Dysoxylon* sp., e- *Diospyros* sp, f- *Ixonanthes icosan-
dra*, g-*Knema* sp., h- 23 other species.

exchange capacity quite high. These soil structures are summarized in
Figure 8.9.

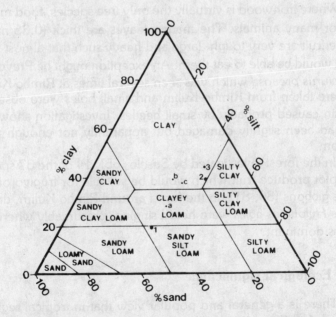

Figure 8.9 The structure of soils under two ironwood forests in Jambi.
Rimbo Kulim soil: 1 — 1-3 cm, —2 — 5-10 cm, 3 — 10-15
cm (soil collected by CRES team). Dusun Aro soil: a - 1—5 cm,
b - 20—30 cm (data from Suselo [69]).

The distribution of ironwood forests shown in Figure 1.10 (section 1.4.2) coincides with areas of red-yellow pozolic soils on folded sedimentary rock shown on the map in BPPP/Soepraptohardjo *et al.* [12]. There are, however, areas with the same soil characteristics in the same climatic zone where ironwood is known not to dominate the forests. Various authors have commented on ironwood's preference for slightly undulating topography but the cause of any such limitation has not been established.

8.3.5 Fauna

Nothing seems to have been written on the fauna of ironwood forest. The birds seen during the CRES visit to Rimbo Kulim seemed similar in diversity and number to those in normal dipterocarp forest. Two groups of the unnamed black and white subspecies of leaf monkey *Presbytis melalophos* (section 1.6.3) were seen but were not observed to feed. Where ironwood is virtually the only tree species, food may be a problem for many animals. The mature leaves are thick (0.35 mm), coarse and the fruit are very tough, large and heavy such that almost no arboreal animal would be able to eat them. An exception might be Prevost's squirrel *Callosciurus prevosti* which was seen several times at Rimbo Kulim. A few fruit were taken from Rimbo Kulim and small holes were observed in the fruit skin caused probably by small beetles. Investigation showed that the seed had been slightly damaged but apparently not enough to halt germination.

In the forest investigated by Suselo [65], 14 of the 37 species found in the plot produce fruit which would be suitable for frugivorous primates such as gibbons [80, 81]. In the forest around Rimbo Kulim, dark-handed gibbons *Hylobates agilis* were heard singing, presumably where ironwood was less dominant.

8.3.6 Ecological significance

There is a general and popular view that in tropical regions where climate and soils are favourable for plant growth, high species diversity in natural ecosystems is the rule is necessary for ecological stability. In section 2.3.1 it was shown that mangroves do not conform to this preconception, and it would seem that the same applies to certain ironwood forests. Indeed, the former ecological tenet of ecosystem complexity leading to stability has been called into question and this is discussed by Pimm [84].

In section 7.4.1. the strategy of gregarious fruiting was described for the dominant, large dipterocarps which at their canopy level at least, form species-poor stands. Janzen suggests that a second type of strategy common in species which occur at relatively high densities, is the production of large and toxic seeds on a more or less continuous basis [35]. Some mangrove species fall into this category and so, apparently, does ironwood. Koopman and Verhoef describe the flowering of ironwood as irregular but with a peak around the middle or end of the dry season [41]. Ripe fruits are found approximately three months after flowering. The results of analyses of ironwood seeds collected by the CRES team are not yet available but the very large numbers of seeds found on the ground, and the very large numbers of seedlings under parent trees (Suselo found 920 saplings per ha [65]) is indicative of very little seed predation. Porcupine damage of ironwood seed-beds mentioned in section 8.3.2 has not been described in detail but it is conceivable that only parts of the seed were eaten and, like the monkeys described eating leaves from trees growing on white-sand soils (section 8.2.4), the benefits of eating a highly nutritious item of food may exceed the costs of ingesting defence compounds. In any case, porcupine damage of seeds in natural situations does not seem to have much effect.

The CRES team also collected leaves but again the analysis results are not yet available. However, their feel suggests a high concentration of fibre (lignin) and the timber itself must be defended very effectively against insect attack for it to be so exceptionally durable. The ecology of a leguminous tree called Mora has recently been studied in Trinidad where it accounts for 40—60% of trees in the forests where it is found. Most of what Janzen proposed as theory for such trees, as described above, fits for Mora. It suffers very little seed predation in comparison with other trees around it. Its major seed predator is a large rat-like rodent Oryzomys but the seeds are generally less than one-third eaten. Indeed, this damage is usually confined to the surface of the cotyledons and the seeds were still able to germinate [55]. It is possible that Mora seeds, and also those of ironwood, are protected by lectins, a group of glycoproteins which are sticky and act as digestion inhibitors. Lectins are very strongly selected against by rodents [36] and this may be the reason porcupines do not do more damage to the abundant ironwood seed crop.

Species-poor ironwood forests would make ideal study areas to try to unravel the reasons why such abundant trees are not exploited or controlled by herbivores. Species-rich forests are incredibly complex and any ecological investigation confronts numerous confounding variables. Ironwood forests have some of these variables controlled and if an understanding of the ironwood ecosystem can be achieved then attempts to understand species-rich forests are more likely to succeed.

Unfortunately, licences continue to be granted for the exploitation of ironwood trees and so it seems that the time remaining to make a thorough investigation of the exceptional forests of Sumatra is severely limited.

8.4 FOREST ON LIMESTONE

8.4.1 Introduction

Sumatra has numerous limestone areas although few exceed ten square kilometers in area (Figure 8.10). Limestone forms a characteristic landscape called karst which occurs in two forms, cockpit (or labyrinth) karst and tower karst, both of which are found in Sumatra. Cockpit karst such as at Lho'Nga, North Aceh, and in the hills near Payakumbuh has a regular series of conical of hemispherical hills and hollows with moderately steep sides (30—40°C). Tower karst such as is found in the river plants near Payakumbuh consists of low (± 300 m) isolated hills with precipitous sides (60—90°) and often riddled with caves, separated by flat depressions [37, 73]. The surface of the limestone may be either rocky or covered with intricately scluptured, razor-sharp pinnacles as at Lho'Nga.

8.4.2 Soils

On moderate limestone slopes and hollows, brownish-red latosols would be expected to be formed which are clay-rich and leached. As might be predicted from the parent material, the soils are often richer in bases, particularly calcium and magnesium, with a higher cation exchange capacity than oils in similar situations but on other parent materials. On limestone crests and shelves an acid, humus-rich, peat-like soil can

Karst scenery near Payakumbuh.

Padang vegetation, Bangka Island.

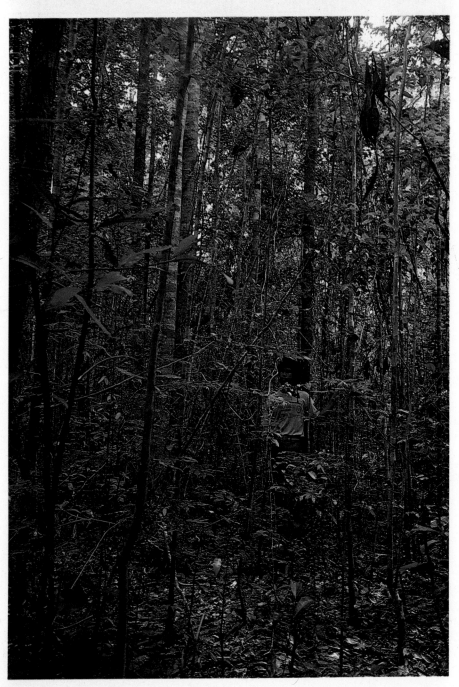

Heath forest; Bangka Island.

develop directly on top of limestone rock, but this has not been reported (as far as could be determined) from Sumatra. On steep slopes, of course, soil cannot form except in very small quantities in fissures and cracks [17]. Soils over limestone can be very variable depending on the purity of the parent material and the topography. [20].

The soil beneath the forest on limestone examined by Proctor *et al.* in Mt. Mulu National Park, Sarawak, lay on a 25—30° slope and was extremely shallow (average 11 cm, range 0—55cm), and highly organic (80% weight lost on ignition) [54]. Its base saturation was 32% compared with 1.6% in dipterocarp forest and 2.9% in heath forest. Similarly, its cation exchange capacity was 210m-equivalents/100g, compared with 37 in dipterocarp forest and 110 in heath forest. Despite the high organic content of the soil on limestone, its pH was 6.1, the highest recorded from the forests on Mt. Mulu.

Soil collected by a CRES team from small ledges on the rock walls outside Kutabuluh Cave, Tanah Karo, was basic and had very high concentrations of calcium and magnesium (Table 8.5).

Table 8.5 **Result of analyses made on soil samples from outside the cave at Kutabuluh.** Soil collected by a CRES team.

Sand	Silt	Clay	pH H_2O	C (%)	N (%)	C/N
\
FRACTION (%)						
52	31	17	7.2	6.43	0.87	7.4

P-av (ppm)	K	Na	Ca	Mg	T.E.B. (m.e./100gr)	C.E.C (m.e./100g)	B.S. (%)
	\
Exchangeable (m.e./100g)						
177	1.82	0.34	51.01	5.32	58.49	50.64	116

8.4.3 Vegetation

No publication describing limestone vegetation in Sumatra has been located. Anderson identified a range of habitats influenced by limestone in Sarawak [3].

a) At the base of limestone hills the soils, although derived from other parent material, are influenced by the water running off the limestone

Figure 8.10 The distribution of limestone in Sumatra. (Adapted from Verstappen [74]).

and by eroded limestone fragments. The relatively base-rich, fertile soils support a number of characteristics tree species but cultivation often extends to the very base of the hill.

b) Characteristic species can also be found at the base of limestone hills where the base itself is also over limestone.

c) The steeper slopes can support an untidy forest of trees whose roots cling to the rough surface or penetrate the rocks to emerge in caves below. Where the slope is too steep small herbs thrive, many of which are not found in any other habitat. Many of these plants are subject to repeated water stress because the volume of the meagre soil in which they grow does not have sufficient water capacity. As a result they exhibit 'poikilohydry' - the ability to lose most of their water except that in their protoplasm which resists drying out, and then to revive on rewetting [78].

d) Small scree slopes also support a characteristic flora.

e) Forest of the moderate slopes and summits of limestone hills grow in the peat-like humus described in the previous section, and has certain similarities between in species and those of heath forest and inner peatswamp forst (see Anderson [3] for details).

This was one type of forest examined as part of the study by Proctor *et al.* [53, 54]. In their one-hectare plots they found only 74 tree species in forest on limestone, compared with 215 in dipterocarp forest and 122 in heath forest. Forest on limestone also has a relatively low density of trees, small total basal area and mean basal area per tree, low tree height and total biomass. Also a larger percentage of trees in forest on limestone had trunk diameters of 10−20cm. Dipterocarpaceae was the most important plant family. The phenolic content of leaf litter from forest on limestone was also measured by Proctor *et al.* but the results are not easily interpreted, possibly because leaf litter rather that leaves taken directly from the parent plant were examined.

Limestone hills are peculiar in their discontinuous distribution, their relatively base-rich soils, the high levels of calcium in the rock, and their very steep or sheer slopes, which can become periodically very dry. It is not surprising, then, that some plants are confined to them. For example, of 1216 plant species recorded on limestone hills in Peninsular Malaysia, 254 species (21%) are found only on limestone hills and 130 of these species are only found in Peninsular Malaysia [19]. Considering the greater extent of karst limestone in Sumatra it would be safe to suggest that an even greater number of plants are endemic to Sumatran limestone. About 10% of the plant species found on, but not restricted to, limestone in Peninsular Malaysia are specialized to living in crevices [32]. Peninsular Malaysian limestone hills also represent the only known habitat of a genus of small serdang palms *Maxburretia* [22, 78, 79] and similar plants should be looked for in any ecological surveys of limestone hills in Sumatra. For example, the CRES team visiting the Lho'Nga limestone in North Aceh found a species of pigeon cane palm *Rhapis* which until then was a genus unknown in the Malesian region.

8.4.4 Fauna

The only fauna restricted to limestone habitats are certain molluscs.

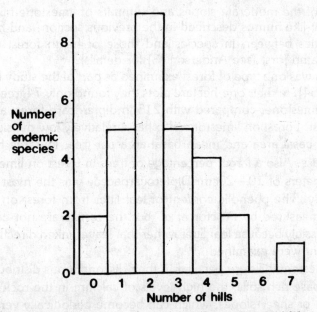

Figure 8.11 The distribution of endemic species of snails of different numbers of limestone hills (Based on data from Tweedie [69]). **Thus, four hills had a total of four endemic snail species, and seven hills had only one endemic species.**

This was first recognized in the last century but the only thorough account of the pheomenon for the Sunda Region appears to be by Tweedie [69]. He examined the mollusc fauna of 28 more-or-less isolated limestone hills in Peninsular Malaysia and found a total of 108 species. The most remarkable finding was that 70 (66%) of these species were restricted to just one limestone hill. One hill even had seven mollusc species not found on any of the other hills (Figure 8.11). These endemic species must be extremely intolerant of living away from their limestone environment. Strangely, other species from the same genera as the endemic species were found on a wide range of hills; one such was collected from no less than 19 of the 28 hills. Some of these wider ranging species have indeed been found in areas between the limestone hills, but others must be present in those inhospitable (for a mollusc) intervening habitats in such low numbers that transfers between hills are extermely rare occurrences.

Similar situations as the above doubtless exist for the isolated limestone outcrops in Sumatra. Obviously, those hills supporting more endemic species would be more worthy of protection from use as, for example, limestone quarries. Anyone interested in pursuing such a line of study should consult Benthem Jutting [7] as the first step.

REFERENCES

1. Addicott, J.F. (1974). Predation and prey community structure: an experimental study of mosquito larvae on the protozoans of pitcher plants. *Ecology* 55: 475—492. (12.4.20)
2. Afriastini, J. (1982). Kayu bawang. *Suara Alam No. 15:* 20—21. (12.1.95)
3. Anderson, J.A.R. (1965). Limestone habitat in Sarawak. In *Proc. Symp. Ecol. Res. Humid. Trop. Veg.*, pp. 49—57. UNESCO, Paris. (12.10.49)
4. Asthon, P.S. (1971). The plants and vegetation of Bako National Park. *Malay. Nat. J.* 24: 151—162. (12.10.58)
5. Beaufort, L.F. de (1939). On a collection of freshwater fishes of the island of Billiton. *Treubia* 17: 198—198. (12.5.27)
6. Beaver, R.A. (1979). Biological studies of the fauna of pitcher plants (*Nepenthes*) in West Malaysia. *Annals soc. ent. Fr. (N.S.)* 15: 3—17. (12.4.18)
7. ＿＿＿＿＿＿. (1979). Fauna and foodwebs of pitcher plants in West Malaysia. *Malay. Nat. J.* 33: 1—10. (12.4.19)
8. ＿＿＿＿＿＿. Personal communication.
9. Beekman, H.A.J.M. (1949). *Houttelt in Indonesia*. H. Veenan and Zonnen, Wageningen. Referred to in Suselo (1981).
10. Benthem Jutting, W.S.S van (1959). Catalogue of the nonmarine mollusca of Sumatra and of its satellite islands. *Beaufortia* 7: 41—191. (12.3.30)
11. Berkhout, A.H. (1895). Boschbouwkundige beschrijring v.h. eiland Banka. *Tijd. v. Nijverh. en Landb. in Ned. Indie.* 50: 11—66. (12.10.23)
12. BPPP/Soepraptohardjo, M., Soekardi, M., Kurnia, H.D. and Suharjo, S. (1979). *Sumber daya lahan/tanah dan potensinya di Pulau Sumatera*. Konsultasi Penelitian Pertanian Menunjang Pembangunan Sumatera 28 Nopember—3 Desember 1979. Lembaga Penelitian Tanah, Bogor. (23.4.14)

13. Brunig, E.F. (1965). A guide and introduction to the vegetation of the kerangas forests and the padangs of the Bako National Park. In *Proc. Symp. Ecol. Res. Humid. Tropics Veg.*, Kuching, UNESCO, Kuching. (12.10.60)

14. ——————. (1969). Forestry on tropical podzols and related soils. *Trop. Ecol.* 10: 45—58. (9.1.20)

15. ——————. (1970). Stand structure, physiognomy and environmental factors in some lowland forests in Sarawak. *Trop. Ecol.* 11: 26—43. (12.10.52)

16. ——————. (1973). Species richness and stand diversity in relation to site and succession of forests in Sarawak and Brunei (Borneo). *Amazoniana* 4: 293—320.

17. Burham, C.P. (1975). Soils. In *Tropical Rain Forests of the Far East* (oleh T.C. Whitmore), pp. 103—120. Clarendon, Oxford. (12.10.8)

18. Chasen, F.N. (1937). The birds of Billiton Island. *Treubia* 16: 205—238. (12.).11)

19. Chin, S.C. (1977). The limestone hill flora of Malaya. Part I. *Gdns' Bull. S'pore* 30: 165—220. (12.1.115)

20. Crowther, J. (1982). Ecological observations in a tropical karst terrain, West Malaysia. I. Variations in topography, soils and vegetation. *J. Biogeogr.* 11: 65—78. (12.10.112)

21. De Wit, (1949). A note on *Eusideroxylon* T. and B. (Laur.) *Bull. Bot. Gard. Buitenzorg* 18: 200—208. (12.1.42)

22. Dransfield, J.: Personal communication.

23. FAO/MacKinnon, J.R. (1982). *Sumatra. Volume VIII of A National Conservation Plan for Indonesia.* FAO, Bogor. (10.2.15)

24. Franken, N.A.P. and Roos, M.C. (1981). Studies in lowland equatorial forest in Jambi province, central Sumatra. Unpubl. report, BIOTROP, Bogor. (12.10.103)

25. Frey-Wijssling, A. (1933). Over de zandsteppen van Kota Pinang ter Oostkust van Sumatra. *Trop. Natuur* 22: 69—72. (12.10.55)

26. Glass, A.D.M. (1973). Influence of phenolic acids on ion uptake. I. Inhibition of potassium absorption. *J. Exp. Bot.* 25: 1104—1113. (12.1.36)

27. ——————. (1974). Influence of phenolic acids on ion uptake. II. Inhibition of phosphate uptake. *Plant Physiol.* 51: 1037—1041. (9.1.23)

28. Greeser, E. (1919). Bijdragen Resumeerend Repport over het voor-komen van ijzerhout op de olieterreinen Djambi I *Tectona*. 12: 283—304. (9.1.23)

29. Hanski, I. (1983). Distributional ecology and abundance of dung and carrion eating beetles (Scarabaeidae) in tropical rain forests in Sarawak, Borneo. *Acta Zool. Fenn.* 167: 1—4. (12.4.51)

30. Hardon, H.J. (1937). Padang soil, an example of podzol in the tropical lowlands. *Proc. Kon. Akad. Wet.* 40: 530—538. (23.4.4)

31. Harrison, T. (1965). Some quantitative effects of vertebrates on the Borneo flora. In *Symp. Ecol. Res. Humid Trop. Vegetation, Kuching, Sarawak, 1963*, pp. 164—169. UNESCO, Paris. (12.13.7)

32. Henderson, M.R. (1939). The flora of the limestone hills of the Malay peninsula. *J. Malay. Br. R. Asiat. Soc.* 17: 13—87. (12.10.50)

33. Huxley, C.R. (1978). The ant-plants *Myrmecodia* and *Hydnophytum* (Rubiaceae), and the relationships between their morphology, ant occupants, physiology and ecology. *New Phytol.* 67: 231—268. (12.1.17)

34. Janzen, D.H. (1974). Epiphytic myrmecophytes in Sarawak: Mutualism through the feeding of plants by ants. *Biotropica* 6: 237—259. (12.1.18)

35. _____. (1974).Tropical blackwater rivers, animals and mast fruiting by the Dipterocarpaceae. *Biotropica* 6: 69—103. (12.10.59)

36. _____. (1981). Lectins and plant-herbivore interactions. *Recent Advances in Phytochemistry* 15: 241—258.

37. Jennings. J.N. (1972). The character of tropical humid karst *Z. Geomorph.* 16: 336—341. (23.3.3)

38. Kartawinata, K. (1978). The 'kerangas' heath forest in Indonesia. In *Glimpses of Ecology* (ed. J.S. Singh and B. Gopal), pp. 145—153. (12.10.17)

39. _____. Unpublished.

40. _____. Personal communication

41. Koopman, M.J.F. and Verhoef, L. (1938).*Eusideroxylon zwageri T.* and B. Het ijzerhout van Borneo en Sumatra. *Tectona* 31: 381—399. (9.1.22)

42. Kostermans, A.J.G.H. (1979). *Potocylon*, a new Bornean genus of Lauraceae. *Malay. Nat. J.* 32: 143—148. (12.1.41)

43. _____. Personal communication.

44. Laan, E van der (1925). De boschen van de Zuider en Ooster-afdeeling van Borneo. *Tectona* 18: 925—952. (12.10.62)

45. Leeuw, H.A.L. de (1936). Het boschbedrijf, meer in het bijzonder de boschverjonging op Bangka en Billiton. *Tectona* 29: 915—928. (9.1.33)

46. Lloyd,M., Inger, R.F. and King, F.W. (1968). On the diversity of reptile and amphibian species in a Bornean rain forest. *Am. Nat.* 102: 497—515. (12.6.8)

47. McKey, D. (1978). Soils, vegetation, and seed-eating by black colobus monkeys. In *The Ecology of Arboreal Folivores* (ed. G. Montgomery), pp. 423—437. Smithsonian Institution Press, Washington, D.C. (12.8.27)

48. McKey, D. Waterman, P.G., Mbi, C.N., Gartlan, J.S., and Struhsaker, T.T. (1978). Phenolic content of vegetation in two African rain forests: ecological implications. *Science* 202: 61—64. (12.1.34)

49. Mani, M.S. (1972). *General Entomology*. Oxford IBH Publishing Co., New Dehli.

50. Manullang, B.O. (1980). Kantong semar, tumbuhan pemakan serangga. *Suara Alam* 9: 45—47. (12.1.114)

51. Mohr, E.C.J. and Baren, F.A. van (1954). *Tropical Soils*. Mouton, The Hague. (23.4.6)

52. Peace, W.J.H. and MacDonald, F.D. (1981). An investigation of the leaf anatomy, foliar mineral levels, and water relations of trees of a Sarawak forest. *Biotropica* 13: 100—109. (12.1.33)

53. Proctor, J., Anderson, J.M., Fogden, S.C.L. and Vallack, H.W. (1983). Ecological studies in four contrasting lowland rain forests in Gunung Mulu National Park, Sarawak. I. Forest environment, structure and floristies. *J. Ecol.* 71: 237—260. (12.10.22)

54. Proctor, J., Anderson, J.M., Chai, P., and Vallack, H.W. (1983). Ecological studies in four contrasting lowland rain forests in Gunung Hulu National Park, Sarawak. I. Forest environment, structure and floristics. *J. Ecol.* 71: 237—260. (12.10.22).

55. Rankin, J.M. (1978). *The influence of seed predation and plant*

competition on tree species abundances in two adjacent tropical rain forest communities in Trinidad, West Indies. PhD thesis, University of Michigan, Michigan.

56. Richards, P.W. (1941). Tropical forest podzols. *Nature, Lond.* 148: 129—131.

57. Riswan, S. (1981). Natural regeneration in lowland tropical forest in East Kalimantan, Indonesia (with reference to kerangas forest.) *BIOTROP Spec. Publ.* 13: 145—152. (10.4.18)

58. _____. (1982). *The Ecology of heath forest (kerangas) in East Kalimantan, Indonesia.* Ph.D. thesis, University of Aberdeen, Aberdeen.

59. Sobrado, A. and Medina, E. (1980). General morphology, anatomical structure, and nutrient content of schlerophyllous leaves of the 'Bana' vegetation of Amazonas. *Oecologia* 45: 341—345. (12.1.28)

60. Soedibja, R.S. (1952). Penyelidikan tentang tumbuh dan ekologi kaju besi (*Eusideroxylon zwageri* T. and B.) di lingkungan hutan Semandai (Palembang). *Rimba Indonesia* (1952): 215—223. (9.1.21)

61. Soepraptohardjo, M. and Barus, A. (1974). *Pra-Survey untuk Penelitian Tanah Kolong (tin tailing soil).* Lembaga Penelitian Tanah, Bogor. (10.4.11)

62. Specht, R.L. and Womersley, J.S. (1979). Heathlands and related shrublands of Malesia (with particular reference to Borneo and New Guinea). In *Heathlands and Related Shrublands* (ed. R.L. Specht), pp. 321—378. Elsevier, Amsterdam. (12.10.20)

63. Steenis, C.G.G.J. van (1932). Botanical results of a trip to the Anambas and Natoena Islands. *Bull. Jard. Bot. Buitenzorg, ser. III* 12: 151—211. (12.10.53)

64. _____. Personal communication.

65. Suselo, T.B. (1981). *Preliminary report on ecological studies of Eusideroxylon zwageri T. and B. in Jambi, Sumatra.* BIOTROP, Bogor. (12.1.40)

66. Thienemann, A. (1932). Die Tierwelt der *Nepenthes*-Kannen. *Arch. Hydrobiol. Suppl.* 11:1—54.(12.4.30)

67. _____. (1934). Die Tierwelt der tropischen Pflanzengewasser. *Arch Hydrobiol., Suppl.* 13:1—91. 612.1.45)

68. Tuyt, P. (1939). Oorspronkelijke Bijdragen. Schaduwrijen cultuur van ijzerhout in de Resedensie Palembang. *Tectona* 32: 808—828. (9.1.20)

69. Tweedie, M.W.F. (1961). On certain Mollusca of the Malayan limestone hills. *Bull. Raffles Mus.* 26: 49—65. (12.3.5)

70. Ungemach, H. (1969). Chemical rain studies inthe Amazon basin. In *Simposio y Foro de Biologia Tropical Amazonica,* pp. 354—358. (Referred to in Janzen, 1974)

71. Valeton, TH. (1908). Lindeniopsis. Een nieun subgenus der Rubiaceae. *Verh. Kon. Akad. Wet. Amst.* 17: 120—126. (12.10.57)

72. Verbeek, R.D.M. (1897). Geologie van Bangka. *Jaarb. Mijnw. Ned. O. Indie* 26: 60—61. (23.5.1)

73. Verstappen, H.TH. (1960). Some observations on karst development in the Malay Archipelago. *J. Trop. Geogr.* 14: 1—10. (23.3.2)

74. _____. (1973). *A Geomorphological Reconnaisance of Sumatra and Adjacent Islands (Indonesia).* Wolters-Noordhoft, Groningen. (23.3.1)

75. Wallace, A.R. (1869). *The Malay Archipelago: The Land of the Orang-utan and the Bird of Paradise. A Narrative of Travel with Studies of Man and Nature.* Republished by Dover, New York, 1962. (23.7.12)

76. Waterman, P.G.: Personal communication.

77. Westermann, J.H. (1942). Snakes from Bangka and Billiton. *Treubia* 18: 611—619. (12.6.7)

78. Whitmore, T.C. (1975). *Tropical Rainforests of the Far East.* Clarendon, Oxford. (12.10.8)

79. _____. (1977). *Palms of Malaya.* Oxford Univ. Press, Oxford. (12.1.3)

80. Whitten, A.J. (1982). Diet and feeding behaviour of Kloss gibbons on Siberut Island, Indonesia. *Folia primatol.* 37: 177—208. (12.8.6)

81. _____. Personal observation.

82. Witkamp, H. (1925). De ijzerhout als geologische indicator. *Trop. Natuur* 14: 97—103. (23.4.7)

83. Wyatt-Smith, J. (1963). Manual of Malayan silviculture of inland forests. *Malay. For. Rec. No. 23* (9.1.17)

CHAPTER 9

MOUNTAINS

9.1 INTRODUCTION

Sumatra has a large number of mountains, some, such as most of those in the Barisan range, formed by uplift of sedimentary deposits and others, such as Mt. Kerinci, Mt. Sinabung, Mt. Merapi and Mt. Singgalang, formed by volcanic action. The physical environment changes up a mountain, thus providing a gradual change of conditions against which the fauna and flora can be examined. These differences between the montane ecosystems and the luxuriant, hot and humid lowland forest ecosystems are stimulating subjects for study.

The mountain about which most is known, Mt. Kerinci (3800m), is also the highest. It was the object of a large collecting expedition in 1914 and about 30 papers were published on different groups of animals and plants in the *Journal of the Federated Malay States Museum* between 1918 and 1931 [73]. These papers are most useful for taxonomists, but for understanding the changes occurring with altitude more informative papers are available on Mt. ni Telong [27], the mountains in the Mt. Leuser National Park [83], Mt. Singgalang [17] and Mt. Kerinci [28, 44, 72]. A CRES team climbed Mt. Kemiri (3340m) in the Mt. Leuser National Park and Mt. Kerinci as part of the preparation for this book.

9.2 CLIMATE

9.2.1 Temperature

There is a mountainward current of air blowing during the day which is caused by air warming in the lowlands and thus expanding and rising. As any gas rises and expands in response to lower pressure, so its temperature falls because the wider-spaced gas molecules, which move about in response to energy from the sun, collide less frequently and therefore create less heat. The montane environment does warm up in the same manner as the lowlands because of the reduced air pressure (caused by the shorter and therefore lighter column of air above the mountain), the low density of water vapour, and the generally clearer air. These three factors result in less retention of infra-red (warming) radiation in the mountain air, even though the intensity of radiation is greater on mountains for the same reasons as above. Similarly, during the night, heat is lost quickly and the daily change of temperature at about 3000 m can be as much as 15 to 20°C, but this depends on cloud cover.

The rate of temperature decrease is generally about 0.6°C per 100 m but this varies from place to place, with season, time of day, water vapour content of the air, etc. Readings of minimum temperature were taken on five consecutive nights during the ascent of Mt. Kemiri and the results are shown in Figure 9.1. The four uncircled points, recorded when the sky was cloud-covered early in the morning, indicate a lapse rate of 0.63°C per 100 m and suggest that snow would settle at 4200 m if such a montain existed. The permanent snow line would be still higher than this and occurs at about 4700 m in Irian. The circled reading was recorded after a totally cloudless night. The regression coefficient of the four uncircled points is 0.99 but this may be artificially high because other writers have found two lapse rates the first up to the cloud or condensation level (about 2500 m) of 0.6°C/100 m, and the second above that of 0.5°C [85, 86, 95]. Interestingly, however, the regression coefficient calculated from the many temperature readings made by van Beek up a number of mountains in the Mt. Leuser National Park was much higher when all the points were taken together than when they were divided at the cloud level [2].

Of considerable importance to understanding some aspects of

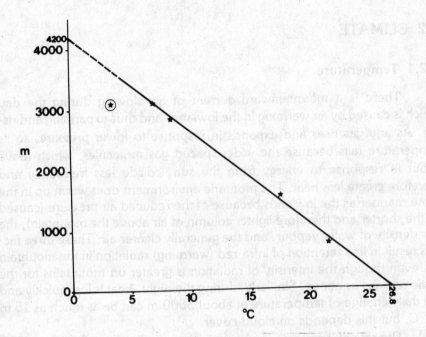

Figure 9.1 Minimum temperature readings on successive nights during the ascent of Mt. Kemiri by a CRES team.

mountain ecology is the Massenerhebung effect which was first noticed in the European Alps. It describes the phenomenon that vegetation zones on a large mountain or the central parts of large mountain ranges (such as the Barisan range) are higher than they are on a small mountain or outlying spurs [33]. This must be remembered when reading about mountains in, for example, Peninsular Malaya (highest peak 2200 m) or Irian (highest peak 5300m) because zones of vegetation and fauna will be lower in the former and higher in the latter compared with the majority of mountains in Sumatra.

9.2.2 Relative humidity

The percentage saturation of a mass of air increases as its temperature falls. The dew-point (the temperature at which condensation occurs and clouds or drops of dew form) at different altitudes depends therefore on the temperature and the initial moisture content of the air. The forests of higher altitudes experience a very high relative humidity, particulary at night when the temperature falls, and the dew point is frequently passed so that water condenses on the leaves. During dry spells at altitudes above the main cloud layer, however, the relative humidity can be quite low during the day, leading to wide daily extremes.

9.2.3 Clouds

Clouds originate where ascending air reaches its dew point (see relative himidity). Once water droplets have been formed they tend to act as 'seeds' and more water condenses on them. During the wettest months, the slopes and peaks of mountains can be enveloped in clouds for days on end, but during the drier months, when the air is not saturated with water vapour, it is common for a belt of clouds to form around a mountain, often at about 2000 m. As experienced mountain climbers know, a low, even continuous, layer of cloud at 2000 m does not always mean that any cloud is present at 3000 m or above.

9.2.4 Rainfall

Rainfall is generally greater on the windward (western) slopes of the Barisan Range and other mountains than on the lee (eastern) slopes (section 1.3.2). There is, however, considerable local variation and there seems to be no guiding principle relating rainfall to elevation [57]. Rainfall on mountain slopes up to about 2000 m will generally be higher than on the surrounding lowlands. At the cloud level, rainfall measurements are not particularly useful ecologically because water droplets in the air are utilized by the plants. Above the main cloud level, it seems reasonable to suggest that rainfall is less than below it because of the lower incidence of cloud cover.

9.2.5 Frost

Although the peaks of Sumatran mountains are not covered with permanent ice they almost certainly occasionally experience frost in the hours before sunrise. Radiation of heat from the ground occurs both by day and by night but at night is not compensated for by radiation from the sun (section 9.2.1). Thus as warm surfaces of plants, soil, rock, etc. cool so the thin layer of air immediately around them cools. Cold air is heavier than warm air and so if there is not a slope for it to flow down or a wind to push it away, it will become progressively colder. Since heat loss from the earth is hampered by dust, fog and clouds the lowest temperatures will be reached on clear, dry nights. Maximum cooling will be from non-conductive surfaces such as dead twigs or grasses and dry sandy soil rather than from conductive surfaces such as rocks, water and living vegetation. Thus frost is most likely to occur on calm, dry, clear nights in flat hollows [85]. Such places are called frost pockets and can occur in silted-up small lakes or in the glaciated topography at the tops of the major mountains in the northern Barisan Range.

9.2.6 Ultra-violet radiation

It has been suggested that ultra-violet radiation on tropical mountains is probably more intense than on mountains in any other region on earth [53]. This is due to the amount of ozone which absorbs ultra-violet radiation in the stratosphere being appreciably less near the equator, and to the atmosphere at low altitudes being more turbid and dense and thus more capable of absorbing or reflecting this radiation. Climbers must therefore protect their skins or rapidly suffer the effects of sunburn.

9.3 SOILS

The considerable changes in climate with altitude are reflected in the soils. Unfortunately the difficulty of identifying a consistent pattern parallels the confused pattern in rainfall which is influenced by local topography. Further variation obviously occurs due to the nature of the parent material. However, it is generally observed that the soils up to 1000 m are more or less the same as the lowland soils, i.e. latosols and red-yellow podzolic soils. Between 1000 m and the cloud zone at about 2000 m (on the higher mountains) the increase in water supply leads to leaching, podzolization or water-logging. In addition, chemical weathering and biological activity are retarded by the lower temperatures. During the CRES expedition up Mt. Kemiri no termites were seen above about

Padang vegetation, Bangka Island.

Discidia.

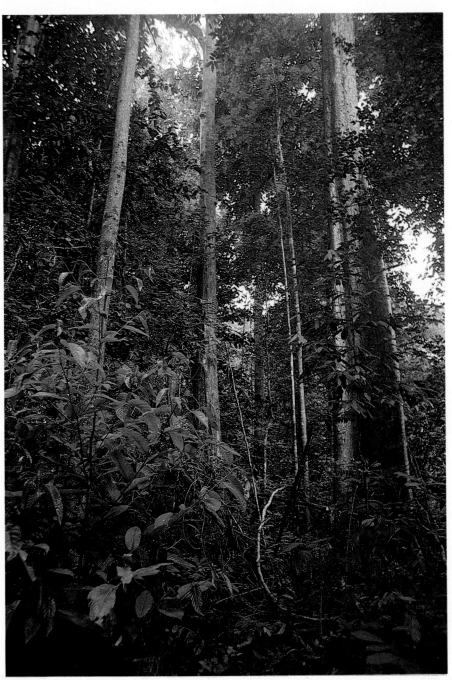

Ironwood forests; Rimbo Kulim, Muara Tembesi.

1500 m and earthworms apparently become scarcer as well (section
9.5.1). These features are accentuated in the cloud zone where the more
or less continuously saturated air causes peat to be formed in blankets up
to 1m deep. The pH is often very low (pH 2.5—4.0). Above the cloud
level, the peat layer remains but it is less thick and the soil is generally less
wet [5, 6, 96]. On Mt. Kemiri the percentage of carbon and the carbon :
nitrogen ratio rose from 2.8 to 42.6% and from 10 to 24.6 respectively
from 880 m to 3310 m. Mountain soils are frequently very poor in calcium
and on Mt. Kemiri most of the soil samples collected by the CRES team
had levels of only 0.11 m.eq/100 g or less. Similarly, many of the mountain soils examined by van Beek had no or very little calcium. These are indeed low compared with figures of 0.9 and 1.8 m.eq/100 g for the top 15
cm of lowland soils less than 100 m above sea level in North Sumatra [2].
Soils on young volcanic debris are clearly very poor. A soil sample collected on the outer rim of the fuming Mt. Sibayak was, as expected, very
low in bases (Table 9.1). The important influence of soil nutrients on the

Table 9.1 Soil analysis of a sample from the outer unvegetated slope of the
summit of Mt. Sibayak (Tanah Karo). Soil collected by a team from
CRES

pH H₂O	C (%)	N (%)	C/N	p-av (ppm)	Exchangeable (m.eq/100g)				T.E.B (m.eq /100g)	C.E.B (m.eq. /100g)	B.S. (%)
					K	Na	Ca	Mg			
3.4	0.22	0.02	11.0	22	0.13	0.08	0.23	0.51	0.95	10.82	9

growth of mountain plants is discussed in section 9.4.7 and the cycling of
minerals is described in section 9.4.6. Volcano soils are discussed in section 9.4.9.

9.4 VEGETATION

9.4.1 Introduction

A greater variety of plant communities is encountered on most tropical mountains than in any other area of comparable size in the World. Indeed, the vegetation changes observed when climbing a tropical mountain mimic the changes seen when travelling from the equator towards the poles. The tops of some Sumatran mountains are really very similar to, for example, Scottish moors in general appearance and some of the plants are even in the same genus. In fact, the plants of the high regions of tropical mountains have closer taxonomic links with plants of distant temperate regions than with the 'sea' of lowland forest plants that surrounds them.

The forest on the lower slopes of a Sumatran mountain seems indistinguishable from 'normal' lowland forest but then, with increasing altitude, the trees become shorter and epiphytes, climbers and other features change in abundance. This zone is called lower montane forest. There then occurs a much more striking change when the tree canopy becomes even, the trees are even shorter, squat and gnarled, the leaves are thick and small, and mossy epiphytes are common. This zone is upper montane forest. Beyond this lies the subalpine forest, a complex of grassy, heathy and boggy areas. The grassy mountain tops of the subalpine zone have probably been caused by occasional fires-possibly lit by men for generations in their attempt to hunt animals such as deer and pig [86]. Analyses of soil samples taken in the subalpine zone of Mt. Kemiri by the CRES team revealed levels of potassium as high as 1.29 m.eq/100g, levels which in such poor places could have been caused only by fires. It has been suggested that the grassy slopes and valleys are caused by soil factors. In the wet grassy valleys near the summit this is more or less true because there is no tree species in the whole floral area of Malesia which can stand permanent inundation at high altitude [87]. The soil of the grassy slopes is, however, indistinguishable from the soil under the forest (unburnt) adjacent to it [87]. The question of regeneration of mountain vegetation after fire is discussed in section 11.11.

The general characteristics of the forest types on mountains is shown in Table 9.2. During the ascent of Mt. Kemiri by the CRES team, the frequency of different forms of plant life were recorded at various altitudes and these are shown in Table 9.3. In both these tables, the gradual decrease in height (illustrated in Figure 9.2) is recorded. This is not, however, accompanied by a proportional decrease in bole diameter which tends to increase with altitude for a given height of tree (Figure 9.3). The changes in vegetation structure up Mt. Kerinci have been

Table 9.2 Characteristics of four types of forest found on mountains; the most useful characters in italics. (After Whitmore [95] and Grubb [35]). * — the leaf-size classes refer to a classification of leaves devised by Raunkier and modified by Webb [93]. The definitions are: mesophyll — 4500—18225 mm^2, notophyll — 2025—4500 mm^2, microphyll — 225—2025 mm^2, nanophyll — less than 225 mm^2. An approximate measure of leaf area is 2/3 (width x length).

	lowland forest	lower montane forest	upper montane forest	subalpine forest
Canopy height (m)	25—45m	15—33m	1.5—18m	1.5—9m
Height of emergents (m)	67m	45m	26m	15m
Leaf size class	*mesophyll*	*notophyll/ mesophyll*	*microphyll*	*nanophyll*
Tree buttresses	*common and large*	*not common or small on both*	usually absent	absent
trees with flowers on trunk or main branches (cauliflory)	common	rare	absent	absent
compound leaves	*abundant*	present	rare	absent
leaf drip tips	*abundant*	present or comon	rare or absent	absent
large climbers	*abundant*	usually absent	absent	absent
creepers	usually abundant	common or abundant	very rare	absent
epiphytes (orchids etc.)	common	abundant	common	very rare
epiphytes (moss, lichen, liverwort)	present	present or common	*usually abundant*	*abundant*

Table 9.3 Frequency of plant lifeforms found in 10 × 10 plots at 10 locations on Mt. Kemiri. Location 1 is at the near-by Ketambe Research Station. Figures are means from three plots at each location.

Forest type	Lowland forest			Lower montane forest		Upper montane forest				Subalpine forest	
Forest sub-type		hill	hill					moss forest			
Number	1	2	3	4	5	6	7	8	9	10	11
Altitude	300	985	1130	1500	2250	2750	3200	3050	3100	3080	3200
No. trees over 10 cm diameter	7	8	9	10	12	2	1	7	4	3	0
No. trees 2–10 cm diameter	18	10	14	12	16	6	15	12	6	6	0
Saplings	100s	400	100s	100s	100s	20	40	40	13	25	0
Creepers	3	0	3	6	6	0	0	1	0	0	0
No. climbers over 10 cm diameter	2	0	2	0	0	0	0	0	0	0	0
No. climbers 1–10 cm diameter	8	4	4	2	3	0	0	0	0	0	0
Herbs and grass	0	0	0	0	0	+	common	0	common	abundant	very abundant
Epiphytes (orchids)	+	+	+	many	many	0	0	+	0	0	0
Epiphytes (large ferns)	1	2	2	1	0	0	0	0	+	0	0
Epiphytes (small ferns)	+	+	+	+	100s	0	+	rare	+	0	0
Epiphytes (moss, lichen, liverwort)	0	0	0	0	+	abundant	abundant	very abundant	abundant	abundant	0
Tree ferns	0	0	0	0	3	0	0	0	0	0	0
Pinang palms	0	0	0	0	8	0	0	3	4	4	0
Canopy height	30–45	25–35	20–35	20–30			4	9	4	2.5	0

Figure 9.2. Cross-sections of: a - lowland forest; b - lower montane forest (low levels); c - lower montane forest (high levels); d - upper montane forest, to show decrease in tree height and simplification of structure. (Adapted from Robbins and Wyatt-Smith [76]).

382

Figure 9.3. Relationship between tree height and trunk diameter at breast height in four montane forest types on Mt. Kemiri. Data collected by a CRES team. a - lower montane, b and c - upper montane, d - sub-alpine.

described in general terms [28, 44, 72].

The division of montane vegetation into forest types is based on both floristics [86], and on general structure. Many plant species cross the ecotones (transition areas between two types of forest or other ecosystems), but occur in different forms. For example, in the subalpine zone at 3250 m on Mt. Kemiri, the CRES team found a flowering *Leptospermum flavescens* which was only 15 cm high, but 300 m lower down the same species was a common tree about 4 m high. The dwarfed specimen had a massive root and this illustrates the fact that the measure of biomass called root-to-shoot ratio (ratio of dry weight of below-ground parts to above-ground parts) tends to increase with elevation. In the lower montane forest studied by Edwards the ratio was 0.1 [21], but in harsh, cold habitats such as the subalpine zone the figure is often 3.0—4.0 [74].

Leaf size and thickness change between lowland forest and

subalpine forest. The CRES team measured the thickness of leaves from ten species of trees/shrubs from the subalpine zone at 3000 m and the mean thickness was 0.5 mm (range 0.3—0.85). The equivalent figures for a sample of leaves from lowland forest (Ketambe Research Station) were 0.2 mm (range 0.1—0.25). The thicker leaves of montane forests have been called 'pachyphylls' by Grubb [34, 35], which differ from other leaves chiefly in the thickness of their palisade layer (the long, photosynthetic cells of the leaf mesophyll) and the high frequency of a hypodermis (a layer immediately beneath the epidermis, often strengthened, forming an extra protective layer). See also the paper by Tanner and Kapos [89].

The average heights at which the various forest zones in Sumatra are as follows:

0 — 1200m	lowland forest
1200 — 2100m	lower montane forest
2100 — 3000m	upper montane forest
3000m +	subalpine forest

Temperature and cloud level are the major determinants of these forest zones (section 9.4.7) but the vegetation zones are compressed on smaller mountains (the Massenerhebung effect - Figure 9.4). The presence of a montane plant does not necessarily correlate with altitude for reasons other than the Massenerhebung effect and this is represented by wavy lines in Figure 9.4. From the locations where a particular species thrives, dispersion to other areas is achieved by upward and downward movement of its fruits, seeds or spores. Conditions of higher altitudes are mimiced by frost pockets (section 9.2.5), beside mountain streams, on bare soil and near water-falls, and the lowest parts of a species' range, the individual plants are usually sterile. The population of a particular species in such an area therefore depends on seeds or spores being carried or blown down from above for its maintenance. A similar mechanism operates up the mountain. Thus it had been proposed by van Steenis that there is a zone of permanent occurrence which 'feeds' the populations of the upper and lower zones of temporary localities [85, 86] (Figure 9.5). Thus a mountain may lack a species of plant even though at the same height on a higher mountain (with a zone of permanent occurrence) that plant may be present.

384

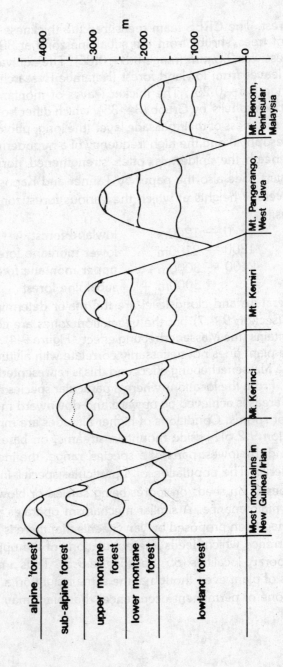

Figure 9.4. Vegetation zones on five mountains to show the compression found on smaller mountains.

Figure 9.5. The zone of permanent occurrence on mountains and its significance for the distribution of species. Stippled areas represent localities where a hypothetical species is found.

9.4.2 Characteristic plants

Whereas lowland forests are often characterized by trees of the family Dipterocarpaceae (section 7.2.3), the lower montane forests are characterized by the occurrence of the families Fagaceae (oaks) and Lauraceae (laurels). Both these families are also present at lower levels and their apparent dominance is caused largely by dipterocarps becoming increasingly uncommon. Fagaceae are forest trees and are recognizable by their fruit which consist of a hard nut (containing the seed) sitting in an open or closed, usually spiky, cup. The fruit of various species of *Lithocarpus*, one of the commonest genera found in Sumatra, are shown in Figure 9.6. A useful key to many *Lithocarpus* species found in Sumatra has been

Figure 9.6 Fruits from trees of the genus *Lithocarpus* (Fagaceae) found in Sumatra: a-*L. conocarpus*, b-*L. hystrix*, c-*L. lamponga*, d-*L. rassa*, e-*L. blumeana*, f-*L. encleisacarpa*. (After Corner [114].

written by Corner [14][1]. Lauraceae (the family containing cinnamon

---

1. *Lithocarpus* is called by its old name *Quercus* in Corner's book. A recent but complex key to Fagaceae has been constructed by Soepadmo [80].

Cinnamomum burmansea and avocado pear *Persea americana*) is represented in the mountain forest primarily by the genus *Litsea*. This genus has fruits which also sit in a cup but the cup is not woody and the fruit is soft and pulpy.

Tree ferns are also common in lower montane forests. All but one of the tree fern species in Sumatra belong to the genus *Cyathea* (the exception being a montane species of *Dicksonia*) and the identification of species is based on the form of reproductive parts and on the fine brown scales found covering young coiled leaves and the bases of older leaves [42]. A simplified identification key to some of the species found in Sumatra is given by Holttum and Allen [43]. A recent demographic and growth study of *Cyathea* tree ferns in Jamaica has shown that a trunk can grow about 1m per fifteen years. A tree fern 1m high will, however, be considerably more than fifteen years old because many years elapse between the first growth of a young fern and the stage at which upward growth (formation of a trunk) begins [88].

The upper montane forest is characterized by the order Coniferae (the pines and related trees) particularly *Dacrycarpus imbricatus* [51], and the families Ericaceae (e.g. bilberries *Vaccinium*, *Rhododendron*), and Myrtaceae (the family to which *Eucalyptus*, clove *Eugenia aromatica*, and paperbark *Melaleuca* belong) particularly *Leptospermum flavescens*. These trees are often quite low, crooked and gnarled, and because of their mysterious shapes this part of the zone has earned the name of elfin forests. On ridge tops and in the upper regions of upper montane forest the conditions are quite dry and the commonest and most conspicuous epiphytes here are the beards of the bright yellow-green lichen *Usnea*. In the valleys and in the lower regions of this same forest more or less the same tree community is found but virtually every available space on the trees and on the ground is covered with carpets of thick liverworts and moss. This is commonly called moss forest and coincides with the most frequent level at which clouds form (section 9.2.3).

The subalpine zone is characterized by dwarf specimens of upper montane forest species and by grasses (e.g. *Agrostis*, *Festuca*), rushes and sedges, (*Juncus* of Juncaceae, *Carex*, *Scirpus* and *Cyperus* of Cyperaceae), and small herbs often with colourful flowers.

Many subalpine plants form rosettes of leaves just above the ground. These rosettes are caused by the distance between successive leaves being extremely short and only the flower stalk rises any distance above the ground, presumably to decrease water loss and to facilitate pollination or seed dispersal. The leaf under-surface of some species with rosette leaves and some other species are covered with dense, silky, white hairs (see section 9.4.3).

It has been suggested that the high levels of ultra-violet radiation received by subalpine and alpine zones on high tropical mountains (section 9.2.6), together with altitudinal shifts in vegetation zones during the Pleistocene (section 1.4.1) may have led to accelerated rates of mutation and speciation [53]. This may be a cause of high levels of endemism found in tropical subalpine and alpine plant communties. Figures have not been calculated for Sumatran mountains but 37% of the plant species on the higher parts of Irian Jaya mountains are not found in Papua New Guinea [79], and 40% of the subalpine plants on Mt. Kinabalu, Sabah, grow only on that mountain [78].

Repeated freezing of dead plant parts is thought by van Steenis to result in mummification [86]. The dead material becomes an ashy-grey colour and when touched is easily reduced into fine grey dust. This was observed on Mt. Kerinci by Jacobs [44] and by the CRES team on Mt. Kemiri.

9.4.3 Leaf adaptations to temperature and radiation

In theory, structures lose heat by convection most rapidly at their edges where wind currents disrupt insulating boundary layers of still air; the more edges (or smaller), the cooler the leaf and the lower the water loss [74]. Although there are exceptions and effects opposing the theory, this is the general pattern found in the shrubs and small trees of the subalpine and upper montane zones where midday temperatures can be high and where water availability is low. The same plants however need to cope with night-time temperatures approaching zero. The cooling effect of small leaves appears to be balanced by their close arrangement on the end of twigs, their dark colour and compact crown structure. Thus a compromise structure seems to have developed whereby the leaves will warm up quickly in the early morning sun so that efficient photosynthesis can begin as soon as possible before either clouds form or the solar radiation becomes too intense. The closensess and often vertical position of these small leaves have also been interpreted as a means of 'fog-stripping'. Water saturated air or fog would be temporarily caught within the leaves on the end of a twig with a greater likelihood of water condensing on the plant and falling to the ground. The leaves of subalpine and dry parts of the upper montane zones probably experience longer periods of lower relative humidity than do leaves in the cloudy upper montane forest and so will run less risk of encouraging epiphyllae to grow on their leaf surfaces. Many leaves of the upper montane and sub-alpine zone plants have characteristics normally found in areas subject to periodic drought: that is, xeromorphic characters. In fact, however, the mountain plants are not particularly efficient in restricting water loss [4].

The wooly hairs of some subalpine plants have been variously attributed with the ability to protect against high temperatures [53], intense ultraviolet raditon [59] and frost/freezing [77, 86]. Maybe they play a role in all three. For plants with leaf rosettes on the ground such as the silverweed *Potentilla borneensis*, however, the wooly hairs are on the lower surface and petioles only. This would make sense as frost protection but not against ultra-violet radiation or high temperatures. Other plants provide their growing buds and perennial parts with thermal insulation by retaining old leaves, and by having tufted branches and persistent scales. Such protection is necessary because the 'cost' to a subalpine plant of replacing a leaf is much greater than for plants growing in the more hospitable environments lower down the mountain or in the lowlands. Lee and Lowry have listed the adaptations of leaves to intense ultraviolet radiation as thick cuticles, wax deposits, and high concentrations of red, protective leaf pigments called anthocyanins in young leaves [53].

9.4.4 Origin and dispersal of the flora

The mountain flora of Sumatra is derived from two sources: those which originated locally (autochthonous) and those for which the centre of origin is outside the area concerned (allochthonous) [86]. The local source is itself divisible into two groups: those which are characteristic of equatorial lowland forest, such as members of the families Dipterocarpaceae, Bombacaceae (e.g. durian) or the genus *Ficus* (figs), and those which have a wide latitudinal distribution throughout the globe and a wide altitudinal distribution in the tropics, such as Pinaceae (e.g. *Pinus*),

Cruciferae (e.g. mustard), Theaceae (e.g. tea) and tree ferns. Of the first group very few are found over 2000m and most are found below 1000m. Genera and families of the second group, however, have wide tolerances of temperature and have both low- and high-temperature adapted (microtherm and megatherm) species. The low-temperature adapted species could possibly have originated outside the tropics and migrated towards Sumatra but they are equally likely to have evolved in or near Sumatra. None of the autochonous plants are therefore very useful in deciding how Sumatra gained its mountain flora.

The allochthonous flora, however, although a minority of the total mountain flora, do allow hypotheses regarding their origin to be formed. This part of the flora belongs to genera whose species are only found in cold climates (i.e. microtherm species), and in the tropics they are never found below 1000m and thus are generally found only in the subalpine forests on mountains 2000-2500m high (see principle of the zone of permanent occurrence, section 9.4.1). These genera, such as *Rhododendron*, the grass *Deschampsia* and the coloured herbs *Gentiana* and *Primula*, are found in many tropical and subtropical countries yet none can tolerate a hot climate.

Wallace worked out more or less how the mountains of the Sunda region had received their flora - that is, by dispersal at lower levels during cooler glacial periods when the Sunda Region was a single land mass [92]. Van Steenis made exhaustive studies of the region's microtherm allochthonous flora and revealed numerous intersting patterns of distribution [82, 83, 85, 86]. Plants must have extended their ranges hopping by one means or another along mountain chains. Some of the 'chains' of passage are still quite complete. For example, the prostrate, branched herb with small white flower called *Haloragis micrantha* is found from New Zealand to Japan to the top of the Bay of Bengal as well as on the top of Mt. Papandayan in West Java. It does not seem to have crossed over the relatively short gap to Sumatra (Figure 9.7). Conversely, the stately herb with up to five layers of bright yellow flowers called *Primula prolifera* shows an enormous gap in its distribution (Figure 9.8). Soils seem to have little or no influence on the distributions since a single species will be found on soils originating from igneous, sedimentary or recent volcanic paent material. The age of the rocks does seem to have an effect though, with some species not being present on recent volcanic soils [86] (section 9.4.9).

Figure 9.7 The distribution of *Haloragis micrantha*. **(After van Steenis [86]).**

Figure 9.8 The distribution of *Primula prolifera*. **(After van Steenis [86]).**

Figure 9.9 The three tracks by which microtherm allochthonous flora reached Sumatra. (After van Steenis [86]).

From his analysis of the distribution of about 900 cold-adapted mountain species, van Steenis concluded the existence of three tracks by which plants arrived in Sumatra and other parts of the Sunda Region during some period or periods in the geological past [86]. These three tracks are shown in Figure 9.9. Continuous ranges of high mountains do not, of course, exist along the entire lengths of these tracks. During the coldest times of the Pleistocene the mean temperature dropped only about 2°C (section 1.3.1) which, with rates of temperature change of 0.5-0.6°/100m (not necessarily applicable at that period) is equivalent to a drop in the levels of the forest zones of 350-400m. The locations of mountains over 2500m high, and of mountains 2000-2500m high (Figure 9.10) illustrates how the number of viable 'stepping stones' would have increased for microtherm plants during the coldest periods of the Pleistocene.

There seem to be no easy answers to the problem of how plants actually dispersed (and currently disperse) themselves between their small

Forest on limestone, Lho'Nga, North Aceh.

Seven species of snail found in $2m^2$ of forest floor. Lho'Nga, North Aceh.

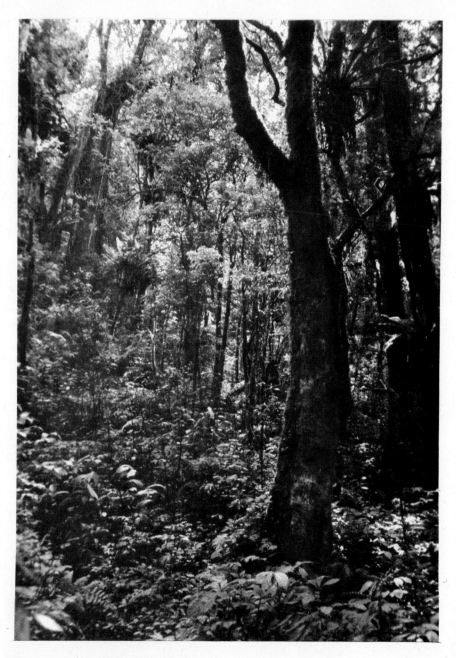

Lower montane forest on Mt. Kerinci.

Figure 9.10 Location of mountains of 2500m and over (circles) and of 2000-2490m (squares) on Sumatra.

islands of suitable habitat. There are four main ways in which plants disperse their fruit and seeds, or, in the case of ferns, mosses, fungi etc., their spores:

a) in water;
b) by wind;
c) by sticking to, being eaten but not destroyed or being removed for later ingestion but then forgotten by terrestrial mammals;
d) by sticking to or being eaten and not destroyed by birds or bats.

The first and third of these are clearly of no significance in explaining the distribution of microtherm plants. Water only flows downstream to unfavourable habitats, and the distances between high mountain tops are too great for terrestrial mammals to complete before either the seed is excreted or is rubbed off.

Wind seems a likely candidate for the dispersion of the minute, dust-like seeds of orchids, spores, or the light, parachute-like, plumed seeds (achenes) of the many montane species of Asteraceae (formerly Compositae—section 9.4.9). Wind must indeed transport such seeds over quite long distances but plumes only open in low humidity, and van Steenis points out that the expected wide distributions of such species is not always found to be the case [86].

Many of the shrubs and small trees in the upper montane and subalpine forests bear berries which, if not exactly tasty, are quite edible and form an important source of food for birds and mammals.[2] Many of the seeds in these juicy berries pass through bird intestines without harm. However, since the time to pass through the intestine is little more than an hour, there is very little possibility of transfering seeds to mountain tops more than about 30 km away and, in addition, birds of mountain tops are mostly sedentary. Sticky or adherent seeds or fruits may attach themselves to feathers or legs, but before a long flight birds will generally preen themselves throroughly so that their feathers give maximum flying efficiency.

If one assumes, however, that occasional, unusual dispersion of seeds occurs between neighbouring mountains by wind or by birds, it would be natural to expect that the percentage of plant species dispersed in these ways would increase up mountains in comparison with species

---

2. It has been suggested that the famous humanoid creatures of the Himalayas called Yetis (if they exist) may subsist on such foods.

whose seeds have no obvious dispersal device or are too heavy for wind dispersal. Although this has not been investigated in Sumatra, it has been investigated for Mt. Kinabalu in Sabah [86] and Mt. Pangorango in West Java [18]. The results show that the opposite is true.

The question of dispersal is further complicated by the observation that communities of plants having a variety of dispersal mechanisms have exactly overlapping ranges on different mountains as though means of dispersal was immaterial. In addition, limited experiments were conducted on Javan mountains to introduce a species not found on a particular mountain to grow there. They met with singular failure. Even if a species grew from a seed and survived, it was not dispersed [86].

As stated above, the lowering of forest zones during the Pleistocene would have made chance dispersal easier if only because more mountain tops would have become suitable habitat. But even then, large gaps would have existed and it is clear that the means by which plants or groups of plants effected their dispersal is not yet fully understood.

9.4.5 Biomass and productivity

There appear to be no estimates of biomass or productivity in montane forests of the Sunda Region, but Grubb has sumarized the trends he found from examining data for montane forests in all parts of the tropics [34]. Thus:

a) biomass decreases proportionally less than height on passing from lowland forest to upper montane forest (see Figure 9.3, section 9.4.1);

b) production of woody parts declines from lowland forest (3-6 t/ha/yr) to upper montane forest ($\pm$ 1 t/ha/yr);

c) production of litter, particularly leaf litter, decreases proportionally much less than biomass or, it seems, production of woody parts;

d) the standing crop of leaves declines proportionally much less than the overall biomass;

e) the mean life span of leaves seems to lengthen only slightly from lowland forest to upper montane forest;

f) the leaf area index (m^2 of leaves per m^2 of ground) decreases proportionally much more than leaf standing crop because the leaves become thicker and harder. Thus the area of leaf per gram decreases from $90-130$ cm^2/g in lowland forest, to ± 80 cm^2/g in upper montane forest.

It appears then, that as total production falls the montane plants invest relatively more of their production in making leaves, and so it is important to understand what advantages accrue to a plant from having thick, 'expensive' leaves which may last no longer than the thinner, 'cheap' leaves of the lowlands.

9.4.6 Mineral cycling

In any type of forest there are two types of mineral turnover:
a) the rapid cycling in the small litter (leaves and twigs) and in throughfall (rain reaching the forest floor), and
b) the much slower cycling in the large woody parts of trees.

As stated in section 9.4.5, in going from lowland to montane forests, the production of woody parts decreases proportionately more than does the production of leaves. The concentration of nutrients in leaves from upper montane forest are roughly half the concentration found in leaves in lowland forests. This reduction is compounded because trees of upper montane forests seem to absorb half of the minerals from their leaves before shedding them, compared to about a quarter for trees of lower montane forests [98]. Thus, lower quantities of minerals cycle through leaves in montane forests than in lowland forest, and much lower quantities through woody parts.

The most detailed study of mineral cycling in montane forest close to the Sunda Region is by Edwards in Papua New Guinea [19, 20, 21, 37]. In the final paper of the series, Edwards summarized the major findings of the preceding papers [19]. The major external input of minerals into the montane forest was from the rain, and these minerals may have been released into the atmosphere from fires [91]. Surprisingly, perhaps, not all the rain reaches the forest floor (a certain percentage soaks into bark, evaporates, or gets trapped) and the percentage which reaches the ground, the throughfall, varies with rain intensity, being greater when the rainfall is heavier (Figure 9.11). This throughfall contains minerals leached from the leaf and bark surface and from decomposition products so that the mineral concentration in rain reaching the forest floor is considerably higher than that reaching, say, a neighbouring cultivated field. In addition

Sphagnum lake near the summit of Mt. Kemiri.

Nepenthes gymnamphora pitcher plant; 2500m, Mt.Kemiri.

Figure 9.11 Percentage of rain falling over a lower montane forest that actually reaches the forest floor. (After Edwards [19]).

to the throughfall, the other source of minerals falling to the forest floor is the litterfall. The proportions of minerals in the litterfall is affected somewhat by the withdrawal of minerals from leaves before abscission i.e. the parting of leaf and twig. Edwards compared mineral concentrations in healthy leaves with leaves in the litterfall, and found that calcium and magnesium did not seem to be absorbed, but that nitrogen and phosphorus were respectively 15% and 31% lower in the litterfall [19]. The recycling of these two minerals may indicate that they were limiting in the soil (see section 9.3.7). Potassium is very mobile in soil and quickly resorbed by plants so its retention is less important. The calcium levels in the top soil layers of the forest examined were extremely high (16-40 meq./100 g) [21] compared to the levels in many mountain soils in Sumatra (section 9.3) and elsewhere in the western Sunda Region. It would be interesting to determine whether calcium is absorbed before abscission in Sumatran mountain plants and thus gain an indication of the limiting role of calcium in its mountain forest.

A summary of mineral cycling in the Papua New Guinea montane forest is shown in Figure 9.12.

398

Figure 9.12 Summary of mineral cycling in a lower montane forest. Data in boxes are expressed in kg/ha. Complete arrows represent major pathways of mineral transfer and data are expressed in kg/ha/year. Dashed arrows represent presumed pathways for which no data are available. (After Edwards [19]).

9.4.7 Limitations on forest distribution and growth

The lower limit of a particular type of montane forest is probably set, not by temperature, but by the ability of its species to compete with species of the lower formation. The upper limit of a forest formation, however, is set by some factor related to temperature [35]. The Massenerhebung effect section 9.2.1) appears to act on plants through the height at which cloud habitually settles and this is clearly related to temperature. The most important effect of cloud is that it prevents bright sunlight from raising the temperature of leaves of plants. Those not adapted to living in the cloud zone may not reach their optimum temperature for photosynthesis. The amount of radiation available for photosynthesis is also reduced by cloud [34]. The decrease with altitude of biomass, productivity, number of life forms and number of species can also be attributed to these factors.

Although temperature and radiation are the factors primarily responsibly for limiting montane forest distribution and growth, the mineral supply is also highly important. Without conducting soil analyses or productivity studies, it can be seen that:

a) the crooked and gnarled growth of many montane trees is similar to growth of trees on infertile lowland soils or to the miniature bonsai trees deliberately grown in nutrient-poor soils;

b) the slow rate of litter decay and the subsequent humus mineralization may be assumed to lock up plant nutrients (especially nitrogen and phosphorus) in forms unavailable for plant growth;

c) forest types are found at lower levels and forest growth is less on sites most likely to be poor in nutrients, i.e. ridges;

d) the most dwarfed forests are found on peaty soils of very low pH which are likely to be too infertile for most plants;

e) some of the species found on peat soils in upper montane forest, are found also in the similarly acid, infertile heath forests of the lowlands;

f) the insectivorous pitcher plants *Nepenthes* (section 8.2.4) are often abudant in peaty upper montane forest [35].

Quantities of nutrients in leaves (see section 8.2.3) reflect to some degree the nutrients available in the soil and so analysis of leaf nutrients is standard practice in investigative agriculture. Grubb examined both his own and other data on nutrient levels in leaves of montane species and found considerable variation within the forest types, but was able to conclude that the supply of phosphorus seemed particularly deficient in peaty upper montane forest. This supports the suggestion that phosphorus is the factor underlying the observations d), e), and f) above [35]. Interestingly, Grubb also analysed the nutrients in leaves of pitcher plants *Nepenthes* to determine how similar they were to the surrounding vegetation that was not able to catch or digest insects. The results showed that nearly three times as much phosphorus and almost twice as much potassium was present in *Nepenthes* leaves compared with nearby trees and shrubs [34].

The major limitation on leaf life in the upper montane subalpine forests is probably not, as in most other forests, the destruction by insects, but the high humidity. This allows invasion by fungi and bacteria, and by epiphyllous lichens and mosses which are able to puncture the leaf's cuticle. The very thick outer walls of pachyphylls may be an adaptation to minimize such unwanted penetration [35].

In section 7.2.1 it was argued that drip tips on leaves allow water to flow rapidly off the leaves and so prevent, or at least slow down, the growth of epiphylls. If that is so then why do montane forest plants invest in much more expensive thick leaves? Grubb has suggested that whereas drip tips are effective under conditions of alternating heavy rains and sun, they would not be so effective where the dampness of leaf surfaces is caused by very high humidity and very fine water droplets from clouds or fog [35].

9.4.8 Similarities between upper montane forest and heath forest

The impoverished, acid soils of some higher mountain zones might lead to an expectation that upper montane and heath forests (section 8.2) might be somewhat similar. The structure of the forests are indeed rather similar with both of their canopies being even and appearing rather pale (high albedo). The trees tend to have dense crowns, usually with microphyll leaves (section 9.4.1) which are often held obliquely vertical and closely placed on the twigs. Large woody climbers are more or less absent and biomass and productivity also seem to be low (section 9.4.4).

They also share some tree and shrub species which do not (or only very rarely) exist in other types of forests. Examples are sesapu *Baeckia frutescens* (section 8.1.3), and species of bilberry *Vaccinium* and

Rhododendron.

9.4.9 Volcanoes

Near volcanic craters the ground surface is generally rocky, dry, sterile, acid, exposed, lacking in organic matter, and often warm or hot from the gases beneath. The air contain such potentially toxic gases as sulphur dioxide (SO_2) and hydrogen sulphide (H_2S) (the smell of rotten eggs) as well as carbon monoxide (CO), nitrous oxide (NO), and chlorine (Cl_2) [86]. Water flowing out of craters is commonly little more than a stream of sulphuric acid. These are hardly conditions that favour plant growth but van Steenis reports finding the tussock-forming sedgelike *Xyris capensis* (a species ranging from Central Africa to Australia) in a North Sumatran crater stream the pH of which was 2.9 [86]. Blue-green algae are also commonly found in hot, sulphurous acid water.

Ash produced by eruptions occurs in screes on the tops of volcanoes, such as Mt. Kerinci, which have been active in the recent past. They are barren, pervious, sterile and unstable, moving downhill particularly during heavy rains. The only plants able to colonize such ground must have long, deep roots for anchorage and to find moisture. Grasses (e.g. *Agrostis*), sedges (e.g. *Carex*) and the composite *Senecio sumatrana*, are among the first pioneers on Mt. Kerinci but the highest-growing plant of all is a small fern [28]. *Melastoma* and pandans are common on the sulphurous screes of Mt. Sibayak and Mt. Sinabung. Tanah Karo, but they are absent from the non-sulphurous screes on Mt. ni Telong, Central Aceh [27].

The magnificent edelweiss *Anaphalis javanica* is one of the very few plants confined to volcanoes and is known only from central and southern Sumatra. It is a long-lived pioneer of volcanic ash screes and crater soils and is frequently gregarious. It usually grows to about 4 m (sometimes to 8 m) with it stem as thick as a man's wrist [86]. The stem has fine, velvety white hair and the abudant flowers appear white too, except for a central yellow disk. Most mountain plants have become dwarfed but the edeweis is one of the giant, white-haired members of the Asteraceae (formerly Compositae) which, in height at least, dominate the generally short subalpine vegetation on tropical mountains. Its equivalent on East African mountains are giant species of *Senecio* and in the Andes the 9m tall *Espeletia* [59]. The edelweiss has traditionally been regarded as a gift from heaven in some areas and climbers have taken small pieces with them when they descend. The habit has turned to vandalism on some mountains, such as Mt. Singgalang and Mt. Kerinci, where this strikingly beautiful plant does not have just a portion removed but is dug up completely in the naive hope that it might grow in the lowlands.

On volcanic scree such as on Mt. Kerinci [44] the fern *Gleichenia arachnoidea* forms dense prickly thickets. This and the common mountain fern *Dipteris* (Figure 9.13) are of interest because fossils of seemingly identical plants have been found in Greenland and Britain dating from the Cretaceous Period, 65-135 million year ago [42].

9.4.10 Mountain lakes

Mountain lakes in Sumatra are generally of two types: lakes in extinct volcanic craters such as Lake Maninjau (±600m a.s.l) and Lake Tujuh (1996m a.s.l) [23] and marshy lakes in small depressions formed by glacial action (see section 1.3.1).

After volcanic activity ceases, water begins to accumulate in the craters. At first the sulphurous content of the water prevents colonization

Figure 9.13 *Gleichenia* and *Dipteris* **ferns of the higher mountain zones.** (After Holttum [42]).

by most plants, but as these harmful substances are either leached away or incorporated into sediments, marshy plants can begin to grow. The depth of a crater lake obviously depends on the height above the lake floor of an outlet, but is usually quite considerable. The flora and fauna of high, deep, cold, oligotrophic (nutrient-poor) lakes is impoverished and, since the sides are generally steep there is little or no characteristic fringe habitat.

Of more interest, however, are the marshy fringes of shallow lakes in glacial hollows such as the one at 3000m on Mt. Kemiri. The rushes, sedges and grass such as *Juncus, Carex, Scirpus mucronatus* form clumped mats while nearer the water's edge the white, round-flowered *Eriocaulon browniana* is commonly found in hummocks. The most characteristic plant, however, is the moss *Sphagnum* which is sometimes also found in moss forest [9]. This genus has a world-wide distribution and is generally found in shallow , cold, usually acid, nutrient-poor water or in similar water-logged soil where few other plant species thrive. *Sphagnum* productivity varies between 100-600 $g/m^2/year$ depending on environmental conditions [11]. Sumatran *Sphagnum* is very poorly known, but Johnson reports one species, *S. junghuhnianum* from mountain tops in Peninsular Malaysia and from China, Japan and Taiwan which is also found on Sumatran mountains [49].

Sphagnum grows like other mosses but the dead parts decay very slowly (even though the leaves are only one cell thick) and form the basis of much of the peat in temperate regions. The reasons for this slow decay are perhaps two fold: the very low nitrogen content ($\pm 1\%$ of dry weight) makes it an unattractive to decomposing organisms, and the acid conditions and the low oxygen levels in the water enclosed within the carpets of the moss, also create unfavourable conditions for breakdown. *Sphagnum* may be just a lowly moss but it is extremely successful: virtually nothing eats it, it covers at least 1% of the earth's surface, and its bulk of living and decomposing parts is probably greater than any other plant genus in the world [11].

The fauna associated with *Sphagnum*-dominated lakes is poor and at the lake on Mt. Kemiri the only animals found were a few bloodworms (larvae of chironomid midges) which feed on detritus, hunting spiders which can walk on the water surface between clumps of *Sphagnum* and probably prey on emerging midges, and predatory larvae of libellulid dragonflies.

9.5 ANIMALS AND THEIR ZONATION

9.5.1 Invertebrates

The number of invertebrates declines with altitude. On Mt. Mulu, Sarawak, for example, the decrease in soil macroinvertebrates was accounted for largely by the gradual reduction in the abudance of ants and termites. Biomass, however, reached a maximum in the peaty soils of the taller parts of upper montane forest where beetle larvae took over from termites as the major detritivores. At higher altitudes centipedes and spiders took over from ants as the major predators [12, 13]. A disjunction in the distribution of beetles was found up the mountain such that no beetle species found below 500m (lowland forest) was found above 1500m (upper montane forest) [38, 39]. The highland beetles were thus a distinct association of species. A study of large moths in Papua New Guinea showed that the total number of species dropped from 774 at 2200m (lower montane forest) to 379 at 2800m (upper montane forest) [40].

Whereas in the lowlands the most conspicuous bees are the carpenter bees (Xylopodidae) these are rare above 1500m. During sunny periods in the subalpine forest bumble bees *Bombus* sp. (Apidae) are a common sight as they visit flowers for pollen and for nectar. It must be remembered that a visit to a flower by a potential pollinator (birds, bats, moths, butterflies, wasps, bees, ants, flies or beetles) does not necessarily constitute actual pollination. Notes have been made on mountain plant pollination by van Steenis [86], and for detailed, fascinating information on pollination ecology see Faegri and van der Pijl [22].

It is well known to entomologists that moths and many other insects such as winged ants, beetles and flies exhibit the phenomenon of summit-seeking in which they fly up mountains and sometimes congregate in large numbers. The basic factors underlying this behaviour are not known and a bewildering variety of explanations have been proposed [60].

9.5.2 Reptiles and amphibians

Nothing seems to be known about the altitudinal limits of reptiles and amphibians of Sumatran mountains but these were investigated up Mt. Benom, an isolated, granitic mountain in Peninsular Malaysia. No

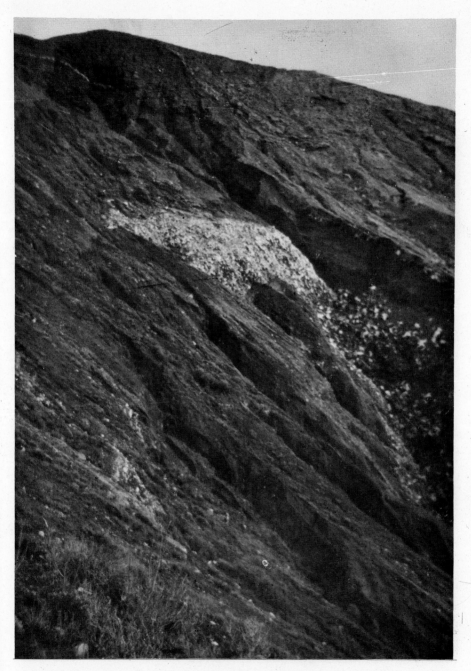
The eroding ash cone above the tree line on Mt. Kerinci.

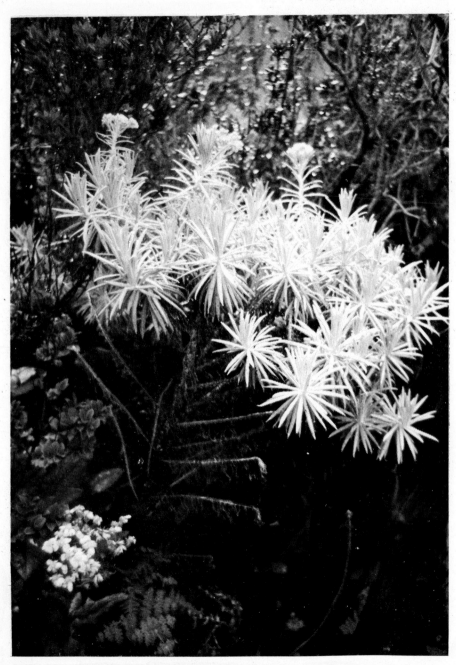

Sumatran edelweiss on Mt. Kerinci.

lizards were found above 1000m but five snakes were. Only one of these was found beyond 2000m. Similarly, seven species of frogs or toads were found above 1000m but only one was found above 2000m [32]. None of the montane species found on Mt. Benom are known from Sumatra but a similar type of reduction in species would be expected on Sumatran mountains.

9.5.2 Birds

As part of their report on a collection of birds from Aceh, Chasen and Hoogerwerf list the species found in different habitats and at different altitudes [9]. Thus, in the primary and dense secondary growth between 300 and 1200m, 134 species were found. In the upper montane forest they found only nine, but eight of these were also found lower down. In the subalpine zone, however, eleven species were found, but only two of these were found in either the lowlands or in the upper montane forest. This illustrates that the montane avifauna is also not just an impoverished selection of hardy species but is a distinct community of species.

Similarly, on Mt. Benom, only 3% of the lowland birds reached 1200m (the lower region of Fagaceae/Lauraceae forest in lower montane forest) and the species of the upper parts of lower montane forest and of upper montane forest were quite distinct from the lowland species [65]. Similar results were found for the birds of Mt. Mulu [15, 94]. Characteristic and conspicuous birds of Sumatran mountain tops are the medium-size (±30cm) Sunda Whistling Thrush *Myiophoneus glaucinus*, Shiny Whistling Thrush *Myiophoneus melanurus*, Scaly Thrush *Zoothera dauma* and Island Thrush *Turdus poliocephalus* [51, 88]. Perhaps because humans are so rarely seen on high mountains, many of these birds are very tame, and can easily be watched eating *Vaccinium* berries and similar foods. Above the summit of Mt. Kemiri, the CRES team observed a crested serpent eagle *Spilornis cheela* and a high-flying swift *Apus* sp. Large mountains clearly are no barriers to these master flyers.

In Papua New Guinea, Kikkawa and Williams found that a distinct discontinuity of bird species occurred at about 1500-2200m, which corresponds to the change from lower to upper montane forest, They continued their analysis to examine the differences in the niche occupancy of birds at high altitudes [50]. Thus, with increasing altitude:

406

- the proportion of tree-nesting insectivorous species increased;
- the proportion of tree-nesting frugivorous species decreased;
- the proportion of tree-nesting omnivorous species stayed roughly the same;
- the proportion of predatory birds decreased; and
- the proportion of ground-living birds increased.

9.5.4 Mammals

At least eleven species of mammals found in Sumatra are more or less restricted to the mountains:

a) Grey shrew *Crocidura attenuata* known from subalpine zones of Mt. Leuser, Mt. Kerinci and one was caught by the CRES team on Mt. Kemiri. Also known from the highest mountain in Peninsular Malaya, Mt. Gede in West Java and lowland areas of northern Indo-China and southern China [8, 48, 54].

Figure 9.14 The Sumatran rabbit *Nesolagus netscheri*

b) Grey fruit bat *Aethalops alecto,* known only from mountain forests above 1000m in Sumatra, Peninsular Malaysia and Kalimantan [24].

c) Sumatran rabbit *Nesolagus netscherii,* known only from Mt. Kerinci and the Padang Highlands [46, 47] (Figure 9.14). This species has not been reported since 1937 but the CRES team found that some farmers on the lower slopes of Mt. Kerinci still see it very occasionally.

d) Volcano mouse *Mus crociduroides,* known only from 3000m on Mt. Kerinci and 2400m on Mt. Gede in West Java [8, 64, 74]. Other localities may yet be discovered.

e) Giant Sumatran rat *Sundamys infraluteus,* known from the length of the Barisan Mountains between 700 and 2500m and also on Mt. Kinabalu, Sabah. This species is known on Sumatra from only six specimens [71].

f) Edward's rat *Leopoldamys edwardsi,* which is widely distributed and rarely found below 1000m [65, 71].

g) Hoogerwerf's rat *Rattus hoogerwerfi,* known only from 800m near Blangkejeren, Aceh [8, 71].

h) Kerinci rat *Maxomys hylomyoides,* known only from 2200m on Mt. Kerinci [22, 70, 71, 75].

i) Kerinci rat *Maxomys inflatus,* known only from 1400m on Mt. Kerinci [22, 70, 71, 75].

j) Kinabalu rat *Rattus baluensis,* known only from 2200m on Mt. Kerinci and from 2500m on Mt. Kinabalu, Sabah [24, 70, 71, 75].

k) Mountain spiny rat *Niviventer rapit,* known from 1400m on Mt. Kerinci and between 1000 and 2600m on widely separated peaks in northern and southern Thailand, Peninsular Malaysia and Sabah [63, 66, 71]. The distribution of these last two species (shown in Figure 9.15) is particularly interesting. More localities in Sumatra may yet be discorvered.

l) Serow, or Mountain goat *Capricornis sumatraensis,* known from 200m to the vegetated summits of mountains in Sumatra, Peninsular Malaysia and north to the Himalayas of India. In Sumatra this agile animal also lives on forested limestone hills with nearly vertical sides even though the hills may be surrounded by cultivation. It

408

leaves characteristic piles of faeces in small caves or the entraces to larger caves [45, 54].

The mammal fauna of Mt. Benom became markedly impoverished above 1200m (the lower level of Fagaceae/Lauraceae forest) [65]. This same depauperization has been recorded for Sumatran mountains by Robinson and Kloss [75]. and WWF/van Strien [97], and by the CRES expedition to Mt. Kemiri. Those mammals with a wide altitudinal range tend to be large—thus above 2500m in the subalpine and upper

Rattus baluensis   *Niviventer rapit*

Figure 9.15 Distribution of two Sumatran rat species. (After Marshall [63]).

montane zones on Mt. Kemiri signs (tracks or faeces) were found of Sumatran rhino *Dicerorhinus sumatrensis*, tiger *Panthera tigris*, bear *Helarctos malayanus*, pig *Sus* sp., serow *Capricornis sumatraensis*, and barking deer *Muntiacus muntjak*.

The most surprising mountain mammal is probably the grey shrew. This is one of the smallest mammals on Sumatra, having a body length of only about 8cm, and a cold mountain top is the least likely habitat to find such an animal. Small mammals lose body heat very quickly (a problem

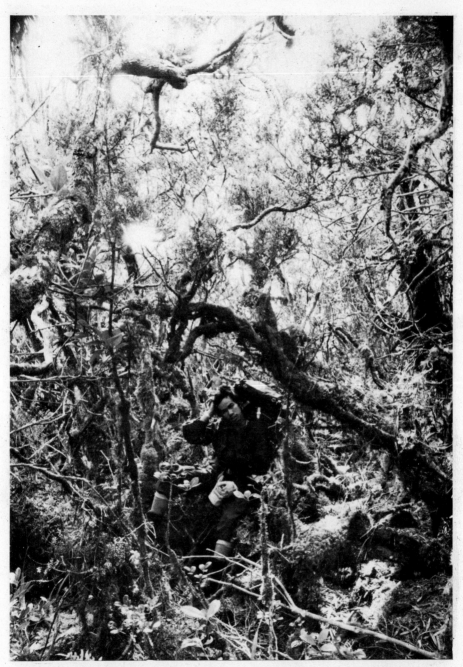

Upper montane forest on Mt. Kemiri.

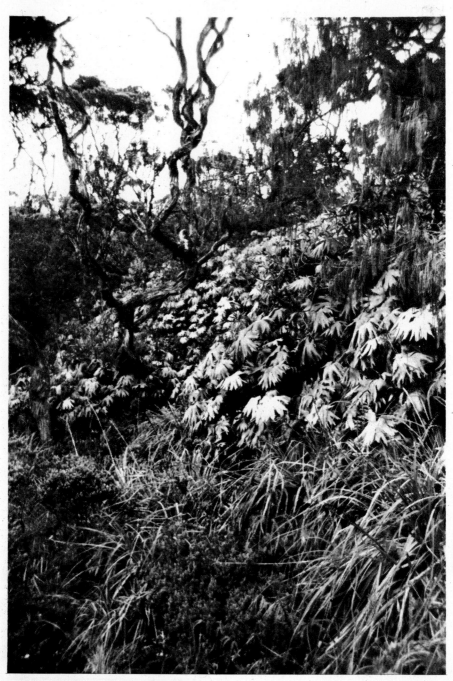

Subalpine forest on Mt. Kemiri.

exacerbated in cold regions) because the surface area:body weight ratio is very high and the heat loss must be compensated by high energy intake in food. Shrews are almost entirely carnivorous and eat small insects, snails, earthworms, millipedes, centipedes and spiders; resources which are largely scattered, not storable and often unpredictable. Shrews therefore have to spend a great deal of time searching for food, which itself uses up energy. It is not surprising then that shrews eat about their own body weight in food each day and are active at most times of day although they rest briefly every few hours. If more than a few hours pass without a meal, a shrew will starve to death. Shrews make underground burrows in which they build a nest and during the cold nights the temperature there is probably significantly higher than outside.

The volcano mouse experiences similar conditions but its diet is primarily vegetable, the sources of which are generally quite large (for a mouse) and storable. Mice will eat small invertebrates when they can catch them.

Figure 9.16 Changes in biomass of four primate species up Mt. Benom. (After Caldecott [7]). a-white-handed gibbon, b-siamang, c-banded leaf monkey, d-dusky leaf monkey.

The only detailed study that seems to have been conducted on altitudal effects on mammals in the Sunda Region is by Caldecott and concerns the altitudinal limits of monkeys and gibbons on Mt. Benom (2108m). From his repeated censuses conducted from 150m to the summit he found that the changes in biomass of the six species present varied up the mountain [7] (Figure 9.16). He asked two questions:
— why are the species limited by altitude?
— why are the species limited at different altitudes?

The answer to the first question is a combination of energetics and food supply. As described in section 9.4.1, with increasing altitude the forest becomes shorter and more crooked and gnarled. There are also few large boughs. Thus, at higher altitudes, the gibbons, which normally travel by swinging below boughs and branches, would experience increasing difficulty and thus greater energy costs in moving through the tree canopy. In addition, because productivity levels are lower at higher altitudes (section 9.4.5) the young leaves and fruit eaten by leaf monkeys and gibbons would not be available in the same quantity as in the lowlands. Also, few tree species with leaves or fruit eaten by primates in the lowlands are found in the higher zones. Although no data exists it may be that leaves of the higher forest types (on acid, nutrient-poor soils) contain high concentrations of defence compounds (section 5.5, 7.6.1, 8.2.4).

The answer to the second question (why are species limited at different altitudes?) is a combination of food preferences, body size and morphology. The altitudinal limit for white-handed gibbons, which are primarily frugivorous, is lower than for siamang which, although still mainly frugivorous, eat a larger proportion of leaves. This represents the differences in altitude at which these two species could reliably collect the different types of food they require to support the energy expended during food collection. The larger body size of the siamang (10-12 kg compared with 5-6 kg for the white-handed gibbon) and its thicker fur would also decrease the relative energetic costs of keeping warm at higher (colder) altitudes [7]. The dark-handed gibbon *Hylobates agilis* found south of Lake Toba is ecologically equivalent to the white-hand gibbon [30, 31], and so the ecological separation from the siamang decribed above would doubtless also occur in southern Sumatra.

The two leaf monkeys weigh about the same (about 7 kg) [10], but during a study of their comparative ecology, Curtin recorded 137 food species for the banded leaf-monkey and only 87 food species for the dusky leaf-monkey [16]. The apparently greater dietary versatility of the banded leaf-monkey may be one reason it is able to live at higher altitudes than the dusky leaf-monkey. Another possible reason is that the morphology and muscular anatomy of the banded leaf-monkey is more adapted to the use of smaller supports and travelling on the ground (both of advantage in montane forest) than that of the dusky leaf-monkey which seems to depend on larger branches in the forest canopy [25, 26]. Similar reasoning can be applied to the two macaque species - the long-tailed macaque *Macaca fascicularis* and the pig-tailed macaque *Macaca nemestrina*. The former is an arboreal frugivore which is generally found beside rivers below 300m a.s.l. [1], whereas the pig-tailed macaque eats a varied diet including many terrestrial arthropods, and its morphology is dog-like and thus suitable for travel on the ground [7].

Finally, there are many traditions which hold that mammals climb mountains to die, Mt. Leuser in the Gajo language means the mountain where animals go to die. Jacobson [46] and van Steenis [84] report often finding dead or dying flying squirrels on barren mountain summits and Gisius [29] and van der Bosch [3] report similar observations for other animals. There are no data to negate the hypothesis but is should be remembered that:

- all animals (dead or alive) are far more conspicuous on bare mountains than in forest;
- scavenging beetles etc. are rare at high altitudes, and
- rates of microbial decay are much slower at low temperatures and so corpses will remain for a longer time.

REFERENCES

1. Aldrich-Blake, F.P.G. (1980). Long-tailed macaques. In *Malayan Forest Primates: Ten Year's Study in Tropical Rain Forest* (ed. D.J. Chivers), pp. 147—165. Plenum, New York. (12.8.25)

2. Beek, C.G.G. van (1982). *A geomorphological and pedological study of the Gunung Leuser National Park, North Sumatera, Indonesia.* Wageningen Agricultural University, Wageningen. (23.3.5)

3. Bosch, A.C. van der (1938). Het verdwalen van dieren op bergtoppen. *Trop. Natuur* 27: 169—172. (12.8.17)

4. Buckley, R.C., Corlett, R.T. and Grubb, P.J. (1980). Are the xeromorphic trees of upper montane rain forests drought-resistant? *Biotropica* 12: 124—136. (12.1.39)

5. Burnham, C.P. (1974). The role of the soil forming factors in controlling altitudinal zonation on granite in Malaysia. In *Altitudinal Zonation in Malesia* (ed. J.R. Flenley), pp. 59—74. University of Hull, Hull. (12.10.44)

6. _____. (1975). Soils. In *Tropical Rain Forests of the East* (oleh T.C. Whitmore), pp. 103—120. Clarendon, Oxford. (12.10.8)

7. Caldecott, J.O. (1980). Habitat quality and populations of two sympatric gibbons (Hylobatidae) on a mountain in Malay. *Folia primatol.* 33: 291—309. (12.8.12)

8. Chasen, F.N. (1940). The mammals of the Netherlands Indies Mt Leuser Expedition 1937 to North Sumatra. *Treubia* 17: 479—502. (12.8.13)

9. Chasen, F.N. and Hoogerwerf, A. (1941). The birds of the Netherlands Indies Mt Leuser Expedition 1937 to North Sumatra. *Treubia* 18 (suppl.): 1—125. (12.7.12)

10. Chivers, D.J. and Davies, A.G. (1978). Abundance of primates in the Krau Game Reserve, Peninsular Malaysia. In *The Abundance of Animals in Malesian Rain Forests* (ed. A.G. Marshall), pp. 9—36. University of Hull, Hull. (12.8.22)

413

11. Clymo, R.S. and Hayward, P.M. (1982). The ecology of *Sphagnum*. In *Bryophyte Ecology* (ed. A.J.E. Smith), pp. 229—289. Chapman and Hall, London. (12.1.19)

12. Collins, N.M. (1979). Soil invertebrates from Mulu's forests. Paper presented at Gunung Mulu Symposium, 1979, Royal Geographical Society, London. (12.4.17)

13. ——————. (1980). The distribution of soil macrofauna on the west ridge of Gunung (Mount) Mulu, Sarawak. *Oecologia* 44: 263—275.

14. Corner, E.J.H. (1952). *Wayside Trees of Malaya*. 2 vols. 2nd Ed. Government Printer, Singapore. (12.1.15)

15. Croxall, J.P. (1979). The montane birds of Gunung Mulu. Paper presented at Gunung Mulu Symposium, 1979, Royal Geographical Society, London. (12.7.15)

16. Curtin, S.H. (1980). Dusky and leaf monkeys. In *Malayan Forest primates: Ten Years' Study in Tropical Rain Forest* (ed. D.J. Chivers), pp. 107—145. Plenum, New York. (12.8.25)

17. Docters van Leeuwen, W. (1920). Naar de top van de Singgalang bij Fort de Kock. *Trop. Natuur* 9: 97—104.

18. ——————. (1933). Biology of plants and animals occuring in the higher parts of Mount Pangrango-Gedeh in West Java. *Ver. Kon. Akad. Wet. Amst.* 31: 1—1278. (12.13.7)

19. Edwards, P.J. (1982). Studies of mineral cycling in a montane rain forest in New Guinea. V. Rates of cycling in throughfall and litter fall. *J. Ecol.* 70: 507—828. (12.10.26)

20. Edwards, P.J. and Grubb, P.J. (1977). Studies of mineral cycling in a montane rain forest in New Guinea. *J. Ecol.* 65: 243—969. (12.10.24)

21. ——————. (1982). Studies of mineral cycling in a montane rain forest. IV. Soil characteristics and the division of mineral elements between the vegetation and soil. *J. Ecol.* 70: 649—666. (12.10.25)

22. Faegri, K. and Pijl, L. van der (1979). *The Principles of Pollination Ecology*. 3rd rev. ed. Pergamon, Oxford. (12.1.27)

23. FAO/Wulf, R. de, Djoko, S., Kurnia, R. (1981). *Usulan Taman Nasional Kerinci-Seblat: Rencana Pengelolaan Pendahuluan 1982—1987*. UNDP/FAO National Parks Development Project, Bogor. (10.2.11)

24. FAO/Zon, A.P.M. van der (1979). *Mammals of Indonesia*. FAO. Bogor (12.8.36)

25. Fleagle, J.G. (1978). Locomotion, posture, and habitat utilization in two sympatric, Malaysian leaf-monkeys (*Presbytis obscura* and *Presbytis melalophos*). In *The Ecology of Arboreal Folivores* (ed. G.G. Montgomery), pp. 243—251. Smithsonian Institution, Washington. (12.8.19)

26. _____. (1980). Locomotion and posture. In *Malayan Forest Primates: Ten Years' Study in Tropical Rain Forest*. (ed. D.J. Chivers), pp. 191—207. Plenum, New York. (12.8.25)

27. Frey-Wyssling, A. (1931). Over de vegetatie van den Boer Ni Telong en omstreken in Gajolanden (Noord Sumatra). *Trop. Natuur* 20: 37—49.

28. _____. (1933). Over de flora van den pick van Kerintji (3800m). *Trop. Natuur* 22: 1—10.

29. Gisius, A. (1930). Het sterven der dieren in de wildernis. *Trop. Natuur* 19: 197—198. (12.8.18)

30. Gittins, S.P. (1979). *The Behaviour and Ecology of the Agile Gibbon (Hylobates agilis)*. Unpubl. thesis, University of Cambridge, Cambridge. (12.8.26)

31. Gittins, S.P. and Raemaekers, J.J. (1980). Siamang, lar and agile gibbons. In *Malayan Forest Primates: Ten Years' Study in Tropical Rain Forest* (ed. D.J. Chivers), pp. 63—105. Plenum, New York. (12.8.25)

32. Grandison, A.G.C. (1972). The Gunong Benom Expedition 1967. Reptiles and amphibians of Gunung Benom with a description of a new species of *Macroca*. *Bull. Brit. Mus. Nat. Hist. (Zool.)* 23: 43—107. (12.6.6)

33. Grubb, P.J. (1971). Interpretation of the 'Massenerhebung' effect on tropical mountains. *Nature* 229: 44—46. (12.10.45)

34. _____. (1974). Factors controlling the distribution of forest types on tropical mountains: new factors and a new perspective In *Altitudinal Zonation in Malesia*. (ed. J.R. Flenley), pp. 13—46. University of Hull, Hull. (12.10.27)

35. _____. (1977). Control of forest growth and distribution on wet tropical mountains with special reference to mineral nutrition. *Ann. Rev. Ecol. Syst.* 8: 83—107. (12.10.28)

415

36. _____. Personal communication.
37. Grubb, P.J. and Edwards, P.J. (1982). Studies of mineral cycling in a montane rain forest in New Guinea. III. The distribution of mineral elements in the above-ground material. *J. Ecol.* 70: 623—648. (12.10.29)
38. Hammond, P.M. (1979). Distribution and diversity of Coleoptera in relation to forest type and altitude. Paper presented at Gunung Mulu Symposium, 1979, Royal Geographical Society, London. (12.4.18)
39. Hanski, I. (1983). Distributional ecology and abundance of dung and carrion feeding beetles (Scarabaeidae) in tropical rain forest in Sarawak, Borneo. *Acta Zool. Fenn.* 167: 1—45. (12.4.51)
40. Hebert, P.D.N. (1980). Moth communities in montane Papua New Guinea. *J. Anim. Ecol.* 49: 593—602. (12.4.14)
41. Holttum, R.E. (1963). Cyathaceae. *Flora Malesiana II* I: 65—176.
42. _____. (1977). *Plant Life in Malaya*, 2nd Ed. Longman, Kuala Lumpur. (12.1.14)
43. Holttum, R.E. and Allen, B.M. (1963). The tree-ferns of Malaya. *Gdns' Bull. S'pore* 22: 41—51 . (12.1.31)
44. Jacobs, M. (1958). Contribution to the botany of Mt. Kerintji and adjacent area in West Central Sumatra — I. *Ann. Bogorienses* 3: 45—79. (12.10.38)
45. Jacobson, E. (1918). De kambing oetan. *Trop. Natuur* 7: 129—134.
46. _____. (1921). Notes on some mammals from Sumatra. *J. Fed. Malay. States Mus.* 10: 235—240. (12.8.14)
47. Jacobson, E. and Kloss, C.B. (1919). Notes on the Sumatran Hare. *J. Fed. Malay. States Mus.* 7: 293—297. (12.8.15)
48. Jenkins, P.D. (1982). A discussion of Malayan and Indonesian shrews of the genus *Crocidura* (Insectivora: Soricidae). *Zool. Med.* 56: 267—269. (12.8.15)
49. Johnson, A, (1960). Variations in *Sphagnum junghuhnianum* subsp. *junghuhnianum* Dz. & Molk. *Trans. Br. bryol. Soc.* 3: 725—728. (12.1.100)
50. Kikkawa, J. and Williams, W.T. (1971). Altitudinal distribution of land birds in New Guinea. *Search* 2: 64—65. (12.7.12)
51. King, B., Woodcock, M. and Dickinson, E.C. (1975). *A Field Guide to the Birds of S.E. Asia.* Collins, London. (12.7.45)

52. Laubenfels, D.J. de (1969). A revision of the Malesian and Pacific rainforest conifers, I. Podocarpaceae, in part. *J. Arn. Arb.* 50: 274—369. (12.1.11)

53. Lee, D.W. and Lowry, J.B. (1980). Solar ultraviolet on tropical mountains: Can it affect plant speciation? *Am. Nat.* 115: 880—883. (12.1.23)

54. Lekagul, B. and McNeely, J.A. (1977). *The Mammals of Thailand.* Association for the Conservation of Wildlife, Bangkok. (12.8.21)

55. Loveless, A.R. (1961). A nutritional interpretation of schlerophylly based on differences in the chemical composition of schlerophyllous and mesophytic leaves. *Ann. Bot.* 25: 168—184. (12.1.20)

56. _____. (1962). Further evidence to support a nutritional interpretation of schlerophylly. *Ann. Bot.* 26: 551—561. (12.1.21)

57. McVean, D.N. (1974). Mountain climates of the south-west Pacific. In *Altitudinal Zonation of Forests in Malesia.* (ed. J.R. Flenley), pp. 47—57. University of Hull, Hull. (1.1.2)

58. Maloney, B.K. (1983). The plant ecology of forest remnants on the Toba plateau of North Sumatra. *Indonesia Circle* 31: 23—37.

59. Mani, M.S. (1980). The vegetation of highlands. In *Ecology of Highlands.* (ed. M.S. Mani, and L.E. Giddings), pp. 127—139. Junk, The Hague. (12.10.30)

60. _____. (1980). The animal life of highlands. In *Ecology of Highlands.* (ed. M.S. Mani, and L.E. Giddings), pp. 141—159. Junk, The Hague. (12.13.5)

61. Manokaran, N. (1979). Stemflow, throughfall, and rainfall interception in a lowland tropical rainforest in Peninsular Malaysia. *Malay. Forester* 42: 174—201. (12.10.44)

62. _____. (1980). The nutrient contents of precipitation, throughfall and stemflow in a lowland tropical rainforest in Peninsular Malaysia. *Malay. Forester* 43: 266—289. (12.10.46)

63. Marshall, J.T. (1977). Family Muridae. In *Mammals of Thailand* (ed. B. Lekagul and J.A. McNeely), pp. 397—494. Association for the Conservation of Wildlife, Bangkok. (12.8.21)

64. _____. (1977). A synopsis of Asian species of *Mus* (Rodentia, Murridae). *Bull. Amer. Mus. nat. Hist.* 158: 173—220. (12.8.82)

65. Medway, Lord (1972). The Gunong Benom Expedition 1967. 6. The distribution and altitudinal zonation of birds and mammals on Gunong Benom. *Bull. Brit. Mus. Nat. Hist. (Zool.)* 23: 105—154. (12.13.6)

66. _____. (1977). The Mammals of Borneo. *Monogr. Malay. Br. Royal As. Soc.* No. 7: (12.8.23)

67. Meijer, W. (1982). Checklist of the flora of Mt. Sago, West Sumatra. Unpubl. Report, University of Kentucky. (12.10.33)

68. Merrill, E.D. (1940). Botanical results of the George Vanderbilt Sumatran Expedition, 1939. Plants from Mt. Leuser. *Notula Naturae* 47: 9 (12.10.42).

69. Morley, R.J., Flenley, J.R., and Kardin, M.K. (1973). Preliminary notes on the swamps and small lakes of the central Sumatran highlands. *Sumatra Res. Bull.* 2: 50—60.

70. Musser, G.G., Marshall, J.T., and Boeadi (1979). Definition and contents of the Sundaic genus *Maxomys* (Rodentia, Muridae). *J. Mammal.* 60: 592—606. (12.8.28)

71. Musser, G.G. and Newcomb, C. (1983). Malaysian murids and the giant rat of Sumatra. *Bull. Amer. Mus. nat. Hist.* 174: 327—598. (12.8.107)

72. Ohsawa, M. (1979). *Tentative report of forest ecological survey in Mt. Kerinci, Central Sumatra.* Unpubl. Report, BIOTROP, Bogor. (12.10.102)

73. Pendelbury, H.M. (1936). An expedition to Kerinchi Peak, Sumatra, carried out in 1914 by Messrs. H.C. Robinson and C. Boden Kloss. *J. Fed. Malay States Mus.* 8: 1—31.

74. Ricklefs (1979). *Ecology.* Chiron, London. (12.10.85)

75. Robinson, H.C. and Kloss, C.B. (1918). Results of an expedition to Korinchi Peak, Sumatra, 1. Mammals. *J. Fed. Malay. St. Mus.* 8: 1—80. (12.8.20).

76. Robbins, R.G. and Wyatt-Smith, J. (1964). Dry land forest formations and forest types in the Malay Peninsular. *Malay. Forester* 27: 188—217. (12.10.48)

418

77. Smith, A.P. (1979). Function of dead leaves of *Espeletia schultzii* (Compositae), an Andean caulescent rosette species. *Biotropica* 11: 43—47. (12.1.38)
78. Smith, J.M.B. (1970). Herbaceous plant communities in the summit zone of Mount Kinabalu. *Malay. Nat. J.* 24: 16—29. (12.1.30)
79. _____. (1975). Notes on the distribution of herbaceous angiosperm species in the mountains of New Guinea. *J. Biogeogr.* 2: 87—101. (12.1.29)
80. Soepadmo, E. (1972). Fagaceae. *Flora Malesiana I* 7: 265—403.
81. Specht, R.L. (1979). Heathlands and related shrublands of the world. In *Heathlands & Related Shrublands* (ed. R.L. Specht), pp. 1—18. Elsevier, Amsterdam. (12.10.37)
82. Steenis, C.G.G. (1934). On the origin of the Malaysian mountain flora. Part 2. Altitudinal zones, general considerations and renewed statement of the problem. *Treubia* 13: 289—417. (12.10.34)
83. _____. (1934). On the origin of the Malaysian mountain flora. Part I. *Treubia* 13: 135—262. (12.10.35)
84. _____. (1938). Exploratie in de Gajo-Landen. Algemeene resultaten der Loser-expeditie 1937. *Tijdschr. Kon. Ned. Aardr. Genootschap* 55: 728—801. (12.10.39)
85. _____. (1962). The mountain flora of the Malaysian tropics. *Endeavour* 21: 183—193. (12.10.31)
86. _____. (1972). *The Mountain Flora of Java.* Brill, Leiden. (12.10.43)
87. _____: Personal communication.
88. Strien, N.J. van (1977). *Sumatran Birds: Supplement to the Field Guide to the Birds of South-east Asia.* Agriculture Dept., Wageningen. (12.7.45)
89. Tanner, E.V.J. (1983). Leaf demography and growth of the tree fern *Cyathea pubsecens* in Jamaica. *Bot. J. Linn. Soc.* 87: 213—227. (12.1.32)
90. Tanner, E.V.J. and Kapos, V. (1982). Leaf structure of Jamaican. upper montane rainforest trees. *Biotropica* 14: 16—24 (12.1.74)
91. Ungemach, H. (1969). Chemical rain studies in the Amazon region. In *Simposio y Foro de Biologia Tropical Amazonica*, pp. 354—358. Association pro Biologia Tropical.

92. Wallace, A.R. (1869). *The Malay Archipelago: The Land of the Orang-utan and the Bird of Paradise. A Narrative of Travel with studies of Man & Nature.* Reprint edition 1962, Dover, New York. (23.7.12)
93. Webb, L.J. (1959). A physiognomic classification of Australian rain forests. *J. Ecol.* 47: 551—570.
94. Wells, D.R., Halls, C.J. and Hails, A.J. (1979). Birds of the forests of the lowlands and lower hill slopes on Gunung Mulu. Paper presented at Gunung Mulu Symposium, 1979, Royal Geographical Society, London (12.7.14)
95. Whitmore, T.C. (1975). *The Tropical Rain Forests of the Far East.* Clarendon, Oxford. (12.10.8)
96. Whitmore, T.C. and Burnham, C.P. (1969). The altitudinal sequence of forests and soils on granite near Kuala Lumpur. *Malay. Nat. J.* 22: 99—118. (12.10.36)
97. WWF/Strien, N. (1978). Proposed Gunung Leuser National Park Management Plan 1978/9—1982/3. IUCN/WWF, Bogor. (10.2.10)

CHAPTER 10
CAVES

10.1 INTRODUCTION

Very few studies have ever been conducted in Sumatran caves. Musper explored a number of caves in the hills around Gumai (near Lahat) [30], and Bronson and Asmar describe a little of the biology of Tiangko Panjang cave in Sarko, Jambi [3] (section 1.7.1). Some brief studies of a few caves in northern Sumatra have been conducted by teams from CRES but the most detailed collecting work was undertaken by Meer Mohr, also in North Sumatra [29]. He describes the fauna of two caves south of Medan (also visited by a CRES team) and one near Balige, south of Lake Toba.

Most caves are found in limestone areas (Figure 8.9) but 'caves' were created during the Japanese occupation when tunnels were constructed. These have many of the same features as natural caves and are not without interest. For example, the moss-nest swiftlet *Aerodramus vanikorensis* was found for the first time in Sumatra in a tunnel in the famous Ngarai Simanuk gorge near Bukittinggi [39]. Even road tunnels, such as that between Kota Panjang and Bangkinang, Riau, support populations of bats and swiftlets.

10.2 CAVE STRUCTURE

Rainwater contains carbon dioxide from the atmosphere and is therefore slightly acid. This weak acid dissolves calcium carbonate (the main constituent of limestone) and forms channels which, in time, achieve the dimensions of caves, often with a stream running through them. Water dripping from the roof in the main chamber of the Quarry Cave, Lho' Nga, North Aceh had a pH of 5.0. Dry caves exist where the stream flow has been diverted or where the limestone has been raised or tilted relative to the surrounding land. In Sumatra, most of the limestone emerges at intervals along the length of the Barisan Range and dates from the early and late Tertiary. The caves themselves can date from anytime between then and the present.

Two of the commonest features within a cave are stalactites and stalagmites which are columns of calcium carbonate with various impurities (which are the cause of the wide range of colours found). Their formation is described in Figure 10.1. The surface of stalactites and stalagmites increases the surface area of a cave and therefore the living area available to its inhabitants.

The nature and depth of cave deposits and the manner in which they lie on one another can provide information on the past history of the cave and the surrounding area. Pollen grains may be found in organic and inorganic deposits and these too can help us to reconstruct the conditions of palaeo-environments.

10.3 THE CAVE AS A HABITAT

The salient features of a cave are its definable limits, its enclosed nature and the consequent reduction of light and comparative stability of climatic factors such as temperature, relative humidity and air flow [4]. Variations in these features create a surprisingly wide range of effects which determine the type and number of animals which can inhabit a cave. Cave animals can be divided into three ecological groups: (a) troglobites, obligate cave species unable to survive outside the cave environment; (b) troglophiles, facultative species that live and reproduce in caves but that are also found in similar dark, humid microhabitats outside the cave; and (c) trogloxenes, species that regularly inhabit caves for refuge but normally return to the outside environment to feed. Some other species wander into caves accidentally but cannot survive there [15].

The floor of most dry caves is composed largely of a layer of material formed from waste products and bodies of animals. A sample of 'soil' was taken from Kotabuluh Cave, Tanah Karo, and the analysis

Table 10.1. Results from an analysis of guano from Kotabuluh cave.

pH H$_2$	C (%)	N (%)	C/N	P-av (ppm)	Exchangeable (m.e/100g)				T.E.B. (m.e./ 100 gr)	C.E.C. (m.e./ 100 gr)	B.S. (%)
					K	Na	Ca	Mg			
3.7	0.21	0.03	7.0	160	0.96	0.12	0.76	0.50	2.34	14.20	16

(Table 10.1) showed very low levels of carbon and nitrogen, but a high level of potassium and an extremely high level of phosphorus. Not surprisingly, local villagers are extracting this 'guano' to sell as fertilizer (see also the paper by Khotbet [16]).

10.3.1 Darkness

Exclusion of photosynthesising plants
Since light is essential for photosynthesis, it would be reasonable to expect that green plants are excluded from the dark parts of caves. This is essentially true for almost all caves but a form of 'lichen' consisting of a colony of gram-positive bacteria with a few blue-green algae between it and the substrate, has been reported from a cave wall in 'absolute' darkness in Nepal [40, 41]. The blue-green algae had high densities of thylakoids (the membranes on which photosynthesis occurs) and increased thylakoid density leads to greater photosynthetic efficiency. Interestingly, what appears to be a very similar 'lichen' has recently been found at Kotabuluh Cave by a CRES expedition. The results of specialist examination of the specimens are awaited with interest. The most important effect of this virtually total exclusion of green plants is to make all cave dwellers dependent on material brought in from the outside and to exclude all animals which feed directly on the above-ground parts of green plants. Plant roots can penetrate fissures above a cave and these can commonly be seen attached to or hanging from the cave roof. Fungi and bacteria are not, of course, dependent on light and their role in caves is discussed below.

Vision
In near or total darkness a cave-dweller becomes reliant on senses other than sight to detect food or enemies. This is not peculiar to cave

423

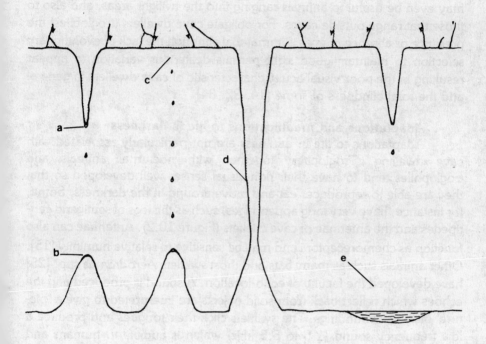

Fig. 10.1. The formation of stalactites and stalagmites. a - water evaporates from drips leaving deposits of calcium carbonate and impurities thereby forming a stalactite; b - water evaporates also leaving a deposit but forming a squatter stalagmite; c - where water drips quickly no stalagtite is formed; d - stalactite and stalagmite eventually join to form a single column; e - where the drips from a stalactite fall (or fell) into a river, no stalagmite is formed.

animals - many nocturnal and cryptic animals depend almost exclusively on hearing, smell and touch [4]. Clearly, however, diurnal animals can live in a cave provided their other senses are sufficiently acute, and sight may even be useful to animals ranging into the twilight areas, and also to those that range outside caves. For obligate cave dwellers (troglobites) the presence or absence of eyes is immaterial although the lack of evolutionary selection to maintain good sight permits deliterious variation to appear resulting in the poor visual acuity characteristic of cave dwellers in general and the total blindness of some [14, 32, 34].

Adaptations and modifications to life in darkness

Adaptations to life in darkness are not particularly associated with cave dwelling. Troglobites, together with nocturnal animals and troglophiles tend to have their non-visual senses well developed so that they are able to reproduce, eat and move around in the darkness. Some, for instance, have very long appendages, such as the legs of scutigerid centipedes and the antennae of cave crickets (Figure 10.2). Antennae can also function as chemoreceptors and may be sensitive to relative humidity [15]. Other animals such as many bats and most swiftlets *Aerodramus* spp. [25] have developed the faculty of echo-location. A sound is produced and the echoes which reflect back from solid objects are interpreted to give a 'picture' of the surroundings. The swiftlets click their tongues and produce a low frequency sound (1.5 to 5.5 kHz) which is audible to humans and sounds like a wooden rattle. This enables them to detect large objects, allowing them to navigate, nest and breed within a totally dark cave, but is not sufficiently accurate to enable them to catch insects at night [28]. It might be thought that the different activity periods of bats and swiftlets would represent temporal partitioning of a common food resource. In fact, swiftlets feed mainly on small wasp-like insects (Hymenoptera) [13, 25], whereas insectivorous bats concentrate on various moths and beetles [11, 42]. Bats do interact ecologically with nocturnal birds and this is described elsewhere [9].

Echo-location in bats has evolved independently at least twice, but in each case it is characterized by high frequency sounds (20—130 kHz), above the threshold of human hearing originating from the larynx or speech-box, and the reception of echoes in complex and often large ears.

Mouse-eared bats (Verspertilionidae) use a predominantly

Epigenium pulchellum orchids; 3300 m, Mt. Kemiri.

Viola biflora violet; 3250m, Mt. Kemiri.

Grey shrew on Mt. Kemiri.

cm

0   4

Fig. 10.2   A cave cricket showing its extremely long antennae.

frequency-modulating (FM) system; that is, the frequency of the sound they emit through their mouth varies and is given in very short pulses. When cruising in the open a pulse is emitted and some time is spent listening for echoes. When closing in on the prey, however, pulses are emitted rapidly so that the exact locations for the flying insect can be determined. A flying mouse-eared bat can detect objects less than 1mm across.

Horseshoe bats (Rhinolophidae and Hipposideridae) mainly use a single rather than a variable frequency and each species uses a characteristic frequency. Instead of emitting the sound through their mouth, these bats keep the mouth shut and emit the sound through their nostrils which are positioned half a wavelength apart to give a stereo impression. The peculiar 'horsehoe' around the nostrils has the function of a megaphone, 'causing the sound to be emitted in a concentrated beam.

It used to be thought that bats using echo-location had no difficulty catching their insect prey, but it now appears that some moths can detect bats from 40m away and before the bat has detected the moth. These moths have developed the ability to utter clicks which confuse the bat. Other moths have a variety of responses which themselves make it difficult for the bats to predict their behaviour. Some bats in their turn do not keep their echo-locating system 'switched-on' continuously so as to give as little warning as possible to the moths, while others emit frequencies above the moth threshold of hearing [10].

Whereas the bats mentioned above catch flying insects, false vampires (Megadermatidae) feed by picking insects off leaves, or lizards, frogs and small rodents off the ground. They have also been known to eat bats caught in mist-nets without themselves getting caught in the net [27]. To avoid swamping the echoes from their prey they 'whisper' their sounds which are FM like those of mouse-eared bats. Sometimes false vampires locate their prey solely by homing in on sounds made by the prey itself. This is similar to a frog-eating bat which has been studied in Panama and which can differentiate between the calls of edible and poisonous frogs and between the calls of small frogs and frogs too big to capture. Its efficiency at catching frogs has probably led to adaptations in the frogs calls so that the males still call to attract females but in such a way as to reduce their chances of being caught [38].

Finally, the only fruit bat to echo-locate, the cave-dwelling rousette bat *Rousettus,* uses a tongue-click like swiftlets [10, 42].

As well as the loss of eyes, many troglobite invertebrates have also lost cuticle pigments [29] and wings. Some have developed a thinner cuticle, a larger more slender body than their relatives outside the cave, adaptations to their feet allowing them to walk on wet surfaces and also a lower metabolic rate [1, 15].

Diurnal rhythms

Most animals have a clearly defined daily cycle of activity. Nocturnal species are active at night, diurnal species during the day, and crepuscular species around dawn and dusk. Such cycles are obviously associated with daylight and darkness and thus may not occur in a cave community. There are, however, certain events within a cave which may impose a daily rhythm on the inhabitants. The most important of these is the departure, and later return, of the bats. In their absence, food is not available for the predators and free-living ectoparasites in the roosts, and there is a halt to the rain of fresh faeces from the roof [4]. Although data are lacking, it is probable therefore that a diurnal rhythm exists despite the absence of night and day.

10.3.2 Temperature, humidity and air flow

The insulating role of the walls and roofs of caves effectively buffer the wide daily variations in temperature and humidity of the outside world. During the CRES expedition to the dry cave near Batu Katak, Langkat, it was found that the humidity in the cave did not fall below 97% although the outside humidity at midday was about 75%. Similarly, the temperature in the cave varied between 24° and 25° C although the range outside was 24°—32°C. As would be expected the maxima and minima of humidity and temperature in the cave occurred some time after those outside. Conditions thus remain fairly stable from day to day, but there are still seasonal changes which can greatly alter conditions in caves. For example, during a rainy period the humidity and amount of free water within a cave tends to increase. Thus a chironomid midge which requires free water for breeding may only be able to reproduce when seasonal pools are full of water, while at other times the pools are dry and its number dwindle. Fluctuations also occur in other insect and bat numbers; some bats show distinct periodicity in breeding and mortality rates, but there is no actual evidence that this is caused by changes in the environment [19]. These bat cycles affect other organisms: heavy mortality of bats permits a rapid increase in corpse-feeding organisms which would diminish later in the year due to lack of food.

Air movement is also buffered by the cave walls but still occurs as air is drawn out of the cave during the day when the air outside is warmer and lighter. This air movement follows a regular pattern but leaves pockets of stagnant air where spiders can weave delicate and complex webs, and preserves pockets of high humidity. Under such stable conditions the air disturbance caused by the approach of predators or prey may be discerned.

The constant high humidity in the deeper parts of caves appears to have led to many troglobite arthropods becoming morphologically similar to aquatic arthropods. In these deeper areas, the carbon dioxide levels may become relatively high if there is no inflow of air except from the cave mouth. Howarth has suggested that the lower metabolic rate of some troglobite arthropods may be a physiological response to this high carbon dioxide concentration. Many, if not most, of these troglobites can survive long periods of starvation, gorging themselves when food is available and storing a large amount of fat [15].

10.4 FOOD

As noted in section 10.3, all cave dwellers are dependent for food on material brought into the cave from outside. Some animals feed on the plant roots attached to the cave roof, wood and other material washed in during floods (if the cave has a river running through it), or the organic matter percolating through from the surface. In Sumatra, however, the major providers of food are the bats and swiftlets which roost and breed in the cave but feed outside. Other cave shelterers such as porcupines may also contribute but to a negligible extent in most caves.

Bats and swiftlets supply food in a number of ways:
- during their lives they produce faeces, collectively known as 'guano', which has nutritive value and is fed upon by various animals (coprophages) as well as providing a source of nourishment to fungi and bacteria;
- as live animals they are hosts to many parasites, both internal and external, and provide food for predators;
- they moult hair and feathers and shed pieces of skin;
- they produce progeny which may be susceptible to different predators and parasites. For instance, eggs of swiftlets are attacked by a cave cricket *Rhaphidophora oophaga* which does not attack the birds themselves [5].
- when the bats and swiftlets die, their bodies form a source of food for various corpse-feeding organisms (necrophages).

Almost all animals provide food for others in these five ways, but within the cave ecosystem, in the absence of green plants, these are the *only* major sources of food.

The bats themselves roost on the roof and walls and form the basis of one community; their faeces and dead bodies fall to the cave floor and form the basis of another. Thus there is a distinct division of the animals into a roof community and a floor community [4].

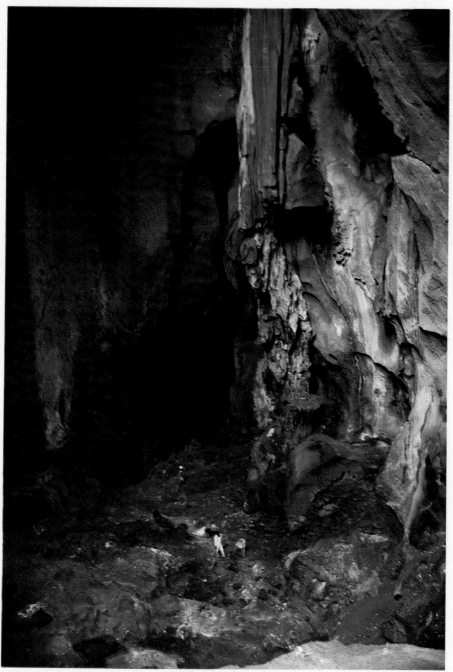

Green Cave, Lho'Nga; note men on cave floor.

Quarry cave, Lho'Nga, North Aceh.

'Lichen' from Kotabuluh cave, Tanah Karo.

10.4.1. Roof community

The roof community includes all those animals which feed on live bats and swiftlets. These include only one major predator, the snake *Elaphe taeniura*. The snake waits, coiled in a crevice, until a bat alights nearby. Then, bracing itself with part of its body within the crevice, the snake lunges out and captures its victim, which is crushed in a quick coil and swallowed before the snake withdraws into the crevice. The only other major predator on bats is the bat hawk *Macheiramphus alcinus* which roosts near large caves [8].

There are many parasites, some internal, but mostly external. Some such as the wingless nycteribiid flies [20] live almost their entire lives on bats, others such as streblid flies and chigger mites (Trombiculidae) spend only part of their life cycle on bats, while some such as the soft tick *Ornithodoros* attach themselves to bats only when they are hungry (Figure 10.3). Most of these suck blood but the large earwigs of the family

Figure 10.3. **Common parasites of bats: a)** *Ornithodoros* - a soft tick; b) a nycteribiid fly; and c) a streblid fly. (After Lekagul and McNeely [17]).

Arixeniidae eat skin debris. These earwigs are quite large - equivalent to an insect 32 cm long on an average Sumatran man. A survey of parasites on bats in Thailand revealed no less than 116 species belonging to 13 families of insects and mites [17]. It has been suggested that the great majority of insect species parasitic on tropical bats do in fact have only one species as a proper host [21]. In caves containing nests of swiftlets, the community becomes even more diverse for these birds are also hosts to a variety of mites and insects.

The parasitic insects on bats show considerable convergence in many characteristics although six families from four orders are represented. Many of them are flattened, some vertically and some horizontally, to ease their movement between the bat hairs. Most of the insects have tough but expandable 'skin' which allows for large meals of blood from the host. The skin often bears backward-pointing spines which lessen the chance of being dislodged by a scratching bat. They also have well-developed grasping claws. Wings have been lost in species belonging to all but one of the insect families concerned. The loss of wings and general lack of light have led, not surprisingly, to the loss or reduction of eyes in these parasitic insects [21].

10.4.2 Floor community

On the cave floor the coprophages and necrophages predominate. It is difficult to distinguish between these two; although a few forms are exclusively necrophagous, many of the coprophages will include dead bats or swiftlets in their diet. The majority of cave-dwelling bats are insect-eating and the faeces they produce are hard and dry and readily exploited by coprophages such as woodlice, cocoon-encased caterpillars of Tinea moths, flies and beetles. The faeces produced by the few species of fruit-eating bats that roost in caves, however, are amorphous and wet and are not generally utilized by coprophages. In this case, cockroaches ingest the faeces and the general coprophages feed in turn on the faeces of the cockroaches [6]. Fungi and bacteria develop on the faeces and some coprophages exploit this food resource too. The cave crickets and small Psocoptera flies may feed on fungi [19].

The floor community includes many predators such as the scutigerid centipede, assasin bug Bagauda, and medium-sized spiders which feed on the coprophages and the small *Tinea* moths. Some of these predators, and others such as large spiders, live on the walls and wait for wandering coprophages to come to them, or only venture to the ground when hungry. Small predators may also enter the diet of the larger predators such as shrews *Crocidura*, the toad *Bufo asper* and the spider *Liphistius*. *Liphistius* is the world's most primitive spider as shown by its abdomen which, unlike that of other spiders', is still segmented. One species lives on dry stalactites, and builds large web-cases 4—5 cm long with a door about 2 cm across. These are loosely constructed, decorated with debris from the surrounding area, and the inside is lined with smooth white silk. The hinged flap of the door is held partly open by the spider crouching behind it. Radiating from the entrance in a semicircle are six to ten strands of silk 12 to 15 cm long. If a small insect touches one of these the spider races out, catches the prey and returns [19]. No species of *Liphistius* has yet been collected in Sumatran caves but the larger *Liphistius sumatranus* can be found on roadbanks near Bukittinggi [2].

10.4.3 Food webs and pyramids

The various relationships described above may be drawn as a food web (Figure 10.4). As the understanding of a cave ecosystem grows, so its food web becomes more and more complicated. For instance, for simplicity's sake, Figure 10.4 omits the role of certain wasps parasitic on the tinaeid moths which themselves must be preyed upon by one of the predators. As food webs become more complicated (and it should be remembered that caves probably represent Sumatra's *simplest* ecosystem), there is good reason to produce generalized representations or models of food webs. In 1927, Charles Elton. one of the 'fathers' of ecology, noted that the animals at the base of a food chain are relatively abundant while those at the top end are relatively few in number, with a progressive decrease between the two extremes. This 'pyramid of numbers' is found in ecosystems all over the world and provides a useful means of comparing communities. To construct the pyramid, species are grouped together according to their food habits. Thus all the autotrophs (plants) are called primary producers, herbivores are called primary consumers, predators on herbivores are called secondary consumers, predators on secondary consumers are called tertiary consumers, etc. Generally, in a defined area,

Figure 10.4 Simplified food web of a cave ecosystem

Figure 10.5. Pyramids of numbers: a) with a large number of primary producers, b) with a single primary producer, c) the case of parasites and hyper-parasites. (After Phillipson [33]).

a large number of primary producers support a smaller number of primary consumers supporting an even smaller number of secondary consumers supporting one or two tertiary consumers (Figure 10.5a). Variations of the pyramid shape occur when, for instance, a single tree is considered (Figure 10.5b). An inverted pyramid can be formed if one considers a single animal, such as a bat, or a plant, which carries a large number of parasites, which are themselves parasitized by an even larger number of hyper-parasites (Figure 10.5c).

The information contained in a pyramid of numbers permits us to state the number of herbivores supported by a certain number of plants and so on. But for comparisons between ecosystems a better approach is to use the weight of organisms (biomass) rather than numbers, and to show this as a 'pyramid of biomass' which usually has a similar shape to the pyramid of number [33].

In Liang Pengurukan near Bohorok, Langkat, a team from CRES counted all the animals in 25m² of cave floor (or, in the case of woodlice several 1m² samples within that area), and samples of these animals were later weighed. The total biomass of the 25m² was 63.38g (2.5g/m²), 90% of which was contributed by a single species of woodlouse which also accounted for over 99% of the animals found. The heaviest animal, a cave cricket, was 900 times heavier than the lightest, the woodlouse. A pyramid of numbers would overemphasize the woodlice, but a pyramid of biomass (Figure 10.6) demonstrates in a comprehendible fashion the relationship between the 'amount' of primary and secondary consumers. Note the absence of producers. Tertiary consumers such as large spiders were seen in the vicinity but not in the sample area.

Figure 10.6   Pyramid of biomass using data from Liang Pengurukan.

10.5 DIFFERENCES WITHIN CAVES

Although a cave at first sight appears to be a fairly uniform habitat, this is not the case. One of the chief factors causing variation in the cave habitat is the distribution of bats, the producers of guano. Cave maps produced by CRES and by Doyle [6] (Figure 10.7) show that the occupation of the roof by bats is very patchy. Physical factors also vary from place to place in the cave. Thus, during a rainy period, standing water will accumulate in one part but not another. Similarly, some parts are subject to air movement, others are not.

Figure 10.7. **Maps of caves to show distribution of bats: a) plan of Gua Pondok, Malaysia (After Doyle [67]); b) a plan of Liang Pengurukan; c) an elevation of Liang Pengurukan taken between points A and B.**

It is differences such as these that make different parts of the cave suitable for different species. Such factors probably explain the occurrence in Batu Caves, Selangor, Malaysia, of no less than eleven species of Psychodidae [18], a family of moth-like flies (Figure 10.8). (Outside of

Figure 10.8 A psychodid fly

caves the larvae of this family are important in sewage purification because they feed on micro-organisms which would otherwise block the filter beds of the sewage plant). The co-existence of this number of species in a cave requires that they each exploit a different set of limiting resources or, possibly, a similar set of limiting resources to different intensities. This is the Principle of Competitive Exclusion, or Gause's Theorem (named after the Russian scientist who first tried to make closely-related species co-exist on the same nutritive medium in the laboratory). Many closely related species cannot live in the same place because their ecology and behaviour are too similar - that is, they compete for the same limiting resource to the exclusion of one or more of the species. This is illustrated by the exclusive distribution of three ecologically and behaviourly similar species of leaf-monkey on Sumatra for which no area of overlap is known (section 1.6.2), and of the two species of freshwater crayfish described in section 4.8.5. The word 'limiting' is included in the statement of the competitive exclusion principle because only resources that limit population growth can provide the basis for competition. Non-limiting resources, like atmospheric oxygen, are superabundant compared to the needs of organisms, and their use by one organism does not preclude their use by another organism. So, although the eleven species of Psychodidae are all blood-suckers they must, somehow, be successfully dividing up the limiting resources between themselves.

False vampire.

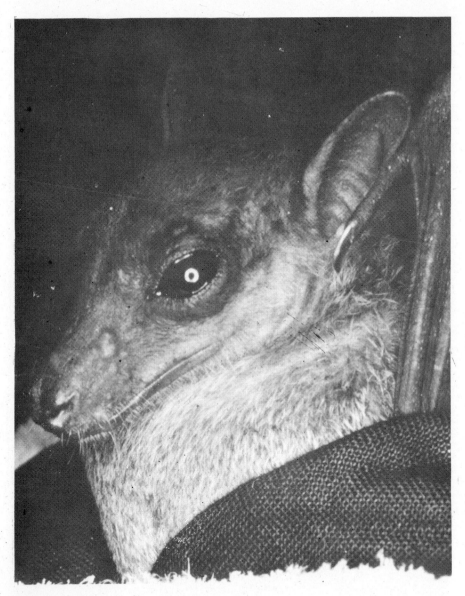

Cave fruit bat.

10.6 DIFFERENCES BETWEEN CAVES

If different caves are considered, conditions vary still further - one may be well-drained while another may have a river running through it; one may contain swiftlets, another may not. There are almost no data by which the fauna of different Sumatran caves can be compared (there is not yet an inventory of caves although one is being started), but some data were collected by CRES for the caves around Batu Katak. Although not exhaustive, the lists (Table 10.1 and 10.2) serve to show considerable differences.

A knowledge of comparative cave fauna richness is of great value because it provides a useful biological input to environmental impact assessments for limestone mines (such as at Lho' Nga and Indarung). In most cases it would be possible to avoid disturbing a particularly rich cave and to exploit another area. It should be remembered that the disappearance of a cave fauna can affect an area far wider than the cave itself. For instance, people would no longer be able to exploit (in a controlled, ecologically sustained manner) the extremely rich guano for fertilizer; the loss of insectivorous bats would mean an increase in local insect populations; and the loss of the cave fruit-bat *Eonycteris spelaea* would result in fewer durians *Durio zibethinus* which they pollinate.

Durian trees usually have two flowering and fruiting periods each year, although the timing of these varies between localities. Durian flowers are large, feathery and white with copious nectar and give off a heavy, sour and buttery odour. These features are typical of flowers which are pollinated by certain species of bats while they eat the nectar and pollen. From research conducted in Peninsular Malaysia it appears that durians are pollinated almost exclusively by cave fruit-bats [35] - and thus we owe the production of durians to these bats and thence to the limestone caves in which they live.

When durian trees are in flower, cave fruit-bats feed enthusiastically upon them, but they also feed on and assist the pollination of other food trees such as banana, mango, petai bean, jackfruit and rose-aple [23, 24, 31, 36]. They also feed on the flowers of a common tree of mangrove forests *Sonneratia alba*, and studies of pollen remains in the faeces of cave fruit bats in Batu Caves near Kuala Lumpur have revealed that these bats

438

Table 10.2 List of invertebrates found in various caves in North Sumatra.
(Data from CRES expeditions and from Meer Mohr [29]).

Class	Order	Family	Genus and species	Liang Pengurukan upper	Liang Pengurukan lower	Batu Katak	Liang Rampah	Liang Terusan	Si-pegeh	Kotabuluh major	Kotabuluh minor
Mollusca	Stylommatophora (snails)	Subulinidea/Stenogyridae	Opeas gracile				X	X	—		
			Prosopeas achatinaceum				X	X	—		
			Prosopeas paioense				—	—	X		
Crustacea	Isopoda (woodlice) (sowbugs)	?Oniscidae	Sp. A		—	X	—				
		Porcellionidae	Porcellio pruinosus					—	X		
		Armadillidiidae	Armadillo thienemanni					—	X		
			Cubaris meemohri					X	—		
Arachnida	Scorpiones (scorpions)	?	Mormurus australasiae				X				
	Pseudoscorpiones (pseudoscorpions)	?	Megachernes grandis			—	—	—	—	—	X
	Araneae (spiders)	?	Sp.A			X				—	—
		?	Sp.B			X				X	—
		?	Sp.C				X			X	—
		?	Sp.D							X	X
		Lyosidae	Trochosa inops				X	X	—		
		Amaurobiidae	Titanoeca fulmeki				X	X	—		
	Opilones (harvestmen)	?	Stylocellus weberi				X	X	—		
		?	Beloniscus quinquespinosus				—	X	—		
Chilopoda (centipedes)		?	Sp.A			—	X	X			
		?	Sp.B			—	X	X			
		?	Sp.C				X	X			
	Scutigeromorpha (scutigerids)	Scutigeridae	Sp.A				X	X	X	X	—
			Sp.B			X	—				

Table 10.2 (continued).

ass	Order	Family	Genus and species	Liang Pengurukan upper	lower	Batu Katak	Liang Rampah	Liang Terusan	Si-pegeh	Kotabuluh major	minor
iplopoda (iillipedes)			Sp.A					X			
			Sp.B		−	X	X				
secta	Thysannura (silverfish)		Sp.A etc				X	X	−		
	Collembola (thrips)		Sp.B etc				X	X	−		
	Orthoptera (crickets, grasshoppers, etc.)	Stenopelmatidae	*Rhapidophora fulva*	−	X	X	−	−	−	−	−
		Gryllacidae	*Diastremmena vandermeermohri*				X	X	−		
		Gryllidae	*Parendacusta cavicola*	−	−	−	−	−	X	−	−
			Parendacusta Sp.A	−	−	−	−	−	−	X	X
	Dictyoptera (cockroaches)	Polyphagidae	Sp.A								
		Pycnoscelliddae	*Symploce cavernicola*	−	−	−	X	X	−	−	−
			Pycnoscellus Sp.A	−	−	−	−	−	−	X	−
			Pycnoscellus Sp.B	−	X	−	−				
			Pycnoscellus cf *surinamensis*	−	X	−	−				
	Hemiptera (bugs)	Reduviidae	*Bagauda* cf *lucifugus*				−	X			
			Reduvius cf *gua*				−	X			
			Sp.A	−	X	−				−	
	Diptera (flies)	Milichiidae	*Phyllomyza* sp.		−		X	−	−	X	−
	Coleoptera (beetles)	Aderidae	*Aderus kempi*				X	X	X		
		Carabidae	*Anaulacus fasciatus*				X	X	−		
	Lepidoptera (moths and butterflies)	Tinaeidae	*Tinea palaechrysis*	−	X	−	X	X	−	−	−
			Tinea sp.A.	−	−	−	−	−	X	−	−

Table 10.3 List of vertebrates found in various caves in North Sumatra. (Data from CRES expeditions and from Meer Mohr [29]).

Class	Order	Family	Genus and species		Pengurukan upper	Pengurukan lower	Batu Katak	Liang Rampah	Liang Terusan	Sipegeh	Kotabuluh major	Kotabuluh minor
Amphibians	Anura	Bufonidae	Bufo asper	black toad	—	—	X	—	—	—	—	—
Birds	Apodiformes	Apodidae	Collocalia esculenta	white-bellied swiftlet	X	—	—	—	—	—	X	—
			Aerodramus maxima	black-nest swiftlet	X	—	—	—	—	—	X	—
Mammals	Chiroptera	Pteropidae	Cynopterus brachyotis	common dog-faced fruit bat	—	—	X	—	—	—	—	—
			Eonycteris spelaea	cave fruit bat	—	—	—	X	—	—	X	X
		Rhinolophidae	Rhinolophus stheno	intermediate horseshoe bat	—	—	—	—	X	—	—	—
			Rhinolophus affinis	horseshoe bat	X	X	—	—	—	—	—	—
		Hipposideridae	Hipposideros larvatus	lesser round-leaf horseshoe bat	—	—	—	—	—	X	—	—
			Hipposideros galeritus	diadem round-leaf horseshoe bat	X	—	X	—	—	—	—	—
			Hipposideros diadema	bat	X	X	—	—	—	—	—	—
		Megadermatidae	Megaderma spasma	false vampire bat	—	—	X	—	—	—	—	—
		Vespertilionidae	Miniopterus schreibersi	greater bent-winged bat	X	—	—	X	—	X	X	—
			Miniopterus pusillus	lesser bent-winged bat	X	—	—	—	—	—	—	—
Rodentia	Histricidae		Atherurus macrourus	brush-tailed porcupine	—	—	X	—	—	—	—	—

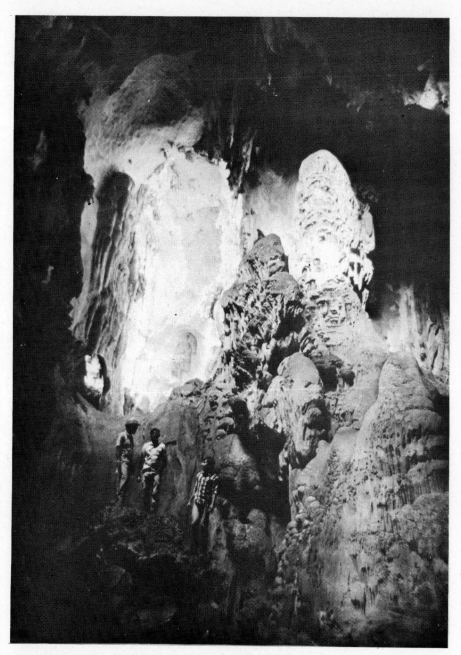

Part of Green Cave, Lho'Nga, North Aceh.

Roundleaf horseshoe bat *Hipposideros diadema.*

Horseshoe bat *Rhinolophos affinis.*

regularly fly to mangrove areas nearly 40 km away [23, 37].

Only two roosts of cave fruit-bats have been recorded in North Sumatra, both of them discovered by teams from CRES. The first roost was found in one of the caves, Liang Rampah, near Penen south of Medan, and contained an estimated 1000—2000 individuals; none of the other five caves in the area being inhabited by this species. Interestingly, this bat does not seem to have been present when Meer Mohr visited the cave in 1935 [29]. A colony of similar size was found at Kotabuluh Cave. Assuming that these bats can also fly at least 40 km to a food source at night, the areas they cover ($\pm$ 1,250 km^2 per roost) include the famous durian-growing area around Sembahe/Sibolangit. However, only the Penen bats are likely to visit the other famous durian farm around Binjai. (Figure 10.9). Although there may well be other roosts of this bat in the area, it is not unreasonable to assume that Penen cave is the only source of cave fruit bats for at least some of the area shown. If the value of the intact, undisturbed cave is to be estimated we would need to assess the value of durians for durian-orchard owners, small-scale owners and collectors, roadside vendors, wholesalers, distributors and town vendors. It has been estimated that an owner of one hectare of good quality durian trees can easily earn Rp. 2.5—4 million per year.

Some people may believe that cave fruit-bats are 'only bats' and do not deserve protection, but our choice is clear: leave the bat roost undisturbed and enjoy durians, or destroy the roosts and be content to have only the rarest taste of the fruit. There is almost no chance of successfully translocating bat colonies because, although we know that the cave fruit-bat inhabits very few of the available caves, we do not know precisely what cave qualities it requires.

10.7. CAVES AS ISLANDS

For some cave animals such as some species of cockroach and scutigerid centipede, the outside world is an acceptable living place, and they merely move into a cave when the opportunity arises. But many cave animals, such as species of the primitive spider *Liphistius*, the cave cricket and the assasin bug *Bagauda*, are more or less confined to caves. Their caves, then, represent habitat islands set among inhospitable habitat seas

442

Figure 10.9 Areas within which cave fruit-bats from Kotabuluh and Penen caves could pollinate durian flowers.

or, perhaps, barely hospitable habitat seas occupied by unhospitable animals.

As with other forms of islands, dispersal of animals between them represent a serious problem. Parasitic animals on bats can be transferred between caves if they move off their host when it is visiting a food source and then attach themselves to a new bat from another cave when it in turn visits the food source [36], or when the host changes roosts. Some species of non-parasitic cave animals are quite widely distributed but they are poor competitors in the outside world and their means of dispersal is not known. It may be that generations ago they had a means of dispersal (such as strong flight) but this has been lost through a lack of evolutionary pressure to select for it. Thus each cave or group of caves may contain a population isolated from others of the same species which is gradually shifting or has shifted away from the species type to evolve distinct sub-species or even species. Nowhere in the Sunda region has sufficient work been conducted to show if certain caves have endemic fauna but this is extremely likely.

Another respect in which caves are like islands is in the relationship between cave size and number of species. This was studied in Greenbrier Valley (West Virginia, U.S.A) where a series of seven limestone exposures are set amid other rocks or divided by rivers. Thus cave-dwelling animals could move within a limestone block with relative ease but not between the blocks. The number of terrestrial species was significantly correlated with 'island' area, but there was no correlation between 'island' size and species number for the aquatic animals. These species, unlike the terrestrial ones, were often found near cave mouths, for example in pools formed by drips from the top of the entrance, and thus had more chance of dispersal. In addition, there were probably sub-terranean aquatic connections between the caves meaning that the caves do not form truly isolated islands for these species [12].

REFERENCES

1. Barr, T.C. Jr. (1968). Cave ecology and the evolution of troglobites. In *Evolutionary Biology* (ed. T. Dobzhansky, M. Hecht and W. Steere), vol. 2, pp. 35—102. Appleton-Century-Crofts, New York. (12.13.4)
2. Bristowe, W.S. (1976). A contribution to the knowledge of liphistiid spiders. *J. Zool., Lond.* 178: 1—6. (12.4.11)
3. Bronson, B. and Asmar, T. (1976). Prehistoric investigations at Tiangko Panjang cave, Sumatra: An interim report. *Asian Perspectives* 18: 128—145. (23.7.4)
4. Bullock, J.A. (1966). The ecology of Malaysian caves. *Malay. Nat. J.* 19: 57—63.
5. Chopard, L. (1929). Fauna of Batu Caves, Selangor. xii Orthoptera and Dermaptera. *J. Fed. Malay. States Mus.* 14: 366—371.
6. Doyle, M.E. (1969). Factors affecting the distribution of fauna in Gua Pondok. *Malay. Nat. J.* 23: 21—26. (12.4.9)
7. Dunn, F.L. (1965). Gua Anak Takun: Ecological observations. *Malay. Nat. J.* 19: 75—87. (12.4.8)
8. Eccles, D.H., Jensen, R.A.C. and Jensen, M.K. (1969). Feeding behaviour of the bat hawk. *Ostrich* 40: 26—27.
9. Fenton, M.B. and Fleming, T.H. (1976). Ecological interactions between bats and nocturnal birds. *Biotropica* 8: 104—110. (12.7.8)
10. Fenton, M.B. and Fullard, J.H. (1981). Moth hearing and the feeding strategies of bats. *Amer. Scient.* 266—275. (12.8.11)
11. Gaisler, J. (1979). The ecology of bats. In *Ecology of Small Mammals* (ed. D.R. Stoddart), pp. 281—342. Chapman and Hall, London. (12.8.20)
12. Gorman, M. (1979). *Island Ecology*. Chapman and Hall, London. (23.2.14)
13. Hails, C.J. and Amiruddin, A. (1981). Food samples and selectivity of white-bellied swiftlets *Collocalia esculenta*. *Ibis* 123: 328—333. (12.7.40)

14. Holthuis, L.B. (1979). Caverniculous and terrestrial decapod curstaceans from northern Sarawak, Borneo. *Zool. Verh. Leiden* No. 171: 1—47. (12.3.34)

15. Howarth, F.G. (1983). Ecology of cave arthropods. *Ann. Rev. Entomol.* 28: 365—389. (12.4.6)

16. Khobkhet, O. (1980). Research on bats in Thailand: a bird's eye view. *BIOTROP Spec. Publ.* 12: 109—120. (11.1.6)

17. Lekagul, B. and McNeely, J.A. (1977). *The Mammals of Thailand.* Association for the Conservation of Wildlife, Bangkok. (12.8.21)

18. McClure, H.E. (1965). Microcosms of Batu Caves. *Malay. Nat. J.* 19: 65—74. (12.4.7)

19. McClure, H.E., Lim B.L., and Winn, S.E. (1967). Fauna of the Dark Cave, Batu Caves, Kuala Lumpur, Malaysia. *Pac. Insects* 9: 399—428. (12.4.10)

20. Marshall, A.G. (1971). The ecology of *Basilla hispida* (Diptera: Nycteribiidae) in Malaysia. *J. Anim. Ecol.* 40: 141—154. (12.4.22)

21. _____. (1980). The comparative ecology of insects ectoparasitic upon bats in West Malaysia. In *Proc. 5th Int. Bat Res. Conf.* (ed. D.E. Wilson and A.C. Gardner), pp. 135—142. Texas Tech. Press, Lubbock, Texas. (12.4.23)

22. _____. (1982). The ecology of insects ectoparasitic on bats. In *Ecology of Bats* (ed. T.H. Kunz), pp. 369—397. Plenum, New York.

23. _____. (1983). Bats, flowers and fruit: evolutionary relationships in the Old World: *Biol. J. Linn. Soc.* 20: 115—135.

24. _____. (1984). Old World phytophagous bats (Megachiroptera) and their food plants: A Survey. *Biotropica* 16.

25. Medway, Lord (1962). The swiftlets (*Collocalia*) of Niah Cave, Sarawak. *Ibid* 104: 228—245. (12.7.9)

26. _____. (1966). Field characters as a guide to the specific relations of swiftlets. *Proc. Linn. Soc. Lond.* 177: 151—172. (12.7.4)

27. _____. (1967). A bat-eating bat, *Megaderma lyra* Geoffrey. *Malay. Nat. J.* 20: 107—110. (12.8.26)

28. _____. (1969). Studies on the biology of the edible nest swiftlets of South-east Asia. *Malay. Nat. J.* 22: 57—63. (12.7.10)

29. Meer Mohr, J.C. van der (1936). Faunistisch onderzoek van eenige grotten op Sumatra's Oostkust en Tapanoeli. *Trop. Natuur Jub. Vitg.*: 60—67.

30. Musper, K.A.F.R. (1934). Een bezoek aan de grot Soeroeman Besar in het Goemaigebergte (Palembang, Zuid Sumatra). *Tijds. Kon. Ned. Aardr. Gen.* 51: 521—531.

31. Nur, N. (1976). Studies on pollination in Musaceae. *Ann. Bot.* 40: 167—177. (12.1.25)

32. Peck, S.B. (1981). A new cave-inhabiting *Ptomaphaginus* beetle from Sarawak (Leiodidae: Cholevinae). *Syst. Entomol.* 6: 221—224. (12.4.12)

33. Phillipson, J. (1966). *Ecological Energetics*. Studies in Biology No. 1. Edward Arnold, London. (23.2.8)

34. Roth, L.M. (1980). Cave dwelling cockroaches from Sarawak, with one new species. *Syst. Entomol.* 5: 97—104. (12.4.13)

35. Soepadmo, E. and Eow, B.K. (1977). The reproductive biology of *Durio zibethinus*. *Gdns'. Bull. S'pore* 29: 25—34. (12.1.68)

36. Start, A.N. (1974). More cave earwigs transported by a fruit bat. *Malay. Nat. J.* 27: 170. (12.4.61)

37. Start, A.N. and Marshall, A.G. (1975). Nectarivorous bats as pollinators of trees in West Malaysia. In *Tropical Trees: Variations, Breeding and Conservation* (ed. J. Burley and B.T. Styles), pp. 141—150. Academic, London. (12.8.37)

38. Tuttle, M.D. and Ryan, M.J. (1981). Bat predation and the evolution of frog vocalizations in the Neotropics. *Science* 214: 677—678. (12.8.29)

39. Wells, D.R. (1975). The moss-nest swiftlet *Collocalia vanikorensis* Quoy and Gaimard in Sumatra. *Ardea* 63: 148—151. (12.7.32)

40. Wilson, J.M. (1981). Plants underground. In *Himalaya Underground* (ed. G.A. Durrant, C.M. Smart, J.E.K. Turner, J.M. Wilson), pp. 33—34. Southampton University, Southampton.

41. _____. (1977). Cave ecology in the Himalaya. *Studies Speleol.* 3: 66—69, 4: 84.

42. Yalden, B.W. and Morris, P.A. (1975). *The Lives of Bats*. David and Charles, London. (12.8.16)

PART C

MAN-MADE ECOSYSTEMS

Natural ecosystems do not hold exclusive rights to ecology, and ecological study is not the prerogative of those who gain pleasure from working in the grandeur of Sumatra's wild areas. Disturbed, agricultural and urban areas have biological components which interact, change in abundance, adapt to physical constraints and impinge upon human life according to the same principles described in the preceding chapters. There is no reason, for example, for people in Lampung, one of the most disturbed provinces in Indonesia, to regard ecology as an irrelevant science. Thus the Government of Indonesia now employs ecologists to work in transmigration areas.

As will be described in Chapter 11, a characteristic of man-made ecosystems is their relative simplicity. This in itself should encourage those people who have been surprised at the complexity of the ecology of Sumatra's natural ecosystems to gain an understanding of how a simple ecosystem works. Valuable studies can be made of a pond, a street, a rice field or a cattle pasture. Although these may not appear at first sight to be very exciting, a short acquaintance with the areas and the first attempts to understand what eats what, when, how, in what quantities and why, are likely to produce enthusiasm to learn more and to apply the knowledge gained to increasingly complex systems.

Few of the present or planned industrial developments in Sumatra have major impacts on entirely natural ecosystems because they tend to be sited near road or rail networks and near centres of population which can provide the necessary manpower. Large scale developments are not required by law to be preceded by an environmental impact assessment. This cannot be effectively conducted until a data base exists concerning the distribution and movements of species, their yearly (or longer) population cycles, species food and reproductive requirements, competition, predators, prey, etc. Possible impacts can then be judged against the *status quo*. If monitoring starts when an industrial project begins to be built many ecological 'impacts' might be detected. However, these changes may be nothing more than normal fluctuations. The time to start some limited form of ecological monitoring is now.

Consider the efforts of the Meteorological Department. The actual recording of one day's weather details is not in itself particularly useful- no one needs to be told that his town has just experienced floods or extremely high temperatures. The value of the information derives from the data being recorded regularly. Yearly patterns can be established, and frequency of extreme records and trends, can be calculated. Agriculture benefits most from such information because planting times can be geared to maximum productivity. Ecological monitoring should be seen in the same light and should be undertaken as normal practices by departments concerned with different aspects of the biological and physical environment.

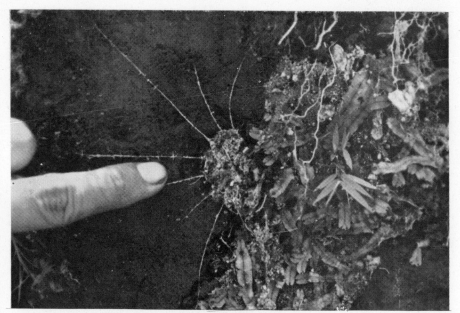

Tube web of *Liphistius sumatrana*, near Bukittinggi.

Liphistius sumatrana behind its hinged door.

Traditional shifting agriculture is not a threat to the forest.

CHAPTER 11

EFFECTS OF DISTURBANCE

11.1 INTRODUCTION

Natural ecosystems are not static. The plants and animals within them die and others are born to replace them. Energy and nutrients pass through the organisms and are removed from the system in water, by emigrations or by 'visitors'. If part of an ecosystem is destroyed in some way, the biotic community and the physical features of the soil will generally be rebuilt. This can take decades or even a thousand years depending on the ecosystem and the extent of the disturbance. The disturbed area is colonized by pioneer species which are gradually replaced by others until an ecosystem closely resembling the original is formed. This sequence of changes is called succession. In areas where repeated disturbance occurs or where the process of succession is halted, an ecosystem may never reform.

Where plants colonize a newly-formed substrate, primary succession is said to occur. This has already been described for coastal mud (sections 2.4.2, 2.5) and sandy beaches (section 3.2.1), and the primary succession of plants on the remains of Mt. Krakatau is described in section 11.3.

The return of an area to its natural state following major disturbances, such as tree falls and landslides on steep, unstable slopes, form part of the natural pattern of ecosystem functioning. These disturbances are the major cause of the mosaic of gap, building and mature phases in forests described in section 7.2.2. The disturbances envisaged in this chapter are of a large scale, probably caused by man, possibly repeated and relatively unselective in their effects.

Four basic ecological principles can be formulated from the study of succession [113].
1) Succession proceeds in only one direction. That is, fast-growing, tolerant colonizers are replaced by slower-growing species with more specific requirements but with great competitive ability where those requirements are met.
2) As new species colonize an area, they will inevitably alter the environment by their presence. The new conditions are generally less suitable for their own seedlings but more suitable for those of other species; hence the succession continues.
3) The understanding of a climax community should not be too rigid. A particular 'climax' vegetation is probably just one of a continuous range of possible 'climaxes' for that area. The actual climax which is formed is determined by local climate, soil, topography, the nature and duration of the preceding disturbance and the completeness of the community of herbivores and seed-dispersing animals.
4) A climax is itself a mosaic of successional stages (section 7.2.2).

In the following sections disturbance is discussed with reference to all the natural ecosystems discussed in previous chapters. For some, it has been difficult to find any relevant information; for others, such as lowland forest, there is a great deal known, albeit not enough. No study of the effects of disturbance to a tropical lowland forest can even be compared to the detailed work at Hubbard Brook in the U.S.A. [23, 85] but many of the principles are common to both tropical and non-tropical forests [20, 153]. It is unlikely that an equivalent study will have been completed in the Sunda Region, let alone Sumatra, before the end of this century and because of this, research must be aimed at understanding particular problems. There is no shortage of problems.

11.2. GENERAL EFFECTS OF DISTURBANCE ON FORESTS

11.2.1 Introduction

In brief, the effects of large-scale disturbance on forested ecosystems

are:
1) the creation of open, hot, simple habitats containing relatively few, small, widespread species with broad niches and great reproductive potential. These species are rarely, if ever, found in mature ecosystems;
2) a huge decrease in biomass ($\pm$ 30 kg dry weight/m² in lowland forests to 0.2 kg dry weight/m² in alang-alang plains);
3) the temporary or permanent impoverishment of the soil;
4) the creation of increasingly small and isolated patches of natural vegetation whose animal and plant diversity also progressively declines;
5) virtually all the rainfall reaches the soil surface and far more rapidly than in a forest (section 9.4.6) but less enters the groundwater and more flows in the surface runoff. This can lead to a loss of soil, a decrease in ground water supplies and an increased propensity to flooding.

These ecological effects can be observed whether the disturbed area becomes wasteland or valuable agricultural land.

The major effect of less intense disturbance (where the forest retains at least some of its former structure) is a simplification of the ecosystem caused by deleterious changes to the soil, hydrology and microclimate as well as by the actual removal of plant material such as logs. As the taller trees are removed, so the volume of living space available to the forest biota is considerably reduced [102]. There is also less substrate available for use as nest sites, aerial pathways or growing sites for epiphytes and climbing plants. In addition, there is obviously also the loss of resources, particularly food.

11.2.2 The relevance of island biogeographic theory

As the disturbance of natural ecosystems proceeds, so smaller and smaller pockets of pristine vegetation are formed and these contain reduced populations of animals and plants. The study of island biogeography (section 1.6.3) is not yet twenty years old and academic arguments continue over what predictions the mathematical models can actually make about the extinction and colonization of species in different sized areas of land, and therefore what shapes are theoretically best for nature reserves [33, 88, 165, 166]. Despite this, a number of important principles concerning the remaining 'islands' of natural habitats can be agreed.
1) The smaller the area of a particular habitat type, the higher will be the

rate of extinction.

2) Even the largest nature reserves ($\pm$ 10,000 km^2) will lose about half their larger mammal species and many of their bird species over the next 1000 years or so, through natural extinction.

3) 'Corridors' of suitable habitat linking reserves or the close proximity of two or more reserves will increase the effective population for only a proportion of species. Others are distinctly averse to travelling through or over open or disturbed areas.

Corridors may also permit the transmission of diseases and the risk of epidemics should not be underestimated. If a fatal disease were to be introduced to the wild orang-utan population through orang-utans released from a rehabilitation station, it could reduce the population to such a low level that extinction would soon follow. Virtually all the areas of forest occupied by Sumatran orang-utans are connected and any areas unaffected by the disease would not contain enough animals for a viable breeding population. It is conceivable that the road to Blangkejeren which is splitting the Mt. Leuser National Park in two might one day be seen as a blessing if an epidemic were to occur - but this is no argument for dividing up Sumatra's reserves! As domestic plants and animals - both major reservoirs of contagious diseases - press ever more heavily against natural ecosystems, the risk of epidemics becomes ever greater. The extinction of certain species which play key roles - such as dipterocarp trees, fig wasps, and animals which are the major dispersers of particular fruit - would have disproportionate effects on the remaining biota [47].

As far as Sumatra is concerned, the subject of nature reserve design is largely one for academic debate. The question of what percentage of species will become extinct in different shaped reserves in 50, 500 or 5000 years is not of great relevance when it is by no means certain how much land will still be covered by natural vegetation in even 25 years. The shape of Sumatran reserves do not generally conform to the neat models of the theories (see Gorman [51]) because the rationale behind the establishment of reserve boundaries has been set primarily by human settlement patterns. In Sumatra today the major priority is simply maintaining the integrity of reserves against the pressure of legal and illegal forms of habitat disturbance. Every day the natural ecosystems are being destroyed at a vastly faster rate than they are being added to by succession. Anyone acquainted with the major Sumatran reserves knows that not only non-reserved area are being destroyed, but that incursions into reserved areas occur also, in the form of logging, settlement, and wood cutting.

11.2.3 Genetic erosion and conservation

Destruction of tropical forests, and particularly lowland forest, represents an extremely serious global loss of plant and animal genetic resources. These play a vital role in the improvement of crop species, and in the development of industrial and medicinal products, and as such play an essential role in world economic productivity. If their availability and diversity are reduced or lost, the effects on man and his many and growing needs will be severely felt. Anyone who has the slightest doubt that conservation of Sumatra's and other tropical genetic resources is one of the highest environmental priorities should consult some of the many papers and books on the subject [3, 12, 13, 40, 42, 47, 62, 100, 101, 105, 123, 124, 125, 126].

As stated in the previous section, reduced forest area leads to a reduced number of species as well as a reduced number of individuals. The resultant inbreeding of organisms often reduces their 'fitness' (adaptability, genetic stability and variation) and can fix deleterious traits in a population which can lead to extinction. Many social mechanisms exist in Man and other animals to prevent inbreeding but for animals 'trapped' in a small population within a patch of forest there may be no choice.

How large should a population of animals be to prevent disastrous inbreeding? There is no hard and fast rule but it has been suggested that an 'effective population' of 50 is the absolute minimum possible before deleterious characters begin to become fixed and that a minimum of 500 individuals should be the goal. An 'effective population' of 50 is not the same as 50 individuals nor necessarily the same as 25 breeding animals of each sex. As explained in section 7.8.1. many animals live in social groups which are not simply pairs of adults. The effective population number, N_e, can be calculated as follows:

$$N_e = \frac{4 N_m N_f}{N_m + N_f}$$

where N_m and N_f are the number of breeding males and breeding females respectively [47]. Thus for tigers, in which one breeding male may reproduce with three females, 17 males and 51 females are required for an effective population of 50. These 68 adult animals will require 340 km^2 or 3,400,000 ha. This is somewhat depressing because each of the three largest reserve areas in Sumatra of the proposed Kerinci-Seblat National Park ($\pm$ 1,000,000 ha), Mt. Leuser National Park ($\pm$ 800,000 ha) and South Sumatra I (356,800 ha - much destroyed) are clearly too small to retain a fully functioning population of tigers. At present, however, the area of habitat used by tigers extends outside the reserves, and those at Kerinci could conceivably walk to South Sumatra I. How much longer it will be before the tigers are confined to reserves, and disturbed reserves at that, is a matter for those in positions of authority.

It is therefore clear that Sumatra's reserves and other areas where the natural biota can still be found are too small for all the components to survive if left on their own. For this reason, genetic management will one day become essential and the theory and practice of this are described by Frankel and Soulé [47].

11.2.4 Atmospheric and climatic changes

The destruction of forests and changes in land use is sometimes suggested as a cause of the rise in atmospheric carbon dioxide levels. The argument is that forests fix a great deal more carbon dioxide than grasslands or other secondary growth. Levels of carbon dioxide have been increasing over the last 100 years or so and if present trends persist the concentration will have doubled from 0.03% in the middle of last century to 0.06% in the middle of next century. Although still a small proportion of the atmosphere, the increase could well cause major climatic changes.

In fact, the majority of the rise in carbon dioxide levels is the result of burning fossil fuels and the increase to date has not caused any noticeable climatic changes [160, 161]. Thus, the effect on global climate of complete deforestation of tropical forests is most likely to be extremely small [38]. That should not lead to any complacency, however, because the effects on a regional basis would be much more noticeable. It is very difficult to collect data on this, but two studies using computer models indicated that large-scale deforestation could change mean temperatures in those areas by as much as 1 or 2°C and cause rainfall changes of up to 10% [38]. These may not sound very great, but they could greatly disrupt crop growth, harvesting, river flow (and thus irrigation) and the viability of certain crops. Local climatic changes in the Musi-Banyuasin area are described by Chambers and Manon [30].

It has been estimated that termites (section 7.7) are 8—10 times more common in land disturbed by human activities than they are in natural ecosystems. Recent research has shown that termites produce about 150 million tons of methane each year, compared with a total global input of between 350 and 1210 million tons. Termites produce methane as a by-product of their anaerobic digestive processes. The level of atmospheric methane is increasing at about 2% per year and most of the increase appears to originate from tropical areas disturbed by development [170]. The potential environmental impact of the increased level of atmospheric methane has yet to be assessed but it is clearly worthy of study.

11.3 PRIMARY SUCCESSION - THE CASE OF KRAKATAU

Krakatau is the name of a group of four islands in the Sunda Straits half-way between Tanjung Karang and Labuan (Figure 11.1). These islands represent the visible remains of Mt. Krakatau, the whole cone of which is thought to have once been above the sea surface. Periods of volcanic activity have altered the shape of the islands and its was only in 1930 that Anak Krakatau Island emerged from beneath the sea after three years of activity (Figure 11.2) [59, 107].

It was the massive eruption of 1883 that made Krakatau famous. The force of the explosion was equivalent to 2000 Hiroshima bombs, and it was heard as far away as Sri Lanka, The Philippines and Australia. Pumice and ash shot up to 80 km above the earth and this dust darkened the sky so much that lamps had to be used during the day in Jakarta and Bandung. Enormous tidal waves claimed 36,000 lives along the Sunda Strait and were detected in Alaska, San Francisco and South Africa [59].

The explosion of 1883 made Krakatau very important ecologically. Not only was all the vegetation burned, but it is almost certain that the entire land surface was sterilized [155]. Thus it is possible to observe the ways in which plants and animals colonize virgin land - a natural laboratory was

456

Figure 11.1 The Krakatau Islands showing contours every 100 m and (dotted line) the coastlines in 1883. (After Richards [112]).

The destruction caused by the River Mengkudu was out of all proportion to its normal size.

Logging roads cause serious damage to soil, the forest and hydrology.

Selective logging causes more damage and results in more wood waste than is generally realized.

It would take centuries before this log yard on Siberut Island where covered with lowland forest again. (Photograph by Gerard Persoon).

457

Figure 11.2   The geological history of the Krakatau Islands. a - the original volcanic cone of Mt. Krakatau in prehistoric times; b - the three small islands left after a prehistoric eruption; c - the growth of Rakata as a result of prehistoric volcanic activity; d - Krakatau before 1883; e - Krakatau in 1930 (it was not until this year that Anak Krakatau emerged). (After Richards [112]).

458

formed in which to study primary succession.

The first botanical expedition to visit Krakatau after the explosion was in 1886 and irregular surveys of varying thoroughness continued up to 1951. It was in 1979 that the latest, major botanical survey was conducted.

The total number of plant species found in 1979 was about 200 and this was similar to the total found by the previous comprehensive survey in 1934. This does not, however, indicate a *static* equilibrium because the total number of species recorded from the islands is increasing (Figure 11.3).

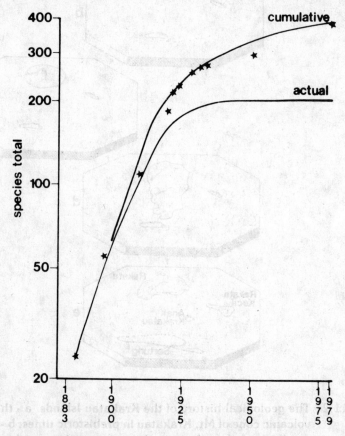

Figure 11.3 The cumulative total number of plant species recorded on Krakatau since the eruption of 1883 and the total of plant species actually present on the islands. (After Whittacker and Flenley [155]).

That is, not all species found in the past appear to be present now, suggesting a turnover of species. It has been calculated that over the last 50 years new species have been appearing on the islands at an average of 2.28 to 2.60 species per year, representing an immigration rate of 1.14—1.30% per year. At the same time, however, extinctions have been occurring at 1% per year and so the net increase in plant species actually present on the islands is between 0.14 and 0.30% per year. Thus, very roughly, a new plant species arrives every two years [155].

So, a dynamic equilibrium appears to have been reached of about 200 species. This is, perhaps, surprising because within about 150 km of the islands there are areas of little disturbed forests containing thousands of plant species. A problem with interpreting the data may be the time scale we are imposing. There is a nagging feeling that more species should have arrived in the second period of fifty years since the major eruption. In fact, as was stated above, the number of species is not at a perfect equilibrium because one new species appears every two years or so. That is equivalent to about 50 species per century. The flattening of the curve in Figure 11.3 may just be because the r-selected (section 7.1.1 and 12.3.2) species of the pioneer and building phases (section 7.2.2) are coming to the end of their domination. We may now be witnessing the slow arrival of K-selected species which will contribute to the mature phase of forest development. Only one tree typical of primary forest has so far been recorded on Krakatau [155]. It may well take a thousand years or more before the forest on Krakatau becmes properly mature but, at the present rates of destruction, there is no evidence to suggest that a pool of 'parent' primary lowland forest trees will exist anywhere in Lampung, South Sumatra or West Java in even 100 years time.

11.4 MANGROVES

The management of mangrove forest for sustained yield forestry is possible but there is very little known about natural regeneration rates or processes [4]. Unless great care is taken the result of large-scale disturbance is not the regeneration of productive forest but rather the appearance of a degraded type of vegetation. This is typically dominated by nipah [39] or *Avicennia*, or ferns *Acrostichum aureum* and sea holly *Acanthus ilicifolius*. Mangrove soils cannot be used for successful agriculture except when careful land management practices have been followed [15, 21, 54, 79].

Large-scale disturbance of mangroves can lead to coastal erosion because the shoreline is no longer protected by trees. The shore may be reduced to a narrow sandy beach or to inhospitable salt pans. The coastal population centres are then more susceptible to the effects of storms such as flooding.

The replacement of mangrove with tambak ponds (for prawn and fish production) is increasing along the north-eastern coast of Sumatra. As described in section 2.3, mangroves are vital for the continuance of coastal fisheries [78, 92], but the establishment of tambak necessitates the removal of mangrove. In moderation this can be successful but in some areas a situation is developing which has been called the 'Tragedy of the Commons' [56]. The 'commons', or unowned useful resource, in this case is a mangrove forest. One person establishes an area of tambak in order to provide an income. Other people are attracted to the idea of owning tambak and more mangrove is felled. Yields stay more or less the same for a while but then they begin to drop. Tambak owners increase the area of their tambak to compensate and to increase their income, and this is achieved by clearing more mangrove. The first tambak is now some way from the source of the fish fry and young prawns (i.e. the mangroves) and the first owner may try to move towards the fringes of the tambak area (nearer the mangroves) where yields are higher. The first tambak is taken over by ferns and other scrub. Other owners experience the same drop in yields and so the process continues. Avoidance of this situation requires either a strong environmental ethic among the tambak owners, or strong enforcement of land use regulations. In fact, some tambak owners have learned, and others are discovering, that the area suitable for tambak is limited by certain conditions of tidal range, shore elevation and soil characteristics [15].

The 'Showa Maru' oil tanker accident of 1975 showed just how sensitive mangroves are to oil pollution [15, 164, 171]. The oil probably acts by clogging the trees' pneumatophores which act as organs of gas exchange, raising the water temperature and lowering the dissolved oxygen levels; leaves may also be easily damaged by oil [87, 93]. Mangroves that survive exhibit signs of chronic stress such as reduced productivity and gradual leaf loss [87, 119]. A covering of oil on the mangrove mud would obviously have extremely adverse effects on the mangrove. The susceptibility of mangroves to other industrial and domestic pollutants requires more study [26], and although many mangrove species may be resistant to particular types of pollution, the equilibrium of the system will probably be upset [119].

Some palm oil and rubber factories discharge their effluents into rivers near the coastal zone. No study into the possible problems this causes for the biota has been conducted in Sumatra but one such study has been completed just across the Malacca Straits along the Puloh River near the estuary of the Kelang River, the river that flows through Kuala Lumpur. The head of the Puloh River was the site of a plantation factory outfall and Seow monitored the macrofauna composition and various water parameters at different locations along the river through the mangrove [130]. The water quality near the outfall was obviously the least conducive to aquatic life because it had hardly been diluted by the river water. The effluent had caused several species of fish to disappear from the estuary and others had moved downstream from the outfall. Unfortunately, no observations were made of the effects of the effluent on the surrounding vegetation.

11.5 OTHER COASTAL ECOSYSTEMS

11.5.1 Beach vegetation

Destruction of fringing coral reefs (see section 11.4.4) and the commercial exploitation of sand (such as near Banda Aceh) can almost totally destroy beach vegetation. By their pioneer nature, however, the smaller plants can recover quickly, particularly in the pes-caprae association (section 3.2.1). The Barringtonia association (section 3.2.2) has been replaced in most areas with coconut plantations and other types of agricultural areas. Where she-oak forest has been felled near Singkil, South Aceh, the vegetation has become dominated by the sensitive plant *Mimosa pudica*, *Melastoma* and various rushes, sedges and grasses.

The removal of beach vegetation may not be regarded as a particularly serious loss in itself, but its ability to hold together a loose sandy substrate means that in its absence more or less continuous coastal erosion occurs. The erosion and the impact on human settlements are particularly serious during bad storms, because the power of the wind and waves is no longer countered by deep-rooted vegetation.

Oil pollution of sandy beaches in Sumatra is not generally a serious problem but it does occur. Even on the remote western coast of Siberut Island, patches of tar have been found [157]. Organic pollution by, for example, domestic waste can reduce the depth of the aerated layer of sand and so affect the zonation of beach biota. Serious pollution by oil or other organic wastes effectively removes the fauna and the processes of soil formation in which they play an important role are greatly slowed.

The overexploitation of turtle eggs and adults for food makes the problem of survival for the rest of the turtle population progressively harder because the mass nesting behaviour of turtles is ecologically akin to the gregarious fruiting behaviour of dipterocarps (section 7.4.1). Both act to satiate the appetites of their predators with the result that at least some of their eggs or seeds will get the chance to develop. The smaller the population of turtles, however, the larger the proportion of eggs destroyed.

11.5.2 Brackish water forest

The disturbance of this forest generally results in a great simplification and the effective domination by nipah palms. No account of other effects specifically concerning brackish water forest has been found.

11.5.3 Rocky shores

Rocky shores are not usually subject to disturbance because the waves, strong currents and ruggedness and steepness of terrain are not compatible with agriculture or other forms of development.

11.5.4 Coral reefs

Coral reefs experience different scales of disturbance. One of the most common forms of serious disturbance is caused by the mining of reefs for limestone either for lime or for road fill [15]. Mining wipes out the entire ecosystem and the fisheries that depend on it becuase the other components depend on the biological and physical features of the coral for

Figure 11.4 The consequences of destroying living coral reefs which protect the coast and of clearing coastal forest are that the land suffers from erosion, the coral no longer supports fish and other animals, the water is turbid, and fishing becomes less successful. (After Odum [104]).

464

their existence (section 3.5.1). Natural disturbances may be equally devastating; corals were more or less wiped out around Krakatoa following the eruption of 1883.

Destruction of reefs also occurs when fishermen 'cheat' and catch fish using explosives. Explosions are totally unselective in the species and size of fish they kill and can reduce live coral to mere rubble [130]. Recovery of the coral, if it occurs at all, is very slow [106]. The rubble is, of course, a 'habitat' of sorts but the biomass of plankton in such areas is little greater than over plain sand [108]. When considering different impacts on coral it is worth remembering that most coral has a radial growth rate of between only 1 and 10 mm per year [15].

Waves generally break over a fringing reef thereby dissipating the wave energy and leaving the sea between the reef and the shore relatively calm. Destruction of the reefs allows waves to break with their full force against the shore (Figure 11.4) and the land erosion this causes has been described for the north coast of Java [109].

Figure 11.5 The distribution of living and dead coral around a logging company pier on Siberut Island. (After Whitten [11, 158]).

Land use which increases the sediment load of rivers and thus coastal waters can have a negative impact on corals because the polyps are suffocated by a rain of silt. This distribution of dead and live coral around a log-loading pier on Siberut Island is shown in Figure 11.5. Many hectares of muddy logging roads and log-ponds caused extremely muddy water to flow into the sea. The disturbance of reef communities by changes in patterns of sediment deposition caused by the construction of a pier near Padang is described by Umbgrove [147]. The land uses which increase sediment load in rivers also increase the seasonality of water flow (section 4.3.1.). Thus, at times of flood, large quantities of fresh water are discharged into the sea and the salinity level may fall so that certain corals die.

Changes in the community structure of coral reef fishes caused by different types of fishing methods can affect the composition and growth of corals. This subject is reviewed by Parrish [106].

The detailed effects of domestic and industrial pollution on corals have not been investigated but they are clearly deleterious [15].

Corals have been observed to exhibit a 'shutdown reaction'. When they are stressed in some way, for example by the effects of reduced water quality or explosions, they are weakened to such an extent that they may die if another stress is imposed, even though the second stress alone would not have caused their deaths. This means that the total cumulative disturbances on coral should be assessed in a study of potential environmental impact, not just the likely stresses caused by one particular development [14].

11.6 RIVERS AND LAKES

11.6.1 Introduction

Disturbance of aquatic ecosystems can, as with clearance of forest, be deleterious to some species but also extend the habitat of other more opportunistic species.

Disturbance can occur in a variety of different ways. Industrial and domestic pollution reduce the water quality with consequent effects on the whole biota: fish poisons and bombs cause indiscriminate fish death; overexploitation of fish stocks to supply the aquarium trade can have devastating effects; introduced fish can cause the demise of indigenous species; and forest clearance causes changes in temperature, turbidity, insolation, stream flow, water input, etc. thereby altering the habitat of many species.

11.6.2 Industrial and domestic pollution

Pollutants of water have been divided into four categories - pathogens, toxins, deoxygenators and nutrient enrichers [110]. Pathogens include a wide range of bacteria, protozoa and parasitic worms harmful to man and other organisms. These are all associated with untreated sewage. Toxins derive from industrial waste and from agricultural chemicals. Their effects can be both dramatic and accumulative and affect not only aquatic animals but also plants and, of course, man. Deoxygenation is caused by bacterial and fungal decay of organic matter and by animal and plant respiration. It can also be related to certain weather conditions [70]. Where large quantities of organic wastes are disposed, deoxygenation and the subsequent death of animals by suffocation can be expected.

Nutrient enrichment is known as eutrophication. Eutrophic habitats are excellent for fisheries because of their high productivity. Indeed, lakes and ponds are often artificially fertilized to increase fish production. In the Philippines, for example, yields of over 1000 kilograms per ha per year can be expected from such habitats, whereas a normal, medium-sized oligotrophic lake might produce only one-hundredth of this yield [113]. Primary production of the phytoplankton is similarly affected.

Eutrophication is not, of itself, a major problem for aquatic ecosystems. Naturally eutrophic systems are usually well-balanced but the addition of artificial nutrients can upset this balance and cause devastating results. Algae 'blooms' are the most spectacular of these effects and the combination of high nutrient levels, favourable conditions of temperature and light stimulate rapid algal growth. These blooms are a natural response of algae to the environment, but when the environment changes and can no longer support such high algae populations, the algae that accumulate during the bloom then die and decay. The ensuing rapid decomposition of organic debris by bacteria robs the water of its oxygen, sometimes to the extent that fish and other aquatic organisms suffocate.

Various studies (e.g. Schindler [129]) have shown that phosphorus is usually the limiting factor in eutrophication (rather than nitrogen or potassium which might have been suspected) and 0.01 mg phosphorius per litre of water has been sugested as the figure above which algal blooms are likely to occur in North America. Research is needed to determine the appropriate level for Sumatran lakes, so that it can be used for the establishment of rational effluent control standards.

In spite of the disturbing effects of artificially enriching lakes to such high levels, such lakes can recover their original condition if the artificial inputs cease. Sediments at the bottom of most lakes have a high affinity for phosphates which are 'locked' into the sediment even if there is an overturn (section 4.7.6). The classic example of this is Lake Washington which in 1963 was receiving 75,600 m^3 of phosphate-rich human waste from the city of Seattle each day; it stank, algal blooms occurred and the fish died. Six years after the human waste was diverted, the phosphorus levels had fallen to those measured before Seattle became a city [41].

Sumatra has yet to experience serious, large-scale, artificial eutrophication of lakes but it has been reported from a Malaysian reservoir [16]. It is important, however, to know and understand the processes involved in order to prevent any such occurrence. Lake Kerinci is perhaps the most likely place to experience such eutrophication given its area, and relatively dense surrounding human population. Saravanamuthu and Lim describe how algae can be used as indicator plants to determine the trophic status of freshwater [121].

Chemical, physical and microbiological parameters were studied at points along the Kelang River (which passes through Kuala Lumpur) and the results were examined against fish catches at the same locations [84, 99]. The species diversity, richness and the number of fish per m^2 were much higher in stations above Kuala Lumpur than in the city itself or downstream. In the worst polluted places only the guppy *Poecila reticulata* (section 13.5) was found. Downstream of Kuala Lumpur the water was unsuitable for most freshwater fishes but a few air-breathing fish species were found. The primary causes of the change in fish abundance and variety were heavy siltation, low pH and high biological oxygen demand. Heavy silt load kills certain fish by clogging their gills, thereby causing suffocation.

Lakes and rivers in North America and Europe are experiencing the serious environmental effects of acid rain. Under completely natural conditions rain is in fact slightly acid, about pH 5.7, because atmospheric carbon dioxide dissolves to form carbonic acid. Acid rain is understood to be rain which is more acid than this. The increased acidity of rain has been caused primarily by gaseous nitrogen and sulphur oxides which form nitric and sulphuric acids. These gases are waste products from the combustion of oil and coal, from metal smelting and from other industrial processes. Most water bodies have some buffering capacity but these are limited and so eventually their acidity will increase. At pHs below 5.0 most fish will die, and almost all other aquatic organisms are affected in some way. The problem is worsened because when the acid rain percolates through soil it releases certain metals, particularly aluminium, which are toxic to most organisms, even at very low concentrations. Acid rain is not an environmental problem in Sumatra and is unlikely to become one in the near future. However, acid rain is a trans-national problem - that is, industrial processes in one country can produce waste gases which fall as acid rain in another. Sumatran environmental scientists should be aware of the problems of acid rain and it would be useful to begin a low-key, long-term monitoring program of water bodies. Clear statements of the acid rain problem have been written by Cowling and Linthurst [35] and Haines [51].

11.6.3 Poisons and bombs

The most common traditional fish poison is 'tuba', made from the roots of the climber *Derris* (various species) in which the active, identifiable chemical is rotenone [133]. Other poisons, typically commercial insecticides, are also commonly used. Poisons and bombs are very effective and kill or debilitate large numbers of fish (the very reasons they are used), and because of this many urban rivers, such as the Deli and Babura in Medan, have virtually no fish left in them. Bombs are even used in rivers within reserves such as the Alas, Bohorok and their tributaries around the Mt. Leuser National Park. Apart from any other arguments against the use of poisons and bombs, these forms of fishing are selfish, needlessly destructive and, in the case of poisonous insecticides, can cause sickness in humans.

11.6.4. Aquarium and food trade

The keeping of freshwater fish in aquaria is a popular, lowcost hobby the world over. Most of these fish originate from the tropics, and Southeast Asia is a source of many popular species. Most of the indigenous species seen in aquaria in Sumatra or exported are caught in the wild rather than bred in captivity. The scale of the trade is hard to gauge but in Peninsular Malaysia and in Singapore uncontrolled collecting has completely robbed small rivers of some of their species [70, 73] with unknown effects on the river ecosystem.

Similarly, the effect of catching certain species of fish for the food trade has not been investigated. In Medan, large featherbacks *Notopterus chitala* (Figure 11.6) can be seen being sold by roadside traders. They are especially esteemed for making fish krupuk [3]. Featherback females lay their eggs on submerged timber in slow moving water and these are then jealously guarded by the male. During this time he is extremely easy to catch and without his protective presence the eggs will be eaten by smaller fish and other animals.

Figure 11.6 Featherback *Notopterus chitala*. (After Tweedie and Harrison [144]).

11.6.5 Introduced species

Introduced fish can have detrimental effects on the natural ecosystems of rivers and lakes, but this does not seem to be documented for Sumatra. The tilapia *Sarcotherodon mossambica* is an extremely productive pond fish but where stock is uncontrolled it can enter waterways. They are aggressive fish and compete very successfully (both by exploitation and interference competition - section 4.8.5) to the detriment of the indigenous fish fauna [110].

11.6.6 Forest clearance

Forest clearance is by far the most serious threat to natural river and lake ecosystems. Many aquatic animals depend on allochthonous material (material falling into the river - section 4.9.1) for their existence, for they feed directly or indirectly on dead leaves and other vegetable matter. If forest around the river is cleared, plant matter fails to accumulate regularly in sufficient quantities and many organisms such as loaches, catfish, prawns, crabs and dragonfly nymphs die even if other conditions are still suitable [72].

The species that are least resistant to such changes tend to be the specifically Sumatran or Sunda species with restricted ranges and they are ousted by species with wider ranges more typical of northern South-east Asia where open habitats occur naturally.

No systematic explanation of the effect of forest clearance on the aquatic ecosystems of Sumatra appears to have been published but it is certain that the experience in Singapore [5] and Peninsular Malaysia [37, 72] (section 4.8.3) is extremely relevant. Unforested streams may indeed have considerable numbers of fish but few species are represented and these tend to be widely-distributed or introduced species. Those species which are exclusive to Sumatra will generally be lost.

11.7 PEATSWAMP FOREST

In areas where this forest is disturbed on a small scale, such as where careful controlled logging occurs, regeneration of timber trees is successful and weed trees (list in Whitmore [153]) dominate the regrowth along the heavily-disturbed roads.

The patterns of secondary growth on peat soils after large-scale disturbance in Sumatra and Kalimantan are described by Kostermans [81]. Fire often prevents the natural succession and instead paperbark *Melaleuca cajuputih* develops extensive and virtually single-species stands in areas where its roots can reach the mineral soil beenath the peat. Fire occurs most years in southern Sumatra where peat has been drained for transmigration projects. Paperbark occurs naturally in peatswamp forest but generally in the drier, better drained parts. In areas where the peat is too thick for paperbark, *Macaranga maingayi* (section 11.9.8) forms extensive, almost pure stands [168] such as observed on the CRES expedition to peatswamp areas of Labuhan Batu. In the areas where the peat itself has burned, small, shallow lakes have formed. Some of these are almost completely covered with floating or semi-floating islands of grasses and herbs. This has been paralleled by farmers who grow young rice on floating rafts [148].

In the areas of deeper peat, plants of the early stages of succession commonly include sedges and grasses and occasional trees of *Combretocarpus rotundatus* and *Campnosperma macrophylla* amongst others. In the inner regions of the swamp where nutrients are poor and the tree growth stunted, the predominant tree is *Tristania obovata* (section 5.4.1) and this persists in the secondary growth as smaller, thinner trees. The secondary growth is also characterized by pitcher plants *Nepenthes* being even more abundant.

11.8 FRESHWATER SWAMP FOREST

The only source of information concerning disturbance in freshwater swamp is the management plan for Way Kambas Reserve [45]. Apart from large-scale logging (especially between 1968—74) there have been several large fires (1972, 1974, 1976, 1982). These disturbances and the wide yearly fluctuations in water level hinder regeneration of the original vegetation types, and areas of swamp grass and bush grow in their place. If these were left undisturbed, it would still take several centuries for a vegetation similar to the primary forest to form. The alang-alang grass and bush would probably first form a forest dominated by legumes and oaks with *Commersonia bartramia* (Sterculiaceae), a common 10 m tree of secondary forest. Dipterocarp seedlings are not light-tolerant and so can only grow once a secondary forest has grown up. The seeds cannot last many years in or on the soil, so dipterocarps may have to spread from parent trees. Also, since dipterocarp trees may be 100 years old before they fruit, and seeds rarely fall more than 100 m from the parent, the replacement of these economically important trees would be painfully slow.

The opening up of the swamp forests has allowed weeds such as the aggresive, shade intolerant, creeper *Mikania micrantha* to form dense mats over grass and bush. In addition, the small fern *Salvinia molesta* and water hyacinth *Eichhornia crassipes* form thick mats on some of the waterways.

In Peninsular Malaysia, and possibly in parts of Sumatra, paperbark is a common secondary growth tree in freshwater swamps [153, 168]. The papery bark peels off and, with the resin-rich leaf litter, forms a highly inflammable soil cover. When burning occurs the paperbark tree itself is relatively resistant but not so the other trees of the secondary growth. Grass will burn down to the soil, but the rhizomes will remain alive.

11.9 LOWLAND FOREST

11.9.1 Introduction

It is often stated that after forest clearance the loss of soil fertility and the loss of nutrients in plant biomass pose a serious threat to the integrity of most natural ecosystems in the Sunda Region. While this is certainly true for heath forest, mountain vegetation and certain peatswamps, there are no descriptions of disturbance to other types of forest resulting in succession which is not directed towards the re-establishment of 'primary' forest where continued disturbance is absent. Unfortunately, once disturbed, most forests in Sumatra experience a long series of destructive disturbances which never allow the succession to progress. Effects which are sometimes attributed to the loss of nutrients from soils, may possibly be due to competitive interaction between plants. Studies have shown that the fertility of soil does indeed decline following forest removal, but the evidence of short-term loss in soil fertility is usually accompanied by evidence that the successional vegetation is remarkably good at regenerating soil fertility [19, 55, 136]. This is not an argument against taking all possible precautions to reduce nutrient loss, but it indicates that further studies are required to elucidate the situation.

A detailed comparison of soil chemistry, soil respiration, seed storage and plant growth between soils of primary forest, cut-over forest, and cut-over and burned forest both before and after rain, has produced many interesting results [44]. Amongst these it was noted that after the

Macaranga triloba.

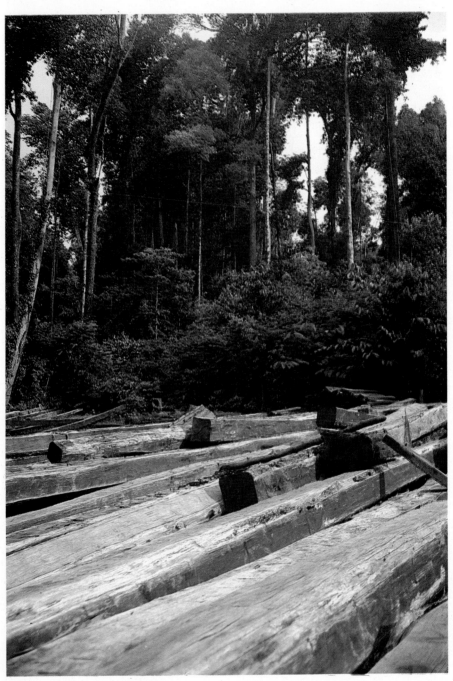
Ironwood logs, Rimbo Kulim.

disturbed vegetation had been burned, 57% of the initial amount of nitrogen and 39% of the initial amount of carbon remained in the soil. The number of viable seeds in the forest soil (the seed bank) was 8000 seeds/ m^2 (67 species) but 3000 seeds/m^2 (37 species) after the burn. Thus vigorous and relatively diverse growth followed the burn because only a proportion of the seeds were killed by the burn. Mycorrhizal fungi (section 7.3.1.) survived, and nutrients were released from the burnt material. The 5000 seeds that did not survive the fire may have either been killed in the heat of the fire or, as might be expected for primary forest trees, be dependent on high humidity for germination [102]. If this is not available for a certain length of time, the seeds will die.

A 1 ha plot of Queensland lowland forest (which contains many genera found in Sumatran lowland forest) was felled and then burned shortly afterwards. Two years afterwards the regeneration of the tree species which had reappeared were studied [139]. All of the 82 tree species present had regenerated in one or more ways: 74 had formed shoots from the base of the old trunk, 10 had formed shoots from roots, and 34 had germinated from seed. This last category appeared to have the greatest growth rate, but frequency of shoots from old trunks shows that this is an extremely important mode of regeneration. The ability of these trees to form shoots is probably limited, however, and repeated cutting or repeated burning may give smothering, light-demanding creepers the advantage and prevent regeneration from taking this form.

When forest is cut selectively for timber, recovery is relatively rapid because the seed bank has many types of viable seeds and many tree species have the ability to sprout from stumps. The silvigenetic cycle has been described in section 7.2.2. When forest is cut, dried and burned and then abandoned, the succession proceeds more slowly because part of the seed bank has been destroyed and because some of the sprouting species are not resistant to fire [145].

Thus, when forests are cut, burned, farmed, weeded or burned and farmed again, recovery of the forest (if allowed) is extremely slow. In places where the only remaining stands of primary forest (source of seeds) are some kilometers away, full regeneration will take hundreds if not thousands of years [145]. Even if a few mature trees have been left to stand there is no guarantee that these will regenerate successfully because some species have seeds which have to pass through an animal intestine before they will germinate [102]. These areas should not, however, be regarded as ecological deserts or without interest [7, 46, 66], particularly since their rehabilitation to useful land needs ecological approaches. Ideas for ecological experiments to achieve successful rehabilitation have been suggested by Mendoza [97].

The vegetation that grew up during the seven years fallow period between tobacco crops in the Deli area has been described in detail by Jochems [67]. Its composition remained quite constant in that it contained those species which were able to fruit within seven years and whose seeds could remain viable for at least one year. The shorter fallow period allowed nowadays has presumably reduced the diversity of the secondary vegetation but it still avoids the invasion of the pernicious alang-alang grass. A great deal is written about alang-alang but the symposium organized by BIOTROP [22] remains an excellent sourcebook.

A common strategy in reafforestation programs for wastelands is to plant pines or other plantation trees. Where there is a local human population these programs do not always succeed. It has recently been suggested that assisted natural regeneration might, in the long-term, produce a larger yearly biomass increment than plantations, particularly in areas where financial resources were limited [74]. Assisted natural regeneration would require strips or other shaped areas to be planted with a range of good, light-tolerant timber trees and other species. One likely candidate is *Anthocephalus chinensis*. Regeneration of neighbouring areas would then occur outwards from these centres.

The typical (but not inevitable) vegetation types caused by different forms of disturbance are summarized in Figure 11.7.

11.9.2 Shifting cultivation

Shifting cultivation, in its purest sense, is the repeated use of a patch of forested land for agriculture, characterized by long fallow periods between short periods of intensive production. An area of forest is cleared, the remains are left to dry and are then burned. Crops are subsequently sown in the ashes between the tree trunks which were too large to burn.[1]

---

1. On Siberut Island, the shifting agriculture traditionally practised does not include a burn; instead, fruit trees are planted amongst the fallen vegetation which remains to protect the soil until it rots down, slowly releasing nutrients to the soil. This 'wise' land practice is probably a result of the very high rainfall which makes a large burn difficult, and of the fact that the people do not traditionally grow hill rice [11, 157].

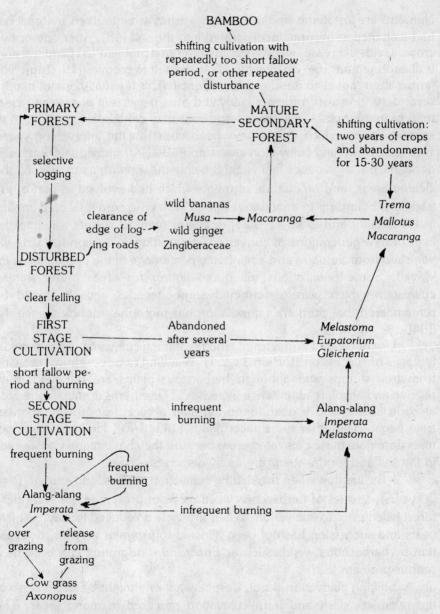

BAMBOO

shifting cultivation with
repeatedly too short fallow
period, or other repeated
disturbance

PRIMARY
FOREST

MATURE
SECONDARY
FOREST

shifting cultivation:
two years of crops
and abandonment
for 15-30 years

selective
logging

clearance of
edge of log-
ing roads

wild bananas
Musa
wild ginger
Zingiberaceae

Macaranga

Trema
Mallotus
Macaranga

DISTURBED
FOREST

clear felling

FIRST
STAGE
CULTIVATION

Abandoned
after several
years

Melastoma
Eupatorium
Gleichenia

short fallow pe-
riod and burning

SECOND
STAGE
CULTIVATION

infrequent
burning

Alang-alang
Imperata
Melastoma

frequent burning

frequent
burning

Alang-alang
Imperata

infrequent burning

over
grazing

release
from
grazing

Cow grass
Axonopus

Figure 11.7 Land-use and forest succesion. (After Tanimoto [142], Whitten
[158] and Wyatt-Smith [168]).

Nutrients are lost in the smoke and rain washes ash into rivers before it has had a chance to become incorporated into the soil [48]. After one or two crops, yields decrease, weeds become a serious problem [31] and the area is abandoned for 15—30 years to allow the soil to recover [19, 136]. The farmer then moves to another area of forest. This is usually one of mature secondary forest on a former cultivated area because it is easier to clear than primary forest. This secondary forest may contain mature fruit trees such as durian which would have been visited in the intervening years. This form of shifting cultivation can support 30—40 individuals/km^2 and depends on subsistence agriculture being the predominant use of the cleared areas, and on cultural restraints which had evolved as part of the traditions bound up in animistic religions. The environmental care implicit in Christianity and Islam [2, 128] does not seem to find its way into the lives of new generations of converts. True shifting cultivation has virtually vanished from Sumatra and a miniscule percentage of the population is involved. Some publications still quote figures for areas under shifting cultivation which were determined some decades ago. It should be remembered that Sumatra's population has more than doubled since the 1940s.

Use of cleared and burned land for shifting cultivation alters the early stages of succession (section 11.2.1). Weeding removes shoots growing from tree stumps and although herbaceous plants are removed, their relative and absolute abundance increases. These herbs dominate the area as soon as the land is abandoned but after a year, fast-growing pioneer trees begin to smother the smaller plants [141, 146]. Herbs and pioneer trees dominate these cultivated areas because they have many viable seeds in the soil and/or the seeds are easily dispersed.

It is clear that when the shifting cultivation cycle is long enough (e.g. 30 years), species of herbaceous weeds are not present in the secondary forest felled prior to cultivation. When the cycle is reduced to, say, just five years and succession has not been allowed to progress very far, domination by herbaceous weeds such as *Eupatorium odoratum* can become a serious problem [82].

Shifting cultivation *is not*, despite what one might be led to believe, the relentless slash and burn cultivation practised in many areas. The distinction is illustrated in Figure 11.8. Slash and burn is practised with almost no cultural or social restraint and the cultivation of cash rather than

| 1° forest | Fields | Scrub | 2° forest | Weed lands |

Figure 11.8 The distinction between traditional shifting agriculture (a) and the now prevalent slash-and-burn agriculture (b) which is endangering so many of Sumatra's natural ecosystems. (After Rijksen [114]).

subsistence crops is the major use of cleared land. The change from shifting cultivation to slash-and-burn is caused largely by population increase [48], whereby rested land is virtually non-existent and primary forest is cleared when the former cultivated area is exhausted or when alang-alang grass can be kept at bay no longer by simple (cheap) weeding. Regeneration of forest in such areas would take many centuries.

11.9.3 Effects of logging on the soil

The damage that logging causes to soil has barely been studied in Indonesia but the general subject has been reviewed by Kartawinata [76]. The major problems are soil removal by bulldozers when making roads, soil compaction caused by heavy vehicles, and soil loss due to rain striking the ground with its full force and the greater quantity of rain reaching the soil. The removal or destruction of trees also reduces litter fall and hence the organic inputs to the soil, but in areas where the soil has not been too greatly damaged, soil nutrient levels and microorganisms can recover within a few years. Since only the larger portions of the tree trunks are removed, and most of a tree's nutrients are in its leaves and roots, the loss of biomass after logging is proportionally greater than the loss of nutrients.

11.9.4 Effects of logging on hydrology

A study of the effect of logging and other forms of forest clearance on hydrology is also beset by inadequate data and differences in interpretation [103]. It is obvious, however, from a brief visit to a logging camp or a flight over areas where logging occurs that a great deal of water runs off the roads, carrying soil with it. This has been quantified by Hamzah who measured the silt content:

a) of a river near, but not influenced by, a particular logging area,
b) from a river in the logging area, and
c) from a ditch by a logging road [53].

The silt contents were 0.01, 0.05 and 0.1% respectively—a ten-fold increase. The increased silting of Sumatra's main rivers could probably be traced to logging as well as other forms of unprotective land use.

In the lower stretches of major rivers the actual volume of water is probably not greatly affected by forest clearance, but it is in the higher river regions, before high water levels can be dampened, that dramatic effects are noticed. For example, the consequence of clearing just 10 ha of forest for fields on slopes above the Mengkudu River near the edge of the Mt. Leuser National Park in May 1981 was that 13 people died [116, 117]. The Mengkudu River is normally only one metre wide and 8—15 cm deep but landslides on the steep, deforested slopes and the increased surface runoff, both caused by the 10 ha ladang, turned the Mengkudu into a river capable of moving $1-3$ m^3 boulders. A nearby river also flooded and destroyed new bridges and roads (which took months to repair), ricefields and most of a town and by luck claimed only one more life. Few floods in Sumatra have been so well documented as these but they are commonly reported in the newspapers. The floods are generally attributed to illegal or irresponsible logging or other forest clearance.

11.9.5 Effects of logging on the forest

The felling of trees and extraction of logs are the primary causes of disturbance during a logging operation. Felling damages tree crowns, boles and saplings, exposes wood making it susceptible to fungus damage and also covers seedlings. Extraction of the logs exposes bare soil and damages large areas of the forest floor [76].

Selective logging sounds a very mild and benign activity to many people who have not visited or worked in a logging concession and it comes as a surprise to learn how much damage is caused to the forest as a whole. One estimate is that five times more timber is destroyed or badly damaged than is extracted [28]. Another illustration is that for every large tree felled, 17 similar- or smaller-sized ones are destroyed [1].

Most of the destruction is caused by the access roads which remove all cover from the soil and form channels which are further scoured by water during storms. It has been estimated that 20—30% of a logged area is completely bare, being composed of roads and logyards [76, 96]. Some of the roads cut across small rivers, acting as dams, and the subsequent flooding kills most of the inundated trees and other plants [12, 76]. The lorries used to drag logs out of the forest cause compaction of the soil surface and this disturbance is traceable in some forests by the occurrence of the pioneer tree *Anthocephalus chinensis* even 40 years after the logging. By this time other pioneer trees such as *Trema*, *Macaranga* and *Homolanthus* have died or become rare as different genera take over in the succession. The soil compaction caused by lorries is, however, only a fraction of that caused by the bulldozers used to make the roads. Additional disturbance is caused when trees are felled on both sides of the main logging roads to hasten the drying of the road surface after rain. These 'daylighting' areas have been estimated as occupying 8 ha per km of road [53].

A very thorough study of the effects of logging on the forest was conducted on South Pagai Island in the Mentawai Islands, West Sumatra [9]. A total of 2416 trees (20 cm diameter and over) originally stood in the 15 1 ha plots, half of which were commercial species and half non-commercial species. A total of 194 trees (13/ha) were felled and extracted. On average, about half of the remaining trees had been noticeably damaged, broken or knocked down, and the other half had escaped damage (Figure 11.9). This proportion seems to be relatively consistent

480

Figure 11.9 The effect of extracting 8% of the trees by selective logging on an area of forest on South Pagai Island (Mentawai). The other categories are undamaged forest, totally destroyed, seriously broken, and badly damaged crowns and stripped bark. (From data in Alrasjid and Effendi [9]).

between studies [1, 28, 143]. In areas of South Pagai Island where many trees were extracted, over 70% of the remaining trees had been damaged or killed. Damage to saplings and seedlings was also extremely high.

Damage to a forest during logging can be reduced if all climbing plant stems are cut. When a tree is felled the tangle of these stems often

The plains of Padang Lawas, South Tapanuli, may once have been covered with heath forest.

Tin tailings backed by heath forest; Bangka Island.

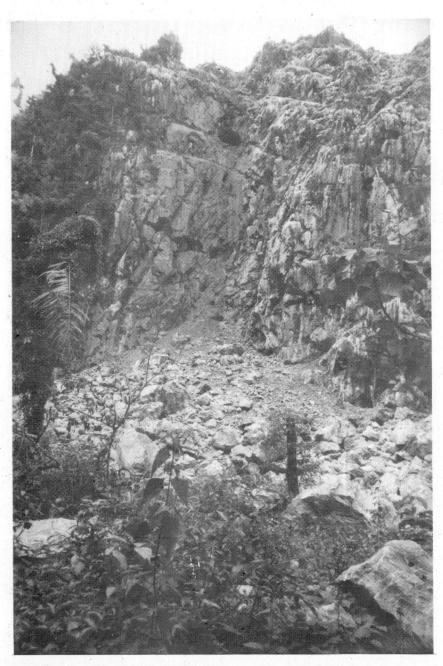

Limestone mining obviously destroys cave ecosystems.

pulls other trees over and the climbers also compete with the trees for light, water and nutrients. This cutting may be sound forestry but their death must have a significant effect on frugivorous animals. For example, 25% of the food plants of orang-utans are climbers [114], as are 42% of the food plants of Mentawai gibbons [156].

The cutting of climbers is obviously disastrous for the famous *Rafflesia* and other members of its family (section 7.3.7), all of which are rare enough as it is, because they live only as non-deleterious parasites on the stems and roots of *Tetrastigma* climbers. In addition, the climbers of the genus *Aristolochia* have spectacular flowers and the leaves are the sole food of some of the larger (and saleable) butterflies and moths.

It is difficult to resolve the conundrum of whether to cut or not to cut climbers. The answer will probably have to be total and enforced protection of such plants in reserves since they are unlikely to survive otherwise.

Selective logging is, in theory, a repeatable exercise in any given area. After the largest commercial trees have been extracted the area should be left for about 70 years when the next timber crop can be harvested. The average volume of dipterocarp timber in a forest logged forty years before is only half the volume found in adjacent unlogged forest [96]. Logging of a forest at intervals of less than about 70 years is unsound forestry practice but as more species become economically worth exploiting and when timber prices increase, and when smaller and smaller trees are permitted to be cut, repeated logging occurs. Over a hundred species of Sumatran trees are probably commercially exploited but a tree species which is non-commercial today can easily become commercial tomorrow if a particular use is found for its timber properties or if supplies of better species are insufficient to meet the demand. Each time logging occurs plant succession is set back a step, the forest becomes progressively poorer in desirable species and progressively richer in 'weed' species [153, 168].

The microclimatic changes caused by logging are obvious - it is hotter, lighter and drier in logged-over forest. These changes result in the dieback of crowns, scalding of intolerant trunk and branches, water stress and even an increased likelihood of insect attack, any one of which might lead to the death of a tree [76].

While selective logging clearly has many advantages, its also removes the best individual trees leaving only inferior ones to produce seeds for future 'crops'. This genetic erosion is potentially extremely serious for future forestry [17, 76, 127, 153] but in many logged areas it is doubtful whether in fact a full cycle of regeneration will ever be allowed to occur.

The regeneration of lowland forests in natural gaps has been described in section 7.2.2. Regeneration after selective logging takes a similar course and has been studied in parts of West Sumatra, Jambi, South Sumatra and Lampung [49, 50, 60, 61]. Plots studied one, three, four, and ten years after logging each had distinctly different structure and species composition (Table 11.1). After ten years it was generally found that the secondary forest was forming a layered canopy and entering the building phase [49, 50]. It seems unlikely that regenerated forests will grow to their original heights and Ng has suggested that a height decrease of 25—50% would not be surprising [102].

The daylighting areas at the sides of the roads are quickly colonized by wild bananas (although in some areas these appear to be quite rare), smaller weed trees and various members of the ginger family (Zingiberaceae). This early community plays an important role in stabilizing otherwise vulnerable soil.

11.9.6 Effects of disturbance on the fauna

About 70% of the mammal and bird species found in the Sunda Region are dependent on more or less intact primary lowland forest [95, 151]. Considering the very large number of insects which are restricted to a single species of plant (section 7.1.2) the percentage of the region's insects dependent on undisturbed forest is probably even greater. In view of this, there is clearly a need to know what effects different types of disturbance have on Sumatra's fauna. The trends and general patterns, at least for mammals and birds, are now however quite well understood. The forest fauna is affected by disturbance in at least three ways:

(1) the noise and shock of disturbance may cause immediate change in behaviour;

(2) the actual removal of parts of the forest canopy will alter ranging patterns and diet which may in turn affect social behaviour and population dynamics;

(3) the slow regeneration rate may cause permanent changes in population density [69].

Table 11.1. Structure and composition of trees in four study plots in selectively logged forest in South Sumatra. (After Geollegue and Huc [50]).

	one-year old plot	three-year old plot	four-year old plot	ten-year old plot
Sylvigenetic phase	Pioneer	Pioneer	Pioneer	Building
Characteristics	-presence of decaying logs -seedlings of pioneers -dense crown cover	-logs in advanced decay -presence of vines and saplings of pioneers -heterogeneous but closed crown cover	-decaying logs still present -vines on top of canopy -clear understorey	-decaying logs absent -vines in lower canopy only -crown stratified into three layers
Mean height of dominant trees (m)	2	4	8	22
Mean trunk diameter of dominants (cm)	2	5	10	35
Dominant species	*Macaranga gigantea* (Euphorbiaceae) *Alchornea villosa* (Euphorbiaceae)	*Macaranga trichocarpa* *Croton laevifolius* (Euphorbiaceae) *Anthocephalus villosa* (Rubiaceae) *Shorea ovalis* (Dipterocarpaceae) *Shorea leprosula* *Shorea escimia* *Quercus gemelliflora* (Fagaceae)	*Anthocephalus chinensis* *Macaranga gigantea* *Macaranga trichocarpa* *Macaranga hypoleuca* *Glochidion sericeum* (Euphorbiaceae)	Upper Storey: *Anthocephalus chinensis* *Sapium discolor* (Euphorbiaceae) Middle Storey: *Vitex vestita* (Verbenaceae) *Glochidion* sp. *Euodia alba* (Rutaceae) *Tetrameles nudiflora* (Dattiscaceae) Lower Storey: *Buchania sessifolia* (Anacardiaceae) *Polyalthia rumphii* (Annonaceae) *Macaranga trichocarpa* *Anthocephalus villosa*

484

Different species show different degrees of tolerance to disturbance and some animals will usually be found even in the most disturbed areas. A long-term study of terrestrial mammals in different habitats ranging from primary forest to an area of alang-alang grass showed, not surprisingly, that the total number of species decreased. It also demonstrated that the proportion of introduced species (rats) increased from 0—100% [57] (Figure 11.10). Similar results were reported by Yong [169]. Surveys for

Figure 11.10 The total number of non-flying mammal species in six types of vegetation and the percentage of introduced species. (From data in Harrison [57]).

noticeable animals along transects in forest with different levels of disturbance in the Sekundur Reserve (Langkat) also showed a dramatic decrease in species present with increasing disturbance [114] (Table 11.2).

Properly executed selective logging is not disastrous for much of the forest fauna although some squirrels and birds fare badly [68, 69, 90, 91, 162, 163]. 'Properly executed' in the ecological sense used here means an average of 8—10 and an absolute maximum of 15 trunks removed per hectare, no relogging for at least 50 and preferably 70 years (section 11.9.5), no replanting with foreign tree species, and an adjacent area of

Table 11.2 Direct observations (observations/km) (a) and indirect observations (signs/km) (b) of animals encountered along transects of different lengths in four forests in the Sekundur Reserve, Langkat. (After Rijksen [114]).

		Secondary vege-tation (5 km)	Forest being logged (4 km)	Slightly disturbed forest (14 km)	Undisturbed primary forest (7 km)
a)	Siamang *Hylobates syndactylus*	—	—	0.07	0.14
	White-handed gibbon *Hylobates lar*	—	—	0.35	0.57
	Long-tailed macaque *Macaca fascicularis*	—	—	0.14	0.14
	Pig-tailed macaque *Macaca nemestrina*	—	—	0.07	0.14
	Thomas' leaf monkey *Presbytis thomasi*	—	0.25	0.07	0.29
	Silvered leaf monkey *Presbytis cristata*	0.6	—	—	—
	Elegant flying squirrel *Hylopetes elegans*	—	0.25	—	—
	Horse-tailed ground squirrel *Sundasciurus hippurus*	—	—	0.21	0.57
	Slender squirrel *Sundascriurus tenuis*	0.2	0.25	0.28	0.57
	Common treeshrew *Tupaia glis*	—	—	0.21	0.28
	Flying lemur *Cynocephalus brachyotis*	—	—	—	0.14
	Pig *Sus scrofa*	—	—	0.14	0.14
	Argus pheasant *Argusianus argus*	—	0.25	0.64	0.71
	Helmeted hornbill *Rhinoplax vigil*	—	—	0.14	0.86
	Rhinoceros hornbill *Buceros rhinoceros*	—	—	—	0.42
	Bushy-crested hornbill *Anorrhinus galeritus*	—	—	0.14	0.14
	TOTAL	0.8	1.00	2.46	5.11
b)	Orang-utan nests	—	—	0.28	1.57
	Elephant tracks	0.4	—	0.21	0.14
	Deer tracks	0.4	0.25	0.28	0.28
	Pig tracks	1.0	0.50	0.86	0.57
	TOTAL NUMBER OF SPECIES	5	6	15	17

primary forest from which fruits can be dispersed into the logged area. If such practices are adhered to, there is no reason why nature conservation and forestry should conflict. Logged forest supports a lower species diversity but is able to maintain viable populations of many species.

The initial effects of selective logging are probably the most serious and Johns found a lower birth rate and a greater mortality amonst infant primates in such areas [68]. These effects were temporary and the populations eventually began to return to normal. It is likely, however, that the effects of disturbance will last several decades because it takes that long for the lost resources such as food sources, nest sites, etc. and for microclimatic conditions to recover.

The effects of disturbance depend in part on the social system and diet of the species concerned. Territorial species are worst affected because they are unable, even temporarily, to move out of the disturbed area because they will probably be surrounded by defended territories of the same species. Non-territorial species may be able to withstand some temporary crowding before moving back into the disturbed forest (Figure 11.11).

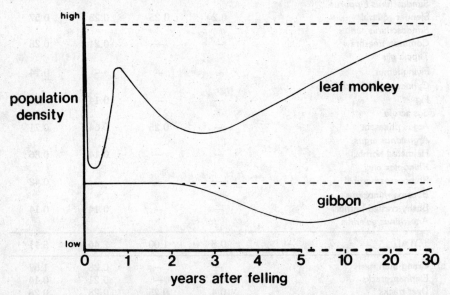

Figure 11.11 Changes in population density of leaf monkeys (non-territorial) and gibbons (territorial) after selective logging. (After Marsh and Wilson [90]).

Species with relatively specialized diets (e.g. section 7.8.3) would be expected to fare rather worse in disturbed forest than unspecialized species.

Some indigenous animals, such as bulbuls *Pycnonotus*, tapirs and, to some extent, elephants actually seem to benefit from selective logging because they favour the r-selected (section 7.1.2 and 12.3.2) foods which are abundant in disturbed areas.

When forest is completely cleared for large-scale agriculture or other purposes the animals that once lived in it will eventually die. The territorial species are very unlikely to be able to find unoccupied areas in the neighbouring undisturbed areas, and the non-territorial species may be able to move into adjacent forests (assuming there are any) but sooner or later the food resources will limit the population to more or less its original level.

It is worthwhile to quantify roughly the losses in order to make the effects more understandable. If 10,000 ha of lowland forest were felled for, say, an oil palm plantation, the following would be among the subsequent deaths:

30,000	squirrels
5,000	monkeys
15,000	hornbills
900	siamang
600	gibbons
20	tigers
10	elephants

More than these would be affected by the disturbance, but some may later be able to exploit the plantation in some way.

Those people involved with logging or forest clearance and those who remain behind after the initial disturbance occasionally see the animals whose habitat has been disturbed. Some of these are shot by hunters and others are caught (often illegally) and sold. The trade in young orang-utans has decreased enormously because of the efforts of the Directorate-General of Nature Conservation but the problem of what to do with these displaced animals is not easily solved.

Rehabilitation of animals displaced by forest clearance or caught and sold as pets is not really an answer because most of them found themselves homeless because of forest destruction. Rehabilitation centres for orang-utans, such as at Bohorok (Langkat), are wonderfully valuable as sites for

488

conservation education [18] but in terms of long-term conservation of orang-utans their role is doubtful for two main reasons:

(a) The surrounding forests have their own resident population of orang-utans, and their birth-rates in areas close to logging operations (that is, near the forest edge) are lower than average indicating that they are suffering from stress [89]. Introducing rehabilitant orang-utans into this already disturbed population could have any number of consequences.

(b) There is the danger that diseases contracted from humans during the time the orang-utans were in captivity could spread to the wild population with possibly disastrous effects. The orang-utans are kept in quarantine for a while but this will not necessarily reveal those diseases with a long incubation period or animals which are 'carriers' of the disease but do not show any symptoms.

Orang-utans are particularly amenable to rehabilitation because they do not live in social groups. Other Sumatran primates are social, however, and attempts to introduce a monkey into an established group are quite likely to lead to the new animal being killed, probably by the adult male. There is no reason why the adult male should bother to defend his group or territory for any individual except his mate(s) and offspring, because the introduced animal will not increase the adult male's genetic legacy.

11.9.7 Bamboo

Repeated disturbance of an area of lowland forest allows various species of bamboo to gain a toehold and they can form a more or less permanent vegetation cover. Many species are shade-tolerant and so persist even when forest has grown around and above them. Patches of bamboo in the forest almost invariably indicate sites disturbed intensively by man at some time in the past. Bamboos are giant members of the large grass family, Poaceae (formerly Graminae), which includes rice, sugar cane, alang-alang and maize. Like rice, bamboo dies after flowering and fruiting, but it can take over a century for flowering to occur [65, 134]. Stranger than this, however, is that under natural conditions most species flower simultaneously over wide areas. This is similar to the phenomenon of gregarious flowering found in dipterocarp trees (section 7.4.1) and pigeon orchids (section 13.2) but in these cases flowering is mainly governed by environmental factors. The flowering of bamboo is not. Even when individual plants of some bamboo species are grown in different parts of the world with different climates, the species will still flower simultaneously [65].

Why should bamboos behave in this way and how are the cycles maintained? The reasons are in essence the same as for the dipterocarps. That is, long gaps between fruiting periods allow reserves to be accumulated so that very heavy fruiting occurs and this satiates the available seed predators so that at least some seeds are left to form the next generation. If the plants did not synchronize the fruiting, heavy fruiting would simply result in large populations of seed predators. Bamboos provide very attractive food:

1) Bamboo seeds are extremely nutritious, having a nutrient quality slightly greater than either rice or wheat [65, 111].
2) There is no evidence to suggest that bamboo seeds are defended chemically against predation.
3) The fallen seeds are easily found beneath the clumps of bamboo because the dense shade produced by the bambo stems and leaves precludes most other plants from growing beneath them.

Bamboo seeds therefore form an easily harvestable, nutritious but periodic food source. The seeds are eaten by a wide range of opportunistic vertebrates such as rats, pigs,porcupines, pheasants, jungle fowl, doves and parrots. None of these animals form defended territories and so can range widely around forests in search of food. They also have r-selected reproductive strategies; that is, they can increase dramatically in numbers in response to an abundant source of food which, in the case of bamboos, may last for two years. It has been hypothesized by Janzen that the above animals would have been effective at devouring the majority of seeds produced by clumps of bamboo fruiting out of phase of at the very beginning or very end of a fruiting period [65]. Conversely, when bamboo fruit was most abundant, the animals would eat proportionately less of the crop. Since the determination of the inter-fruting period appears to be largely genetic rather than environmental, such 'weeding out' of those plants behaving independently would favour increasingly synchonous behaviour.When the fruiting period is over, the swollen population of certain animals, such as rats, often turn their attention to growing or stored crops.

Man disrupts this synchrony in three ways:

490

1) He removes (by hunting or habitat change) the animals which are the agents of selection.

2) He moves bamboos around deliberately, mixing different species or cohorts of the same species [134]. He does this because of the many and varied uses of bamboo [131, 134, 159].

3) He harvests (or harvested) the larger bamboo seeds when they are most abundant and so his impact is most when the other animals' impact is least. This is largely becuase it is not worth his while putting effort into collecting the seeds unless there are considerable quantities available. Conversely, a foraging animal would be able to occupy a bamboo area and gradually increase its intake of bamboo seeds.

Bamboo deserves more attention particularly now it is being grown as a minor plantation crop in Sumatra for use in the oil-palm industry [159].

11.9.8 Macaranga

One of the most common genera of pioneer trees found in disturbed lowland forest (and peatswamp - section 11.7) is *Macaranga* (Euphorbiaceae). This genus contains over twenty species found in Sumatra and the vast majority are shade intolerant and are only found in open conditions. Keys to the species have been prepared by Corner [34] and Whitmore [15], of which the second is the more useful.

About one third of the species of *Macaranga* are peculiar in having hollow twigs in which live colonies of ants. Winged females bite their way into the twigs of young seedlings and subsequent holes are made by other members of the growing colony.

It is usually the case that every branch of a tree will be occupied and only rarely is an 'ant-species' of *Macaranga* found without ants. Only one species of ant *Cremastogaster borneensis macarangae* occupies *Macaranga* in Peninsular Malaysia [152] and it is likely that the same species is found on Sumatra.

The ants bring young scale insects (generally a species of *Coccus* [77]) into the twigs where the scale insects suck sap from the tree tissue. The scale insects excrete sugary fluid (honey-dew) on which the ants feed. *Macaranga* does not only provide the ants with a safe place to keep their 'cattle' but it also forms small, white, oily food bodies on the stipules (small leaf-like extension at the base of the petiole) which are utilized by the ants [34].

While it is clear how the ants benefit from the *Macaranga,* no thorough investigation has been made of the other side of the relationship. It is presumed, however, that the ants protect the tree from caterpillar and other pest damage. It would be easy enough to test this hypothesis by comparing insect damage on two sets of trees of the same species in which one set had had the ants systematically killed and the other set was left alone as a control.

11.10 UNCOMMON LOWLAND FORESTS

11.10.1 Heath forest/padang vegetation

Disturbance of heath forest results in impoverished vegetation. Repeated disturbance results in vegetation which, because of the extremely low mineral status of the soil, appears unable to develop back into heath forest [98] (section 8.2.3). Disturbance to padang vegetation, which may possibly be a natural ecosystem (albeit improverished) in its own right, results in even poorer padang, easily burned and increasingly slow to recover. It has been suggested that the large sandy area of impoverished vegetation near Gunung Tua (Labuhan Batu/South Tapanuli) used to be heath forest [149].

The only study on the effects of disturbance on heath forest in Indonesia was conducted by Riswan in East Kalimantan [115]. He clearfelled two 0.5 ha plots in primary heath forest, burned the vegetation in one and removed all the surface vegetation from the other without burning. Transects 100×1 m were established and divided into 100 1×1 m quadrats and the regrowth was monitored. After 18 weeks all the quadrats in the unburnt plot were occupied by some living vegetation. There were only two seedlings (two species) but 29 species had sprouted from the base of the felled trunks. In contrast, 13 of the quadrats in the burnt plot remained bare after the same time period. In the other 87 quadrats there were five seedlings of one species but only 19 species were sprouting from felled tree bases. in a nearby 'mature' disturbed heath forest there were only eight tree species present compared with 27 species in an adjacent primary heath forest. Riswan joined virtually all other authors who have experience of heath forest in strongly recommending that:

- all heath forests should be retained in its natural state and classified as conservation areas; and that
- they should be used for education, research and recreation [115].

Reclamation of the bare, sandy, glaring-white tin mine tailings, which are in areas probably once covered with heath forest, presents a considerable challenge to a plant ecologist. Soepraptohardjo and Barus write, "Because of the low potential of tin tailings, they are generally forgotten about, becoming mounds of white in an otherwise green landscape. It is the responsibility of P.T. Timah (the major tin-mining company) to seek ways of rehabilitating the tailings [135]." Similar views were expressed in the environmental impact assessment of the P.T. Koba Tin operation [83]. Reclamation experiments with various foreign shrubs and trees have been started [132] but tree species from heath forest may represent an important element in any such reclamation. Brunig estimated that a total of 849 species of tree from 428 genera lived in the heath forests of Sarawak and Brunei [25]. The area of heath forest on Bangka and Belitung Islands is much less, so a correspondingly lower number of species would be expected. However, it is these trees which have adapted to atrociously poor soils that should be used in trials aimed at reclamation. Van Steenis has suggested *Ploiarium*, *Rhodamia* and *Rhodomyrtus* as possible trial genera [138]. There is little hope of recreating heath forest [98] but the use of local species is likely to meet with much more success than the use of foreign species adapted to quite different conditions. Enormously successful reclamation of kaolin soils in S.W. England has been achieved through soil conditioning and the careful choice of appropriate indigenous plants [6].

Considering the size and influence of P.T. Timah on Bangka and Belitung Islands, it is recommended that they make strenuous efforts to protect heath forest in and around their concession areas, and to begin a program of identifying tree species suitable for use in reclamation projects.

11.10.2 Ironwood forest

Nothing appears to have been documented about effects of

disturbance in ironwood forest. One of the characteristics of ironwood trees is that after being felled large numbers of suckers grow freely from the base of the trunk. It is not clear how many, if any, of these survive to become mature trees. These suckers grow vigorously even in full light, such as at the side of logging roads. This, plus the initial predominance of ironwood (seeds and saplings) in the forest probably means that ironwood would regenerate quite successfully in the long term. For notes on germination requirements for ironwood seed see Koopman and Verhoef [80] and section 8.3.2.

11.10.3 Forest on limestone

Limestone hills are generally drier than hills consisting of other rock, and fires, either natural or deliberate, are the chief causes of the destruction of forest on limestone. The thin soil is highly organic and can itself burn in the fires and so regeneration may be very slow. Bare rock is colonized first by bryophytes and ferns and then eventually clumps of shrubs and small trees grow where litter has accumulated [10]. Forest on limestone has few commercially important tree species but is destroyed by mining.

11.11 MOUNTAINS

During the ascent of Mt. Kemiri by a CRES team it was repeatedly remarked that signs of prior expeditions were extremely obvious particularly in the upper montane and subalpine zones. A ditch and a soil pit dug by a geomorphological expedition two years before still had sharp edges and the piles of earth at their sides were still quite loose. There can have been hardly any heavy rain to smooth the edges or to wash the piles of earth back into the ditch. Campsites used by army expeditions in the 1940's were still largely clear of vegetation. Van Steenis remarked on the flattened empty biscuit tins at the summit left by the expedition which set up the triangulation pillar six years before his 1937 expedition. In 1982 these tins were still there although they were slightly rusty. Lastly, the burnt slopes, although almost certainly not burned since the description by van Steenis, were essentially unchanged in character from the photographs at the end of his paper.

Most people in Sumatra live in climates where vegetation can grow vertically as much as eight metres in three years. It is important, therefore, that those people who climb Sumatra's mountains for recreation or study should remember just how long-lasting the effects of disturbance can be. The campsite at about 3200 m on Mt Kerinci was, at the time that it was visited by a CRES team, littered with tins, paper and plastic wrappings and there were signs of fires which had got out of control. An untended fire on Mt Sinabung destroyed most of the upper zone vegetation there in 1981.

The only known detailed studies of regeneration of tropical vegetation at high altitudes were both conducted in Costa Rica. The regeneration of subalpine vegetation studied by Janzen followed a fire three years previously and he describes fire ecologically as a generalist herbivore [64]. The two shrubs he studied in detail were a *Vaccinium* and a *Hypericum*, both of which have species occurring on Sumatran mountains. The fire killed the above ground parts of the shurbs but suckers had shooted from the base of the plants. On average, the suckers had grown less than 50 cm in the three years. The soil surface exposed by the fire did not, as one would expect in lowland areas, become covered with fast growing pioneer species. Instead, much of the bare soil remained unvegetated. In other places liverworts and mosses had started to grow. Very few seedlings of the surrounding plants were found.

Three years after the fire, dead stems of plants were still standing and even those that had fallen to the ground showed no signs of decay. This extremely slow rate of decomposition is caused partly by the low temperatures but also by the absence of (or extreme lack of) most of the lowland decomposers such as ants, termites, and earthworms. This in turn may be due to the extremely very moist condition of the soil, branches, and logs which never warm up to any great extent [64].

Regeneration of Costan Rican oak forest, which is similar to that found in Sumatra from 1500—2000 m, was also found to be extremely slow [43]. Repeated cutting would deplete the seed stocks irrevocably and it was concluded that montane forests are "truly the tropics' most fragile ecosystems." Disturbance of oak/laurel forest in Peninsular Malaysia leads to a vegetation dominated by tree ferns and the scrambling fern *Gleichenia* [168].

The Sumatran pine *Pinus merkusii* is an indigenous tree occasionally found at about 1000—1600 m in lower montane forest in northern and western Sumatra. Trunks of large specimens can reach a metre in diameter, considerably larger than most of the trees of the same species seen in plantations, such as around Lake Toba, the first of which were planted in 1927 [8]. Young pines in primary forest are generally found growing as pioneers on, for example, landslides. Large areas (possibly 150,000 ha) of unplanted pine forests occur in parts of central Aceh and these are sometimes thought to be natural. In fact, they have been caused by man. Felling and repeated burning of lower montane forest has increased the area of suitable habitat for the pioneer pines. Once over 3 m tall the trees are quite resistant to fires [153], unlike most of the broad-leaf trees with which they had once shared the land. These pine forests are maintained by the cattle owners who burn the undergrowth to encourage the growth of tender young grass for the cattle to graze.

Eighteen species of birds were recorded in the pine forest of the Gayo and Alas lands of South-east Aceh by Chasen and Hoogerwerf, compared with eight on cleared, grass and fern-covered mountain slopes where pines had not yet become established [32]. The two sets of species were completely different. The primary forests between 300 and 1200 m shared only 3.5% of its bird species with the species in pine forests and none with the species of grassy slopes. It is thus clear that disturbance of montane forest causes a great reduction in bird species and most of the species that are seen are not primary forest birds.

11.12 CAVES

The study of the effects of disturbance on caves in an open book. At one extreme, it is clear that opening up a cave by mining the limestone and allowing the sunlight in will utterly destroy the specialized cave communities. There is no such thing as regeneration of cave life. Instead, a succession of plants from the limestone flora (section 8.4.3) will colonize the rocks where light newly penetrates.

The resilience of the cave fauna to disturbance is unknown. The extraction of insectivorous-bat guano should not be complete, to avoid endangering the cave floor community. This sort of exploitation would obviously be better undertaken after an ecological survey and assessment of the possible impacts of different collection techniques. Similarly, the harvesting of swiftlet nests for food should be conducted so as to cause as little disturbance as possible to the birds. A nest harvesting plan has been worked out for Niah Cave in Sarawak where some 4,000,000 swiftlets nest [94].

It is interesting that Ngalau Indah near Payakumbuh, the only Sumatran cave where tourists are catered for, still seems to have sizeable populations of bats and swiftlets despite the almost daily disturbance. It is not known, however, if some less resilient species have abandoned the cave.

Bats are sensitive to disturbance and when caves are visited during daylight hours, strong lights and loud noises should be avoided in the darker chambers. Catching bats requires skill and practice and should not be attempted except with good reason. Scientific collecting of bats should be conducted in moderation and other studies should cause as little disturbance as possible. The consequences of bats abandoning caves are described in section 10.6.

Limestone mining can cause a variety of disturbance, even if it is not immediately adjacent to a cave. For example, explosions used to break rock free can cause shock waves that break stalactites and stalagmites or cause thin cave roofs to cave-in [120, 122]. Even so, there are still quite a number of bat species roosting in the Quarry Cave at Lho'Nga but, again, it is not known what species were present before quarrying began.

REFERENCES

1. Abdulhadi, R., Kartawinata, K. and Sukardjo, S. (1981). Effects of mechanized logging in the lowland dipterocarp forest at Lempake, East Kalimantan. *Malay. Forester* 44:407—418.
2. Achmad, A.G. (1979). Menyadarkan masyarakat untuk keberhasilan dalam lingkungan hidup ditinjau dari sudut agama. In *Lokakarya Membudayakan Kesadaran Lingkungan Hidup di Masyarakat*, pp. 168—178. Pusat Kajian Lingkungan Hidup, Universitas Sumatera Utara, Medan. (20.2.26)
3. Adisoemarto, S. and Sastrapradja, S. (1977). *Sumber Protein Hewani*. Lembaga Biologi Nasional, Bogor. (9.2.2)
4. Aksornkoae, S. (1981). Distribution, growth and survival of seedlings of mangrove forest in Thailand. *BIOTROP Spec. Publ.* 13: 23—27. (10.4.18)
5. Alfred, E.R. (1966). The freshwater fishes of Singapore. *Zool. Verh. Leiden* 78: 1—68. (12.5.28)
6. Allaby, M. (1983). The greening of the Cornish Alps. *New Scient.* 98: 138—141. (10.1.2)
7. Allen, B. (1954/5). Some common ferns of the open country. *Malay Nat. J.* 8: 95—110, 133—151. (12.1.90)
8. Alphen de Veer, E.J. van (1953). Plantations of *Pinus merkusii* as a means of reafforestation in Indonesia. *Tectona* 43: 119—130. (10.1.3)
9. Alrasjid, H. and Effendi, R. (1979). *Pengaruh eksploitasi dengan traktor terhadap kerusakan tegakan sisa di kelompok hutan hujan tropis Pulau Pagai Selatan, Sumatera Barat*. Laporan No. 293, Lembaga Penelitian Hutan, Bogor. (9.1.13)
10. Anderson, J.A.R. (1965). Limestone habitat in Sarawak. In *Proc. Symp. Ecol. Res. Humid Trop. Veg.*, pp. 49—57. UNESCO, Paris. (12.10.69)
11. Anon. (1980). *Penyelamatan Siberut: Rencana Induk Konservasi*. World Wildlife Fund, Bogor. (10.2.1)

12. Anon. (1980). *World Conservation Strategy: Living Resource Conservation for Sustainable Development*. International Union for the Conservation of Nature and Natural Resources, Gland. (20.3.11)

13. _____: (1981). Conclusions and recommendations from the BIOTROP symposium on forest regeneration in Southeast Asia. *BIOTROP Spec. Publ.* 13: 224-226. (10.4.18)

14. Antonius, A. (1977). Coral mortality in reefs a problem for science and management. *Proc. Third Intnl. Coral Reef Symp.* 2: 617-623. Referred to in Parrish (1980).

15. Aprilani Soegiarto and Polunin, N.V.C. (1980). *The Marine Environment of Indonesia*. IUCN, Gland. (2.5.3)

16. Arumugan, P.T. and Furtado, J.I. (1981). Eutrophication of a Malaysian reservoir: effects of agroindustrial effluents. *Trop. Ecol.* 22: 271-275. (25.1.18)

17. Ashton, P.S. (1980). The biological and ecological basis for the utilization of dipterocarps. *BioIndonesia* 7: 43-53. (9.1.25)

18. Aveling, R.J. and Mitchell, A. (1982). Is rehabilitating orang utans worthwhile? *Oryx* 16: 263-271. (12.8.65)

19. Baren, F.A. van (1975). The soil as an ecological factor in the development of tropical forest areas. In *The Use of Ecological Guidelines for Development in Tropical Forest Areas of South East Asia*, pp. 88—98. IUCN, Gland. (20.1.14)

20. Bazzaz, F.A. and Pickett, S.T.A. (1980). Physiological ecology of tropical succession: a review. *Ann. Rev. Ecol. Syst.* 11: 287-310. (12.10.92)

21. Beers, W.F.J. van (1962). *Acid Sulphate Soils*. Veenan and Zonen, Amsterdam. (10.3.3)

22. Biotrop (1976). *Proceedings of Biotrop Workshop on Alang-alang, Bogor, 27-29 July 1976*. BIOTROP, Bogor.

23. Bormann, F.H. and Likens, G.E. (1981). *Pattern and Process in a Forested Ecosystem*. Springer-Verlag, New York. (12.10.94)

24. BPPP/Soepraptohardjo, M., Soekardi, M., Kurnia, H.D. and Suharjo, S. (1979). *Sumber daya lahan/tanah dan potensinya di Pulau Sumatera*. Konsultasi Penelitian Pertanian Menunjang Pembangunan Sumatera 28 Nopember 1979. Lembaga Penelitian Tanah, Bogor. (23.4.14)

25. Brunig, E.F. (1973). Species richness and stand diversity in

relation to site and succession of forests in Sarawak and Brunei (Borneo). *Amazoniana* 4: 293 - 320. Referred to in Whitmore (1975).

26. Bunt, J.S. (1980). Degradation of mangroves. In *Marine and Coastal Processes in the Pacific: Ecological Aspects of Coastal Zone Management.* UNESCO, Jakarta. (2.4.33)

27. Burbridge, P.R. (1982). Problems and issues of coastal zone management. In *Man, Land and Sea* (ed. C. Soysa, L.S. Chia and W.L. Collier) pp. 309-320. Agricultural Development Council, Bangkok. (2.4.26)

28. Burgess, P.F. (1971). The effect of logging on hill dipterocarp forests. *Malay. Nat. J.* 24: 231-237. (9.1.29)

29. Chapman, E.C. (1975). Shifting agriculture in tropical forest areas of south-east Asia. In *The Use of Ecological Guidelines for Development in Tropical Forest Areas of South-east Asia,* pp. 120-135. IUCN, Gland. (20.1.14)

30. Chambers, R.E. and Manan, M.E. (1978). *Agroclimatology of the Musi-Banyuasin Coastal Zone, South Sumatra.* Research Report 005, PSPSL, Bogor. (1.1.3)

31. Chapman, E.C. (1975). Shifting agriculture in tropical forest areas of south-east Asia. In *The Use of Ecological Guidelines for Development in Tropical Forest Areas of South-East Asia,* pp. 120-135. IUCN, Gland. (20.1.14)

32. Chasen, F.N. and Hoogerwerf, A. (1941). The birds of the Netherlands Indian Mt. Leuser Expedition 1937 to North Sumatra. *Treubia* 18 (suppl.): 1-125. (12.7.12)

33. Cole, B. (1981). Colonizing abilities, island size and the number of species on archipelagos. *Amer. Nat.* 117: 629-638. (12.11.4)

34. Corner, E.J.H. (1952). *Wayside Trees of Malaya.* 2 vols. 2nd ed. Government Printer, Singapore. (12.1.15)

35. Cowling, E.B. and Linthurst, R.A. (1981). The acid precipitation phenomenon and its ecological consequences. *BioScience* 31: 649-654. (25.7.11)

36. Cremer, M.C. and Duncan, B.L. (1979). *Brackish Water Aquaculture Development in Northern Sumatra, Indonesia.* Auburn University, Auburn. (2.2.14)

37. Crowther, J. (1982). The thermal characteristics of some West

Malaysian rivers. *Malay Nat. J.* 35: 99-109. (3.2.18)

38. Dickinson, R.E. (1981). Effects of tropical deforestation on climate. In *Blowing in the Wind: Deforestation and Long-range Implications*, pp. 411-441. College of William and Mary, Williamsburg. (10.4.16)

39. Dinas Kehutanan Propinsi Dati I Riau (1979). Hutan mangrove di Propinsi Riau. In *Prosiding Seminar Ekosistem Hutan Mangrove* (ed. S. Soemodihardjo, A. Nontji, A. Djamali) pp. 176-185. Lembaga Oseanologi Nasional, Jakarta. (12.9.2)

40. Djajasasmita, M. and Sastraatmadja, D.D. (1981). *Penelitian Peningkatan Pendayagunaan Sumber Daya Hayati*. Lembaga Biologi Nasional, Bogor. (9.2.6)

41. Edmondson, W.T. (1970). Phosphorus, nitrogen and algae in Lake Washington after diversion of sewage. *Science* 169: 690-691 (3.1.10)

42. Ehrlich, P.R. and Ehrlich, A.H. (1981). *Extinction: The Causes and Consequences of the Disappearance of Species*. Victor Gollancz, London. (9.2.13)

43. Ewel, J. (1980). Tropical sucession: manifold routes to maturity. *Biotropica (Tropical Succession Suppl.)* pp. 2-7. (12.1.89)

44. Ewel, J., Berish, C., Brown, B., Price, N., and Reach, J. (1981). Slash and burn impacts on a Costa Rican wet forest site. *Ecology* 62: 816-829. (10.4.13)

45. FAO/Wind, J., Soepomo, D. and Isnan, W. (1979). *Way Kambas Game Reserve Management Plan 1980/81 - 1984/85*. Field Report No. 5, INS/78/061, FAO, Bogor. (10.2.9)

46. Frey-Wyssling, A. (1931). Over de struikwildernis van habinsaran. *Trop. Natuur* 20: 194-198. (12.1.103)

47. Frankel, O.H. and Soulé, M.E. (1981) *Conservation and Evolution*. Cambridge University Press, Cambridge. (12.12.7)

48. Geertz, C. (1963). *Agricultural Involution: The Processes of Ecological Change in Indonesia*. University of California Press, Berkeley. (23.7.10)

49. Geollegue, R.T. (1979). Notes on sylvigenesis in the tropical lowland primary rainforest and loggedover areas in Semangus, South Sumatra. Unpubl. report, BIOTROP, Bogor. (9.1.31)

501

50. Geollegue, R.T. and Huc, R. (1981). Early stages of forest regeneration in South Sumatra. BIOTROP Spec. Publ. 13: 153—161. (10.4.18)

51. Gorman, M. (1979). Island Ecology. Chapman and Hall, London. (23.2.14)

52. Haines, T.A. (1981). Acidic precipitation and its consequences for aquatic ecosystems: A review. Trans. Amer. Fish. Soc. 110: 669-707. (25.1.17)

53. Hamzah, Z. (1978). Some observations on the effects of mechanical logging on regeneration, soil and hydrological conditions in East Kalimantan. BIOTROP Spec. Publ. 3: 73—78. (9.1.32)

54. Hanson, A.J. and Koesoebiono (1977). Settling coastal swamplands in Sumatra: a case study for integrated resource management. PSPSL Research Report 004, Institut Pertanian Bogor. (10.4.8)

55. Harcombe, P.A. (1980). Soil nutrient loss as a factor in early tropical secondary succession. Biotropica 12 (Tropical Succession Suppl.): 8-15. (12.10.97)

56. Hardin, G. (1968). Tragedy of the Commons. Science 162: 1243-1248. (10.4.15)

57. Harrison, J.L. (1968). The effect of forest clearance on small mammals. In Conservation in Tropical Southeast Asia. IUCN, Morges. (12.8.71)

58. Hartono, W., Soeroso, S. and Bambang, S. (1979). Pengelolaan hutan payau Cilacap. In Prosiding Seminar Ekosistem Hutan Mangrove (ed. Subagjo, S., Nontji, A. and Asikin, D.J.), pp. 72-80. Lembaga Oseanologi Nasional, Jakarta. (12.9.2)

59. Hehuwat, F. (1982). Krakatau: Punah dan lahirnya sebuah Gunung Api. Suara Alam No. 15: 29-31 and 34. (23.3.9)

60. Huc, R. (1981). Preliminary studies on pioneer trees in the dipterocarp forest of Sumatra. Unpubl. report, Biotrop, Bogor. (12.10.104)

61. Huc, R. and Rosalina, U. (1981). Aspects of secondary forest succession in logged-over lowland forest areas in East Kalimantan. Unpubl. Biotrop report. (12.10.96)

62. Jacobs, M. (1982). The study of minor forest products. Flora

502

Malesiana Bull. 35: 3768-3782. (9.2.12)

63. Janos, D.P. (1980). Mycorrhizae influence tropical succession. Biotropica 12 (Tropical Succession Supplement): 56-64. (12.1.62)

64. Janzen, D.H. (1973). Rate of regeneration after a tropical high-elevation fire. Biotropica 5: 117-122. (12.10.42)

65. _____: (1976). Why bamboos take so long to flower. Ann. Rev. Ecol. Syst. 7: 347-391. (12.1.134)

66. Jochems, S.C.J. (1926). De Westenenk-paadjes van Brastagi. Trop. Natuur 15: 65-71. (10.4.21)

67. _____: (1928). De begroeiing der tabakslanden in Deli en hare betehenis voor de tabakscultur. Med. Deli-Proefstation No. 59. (11.4.22)

68. Johns, A.D. (1981). The effects of selective logging on the social structure of resident primates. Malays. appl. Biol. 10: 221-226. (12.8.76)

69. _____: (1983). The Effects of Selective Logging on a Malaysian Rain-forest Community. Ph.D. thesis, University of Cambridge, Cambridge.

70. Johnson, D.S. (1961). Freshwater life in Malaya-its conservation. Malay. Nat. J. CN: 232-236. (12.13.24)

71. _____. (1961). An instance of sudden large-scale mortality of fish in a natural habitat in S. Malaya. Malay. Nat. J. 15: 160—162. (3.2.34)

72. _____: (1973). Equatorial forest and the inland aquatic fauna of Sundania. In Nature Conservation in the Pacific (ed. A.B. Costin ʻand R.H. Groves), pp. 111-116. IUCN, Gland. (3.2.26)

73. Johnson, D.S., Soong, M.H.H. and Wee, B.T. (1969). Freshwater streams and swamps in the tree country of southern and eastern Malaya with special reference to aquarium fish. In Natural Resources of Malaysia and Singapore (ed. B. Stone), University of Malaya, Kuala Lumpur. (3.2.33)

74. Jordan, C.F. and Farnworth, E.F. (1982). Natural vs. Plantation forests: a case study of land reclamation strategies for the humid tropics. Env. Manage. 6: 485—492. (10.3.13)

75. Kartawinata, K. (1978). Biological changes after logging in lowland

503

dipterocarp forest. *BIOTROP Spec. Publ.* 3: 27-34. (9.1.32)

76. _____: (1980). The environmental consequences of tree removal from the forest in Indonesia. In *Where Have All the Flowers Gone? Deforestation in the Third World,* pp. 191-214. College of William and Mary, Williamsburg. (10.4.17)

77. Khoo, S.G. (1974). Scale insects and mealy bugs: their biology and control. *Malay. Nat. J.* 27: 124-130 (11.1.13)

78. Koesoebiono and Chairul, M. (1980). *Prospects for Fisheries Development in the Musi Banyuasin Coastal Zone of Southeast Sumatra.* PSPSL Research Report 006, Institut Pertanian Bogor. (2.2.3)

79. Koesoebiono, Collier, W.L. and Burbridge, P.R. (1982). Indonesia: Resources' use and management in the coastal zone. In *Man, Land and Sea* (ed. C. Soysa, L.S. Chia and W.L. Collier) pp. 115-133. Agricultural Development Council, Bangkok. (2.4.35)

80. Koopman, M.J.F. and Verhoef, L. (1938). *Eusideroxylon zwageri* T. and B. Het ijzerhout van Borneo en Sumatra. *Tectona* 31: 381-399. (9.1.22)

81. Kostermans, A.J.G.H. (1958). Secondary growth on areas of former peat swamp forest. In *Proc. Symp. Humid Tropics Veg., Tjiawi, 1958,* pp. 155-169. UNESCO, Jakarta. (12.10.90)

82. Kushwaha, S.P.S., Ramakrishnan, P.S. and Tripathi, R.S. (1981). Population dynamics of *Eupatorium odoratum* in successional environments following slash and burn agriculture. *J. appl. Ecol.* 18: 529-535. (12.1.91)

83. LAPI-ITB (1980). *Environmental impact analysis of the Koba tin mining operation on Bangka Island, Indonesia.* Lembaga Afiliasi Penelitian dan Industri, Institut Teknologi Bandung, Bandung. (20.2.3)

84. Law, A.T. and Mohsin, Moh. A.K. (1980). Environmental studies of Kelang River. I. Chemical, physical and microbiological parameters. *Malay. Nat. J.* 33: 175-187. (3.2.24)

85. Likens, G.E., Bormann, F.H., Pierce, R.S., Eaton, J.S., and Johnson, N.M. (1977). *Biogeochemistry of a Forested Ecosystem.* Springer-Verlag, New York. (12.10.93)

86. Lugo, A.E. and Snedaker, S.C. (1974). The ecology of mangroves. *Ann. Rev. Syst. Ecol.* 5: 39-64. (12.9.9)

87. Lugo, A.E. Cintron, G. and Geonaga, C. (1978). Mangrove ecosystems under stress. In *Stress Effects on Natural Ecosystems* (ed. G.W. Barrett and R. Rosenberg), pp. 1—32. (12.9.19)

88. McCoy, E.D. (1982). The application of island-biogeographic theory to forest tracts: Problems in the determination of turnover rates. *Biol, Conserv.* 22: 217-227. (12.13.27)

89. MacKinnon, J.R. (1974). The behaviour and ecology of wild orang-utans *(Pongo pygmaeus). Anim. Behav.* 22: 3-74. (12.8.53)

90. Marsh, C.W. and Wilson, W.L. (1981). *A Survey of Primates in Peninsular Malaysian Forests.* Universiti Kebangsaan Malaysia, Bangi. (12.8.9)

91. Marsh, C.W., Johns, A.D. and Ayres, J.M. (in press). Effects of disturbance on rain forest primates. In *Primate Conservation in Tropical Rain Forest* (ed. S.J. Gartlan, C.W. Marsh and R.A. Mittermeier). (12.8.77)

92. Martosubroto, P. (1979). Sumbangan hutan mangrove terhadap perikanan. In *Prosiding Seminar Ekosistem Hutan* (ed. S. Soemodihardjo, A. Nontji, and A. Djamali), pp. 109-113. Lembaga Oseanologi Nasional, Jakarta. (12.9.2)

93. Mathias, J.A. (1977). The effect of oil on seedlings of the pioneer *Avicennia intermedia* in Malaysia. *Mar. Res. Indonesia* 18:17. (25.5.33)

94. Medway, Lord (1957). Birds' nest collecting. *Sarawak Mus. J.* 8: 252-260. (9.2.14)

95. _____: (1971). The importance of Taman Negara in the conservation of mammals. *Malay. Nat. J.* 24: 212-214.

96. Meijer, W. (1970). Regeneration of tropical lowland forest in Sabah, Malaysia, forty years after logging. *Malay. Forester* 33: 204-229. (9.1.30)

97. Mendoza, V.B. (1978). Some ecological considerations in the rehabilitation of Philippine grassland areas. *Philippine Lumberman* 24: 8-11. (10.3.12)

98. Mitchell, B.A. (1963). Forestry and tanah beris. *Malay. Forester* 26: 160-170. (9.1.19)

99. Mohsin, Moh. A.K. and Law, A.T. (1980). Environmental studies of Kelang River. II. Effects on fish. *Malay. Nat. J.* 33: 189-199. (3.2.25)

100. Myers, N.M. (1979). *The Sinking Ark: A New Look at the Problem of Disappearing Species.* Pergamon, New York. (12.12.8)

101. _____: (1980). Deforestation in the tropics: Who gains who loses? In *Where Have All the Flowers Gone? Deforestation in the Third World,* pp. 25-44. College of William and Mary, Williamsburg. (10.4.17)

102. NG, F.S.P. (1983). Ecological principles of tropical lowland rain forest conservation. In *The Tropical Rain Forest* (ed. A.C. Chadwick, S.L. Sutton and T.C. Whitmore), pp. 359-376. Blackwell, Oxford.

103. Nordin, C.F. and Meade, R.H. (1982). Deforestation and increased flooding of the upper Amazon. (Followed by reply by A.H. Gentry and J. Lopez-Parodi). *Science* 215: 426-427. (10.4.19)

104. Odum, W.E. (1976). *Ecological Guidelines for Tropical Coastal Development.* IUCN Publ. N.S. No. 42, IUCN, Gland. (2.4.29)

105. Oldfield, M.L. (1981). Tropical deforestation and genetic resources conservation. In *Blowing in the Wind: Deforestation and Long-range Implications,* pp. 277-345. College of William and Mary, Williamsburg. (10.4.16)

106. Parrish, J.D. (1980). Effects of exploitation upon reef and lagoon communities. In *Marine and Coastal Processes in the Pacific: Ecological Aspects of Coastal Zone Management.* UNESCO, Jakarta. (2.4.33)

107. Partomihardjo, T. (1982). Sepuluh hari di Anak Krakatau. *Suara Alam* No. 15: 32-33. (23.3.11)

108. Porter, J.W., Porter, K.G. and Batac-Catalan, Z. (1977. Quantitative sampling of Indo-Pacific demersal reef plankton. *Proc. Third Intnl. Coral Reef Symp.* 1: 105-112. Referred to in Parrish 1980.

109. Praseno, D.P. and Sukarno (1977). *Mar. Res. Indonesia* 17: 59-68.

110. Prowse, G.A. (1968). Pollution in Malayan waters. *Malay. Nat. J.*

506

21: 149-158. (25.1.16)

111. Rao, P.S. Jacob, C.M. and Ramasastri, B.V. (1969). Nutritive value of bamboo seeds. *J. Nutr. Diet.* 6: 192. (12.1.119)

112. Richards, K. (1982). Introduction. In *The Krakatoa Centenary Expedition* (ed. J.R. Flenley and K. Richards), pp. 1-8. University of Hull, Hull). (12.1.92)

113. Ricklefs, R.E. (1979). *Ecology.* Chiron, London. (23.2.1)

114. Rijksen, H.D. (1978). *A Field Study on Sumatran Orang Utans* (Pongo pygmaeus abellii *Lesson 1827*): *Ecology, Behaviour and Conservation.* Veenman and Zonen, Wageningen. (12.8.88)

115. Riswan, S. (1981). Natural regeneration in lowland tropical forest in East Kalimantan, Indonesia (with reference to kerangas forest). *BIOTROP Spec. Publ.* 13: 145—152. (10.4.18)

116. Robertson, J.M.Y. and Soetrisno, B.R. (1981). Penebangan hutan, lerengan, erosi, bendungan dan kematian di Lembah Alas. Unpubl. (10.4.14)

117. _____: (1982). Logging on slopes kills. *Oryx* 16: 229-230. (8.1.2)

118. Rosen, B.R. (1983). The recovery of the corals of the Krakatoa region. Paper given at the symposium 'Krakatoa: 100 Years On', British Museum (Natural History), 21 September 1983.

119. Saenger, P., Hegerl, E.J. and Davie, J.D.S. (ed.) (1981). *First Report on the Global Status of Mangrove Ecosystems.* Commision on Ecology, IUCN, Gland. (12.9.23)

120. Sani, S. (1976). Notes on dustfall in and around Batu Caves, Selangor. *Malay. Nat. J.* 29: 168-175. (25.7.10)

121. Saravanamuthu, J. and Lim, R.P. (1982). A preliminary limnological survey of a eutrophic pond. Taman Jaya Pond, Petaling Jaya. *Malay. Nat. J.* 35: 83-97. (3.1.14)

122. Sardar, Z. (1980). Quarrying blasts Malaysia's underground past. *New Scient.* 88: 352. (5.1.3)

123. Sastrapradja, S. (ed.). (1977). *Sumber Daya Hayati Indonesia.* Lembaga Biologi Nasional, Bogor. (9.2.3)

124. _____: (ed.). (1978). *Tanaman Obat.* Lembaga Biologi Nasional, Bogor. (9.2.5)

125. _____: (ed.). (1978). *Tanaman Industri*. Lembaga Biologi Nasional, Bogor. (9.2.4)
126. Sastrapradja, S. and Rifai, M.A. (1975). Exploration and conservation of the undeveloped genetic resources in Indonesian forests. *BioIndonesia* 1: 13—83.
127. Sastrapradja, S., Soenartono, A., Kartawinata, K. and Tarumingkeng, R.C. (1980). The conservation of forest animal and plant genetic resources. *BioIndonesia* 7: 1—42 (12.13.10)
128. Schaeffer, F.A. (1970). *Pollution and the Death of Man: The Christian View of Ecology*. Tyndale House, Wheaton. (23.2.5)
129. Schindler, D.W. (1974). Eutrophication and recovery in experimental lakes: implications for lake management. *Science* 184: 897—899. (3.1.12)
130. Seow, R.C.W. (1976). *The Effect of a Mixed Organic Effluent on the Distribution of Pelagic Macrofauna at Sungai Puloh with Special Reference to Water Quality*. B.Sc. thesis, University of Malaya, Kuala Lumpur (2.5.14)
131. Sharma, Y.M.L. (1980). Bamboos in the Asia-Pacific region. In *Bamboo Research in Asia* (ed. G. Lessard and A. Chouinard), pp. 99—120. International Development Research Centre, Ottawa. (12.1.94)
132. Siagian, Y.T. and Harahap, R.M.S. (1981). *Preliminary Result of Species Trial on Tin Mine Tailing Land in Dabo Singkep*. Balai Penelitian Hutan, Report No. 384, Bogor. (10.1.4)
133. Sinnappa, S. and Chang, E.T. (1972). Identification of rotenone in fish poisoned by derris root resin. *Malay. Agric. J.* 48: 20—24. (6.1.4.)
134. Soderstrom, T.R. and Calderon, C.E. (1979). A commentary on the bamboos (Poaceae: Bambusoideae). *Biotropica* 11: 161—172. (12.1.99)
135. Soepraptohardjo, M. and Barus, A. (1974). *PRA-Survey untuk penelitian tanah kolong (tin-tailing soil)*. Lembaga Penelitian Tanah, Bogor. (10.4.11)
136. Soerianegara, I. (1970). Soil investigation in Mount Hondje Forest Reserve, West Java. *Rimba Indonesia* 15: 1—16. (23.4.5)

137. Steenis C.G.G.J. van (1938). Exploraties in de Gajo-Landen. Algemeene resultaten der Löser-expeditie 1937. *Tijdschr. Kon. Ned. Aardr. Genootschap* 55: 728—801. (12.10.39)

138. _____ : Personal communication.

139. Stocker, G.C. (1981). Regeneration of a North Queensland rain forest following felling and burning. *Biotropica* 13: 86—92. (12.10.100)

140. Sumadhiharga, O.K. (1977). A preliminary study on the ecology of the coral reef of Pombo Island. *Mar. Res. Indonesia* 17: 29—49. (2.5.18)

141. Symington, C.F. (1933). The study of secondary growth or rain forest sites in Malaya. *Malay. Forester* 2: 107—117. (12.10.118)

142. Tanimoto, T. (1981). Vegetation of the Alang-alang grassland and its succession in the Benakat District of South Sumatra, Indonesia. *Bull. For. For. Prod. Res. Inst.* 314: 11—19. (10.3.14)

143. Tinal, U.K. and Palinewan, J.C. (1978). Mechanical logging damage after selective cutting in the lowland dipterocarp forest at Beloro, East Kalimantan. *BIOTROP Spec. Publ.* 3: 91—96. (9.1.32)

144. Tweedie, M.W.F. and Harrison, J.L. (1970). *Malayan Animal Life.* Longman, Kuala Lumpur. (12.13.2)

145. Uhl, C., Clark, K., Clark, H. and Murphy, P. (1981). Early plant succession after cutting and burning in the upper Rio Negro region of the Amazon basin. *J. Ecol.* 69: 631-649. (12.10.98)

146. Uhl, C., Clark, H., Clark, K. and Maquirno, P. (1982). Successional patterns associated with slash-and-burn agriculture in the Upper Rio Negro region of the Amazon basin. *Biotropica* 14: 249—254. (12.10.99)

147. Umbgrove, J.H.F. (1947). Coral reefs of the East Indies. *Bull. geol. Soc. Am.* 58: 729—778. (23.3.13)

148. Vaas, K.F., Sachlan, M. and Wiraatmadja, G. (1953). On the Ecology and fisheries of some inland waters along the rivers Ogan and Komering in South-East Sumatra. *Contr. Inl. Fish. Res. St.* 3: 1—23. (3.2.23)

149. Voort, M. van der (1939). De merkwaardige Padang Bolak. *Trop. Natuur* 28: 201—209.

150. Walsh, G.E. (1974). Mangroves: a review. In *Ecology of Halophytes* (ed. R.J. Reimold and W.H. Queen), pp. 51-174. Academic, New York. (12.1.98).

151. Wells, D.R. (1971). Survival of the Malaysian bird fauna. *Malay. Nat. J.* 24: 248—256. (12.7.39).

152. Whitmore, T.C. (1967). Studies in *Macaranga,* an easy genus of Malayan wayside trees. *Malay. Nat. J.* 20: 89—99. (12.1.118).

153. _____. (1975). *Tropical Rain Forests of the Far East.* Clarendon, Oxford. (12.10.8).

154. _____. (1982). On pattern and process in forests. In *The Plant Community as a Working Mechanism* (ed. E.I. Newman), pp. 45—59. Blackwell, Oxford. (12.10.70).

155. Whittacker, R. and Flenley, J.R. (1982). The flora of Krakatau. In *The Krakatoa Centenary Expedition* (ed. J.R. Flenley and K. Richards), pp. 9—53. University of Hull, Hull. (12.1.92).

156. Whitten, A.J. (1982). Diet and feeding behaviour of Kloss gibbons on Siberut Island, Indonesia. *Folia primatol.* 37: 177—208. (12.8.6).

157. _____: (1982). *The Gibbons of Siberut.* J.M. Dent, London. (12.13.3).

158. _____. Personal observation.

159. Widjaja, E.A. (1980). Indonesia. In *Bamboo Research in Asia* (ed. G. Lessard and A. Chouinard), pp. 63—68. International Development Research Centre, Ottawa. (12.1.94).

160. Wigley, T.M.L. and Jones, P.D. (1981). Detecting CO_2-induced climatic change. *Nature* 292: 205—208. (1.2.3).

161. Wigley, T.M.L., Jones, P.D. and Kelly, P.M. (1980). Scenario for a warm, high CO_2 world. *Nature* 283: 17—21. (1.2.2).

162. Wilson, C.C. and Wilson, W.L. (1975). The influence of selective logging on primates and some other animals in East Kalimantan. *Folia primatol.* 23: 245—274. (12.8.72).

163. Wilson, W.L. and Johns, A.D. (1982). Diversity and abundance of selected animal species in undisturbed forest, selectively

logged forest and plantations in East Kalimantan, Indonesia. *Biol. Conserv.* 24: 205—218. (12.8.79).

164. Wisaksono, W. (N.D.). *Pencemaran minyak oleh kapal super tanker 'Showa Maru'*. Lemigas, Jakarta. (25.5.7).

165. Wright, S.J. (1981). Intra-archipelago vertebrate distributions: the slope of the species-area relation. *Am. Nat.* 118: 726—748. (12.13.25).

166. Wright, J.S. and Biehl, C.C. (1982). Island biogeographic distributions: testing for random, regular, and aggregated patterns of species occurrence. *Am. Nat.* 119: 345—357. (12.13.26).

167. Wyatt-Smith, J. (1955). Changes in composition in early natural plant succession. *Malay. Forester* 18: 44—49. (11.4.24).

168. _____: (1963). Manual of Malayan silviculture for inland forests (2 vols.). *Malay. For. Rec.* No. 23. (9.1.17).

169. Yong, H.S. (1978). Mammals of virgin and logged forests in Peninsular Malaysia. *BIOTROP Spec. Publ.* 3: 153—158. (9.1.32).

170. Zimmerman, P.R., Greenberg, J.P., Wandiga, S.O. and Crutzen, P.J., (1982). Termites: a potentially large source of atmospheric methane, carbon dioxide and molecular hydrogen. *Science* 218: 563—565. (1.2.1)

171. Baker, J.M. (1982). Mangrove swamps and the oil industry. *Oil Petrochem. Poll.* 1:5—22.

CHAPTER 12
AGRICULTURAL ECOSYSTEMS

12.1 INTRODUCTION

This chapter is concerned largely with pests and the important role ecology can play in their control. It does not attempt an exhaustive review of all the different agricultural ecosystems found on Sumatra, or an analysis of ecological constrains to tropical agriculture (for which see Janzen [34]). Nor does this chapter discuss the fascinating home garden ecosystems which cover 20% of the available arable land in some areas of Indonesia, particularly Central Java [47, 51, 62]. Elsewhere, where Javanese have been settled for twenty years or so, home gardens can also be found but they do not yet cover a significant area of the arable land of Sumatra.

Most of the ecological studies conducted in agricultural ecosystems will aim to solve problems but, as with urban ecology, a great deal can be learned from studies in simple ecosystems on apparently insignificant creatures. An excellent example of such a creature is the ant lion, which builds its characteristic funnel-shaped holes under buildings resting on stilts in rural areas. It is a common and interesting organisms from which many ecological principles can be learnt [35, 42, 63], and teachers and students should be encouraged to investigate common animals and plants even though they may not be of major economic importance. When opportunities arise to conduct ecological studies of pests, the person equipped with a personal knowledge of how at least one organism adapts to and exploits its environment will find it much easier to understand the ecology of another organism, however different.

12.2 ECOLOGICAL PROBLEMS IN AGRICULTURE

Over 400 species of insects, mites and ticks have developed resistance to one or more pesticides. The resistance spreads through populations because individuals which avoid the effects of the pesticide by behavioural, biochemical or physiological means, survive pesticide applications and their genes are therefore passed on to the next generation. Repeated applications thus lead to the entire population becoming resistant. There is a greater tendency for species with a high intrinsic rate of population increase (the r-strategists - section 7.1.1) to develop resistance, but the main determining factor is frequent application of high concentrations of pesticides. Once a species has developed resistance to a pesticide - and resistance has developed to all chemical groups - the state is more or less irreversible. It is therefore conceivable that certain insect strains could develop resistance to all known insecticide groups [12].

Resistance does not pose an immediate threat to world food production but it can cause extremely serious problems on a local level. In one of the latest reviews of pesticide resistance, Asia is identified as the area most likely to suffer crises of pest resistance, if the use of pesticides grows to the high levels currently used in countries such as Japan [12]. This resistance is most likely to occur in the diamond-backed moth *Plutella xylostella* on cabbage and other brassica crops, and in major rice pests, particularly the green rice leafhopper *Nephotettix cinciteps*, brown plant hopper *Nilaparvata lugens* [16] and Asiatic stem borer *Chilo suppressalis* [12].

It is beyond the scope of this book to deal comprehensively with pest ecology. For particular pest species readers should consult the agriculture literature, but for succinct accounts of general pest ecology and control, Conway [11], van Emden [17] and Wratten and Watt [66] are recommended.

It is generally true that species which become agricultural pests are present at relatively low densities in natural ecosystems. They tend to have specialized and ephemeral niches and their populations never reach pest proportions. With a change in land use, however, a once restricted niche

Soil loss after logging or forest clearance can be quite dramatic.

Plantations do not 'mimic forest' at all stages of their growth.

The ecology of rice fields is not fully understood; near Porsea, North Tapanuli.

House swifts nest on many types of buildings, Medan.

can become available continuously over wide areas. Natural predators on the pest may not be able to hold the growing population in check if suitable habitat or other vital resources are not available. An insect predator may be dependent, for example, on certain plants on which its larvae have to feed.

The best known and, most frequently used form of pest control in Sumatra is the use of toxic chemicals or pesticides. During the 1960s and early 1970s the potential dangers and undesirable effects of pesticides were brought to the notice of the general public. Much was overstated or biased and it was impractically suggested that controlling pests by biological means was the only reasonable path to follow. Biological control is a term used for pest control by predators, parasites, pathogens, hormones which change insect behaviour, sterilization of male pests, or by using resistant crop varieties. Most biological controls are highly selective and pest problems therefore should not be intensified and new problems should not be created.

Other advantages are that a controlling organism can seek out its prey in a way chemicals cannot, can increase in number and spread, and resistance is either slow or impossible to develop. Disadvantages are that control is slow, pests are almost never wholly exterminated, patterns of control are often unpredictable, techniques are expensive to develop properly and to apply, and expert supervision is required. In addition, problems can occur when pathogens are imported along with a controlling predator or parasite or when the agent is less specific than was hoped. These disadvantages were not emphasized during the early chemical scares and society was presented with an unrealistic choice between pesticides on the one side and apparently benign biological control on the other. Fortunately, agriculturalists did not make such simplistic choices and instead have developed the concept of integrated control.

Integrated control was defined over two decades ago as "applied pest control which combines and integrates biological and chemical control. Chemical control is used as necessary and in a manner which is least disruptive to biological control" [59]. Chemical control is the only feasible solution to certain pest problems but other methods, such as making the agricultural environment as favourable as possible to predators and as unfavourable as possible to pests, and the various forms of biological control described above can serve to keep most pest populations within bounds for most of the time. However, when pest populations reach a certain, predeterminated level which could precipitate serious economic loss, selective chemicals need to be used. The brown planthopper (or rather the two virus diseases it transmits) is considered to be Indonesia's major insect pest and the greatest challenge for plant protectionists. An integrated approach to its control has begun using resistant rice varieties, cultural controls (synchronized planting, etc.), natural enemies, pest surveillance and different modes and patterns of insecticide use [9, 25, 45, 46]. These types of approaches will also reduce the likelihood of resistance crises.

It is notable that accounts of pests and the problems they cause often close with the remark that if the ecology of the particular pest organism and the ecology of the crop (or of wild species related to the crop [50]) were better understood, better control measures could be developed. In theory, if the pest is thoroughly understood then accurate predictions can be made on the probable effects of different forms of control. The gathering of data which could genuinely achieve such ends for just a single pest species could take many years [17, 30], during which serious increases in population levels could occur. Thorough documentation and analysis of the different ecological responses of pest populations to different forms of control should lead to selection of control mechanisms, the effects of which can be predicted with increasing accuracy [3]. In this way, ecological knowledge of the organisms concerned will lead to environmentally sound and effective pest control.

Much of the above concerns the control of insect pests, but rats and birds are ubiquitous pests which also cause considerable damage. Soerjani considers that rats are the most important group of pests hindering agricultural production in South-east Asia [53]. Rats are known to occur in almost all agricultural crops and to damage many stored products [7, 14, 19, 44, 52]. They present the additional hazard of being a health risk to humans; the organisms causing scrub typhus, meningo-encephalitis, plague and leptospirosis are all known to be carried by parasites of agricultural or urban rats [41, 60]. Luckily, even though the disease and the organisms may be found close to where humans work or live, the disease does not necessarily break out. The environmental conditions required for the disease to be transmitted are not known, but it is clear that detailed ecological knowledge of rats should be collected now, rather than once an epidemic has begun.

The number of bird species inhabiting rice fields, plantations and other areas of permanent agriculture is quite considerable. For example, 72 species were observed in these areas in Aceh by Chasen and Hoogerwerf [8]. This represents about half the number of bird species observed in primary and mature secondary lowland forest, but in fact only two species or 1% of the combined species list were seen in both areas. Seventy-five species were seen in clearings, pastures and young secondary growth, but when compared with those seen in agricultural areas only 23 (19%) were common to both lists. This serves to demonstrate how few of the forest birds can survive in disturbed areas. The birds of agricultural areas tend to have large geographic distributions and many can become pests.

Among the more serious pests are:

White-rumped munia	- *Lonchura striata*
White-headed munia	- *Lonchura maja*
Baya weaver	- *Ploceus philippensis*
Red avadavat	- *Amandava amandava*
Pin-tailed parrotfinch	- *Erythrura prasina*

all of which are members of the sparrow family (Ploceidae).

Bird control poses considerable problems since birds generally range far wider and into more habitats than insect pests. Poisoning does not seem to be a viable control method because effective poisons are usually toxic against other animals, including man. Alternative methods, such as destroying communal roosts of weaver birds, can have temporary, local effects. The quelea, an African relative of the weaver birds, has been controlled in the past using the rather spectacular method of setting a small gelignite charge next to a 200 litre drum of petrol or diesel underneath a tree used for nesting. Up to five million birds could be destroyed in a single explosion, but despite decades of control by destruction the quelea is still a major pest. In his account of bird pests, Adisoemarto repeatedly states that more ecological information is required for effective control programs [1].

A locally problematic group of pests on a wide range of fruit trees is bats. Village-level control programs are rarely sufficiently selective and confront the problem that whereas some bats cause economic losses to fruit harvests [1], others are essential to the fruit harvest in their role as pollinators [33] (section 10.6). The flying fox *Pteropus vampyrus* is easy to shoot because of its size, but although it does eat fruit, it also pollinates durian [22]. An ecological cost-benefit analysis is necessary to determine what level of control, if any, is required.

12.3 RICE FIELDS

12.3.1 Introduction

No comprehensive ecological study of rice fields ever seems to have been conducted in the Sunda Region. In addition, no attempt seems to have been made to bring together the results of the hundreds of disparate studies in different disciplines in order to show how the system as a whole works. An integrated study of rice fields has, however, been conducted in the seasonal part of northeast Thailand [28] and could serve as a model for a similar study in Sumatra.

The changing water levels, the variety of plant species which seek to share the sawah, the fixing of atmospheric nitrogen by blue-green algae, the air-breathing fish that survive the harvesting and ploughing by various strategies [54, 55, 56], the life histories of the insect pests, the insect-eating frogs and toads [5, 6, 67], the ever-present threats to yields by birds and rats (see below), the effect of predatory birds, and the interactions and interdependencies between all these make rice fields extremely interesting. An ecological review would be feasible and extremely useful, but it is beyond the scope of this book.

12.3.2 The ecology of rice-field rats

Rats cause the loss of at least 12 million tons of rice each year worldwide, and it is possible that rats and birds combined may have more serious impacts on rice crops than all other types of pests [13]. In the Sunda Region rats are probably responsible for a 5—6% overall loss of rice yield, but losses in individual fields can be much more than this.

Rice fields in Sumatra are inhabited to different extents by at least eight species of rodent. The most serious pest among them is the rice field rat *Rattus argentiventer* which damages rice crops throughout South-east Asia, although the wood rat *R. tiomanicus* and Whitehead's rat *Maxomys whiteheadi* are locally the dominant species [1, 39, 52]. Two species of mice, the ryukyu mouse *Mus caroli* and the fawn-coloured mouse *Mus cervicolor*, have been introduced into the northern half of Sumatra where they are confined to rice fields [43]. It is possible that the large bandicoot *Bandicota indica*, which can measure 50 cms (head to tail) and weigh half a kilogram, has increased its range through introduction by man, because its flesh is commonly eaten. Two further species, the little rat *Rattus exulans* and the house rat *Rattus rattus diardi* are generally found in peripheral areas but will enter rice fields to feed. These species are usually only found close to man's buildings or farms.

Analysis of stomach contents of these rodents has shown that they all eat insects and snails, and that the amount of plant material they ingest depends on the type of habitat and varies between species [39]. Rats eat rice at all stages of its development and although the theft of ripening rice grains is a direct loss from the harvest, the shredding of growing stems to eat the tender growing shoot does more absolute damage. A single, ripe seed head may represent a rat's daily food requirement, but the same rat may eat 100 growing shoots in a day before it is satisfied.

The reproduction of these rats clearly follows an r-strategy. The gestation period of the rice field rat, for example, is 21 days, a litter generally numbers seven, and about eight litters are produced per female per year. Females could theoretically have more litters but reproduction tends to occur only when an abundant food supply is available, that is, towards the end of the rice-growing cycle. Male rats are capable of breeding at two months of age and female rats at 1½ months [36]. The mean life span of the rats is only about 4—7 months [26], but even by seven months a single female could have raised about 20 young.

The very high intrinsic rate of growth among rats is the major reason why attempts to exterminate them using traps or poisons are effective only locally or for short periods. If any rats are left, their litter size is likely to be larger than normal (up to 11) because competition for food is less and so the population will increase quickly. If, as rarely happens, all the rats in an area are killed, the unoccupied rice fields represent a wonderful opportunity for rats from other areas to colonize. If one thinks of an animal's niche as its 'profession', then when rats have been exterminated from a field, hundreds of 'jobs' become vacant. It should be remembered that rats do not produce large numbers of offspring for the good of the species or because that many are needed to fill all vacant 'jobs'. They are produced because rats are locked into their r-strategy and each female has to produce as many fast-growing, healthy young as she can, so that her hereditary line is not smothered by others. Many of the rats die young (as is shown by the life span figures above) but this is a consequence of the r-strategy. If the mother rat produced just a few offspring to whom she devoted her time in fetching food and defending them, the available jobs would have been filled by the larger number of other rats from other mothers.

Thus, control of rats in the long-term has to be centred on land management. We can take an ecological lesson from the dipterocarps, the family of relatively common trees in lowland forest (section 7.2.3). These trees avoid undue loss of their seeds by all fruiting together with long intervals between fruiting periods. This prevents any particular seed predators maintaining a population of a size that would pose a serious problem to the dipterocarps. Rats can live for only a few days on a diet of just rice stems [13] and this may be the only food at certain times, particularly if insect populations are also controlled in some way. Thus, if rice is planted and therefore harvested at the same time over large areas, and if scrub and other neighbouring habitats, where rats could find alternative foods when rice grain was not available, were removed or utilized, rat populations could be kept within bounds. These are thus two of the main methods of rat control encouraged by the Department of Agriculture, the others being the digging out of rat holes and poisoning [52].

The niches of the different rodent species in rice fields clearly overlap - they share a major food item and many of them make their burrows in the banks between the fields. Each species must compete in some way with the others and this must be important in determining the relative abundances of the species and therefore the amount and type of rice damage. Very little is known about the actual ecology of these animals and detailed studies of their movements [27, 61], food [39] and inter-specific relations could be of considerable economic benefit.

12.4. PLANTATIONS

12.4.1. Introduction

It is sometimes said, without a great deal of evidence, that plantations (monocultures of trees) mimic the functions of natural forest ecosystems. This analogy contains a certain amount of truth but should not be taken too literally. Mature plantations certainly protect the soil, water and a few of the indigenous biota more than, say, rice fields, but they cannot approach the efficiency of mature natural forest. There is tremendous soil loss, for example when forest or old plantations are laid bare prior to planting. Unfortunately the myth that plantations are as good as forest in many aspects is perpetuated and is sometimes used as an excuse for extensive forest clearance.

The two main plantation crops in Sumatra, rubber *Hevea brasiliensis* and oil palm *Elaeis guineensis*, have rather different ecological characteristics.

1) Rubber is intolerant of swampy conditions and, in the past, poorly-drained areas within a plantation were left as forest or secondary growth from which various forms of wildlife could make sorties into the plantations. Conversely, under natural conditions, oil palm is a tree of riverine forests, but those now in cultivation are tolerant of drier conditions. Almost no residual areas of forest are left in an oil palm plantation because virtually all the land can be utilized.

2) The branches of rubber form a stable and long lasting substrate on which nests of squirrels and birds can be built. Large bird-nest ferns *Asplenium nidus* and other epiphytic ferns are common on old trees. The leaves of oil palm, however, continually change their position - from the vertical young spear to the dangling dead leaf. Only a few animals, such as weaver birds, are able to make nests on these leaves. The dead leaf bases remaining on the tree are colonized by various epiphytic ferns which, because of the generally very moist air, are extremely abundant (Figure 12.1). A useful guide to epiphytic ferns has been written by Piggott [48].

3) Harvesting the rubber latex usually disturbs nothing above head height, whereas the cutting of the infructescence away from the crown of the oil palm disturbs the only place where animals could set up a permanent base. The only animals that seem to be tolerant of this more or less weekly disturbance are squirrels [68] and rats, and the control of the latter is discussed below.

4) Rubber has one major fruiting season each year. The fruit are hard and have limited appeal to wildlife. Oil palm produces oil-rich, brightly coloured fruit which are obviously far more attractive as a food source [15].

520

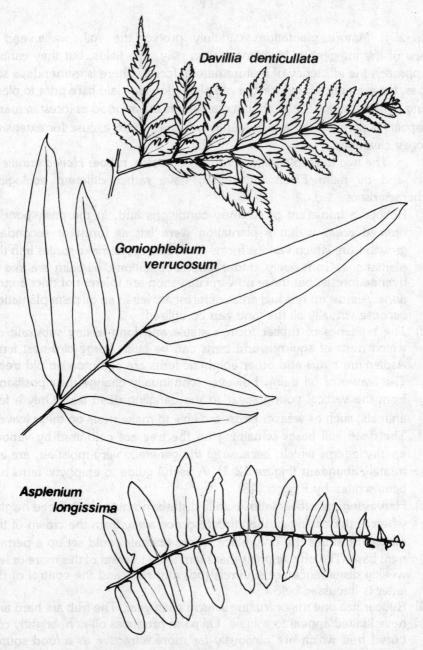

Davillia denticullata

Goniophlebium
verrucosum

Asplenium
longissima

Figure 12.1. Three species of epiphytic fern commonly found in plantations.

The plant species covering the ground between the oil palm or rubber trees also influence the general abundance of animals [2]. For example, ferns and long grass between short oil palms provide an excellent environment for rats. Poorly-kept smallholder estates where rubber trees are densely planted and many other plants are allowed to grow have a more diverse biota but do not make economic sense.

12.4.2 Large pests

The major reason that plantations sustain a very low diversity of wildlife is the highly restricted floral diversity (section 7.1.2). A walk of 500 m through a well-maintained estate is unlikely to reveal more than 15 plant species (including ferns). This leads to an impoverished fauna of pollinators, leaf-eaters, parasites on other insects, etc. The impression gained in certain areas is that monkeys and other animals live in plantations. These have almost always come from an area of neighbouring forest or an isolated forest block [4], or are immature animals seeking unoccupied forest to avoid personal extinction. Visits by large animals to plantations, particularly young oil palm plantations, can cause severe economic loss. The main offenders are elephants and forest pigs. In these cases, which are reported almost every month and are a continual threat in certain places, it is pointless to blame the animals. The situation is almost always caused by careless land-use planning. If a favoured elephant food (such as sugar cane or young oil palm) is planted next to elephant habitat or across a traditional elephant pathway [23, 24, 29], of course the elephants will eat the food and there are few effective ways of dissuading elephants from their avowed intention.

The answer to the elephant (bear/pig/tiger) problem lies in the formation of buffer zones around forested natural ecosystems. These zones aim to:

1) contain plant species which are low-grade food items for potential agricultural pests so that the animals are not attracted to the area and this in turn will make their predators search elsewhere for food; and
2) provide local inhabitants with products they had traditionally taken from the forest (timber, rotan, medicine, firewood), or provide a cash income to enable the people to buy these products.

Buffer zones and the merits of different potential crops are discussed by MacKinnon [20].

12.4.3 Rats and their predators

As described in section 11.9.6 and 12.2, one of the consequences
of forested land being converted to other forms of land use is that some
species of birds have increased in number or have entered and colonized
new areas. One such is the barn owl *Tyto alba*, one of the world's most
widely distributed birds, which has spread from Java into southern
Sumatra [31] and has thence spread quickly into northern Sumatra. A
similar population explosion of this bird has also been witnessed in Peninsular Malaysia and it has been turned to good use in certain oil palm plantations.

In other parts of its range, the barn owl eats a range of small animals
but in Peninsular Malaysia it appears to feed almost entirely on rats particularly the wood rat. The diet of owls is easy to determine because they
regurgitate pellets containing the fur and bones of their prey about 8 to 12
hours after a meal. These pellets may be collected from beneath the roosts.
Of 2839 pellets examined, 90% contained remains of rats and the rest
were composed of insects, shrews and frogs [37]. More than half (55%) of
the rats were rice field rats, a third (32%) were wood rats and the remainder (13%) were little rats. Whether this reflects the actual relative
abundance of the rats is unknown. The rats have different activity patterns
and some may successfully avoid owls in this way. For example, house rats
and rice field rats have finished most of their activity by midnight, but wood
rats maintain moderate activity all night long. House rats start becoming
active before dusk, rice field rats at about dusk and wood rats after dusk
[2].

The owls reproduce rapidly; the clutch size averages 6.6 eggs per
nest and two or three broods can be raised per year. At this level of production an adult pair accounts for about 1300 rats per year in the feeding
of themselves and their young [38].

Rats in oil palm plantations live at considerable densities - an estimate for just one species, the wood rat, is 250/ha [64] and so barn owls
could be an extremely important control agent. Nest sites for barn owls in
oil palm plantations are limited and so nest boxes (0.5 × 0.5 × 1 m) on
the top of telegraph poles have been provided. There is a limit to how close
adult pairs can live to other pairs and 20 ha has been suggested as the
minimum area required. This area could contain 5000 rats so that the owls

could be responsible for the removal of about a quarter of the standing crop of rats per year. (It should be remembered this is less than a quarter of all rats that live in an area during any period because rats are continually reproducing and dying). In a study of the effects of owl predation on small mammal populations in England, it was found that 20—30% of the standing crop of mice was taken every two months [58].

Snakes also appear to be significant predators on rats in oil palm plantations and for this reason plantation managers make little effort to control them. The stomach contents of five snakes species from an oil palm plantation in Peninsular Malaysia were examined and the results are shown in Table 12.1. The vertebrates other than rats found in the stomach

Table 12.1 Results of stomach analyses of five snake species in a plantation (After Lim [40]).

	Total examined	% containing only rat remains	% containing rat and other remains	% containing only other remains	empty
Common cobra *Naja naja*	62	32	11	14	43
Indo-Chinese rat snake *Ptyas korros*	42	24	2	4	70
Brown snake *Xenalaphis hexagonotus*	35	40	3	3	54
White-bellied rat snake *Zaocys fuscus*	20	20	—	5	75
Keeled rat snake *Zaocys carinatus*	5	20	—	—	80

were frogs, lizards and birds. Five live individuals of each of the five species were kept in cages and for one year five wood rats were placed in each cage at the start of each week. On the seventh day any remaining rats were removed prior to a new set being provided.

To calculate how many rats a snake of each species would devour in nature, where the whole range of prey would be available, the figures have to be adjusted. Thus the experimental feeding rate is multiplied by the

524

percentage of dead snakes examined which had rats in their stomachs (Table 12.2). So, if an average rat-eating snake eats 1.5 rats per week, it would consume 78 rats per year. The density at which these snakes live is not known but 2/ha would not be unreasonable. With a standing crop of 250 rats/ha, it can be seen that the snakes do take a considerable proportion [40].

Table 12.2 Estimates of the number of rats eaten by snakes. (After Lim [40]).

	Average number of rats eaten per snake per week while caged	Average number of rats eaten per snake per week if free
Common cobra	3.5	1.1
Indo-Chinese rat snake	5.1	1.2
Brown snake	4.6	1.9
White-bellied rat snake	5.6	1.1
Keeled rat snake	6.5	1.3

12.4.4 Pest control by predators

Caution is needed before one concludes that a predator, particularly a vertebrate predator, is actually controlling the number of its prey [18]. Tigers and other large forest predators certainly do not control the numbers of deer, pigs, mouse deer or other common prey species. Detailed studies of large predators have dispelled the myths that these are master killers from which a prey animal, once detected, has no chance of escape. Instead, these large predators tend to take the young, the old and the sick. The remainder can successfully outrun, outwit or intimidate the predators such that a relatively small percentage of hunting attempts end with a kill.

Many insect predators, however, certainly do control the numbers of their prey species. This was clearly demonstrated in the 1960s and early 1970s when DDT and other long-lasting poisons were used to combat pests such as bagworms (a common pest on perennial crops) in oil palm plantations. In many cases the pests escaped the spraying because of behavioural characteristics. In the case of bagworms, the worst of the pests, for example, the larvae, pupae and adult females are protected by the bags they construct around themselves (Figure 12.2). In contrast, the 20 or so species of wasps that laid eggs in the young bagworms, and the larvae of which slowly ate the bagworm from the inside, had no such protection and were killed by the chemicals. The result was an increase in the bagworm population. A cessation of spraying resulted in an increase in predators and a decrease in bagworms [10, 11]. Thus the wasps were truly controlling the bagworm population.

The major distinction between tigers and parasitic wasps in the way they predate is that only the wasp will certainly kill its prey every time it attacks. In addition, the tiger's prey can try to evade the tiger by running away but the wasp's prey cannot. Even with this efficiency, the wasps are

Figure 12.2 **Bagworms (Psychidae) are serious potential pests on a range of perennial crops. The caterpillars make bags of silk which they cover with twigs etc. (species differ in the material used). When moving, only the head, thorax and legs are exposed but if disturbed all these are pulled inside the bag which is then closed. The caterpillars pupate inside the bag and the male emerges as a typical grey/brown moth. The female emerges as a degenerate, wingless adult, capable of little more than building her own bag and producing eggs. The male copulates with her through the open end of her bag and the newly hatched caterpillars leave the parental bag and start making their own bags, often using material from the parental bag. The adult female dies inside her bag.**

highly unlikely to reduce bagworms to extinction because the more they predate upon the bagworms the harder it is for the wasps to find the remaining individuals or populations.[1] If prey are hard to find, the population of wasps will decrease, which therefore reduces the pressure on the bagworms, thereby allowing them to increase, and so on. Thus, after the wasps have reduced the bagworm population to a certain level, it is the numbers of prey that control the numbers of predators. The relationship between owls and rats is similar to that between tigers and deer.

In section 12.4.3 it was stated that pairs of barn owls are unlikely to live in areas of less than 20 ha, even if the prey density increases. Territory size for animals is partly related to abundance of available resources but there are strict upper and lower limits. Detailed studies of owls and their prey in temperate and arctic regions, where the size of rodent populations exhibit considerable natural fluctuations, have shown that the resident population of owls remains more or less the same, but the number of young birds raised varies considerably depending on the availability of prey [49, 51]. This is a reflection of the innate desire to maximize reproductive success. Insufficient studies have been conducted in plantations and other relatively constant ecosystems in the Sunda Region to know whether similar natural fluctuations occur in their rodent populations [21]. Fluctuations are created in plantations, however, by the rat poisoning programs which usually severely reduce the populations and the number of eggs laid by the owls, and the number of young raised would be expected to reflect these population changes.

Owls are not going to defeat the rat problem but they may be seen as a means by which the period between rat poisoning programs can be lengthened because owls can slow the rats' population growth. Poisoning is expensive but the only cost involved with the owls is the provision of nest boxes. The economics appear very attractive [37, 38].

---

1. For the reader to prove this to himself: put 90 sweets (or something of similar size) of one colour in a bag or pillow case. Add 10 sweets of the same type but a different colour. The 10 sweets represent trees infected with bagworms, the 90 sweets represent those trees with no bagworms. Mix up the sweet and, without looking ,take out a sweet. This is the action of a predator. If the sweet is the common colour, put it back. If it is the rare colour, take it out and replace it with a sweet of the common colour. Count how many 'hunts' are needed to replace all the infested trees.

REFERENCES

1. Adisoemarto, S. (1980). *Binatang Hama.* Lembaga Biologi Nasional, Balai Pustaka. (11.1.4)
2. Ahmad, I. (1980). *Tinjauan umum tentang beberapa aspek ekologi dan lakuan tikus liar dari ladang kelapa sawit.* Tesis Sarjana Muda, Universiti Kebangsaan Malaysia, Kuala Lumpur. (12.8.80)
3. Altieri, M.A., Martin, P.B. and Lewis, W.J. (1983). A quest for ecologically based pest management systems. *Env. Manag.* 7: 91–100. (11.1.16)
4. Bennett, E.L. and Caldecott, J.O. (1981). Unexpected abundance: the trees and wildlife of the Lima Belas Estate Forest Reserve, near Slim River, Perak. *The Planter* 57: 516–519. (10.2.14)
5. Berry, P.Y. (1965). The diet of some Singapore Anura (Amphibia). *Proc. Zool. Soc. Lond.* 144: 163–174.
6. Berry, P.Y. and Bullock, J.A. (1962). The food of the common Malayan toad *Bufo melanostictus* Schneider. *Copeia* 1962: 736–741.
7. BIOTROP (1980). *Symposium on Small Mammals: Problems and Control.* BIOTROP Special Publication No. 12, BIOTROP, Bogor. (11.1.6)
8. Chasen, F.N. and Hoogerwerf, A. (1941). The birds of the Netherlands Indian Mt Leuser Expedition 1937 to Norh Sumatra. *Treubia* 18 (Suppl.): 1–125. (12.7.12)
9. Chiu, S.C. (1979). Biological control of the brown planthopper. In *Brown Plant Hopper: Threat to rice production in Asia,* pp. 335–355. International Rice Research Institute, Los Banos.
10. Colinvaux, P.A. (1973). *Introduction to Ecology.* Wiley, New York. (23.2.3)
11. Conway, G.R. (1972). Ecological aspects of pest control in Malaysia. In *The Careless Technology* (ed. M.T. Farvar and J.P. Milton), pp. 467–488, Natural History Press, New York.

12. ⎯⎯⎯⎯⎯⎯⎯⎯⎯. (1982). (ed.) *Pesticide Resistance and World Food Production*. Imperial College, University of London, London. (11.4.27)

13. COPR (1976). *Pest Control in Rice*. Centre for Overseas Pest Research, London. (11.1.2)

14. ⎯⎯⎯⎯⎯⎯⎯⎯⎯. (1978). *Pest Control in Tropical Root Crops*. Centre for Overseas Pest Research, London. (11.1.3)

15. Duckett, J.E. (1976). Plantations as a habitat for wild-life in Peninsular Malaysia with particular reference to the oil palm (*Elaeis guineensis*). *Malay. Nat. J.* 29: 176—182. (11.3.6)

16. Dyck, V.A. and Thomas, B. (1979). The brown planthopper problem. In *Brown Planthopper: Threat to rice production in Asia*, hal. 3—17. International Rice Research Institute, Los Banos.

17. Emden, H.F. van (1974). *Pest Control and Its Ecology*. Edward Arnold, London. (11.18)

18. Erlinge, S., Göransson, G., Hogstedt, G., Jansson, G. Liberg, O., Loman, J., Nilsson, I.N., Schantz, T. von. and Sylven, M. (1984). Can vertebrate predators regulate their prey? *Am. Nat.* 123: 125—133.

19. Estioko, B.R. (1980). Rat damage and control in Philippine sugar cropping. *BIOTROP Spec. Publ.* 12: 159—168. (11.1.6)

20. FAO/MacKinnon, J. (1981). *National Conservation Plan for Indonesia, Vol. VIII: National Park Development and General Topics*. FAO, Bogor. (10.2.15)

21. Flemming, T.H. (1975). The role of small mammals in tropical ecosystems. In *Small Mammals: Their Productivity and Population Dynamics* (ed. F. Golley, K. Petrusewicz and L. Ryszkowski), pp. 269—298. Cambridge University Press, Cambridge. (12.8.81).

22. Gould, E. (1977). Foraging behaviour of *Pteropus vampyrus* on the flowers of *Durio zibethinus*. *Malay. Nat. J.* 30: 53—57. (12.8.87)

23. Groeneveldt, W. (1936). Beschouwingen over wild en landbouw. *Ned.-Ind. Ver. Natuurbesch.* 1935: 143—151.

24. ⎯⎯⎯⎯⎯⎯⎯⎯⎯. (1938). Een overzicht van de vaste trekwegen in Zuid Sumatra alsmede enige gegevens over rhinocerossen. *Ned. Comm. Intern. Natuurbesch. Med.* 12: 73—109.

25. Harahap, Z. (1979). Breeding for resistance to brown planthopper and grassy stunt virus in Indonesia. In *Brown Planthopper: Threat to rice production in Asia*, pp. 201—208. International Rice Research Institute, Los Banos.

26. Harrison, J.L. (1956). Survival rates of Malayan rats. *Bull. Raffles Mus.* 27: 5—26.

27. _____. (1958). Range of movement of some Malayan rats. *J. Mammal.* 39: 290—206. (12.8.44)

28. Heckman, C.W. (1979). *Rice Field Ecology in Northeastern Thailand. The Effect of Wet and Dry Seasons on a Cultivated Aquatic Ecosystem.* Junk, The Hague.

29. Heurn, F.C. van (1937). Eerste registratie van de kudden olifanten die voorkommen op Sumatra's Oostkust, Westkust en Tapanoeli en van gegevens, die daarop betrekking hebben. *Ned. Comm. Intern. Natuurbesch. Med.* 11:66—78.

30. Hingkley, A.D. (1973). Ecology of the coconut rhinoceros beetle *Oryctes rhinoceros* (L.) (Coleoptera: Dynastidae). *Biotropica* 5: 111—116. (11.1.12)

31. Holmes, D.A. (1977). Faunistic notes and further additions to the Sumatran avifauna. *Bull. Brit. Orn. Club* 97: 68—71. (12.7.50)

32. Holttum, R.E. (1977). *Plant Life in Malaya*, 2nd Ed. Longman, Kuala Lumpur. (12.1.14)

33. Khobkhet, O. (1980). Research on bats in Thailand: A bird's eye view. *BIOTROP Spec. Publ.* 12: 109—120.

34. Janzen, D.H. (193). Tropical agroecosystems. *Science* 182: 1212—1219. (11.4.23)

35. Kiew, B.H. (1970). The ecology of *Myrmeleon celebensis* McLachlan (Neuroptera: Myrmeleontidae). *Malay. Nat. J.* 24: 11—15. (12.4.47)

36. Lam, T.M. (1983). Reproduction in the rice field rat *Rattus argentiventer. Malay. Nat. J.* 36: 249—282.

37. Lenton, G. (1980). Biological control of rats by owls in oil palm and other plantations. *BIOTROP Spec. Publ.* 12: 87—94. (11.1.6)

38. _____. (1983). Wise owls flourish among the oil palms. *New Scient.* 97: 436—437. (11.3.5)

39. Lim, B.L. (1974). Small mammals associated with rice fields. *MARDI Res. Bull.* 3: 25—33. (12.8.83)

40. _____. (1976). Snakes as natural predators of rats in an oil palm estate. *Malay, Nat. J.* 27: 114—117. (11.1.9)

41. Lim, B.L., Hadi, T.R., Sustriayu and Gandahusada (1980). A preliminary survey of rodents in two transmigration schemes in South Sumatra. *BIOTROP Spec. Publ.* 12: 67—78. (11.1.6)

42. Lucas, J.R. and Brockmann, H.J. (1981). Predatory interactions between ants and ant lions (Hymenoptera: Formicidae and Neuroptera: Myrmeleontidae). *J. Kans. Entomol. Soc.* 54: 228—232.

43. Marshall, J.T. (1977). Family Muridae. In *Mammals of Thailand* by Lekagul, B. and McNeely, J.A., pp. 397—494. Association for the Conservation of Wildlife, Bangkok. (12.8.21)

44. Myllymaki, A. (1979). Importance of small mammals as pest in agriculture and stored products. In *Ecology of Small Mammals* (ed. D.M. Stoddart), pp. 239—279. Chapman and Hall, London. (11.1.14)

45. Oka, I.N. (1979). Cultural control of the brown planthopper. In *Brown Planthopper: Threat to rice production in Asia.* pp. 357—369. International Rice Research Institute, Los Banos.

46. Oka, I.N. (1980). Feeding population of people versus population of insects: The example of Indonesia and the rice brown planthopper. *BioIndonesia* 7:121—134. (11.1.10)

47. Penny, D.H. and Ginting, M. (1980). House gardens - the last resort? Further economic arithmatic from Sriharjo. In *Indonesia: Dualism, Growth and Poverty* (ed. R.G. Garnaut and P.T. McCawley), pp. 487—499. Australian National University, Canberra. (15.2.5)

48. Piggott, A. (1979). *Common Epiphytic Ferns of Malaysia and Singapore.* Heinemann, Singapore. (12.1.105)

49. Pitelka, F.A., Tomich, P.Q. and Treichel, G.W. (1955). Ecological relations of jaegers and owls as lemming predators near Barrow, Alaska. *Ecol. Monogr.* 25: 85—117.

50. Salick, J. (1983). Natural history of crop-related wildspecies: Uses in pest habitat management. *Env. Manage.* 7: 85—90. (11.1.15)

51. Sastrapradja, S. (1979). *Tanaman Pekarangan.* Lembaga Biologi Nasional, Bogor. (11.4.7)

52. Soekarna, D., Partoatmodjo, S., Wirjosuhardjo, S. and Boeadi. (1980). Problems and management of small mammals in Indonesia with special reference to rats. *BIOTROP Spec. Publ.* 12: 35—54. (11.1.6)

53. Soerjani, M. (1980). Status and future needs of small mammal research and training in Southeast Asia. *BIOTROP Spec. Publ.* 12: 237—240. (11.1.6)

54. Soong, M.K. (1948). Fishes of the Malayan padi fields. I. Sepat Siam (Trichogaster pectoralis). *Malay. Nat. J.* 3: 87—89.

55. _____. (1949). Fishes of the Malayan padi fields. II. Aruan: Serpent-headed fishes. *Malay. Nat. J.* 4: 29—31.

56. _____. (1950). Fishes of the Malayan padi fields. III. Keli. Cat-fishes. *Malay. Nat. J.* 5: 88—91.

57. Southern, H.N. (1970). The natural control of a population of tawny owls (*Strix aluco*). *J. Zool.* 162: 197—285.

58. Southern, H.N. and Lowe, V.P.W. (1982). Predation by tawny owls (*Strix aluco*) on Bank voles (*Clethrionomys glareolus*) and Wood mice (*Apodemus sylvaticus*). *J. Zool.* 198: 83—102. (12.8.84)

59. Stern, V.M., Smith, R.F., Bosch, R. van den, and Hagen, K.S. (1959). The integrated control concept. *Hilgardia* 29: 81—101.

60. Sustriayu, N. (1980). Zoonotic diseases transmissible from Indonesian rodents. *BIOTROP Spec. Publ.* 12: 101—108. (11.1.6)

61. Taylor, K.D. (1978). Range of movement and activity of common rats (*Rattus norvegicus*) on agricultural land. *J. appl. Ecol.* 15: 663—677. (12.8.85)

62. Widagda, L.C. (1981). *An ecosystem analysis of West Javanese home gardens.* Working paper, East-West Environment and Policy Institute, Honolulu. (11.4.21)

63. Wilson, D.S. (1974). Prey capture and competition in the Ant Lion. *Biotropica* 6: 187—193. (12.4.48)

64. Wood, B.J. (1969). Population studies on the Malaysian wood rat (*Rattus tiomanicus*) in oil palm, demonstrating an effective new control method and assessing some older ones. *Planter* 45: 510—526.

65. _____. (1971). Investigations of rats in rice fields demonstrating an effective control method giving substantial yield increase. *PANS* 17: 180—193.

66. Wratten, S.D. and Watt, A.D. (1984). *Ecological Basis of Pest Control.* George Allen and Unwin, London.

67. Yap, S.P. (1976). The feeding biology of some padi field anurans. B.Sc. thesis, University Malaya, Kuala Lumpur. (13.6.22)

68. Duckett, J.E. (1982). The plantain squirrel in oil palm plantations. *Malay. Nat. J.* 36: 87—98.

CHAPTER 13

URBAN ECOLOGY

13.1 INTRODUCTION

Sumatran towns are not nearly as interesting ecologically as they could be because their vegetation is largely foreign and therefore suports few birds, squirrels and other animals. Many of the larger animals that are able to live in Sumatran towns are shot as soon as they are in the sights of an air rifle and the DDT used for lack of an alternative in mosquito control presumably takes a heavy toll. Towns in India are often home to large numbers of animals, including monkeys and squirrels, because the human inhabitants have a religious respect for these forms of life. India is used here as an example because the high human population density and the effects of development there cause more serious environmental problems than currently exist in Sumatra.

Urban ecology is an underexploited field of study. For example, some urban animals and plants can be used as indicators of pollution. Some trees are better at exploiting certain urban conditions than others, some urban rats carry transmitable diseases [26], but some trees support a wide range of other harmless plants and animals thereby making the environment more interesting. This type of knowledge should be sought by urban planners for they are charged with the responsibility of creating a healthy and fulfilling human environment.

A great deal of ecology can be taught in towns and cities. Studies of common toads or house geckos (sections 13.5 and 13.3.2) are unlikely to change any national policy, but they are useful for learning about

534

population structure and dynamics which will in turn make the investigators more aware of the way animal populations function. Urban lakes can be used for studying phytoplankton production [49]. Bird-watching is a recreation but records kept over months or years can provide information on seasonality, new invaders, appropriateness of certain city trees, control of birds at airports and adaptations to a man-made environment. Some studies may be economically useful - such as the prevention of algae growing on white-washed and painted walls (section 13.3.1).

As the proportion of Sumatra's population living in town increases, so urban ecologists will face great challenges to provide living space which is functional yet attractive, dynamic, and interesting [8].

13.2 VEGETATION

It may be felt that the vegetation of parts of Sumatran cities is really quite diverse. This is largely because we spend so much time in cities and thereby become familiar with the plants. If we spent an equivalent length of time in any of Sumatra's forested ecosystems it would soon become clear how poor city vegetation is in comparison.

How many tree species are there in Sumatran towns and where do they come from?[1] The ubiquitous acacia *Acacia auriculiformis* comes from Thursday Island in the Torres Strait. The tall mahogany *Swietenia macrophylla* comes from tropical America. The teak *Tectona grandis* comes from Burma and Thailand. The origins of the tamarind *Tamarindus indica* are uncertain but are possibly east Africa and western Asia. Of the common urban trees probably only the she-oak *Casuarina equisitifolia* is indigenous to Sumatra.

The two most common urban trees, acacia and she-oak, were chosen for good reasons. They have strong roots, grow quickly, give shade, require little attention, are evergreen and quite attractive, can grow in dry exposed habitats and both possess the capability of fixing atmospheric nitrogen in root nodules [47]. The last property means that the trees can grow on young soils and help to improve the soil for other trees.

---

1. Corner [16] and van Steenis [51] can be used to identify virtually all the trees planted in towns and villages.

But these advantages are not confined to the two species above. All the leguminous trees fix nitrogen and drought-resisting properties are only necessary in the most open places. If just some of the thousands of indigenous Sumatran trees, including those with fruit eaten by birds, were brought into the towns, the fauna might be rather more interesting (section 13.7). Try identifying roadside and garden trees - the total will probably surprise you - to acquaint yourself with plant characters and the classification of plants. Identifying trees in natural ecosystems will then be much easier. Most of the epiphytic ferns are also quite easily identifiable [44].

The number of species of insect herbivores associated with a particular plant species depends on various factors; such as the plant's geographical range, its taxonomic isolation, growth form, palatability, structural complexity, successional status and also on its relative abundance in the prehistoric past and the length of time it has been available for colonization [58]. The acacia used so much in recent re-greening programs originated on a small Australian island and has only recently been introduced to Sumatra, and so it would not be expected to have many herbivores. This is a point in its favour but native trees survive with perhaps hundreds of associated species of insects. It should be remembered that a herbivore does not necessarily devastate its host. In fact, acacia leaves[2] in Medan are fed upon by larvae of bagworm moths (Psychidae) (section 12.4.4), some of which build their bags from near-entire leaves and others (*Eumeta*) build small conical bags from circles of leaf epidermis removed from the lower leaf surface.

Quite a wide range of urban and rural plants have some form of compound leaves which 'sleep' at night. That is, at night they hang down and/or fold up so that the leaf surfaces are held close or even touching. Common examples are the sensitive plant *Mimosa pudica* and young leaves of cassava *Manihot uttilissima*. In 1880, Darwin suggested that this behaviour protected the plants from chilling but this view did not gain wide acceptance. In section 9.4.3 it was stated that leaves with long edges relative to their length (such as compound leaves) would lose heat faster than simple leaves, and the chilling hypothesis has recently been shown to be valid. By experimentally preventing leaves from 'sleeping' it was

---

2. Acacia 'leaves' are in fact modified petioles or leaf stems and are correctly called phyllodes.

found that the leaves became colder at night than those leaves which were allowed to sleep. The difference was only about 1°C but this could affect growth rates, and plants whose leaves sleep may have a competitive advantage over those plants with simple leaves [20].

One of the most common orchids on big city trees is the pigeon orchid *Dendrobium crumenatum*. It is not frequently seen with flowers but if one plant flowers then all the plants in an area will be flowering too. How is this coordination achieved? Similar gregarious flowering in bamboo was found to be genetic (section 11.9.7) but the gregarious flowering of dipterocarp trees was probably a response to some environmental cue, possibly water stress (section 7.4.1). The major trigger for pigeon orchids is a rapid fall in temperature, such as occurs during a rainstorm. Nine days after that temperature drop all the pigeon orchids will bear the white, sweet smelling flowers. This was demonstrated in Medan during July 1983 and on the nights the stimulus occurred, the temperature fell below 20°C (Figure 13.1). Cold night temperatures alone are not the primary stimulus,

Figure 13.1 Minimum night temperatures in Medan during part of 1983 and the start of flowering in the pigeon orchid.

however, and analyses of meteorological data have been published [6, 17]. The reasons the pigeon orchids flower simultaneously is presumably to increase the likelihood of cross-pollination by the pollinating insects.

Plots of land awaiting development, roadsides, the gardens of unoccupied houses and neglected corners of towns represent opportunities to study plant succession [22]. Which plants colonize open ground? Which are first? How long until the first plants are smothered? How quickly does humus form? Assuming the first plants are grasses and herbs, how long until the first woody plant appears? Measure samples of the above ground biomass at different times. Is the rate of increase constant? Does it show changes related to the seasons? What animals are associated with different stages of the succession?

13.3 LIFE ON WALLS

13.3.1 Algae

White-washed or emulsion-painted walls quickly discolour. Areas of green, black and orange appear in patches or streaks, some in shade, some in the open. The 'stains' are caused by green and blue-green algae and by diatoms (section 4.4.1). In Singapore the distribution of these microscopic plants on buildings has been investigated by Chua et al. [12] and by Lee and Wee [37] who also provide an identification key. The black stains are usually blue-green algae which have caught airborne dust particles in their mucilaginous sheaths. Some of the algae are able to fix atmospheric nitrogen and as more dust and soil particles become attached, so a favourable habitat is formed for higher plants to colonize. This obviously takes time, and regular maintenance prevents succession from proceeding.

Try to establish the ecological requirements for different species of algae. Note the type and age of the substrate, the compass direction it faces, the times it is in the shade, etc. Clear small circles from the middle of a patch of alga and 'transplant' another species. Follow the success of the two species. Reverse the experiment by transplanting some of the first algae into a cleared patch of the second alga. Do certain paints or colours remain free of algae for longer than others? Paint manufacturers would be interested in the results.

13.3.2 Geckos

There are few houses or other buildings in towns without a resident population of geckos. Their ecology is little known and the only studies in the Sunda Region appear to be those of Church [13], Church and Lim [14], and Chou [10, 11]. Geckos are unusual amongst the animals which live alongside man in that they are not, for the most part, regarded as dangerous or undesirable.

It is a frequent matter of debate how geckos manage to climb on vertical surfaces or even walk upside down on a ceiling. The feet do not have suckers but instead have small overlapping flaps of skin (Figure 13.2).

Figure 13.2 The foot of a gecko to show the hair-covered folds of skin.

These flaps are covered with minute, closely-set hairs which make contact with the slight irregularities of a surface and enable geckos to cling where other animals would fall.

Geckos are also known for their ability to shed their tails when caught - a response designed either to enable them to break free if caught by the tail, or to distract the 'predator' with a wriggling tail, or perhaps both. Tail shedding is also known in some snakes and lizards and involves muscular contractions which causes a fracture to occur across a vertebra, not between two vertebrae. The tails which regenerate are not usually as long or as symmetrical as the original; for a discussion of the adaptive strategies and energetic costs involved in tail loss see Vitt *et al.* [52]

There are three main species of geckos in houses over most of Sumatra—the common house gecko *Hemidactylus frenatus*, the flat-tailed gecko *H. platyurus* and the four-clawed gecko *Gehyra mutilata* which has no claw on any of its inner digits. The much larger (35 cm) tokay *Gekko gecko*, although quite common in Java, does not seem to be found in the northern half of Sumatra but would be expected to occur in the south as an introduction from West Java. The spotted gecko *Gekko monarchus* is intermediate in size (about 20 cm) but is not commonly seen. The tokay has a proper voice produced in a larynx but the common gecko call is produced by tongue-clicking. The tongue-clicking serves to space males to prevent overcrowding but has little or no effect on females [40].

Geckos generally feed on insects but the tokay feeds on smaller geckos and even mice and small birds. Geckos in Medan have also been observed licking the juice from mangos which have been part-eaten by bats.

The three commonest house gecko species are more or less the same size ± 11cm)—what forms of competition and niche separation allow them to coexist? Kill several of each species at intervals of several weeks over a period and analyze the stomach contents. Without necessarily identifying the animal food remains to species or even family, it is possible to detect consistent differences in composition of size of prey between the gecko species. Watch the geckos—does one species sit and wait for prey and another species search? Does one species become inactive and another active in the middle of the night? How do species space themselves around light bulbs? Is aggression shown within or between species? Are resting places (in cracks, behind pictures and mirrors, under stones, in atap roofing, in corners of ceilings or behind cup boards) different between species? For clues and guides see Church and Lim [14], Pianka and Huey [42] and Pianka *et al.* [43].

13.4 LICHENS-MONITORS OF POLLUTION

Lichens are not strictly a group of plants but rather the result of a mutually-beneficial relationship, or symbiosis, between a fungus and an alga. The dominant partner is the fungus and it derives its nutritional needs from the alga trapped within its strands. Despite their dual nature they behave like a single organism and for convenience are treated as such (see description of coral polyps in section 3.5.1).

Lichens of the Sunda Region are poorly known but without knowing their specific names they can be divided into various growth forms:

Leprose -   powdery collection of fungal hyphae (root strands) and algal cells with no organization;

Crustose -   crust-like with algae situated below a distinct layer of fungal material;

Squamulose -   crustose but with the margins raised above the substrate surface;

Foliose -   like a leaf with distinct upper and lower layers, often attached by hair-like 'roots' but easily peeled from the substrate;

Fruticose -   erect or beard-like attached to the substrate only at the base (Figure 13.3) [28].

Figure 13.3 Five forms of lichen. (After Hawksworth and Rose [28]).
a. leprose; b. crustose; c. squamulose; d. foliose; e. fructicose.

Lichens are probably the longest living organisms on earth. In the cold wastes of the Arctic, lichens have been found which are over 8,000 year old, and in a part of Antarctica where it is warm enough for growth only 300 hours per year, a lichen of about 10,000 years old has been found. For comparison, the oldest known trees are not quite 5,000 years old.

Even in the tropics, lichens grow slowly - 5 mm of radial growth per year would be a normal rate. Since many species occur on exposed surfaces they have to withstand considerable extremes in environmental conditions. When conditions are moist, photosynthesis and respiration can occur rapidly but when dried out in hot sun, such processes halt because unlike leaves lichens have no protective cuticle. Mineral nutrients are either received from the rain or from the substrate [28].

Lichens occur on tree bark, rock and other substrates in most natural ecosystems and different species or groups of species are confined to particular types of substrate. Tree bark, for example, varies in its acidity and so lichens of different tolerance will be found on different trees. In natural and urban ecosystems lichens are often the only organisms occupying a particular substrate. In towns, for example, lichens are often the sole inhabitants of certain types of wall, exposed tree bark, gravestones, building timber, etc.

The environmental interest in lichens stems from their sentitivity to pollutants and they can thus be used as indicators in programs of environmental monitoring. No organisms are more sensitive to sulphur dioxide than lichens.

Sulphur dioxide is a by-product of combustion of coal and some types of oil, and in its various forms (solutions of sulphate, sulphite and bisulphite ions, sulphurous acid, gaseous sulphur dioxide and sulphur trioxide) affects many plants but particularly lichens. The effect of sulphur dioxide is primarily through disrupting photosynthesis. This can cause a reduction in the reproduction and growth rates or in death. This can be recognized by chlorosis, a bleaching of the lichen, and a tendency for it to peel away from the substrate. The centres of lichens (the oldest parts) generally die first. Whitewash, cement containing lime and certain tree bark tend to neutralize the acidic effects on the lichens they bear, whereas substrates with acidic properties such as some other tree barks and sandstones, will quickly lose much of their lichen flora. Some lichens are more resistant than others to the damaging effects of sulphur dioxide, but the mechanism of this resistance is complex [28]. Thus, if a survey transect is established outwards from a source of sulphur dioxide pollution, the following effects are likely to be found:

- the quantity of sulphur in the lichen tissue will decrease;
- the size of a given species of lichen will increase (Figure 13.4);
- the species assemblage found on a particular type of substrate will change and probably become less diverse.

Lichens show similar accumulation of, and sensitivity to, other pollutants such as fluorides, radionuclides and heavy metals. Many species accumulate heavy metals without overt effects and thus metal content in lichens will generally show a gradual reduction with increasing distance from, for example, a metal smelter.

The study of lichens, let alone their use as pollution monitors, has barely begun in Sumatra or even elsewhere in South-east Asia. It is obviously preferable to know the identity of different lichen species before beginning environmentally-oriented studies. Even if scientific names have

13 14 15 17 20 23 26 30 km

Figure 13.4 Changes in size for a species of lichen at different distances from a source of pollution. (After O.L Gilbert in Hawksworth and Rose [28]).

not been determined, temporary names referring to colour, shape or location, or simple codes, can be given. It is important that a reference collection be made so that, at least within one group of researchers, names can be standardized. Whole specimens, not fragments, should be collected, dried gently, and placed in individual air-tight containers containing silica gel or some other descicant.[3] The containers and specimens should be handled carefully because lichens can be very brittle when dry.

Suggested preliminary studies are as follows:

1) Count the number of lichen species on a single type of substrate. Repeat in other areas or along a transect suspected of being a pollution gradient. Plot the number of species on a graph with distance from a possible pollution source along the horizontal axis. Suitable substrates for study include tombstones, trunks of a single tree species, walls of buildings, roof tiles, milestones. Care should be taken that the samples of substrates chosen are of more or less similar age and aspect to the sun. If it is possible to conduct a number of transects around a possible pollution source, a 'contour' map may be drawn of the number of lichen species.

2) Decide on one particular and relatively abundant species of lichen and measure its concentration of sulphur or metal along a transect from a possible polution source. Display results graphically as in 1.

3) Measure the size of one particular and relatively abundant species of lichen on one substrate of similar age along a transect as above [28]).

Sulphur dioxide levels in Sumatran towns are not particularly high (± 1 ppm was measured in Medan) but lichens on trees are clearly killed by some agent near busy and confined roads. The death of lichens can have unexpected effects as in shown by the following story of the peppered moth. Soot originating from uncontrolled gaseous factory effluent killed many lichens on tree trunks around Britain's industrial centres up to the middle of this century. The death of one particular light-coloured species resulted in interesting changes in the peppered moth *Biston betularia*. This is generally a pale-coloured moth with flecks of black on its wings which afford good camouflage when it rests on certain lichens. Black forms of this species, however, were found to be more common than the normal pale form in the industrial areas where pollution had killed the lichens.

---

3. Tea dried gently in a oven is an effective and extremely cheap descicant.

Experiments by Kettlewell demonstrated that the variation in the abundance of the two colour forms was caused by natural selection, one of the main mechanisms by which evolution occurs [31,32]. He placed equal numbers of light and dark forms onto tree trunks in two forests—one in a polluted area and the other in an unpolluted area. He observed the frequency with which predatory birds caught the moths and found that light forms in the polluted area and dark forms in the unpolluted area were more susceptible to being eaten (Figure 13.5). His results are shown in Table 13.1.

Thus, over a long period, pollution caused changes in the genetic composition of a moth species, and insectivorous birds acted as the agents for the change. Controls of factory emissions in Britain began to come into effect in the early 1950's and, as one might predict, the light form of the moth and the lichen are becoming common again [15].

If Sumatra's lichens have been barely studied, studies of their associated fauna have not even begun. The example above of the peppered moth comes from Europe but it serves to illustrate the perhaps

Figure 13.5 Both forms of peppered moth on unpolluted (left) and polluted (right) bark.

Common toad, Medan.

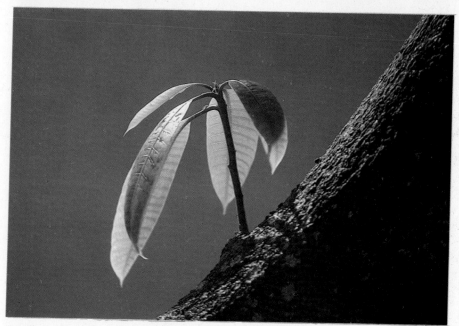

Do trees in towns produce leaves simultaneously?

Pigeon orchid.

Table 13.1 Number of light and dark forms of the peppered moth eaten by birds in unpolluted and polluted forests (From Kettlewell [32]).

	Total of moths eaten by birds	
	pale-coloured moths	dark-coloured moths
Unpolluted forest	26	164
polluted forest	43	15

Figure 13.6 The guppy *Poecilia reticulata;* **female above (about 4 cm), male below (about 2.5 cm). The males found in ditches are very variable but not as fancy as those in aquaria.**

unexpected dependence of one component of an ecosystem on another. Soot is not a serious pollutant in Sumatra but the death of lichens caused by other pollutants might well be expected to have more widespread effects than simply a change in the distribution of that lichen.

13.5 DITCHES

To an engineer, urban roadside drains are simply means of preventing floods are of removing household water to larger water courses. To an ecologist, a ditch is a simple, small river, the life in which can give indications of water quality.

Perhaps the most obvious animal in many ditches is the guppy *Poecilia reticulata* (Figure 13.6). This small fish is a native of South America but was introduced to help control mosquitoes (see section 4.4.4). They are in fact mainly algae eaters but their growth rate is greater if the diet includes animal material such as insect larvae [19]. Guppies do not lay eggs like most fish but give birth to small fry.

Guppies are most obvious in urban ditches when they mouthe at the surface, looking as though they are breathing air. Some fish can use atmospheric oxygen but the guppies, and many other fish which exhibit similar behaviour, are in fact taking in water from the air-water interface [35], where the oxygen concentration is greatest. This aquatic surface respiration is generally only used where oxygen levels are low (such as slow-moving ditch water with a high organic content) and when oxygen levels are raised they respire normally. Aquatic surface respiration does not allow guppies to stay alive for long periods in highly deoxygenated water [36] but it confers an advantage such that guppies can survive where other fishes cannot. Thus guppies can be used as an indicator species.

Investigate different urban ditches, and try to catch one of each of the fish species present. It is more informative if the fishes caught can be given a scientific name [1, 2, 18, 38, 50], but simply the total of different species provides useful data. Plot a graph of the number of species against the biological oxygen demand or the oxygen concentration of the water. Repeat in a different section of town and in irrigation canals. You now have a means of determining approximate oxygen levels in the field using biological indicators instead of resorting to expensive laboratory tests.

Johnson suggests some other organisms which could be used as pollution indicators [30].

Another ubiquitous inhabitant of ditches and their surroundings is the common toad *Bufo melanostictus*. An average-sized garden in Medan can harbour nearly thirty toads and these can be individually recognized by clipping toes and noting colour (variable in this species), weight or length. These data can be used to estimate the population size [7]. Do the toads grow at a constant rate throughout the year? Is there a clear breeding season (as indicated by large numbers of small toads appearing at about the same time) or not? Kill a few and examine the stomach contents—does the diet change through the year? Take a stretch of road and remove toad corpses. Make daily counts of the toads freshly killed. What proportion of the toad population is killed by cars each year [23]? What other forms of mortality are faced?

13.6 BATS

Some cities, such as Medan, have huge populations of resident bats but others, such as Palembang, have rather fewer. Some bats, usually insectivorous ones, often roost in roofs of houses, churches and mosques. Others, both insectivorous and frugivorous species, live amongst palm fronds, particularly the hanging, dead leaves of oil palms, and in tree holes. A Sumatran city is home to probably 15-30 bat species.

At first sight, bats in flight all look the same but with a little patience different groups can be distinguisted [24]. The medium-sized, roof-dwelling, long-winged tomb bat *Taphozuos longimanus* is usually the first to start flying. Before it leaves its roost it becomes quite vocal and this is easily heard in the house below. It and other smaller insectivorous bats fly rather erratically as they swoop to catch insects. Frugivorous bats generally fly in a more direct manner.

Stand outside at dusk and watch for bats and note the time the different types appear. Where do they seem to come from? Finding roosts is sometimes easier at dawn when bats tend to fly round and round their roost. Over a series of days try to pin down the actual roosts. Do the bats emerge at the same time each day? What effect does rain have? Are roosts available all over the city or are they concentrated in one area?

How many bats emerge from each roost? Is it the same number day after day? Take a series of 1 ha plots in a town and collect data to estimate the number of resident bats. From data in Lekagul and McNeely [38] and Medway [41] estimate the biomass.

13.7 BIRDS

13.7.1 Introduction

In general the bird fauna of towns tends to have a lower species richness and diversity than nearby forests, but a higher biomass and density, and a very few dominant species. In addition, the major feeding niche shifts from bark-and canopy-insect eaters to ground feeders [53].

No comprehensive list of birds appears to have been compiled for Sumatran towns despite the ease of observation and data collecting, but lists for Kuala Lumpur and Singapore can be used as indications of what might eventually be recorded (Table 13.2). A two-year study of birds in Kuala Lumpur revealed the presence of 24 species of common resident birds, nine species from rural areas which visited towns irregularly, one species which remained only between April and September, and eight species which were resident only between September and April. In addition to these, about 20 other species were seen only occasionally [39]. A similar number and composition of species was recorded for Singapore and it was noted that the total number of species was lower than for towns in other tropical areas, for instance West Africa [53]. An examination of the natural habitats of urban and sub-urban birds in Peninsular Malaysia and Singapore suggests that over half originate in coastal and riparian vegetation, only about 5% from lowland forest and a similar percentage are normally cliff or cave-mouth nesters. About 25% have been introduced or are recent immigrants. The similarity between cliffs and buildings are obvious and swifts have taken advantage of that. The similarity between coastal and riparian vegetation and towns is not so clear but a common factor is their simple plant communities with few species (section 13.2) [53]. Because of this, generalized foragers are the major town invaders. The most common invader from the above habitat is the yellow-vented bulbul *Pycnonotus goiaveri*. Unlike Africa, the Sunda Region has no large areas of natural open country or savannah which might be

Table 13.2 Common resident garden birds in cities in Sumatra and in Penang and Kuala Lumpur. (Based on McClure [39], Ward [53], and Whitten [57]). This table is clearly incomplete and it is hoped that readers will fill in the gaps and inform the authors of their observations so that they can be included in the second edition of this book.

	Banda Aceh	Medan	Padang	Pekanbaru	Jambi	Palembang	Bengkulu	Bandar Lampung	Penang	Kuala Lumpur
Barred ground dove *Geopelia striata*										+
Spotted dove *Streptopelia chinensis*										+
Pink-necked pigeon *Treron vernans*										+
Long-tailed nightjar *Caprimulgus macrurus*		+								+
White-bellied swiftlet *Collocalia esculenta*	+	+								+
House swift *Apus affinis*		+								+
Palm swift *Cypsiurus balasiensis*		+								+
Crested tree swift *Hemiprocne longipennis*										+
White-breasted kingfisher *Halycon smyrnensis*		−								+
Coppersmith barbet *Megalaima haemacephala*		−								+
Black-naped oriole *Oriolus chinensis*		+								+
Large-billed crow *Corvus macrorhynchos*		−								+

Table 13.2 (continued).

	Banda Aceh	Medan	Padang	Pekanbaru	Jambi	Palembang	Bengkulu	Bandar Lampung	Penang	Kuala Lumpur
House crow										
Corvus splendens	–	–	–	–	–	–	–	–	+	–
Common brown babbler										
Trichastoma abbotti							+			+
Common iora										
Aegithina tiphia										+
Yellow-crowned bulbul										
Pycnonotus zeylandicus										
Yellow-vented bulbul										
Pycnonotus goiaver		+	+	+			+			+
Magpie robin										
Copsychus saularis		–								+
Flyeater										
Gerygone sulphurea										+
Common tailorbird										
Orthotomus sutorius										
Ashy tailorbird										
Orthotomus ruficeps	+									
Rufous-tailed tailorbird										
Orthotomus sericeus		+								
Glossy starling										
Aplonis panayensis		+								
Common myna										
Acridotheres tristis		–							+	+
Brown-throated sunbird										
Anthreptes malaccensis		+								+
Scarlet-backed flowerpecker/										
Dicaeum cruentatum		+						+		
Tree sparrow										
Passer montanus	+	+	+	+	+	+	+	+	+	+
White-headed munia										
Munia maja		+								

expected to form a source of urban birds and so the number of urban birds originating from indigenous natural habitats is limited.

For certain birds from the dryer land north of the Sunda Region, roads, railways, disturbed vegetation and towns present opportunities for colonizing areas which had previously been closed to them because of the intervening large areas of species-rich forests [53, 55]. This has yet to be documented for Sumatra but birds from the dryer more open land in Java are starting to spread into Sumatran towns [27, 29].

Sumatra and Peninsular Malaysia have witnessed a spectacular invasion by the tree sparrow *Passer montanus*. This bird is native of the Paleartic Realm (Figure 1.21, section 1.6.1), that is Europe, Russia and China, and probably arrived at ports aboard ships in the sixteenth and seventeenth centuries. It has now spread to every urban area on Sumatra. A similar spread of a new species may occur if the introduced house crow *Corvus splendens* (not to be confused with the shy forest crow *Corvus enca*) or the common mynah *Acridotheres tristis* spreads from the island of Pinang across the Malacca Straits to northern Sumatra [9]. The crow fills the scavenging niche which in most other tropical regions is also filled by various crows and birds of prey.

Those concerned with environmental affairs in Sumatra should keep an eye open for species new to a region. They are likely to occur first in the coastal urban regions. Even if they are unlikely to compete severely with indigenous birds, they may be considered undesirable for other reasons and the time to undertake a management program is at the beginning of an 'invasion', not when the 'invaders' have established a firm foothold. House crows are somewhat unpopular because of their raucous calls, gregarious nesting habits, fouling of public places, and stealing of food or young chicks [9], but they do process urban waste, which might otherwise be utilized by rats which, unlike crows, harbour and transmit several important diseases [25] (section 12.3.2). Charles has concluded that one of the best ways to control these birds is by controlling the disposal of household waste [9].

The trouble with recognizing new bird species in Sumatra is that regional lists of urban and suburban birds do not yet exist. This would not be hard to rectify.

It is sometimes remarked that the total number of birds, not just the number of species, is low in Sumatran towns. One reason, of course, is the thoughtless shooting by the air-rifle toting, motor-bike riding, urban cowboys on Sunday afternoons. Additional ecological reasons are that few of the urban trees produce fruit suitable for birds and there are few insects able to utilize the 'foreign' trees (section 13.2) and therefore there is less food for insectivorous or partially-insectivorous birds (see section 7.4.2).

Birds represent excellent subjects for a study of urban ecology. Observation conditions are as near ideal as one could wish for and the number of food species and competing bird species are relatively few. The study of an urban bird or bird community in Sumatra is unlikely to be of island-wide environmental significance, but it will furnish those involved in such a study with an awareness of ecological complexity and principles (see, for example, Ward and Poh [54]. Those will be of immediate practical use should they turn next to more complex ecosystem an environmental impact assessment or similar study.

In Medan, at least, gardens support two species of tailorbird: the rufous-tailed *Orthotomus sericeus* and the ashy *O. ruficeps*. These birds are almost exactly the same size, both eat insects, both build nest by sewing leaves together. How do they divide the available resources between themselves so that they can coexist? Is the competition exploitative or disturbance (section 4.8.5)?

Flowers that are pollinated by birds are generally recognisable by the following features:

1) open during daylight;
2) vivid colours, often scarlet or striking contrasting colours;
3) lip or margin absent or curved back;
4) hard flower wall, filaments stiff or united, nectar retained at rear of flower;
5) no odour;
6) abundant nectar;
7) no nectar guides (lines running along the petals indicating nectar source);
8) a relatively large distance between nectar source and sexual parts [20];
9) relatively low sugar concentration ($\pm 25\%$) in the nectar in comparison with nectar in flowers pollinated by bees ($\pm 75\%$)[4].

A common urban flower which fulfils all these criteria is the hibiscus *Hibiscus rosa-sinensis*. It is visited by sunbirds (Nectariniidae) but, because most hibiscus plants are sterile, the plants do not seed [45,46]. What other plants do sunbirds drink nectar from? Do all the plants conform to the characters listed above? Are sunbirds the only birds to visit the flowers? Design experiments to ensure that only sunbirds gain access to certain flowers. Repeat the experiment but exclude all posible pollinators. Are the birds actually pollinating the flowers? Where on the bird's body is pollen-carried and what features of the flower design ensure that pollen is transferred?

13.7.2 Swifts

Swifts and swift-like birds belong to three families: the swifts and swiftlets (Apodidae), treeswifts (Hemiprocnidae), and swallows (Hirundinidae). Only the first and last of these are particularly common in towns and the two most common species can be distinguished from each other as shown in Table 13.3 and Figure 13.7. Other species occur in towns, however, and for proper identification reference should be made to King et al. [33].

Table 13.3 Characteristics of the house swift and barn swallow.

House swift	Barn swallow
black except for white rump and pale throat	black above with orange throat and white belly
wings curved smoothly in flight	wings somewhat bent in flight
tail only slightly forked	tail strongly forked
nest round, and made of mud, built beneath overhanging roofs and frequently in groups	nest like a cup built in inconspicuous places; does not usually breed in Sumatra
roosts on vertical walls or on nest, rarely if ever on telephone wires	roosts, often in large groups, along telephone wires
permanent resident	migrant, appearing in about September and leaving in about March

Figure 13.7 House swift (left) and barn swallow (right) in flight. (After King *et al* [33]).

Swifts are masters of the air. A swift in Africa has been recorded as flying at 170 kilometres per hour and is easily the fastest moving vertebrate. In normal flight however swifts usually fly at about 50 kilometres per hour. Swifts feed, drink, mate and even sleep while flying. As dusk approaches, non-breeding birds rise steadily in the sky and probably reach a few thousand metres above the ground where they sleep and beat their wings irregularly. When a young swift leaves its nest it may be at least two years before it lands again. Some swifts, such as the Pacific swift recently recorded in Sumatra [3,29], migrate to and from the cooler northern climates. The oldest known wild swift was ringed as an adult 15 years before it was found dying in England. It was calculated that it had flown over 7 million kilometres during its life. Swifts normally live about six years [5].

Swifts feed by chasing or filtering insects and airborne spiders from the air. They are, in effect, feeders on 'aerial plankton'. The food that adult European swifts give to their chicks has been examined and produced some surprising figures [5]. A single mouthful collected over half an hour or so might contain over 500 animals of many species. During a fine day a pair of swifts with two or three young to feed may catch up to 20,000 insects and spiders [5]. Under the eaves of the grand Central Post Office in Medan, there are some 100 swift nests which are occupied during the breeding season (approximately April to June). Swift chicks generally leave their nest when about six weeks old and a simple calculation shows that the breeding swifts and their chicks account for about 40,000,000 insects and spiders during that six-week period. It is not difficult to estimate how many insects would be consumed in one year by this one colony of swifts alone and thus how important the birds are to insect control.[4]

If the nest sites chosen in Medan are any indication, it is clear that modern buildings are not favoured. Most of the sites were built at least thirty years ago and are used again and again. When the Medan Central Post Office was repainted in 1982, all the nests were scraped away from the eaves. It was not many months, however, before nests were built again in the same places.

Examine the locations used by swifts for nesting. What features do they have in common? How many nests are there in each location? Is there any correlation between number of nests and age of buildings? Is there any connection between direction faced by the wall and the number of nests? Can you suggest ways in which modern buildings could be made more attractive to swifts? Do the numbers of nests occupied vary from year to year? How many nests are occupied in which months? How does the number of occupied nests relate to rainfall or other patterns? Do the patterns tie in with the cycles discussed in section 7.4.2?

It is hoped that these few examples will instil some enthusiasm in readers to venture into the urban environment with newly-opened eyes, a questioning mind and a notebook. Sumatra desperately needs a wider and deeper data base of ecological information and school teachers and university lecturers and expatriates should take up the challenge now.

---

4. A study of urban swiftlets has recently been published by Langham [36].

REFERENCES

1. Alfred, E.R. (1961). Singapore fresh-water fishes. *Malay. Nat. J.* 15: 1—19. (12.5.20)
2. _____. (1966). The fresh-water fishes of Singapore. *Zool. Verh. Leiden* 78: 1—68.(12.5.28)
3. Anon. (1980). *Penyelamatan Siberut Rencana Induk Konservasi.*
4. Baker, H.G. (1975). Sugar concentrations in nectars from hummingbird flowers. *Biotropica* 7: 37—41. (12.1.117)
5. Bromhall, D. (1980). *Devil Birds: The Life of the Swift.* Hutchinson, London. (12.7.33)
6. Burkill, I.N. (1917). The flowering of the pigeon orchid, *Dendrobium crumenatum* Lindl. *Grdns'. Bull. Straits Settlement* 1:400—405.
7. Caughley, G. (1978). *Analysis of Vertebrate Populations.* Wiley, Chicester. (19.4.3)
8. Chaphekar, S.B. (1978). Urban ecosystems- a challenge for plant ecologists. *Int. J. Ecol. Environ. Sci.* 4: 19—31. (12.1.79)
9. Charles, J.K. (1978). Management of the house crow *Corvus splendens. BIOTROP Spec. Publ.* 8: 191—197. (12.11.2)
10. Chou, L.M. (1975). Systematic account of the Singapore house geckos. *J. Natl. Acad. Sci. Singapore* 4: 130—138.
11. _____. (1978). Some bionomic data on the house geckos of Singapore. *Malay. Nat. J.* 31: 231—235. (12.6.20)
12. Chua, N.H., Kwok, S.W., Tan, K.K., Teo, S.P. and Wong, H.A. (1972). Growths on concrete and other similar surfaces in Singapore. *J. Singapore Inst. Arch.* 51: 13—15.
13. Church, G. (1962). The reproductive cycles of the Javanese house geckos, *Cosymbotus platyurus, Hemidactylus frenatus* and *Peropus mutilatus. Copeia* 2: 262—269. (12.6.30)
14. Church, G. and Lim, C.S. (1961). The distribution of three species of house gecks in Bandung (Java). *Herpetologica* 17:119—201.
15. Cook, L.M., Askew, R.R. and Bishop, J.A. (1970). Increasing frequency of the typical form of the peppered moth in Manchester. *Nature* 227: 1155. (12.4.56)

16. Corner, E.J.H. (1952). *Wayside Trees of Malaya.* 2 vols., 2nd ed., Government Printer, Singapore. (12.1.15)

17. Coster, C. (1926). Periodische Blütterscheinungen in den Tropen. *Ann. Jard. Bot. Buitenzorg* 35: 125—162.

18. Djuhanda, T. (1981). *Dunia Ikan.* Armico, Bandung. (12.5.30)

19. Dussault, G.V. and Krammer, D.L. (1981). Food and feeding behaviour of the guppy, *Poecilia reticulata* (Pisces: Poeciliidae). *Can. J. Zool.* 59: 684—701. (12.5.29)

20. Enright, J.T. (1982). Sleep movements of leaves: In defence of Darwins interpretation. *Oecologia* 54: 253—259. (12.1.88)

21. Faegri, K. and Pijl, L. van der (1979). *The Principles of Pollination Ecology.* 3rd rev. ed., Pergamon, Oxford (12.1.27)

22. Gilbert, O. (1983). The wildlife of Britain's wasteland. *New Scient.* 97: 824—829. (12.13.21)

23. Gittins, S.P. (1983). Road casualties solve toad mysteries. *New Scient.* 97: 530—531. (12.6.19)

24. Gould, E. (1978). Opportunistic feeding by tropical bats. *Biotropica* 10: 75—76. (12.8.18)

25. Hadi, T.R., Atmosoedjono, S., Peenen, P.F. van and Sukaeri (1976). Acarine ecto-parasites of small mammals in Jakarta, Indonesia. *S.E. Asian J. Trop. Med. Public Health* 7: 144—148.

26. Harrison, J.L. (1951). A Kuala Lumpur garden by night. *Malay. Nat. J.* 5: 193—201. (12.8.102)

27. Harvey, W.G. and Holmes, D.A. (1976). Additions to the avifaunas of Sumatra and Kalimantan, Indonesia. *Bull. Brit. Orn. Club* 96: 90—92. (12.7.51)

28. Hawksworth, D.L. and Rose, F. (1976). *Lichens as Pollution Monitors.* Edward Arnold, London. (19.5.19)

29. Holmes, D.A. (1977). Faunistic notes and further additions to the Sumatran avifauna. *Bull. Brit. Orn. Club* 97: 68—71. (12.7.50)

30. Johnson, D.S. (1968). Water pollution in Malaysia and Singapore: some comments. *Malay. Nat. J.* 21: 221—222. (21.1.15)

31. Kettlewell, H.B.H. (1955). Selection experiments on industrial melanism in the Lepidoptera. *Heredity* 10: 287—301. (12.4.24)

558

32. _____. (1959). Darwin's missing evidence. *Sci. Amer.* 200: 48—53.
33. King, B., Woodcock, M. and Dickinson, E.C. (1975). *A Field Guide to the Birds of South-East Asia.* Collins, London. (12.7.45)
34. Kramer, D.L. and McClure, M. (1982). Aquatic surface respiration, a widespread adaptation to hypoxia in tropical freshwater fishes. *Env. Biol. Fish.* 7: 47—55.
35. Kramer, D.L. and Mehegan, J.P. (1981). Aquatic surface respiration, an adaptive response to hypoxia in the guppy, *Poecilia reticulata* (Pisces, Poeciliidae). *Env. Biol. Fish.* 6: 299—313. (12.5.34)
36. Langham, N. (1980). Breeding biology of the edible-nest swiftlet *Aerodramus fuciphagus. Ibis* 122: 447—461. (12.7.5)
37. Lee, K.B. and Wee, Y.C. (1982). Algae growing on walls in Singapore. *Malay. Nat. J.* 35: 125—132. (12.1.77)
38. Lekagul, B. and McNeely, J.A. (1977). *The Mammals of Thailand.* Association for the Conservation of Wildlife, Bangkok. (12.8.21)
39. McClure, H.E. (1961). Garden birds in Kuala Lumpur, Malaya. *Malay. Nat. J.* 15: 111—135. (12.7.36)
40. Marcellini, D.L. (1977). The function of a vocal display of the lizard *Hemidactylus frenatus* (Sauria: Gekkonidae). *Anim.Behav.* 25: 414—417. (12.6.31)
41. Medway, Lord (1969). *The Wild Mammals of Malaya.* Oxford University Press, Oxford. (12.8.98)
42. Pianka, E.R. and Huey, R.B. (1978). Comparative ecology, resource utilization and niche segregation among gekkonid lizards in the southern Kalahari. *Copeia* 1978: 691—701.
43. Pianka, E.R, Huey, R.B. and Lawlor, L.R. (1979). Niche segregation in desert lizards. In *Analysis of Ecological Systems* (ed. D.J. Horn, G.R. Stairs and R.D. Mitchell), pp. 67—115. Ohio State University Press, Columbus. (12.6.5)
44. Piggott, A. (1979). *Common Epiphytic Ferns of Malaysia and Singapore.* Heinemann, Singapore. (12.1.105)
45. Pijl, L. van der (1937). Disharmony between Asaitic flower-birds and American bird-flowers. *Ann. Jard. Bot. Buitenzorg.* 48: 2—26. (12.7.2)

46. Prendergast, H.D.V. (1982). Pollination of *Hibiscus rosa-sinensis*. *Biotropica* 14: 287. (12.1.76)

47. Ratnasabapathy, M. (1974). *Acacia auriculaeformis* and *Casuarina equisetifolia*-the urban invaders. *Malay. Nat. J.* 28: 18—21. (12.1.78)

48. Saanin, H. (1968). *Taksonomi dan Kuntji Identifikasi Ikan*. I and II vols. Binatjipta, Jakarta. (12.5.1 and 12.5.2)

49. Saravanamuthu, J. and Lim, R.P. (1988). A preliminary limnological survey of a eutrophic pond, Taman Jaya Pond, Petaling Jaya. *Malay. Nat. J.* : 83—97. (3.1.14)

50. Schuster, W.H. (1952). *Local Common Names of Indonesian Fishes*. W. van Hoeve, Bandung. (12.5.7)

51. Steenis, C.G.GJ. van (1981). *Flora untuk Sekolah*. Pradnya Paramita, Jakarta, (12.1.75)

52. Vitt, L.J., Congdon, J.D. and Dickson, N.A. (1977). Adaptive strategies and energetics of tail autonomy in lizards. *Ecology* 58: 326—337. (12.6.29)

53. Ward, P. (1968). Origin of the avifauna of urban and suburban Singapore. *Ibis* 110: 239—255. (12.7.34)

54. Ward, P. and Poh, G.E. (1968). Seasonal breeding in an equatorial population of the tree sparrow *Passer montanus*. *Ibis* 110: 359—363. (12.7.35)

56. Wells, D.R. (1974). Resident Birds. In *Birds of the Malay Peninsula*. (by Lord Medway and D.R. Wells). Witherby, London. (12.7.23)

57. Whitten, A.J. Unpublished.

58. Wratten, S.D., Goddard, P. and Edwards, P.J. (1981). British trees and insects: the role of palatability. *Amer. Nat.* 118: 916—919. (12.1.83)

INDEX

A

Acacia auriculiformis 534
Acanthus ilicifolius 459
Aceh 11, 12, 14, 20, 28, 31, 72, 73, 96, 282, 405, 407
East 66
North 360
South 153, 461
South-east 495
acid rain 467, 468
Acridotheres tristis 550, 551
Acrochordonichthys melanogaster 200
Acrossocheilus deauratus 197
Acrostichum aureum 104, 109, 459
Aegithina 49, 304
tiphia 550
Aerodramus fuciphaga 161
maxima 440
vanikorensis 420
Aethalops alecto 407
Africa 250, 287, 297, 554
east 534
north 160
west 84, 548
Aglaia 357
agriculture, early 62, 64
modern 72, 73, 511—526
Agrostis 387, 401
Air Sawan 34
airphotos 30
Akit people 68, 71
Alahan Panjang 33
Alang Besar Island 34
Alangium ridleyi 240
Alas River 72, 169, 468
Alchornea villosa 483

algae, blue-green 170, 177, 422, 516, 537
coralline 163
freshwater 176, 177, 178, 199, 208, 232, 466
alkaloids 112, 296, 297
Alor 56
Alstonia angustiloba 230
Amandava amandava 515
Amazonia 250, 342
America, South 84, 240, 253, 287
Amorphophallus 282—284
titanum 25, 282, 283
amphibians 49
Anambas archipelago 57, 160, 161, 340
Anaphalis javanica 401
Aneuk Laut 31
Anorrhinus galeritus 318, 485
ants 137, 299, 300, 349, 404, 432, 494
Antarctic 541
Anthocephalus chinensis 474, 479, 483
villosa 482
anthocyanins 389
Anthreptes malaccensis 550
Antiaris toxicaria 293
ant lion 511
Aplonis panayensis 550
Apus affinis 549, 553—555
aquarium fish 469, 470
Arabia 160
Arborophila rubirostris 46
Arctic 541
Arctonyx collaris 45
Ardea cinerea 139
purpurea 139
sumatrana 139

579

X

Xenalaphis hexagonotus 523, 524
Xylocarpus granatum 104, 109
  moluccensis 103
  microcephala 344

Z

Zaire 289, 290
Zaocys carinatus 523, 524
  fuscus 523, 524
zone of permanent occurrence 383, 385
zoogeography 52—61
zooplankton 178, 209
Zoothera dauma 405